Supporting Psychological and Emotional Wellbeing Among Entrepreneurs

Muhammad Nawaz Tunio
The University of Sufism and Modern Sciences, Bhitshah, Pakistan

Published in the United States of America by
IGI Global Scientific Publishing
701 East Chocolate Avenue
Hershey, PA, 17033, USA
Tel: 717-533-8845
Fax: 717-533-8661
E-mail: cust@igi-global.com
Website: https://www.igi-global.com

Copyright © 2025 by IGI Global Scientific Publishing. All rights reserved. No part of this publication may be reproduced, stored or distributed in any form or by any means, electronic or mechanical, including photocopying, without written permission from the publisher.
Product or company names used in this set are for identification purposes only. Inclusion of the names of the products or companies does not indicate a claim of ownership by IGI Global Scientific Publishing of the trademark or registered trademark.

Library of Congress Cataloging-in-Publication Data

Names: Tunio, Muhammad Nawaz, 1984- editor.
Title: Supporting psychological and emotional wellbeing among entrepreneurs / edited by: Muhammad Nawaz Tunio.
Description: Hershey PA : Business Science Reference , [2025] | Includes bibliographical references. | Summary: "The objective of this book is to call the attention of the researchers to focus on the psychological, and emotional well-being of entrepreneurs and address the related issues"-- Provided by publisher.
Identifiers: LCCN 2024039272 (print) | LCCN 2024039273 (ebook) | ISBN 9798369336731 (hardcover) | ISBN 9798369350690 (paperback) | ISBN 9798369336748 (ebook)
Subjects: LCSH: Entrepreneurship--Psychological aspects. | Work environment--Psychological aspects. | Businesspeople--Psychology. | Well-being.
Classification: LCC HB615 .S968 2024 (print) | LCC HB615 (ebook) | DDC 658.4/21--dc23/eng/20241108
LC record available at https://lccn.loc.gov/2024039272
LC ebook record available at https://lccn.loc.gov/2024039273

Vice President of Editorial: Melissa Wagner
Managing Editor of Acquisitions: Mikaela Felty
Managing Editor of Book Development: Jocelynn Hessler
Production Manager: Mike Brehm
Cover Design: Phillip Shickler

British Cataloguing in Publication Data
A Cataloguing in Publication record for this book is available from the British Library.

ll work contributed to this book is new, previously-unpublished material.
he views expressed in this book are those of the authors, but not necessarily of the publisher.
This book contains information sourced from authentic and highly regarded references, with reasonable efforts made to ensure the reliability of the data and information presented. The authors, editors, and publisher believe the information in this book to be accurate and true as of the date of publication. Every effort has been made to trace and credit the copyright holders of all materials included. However, the authors, editors, and publisher cannot assume responsibility for the validity of all materials or the consequences of their use. Should any copyright material be found unacknowledged, please inform the publisher so that corrections may be made in future reprints.

This book is dedicated to my elder brother, Professor Dr. Ahmed Nawaz Tunio, from Sindh Agriculture University, Tandojam, Pakistan.

Your unwavering support, wisdom, and guidance have been the cornerstone of my scholarly journey. It is through your encouragement and belief in my abilities that I have been able to contribute meaningfully to the academic world, including the editing of this book. Your dedication to education and the pursuit of knowledge continues to inspire me, and I am forever grateful for your mentorship.

Muhammad Nawaz Tunio
University of Sufism and Modern Sciences, Pakistan

Table of Contents

Foreword xix

Preface xxi

Acknowledgments xxv

Introduction xxvi

Chapter 1
Abusive Work Environment Effect on Female Entrepreneurs' Emotional Wellbeing by Mediation of Social and Moral Values in the Horn of Africa 1
    Metasebia Adula, Bule Hora University, Ethiopia
    Shashi Kant, Bule Hora University, Ethiopia
    Sofi Badi, Bule Hora University, Ethiopia
    Mona Kumari, Government College for Women Bahadurgarh, Jhajjar, India

Chapter 2
Abusive Work Environments and Strategies to Manage the Psychological Well-Being of Entrepreneurs 23
    Retno Lestari, University of Brawijaya, Indonesia
    Heni Dwi Windarwati, University of Brawijaya, Indonesia
    Ridhoyanti Hidayah, University of Brawijaya, Indonesia

Chapter 3
Balancing Work and Life Techniques for Maintaining Emotional Wellbeing in Entrepreneurship 33
    Mustafa Kayyali, HE Higher Education Ranking, Syria

Chapter 4
Career Resilience and the Limitations of Quiet-Quitting in Mike Judge's Office Space 59
    Kelvin Ke Jinde, Xi'an Jiaotong-Liverpool University, China

Chapter 5
Combating Mental Health Stigma With Artificial Intelligence: Improving Societal Understanding ... 75
    Samantha Elaine Loies, Polygence, USA

Chapter 6
Cultivating Emotional Intelligence: A Catalyst for Entrepreneurial Success 93
Deepak Kumar Sahoo, Biju Patnaik University of Technology, Rourkela, India
Anish Kumar, O.P. Jindal Global University, India
Ajay Chandel, Lovely Professional University, India
Hewawasam P. G. D. Wijethilak, University of Colombo, Sri Lanka

Chapter 7
Developing a Mindfulness-Based Intervention for Entrepreneurial Stress Reduction 117
Aayushi Pandey, Lovely Professional University, India
Shashank Mittal, O.P. Jindal Global University, India
Xuan-Hoa Nghiem, Vietnam National University, Hanoi, Vietnam

Chapter 8
Does Entrepreneurial Leadership Influence Employees' Emotional Wellbeing During Crisis? 135
Swati Sisodia, GD Goenka University, India
Sumaira Jan, Humanities, Social Sciences & Management, National Institute of Technology, Srinagar, India

Chapter 9
Entrepreneurial Mindfulness: A Path to Inner Peace and Professional Fulfilment........................... 155
Deepak Kumar Sahoo, Biju Patnaik University of Technology, Rourkela, India
Mohit Yadav, O.P. Jindal Global University, India
Ajay Chandel, Lovely Professional University, India
Majdi Quttainah, Kuwait University, Kuwait

Chapter 10
Evaluating the Impact of Wellness Programs on Entrepreneurial Burnout 173
Thi Minh Ngoc Luu, International School, Vietnam National University, Hanoi, Vietnam
Sandeep Kumar Singh, O.P. Jindal Global University, India
Shivani Dhand, Lovely Professional University, India

Chapter 11
Exploring the Relationship Between Entrepreneurial Success and Personal Well-Being 201
Deepak Kumar Sahoo, Biju Patnaik University of Technology, Rourkela, India
Anish Kumar, O.P. Jindal Global University, India
Ajay Chandel, Lovely Professional University, India
Rohit, Gulf Medical University, Ajman, UAE

Chapter 12
How Work Environments Drive Mental Calm and Entrepreneurial Progress: Building a Sanctuary for Success 229
J. S. Sathyajith, Christ University, India
K. Sudheesh, Christ University, India

Chapter 13
Leadership Behavior That Promotes Psychological Wellness at Work 239
    Hemlata Parmar, Manipal University Jaipur, India
    Utsav Krishan Murari, Sharda University, India

Chapter 14
Mindful Entrepreneurship: Nurturing Mental Well-Being in Business 249
    S. C. Vetrivel, Kongu Engineering College, India
    P. Vidhyapriya, Kongu Engineering College, India
    V. P. Arun, JKKN College of Engineering and Technology, India

Chapter 15
National and Regional Economic Growth and Development Fostered by Entrepreneurship Ecosystems 273
    José G. Vargas-Hernandez, Tecnològico Nacional de Mèxico, ITS Fresnillo, Mexico

Chapter 16
Navigating Entrepreneurial Stress: Effective Techniques for Reducing Burnout Risk 293
    Xuan-Hoa Nghiem, Vietnam National University, Hanoi, Vietnam
    Shashank Mittal, O.P. Jindal Global University, India
    Shivani Dhand, Lovely Professional University, India

Chapter 17
Social Support Networks and Their Role in Entrepreneurial Well-Being 319
    Shashank Mittal, O.P. Jindal Global University, India
    Shivani Dhand, Lovely Professional University, India
    Xuan-Hoa Nghiem, Vietnam National University, Vietnam

Chapter 18
The Effectiveness of Cognitive-Behavioral Therapy for Entrepreneurial Anxiety 345
    Hewawasam P. G. D. Wijethilak, University of Colombo, Sri Lanka
    Sandeep Kumar Singh, O.P. Jindal Global University, India
    Preet Kanwal, Lovely Professional University, India

Chapter 19
The Effects of Financial Stress on Entrepreneurial Mental Health 363
    Mohit Yadav, O.P. Jindal Global University, India
    Preet Kanwal, Lovely Professional University, India
    Majdi Anwar Quttainah, Kuwait University, Kuwait

Chapter 20
The Impact of Entrepreneurial Failures on Psychological Resilience 381
    Deepak Kumar Sahoo, Biju Patnaik University of Technology, Rourkela, India
    Thi M. Le, Vietnam National University, Hanoi, Vietnam
    Anish Kumar, O.P. Jindal Global University, India
    Ajay Chandel, Lovely Professional University, India

Chapter 21
The Role of Emotional Intelligence in Promoting Mental Peace, Healthy Work Environments, and
Emotional Well-Being Among Entrepreneurs 401
    Tiago Manuel Horta Reis da Silva, King's College London, UK

Chapter 22
The Role of Mentorship in Mitigating Entrepreneurial Loneliness 427
    Sandeep Kumar Singh, O.P. Jindal Global University, India
    Preet Kanwal, Lovely Professional University, India
    Thi Minh Ngoc Luu, International School, Vietnam National University, Hanoi, Vietnam

Chapter 23
The Role of Technology in Facilitating Entrepreneurial Mental Health Support 443
    Mohit Yadav, O.P. Jindal Global University, India
    Preet Kanwal, Lovely Professional University, India
    Rohit, Gulf Medical University, Ajman, UAE

Compilation of References 463

About the Contributors 525

Index 531

Detailed Table of Contents

Foreword xix

Preface xxi

Acknowledgments xxv

Introduction xxvi

Chapter 1
Abusive Work Environment Effect on Female Entrepreneurs' Emotional Wellbeing by Mediation
of Social and Moral Values in the Horn of Africa 1
    Metasebia Adula, Bule Hora University, Ethiopia
    Shashi Kant, Bule Hora University, Ethiopia
    Sofi Badi, Bule Hora University, Ethiopia
    Mona Kumari, Government College for Women Bahadurgarh, Jhajjar, India

This chapter investigates the impact of an abusive work environment on the emotional well-being of female entrepreneurs in the Horn of Africa, with a focus on the mediating role of moral and social values. Using a sample of 400 female entrepreneurs, the study assesses whether the dataset is suitable for factor analysis using the Kaiser-Meyer-Olkin (KMO) measure. An exploratory factor analysis (EFA) is used to identify key ideas related to workplace mistreatment, moral and social values, and mental wellness. Next, the factor structure is confirmed and the reliability of the measuring devices is confirmed using Confirmatory Factor Analysis (CFA). Next, using structural equation modeling (SEM), the relationships between these variables are investigated, with an emphasis on the effects of an abusive work environment on emotional well-being and the findings indicate that abusive work conditions have a detrimental effect on the mental health of female entrepreneurs, but that these impacts can be mitigated by strong moral and social values.

Chapter 2
Abusive Work Environments and Strategies to Manage the Psychological Well-Being of
Entrepreneurs 23
    Retno Lestari, University of Brawijaya, Indonesia
    Heni Dwi Windarwati, University of Brawijaya, Indonesia
    Ridhoyanti Hidayah, University of Brawijaya, Indonesia

Commencing an entrepreneurial voyage can be intimidating, and businesspersons might require assistance in dealing with several types of abusive behaviours from their co-founders or inventors. An abusive work environment can hurt both employees and organizational productivity. This hostile atmosphere may arise from various sources, including harassment, discrimination, or intimidation. These harmful experiences can result in high turnover rates and substandard job performance. As a result, employers must be vigilant and proactive in addressing any recurring instances of belittlement, offensive humour, or unwarranted criticism. They must strive to create a workplace environment based on respect and inclusivity. The purpose of this chapter is to provide readers with a comprehensive understanding of the impact of abusive work environments on entrepreneurs' psychological and emotional well-being. It also examines the related issues that arise from such environments.

Chapter 3
Balancing Work and Life Techniques for Maintaining Emotional Wellbeing in Entrepreneurship 33
    Mustafa Kayyali, HE Higher Education Ranking, Syria

Entrepreneurship is generally characterized by long hours, high levels of stress, and the need to make difficult decisions, all of which can significantly affect emotional well-being. This chapter examines the vital need to establish a balance between work and personal life to sustain mental wellness in the entrepreneurial journey. It covers the frequent issues experienced by entrepreneurs, including burnout, stress, and the blurring of boundaries between work and life. Drawing on research and case studies, the chapter discusses practical approaches for establishing work-life balance, such as time management, delegation, mindfulness practices, and the growth of emotional intelligence. The chapter finishes by underlining the necessity for sustainable techniques that not only boost productivity but also support long-term emotional well-being in the challenging world of entrepreneurship.

Chapter 4
Career Resilience and the Limitations of Quiet-Quitting in Mike Judge's Office Space 59
    Kelvin Ke Jinde, Xi'an Jiaotong-Liverpool University, China

This article examines the limitations of quiet-quitting in the American cult comedy Office Space (dir. Mike Judge 1999). It argues that the representations of workers in the film suggest that workers who quietly-quit may run the risk of marginalization and ostracization in the workplace as such actions can affect the performances and morale of fellow colleagues. The significance of this article lies in showing how Office Space functions not only as an allegory of workers' dissatisfaction in a toxic workplace. It also functions as a cautionary tale regarding the limitations of quiet-quitting as a long-term strategy to cope with work dissatisfaction. Lastly, the analysis offers a humanities approach and contribution to the thinking of a more healthy and productive work environment by analyzing the representations and limitations of quiet-quitting in cinema.

Chapter 5
Combating Mental Health Stigma With Artificial Intelligence: Improving Societal Understanding... 75
Samantha Elaine Loies, Polygence, USA

Mental health stigma remains a significant barrier to individuals seeking help and achieving optimal treatment outcomes. The pervasive nature of stigma is known to exacerbate mental health issues and deter individuals from accessing much-needed support. This research project aims to investigate the role of artificial intelligence (AI) in combating mental health stigma and improving societal understanding of mental health disorders. We will explore how AI-driven tools like chatbots, natural language processing, and social media analysis can enhance public awareness, dispel misconceptions, and foster empathy toward individuals with mental health challenges. It begins with a literature review on the current state of mental health stigma, the factors contributing to its perpetuation, and the use of AI in mental health care. The chapter identifies AI-driven interventions that hold promise for addressing mental health stigma, such as public health campaigns and targeted social media content. It analyzes these AI interventions to assess their effectiveness and potential for adoption.

Chapter 6
Cultivating Emotional Intelligence: A Catalyst for Entrepreneurial Success 93
Deepak Kumar Sahoo, Biju Patnaik University of Technology, Rourkela, India
Anish Kumar, O.P. Jindal Global University, India
Ajay Chandel, Lovely Professional University, India
Hewawasam P. G. D. Wijethilak, University of Colombo, Sri Lanka

This chapter explores the vital role of emotional intelligence (EI) in entrepreneurship, highlighting its significance in leadership, team dynamics, customer relations, and overall business success. As the business landscape evolves, particularly with the rise of artificial intelligence (AI), the integration of EI becomes increasingly crucial. The chapter addresses key components of emotional intelligence, the challenges entrepreneurs face in developing these skills, and the measurable impacts on employee performance, engagement, and customer satisfaction. It also discusses future trends that emphasize the synergy between EI and AI, including enhanced collaboration, personalized training, and a focus on employee well-being. Ultimately, fostering emotional intelligence is essential for entrepreneurs seeking to navigate complexities, drive innovation, and cultivate resilient organizations in a rapidly changing environment.

Chapter 7

Developing a Mindfulness-Based Intervention for Entrepreneurial Stress Reduction 117
    Aayushi Pandey, Lovely Professional University, India
    Shashank Mittal, O.P. Jindal Global University, India
    Xuan-Hoa Nghiem, Vietnam National University, Hanoi, Vietnam

This chapter explores developing and implementing mindfulness-based interventions (MBIs) tailored for entrepreneurs to reduce stress and enhance well-being. Recognizing the unique challenges faced by entrepreneurs, the chapter examines the theoretical foundations of mindfulness and its relevance to entrepreneurship. It outlines practical strategies for creating effective MBIs, including considerations for diverse populations and the integration of technology. The chapter also discusses the importance of measuring the effectiveness of these interventions and addresses potential challenges, such as participant resistance and sustainability of practices. By highlighting future directions for research, practice, and policy, this chapter aims to contribute to a deeper understanding of how mindfulness can transform entrepreneurial experiences, foster resilience and promote a healthier entrepreneurial ecosystem.

Chapter 8

Does Entrepreneurial Leadership Influence Employees' Emotional Wellbeing During Crisis? 135
    Swati Sisodia, GD Goenka University, India
    Sumaira Jan, Humanities, Social Sciences & Management, National Institute of Technology, Srinagar, India

Despite the uncertainty in today's competitive business environment, the current study investigates the implicit influence of Entrepreneurial Leadership on workers' emotional well-being in MSME's from the unorganized restaurant sector. The employees of Delhi/NCR based MSME's unorganized restaurant sector are the target population for this research. The study's main goal is to add to the literature on Indian MSMEs unorganized restaurant sector, which is a mostly neglected and under-researched group. The study provides a deeper understanding of the impact of entrepreneurial leadership on emotional wellbeing. This research has discovered that crises can provide opportunities for enterprises to become more robust, to be more proactive, to learn from their mistakes, to engage in building social networks and strengthen the interpersonal relationships so as to improve the overall emotional wellbeing of the employees working in MSMEs.

Chapter 9
Entrepreneurial Mindfulness: A Path to Inner Peace and Professional Fulfilment............................ 155
 Deepak Kumar Sahoo, Biju Patnaik University of Technology, Rourkela, India
 Mohit Yadav, O.P. Jindal Global University, India
 Ajay Chandel, Lovely Professional University, India
 Majdi Quttainah, Kuwait University, Kuwait

This chapter explores the significance of mindfulness for entrepreneurs, emphasizing its role in fostering inner peace and professional fulfilment. It examines the connection between mindfulness practices and enhanced focus, reduced stress, and improved emotional resilience. By integrating mindfulness into their daily routines, entrepreneurs can cultivate a deeper sense of purpose, strengthen interpersonal relationships, and achieve a healthier work-life balance. The chapter also addresses challenges entrepreneurs face in practicing mindfulness, such as time constraints and skepticism, while highlighting future trends, including technological integration and personalized approaches. Ultimately, mindfulness emerges as a transformative tool that empowers entrepreneurs to navigate the complexities of their journeys with greater clarity and satisfaction.

Chapter 10
Evaluating the Impact of Wellness Programs on Entrepreneurial Burnout 173
 Thi Minh Ngoc Luu, International School, Vietnam National University, Hanoi, Vietnam
 Sandeep Kumar Singh, O.P. Jindal Global University, India
 Shivani Dhand, Lovely Professional University, India

This chapter explores the critical impact of wellness programs on entrepreneurial burnout, emphasizing their role in promoting resilience and sustainable business practices. As entrepreneurs face unique pressures that contribute to stress and burnout, effective wellness initiatives become essential for enhancing overall well-being. This study evaluates various types of wellness programs, innovative digital solutions, and their long-term effects on entrepreneurial sustainability. Additionally, it addresses the challenges of implementing these programs and highlights the need for supportive policies and community involvement. Future trends indicate a shift towards personalized, technology-driven wellness solutions that foster holistic health. By prioritizing wellness, entrepreneurs can cultivate healthier work environments, ultimately leading to increased productivity and business success.

Chapter 11
Exploring the Relationship Between Entrepreneurial Success and Personal Well-Being 201
    Deepak Kumar Sahoo, Biju Patnaik University of Technology, Rourkela, India
    Anish Kumar, O.P. Jindal Global University, India
    Ajay Chandel, Lovely Professional University, India
    Rohit, Gulf Medical University, Ajman, UAE

This chapter explores the intricate relationship between entrepreneurial success and personal well-being, highlighting the interplay between ambition, mental health, and fulfilment. It examines how psychological resilience, coping mechanisms, and support systems contribute to both personal and professional outcomes for entrepreneurs. By emphasizing the significance of work-life balance and community networks, the chapter argues that well-being is integral to sustainable entrepreneurial success. Furthermore, it identifies future research directions that can deepen our understanding of this relationship, including the need for longitudinal studies and interdisciplinary approaches. Ultimately, this exploration underscores that personal fulfilment and entrepreneurial achievement are interdependent, advocating for a holistic view that nurtures both aspects to foster a thriving entrepreneurial landscape.

Chapter 12
How Work Environments Drive Mental Calm and Entrepreneurial Progress: Building a Sanctuary for Success 229
    J. S. Sathyajith, Christ University, India
    K. Sudheesh, Christ University, India

This research investigates the important relationship between a healthy work environment and the mental health of entrepreneurs, particularly women. It emphasizes the importance of mental calm in achieving entrepreneurial success and identifies major aspects that influence it. The work environment has a significant impact on emotional, psychological, and total well-being. The paper highlights ways that employers can use to create a healthy work environment, such as encouraging positive connections, effective communication, and mutual respect. It emphasizes the significance of stress management, confronting harassment and abusive behavior, and incorporating social and moral ideals into corporate culture. Organizations can foster mental well-being and entrepreneurial growth by prioritizing these characteristics.

Chapter 13
Leadership Behavior That Promotes Psychological Wellness at Work 239
Hemlata Parmar, Manipal University Jaipur, India
Utsav Krishan Murari, Sharda University, India

In contemporary organizational environments, the role of leadership extends beyond traditional managerial functions to encompass the holistic well-being of employees. It explores the critical behaviors exhibited by leaders that contribute to enhancing workplace well-being. Leadership behavior profoundly influences employees' psychological, emotional, and social health, which affects organizational outcomes such as productivity, job satisfaction, and retention. Leadership behavior that supports workplace well-being is integral to creating a thriving and sustainable organizational environment. By prioritizing empathetic communication, work-life balance, recognition, development, inclusivity, and stress management, leaders can significantly enhance the well-being of their employees, resulting in a more motivated and productive workforce. This study identifies critical leadership behaviors that support workplace well-being and examines their impact through a comprehensive review of existing literature and empirical research.

Chapter 14
Mindful Entrepreneurship: Nurturing Mental Well-Being in Business... 249
S. C. Vetrivel, Kongu Engineering College, India
P. Vidhyapriya, Kongu Engineering College, India
V. P. Arun, JKKN College of Engineering and Technology, India

The landscape of entrepreneurship is dynamic and demanding, often characterized by intense competition, uncertainty, and relentless challenges. In this context, the concept of mindful entrepreneurship emerges as a holistic approach that emphasizes the integration of mindfulness practices into the entrepreneurial journey. This chapter explores the intersection of entrepreneurship and mental well-being, shedding light on the significance of fostering a balanced and resilient mindset for sustainable business success. Mindful entrepreneurship encompasses various practices derived from mindfulness traditions, such as meditation, self-awareness, and cognitive reframing. By incorporating these practices into the entrepreneurial mindset, individuals can cultivate emotional intelligence, stress resilience, and heightened focus. This not only enhances personal well-being but also positively influences organizational culture and performance.

Chapter 15
National and Regional Economic Growth and Development Fostered by Entrepreneurship
Ecosystems 273
José G. Vargas-Hernandez, Tecnològico Nacional de Mèxico, ITS Fresnillo, Mexico

This study aims to analyze the national and regional economic growth and development fostered by entrepreneurship ecosystems. Based on the assumption that entrepreneurship ecosystems theoretical framing has a specific configuration to be applied in national and regional socioeconomic ecosystems for economic growth and development assuming that there is only one to optimize value objectives on terms of economic value and entrepreneurship configuration. The method employed is the descriptive leading to the meta-analytical reflection based on the conceptual, theoretical, and empirical research literature. It is concluded that entrepreneurship ecosystems are powerful means to foster national and

Chapter 16

Navigating Entrepreneurial Stress: Effective Techniques for Reducing Burnout Risk.......................293

Xuan-Hoa Nghiem, Vietnam National University, Hanoi, Vietnam
Shashank Mittal, O.P. Jindal Global University, India
Shivani Dhand, Lovely Professional University, India

This chapter explores effective strategies for managing stress and preventing burnout among entrepreneurs. Given the unique challenges faced in entrepreneurship, understanding the factors contributing to stress is essential. The discussion includes various stress management techniques, such as mindfulness practices, organizational support, and technological tools that enhance productivity and well-being. Future trends, including the integration of artificial intelligence and a focus on holistic wellness, highlight the evolving landscape of stress management. By prioritizing mental health, entrepreneurs can foster resilience, improve work-life balance, and create supportive environments for themselves and their teams. This chapter aims to equip entrepreneurs with actionable insights to navigate their entrepreneurial journey while safeguarding their mental health.

Chapter 17

Social Support Networks and Their Role in Entrepreneurial Well-Being 319

Shashank Mittal, O.P. Jindal Global University, India
Shivani Dhand, Lovely Professional University, India
Xuan-Hoa Nghiem, Vietnam National University, Vietnam

This chapter explores the critical role of social support networks in enhancing entrepreneurial well-being and success. It examines the types of social support, including emotional, informational, and instrumental support, and their impact on mental health, resilience, and business outcomes. The chapter discusses the evolving nature of these networks in the digital age, highlighting the influence of technology and online platforms in fostering connections among entrepreneurs. Additionally, it addresses the challenges faced in building and maintaining meaningful relationships within support networks and provides strategies for cultivating effective connections. Future trends, such as increased digitalization, AI integration, and a focus on diversity and inclusion, are also considered. By understanding and leveraging social support networks, entrepreneurs can create robust ecosystems that contribute to personal and professional growth.

Chapter 18
The Effectiveness of Cognitive-Behavioral Therapy for Entrepreneurial Anxiety 345
Hewawasam P. G. D. Wijethilak, University of Colombo, Sri Lanka
Sandeep Kumar Singh, O.P. Jindal Global University, India
Preet Kanwal, Lovely Professional University, India

Entrepreneurial anxiety is a pervasive issue that impacts the mental health and performance of business leaders, often leading to burnout, impaired decision-making, and reduced productivity. Cognitive-Behavioral Therapy (CBT) has emerged as an effective approach to managing this anxiety by helping entrepreneurs identify and reframe negative thought patterns, develop emotional resilience, and cultivate healthier coping strategies. This chapter explores how CBT techniques can be applied specifically to the challenges entrepreneurs face, such as stress, uncertainty, and isolation. It also discusses the limitations of CBT, particularly the barriers that entrepreneurs encounter in accessing and sustaining therapy. Future directions include leveraging technology to expand access to CBT, integrating mental health strategies into entrepreneurial education, and fostering a supportive entrepreneurial ecosystem that prioritizes mental well-being. By addressing these areas, CBT can continue to play a crucial role in promoting entrepreneurial success and mental health.

Chapter 19
The Effects of Financial Stress on Entrepreneurial Mental Health 363
Mohit Yadav, O.P. Jindal Global University, India
Preet Kanwal, Lovely Professional University, India
Majdi Anwar Quttainah, Kuwait University, Kuwait

This chapter explores the profound effects of financial stress on the mental health of entrepreneurs, highlighting how chronic financial pressures can impair decision-making, foster burnout, and strain personal and professional relationships. Untreated financial stress can lead to long-term mental health issues such as anxiety and depression, adversely impacting both the individual and their business. The chapter examines the role of financial literacy and support systems in mitigating stress, emphasizing the importance of proactive strategies to manage financial challenges. It also discusses the importance of resilience and coping mechanisms in protecting entrepreneurs' mental health and sustaining business performance. Ultimately, the chapter underscores the need for greater awareness and support in addressing financial stress to ensure long-term entrepreneurial success and well-being.

Chapter 20
The Impact of Entrepreneurial Failures on Psychological Resilience 381
    Deepak Kumar Sahoo, Biju Patnaik University of Technology, Rourkela, India
    Thi M. Le, Vietnam National University, Hanoi, Vietnam
    Anish Kumar, O.P. Jindal Global University, India
    Ajay Chandel, Lovely Professional University, India

This chapter explores the profound impact of entrepreneurial failures on psychological resilience, highlighting how setbacks can serve as catalysts for personal growth and innovation. It examines the nature of entrepreneurial failure, the concept of psychological resilience, and the ways in which failure can foster resilience through learning and adaptation. Furthermore, the chapter discusses the psychological impacts of failure, strategies for building resilience post-failure, and the influence of cultural and societal factors. It also emphasizes the role of emotional intelligence in navigating the challenges of entrepreneurship and outlines effective psychological interventions and support systems. By recognizing the importance of mental health and resilience, this chapter underscores the need for a supportive ecosystem that empowers entrepreneurs to overcome obstacles, ultimately contributing to sustainable economic growth and a thriving entrepreneurial community.

Chapter 21
The Role of Emotional Intelligence in Promoting Mental Peace, Healthy Work Environments, and Emotional Well-Being Among Entrepreneurs 401
    Tiago Manuel Horta Reis da Silva, King's College London, UK

Emotional intelligence (EI), defined as the ability to recognize, understand, and manage one's emotions and those of others, is an essential competency for entrepreneurs, influencing both their personal well-being and the health of the workplace they create. Entrepreneurship is often marked by volatility, stress, and emotional highs and lows, making EI a vital tool for navigating these challenges. This chapter explores how EI can contribute to mental peace, create healthy work environments, and foster emotional well-being among entrepreneurs. It also emphasizes the importance of EI in moving and handling procedures, a critical aspect in healthcare industries that entrepreneurs can learn from to promote physical and emotional health in their teams. Finally, the chapter ties these findings to the United Nations' Sustainable Development Goals (SDGs), particularly Goal 3 (Good Health and Well-being) and Goal 8 (Decent Work and Economic Growth), highlighting how EI interventions can support broader global well-being objectives.

Chapter 22
The Role of Mentorship in Mitigating Entrepreneurial Loneliness 427
    Sandeep Kumar Singh, O.P. Jindal Global University, India
    Preet Kanwal, Lovely Professional University, India
    Thi Minh Ngoc Luu, International School, Vietnam National University, Hanoi, Vietnam

The role of mentoring in countering entrepreneurial loneliness, a commonplace problem in the business world, is analyzed in this chapter. It discusses how the entrepreneurial resilience of boosting emotional security, practical advice, and networking opportunities is provided by mentoring. The adoption of mentorship into the digital realm via virtual platforms, matching through AI, and peer-to-peer mentorship are discussed in the chapter. While discussing conflicts such as mismatched expectations and constraints in terms of time, the chapter also throws up the transformational effects that mentorship has on entrepreneurs geared towards helping them through various stages. As the entrepreneurship landscape continues to change, then creating a successful business or individual development, positive mentorship remains a crucial enabler that empowers entrepreneurs to cut across all the complexities of their ventures with confidence.

Chapter 23
The Role of Technology in Facilitating Entrepreneurial Mental Health Support 443
    Mohit Yadav, O.P. Jindal Global University, India
    Preet Kanwal, Lovely Professional University, India
    Rohit, Gulf Medical University, Ajman, UAE

This chapter explores the critical role of technology in facilitating mental health support for entrepreneurs, a demographic facing unique stressors such as financial pressures and long working hours. It examines current technological solutions, including mobile applications, teletherapy platforms, and community engagement tools, that provide accessible and tailored support for mental well-being. The discussion highlights the challenges of integrating technology, such as issues of accessibility, ethical concerns, and the quality of resources, while offering best practices for effective implementation. Looking to the future, the chapter identifies potential innovations, including AI-driven personalization, virtual reality experiences, and data-driven insights, that can enhance mental health support systems. Ultimately, the chapter emphasizes the importance of fostering a resilient entrepreneurial community through thoughtful and responsible technological integration.

Compilation of References 463

About the Contributors 525

Index 531

Foreword

Entrepreneurship is an exhilarating journey filled with both triumphs and challenges. It offers the freedom to innovate, the opportunity to build something meaningful, and the promise of shaping the future. Yet, it also presents an immense mental and emotional toll, a reality often underappreciated in discussions about entrepreneurial success. As someone who has been closely involved with entrepreneurs for many years, I have witnessed firsthand the extraordinary pressure they face—from managing risk and uncertainty to balancing personal and professional lives, all while constantly striving for growth and sustainability.

The book, *Supporting Psychological and Emotional Wellbeing Among Entrepreneurs*, could not be more timely. In a world that places immense value on productivity and innovation, it is easy to forget the human cost of these pursuits. Many entrepreneurs find themselves battling anxiety, isolation, burnout, and self-doubt. Their mental health can sometimes be the silent casualty of their relentless drive to succeed. This book tackles these issues head-on, shining a much-needed light on the emotional and psychological experiences that often go unspoken.

What makes this work especially important is its holistic approach. It does not simply offer coping mechanisms or strategies for managing stress—it delves into the root causes of mental health challenges among entrepreneurs and explores sustainable solutions. The authors and contributors present a diverse range of perspectives, combining academic research with practical insights from seasoned entrepreneurs. This blend of theory and real-world experience makes the book both informative and deeply relatable.

A special acknowledgment must be made to Dr. Muhammad Nawaz Tunio, the editor of this book. His vision, dedication, and deep understanding of both entrepreneurship and mental well-being have made this work possible. Dr. Tunio's ability to curate and bring together such diverse voices has enriched the dialogue on this crucial topic. He has been a steadfast advocate for the importance of supporting entrepreneurs not only in their professional endeavors but also in their personal well being. His commitment to fostering a more compassionate entrepreneurial ecosystem is truly commendable. I extend my heartfelt appreciation to him for leading this important conversation and ensuring that it reaches a broader audience.

In reading through these pages, I found myself reflecting on the many individuals I've worked with over the years. Entrepreneurs are often celebrated for their resilience, their ability to persevere through adversity, and their visionary thinking. But resilience does not mean invulnerability, and no one should have to endure the challenges of entrepreneurship alone or without the proper support. The insights provided here will help entrepreneurs not only recognize the importance of their mental health but also take proactive steps to protect and nurture it.

I believe this book will be a guiding light for entrepreneurs at all stages of their journey, as well as for those who support them—investors, mentors, family members, and mental health professionals. The message is clear: success and well-being are not mutually exclusive. It is possible to build a thriving business while also taking care of one's psychological and emotional health.

I am honored to contribute this foreword to a work that will undoubtedly make a meaningful impact. I hope that as you turn these pages, you find comfort, guidance, and, most importantly, a sense of solidarity in knowing that you are not alone on this journey.

Samreen Tunio
Bahria University, Karachi, Pakistan

Preface

Entrepreneurship is often celebrated for its role in driving economic growth, innovation, and job creation. Yet, behind the success stories of entrepreneurs lies a complex and often overlooked reality: the psychological and emotional challenges they face. While entrepreneurs are frequently depicted as resilient, self-reliant, and adaptable, the pressures they encounter—ranging from financial uncertainty and long working hours to the emotional toll of decision-making and leadership—can have profound effects on their mental health and well-being.

This book, Supporting Psychological and Emotional Wellbeing Among Entrepreneurs, was born out of a desire to address the critical, yet under-explored, aspect of entrepreneurship: the human experience behind the business endeavors. Entrepreneurs navigate uncertain environments, and their success often depends on their ability to handle not only the external demands of their ventures but also their internal emotional landscapes. The mental strain of building and sustaining a business can lead to burnout, anxiety, depression, and other psychological challenges. These struggles are rarely discussed openly, but they are vital for understanding the full scope of entrepreneurship.

Throughout this book, we explore the various dimensions of psychological and emotional well-being that affect entrepreneurs. From stress management and work-life balance to the role of mental health support systems and coping mechanisms, this work aims to shed light on the experiences that often remain in the shadows. Our contributors—researchers, mental health professionals, and successful entrepreneurs—offer insights into the strategies and practices that can foster a healthier entrepreneurial journey.

By addressing these issues, we aim to not only increase awareness but also to encourage dialogue and action around providing entrepreneurs with the psychological support they need to thrive. Entrepreneurship does not need to be synonymous with emotional sacrifice, and it is our hope that this book will inspire entrepreneurs, support networks, policymakers, and educators to prioritize mental well-being in entrepreneurial ecosystems.

The well-being of entrepreneurs is not only crucial to their personal health but also to the sustainability and success of their ventures. This book is a step toward recognizing that caring for the mental health of entrepreneurs is as essential as building a solid business strategy. By nurturing the psychological resilience of entrepreneurs, we pave the way for more innovative, sustainable, and humane business practices.

Chapter Overviews

Chapter 1 delves into the detrimental effects of abusive work environments on the emotional well-being of female entrepreneurs in the Horn of Africa. Through a rigorous analysis involving 400 participants, the chapter employs the Kaiser-Meyer-Olkin (KMO) measure and exploratory factor analysis (EFA) to identify key themes surrounding workplace mistreatment and mental wellness. Following this, confirmatory factor analysis (CFA) validates the reliability of these measurements, while structural equation modeling (SEM) explores the intricate relationships between an abusive work atmosphere, emotional health, and the protective roles of moral and social values. The findings poignantly reveal that while abusive conditions negatively impact mental health, strong moral and social values can mitigate these effects.

Chapter 2 addresses the often intimidating journey of entrepreneurship, particularly in dealing with abusive behaviors from co-founders or investors. It emphasizes the importance of recognizing and addressing various forms of hostility, including harassment and discrimination, that can adversely affect employee morale and organizational productivity. The chapter aims to provide readers with a comprehensive understanding of how such environments impact entrepreneurs' psychological and emotional well-being, urging employers to foster a culture of respect and inclusivity.

Chapter 3 highlights the challenges of maintaining a work-life balance amidst the demands of entrepreneurship. It discusses the common issues of burnout, stress, and blurred boundaries, emphasizing the need for sustainable practices that promote mental wellness. By drawing on research and case studies, the chapter outlines practical strategies such as effective time management, delegation, and mindfulness practices, underscoring the necessity of fostering long-term emotional well-being while navigating the complexities of entrepreneurial life.

Chapter 4 critically analyzes the portrayal of "quiet quitting" in the cult comedy Office Space, arguing that such behaviors risk marginalization and negatively influence workplace morale. The chapter positions the film as both an allegory of employee dissatisfaction and a cautionary tale regarding the limitations of quiet quitting as a coping strategy. Through this lens, it contributes to a broader understanding of workplace dynamics and the pursuit of healthier, more productive environments.

Chapter 5 investigates the pervasive stigma surrounding mental health that hampers individuals from seeking necessary help. This research explores the role of artificial intelligence (AI) in addressing mental health stigma through innovative tools like chatbots and social media analysis. The chapter reviews existing literature on mental health stigma and highlights AI-driven interventions aimed at raising public awareness and fostering empathy, identifying promising strategies for reducing stigma and promoting mental well-being.

Chapter 6 examines the essential role of emotional intelligence (EI) in entrepreneurship, particularly in enhancing leadership effectiveness, team dynamics, and customer relationships. As the business landscape evolves, the integration of EI becomes increasingly critical. The chapter addresses the challenges entrepreneurs face in cultivating EI and discusses its significant impact on employee performance and organizational success. It also explores future trends emphasizing the synergy between EI and artificial intelligence, ultimately advocating for the cultivation of EI to navigate the complexities of entrepreneurship.

Chapter 7 focuses on developing mindfulness-based interventions (MBIs) tailored specifically for entrepreneurs to alleviate stress and improve overall well-being. The chapter presents theoretical foundations of mindfulness and outlines practical strategies for implementing effective MBIs, addressing challenges such as participant resistance and sustainability. By exploring future research directions, the chapter aims to deepen the understanding of how mindfulness can transform entrepreneurial experiences and foster a healthier ecosystem.

Chapter 8 investigates the implicit influence of entrepreneurial leadership on workers' emotional well-being within the unorganized restaurant sector in Delhi/NCR. The research highlights this sector's under-researched nature and emphasizes the potential of crises to strengthen enterprises through enhanced social networks and interpersonal relationships, ultimately contributing to improved employee well-being.

Chapter 9 underscores the significance of mindfulness in entrepreneurship, linking mindfulness practices to enhanced focus, reduced stress, and greater emotional resilience. The chapter identifies common challenges entrepreneurs face in practicing mindfulness and discusses future trends, such as technological integration, while positioning mindfulness as a transformative tool that empowers entrepreneurs in navigating their journeys.

Chapter 10 explores the critical role of wellness programs in combating entrepreneurial burnout, emphasizing their importance in fostering resilience and sustainable practices. The chapter evaluates various wellness initiatives and innovative digital solutions, addressing the challenges of implementation while highlighting the shift towards personalized, technology-driven solutions that promote holistic health.

Chapter 11 examines the intricate relationship between entrepreneurial success and personal well-being, emphasizing the interplay of ambition, mental health, and fulfillment. It highlights the importance of work-life balance and community support systems, advocating for a holistic approach to nurturing both personal fulfillment and entrepreneurial achievement.

Chapter 12 investigates the relationship between a healthy work environment and entrepreneurs' mental health, particularly focusing on women. It identifies key factors that influence mental well-being and emphasizes strategies employers can adopt to create supportive environments, underscoring the significance of stress management and a culture of mutual respect.

Chapter 13 highlights the evolving role of leadership in promoting employee well-being. It explores critical behaviors that enhance psychological, emotional, and social health, arguing that empathetic communication and inclusivity are essential for creating a thriving organizational environment.

Chapter 14 introduces the concept of mindful entrepreneurship, advocating for the integration of mindfulness practices into the entrepreneurial journey. The chapter discusses how such practices foster emotional intelligence, resilience, and a balanced mindset, ultimately contributing to sustainable business success.

Chapter 15 analyzes the role of entrepreneurship ecosystems in driving national and regional economic growth. It emphasizes the importance of a theoretical framework tailored to the unique dynamics of entrepreneurship, concluding that effective ecosystems can optimize value and foster economic development.

Chapter 16 discusses effective strategies for managing stress and preventing burnout among entrepreneurs. It outlines various techniques, including mindfulness and technological tools, while highlighting the importance of prioritizing mental health to foster resilience and supportive environments.

Chapter 17 examines the role of social support networks in enhancing entrepreneurial well-being, exploring the types of support and their impact on mental health. The chapter discusses the challenges of maintaining meaningful connections in a digital age and provides strategies for cultivating effective networks.

Chapter 18 focuses on the pervasive issue of entrepreneurial anxiety and the effectiveness of Cognitive-Behavioral Therapy (CBT) in addressing this challenge. The chapter explores how CBT techniques can be tailored to entrepreneurs and discusses barriers to accessing therapy, advocating for a supportive ecosystem that prioritizes mental health.

Chapter 19 investigates the profound effects of financial stress on entrepreneurs' mental health, examining how chronic pressures can impair decision-making and relationships. It highlights the importance of financial literacy and resilience in mitigating stress, emphasizing the need for increased awareness and support.

Chapter 20 explores the relationship between entrepreneurial failures and psychological resilience, arguing that setbacks can catalyze personal growth. The chapter examines strategies for building resilience and the influence of emotional intelligence in navigating entrepreneurial challenges.

Chapter 21 addresses the importance of emotional intelligence (EI) for entrepreneurs, exploring how EI contributes to personal well-being and healthy workplace environments. The chapter emphasizes EI's relevance in healthcare-related entrepreneurship and ties its findings to global well-being objectives, particularly the United Nations' Sustainable Development Goals.

Chapter 22 analyzes the role of mentoring in alleviating entrepreneurial loneliness, discussing how effective mentorship can bolster emotional security and provide valuable networking opportunities. The chapter highlights the transformative impact of mentorship while addressing potential conflicts and challenges.

Chapter 23 investigates the critical role of technology in supporting mental health for entrepreneurs. It examines current technological solutions and challenges, advocating thoughtful integration to foster a resilient entrepreneurial community and enhance mental well-being.

We trust that readers from all walks of life, entrepreneurs, business leaders, mentors, and mental health professionals, will find this book a valuable resource for understanding and supporting the well-being of those who choose to embark on the entrepreneurial path.

Muhammad Nawaz Tunio
University of Sufism and Modern Sciences, Pakistan

Acknowledgments

The creation of this book, Supporting Psychological and Emotional Wellbeing Among Entrepreneurs, has been a deeply rewarding journey, and it would not have been possible without the support, guidance, and contributions of many individuals and organizations. This work represents a collective effort to address an often-overlooked but critical aspect of entrepreneurship—mental health and well-being.

I would like to extend my gratitude to the contributors and authors who shared their knowledge, experiences, and research for this book. Their insights into the psychological challenges faced by entrepreneurs and the strategies for overcoming them are invaluable. Your work and dedication to supporting the mental health of entrepreneurs will undoubtedly make a lasting impact.

Special thanks go to my family, friends, and colleagues, whose support has been unwavering. Your encouragement, patience, and understanding have allowed me to devote the time and energy necessary to complete this project. You have been my pillar of strength throughout this process.

Finally, I want to acknowledge the entrepreneurs worldwide, whose resilience and determination inspire us all. I hope this book will contribute to creating a more supportive and empathetic entrepreneurial ecosystem that values the mental and emotional well-being of those who dare to dream and build.

Thank you to everyone who played a role in the creation of this book. Your contributions have made this work possible, and I am deeply appreciative of your support.

Muhammad Nawaz Tunio
The University of Sufism and Modern Sciences, Pakistan

Introduction

Entrepreneurship is often portrayed as a thrilling, rewarding, and transformative career path. It promises autonomy, the opportunity to innovate, and the ability to shape the future. Yet, behind the glamour of entrepreneurship lies an equally important, but frequently ignored, aspect—the psychological and emotional challenges that entrepreneurs face on their journey. These challenges can affect the mental health, decision-making, and overall well-being of entrepreneurs in ways that are often difficult to quantify but crucial to understand.

As entrepreneurial ecosystems grow and more individuals venture into the world of business, the pressures and demands on entrepreneurs have intensified. The responsibility of running a business, managing financial risks, leading teams, and meeting customer expectations creates a high-stress environment. For many, this results in significant mental health struggles, including burnout, anxiety, depression, and feelings of isolation. Despite these growing concerns, conversations around the mental health of entrepreneurs have lagged behind, leaving many without the support they need to maintain their well-being while pursuing their business goals.

This book, *Supporting Psychological and Emotional Wellbeing Among Entrepreneurs*, aims to fill this critical gap. It explores the often-overlooked side of entrepreneurship—the emotional resilience required to navigate uncertainty, manage stress, and cope with failure. By providing a platform for entrepreneurs, researchers, and mental health professionals to share their experiences and insights, this book sheds light on the psychological realities that accompany the entrepreneurial journey and offers practical strategies to support the mental and emotional health of entrepreneurs.

The Entrepreneurial Paradox

Entrepreneurs are frequently celebrated for their resilience and ability to overcome adversity. However, this narrative often creates an unrealistic expectation that entrepreneurs must always be strong, self-reliant, and immune to failure. In reality, the entrepreneurial path is fraught with uncertainty, and the pressure to maintain a façade of success can be overwhelming. The paradox is clear: while entrepreneurs are seen as symbols of independence and innovation, they are often isolated from the very support systems that could help them cope with the immense pressures they face.

The failure to address mental health challenges in entrepreneurship can have far-reaching consequences. Entrepreneurs who experience chronic stress or burnout may make poor business decisions, become disengaged from their ventures, or even abandon promising ideas altogether. Moreover, untreated mental health issues can have a ripple effect, impacting employees, investors, and the wider entrepreneurial ecosystem.

Why Mental Health Matters in Entrepreneurship

Supporting the psychological and emotional well-being of entrepreneurs is not just a personal matter; it is also a critical factor in business success. A growing body of research highlights the link between mental health and entrepreneurial performance. Entrepreneurs who actively manage their stress and prioritize their mental well-being are more likely to innovate, build sustainable businesses, and foster positive workplace cultures. In contrast, those who neglect their mental health may face declining productivity, strained relationships, and ultimately, business failure.

This book argues that mental health is an essential component of entrepreneurial resilience. Just as entrepreneurs invest in their business skills and financial knowledge, they must also invest in their mental and emotional well-being. By doing so, they can create a solid foundation for personal and professional success.

A Call to Action

Supporting Psychological and Emotional Wellbeing Among Entrepreneurs is more than just a book; it is a call to action. It urges entrepreneurs, business leaders, policymakers, and mental health professionals to acknowledge the profound impact of mental health on entrepreneurial success. By addressing the psychological needs of entrepreneurs, we can create more resilient, innovative, and sustainable businesses.

Entrepreneurs are the lifeblood of innovation and economic growth. To continue driving positive change, they must be supported not only in their business endeavors but also in their emotional and mental well-being. This book is a step toward recognizing that entrepreneurship is as much about personal growth and emotional health as it is about profit and success. It is our hope that through the insights shared in these pages, entrepreneurs will feel empowered to prioritize their well-being, seek support when needed, and ultimately thrive both personally and professionally.

Muhammad Nawaz Tunio
University of Sufism and Modern Sciences, Pakistan

Chapter 1
Abusive Work Environment Effect on Female Entrepreneurs' Emotional Wellbeing by Mediation of Social and Moral Values in the Horn of Africa

Metasebia Adula
https://orcid.org/0000-0001-5732-2850
Bule Hora University, Ethiopia

Shashi Kant
https://orcid.org/0000-0003-4722-5736
Bule Hora University, Ethiopia

Sofi Badi
Bule Hora University, Ethiopia

Mona Kumari
https://orcid.org/0009-0001-0476-5831
Government College for Women Bahadurgarh, Jhajjar, India

ABSTRACT

This chapter investigates the impact of an abusive work environment on the emotional well-being of female entrepreneurs in the Horn of Africa, with a focus on the mediating role of moral and social values. Using a sample of 400 female entrepreneurs, the study assesses whether the dataset is suitable for factor analysis using the Kaiser-Meyer-Olkin (KMO) measure. An exploratory factor analysis (EFA) is used to identify key ideas related to workplace mistreatment, moral and social values, and mental wellness. Next, the factor structure is confirmed and the reliability of the measuring devices is confirmed using Confirmatory Factor Analysis (CFA). Next, using structural equation modeling (SEM), the relationships between these variables are investigated, with an emphasis on the effects of an abusive work environment on emotional well-being and the findings indicate that abusive work conditions have a detrimental effect

DOI: 10.4018/979-8-3693-3673-1.ch001

Copyright ©2025, IGI Global. Copying or distributing in print or electronic forms without written permission of IGI Global is prohibited.

on the mental health of female entrepreneurs, but that these impacts can be mitigated by strong moral and social values.

INTRODUCTION

The notion of the Condition of cruelty at workplace and its harmful impact on women start-up enterprisers' psychological emotional health, arbitrated by societal and ethical norms, is of remarkable international significance, particularly in communities like the Eastern Africa where indigenous rituals ethos and sex founded agility play a crucial function in deciding workplace involvements. The birth of this notion can be traced back to the growing recognition of the assimilation among environments at workplaces and mental health, especially concerning indigenous inhabitants such as womenfolk's marketplace persons in societies with exclusive socio-indigenous rituals landscapes (Baluku et al., 2023). Existing empirical literature has shed light on the contrary impacts of workplace abuse on persons' emotional health and the function of Condition of cruelty at workplace in safeguarding or worsening these impacts (Tsehayu & Østebø, 2020). However, real-world barriers persist in impassively solving and justifying the outcomes of condition of cruelty at workplaces, especially among women start-up enterprisers in the Eastern Africa. Investigation vacuums remain in understanding the specific mechanisms through which Condition of cruelty at workplace influence the association among workplace abuse and psychological emotional health in this particular context (Mshilla, 2021).

This chapter aims to bridge these vacuums and address the real-world barriers by delving into the interplay among condition of cruelty at workplaces, societal and ethical norms, and the psychological emotional health of women start-up enterprisers in the Eastern Africa. By exploring these associations in-depth, this investigation seeks to offer understandings that can advise future investigators and officials in developing targeted interventions and assist mechanisms to safeguard the mental health of women start-up enterprisers in alike indigenous rituals settings. The central question that motivates this investigation is: *"How does Condition of cruelty at workplace mediate the impact of condition of cruelty at workplaces on the psychological emotional health of women start-up enterprisers in the Eastern Africa, and what implications does this association hold for fostering a assistive and empowering workplace culture in the country?"* This inquiry serves as the guiding inspiration for this investigation attempt, promising to uncover critical understandings that not only contribute to academic discourse but also offer real-world implications for fostering healthier environments at workplaces and promoting the emotional health of women start-up enterprisers in the country and beyond.

Likely, in Ethiopia, Rahel, a determined marketplace woman, grapples with subtle forms of workplace mental abuse and inequality at workplace due to rooted societal norms that undermine women's authority in marketplace. The burden to follow to inflexible sex founded functions while striving for achievement amplifies the emotional strain she involvements, leading to feelings of isolation and burnout (Noordin, 2021). These real-life illustrations underscore the real-world barriers that women start-up enterprisers in the Eastern Africa confront in the face of condition of cruelty at workplaces. The lack of assistive structures, deep-seated indigenous rituals biases, and partial resources aggravate the harmful impacts of workplace abuse on their psychological emotional health, creating barriers to their work life growth and individual fulfillment (King'ong'o, 2022). By exploring the agility of how condition of cruelty at workplace mediates the impact of condition of cruelty at workplaces on women start-up enterprisers' emotional health in the Eastern Africa, this investigation aims to shed light on the intricacies of this complex association. Through a comprehensive analysis of these factors and their interplay, this investigation endeavor seeks to offer actionable understandings and real-world recommendations to address the barriers faced by women start-up enterprisers in the country.

Statement of the Problem

The ideal state envisions a workplace environment where women start-up enterprisers can thrive without fear of abuse, discrimination, or emotional distress. However, contradictory evidence, vacuums in investigation, inconclusive results, and theoretical and real-world barriers hinder the realization of this ideal state (Mshilla, 2021). Contradictory evidence within the existing literature adds complexity to the understanding of how conditions of cruelty at workplaces affect the psychological emotional health of women start-up enterprisers in the Eastern Africa. While some investigations suggest a direct association among workplace abuse and negative mental health outcomes, others propose that Condition of cruelty at workplace may act as protective factors, justifying the impact of abuse. These conflicting outcomes underscore the need for a comprehensive investigation that considers the interplay of multiple factors in deciding women's involvement in the workplace (Guye et al., 2023).

Inconclusive results from previous investigation efforts further contribute to the ambiguity surrounding this situation. The lack of agreement on the mechanisms through which condition of cruelty at workplace influence the association among workplace abuse and psychological emotional health leaves critical questions unanswered. Theoretical and knowledge vacuums persist in understanding the specific pathways through which indigenous rituals norms, societal expectations, and individual norms interact to either exacerbate or alleviate the emotional toll of condition of cruelty at workplaces on women start-up enterprisers in the Eastern Africa (Dsouza & Panakaje, 2023). Contextual vacuums, rooted in the exclusive socio-indigenous rituals landscape of the Eastern Africa, present additional barriers in solving the psychological emotional health of women start-up enterprisers. Indigenous rituals norms, sex founded agility, and traditional beliefs shape the involvements of women in the workplace, influencing their responses to abuse and their access to assist systems. Real-world barriers, such as partial resources, institutional barriers, and a lack of awareness, pose obstacles to implementing interventions that promote healthier environments at workplace for women start-up enterprisers in the country (Kandilige et al., 2023).

This investigation aims to fill these vacuums by conducting a comprehensive investigation into the agility of condition of cruelty at workplaces and their impact on women start up enterprisers' psychological emotional health in the Eastern Africa. By examining the mediating function of Condition of cruelty at workplace in this association, this investigation endeavor seeks to offer a holistic understanding of the factors that shape women's involvements in the workplace. The understandings generated from this investigation will not only contribute to academic knowledge but also offer real-world implications for officials, organizations, and future investigators seeking to create assistive and empowering environments at workplaces for women start-up enterprisers in the country. By solving the complexities of this situation and offering evidence-founded recommendations, this investigation aims to pave the way for positive change and advocacy efforts that prioritize the psychological emotional health and success of women start-up enterprisers in the Eastern Africa.

Theoretical Lenses

Conservation of Resources (COR) theory in examining the impact of condition of cruelty at workplaces on women start-up enterprisers' psychological emotional health, arbitrated by Condition of cruelty at workplace in the Eastern Africa, several related theories can offer valuable understandings into the agility at play. One prominent theoretical lens for this investigation is the Conservation of Resources (COR) theory. According to COR theory, individuals strive to acquire, maintain, and protect valuable resources, including those that are material, individual, or societal. Workplace abuse can be seen as a depletion of these resources, leading to emotional strain and negative outcomes for women start-up enterprisers. Condition of cruelty at workplace may act as resources that buffer the impacts of abuse, aligning with the core tenets of COR theory (De Clercq et al., 2022).

Additionally, Societal Cognitive Theory (SCT) can offer a framework for understanding how women start-up enterprisers in the Eastern Africa observe, model, and learn from the behaviors of others in their societal and indigenous rituals contexts. SCT emphasizes the function of observational learning, self-efficacy, and the interplay among individual, behavioral, and situation-based factors in deciding individuals' responses to workplace barriers. This theory can help elucidate how Condition of cruelty at workplace influence women's perceptions of and reactions to condition of cruelty at workplaces (Sana et al., 2021). Also, the Function Congruity Theory of Prejudice (Eagly & Karau, 2002) is relevant in the context of women start-up enterprisers facing abuse in male-dominated industries. This theory posits that individuals are often judged founded on the extent to which their sex founded functions align with societal expectations. In the Eastern Africa, where traditional sex founded functions may clash with women's aspirations in start-up enterprise, understanding how sex founded stereotypes and function expectations impact women's emotional responses to workplace abuse is crucial (Kandilige et al., 2023).

The main theoretical lens for this investigation is likely to be the Conservation of Resources (COR) theory, given its emphasis on how individuals respond to stressors that threaten their resources and well-being. By applying the COR framework, investigators can explore how condition of cruelty at workplaces deplete emotional resources and how Condition of cruelty at workplace function as protective resources that help women start-up enterprisers in the Eastern Africa cope with and navigate the barriers they face. This theory can offer a comprehensive understanding of the mechanisms through which workplace abuse influences psychological emotional health and how Condition of cruelty at workplace play a crucial function in mediating these impacts, providing a solid theoretical foundation for the investigation's exploration of this complex association.

Definition and Origin of Concepts

Abuse at the Workplace: A Condition of cruelty at workplace refers to a workplace where staffs, in this case, women start-up enterprisers, are subjected to mistreatment, mental abuse, discrimination, or other forms of negative behavior that can harm their well-being and performance. This can include verbal, physical, or emotional abuse, as well as behaviors that undermine individuals' dignity, autonomy, and sense of safety in the workplace (Dsouza & Panakaje, 2023).

Female Enterpriser: A women start-up enterpriser is a woman who organizes and manages a marketplace venture, typically taking on financial risks in the hope of achieving success and creating norm. Women start-up enterprisers play a vital function in economic development and empowerment, facing exclusive barriers and opportunities in the marketplace world due to sex founded-related biases and societal expectations (Zhou et al., 2024).

Psychological Emotional Health: Psychological emotional health encompasses an individual's mental health, emotional resilience, and overall psychological state. It reflects one's ability to cope with stress, maintain a positive outlook, and navigate barriers impactfully. In the context of women start-up enterprisers, psychological emotional health is crucial for their success, satisfaction, and quality of life (De Clercq et al., 2022).

Societal Norms: Societal norms are societal beliefs, norms, and principles that advise individuals' behaviors, interactions, and decisions within a community or culture. These norms influence how people perceive themselves and others, shape their associations, and inform their ethical judgments and priorities in various domains of life (Saleem et al., 2020).

Ethical Norms: Ethical norms are individual principles and beliefs about what is right and wrong, ethical and unethical, just and unjust. These norms govern individuals' conduct, choices, and judgments, reflecting their sense of integrity, fairness, and responsibility towards themselves and other (Saleh et al., 2023).

EMPIRICAL LITERATURE REVIEW

Abusing Workplace and Psychological Emotional Health

Investigation by Adula et al. (2023) reveals a strong association among workplace bullying and decreased psychological emotional health among staffs, highlighting the harmful impacts of long-term exposure to abusive behaviors in the workplace. Their outcomes underscore the significance of solving organizational culture and implementing impactive interventions to mitigate the negative impact of workplace abuse on staffs' mental health. Building on this investigation, a investigation by Asefa et al. (2024) further explores the psychological outcomes of workplace aggression and mental abuse on individuals' psychological emotional health. The investigators emphasize the function of perceived injustice and power agility in exacerbating the negative impacts of abusive behaviors, shedding light on the mechanisms through which workplace abuse can erode emotional resilience and contribute to stress-related disorders.

Moreover, investigation by Dereso et al. (2023) delves into the assimilation among abusive supervision and psychological emotional health, highlighting the harmful impacts of authoritarian leadership styles on staffs' psychological health. The investigation underscores the significance of fostering a assistive and respectful environments at workplace to safeguard staffs' psychological emotional health and promote a culture of trust and well-being within organizations. Furthermore, the results of several studies on workplace abuse and emotional consequences are combined in a meta-analysis, which exposes a pattern of unfavorable correlations between staff members' psychological and emotional well-being and abusive behaviors such mental abuse and rudeness. The researchers stress that in order to address the underlying causes of workplace abuse and safeguard the mental health of employees, comprehensive treatments that focus on both individual and organizational aspects are necessary (Brieger et al., 2024).

Abusing Working Environment and Societal Ethical Norms

Investigation by Neneh (2024) delves into the impacts of organizational toxicity on staffs' ethical reasoning and ethical decision-making, highlighting how exposure to abusive behaviors can erode individuals' commitment to ethical principles and compromise their integrity in the workplace. The investigation underscores the significance of fostering a culture of respect and fairness to uphold Condition of cruelty at workplace within organizations. Expanding on this line of inquiry, a investigation by Ni et al. (2024) explores the influence of workplace incivility on societal cohesion and ethical norms among staff, revealing a negative impact on inter individual trust, cooperation, and ethical behavior within teams. The investigators emphasize the ripple impacts of abusive interactions on group agility and organizational culture, underscoring the need to address toxic behaviors to uphold Condition of cruelty at workplace in the workplace.

Moreover, an investigation by Kant & Adula (2024) investigates the association among abusive supervision and staffs' perceptions of organizational justice and ethical climate, highlighting how authoritarian leadership styles can undermine trust, fairness, and ethical standards within a environments at workplace. The investigation points to the significance of promoting transparency, accountability, and ethical leadership practices to safeguard Condition of cruelty at workplace in the face of abusive behaviors. Additionally, a meta-analysis by Panigrahi et al. (2024) synthesizes outcomes from multiple investigations on workplace aggression and its impact on societal associations and ethical norms, revealing a consistent pattern of negative associations among abusive behaviors and staffs' perceptions of organizational justice and ethical conduct. The investigators stress the function of organizational policies, leadership practices, and intervention strategies in fostering a culture of respect, empathy, and integrity to counteract the corrosive impacts of workplace abuse on societal and ethical norms.

Societal Ethical Norms and Psychological Emotional Health

Investigation by Birhane et al. (2024) delves into the function of situation-based norms in deciding pro-situation-based behaviors, demonstrating how individual beliefs and ethical commitments influence individuals' attitudes towards sustainability and their willingness to engage in situation-based responsible actions. The investigation underscores the significance of cultivating a sense of situation-based leadership and promoting norms that prioritize conservation for enhancing overall situation-based emotional health. Expanding on this investigation, a investigation by Durga et al. (2024) explores the impact of societal norms and norms on collective situation-based engagement within communities, highlighting the power of shared beliefs, normative influences, and ethical imperatives in driving situation-based initiatives and promoting sustainable practices. The investigators emphasize the function of societal cohesion, altruism, and a sense of responsibility towards future generations in fostering a culture of situation-based care and enhancing the emotional health of both individuals and ecosystems.

Moreover, an investigation by Nyoach et al. (2024) investigates the association among ethical reasoning and situation-based decision-making, revealing how ethical principles and ethical norms shape individuals' perceptions of situation-based situations and advise their actions towards sustainable outcomes. The investigation underscores the need to integrate ethical considerations, empathy, and a sense of justice into situation-based policies and practices to promote long-term ecological emotional health and societal equity. Additionally, a meta-analysis by Birhane et al. (2024) synthesizes outcomes from multiple investigations on the influence of ethical norms on situation-based attitudes and behaviors, highlighting the complex interplay among individual norms, indigenous rituals norms, and situation-based outcomes. The investigators emphasize the significance of fostering a norms-founded approach to situation-based education, advocacy, and policymaking to promote a holistic understanding of sustainability and cultivate a sense of interconnectedness among human societies and the natural world.

Abuse at the Workplace, Emotional Well-Being and Societal and Ethical Norms

Investigation by Kant & Adula (2024) offers initial understandings, highlighting the disproportionate barriers faced by women in start-up enterprise in the country, including involvements of workplace abuse that can harmfully affect their mental health and emotional resilience. The investigation underscores the need to explore the function of Condition of cruelty at workplace as potential buffers in justifying the negative impact of condition of cruelty on women start-up enterprisers' psychological emotional health. Building on this foundation, a investigation by Jabo et al. (2024) delves into the psychosocial outcomes of workplace mental abuse and discrimination on women start-up enterprisers in Somalia, emphasizing the interplay among indigenous rituals norms, societal assist networks, and emotional responses to condition of cruelty at workplaces. The outcomes suggest that adherence to ethical norms such as integrity and solidarity can play a crucial function in empowering women to navigate challenging circumstances and preserve their emotional health in the face of adversity.

Also, investigation by Guyo et al. (2024) explores the association among workplace abuse and psychological emotional health among women start-up enterprisers in Ethiopia, highlighting the mediating function of societal norms such as community cohesion and collective empowerment in fostering resilience and coping mechanisms. The investigation underscores the significance of fostering a assistive and inclusive environments at workplace that upholds ethical principles and societal norms to safeguard women start-up enterprisers' psychological emotional health in the country. Additionally, a meta-analysis by Neneh (2024) synthesizes outcomes from multiple investigations on workplace mistreatment and its impact on emotional outcomes among women in the Eastern Africa. The investigation underscores the need for tailored interventions and policy reforms that address the assimilation of condition of cruelty at workplaces, societal and ethical norms, and women start-up enterprisers' emotional health to promote sex founded equity and well-being in the start-up setting.

Conceptual Framework

Figure 1. Conceptual framework

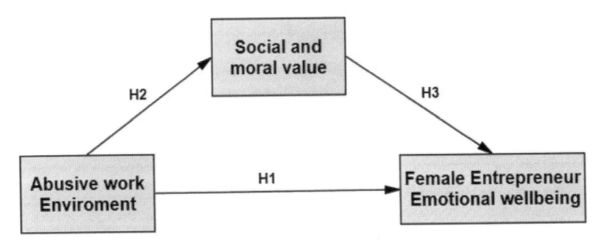

RESEARCH METHODOLOGY

The investigation methodology employed in investigating the impact of a condition of cruelty at workplace on women start-up enterprisers' emotional well-being through societal and ethical norms in the Eastern Africa involved a quantitative investigation approach. The investigation utilized a sample size of 390 participants drawn from the target population. The choice of a quantitative investigation approach allowed for the systematic collection and analysis of numerical information to address the investigation objectives impassively. Initially, the Kaiser-Meyer-Olkin (KMO) measure of sampling adequacy was calculated to assess the suitability of the information for exploratory factor analysis (EFA). The KMO norm helped in determining whether the information was appropriate for further analysis. Subsequently, exploratory factor analysis (EFA) was conducted to identify the underlying factors within the collected information. This step involved examining the associations among observed variables to uncover latent constructs.

Following the EFA, structural equation modeling (SEM) was employed using the AMOS software to test the hypothesized associations among the variables in the investigation model. SEM allowed for the examination of direct and indirect impacts among the variables of interest. This analytical approach offered a comprehensive understanding of how an condition of cruelty at workplace impacts women start-up enterprisers' emotional well-being through the mediating factors of societal and ethical norms in the context of the Eastern Africa. Moreover, the scale development process was undertaken in the past tense to ensure the validity and reliability of the measurement instruments used in the investigation. This involved designing, refining, and validating scales to measure constructs such as condition of cruelty at workplace, emotional well-being, societal norms, and ethical norms among women start-up enterprisers. By conducting scale development in the past tense, the investigation ensured that the measurement tools were rigorously tested and refined before information collection commenced. In conclusion, the rigorous investigation methodology employed in this investigation, encompassing sample selection, quantitative analysis techniques like EFA and SEM using AMOS software, and scale development in the past tense, offered valuable understandings into the intricate association among condition of cruelty at workplace and women start-up enterprisers' emotional well-being arbitrated by societal and ethical norms in the Eastern Africa.

Data Analysis

Table 1. Bartlett's & KMO Test

Sampling Adequacy with Kaiser-Meyer-Olkin Portion		.849
Sphericity with Bartlett's Assessment	Approx. Chi-Square	1420.740
	df	89
	p-worth	.000

Source: Authors

The table 1 results of the Kaiser-Meyer-Olkin (KMO) measure of sampling adequacy and Bartlett's Test of Sphericity indicate that the information set used in this investigation is suitable for factor analysis. The KMO norm of 0.849 surpasses the commonly accepted threshold of 0.7, suggesting that the variables in the information set are sufficiently interrelated to proceed with factor analysis. This indicates that the information set offers an adequate amount of information for meaningful factors to be extracted during analysis. Additionally, Bartlett's Test of Sphericity yielded an approximate chi-square norm of 1420.740 with 89 degrees of freedom and a statistically remarkable p-norm of .000. The significance of the test suggests that associations among variables in the information set are sufficiently different from zero, further assisting with the suitability of the information for factor analysis. This implies that the variables in the information set are not independent and exhibit remarkable inter associations, justifying the use of factor analysis techniques to uncover underlying factors within the information.

Table 2. Total Variance Explained

	Initial Eigen norms			Extraction Sums of Squared Loadings			Rotation Sums of Squared Loadings		
	Total	% of Variance	Cumulative %	Total	% of Variance	Cumulative %	Total	% of Variance	Cumulative %
1	4.5	32.335	32.335	4.5	32.335	32.335	3.0	21.551	21.551
2	1.3	9.787	42.022	1.3	9.787	42.022	2.1	15.591	36.942
3	1.3	9.087	51.110	1.3	9.087	51.110	1.9	14.168	51.110
4	.94	6.782	57.892						

Extraction Method: PCA
Source: Authors

Table 2 presents the Total Variance Explained through different stages of analysis, including Initial Eigen- norms, Extraction Sums of Squared Loadings, and Rotation Sums of Squared Loadings, following a Principal Component Analysis (PCA) extraction method. The results indicate that the first principal component accounts for a substantial portion of the variance, with an initial eigen-norm of 4.5, explaining 32.335% of the total variance. This component retains its significance throughout the extraction and rotation stages, consistently explaining around one-third of the variance. The second and third components also contribute meaningfully to the variance, with initial eigen-norms of 1.3 each, explaining 9.787% and 9.087% of the variance, respectively. By the end of the rotation process, the first three components collectively account for 51.110% of the total variance, indicating that these components capture a remarkable portion of the variability present in the information. The results suggest that the information can be impassively summarized and structured into a smaller set of meaningful components without losing a substantial amount of information.

Confirmatory Factor Analysis

The principle component arrangement of a set of advised proxies is verified using a type of statistics known as confirmatory principle component examination. Founded on the underlying frame job and correlatives among observed proxies, investigations can evaluate hypotheses utilizing CFA. To evaluate the hypothesis that there is a association among the proxies that are being steered and the latent notion that underpin them, the inquiry employed CFA under table 3.

Table 3. Covariances

Covariance			Estimate	S.E.	C.R.	P	Hy.
Societal and Ethical Norms	<-->	Condition of cruelty at workplace	.867	.163	5.310	.00	H2
Societal and Ethical Norms	<-->	Women Start-up enterpriser's Emotional well-being	.566	.185	3.059	.00	H3
Condition of cruelty at workplace	<-->	Women Start-up enterpriser's Emotional well-being	.445	.176	2.52	.00	H1

Source: Authors

Table 3 presents the covariance's among Condition of cruelty at workplace, Emerging innovations, and Women Start-up enterpriser's Emotional well-being, along with their respective estimates, standard errors, critical ratios, p-norms, and hypothesis designations. The covariance estimate among Condition of cruelty at workplace and Condition of cruelty at workplace is reported at 0.854, with a standard error of 0.145. This covariance is statistically remarkable, with a critical ratio (C.R.) of 5.889 and a p-norm denoted as .00 (indicating significance at the 0.001 level), assisting Hypothesis H2. This result suggests a strong positive association among the use of Condition of cruelty at workplace and the adoption of Condition of cruelty at workplace among women start-up enterprisers. Also, the covariance estimate among Condition of cruelty at workplace and Women Start-up enterpriser's Emotional well-being stands at 0.563, with a standard error of 0.154. This covariance is also statistically remarkable, with a critical ratio of 3.655 and a p-norm denoted as .00 (indicating significance at the 0.001 level), assisting Hypothesis H3. This finding indicates a positive association among the utilization of Condition of cruelty at workplace and the work-life balance of women start-up enterprisers.

Lastly, the covariance estimate among Condition of cruelty at workplace and Women Start-up enterpriser's Emotional well-being is 0.374, with a standard error of 0.076. This covariance is statistically remarkable, with a critical ratio of 4.92 and a p-norm denoted as .00 (indicating significance at the

0.001 level), assisting Hypothesis H1. This result suggests a positive association among the adoption of Condition of cruelty at workplace and the work-life balance of women start-up enterprisers. Overall, the remarkable covariance's observed in the analysis offer empirical evidence assisting the interconnections among Condition of cruelty at workplace, emerging innovations, and Women Start-up enterpriser's Emotional well-being, shedding light on the complex agility and influences within this ecosystem.

Table 4. Validity Concern

	CR	AVE	MSV	MaxR(H)	EI	DT	FEEW
AWE	0.732	0.643	0.319	0.852	**0.654**		
SMV	0.758	0.657	0.132	0.763	0.171	**0.665**	
FEEW	0.793	0.603	0.374	0.797	0.383	0.193	**0.684**

Note: AWE= Abuse environments at workplace; SMV= societal and ethical norm; FEEW= Women Start-up enterpriser's Emotional well-being

Source: Authors

Table 4 offers information related to the validity concerns of the constructs in the investigation, including Composite Reliability (CR), Average Variance Extracted (AVE), Maximum Shared Variance (MSV), and Maximum Variance Extracted (MaxR(H)), focusing on the constructs Condition of cruelty at workplace (AWE), Societal and ethical norm (SMV), and Women Start-up enterpriser Psychological emotional health (FEEW). For Condition of cruelty at workplace (AWE), the Composite Reliability (CR) is 0.732, indicating an acceptable level of internal consistency among the items measuring this construct. The Average Variance Extracted (AVE) is 0.643, suggesting that 64.3% of the variance in the observed variables is captured by the latent construct. The Maximum Shared Variance (MSV) is 0.319, which is less than the AVE, indicating convergent validity. The MaxR(H) norm of 0.852 is higher than the AVE, suggesting discriminant validity with other constructs. Regarding Societal and ethical norm (SMV), the CR is 0.758, indicating good reliability. The AVE is 0.657, demonstrating that 65.7% of the variance is explained by the construct. The MSV is 0.132, which is less than the AVE, assisting convergent validity. The MaxR(H) norm of 0.763 suggests discriminant validity. For Women Start-up enterpriser Psychological emotional health (FEEW), the CR is 0.793, indicating strong internal consistency. The AVE is 0.603, showing that 60.3% of the variance is accounted for by the construct. The MSV is 0.374, lower than the AVE, assisting convergent validity. The MaxR(H) norm of 0.797 suggests discriminant validity with other constructs.

Mediating Function Examination

Figure 2. Structure equation model

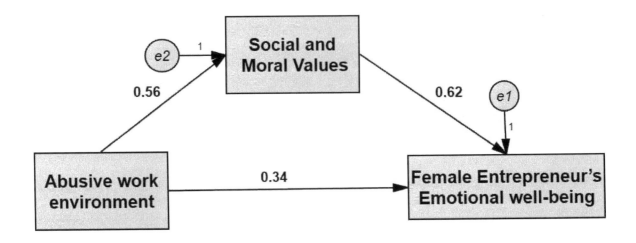

Model Fit Indices

Table 5. Model Fitness

Sig.	Chi-Sq	RMR	Fitness Goodness	Fitness Confirmatory	TLI	RMSEA
0.003	1.067	.034	0.906	0.904	0.902	.031

Source: Authors

Table 5 presents a range of indices used to evaluate the model fit of the information. The statistical significance level of the model is reported as 0.003, indicating that the model's fit is statistically remarkable. The Chi-Square statistic, a measure of the discrepancy among the observed information and the model, is 1.067. A lower Chi-Square norm generally suggests a better fit among the model and the observed information. The Root Mean Square Residual (RMR) norm, which represents the average squared differences among observed and predicted norms, is reported as 0.034. A lower RMR norm indicates a better fit of the model to the information. Regarding goodness-of-fit measures, the Fitness Goodness index is reported as 0.906, suggesting a high level of model fit. The Fitness Confirmatory index, another measure of how well the model fits the observed information, is reported as 0.904. Both norms being close to 1 indicate a good fit of the model to the information.

Additionally, the Tucker-Lewis Index (TLI), which evaluates how well the model reproduces the observed covariance structure, is reported as 0.902, further indicating a strong fit of the model. The Root Mean Square Error of Approximation (RMSEA), a measure of the discrepancy among observed information and the model, is reported as 0.031. A lower RMSEA norm suggests a better fit of the model to the information. Taken together, the results from these fit indices suggest that the specified model fits the information well. The statistically remarkable p-norm, combined with the various fit indices such as RMR, Fitness Goodness, Fitness Confirmatory, TLI, and RMSEA, collectively indicate that the model accurately captures the associations among the variables in the information set, providing a reliable representation of the underlying structure of the information as reported by the authors.

Table 6. Regression Examination

Relative			Approx.	S.E.	C.R.	P	Ass.
societal & ethical norms	<---	Condition of cruelty at workplace	.850	.154	5.519	.00	H2
Societal & ethical norms	<---	Women Start-up enterpriser's Emotional well-being	.427	.142	3.007	.00	H3
Women Start-up enterpriser's Emotional well-being	<---	Condition of cruelty at workplace	.867	.187	4.636	.00	H1

Source: Authors

Table 6 displays the results of the regression analysis examining the associations among Condition of cruelty at workplace, societal and ethical norms, and Women Start-up enterpriser's Emotional well-being. The first regression analysis indicates a remarkable positive association among societal & ethical norms and Condition of cruelty at workplace, with a regression coefficient of 0.850 and a standard error of 0.154. The critical ratio (C.R.) is 5.519, and the p-norm is denoted as .00, assisting Hypothesis H2. This finding suggests that the use of Condition of cruelty at workplace has a substantial impact on the adoption of Condition of cruelty at workplace among Women Start-up enterpriser's Emotional well-being. In the second regression analysis, the results show a statistically remarkable positive association among Women Start-up enterpriser's Emotional well-being and Condition of cruelty at workplace, with a regression coefficient of 0.427 and a standard error of 0.142. The critical ratio is 3.007, and the p-norm is denoted as .00 (indicating significance at the 0.001 level), assisting Hypothesis H3. This outcome implies that the utilization of societal & ethical norm positively influences the Women Start-up enterpriser's Emotional well-being.

The third regression analysis reveals a remarkable positive association among Women Start-up enterpriser's Emotional well-being and Condition of cruelty at workplace, with a regression coefficient of 0.867 and a standard error of 0.187. The critical ratio is 4.636, and the p-norm is denoted as, assisting Hypothesis H1. This result suggests that the adoption of Condition of cruelty at workplace is associated with an improvement in the Women Start-up enterpriser's Emotional well-being. Overall, the regression analysis results offer empirical evidence assisting the associations among Condition of cruelty at workplace, societal ethical and norms, and Women Start-up enterpriser's Emotional well-being as hypothesized by the authors. The outcomes indicate the significance of Condition of cruelty at workplace and societal ethical and norm in influencing and enhancing the Women Start-up enterpriser's Emotional well-being, shedding light on the interconnected agility within this context.

Table 7. Mediating function Impact

	Influence	worth	Path Influence
Condition of cruelty at workplace → Women Start-up enterpriser's Emotional well-being	Direct Influence	.34	Direct influence stated
Condition of cruelty at workplace → Societal ethical & norms → Start-up enterpriser's Emotional well-being	Indirect Influence	56*.62=0.34	Indirect Influence Ensued
	Whole influence	.682	Partial arbitration

Source: Authors

Table 7 presents outcomes related to the mediating function of Condition of cruelty at workplace in the association among Condition of cruelty at workplace and Women start-up enterprisers' work-life balance. The table highlights two key pathways: direct influence and indirect influence. In the case of the direct influence, the association among Condition of cruelty at workplace and Women start-up enterprisers' work-life balance is quantified with a coefficient of 0.34, indicating a direct impact of Condition of cruelty at workplace on the work-life balance of women start-up enterprisers. The table then delves into the indirect influence, which involves the pathway from Condition of cruelty at workplace to Condition of cruelty at workplace and subsequently to Women start-up enterprisers' work-life balance. This indirect pathway has a coefficient of $0.56 * 0.62 = 0.34$, demonstrating that the influence of Condition of cruelty at workplace on Women start-up enterprisers' work-life balance is partially arbitrated by the use of Condition of cruelty at workplace. This indicates that Condition of cruelty at workplace play a remarkable function in mediating the association among Condition of cruelty at workplace and the work-life balance of women start-up enterprisers.

The total influence, represented as 0.68, encompasses both the direct and indirect impacts of Condition of cruelty at workplace on Women start-up enterprisers' work-life balance. The authors classify this as a case of partial arbitration, suggesting that while Condition of cruelty at workplace mediate the association among Condition of cruelty at workplace and Women start-up enterprisers' work-life balance, there may still be additional factors at play that contribute to the overall influence observed. In conclusion, the results from Table 7 suggest a nuanced association where Condition of cruelty at workplace serve as a mediator in the link among Condition of cruelty at workplace and the work-life balance of women start-up enterprisers. These outcomes shed light on the complex interplay among these variables and offer understandings into the mechanisms through which Condition of cruelty at workplace impact the work-life balance of women start-up enterprisers in the context studied by the authors.

Discussion

The tables presented in the investigation shed light on the intricate agility among Emerging innovations, Condition of cruelty at workplace, and Women Start-up enterpriser's Emotional well-being. The regression analysis showcased remarkable associations, with Condition of cruelty at workplace playing a crucial function in influencing both Condition of cruelty at workplace adoption and the Women Start-up enterpriser's Emotional well-being. The results indicated positive associations among Condition of cruelty at workplace and, societal and ethical norm and Women Start-up enterpriser's Emotional well-being, as well as Condition of cruelty at workplace and Women Start-up enterpriser's Emotional well-being, validating the hypothesized connections. Moreover, the mediating function of Condition of cruelty at workplace in the association among societal and ethical norm and Women Start-up enterpriser's Emotional well-being was explored. The outcomes demonstrated a dual impact pathway, with Condition of cruelty at workplace partially mediating the influence of societal and ethical norm on the Women Start-up enterpriser's Emotional well-being. This highlights the significance of technological tools in facilitating the adoption of condition of cruelty at workplace and subsequently enhancing the Women Start-up enterpriser's Emotional well-being in the studied context.

These results have remarkable implications for both investigation and practice. By uncovering the mediating function of Condition of cruelty at workplace, the investigation underscores the transformative potential of technology in empowering women start-up enterprisers and improving their Women Start-up enterpriser's Emotional well-being. Understanding these associations can inform the development of targeted interventions and policies aimed at leveraging technology to assist women start-up enterprisers' emotion in balancing their work life and individual lives more impassively. Overall, the investigation contributes valuable understandings to the existing literature Condition of cruelty at workplace, societal and ethical norms adoption, and Women Start-up enterpriser's Emotional well-being, emphasizing the interconnected nature of these factors. The outcomes underscore the significance of considering technological tools as facilitators of innovation adoption and key drivers of Women Start-up enterpriser's Emotional well-being outcomes for women start-up enterprisers. Future investigation could delve deeper into the mechanisms through which societal and ethical norm mediate these associations and explore additional factors that may influence the agility observed in this investigation.

CONCLUSION

The condition of cruelty at workplace poses a remarkable challenge to the emotional well-being of women start-up enterprisers in the Eastern Africa. Through its harmful impacts on self-esteem, confidence, and mental health, such a hostile workplace environment can severely impact the overall emotional stability and resilience of women striving to succeed in marketplace. The prevalence of abuse, discrimination, and mental abuse in these settings creates a toxic atmosphere that not only hampers work life growth but also takes a toll on individual happiness and fulfillment. Also, the arbitration of this condition of cruelty at workplace exacerbates the emotional strain involvement by women start-up enterprisers. The added layer of navigating and coping with such toxicity while trying to build and sustain a marketplace amplifies feelings of stress, anxiety, and burnout. This arbitration process can further erode self-belief, motivation, and passion, ultimately hindering the ability of women to thrive and excel in their start-up endeavors. In conclusion, the pervasive nature of condition of cruelty at workplaces in the Eastern Africa poses a formidable barrier to the emotional well-being of women start-up enterprisers. The arbitration of abuse within these settings compounds the emotional barriers faced by women striving for success in their marketplaces. Solving and remedying these toxic workplace agility is crucial not only for fostering a more inclusive and assistive start-up ecosystem but also for safeguarding the mental and emotional welfare of women in the country as they navigate the complexities of start-up enterprise amidst adversity.

Managerial Implications

The harmful impact of condition of cruelty at workplaces on the emotional well-being of women start-up enterprisers in the Eastern Africa necessitates urgent managerial intervention and reform. Managers and organizational leaders play a crucial function in creating a safe, respectful, and nurturing workplace environment that assists the growth and success of all staffs, including women start-up enterprisers. Recognizing the pervasive nature of abuse and discrimination in these settings is the first step towards implementing meaningful changes that prioritize the emotional well-being of women start-up enterprisers. Managers must proactively address and eradicate abusive behaviors within the workplace through the implementation of robust policies, training programs, and mechanisms for reporting and solving misconduct. By fostering a culture of zero tolerance for abuse and mental abuse, organizations can create a more inclusive and empowering environment where women start-up enterprisers feel norms, respected, and assisted in their work life endeavors. Additionally, providing resources for mental health assist, counseling services, and stress management programs can help mitigate the emotional toll of condition of cruelty at workplaces on women start-up enterprisers.

Moreover, managers should prioritize diversity, equity, and inclusion initiatives that promote sex founded equality and empower women to thrive in their start-up pursuits. By actively promoting diversity in leadership, mentorship opportunities, and decision-making functions, organizations can create a more equitable and assistive ecosystem that uplifts and champions the contributions of women start-up enterprisers. Investing in training programs that raise awareness about unconscious bias, sex founded stereotypes, and the significance of fostering a respectful workplace culture can further enhance the emotional well-being of women in start-up enterprise.

In conclusion, managerial implications for solving the impact of condition of cruelty at workplaces on the emotional well-being of women start-up enterprisers in the Eastern Africa are paramount.

Practical Implications

The condition of cruelty at workplace's harmful impact on the emotional well-being of women start-up enterprisers in the Eastern Africa, exacerbated by the arbitration of abuse within these settings, calls for real-world implications that go beyond managerial interventions. Real-world solutions are essential to address the systemic situations that perpetuate abusive workplace agility and to assist the emotional resilience of women start-up enterprisers in the country. Real-world implications include the need for community assist networks and resources specifically tailored to assist women start-up enterprisers in navigating and coping with condition of cruelty at workplaces. Establishing mentorship programs, peer assist groups, and counseling services can offer women with the necessary tools and guidance to address emotional barriers, build resilience, and seek help when needed. By fostering a sense of solidarity and empowerment among women start-up enterprisers, these real-world initiatives can offer a lifeline for those facing emotional distress in hostile workplace settings.

Also, enhancing access to legal assist and advocacy services is crucial in protecting the rights and well-being of women start-up enterprisers who involvement abuse and mental abuse in their work life endeavors. Empowering women with knowledge of their legal rights, avenues for seeking redress, and avenues for reporting misconduct can serve as a deterrent to abusive behaviors and ensure accountability for perpetrators. Real-world interventions that strengthen the legal framework and enforcement mechanisms related to workplace mental abuse and discrimination are essential in creating a safer and more assistive environment for women start-up enterprisers to thrive. Additionally, promoting start-up enterprise education and training programs that incorporate modules on emotional intelligence, conflict resolution, and stress management can equip women with the skills and resilience needed to navigate challenging environments at workplaces impassively. By investing in the individual and work life development of women start-up enterprisers, organizations and officials can empower women to assert their boundaries, advocate for themselves, and prioritize their emotional well-being in the face of adversity.

Theoretical Implications

The investigation of the condition of cruelty at workplace's impact on the emotional well-being of women start-up enterprisers in the Eastern Africa, particularly through the arbitration of abuse within these contexts, carries remarkable theoretical implications for investigation and understanding in the fields of psychology, organizational behavior, and sex founded investigations. Firstly, this investigation sheds light on the assimilation of sex founded, start-up enterprise, and workplace agility in the Eastern Africa, highlighting the exclusive barriers faced by women in pursuing start-up ventures in environments rife with abuse and discrimination. By exploring how condition of cruelty at workplaces influence the emotional well-being of women start-up enterprisers, this investigation contributes to a deeper understanding of the complexities of sex founded involvements in the workplace and the implications for mental health and resilience. Secondly, the investigation underscores the significance of considering the mediating function of condition of cruelty at workplaces in deciding the emotional involvements of women start-up enterprisers. By examining how abuse within the workplace amplifies the emotional strain on women striving for success, investigators can further elucidate the mechanisms through which hostile environments at workplaces impact psychological well-being and self-efficacy. This theoretical understanding can inform future investigations on the interaction among workplace agility and individual emotional responses in diverse indigenous rituals contexts.

Moreover, the outcomes of this investigation have implications for theoretical frameworks related to organizational culture, leadership, and staff well-being. Understanding the emotional toll of condition of cruelty at workplaces on women start-up enterprisers can prompt scholars to reexamine theories of workplace behavior, power agility, and resilience through a sex founded-sensitive lens. By integrating understandings from this investigation into existing theoretical frameworks, investigators can advance knowledge on how organizational structures and norms influence emotional outcomes for women in start-up enterprise. In conclusion, the theoretical implications of investigation the condition of cruelty at workplace's impact on the emotional well-being of women start-up enterprisers in the Eastern Africa by mediating abuse offer valuable contributions to interdisciplinary scholarship. By bridging perspectives from psychology, organizational behavior, and sex founded investigations, this investigation enriches our theoretical understanding of the emotional barriers faced by women in start-up contexts and offers a foundation for further inquiry into the complexities of sex founded, work, and well-being in the country.

RECOMMENDATION

Cultivating a assistive workplace culture founded on societal and ethical norms is paramount. Organizations should prioritize empathy, respect, and inclusivity to create an environment where women start-up enterprisers feel norms and understood. By fostering a culture of assist, women can better navigate the emotional barriers posed by condition of cruelty at workplaces, leading to improved well-being and resilience. Implementing norms-founded leadership training programs can empower women start-up enterprisers to uphold societal and ethical norms in the face of adversity. By equipping women with the skills to make ethical decisions and navigate difficult conditions with integrity, organizations can help mitigate the negative impacts of abuse on their emotional health and well-being. Establishing mentorship programs and assist networks specifically tailored to women start-up enterprisers can offer a vital source of emotional assist. These programs offer a platform for women to seek guidance, share involvements, and build connections with like-minded individuals who uphold alike norms. By creating a community of assist, women can find strength and solidarity in challenging times.

Advocating for sex founded equality and inclusivity in the workplace is crucial. Organizations should champion policies that promote diversity, equity, and respect for all staffs. By advocating for a workplace that norms inclusivity and sex founded equality, stakeholders can create a more assistive environment that safeguards the emotional well-being of women start-up enterprisers.

Encouraging ethical leadership practices at all levels of the organization sets a positive illustration for women start-up enterprisers. Leaders who demonstrate integrity, fairness, and compassion can inspire trust and create a culture where societal and ethical norms are upheld. By promoting ethical leadership, organizations can foster a environments at workplace that prioritizes emotional well-being and assists the growth and success of women start-up enterprisers.

FUTURE DIRECTIONS

In solving the impact of condition of cruelty at workplaces on the emotional well-being of women start-up enterprisers through the arbitration of societal and ethical norms, future directions can be shaped by a comprehensive approach. Moving forward, it is crucial to prioritize the development of tailored assist programs that integrate societal and ethical norms into the start-up ecosystem. By fostering a culture of empathy, respect, and ethical conduct, organizations can empower women start-up enterprisers to navigate abusive conditions with resilience and dignity. Collaborative efforts involving stakeholders from various sectors, including government agencies, NGOs, and academia, can drive advocacy for policy reforms that promote a safe and inclusive environments at workplace for women. Embracing technology-driven solutions to offer accessible resources and assist networks can enhance women's ability to seek assistance and connect with peers facing alike barriers. Also, investing in long-term monitoring and evaluation mechanisms will enable stakeholders to assess the interventions and adapt strategies to meet the evolving needs of women start-up enterprisers. By championing societal and ethical norms in start-up enterprise, stakeholders can create a nurturing ecosystem that upholds the emotional well-being and empowerment of women in the face of workplace adversity. Stakeholders can contribute to creating a more inclusive, innovative and assistive ecosystem for women start-up enterprisers in the years to come.

REFERENCES

Adula, M., Birbirsa, Z. A., & Kant, S. (2023). The effect of interpersonal, problem solving and technical training skills on performance of Ethiopia textile industry: Continuance, normative and affective commitment as mediators. *Cogent Business & Management*, 10(3), 2286672. Advance online publication. DOI: 10.1080/23311975.2023.2286672

Asefa, K., & Debela, K. L. "Effect of Transformational Leadership on Organizational Performance: The Mediating Role of Employee Commitment and Expert Systems (AI) Inclusion in Ethiopia," *2023 International Conference on Communication, Security and Artificial Intelligence (ICCSAI)*, Greater Noida, India, 2023, pp. 305-310, https://doi.org/DOI: 10.1109/ICCSAI59793.2023.10421269

Baluku, M. M., Nansubuga, F., Nantamu, S., Musanje, K., Kawooya, K., Nansamba, J., & Ruto, G. (2023). Psychological capital, entrepreneurial efficacy, alertness and agency among refugees in Uganda: Perceived behavioural control as a moderator. *Journal of Entrepreneurship and Innovation in Emerging Economies*, 23939575231194554.

Birhane, M., Amentie, C., Borji, B., & Kant, S. Are Ethiopian Coffee Farmers Proficient to Predict Capital Structure with Mediation of AI Based Knowledge Systems and Asset Liquidity? In *AI in Agriculture for Sustainable and Economic Management* (pp. 199-215). CRC Press. DOI: 10.1201/9781003451648-15

Brieger, S. A., Sonbol, D., & De Clercq, D. (2024). Gender differences in entrepreneurs' work–family conflict and well-being during COVID-19: Moderating effects of gender-egalitarian contexts. *Journal of Small Business Management*, 62(5), 2322–2363. DOI: 10.1080/00472778.2023.2235755

De Clercq, D., Kaciak, E., & Thongpapanl, N. (2022). Happy at home, successful in competition: The beneficial role of happiness and entrepreneurial orientation for women entrepreneurs. *International Journal of Entrepreneurial Behaviour & Research*, 28(6), 1463–1488. DOI: 10.1108/IJEBR-02-2021-0154

De Clercq, D., Kaciak, E., & Thongpapanl, N. (2022). Work-to-family conflict and firm performance of women entrepreneurs: Roles of work-related emotional exhaustion and competitive hostility. *International Small Business Journal*, 40(3), 364–384. DOI: 10.1177/02662426211011405

Dereso, C. W., Kant, S., Muthuraman, M., & Tufa, G. (2023). Effect of Point of Service on Health Department Student's Creativity in Comprehensive Universities of Ethiopia: Moderating Role of Public-Private Partnership and Mediating Role of Work Place Learning. In: Jain, S., Groppe, S., Mihindukulasooriya, N. (eds) Proceedings of the International Health Informatics Conference. Lecture Notes in Electrical Engineering, vol 990. Springer, Singapore. https://doi.org/DOI: 10.1007/978-981-19-9090-8_13

Dsouza, A., & Panakaje, N. (2023). Factors Affecting Women Entrepreneurs' Success: A Study of Small and Medium-Sized Enterprises-A Review. *International Journal of Case Studies in Business* [IJCSBE]. IT and Education, 7(2), 51–89.

Durga, P., Godavarthi, D., Kant, S., & Basa, S. S. (2024). Aspect-based drug review classification through a hybrid model with ant colony optimization using deep learning. *Discov Computing*, 27(1), 19. DOI: 10.1007/s10791-024-09441-w

Guyo, D. M., Kero, C. A., & Kant, S. (2025). Is Marketing Intermediaries' Mediation Required for Livestock and Products Marketing to Improve the Economic Status of Pastoralist Communities in Ethiopia? In *AI in Agriculture for Sustainable and Economic Management* (pp. 216-234). CRC Press.

Guyo, K., & Kero, C. A. "Mediation of Marketing Intermediaries and AI Adoption Between Livestock Products Marketing and Economic Status of Pastoralist in Ethiopia," *2023 International Conference on Communication, Security and Artificial Intelligence (ICCSAI)*, Greater Noida, India, 2023, pp. 311-316, https://doi.org/DOI: 10.1109/ICCSAI59793.2023.10421261

Jabo, B., & Kant, S. "Impact of Technical CRM on Ethiopia Bank Human-Computer Interface and Competitive Advantage as Mediators of Performance," *2024 IEEE International Conference on Computing, Power and Communication Technologies (IC2PCT)*, Greater Noida, India, 2024, pp. 679-682, https://doi.org/DOI: 10.1109/IC2PCT60090.2024.10486237

Kandilige, L., Teye, J. K., Setrana, M., & Badasu, D. M. (2023). 'They'd beat us with whatever is available to them': Exploitation and abuse of Ghanaian domestic workers in the Middle East. *International Migration (Geneva, Switzerland)*, 61(4), 240–256. DOI: 10.1111/imig.13096

Kant, S., & Adula, M. (2024). AI Learning and Work Attitude Mediation Between Reward and Organizational Support in Ethiopia. In Gomathi Sankar, J., & David, A. (Eds.), *Generative AI for Transformational Management* (pp. 109–136). IGI Global., DOI: 10.4018/979-8-3693-5578-7.ch005

Kant, S., & Adula, M. (2024). Mediated by AI-Based Generative Re-Enforcement Learning and Work Attitude: Are Intrinsic Rewards Transforming Employee Perceived Organizational Support? In Gomathi Sankar, J., & David, A. (Eds.), *Generative AI for Transformational Management* (pp. 83–108). IGI Global., DOI: 10.4018/979-8-3693-5578-7.ch004

Kant, S., & Adula, M. (2024). Human-Machine Interaction in the Metaverse in the Context of Ethiopia. In *Impact and Potential of Machine Learning in the Metaverse* (pp. 196–212). IGI Global., DOI: 10.4018/979-8-3693-5762-0.ch008

King'ong'o, G. W. (2022). *Indigenous Entrepreneurship, Post-Conflict Reconstruction And Globalization Dynamics On Economic Development: A Case Of The Micro And Small Livestock Enterprises In Turkana County, Kenya* (Doctoral dissertation, University of Nairobi).

Mshilla, O. (2021). *Access the Role of the Youth in Peace Processes With a Focus in Mediation: a Case of Horn of Africa, Kenya Nairobi County* (Doctoral dissertation, University of Nairobi).

Neneh, B. N. (2024). Why peer support matters: Entrepreneurial stressors, emotional exhaustion, and growth intentions of women entrepreneurs. *Entrepreneurship Research Journal*, 14(3), 985–1019. DOI: 10.1515/erj-2021-0501

Ni, D., Li, N., & Zheng, X. (2024). Why do women entrepreneurs behave dominantly in the workplace, and what does it mean?: A family embeddedness perspective. *Group & Organization Management*, 49(4), 860–901. DOI: 10.1177/10596011221116729

Noordin, M. (2021). *The Impact of Violent Extremism and Radicalization on the Political Economy of the Horn of Africa: a Case Study of Somalia and Eritrea* (Doctoral dissertation, University of Nairobi).

Nyoach, T. D., Lemi, K., Debela, T., & Kant, S. (2024). Does Organizational Commitment Mediate the Relationship between Employee Relationship Management and Bank Performance? The Case of Banks in Ethiopia. *International Journal of Organizational Leadership*, 13(2), 355–376. DOI: 10.33844/ijol.2024.60419

Panigrahi, A., Pati, A., Sahu, B., Das, M. N., Nayak, D. S. K., Sahoo, G., & Kant, S. (2023). En-MinWhale: An ensemble approach based on MRMR and Whale optimization for Cancer diagnosis. *IEEE Access : Practical Innovations, Open Solutions*, 11, 113526–113542. DOI: 10.1109/ACCESS.2023.3318261

Saleem, Z., Shenbei, Z., & Hanif, A. M. (2020). Workplace violence and employee engagement: The mediating role of work environment and organizational culture. *SAGE Open*, 10(2), 2158244020935885. DOI: 10.1177/2158244020935885

Saleh, T. A., Sarwar, A., Khan, N., Tabash, M. I., & Hossain, M. I. (2023). Does emotional exhaustion influence turnover intention among early-career employees? A moderated-mediation study on Malaysian SMEs. *Cogent Business & Management*, 10(3), 2242158. DOI: 10.1080/23311975.2023.2242158

Sana, H. A., Alkhalaf, S., Zulfiqar, S., Al-Rahmi, W. M., Al-Adwan, A. S., & AlSoud, A. R. (2021). Upshots of intrinsic traits on social entrepreneurship intentions among young business graduates: An investigation through moderated-mediation model. *Sustainability (Basel)*, 13(9), 5192. DOI: 10.3390/su13095192

Tsehayu, Y. G., & Østebø, T. (2020). Religious Entrepreneurship and Female Migration: The Case of a Muslim Religious Leader in Masqan, Ethiopia. *Africa Today*, 67(2-3), 63–83. DOI: 10.2979/africatoday.67.2-3.04

Zhou, X., Rasool, S. F., & Ma, D. (2020, September). The relationship between workplace violence and innovative work behavior: The mediating roles of employee wellbeing. [). MDPI.]. *Health Care*, 8(3), 332. PMID: 32927711

KEY TERMS

Abuse at the Workplace: A condition of cruelty at workplace refers to a workplace where staffs are subjected to mistreatment, mental abuse, discrimination, or bullying. This can include behaviors such as verbal abuse, intimidation, threats, sabotage, or discrimination founded on factors like sex founded, race, or age. In the context of women start-up enterprisers, an condition of cruelty at workplace can have harmful impacts on their emotional well-being and overall job satisfaction.

Arbitration: Arbitration is a process of intervention or negotiation aimed at resolving conflicts, disputes, or barriers among parties in a neutral and facilitated manner. In the context of the impact of an condition of cruelty at workplace on women start-up enterprisers' emotional well-being arbitrated by societal and ethical norms, arbitration refers to the function of promoting positive norms, ethical conduct, and assistive associations to mitigate the negative impacts of workplace abuse on women's mental health.

Emotional Well-Being: Emotional well-being encompasses an individual's ability to cope with stress, maintain a positive outlook, and manage their emotions impassively. It relates to feelings of happiness, fulfillment, and contentment in both individual and work life. In the context of women start-up enterprisers, emotional well-being refers to their mental health, resilience, and emotional stability while navigating the barriers of start-up enterprise, including those arising from a condition of cruelty at workplace.

Ethical Norms: Ethical norms are ethical principles and standards that govern individuals' decisions and actions, often founded on notions of right and wrong, justice, honesty, and integrity. In the context of women start-up enterprisers navigating an condition of cruelty at workplace, ethical norms offer a framework for making ethical choices, upholding principles of respect and fairness, and promoting a assistive and inclusive workplace culture that protects women's emotional well-being.

Societal Norms: Societal norms are principles, beliefs, and norms that advise individuals' interactions and behaviors within society. They encompass notions such as respect, fairness, equality, and compassion. In the context of women start-up enterprisers' emotional well-being, societal norms play a critical function in deciding the culture of the workplace and influencing how individuals treat each other, thereby impacting women's mental health and job satisfaction.

Chapter 2
Abusive Work Environments and Strategies to Manage the Psychological Well-Being of Entrepreneurs

Retno Lestari
https://orcid.org/0000-0003-4568-9596
University of Brawijaya, Indonesia

Heni Dwi Windarwati
University of Brawijaya, Indonesia

Ridhoyanti Hidayah
https://orcid.org/0000-0002-7533-4633
University of Brawijaya, Indonesia

ABSTRACT

Commencing an entrepreneurial voyage can be intimidating, and businesspersons might require assistance in dealing with several types of abusive behaviours from their co-founders or inventors. An abusive work environment can hurt both employees and organizational productivity. This hostile atmosphere may arise from various sources, including harassment, discrimination, or intimidation. These harmful experiences can result in high turnover rates and substandard job performance. As a result, employers must be vigilant and proactive in addressing any recurring instances of belittlement, offensive humour, or unwarranted criticism. They must strive to create a workplace environment based on respect and inclusivity. The purpose of this chapter is to provide readers with a comprehensive understanding of the impact of abusive work environments on entrepreneurs' psychological and emotional well-being. It also examines the related issues that arise from such environments.

DOI: 10.4018/979-8-3693-3673-1.ch002

INTRODUCTION

Entrepreneurship demands a superior level of intellectual understanding compared to other vocations, as it entails actively acquiring knowledge of one's field and tackling intricate challenges. This necessitates someone with sharp analytical abilities, exceptional problem-solving skills, and an unwavering willingness to learn continuously (Shepherd & Patzelt, 2018). Accomplished entrepreneurs possess an innate drive for innovation, creativity, and a capacity for critical thinking, all of which enable them to navigate complex business landscapes deftly. Thus, entrepreneurship demands a distinctive set of proficiencies that sets it apart from other professions (Usoro & Brownson, 2024).

Embarking on the entrepreneurship journey is a challenging feat that requires individuals to invest their time, energy, and resources to bring their vision to life (Waite, 2024). Sadly, entrepreneurs are often subjected to various forms of abusive behaviour that can hamper their ability to succeed. Unfortunately, some of these behaviours are subtle and difficult to recognize, making it challenging for entrepreneurs to shield themselves from harm (Brück et al., 2013). One of the most prevalent forms of abusive conduct that entrepreneurs face is financial abuse, which can manifest in various ways. For instance, business partners or investors may exploit an entrepreneur's lack of financial knowledge to manipulate them into making poor financial decisions. A sound understanding of financial management is crucial for entrepreneurs to avoid business failures. Insufficient capital, poor financial management, and misjudgment of risks are common pitfalls that result from a lack of financial knowledge. Hence, entrepreneurs must prioritize enhancing their financial knowledge to make informed decisions that fuel business growth. By grasping financial concepts and principles, entrepreneurs can navigate intricate financial landscapes, make informed investment decisions, and manage risks effectively. Therefore, improving one's financial knowledge is pivotal in establishing sustainable entrepreneurship (Tran et al., 2023). Moreover, entrepreneurs may be coerced into accepting unfavourable business terms, such as low equity stakes or unfavourable loan terms, which can significantly impede their ability to grow their businesses. Another form of abusive conduct that entrepreneurs face is emotional manipulation and bullying. Such behaviour can be detrimental, causing entrepreneurs to feel isolated, unmotivated, and lacking in confidence. The sources of such behaviour may include business partners, investors, clients, or even friends and family members who do not comprehend the unique challenges and pressures of being an entrepreneur. Therefore, entrepreneurs must be mindful of the various forms of abusive conduct they may encounter and take proactive measures to safeguard themselves from harm. This entails seeking out reliable advisors and support systems, educating themselves on financial matters, and being watchful for indications of abusive behaviour from those around them. By doing so, entrepreneurs can improve their chances of success and establish thriving businesses that positively impact their communities.

The study of abusive behaviours in the workplace has captured the attention of researchers in recent years. This includes the phenomenon of workplace bullying, which is characterized by repeated negative behaviour from an individual or group over some time. The surge of mistreatment and emotional abuse in organizations worldwide has made this a popular area of research. The effects of bullying are far-reaching, with organizations spending between $17 to $36 billion annually to combat them. The World Health Organization recognizes bullying as a significant community hazard that demands immediate attention and action (Naseer et al., 2018). Persistent and repeated negative behaviour towards an employee, known as workplace bullying, can take various forms. It can be related to work, such as receiving unwarranted criticism or unrealistic demands, or personal matters, such as being excluded or teased by co-workers (Trepanier et al., 2015; McFarland et al., 2022). Physical intimidation, such as shouting, aggressive remarks, or threats of violence, may also be present. The frequency and persistence of these negative behaviours are crucial characteristics of workplace bullying. Even if they seem minor, these behaviours become increasingly harmful and damaging when they frequently occur (daily or weekly) and persistently (over six months) (Trepanier et al., 2015).

The concept of abusive or hostile work environment was introduced by the Committee of Equivalent Work Opportunities in 1980. Their materials emphasize that all employees have the right to work in an environment that is not hostile, even if such an environment does not directly impact their job responsibilities. In 1994, President Johnson signed a law prohibiting employers from discriminating against individuals based on race, colour, religion, gender, or national origin. Employees may feel marginalized and excluded from decision-making processes when a hostile work environment exists within an organization. This can result in dissatisfaction with work relationships and alienation from the organization (Abbas et al., 2016).

According to the 2023 Work in America Survey, certain demographic and workplace factors are associated with a toxic workplace. The survey revealed that a higher percentage of females (23%) reported experiencing a toxic workplace compared to males (15%). Additionally, employees living with a disability (26%) were more likely to report a toxic workplace than those without a disability (16%). Employees of nonprofit and government organizations also reported higher rates of toxic workplaces (25% and 26%, respectively) compared to those in the private industry (17%). Interestingly, upper management employees (9%) were less likely to report a toxic workplace than middle management (21%), front-line workers (26%), and individual contributors (18%). This raises the question of whether upper management may have difficulty understanding claims of a toxic workplace if they are not directly exposed. The 2023 Work in America Survey revealed that some employees experience a toxic workplace associated with specific demographic and workplace factors. The survey found that more females (23%) reported experiencing a toxic workplace than males (15%). Similarly, employees living with a disability (26%) were more likely to report a toxic workplace compared to those without a disability (16%). Furthermore, nonprofit and government organization employees were more likely to report a poisonous workplace (25% and 26%, respectively) than those working in private industry (17%). Interestingly, upper management employees were less likely to report a toxic workplace (9%) compared to middle management (21%), front-line workers (26%), and individual contributors (18%). This raises the question of whether upper management may find understanding employees' claims of a toxic workplace challenging if they aren't exposed to that aspect.

Employers have a critical role to play in addressing this problem, and several strategies are at their disposal. These strategies include mediation, negotiation, strategic thinking, long-term planning, team building, and conflict management. However, it's important to note that more than these skills are needed to effectively address and prevent the highly stressful situations that employees face. To expand on the current findings, future studies could explore the potential moderating role of these skills. In addition, employers can provide significant support to their employees by developing the abilities above. This can go a long way in addressing and preventing abusive work environments. More broadly, the literature on managers' role in sustaining their employees' performance and well-being highlights the importance of providing training to employers not only on the norms and rules of the work environment but also on psychosocial and managerial practices and methods. By doing so, employers can create a positive work culture that promotes employee well-being and enables them to reach their full potential (Buonomo et al., 2020; Overton & Lowry, 2013; Kazemi et al., 2022)

This chapter examines the impact of abusive work environments on entrepreneurs' mental and emotional well-being and related issues. By creating a workplace free from hostility and enabling real-time monitoring of employee experiences, companies can identify areas for improvement and empower employees to play an active role in shaping their work environment and building a positive and productive workplace culture.

Navigating the Uncertainty of Entrepreneurship

In the business world, uncertainty is a recurring reality that refers to situations where businesses face risks that cannot be accurately predicted or measured. Due to unpredictable or constantly changing events, these situations make it difficult for business workers to evaluate their performance. The political, technological, economic, and environmental landscape is continuously shifting, which can result in a high degree of uncertainty in the business world. For instance, technological advancements can disrupt existing business models, data breaches can compromise sensitive information, natural calamities can disrupt supply chains and operations, and new business regulations can create compliance challenges for businesses. All these factors contribute to an increasingly complex and uncertain business environment, which requires businesses to proactively identify, assess, and mitigate risks to maintain their competitive edge (Deng et al., 2019; Schmitt et al., 2017).

Figure 1. The uncertainty of entrepreneurship (Deng et al., 2019)

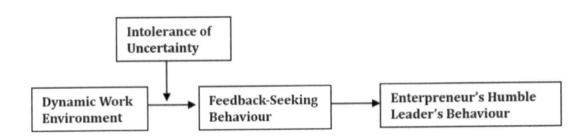

Dynamic environments are characterized by rapid, unpredictable, and turbulent change, creating a challenging work situation. Demand, competition, technology, and regulation change rapidly and discontinuously in highly dynamic settings, leading to a need for more accurate and up-to-date information. This can make entrepreneurs feel uncertain about the outcomes of their decisions and the feedback they receive from the environment. Chinese entrepreneurial teams often face highly dynamic environments due to unpredictable market demand, fierce competition, and sudden changes in legal, political, and economic constraints (Huang et al., 2023). Today's work environments are more dynamic than ever, exacerbating the uncertainty entrepreneurs face. The uncertainty reduction theory suggests that entrepreneurs will engage in specific behaviours to reduce uncertainty, such as seeking new information, experimenting with new products and services, and collaborating with others to develop new ideas and strategies. Navigating highly dynamic environments requires constant vigilance and adaptability. To succeed in these challenging situations, entrepreneurs must remain flexible and open-minded in the face of rapid change. The potential negative effects of dynamic work environments, such as anxiety and information overload, raise questions about their impact on leadership behaviours, particularly among entrepreneurs. Future research should, therefore, explore the "dark side" of dynamic work environments, focusing on their effects on entrepreneurial behaviour.

Our empirical results have yielded significant practical implications for entrepreneurial teams. It is common for entrepreneurs to view dynamic work environments as a substantial obstacle and fear it due to their potential adverse effects. However, our study shows that dynamic work environments can prompt humble leader behaviours among entrepreneurs, leading to positive outcomes for entrepreneurial teams. As such, entrepreneurs should adopt a new perspective on dynamic environments that promotes alertness and stimulates positive behaviours and better performance. Feedback-seeking behaviour can stimulate the display of humble leader behaviours among entrepreneurs. Given the benefits of such behaviours, entrepreneurs and professional human resources training programs should encourage entrepreneurs to seek feedback to cultivate these behaviours. This study highlights the importance of intolerance of uncertainty among entrepreneurs. Given the highly dynamic nature of current environments, it is crucial for entrepreneurial success to react positively to dynamic environments. Entrepreneurs with low intolerance of uncertainty should aim to minimize its adverse effects, while those with high intolerance of uncertainty should carefully consider their decision to become entrepreneurs (Deng et al., 2019).

Abusive Work Environments

Studies indicate that workplace bullying is a growing issue. This type of conduct is characterized by recurrent negative actions from an individual or group over an extended period. Workplace bullying can manifest in various forms, including unwarranted criticism, unrealistic demands, exclusion, teasing, shouting, aggressive remarks, or threats of physical harm. These behaviours can lead to emotional abuse and mistreatment, which can be detrimental to the victim. It is worth noting that even seemingly minor actions can have severe consequences when they occur frequently (daily or weekly) and persistently (over six months). This is a crucial topic of research on a global scale, and it is essential to consider the frequency and persistence of negative behaviours when addressing workplace bullying (Nasir & Can, 2022; Islam et al., 2023; Manga et al., 2023).

Workplace bullying is a serious issue that cannot be ignored. It involves harmful behaviour towards an individual in the workplace, which leads to long-lasting adverse effects on both the victim and the perpetrator. Research has shown that workplace bullying is a widespread problem, affecting millions of American workers. The Workplace Bullying Institute's recent survey revealed that nearly 50 million American workers have fallen victim to direct workplace bullying. This silent and deadly epidemic involves power struggles, verbal and emotional abuse, and a hostile working environment. Victims of workplace bullying often suffer from mental distress, verbal abuse, and even physical illnesses. It's time to take action and end this destructive behaviour in the workplace (Hognas, 2020).

Entrepreneurs often encounter distinct challenges that may trigger stress, burnout, and other mental health issues. Nevertheless, there are effective strategies that entrepreneurs can adopt to manage these hurdles better and cultivate an overall sense of wellness. Entrepreneurs must prioritize their mental health and reach out for assistance whenever necessary to maintain a healthy and sustainable work-life equilibrium.

Strategies to Manage the Psychological and Well-Being of Entrepreneurs

Employers play a crucial role in addressing workplace stress. They can use various skills such as mediation, negotiation, strategic thinking, long-term planning, team building, and conflict management to resolve issues related to work stress. However, it's important to note that these skills alone may not be enough to prevent highly stressful situations. As such, further research is needed to explore these skills' potential benefits and limitations (Rasool et al., 2021; Zhou et al., 2020; Wang et al., 2020).

In addition, employers can support their employees by teaching them these skills. This can help prevent abusive work environments and promote employee wellbeing. Employees can develop their skills and improve their ability to handle stressful situations by offering training and development opportunities. Furthermore, managers play a vital role in creating a positive work culture that fosters employee wellbeing. To achieve this, they should be trained in creating a work environment that is supportive, inclusive, and promotes open communication. By creating a positive work environment, managers can help employees feel more engaged and motivated, leading to better job satisfaction and productivity (Finstad et al., 2019).

Kurt Lewin, a renowned social psychologist, introduced a comprehensive three-phase model of organizational change that aimed to help organizations navigate the complex change process effectively. The model consisted of three stages: unfreezing, moving, and refreezing. During the unfreezing phase, Lewin emphasized the importance of creating awareness among employees about the need for change and breaking down the existing status quo. Employees were encouraged to embrace the changes and develop new working methods in the moving phase. Finally, in the refreezing phase, the latest changes were institutionalized, and the organization was stabilized to ensure that the changes were sustainable in the long run. Throughout the process, Lewin paid close attention to interpersonal interactions and the various forces and factors that could impact the change process, making his model a comprehensive and practical guide for organizations (Burnes, 2019). Miller (2020) explained about Lewin's three-step change model can only be effective if business owners demonstrate and uphold excellent ethical practices. The business owner has a crucial role in creating the necessary momentum for change by ensuring open communication, consistent motivation, and collaboration among employees (Appelbaum et al., 2018; Miller, 2020). Buick et al. (2018) and Wiard (2018) have also highlighted that a lack of transparent, timely, and honest communication can cause fear, anxiety, stress, and uncertainty within the organization. To avoid these negative consequences, business owners must balance the need for change and the fear of change. Doing so will help them communicate the organization's current state, the desired state, and the benefits of the transition to employees, thus creating a sense of stability. By effectively managing the change process through ethical and transparent practices, business owners can improve their chances of success and ensure that their employees remain motivated and committed throughout the transition.

The issue of workplace bullying has been widely discussed in recent years, and research conducted by Stankov et al. in 2022 has shed more light on this phenomenon. The study found that workplace bullying is influenced by various factors, including institutional, legal, organizational, and governmental allowances and the degree of tolerance towards such acts. Moreover, the perception of behaviours that define workplace bullying varies across cultures. Given the seriousness of this issue, small business owners must sensitize their employees about workplace bullying and its various forms. The organizations should educate their employees about the prevention strategies they have in place to mitigate such behaviours. Small business owners should take responsibility for raising awareness about workplace bullying policies and procedures for their employees. To prevent workplace bullying, an open-door policy and zero-tolerance towards such behaviour are essential. This approach ensures transparency and accuracy regarding why workplace bullying occurs and the most effective strategies that business owners can implement to prevent it. Providing employees with knowledge, awareness, education, and leadership is crucial. These are among the most vital aspects of an organization, and organizations should prioritize them to promote a safe and healthy workplace culture.

Effective organizational communication is critical for the prosperity of any organization. In today's fast-paced business environment, where competition is intense, and resources are limited, it's more important than ever to establish a culture of respectful communication to ensure a positive and professional work environment. One of the primary factors that can adversely affect workplace morale and productivity is bullying. Therefore, it is essential to implement strategies to prevent workplace bullying.

Research studies have shown that implementing prevention strategies can significantly increase the value and success of an organization. These strategies have been found to promote active communication, provide knowledge support, and encourage positive behaviours among employees. For instance, Chen and Zhu (2022) argue that effective communication can help foster a sense of community among employees, leading to improved teamwork, higher morale, and lower turnover rates.

Moreover, open communication and prevention strategies can create a positive climate that reduces the need for conflict intervention. According to Rios and Ventura (2022), a positive environment that encourages respectful communication and collaboration can help prevent workplace bullying and other negative behaviours. This, in turn, leads to a more productive and harmonious work environment. Effective organizational communication is critical for the success and prosperity of any organization. Implementing prevention strategies to prevent workplace bullying can significantly increase an organization's value and success by promoting active communication, providing knowledge support, and encouraging positive behaviors.

In summary, employers have a significant responsibility to address workplace stress, and they can do this by using a range of skills, offering training and development opportunities to employees, and creating a positive work culture that promotes employee wellbeing.

REFERENCES

Abbas, A., Abbas Abed Hussein Al-Janabi, A., & Al Hasnawi, H. (2017). The Effect of Hostile Work Environment on Organizational Alienation: The Mediation Role of the Relationship between the Leader and Followers. *Asian Social Science*, 13(2), 140–158. DOI: 10.5539/ass.v13n2p140

Brück, T., Naudé, W., & Verwimp, P. (2013). Entrepreneurship and Violent Conflict in Developing Countries. WIDER Working Paper 2013/028. Helsinki: UNU-WIDER.

Buonomo, I., Fiorilli, C., Romano, L., & Benevene, P. (2020). The Roles of Work-Life Conflict and Gender in the Relationship between Workplace Bullying and Personal Burnout. A Study on Italian School Principals. *International Journal of Environmental Research and Public Health*, 17(23), 8745. DOI: 10.3390/ijerph17238745 PMID: 33255556

Burnes, B. (2019). The Origins of Lewin's Three-Step Model of Change. *The Journal of Applied Behavioral Science*, 56(1), 002188631989268. DOI: 10.1177/0021886319892685

Deng, X., Gao, B., & Li, G. (2019). The Effects of Dynamic Work Environments on Entrepreneurs' Humble Leader Behaviors: Based on Uncertainty Reduction Theory. *Frontiers in Psychology*, 10, 2732. Advance online publication. DOI: 10.3389/fpsyg.2019.02732 PMID: 31920793

Finstad, G. L., Ariza-Montes, A., Giorgi, G., Lecca, L. I., Arcangeli, G., & Mucci, N. (2019). The JDCS Model and Blue-Collar Bullying: Decent Working Conditions for a Healthy Environment. *International Journal of Environmental Research and Public Health*, 16(18), 3411. DOI: 10.3390/ijerph16183411 PMID: 31540020

Högnäs, R., & Magnusson Hanson, L. (2020). Workplace violence and all-cause mortality. *European Journal of Public Health*, 30(Supplement_5), ckaa166.1200. Advance online publication. DOI: 10.1093/eurpub/ckaa166.1200

Huang, X. (2023). The roles of competition on innovation efficiency and firm performance: Evidence from the Chinese manufacturing industry. *European Research on Management and Business Economics*, 29(1), 100201. DOI: 10.1016/j.iedeen.2022.100201

Islam, M. S., Aso, K. A., & Azizzadeh, F. (2023). Workplace Bullying Causes Employee Turnover: A Responsible Human Resource Management Approach. *The International Journal of Organizational Diversity*, 23(2), 17–36. DOI: 10.18848/2328-6261/CGP/v23i02/17-36

Manga, J. P. A. (2023). Workplace Bullying Seen from the Perspective of Bystanders: Effects on Engagement and Burnout, Mediating Role of Positive and Negative Affects. *International Journal of Environmental Research and Public Health*, 20(19), 6821. DOI: 10.3390/ijerph20196821 PMID: 37835092

McFarland, L., Bull, R., Cumming, T., & Wong, S. (2022). Workplace Bullying in Early Childhood Education Settings: Prevalence and Protective Factors. *International Journal of Early Childhood*, •••, 1–22. DOI: 10.1007/s13158-022-00341-y PMID: 36341082

Miller, J., Davis-Sramek, B., Fugate, B. S., Pagell, M., & Flynn, B. B. (2021). Editorial commentary: Addressing confusion in the diffusion of archival data research. *The Journal of Supply Chain Management*, 57(3), 130–146. DOI: 10.1111/jscm.12236

Naseer, S., Raja, U., Syed, F., & Bouckenooghe, D. (2018). Combined effects of workplace bullying and perceived organizational support on employee behaviors: Does resource availability help? *Anxiety, Stress, and Coping*, 31(6), 654–668. DOI: 10.1080/10615806.2018.1521516 PMID: 30200787

Nasir, S., & Can, O. (2022). Workplace Aggression Profiles and Diverse Emotional Responses: Evidence from Pakistan. *Employee Responsibilities and Rights Journal*, 34(3), 335–359. DOI: 10.1007/s10672-021-09392-0

Overton, A. R., & Lowry, A. C. (2013). Conflict Management: Difficult Conversations with Difficult People. *Clinics in Colon and Rectal Surgery*, 26(4), 259–264. DOI: 10.1055/s-0033-1356728 PMID: 24436688

Rasool, S. F., Wang, M., Tang, M., Saeed, A., & Iqbal, J. (2021). How Toxic Workplace Environment Effects the Employee Engagement: The Mediating Role of Organizational Support and Employee Well-being. *International Journal of Environmental Research and Public Health*, 18(5), 2294. DOI: 10.3390/ijerph18052294 PMID: 33652564

Schmitt, A., Rosing, K., Zhang, S. X., & Leatherbee, M. (2017). A Dynamic Model of Entrepreneurial Uncertainty and Business Opportunity Identification: Exploration as a Mediator and Entrepreneurial Self-Efficacy as a Moderator. *Entrepreneurship Theory and Practice*. Advance online publication. DOI: 10.1177/1042258717721482

Shepherd, D. A., & Patzelt, H. (2018). Entrepreneurial Identity. In Shepherd, D. A., & Patzelt, H. (Eds.), *Entrepreneurial Cognition: Exploring the Mindset of Entrepreneurs* (pp. 137–200). Springer International Publishing., DOI: 10.1007/978-3-319-71782-1_5

Stankov, S., Brtka, E., Poštin, J., Ilić-Kosanović, T., & Nikolić, M. (2022). The influence of organizational culture and leadership on workplace bullying in organizations in Serbia. *Journal for East European Management Studies*, 27(3), 519–551. DOI: 10.5771/0949-6181-2022-3-519

Tran, Q. N., Phung, T. M. T., Nguyen, N. H., & Nguyen, T. H. (2023). Financial Knowledge Matters Entrepreneurial Decisions: A Survey in the COVID-19 Pandemic. *Journal of the Knowledge Economy*. Advance online publication. DOI: 10.1007/s13132-023-01137-8

Trépanier, S.-G., Fernet, C., & Austin, S. (2015a). A longitudinal investigation of workplace bullying, basic need satisfaction, and employee functioning. *Journal of Occupational Health Psychology*, 20(1), 105–116. DOI: 10.1037/a0037726 PMID: 25151460

Usoro, I. A., & Brownson, C. (2024). Creative Thinking, Adaptability and Entrepreneurial Development in Nigeria. *British Journal of Management and Marketing Studies*, 7, 69–77. DOI: 10.52589/BJMMS-96UF1ZBT

Waite, R. (2024). Embarking on an Entrepreneurial Journey: Top Advice for Start-Ups. https://www.robinwaite.com/blog/embarking-on-an-entrepreneurial-journey-top-advice-for-start-up-business-success

Wang, Z., Zaman, S., Rasool, S. F., Zaman, Q. U., & Amin, A. (2020). Exploring the Relationships Between a Toxic Workplace Environment, Workplace Stress, and Project Success with the Moderating Effect of Organizational Support: Empirical Evidence from Pakistan. *Risk Management and Healthcare Policy*, 13, 1055–1067. DOI: 10.2147/RMHP.S256155 PMID: 32821183

Zhou, X., Rasool, S. F., & Ma, D. (2020). The Relationship between Workplace Violence and Innovative Work Behavior: The Mediating Roles of Employee Wellbeing. *Healthcare (Basel)*, 8(3), 332. DOI: 10.3390/healthcare8030332 PMID: 32927711

Chapter 3
Balancing Work and Life Techniques for Maintaining Emotional Wellbeing in Entrepreneurship

Mustafa Kayyali
https://orcid.org/0000-0003-3300-262X
HE Higher Education Ranking, Syria

ABSTRACT

Entrepreneurship is generally characterized by long hours, high levels of stress, and the need to make difficult decisions, all of which can significantly affect emotional well-being. This chapter examines the vital need to establish a balance between work and personal life to sustain mental wellness in the entrepreneurial journey. It covers the frequent issues experienced by entrepreneurs, including burnout, stress, and the blurring of boundaries between work and life. Drawing on research and case studies, the chapter discusses practical approaches for establishing work-life balance, such as time management, delegation, mindfulness practices, and the growth of emotional intelligence. The chapter finishes by underlining the necessity for sustainable techniques that not only boost productivity but also support long-term emotional well-being in the challenging world of entrepreneurship.

INTRODUCTION

Entrepreneurship, generally considered a path to freedom and innovation, is loaded with both great potential and tremendous hurdles (Hess, 2006). Entrepreneurs are typically characterized as risk-takers, visionaries, and hard workers, driven by their enthusiasm to bring ideas to life and succeed in competitive markets. However, the drive for success in entrepreneurship often comes at a personal cost, as finding a balance between the demands of work and personal life becomes increasingly hard. This mismatch can have major ramifications on the emotional wellness of entrepreneurs, hurting not only their productivity and decision-making ability but also their personal relationships, physical health, and general mental resilience. The concept of work-life balance is particularly tough for entrepreneurs since the lines between work and life tend to blur more quickly than in regular employment (Nahkamäki, 2018). Entrepreneurs,

DOI: 10.4018/979-8-3693-3673-1.ch003

Copyright ©2025, IGI Global. Copying or distributing in print or electronic forms without written permission of IGI Global is prohibited.

especially in the early years of their businesses, are often deeply involved in every element of their firm, from product creation and marketing to customer service and financial administration. Unlike salaried employees who may enjoy fixed work hours and clear separations between professional and personal lives, entrepreneurs often find themselves working over the clock, spurred by the need to build their firms and stay competitive. This extreme emphasis on work can leave little room for personal life, rest, and emotional recovery, resulting in burnout, chronic stress, and even mental health illnesses such as anxiety and depression.

Despite the prevalent nature of these challenges, the rhetoric around entrepreneurship tends to romanticize the idea of hard effort and sacrifice, fostering the perception that success requires entrepreneurs to push themselves beyond their boundaries. However, recent research in psychology, management, and entrepreneurship has started to shed light on the adverse impacts of disregarding personal well-being in the quest for professional success. Prolonged periods of overwork can corrode an entrepreneur's inventiveness, impair decision-making ability, and weaken resilience, making it difficult to overcome the inevitable failures that come with running a firm. Furthermore, the absence of a healthy work-life balance can impair personal relationships, which are vital support networks for entrepreneurs, compounding feelings of isolation and stress. Achieving a work-life balance is not only about cutting working hours or taking longer holidays; it is about finding techniques to reconcile the demands of both personal and professional domains. In the entrepreneurial environment, this requires a sophisticated strategy that handles the unique constraints entrepreneurs encounter, such as the unpredictability of business cycles, financial uncertainty, and the emotional rollercoaster associated with the successes and failures of a venture. Effective work-life balance for entrepreneurs must be proactive and dynamic, allowing for moments of intense attention on business while maintaining appropriate time for personal activities that replenish emotional energy and nurture well-being.

A healthy work-life dynamic can greatly contribute to an entrepreneur's emotional well-being, which in turn is a major component in long-term business success. Emotional well-being, frequently described as the capacity to manage stress, have a positive outlook, and bounce back from adversity, is vital for entrepreneurs who regularly encounter high levels of uncertainty and risk. Entrepreneurs who invest in their emotional well-being by establishing a healthy balance between work and life are better able to manage the psychological obstacles of entrepreneurship (Stephan, 2018). They are more likely to display resilience, inventiveness, and effective problem-solving skills, which are vital for sustaining innovation and success in their companies. Fostering mental well-being through work-life balance can have a ripple effect beyond the individual entrepreneur. As leaders and role models, entrepreneurs who prioritize their mental health may set a positive example for their staff, encouraging a healthy workplace culture that emphasizes not only productivity but also personal welfare. This transformation can lead to increased employee satisfaction, lower turnover rates, and a more supportive and collaborative work environment, all of which are crucial for the long-term success of any firm. In an age where entrepreneurship is often promoted for its demands and sacrifices, this chapter aims to advocate for a more holistic approach—one that recognizes that psychological well-being and work-life balance are not luxuries, but essential components of a sustainable and successful entrepreneurial journey. By moving the focus from relentless hustling to conscious balance, entrepreneurs can develop cultures where both personal fulfillment and professional performance coexist, leading to healthier individuals, stronger businesses, and a more sustainable entrepreneurial ecosystem.

Challenges Entrepreneurs Face in Balancing Work and Personal Life

Entrepreneurship is often touted as a road to independence, innovation, and financial freedom, but beneath the glamorized picture of entrepreneurial success lies the hard reality of strong demands on time, energy, and emotional resilience. The road to creating and sustaining a business is plagued with problems, many of which can upset the delicate balance between work and family life. Entrepreneurs are uniquely positioned in their professional responsibilities, typically carrying the responsibility of decision-making, risk-taking, and ongoing adaptability to market conditions (Balven et al, 2018). Unlike salaried employees who often have fixed work hours and organized tasks, entrepreneurs must negotiate an uncertain terrain where their obligations are not constrained to a predefined timetable or task list. As a result, the obstacles to striking a healthy balance between work and personal life are both numerous and complex.

1. Blurred Boundaries Between Work and Personal Life

One of the most fundamental issues entrepreneurs confront is the blurring of boundaries between their business and personal life. In the early phases of a business, the entrepreneur often wears multiple hats—overseeing everything from product development and marketing to customer service and financial management (Tahir, 2024). The sheer scope of responsibility makes it tough to separate work from personal time. Unlike regular employees who may "clock out" at the end of the day, entrepreneurs may feel pressured to keep working around the clock, especially if they are operating in a competitive or fast-moving market (Monk, 2023). This blurring of boundaries leads to work intruding on personal time, resulting in fewer possibilities for relaxation, family relationships, or self-care, all of which are crucial to mental wellbeing. Additionally, with the development of technology and the greater interconnection of global markets, entrepreneurs are often "on call" 24/7 (Lubua, 2019). Email notifications, client demands, and business updates can occur at any moment, even during what would usually be considered off-hours. This constant condition of being accessible exacerbates the difficulty of separating personal and business life, causing entrepreneurs to endure mental exhaustion and emotional depletion.

2. Overcommitment and the Reluctance to Delegate

A big hurdle to establishing a work-life balance for many entrepreneurs is the temptation to overcommit. Entrepreneurs, particularly those in the early phases of their companies, sometimes feel the need to take on every duty alone (Lucas et al, 2020). This sense of over-responsibility originates from a fear of losing control or a belief that others may not be able to accomplish particular jobs to the necessary standard. This reluctance to delegate responsibilities can soon lead to overwork, as the entrepreneur tries to manage everything from high-level strategy to day-to-day operations. Overcommitment not only limits an entrepreneur's time and energy but also generates a psychological weight (Gabay-Mariani & Boissin, 2021). Many businesses suffer from the temptation to be continually active, feeling terrible when they take time off for personal reasons. This mindset of always needing to work can contribute to a cycle of stress and burnout, where the entrepreneur's health and personal relationships are neglected in favor of professional duties.

3. Financial Pressure and Uncertainty

Another problem that entrepreneurs frequently confront is the financial pressure that comes with running a business. Unlike salaried employees who have dependable income sources, entrepreneurs sometimes confront shifting financial situations, particularly in the early years of their companies. The need to seek capital, manage cash flow, and maintain profitability can produce tremendous stress, which in turn impacts an entrepreneur's ability to unplug from work. Financial insecurity can also force entrepreneurs to prolong their working hours and neglect their personal life, as they attempt to attain crucial business milestones (Chatrakul Na Ayudhya et al, 2019). The dread of business failure and the high stakes of financial loss can produce an overpowering sense of responsibility, leading to emotional pressure and an inability to take time away from the business. This is especially true for entrepreneurs who have invested personal funds or who are supporting families, as the financial risks they confront may feel extremely personal and serious.

4. Isolation and Lack of Support

Entrepreneurship can sometimes be a lonely endeavor. Many entrepreneurs start their enterprises as solo endeavors or in small teams, where the weight of decision-making lies primarily on their shoulders. The lack of a broader organizational structure or a team of coworkers to share the effort and offer emotional support might leave entrepreneurs feeling isolated. This isolation can be accentuated by the fact that entrepreneurs generally work long hours, limiting their time for social interactions and personal relationships (Becker et al, 2022). The solitude of entrepreneurship can also extend to emotional support systems. Unlike traditional employees who may have access to mentorship, team cohesion, or HR help for mental health, entrepreneurs are frequently forced to negotiate the emotional ups and downs of their company journeys on their own. The emotional toll of running a business—dealing with uncertainty, disappointments, and constant decision-making—can cause feelings of loneliness and overwhelm, making it even more difficult to establish a healthy work-life balance.

5. Burnout and Emotional Exhaustion

Burnout is a serious and prevalent concern that many entrepreneurs experience. Burnout, characterized by emotional weariness, depersonalization, and reduced sense of accomplishment, can develop from protracted periods of overwork and chronic stress. Entrepreneurs, particularly those who are very driven, may push themselves to the point of weariness in the pursuit of success. The constant pressure to meet deadlines, accomplish growth, and manage several tasks can leave little time for rest, rehabilitation, and personal fulfillment (Jiménez-Ortiz et al, 2019). Burnout not only impacts physical health but also inhibits cognitive and emotional performance. Entrepreneurs experiencing burnout may struggle with decision-making, creativity, and problem-solving—key components of business success (McFarland & Hlubocky, 2021). Moreover, burnout can lead to a negative spiral where work becomes increasingly unpleasant, and the entrepreneur's motivation to continue lowers, ultimately harming both personal life and business performance. Emotional weariness can also impact personal connections, as the entrepreneur becomes emotionally unavailable to friends and family.

6. The Myth of the "Always-On" Entrepreneur

Another difficulty in attaining work-life balance in entrepreneurship is the persistent societal notion that entrepreneurs must be "always on" to succeed. Society typically promotes the idea of the workaholic entrepreneur, continuously working and sacrificing personal well-being for business success (Hallonsten, 2023). This myth reinforces the perception that long hours and personal sacrifice are crucial to business performance, causing entrepreneurs to feel that taking breaks or walking away from work is a sign of weakness or failure. This cultural narrative puts great pressure on entrepreneurs to conform to unrealistic standards of performance, continuing the cycle of overwork and emotional distress (Dodd et al, 2023). The promotion of the "always-on" mindset produces a poisonous climate where rest, self-care, and personal leisure are devalued, further diminishing the prospect of attaining a balanced and meaningful life alongside entrepreneurial success.

7. The Impact on Personal Relationships

Balancing business and personal life is particularly tough for entrepreneurs in the context of personal relationships. The hard hours, financial demands, and emotional toll of owning a business may take a considerable toll on relationships with family, friends, and partners. Entrepreneurs may find it difficult to be present in their personal lives, resulting in strained relationships, misunderstandings, and conflict (Kumar et al, 2022). The continual emphasis on the firm can also produce feelings of neglect among loved ones, particularly if the entrepreneur is unable to set aside time for meaningful contact. Moreover, entrepreneurs who are trying to maintain work-life balance may face feelings of shame or irritation when their personal relationships suffer. This emotional struggle can further worsen stress levels, as entrepreneurs feel torn between their professional objectives and their commitments to their loved ones. Over time, this tension can destroy the very support structures that are crucial to an entrepreneur's emotional and mental welfare.

8. Health and Wellbeing Concerns

The pressures of entrepreneurship can significantly influence an individual's physical health, adding to the problems of achieving a work-life balance. The lack of time for rest, exercise, and proper food can contribute to physical tiredness, weight gain, sleep difficulties, and a compromised immune system (Stephan, 2018). These health difficulties, in turn, can contribute to a loss in mental and emotional health, producing a vicious cycle of stress and poor well-being. Entrepreneurs who do not prioritize their health are more likely to have long-term consequences, including chronic illnesses, that can further affect their capacity to manage their firms effectively. Achieving work-life balance is, however, not just about time management but also about ensuring that physical and emotional health are given the care they need to preserve both personal well-being and professional success.

The obstacles entrepreneurs encounter in managing business and personal life are broad and multifaceted. From blurred boundaries and overcommitment to financial demands, isolation, burnout, and cultural myths, these difficulties can adversely influence both personal welfare and company success. Addressing these problems involves purposeful effort, self-awareness, and a commitment to building lasting techniques that create a healthy and meaningful balance between work and life. As entrepreneurs manage the intricacies of their careers, finding balance is not only crucial for their own happiness but also critical to the long-term survival of their companies.

Impact of Imbalanced Work-Life on Emotional Wellbeing

The repercussions of an uneven work-life dynamic on emotional well-being are severe, particularly for entrepreneurs who are actively committed to the success and growth of their firms. The demands of entrepreneurship frequently create an environment where work becomes all-consuming, overshadowing personal life and progressively degrading the mental and emotional health of the individual. The cumulative impact of overwork, stress, and lack of personal time can lead to mental anguish, relational troubles, burnout, and a number of other psychiatric concerns. This section analyzes the multidimensional influence that an uneven work-life connection can have on an entrepreneur's mental well-being and general quality of life.

1. Chronic Stress and Anxiety

One of the most immediate and pervasive repercussions of an uneven work-life dynamic is chronic stress. Entrepreneurs sometimes endure great pressure to succeed, fulfill deadlines, and navigate the uncertainty of business situations. Unlike regular workers who may have a clearer delineation between work and personal time, entrepreneurs are frequently engrossed in work-related problems, often to the point where personal life is disregarded. This persistent exposure to stress can lead to chronic anxiety, a state where the entrepreneur feels perpetually overburdened by commitments and obligations. The worry coming from the desire to manage funds, lead a team, satisfy clients, and stay up with market changes can become devastating (Baker et al, 2024). Many entrepreneurs describe feeling a constant sense of disquiet or dread that they are not accomplishing enough, which can lead to a vicious cycle of overworking to compensate for perceived weaknesses. Over time, this continuous stress can create physical symptoms such as headaches, muscle tightness, insomnia, and high blood pressure, all of which add to emotional tiredness. Anxiety can undermine cognitive skills, such as focus, decision-making, and creativity (Ariyasinghe, 2021). Entrepreneurs who are continually concerned may struggle to think clearly, make educated decisions, and tackle difficulties with the innovative mentality necessary for business success. The accompanying mental pressure can lead to a feeling of helplessness and dissatisfaction, further hurting their emotional state and overall well-being.

2. Burnout and Emotional Exhaustion

Burnout is a common effect of uneven work-life interaction, particularly for entrepreneurs who fail to draw boundaries between their professional and home lives. Burnout is more than simply physical tiredness; it covers emotional and mental malaise that follows from prolonged periods of extreme stress and overwork. For entrepreneurs, burnout may be especially devastating, as it not only impacts their personal health but also threatens the viability of their business. Emotional exhaustion, one of the fundamental components of burnout, is characterized by a feeling of being depleted and unable to cope with the emotional demands of running a business (Sexton & Adair, 2019). Entrepreneurs facing emotional weariness often lose their passion and excitement for their profession. Tasks that formerly brought individuals delight and fulfillment may become sources of irritation or disinterest. This loss of motivation can lead to lower productivity and a drop in the quality of work, generating a negative feedback loop that exacerbates feelings of failure and stress. In addition to emotional tiredness, burnout can lead to cynicism and detachment. Entrepreneurs may come to feel alienated from their firm, their clients, and even their team members (Guercini & Cova, 2018). This emotional detachment is a protective technique to cope with overwhelming stress, but it can further damage relationships both in and beyond the organization. Ultimately, burnout threatens not only the emotional well-being of the entrepreneur but also the long-term health of the business.

3. Depression and Feelings of Isolation

The tremendous pressures of entrepreneurship can also lead to more serious mental health disorders, including depression. Entrepreneurs typically spend long hours in isolation, especially if they are sole firm owners or leading small teams. This solitude, along with the stresses of managing a business, can contribute to feelings of loneliness and separation from others (Ola et al, 2019). Entrepreneurs may believe that they have no one to turn to for assistance or that others, such as family or friends, may not understand the specific obstacles they confront. Depression can show in different ways, including feelings of hopelessness, lack of ambition, and trouble finding joy in activities that once offered pleasure. The emotional load of running a business can become overwhelming, especially when financial pressures or external disappointments increase the stress (Mukherjee, 2023). Entrepreneurs suffering from depression may struggle to get out of bed, focus on work, or even take care of basic personal needs, further contributing to the imbalance between work and personal life. Depression can affect connections with loved ones. Entrepreneurs who are emotionally unavailable or disconnected may unknowingly push away people closest to them, leading to additional isolation. This isolation can intensify feelings of loneliness and exacerbate the symptoms of depression, creating a cycle that is difficult to break without expert care.

4. Strained Personal Relationships

An uneven work-life relationship can have a substantial impact on personal relationships, which are crucial to emotional well-being. Entrepreneurs who are obsessed with their company may struggle to maintain good connections with their family, friends, and partners. The ongoing responsibilities of running a business might leave little time for meaningful connections, resulting in misunderstandings, neglect, and emotional distancing (Hwang & Jung, 2021). Partners of entrepreneurs often bear the burden of this imbalance, feeling that they are competing with the business for attention and affection. This can lead to conflict, resentment, and even the dissolution of relationships. Entrepreneurs may also miss crucial family events, such as birthdays, holidays, or other milestones, which can lead to feelings of guilt and further damage relationships. Over time, the lack of emotional support from personal relationships can leave entrepreneurs feeling lonely and emotionally depleted (Yester, 2019). The impact on relationships extends beyond romantic partners and families. Friendships might also suffer when entrepreneurs emphasize work above social engagements, leading to a sense of detachment from their social groups. Entrepreneurs may discover that they have less and less time for social activities, leading to a contraction of their support network. This isolation can have a detrimental effect on emotional well-being, as the lack of a robust social support system makes it difficult to cope with the challenges of business.

5. Loss of Personal Identity

Another major impact of an uneven work-life interaction on emotional well-being is the potential loss of personal identity. Entrepreneurs often put so much of themselves in their company that their personal identity becomes inseparable from their professional role (Rao & Sharma, 2018). The distinctions between "who they are" and "what they do" blur, and they may begin to measure their self-worth exclusively by the success or failure of their firm (Miller & Cho, 2018). This can be especially destructive at times of business struggles or setbacks, since entrepreneurs may internalize these difficulties and regard them as personal failures. This over-identification with work might lead to a lack of fulfillment in other aspects of life. Entrepreneurs may forsake hobbies, interests, and relationships that once provided them joy because they are fully focused on their firm. As personal identity becomes increasingly related to professional success, entrepreneurs may feel lost or empty when business is not going well, further contributing to emotional discomfort.

6. Decreased Emotional Resilience

An uneven work-life relationship can weaken an entrepreneur's emotional resilience over time. Emotional resilience is the ability to bounce back from stress, hardship, or setbacks. When entrepreneurs are distracted by work and neglect their personal lives, they may not have the required time or space to recharge emotionally (Shapero, 2019). This lack of recovery time makes it more difficult to tackle the unavoidable obstacles and uncertainties of running a business. Without sufficient emotional resilience, entrepreneurs may become more reactive to stress, making poor decisions or indulging in unhealthy coping techniques such as substance addiction or emotional disengagement. The inability to manage stress efficiently can lead to greater emotional strain, harming not just their personal welfare but also their work performance. Entrepreneurs with low emotional resilience may also find it tougher to keep a positive view, which can be damaging to their ability to lead and motivate their colleagues.

7. Impacts on Cognitive Function and Creativity

Cognitive function and creativity, both of which are vital to business success, are also significantly damaged by an uneven work-life relationship (Khalil et al, 2019). The brain requires relaxation and recovery to function efficiently, and when entrepreneurs are overworked, their cognitive abilities might suffer. Chronic stress decreases memory, focus, and decision-making, all of which are necessary for good company management (Aggarwal & Woolley, 2019). Creativity, the lifeblood of entrepreneurship, also weakens when work-life balance is interrupted. Entrepreneurs who are continuously in "survival mode," focused entirely on urgent duties and challenges, may struggle to think creatively or innovate. The lack of time for relaxation, introspection, and exploration inhibits their capacity to tackle difficulties with a fresh perspective. Over time, this reduction in cognitive function and creativity can limit business growth and leave entrepreneurs feeling stuck and unhappy.

8. Physical Health and Its Effect on Emotional Wellbeing

Finally, the impact of an uneven work-life dynamic on physical health might also lead to mental suffering. Entrepreneurs who disregard their physical well-being due to overwork may encounter several health concerns, including exhaustion, sleep disturbances, weight gain, and compromised immune systems (Hernandez et al, 2018). These physical ailments not only limit their capacity to perform at work but also have a direct impact on emotional well-being. Poor physical health can worsen emotions of stress, worry, and depression, creating a negative feedback loop where emotional and physical health decline simultaneously. Entrepreneurs who are physically unwell are less likely to have the energy or emotional ability to engage in good coping mechanisms, such as exercise, socializing, or pursuing hobbies, thus exacerbating the imbalance between work and life.

In summary, the influence of an uneven work-life dynamic on emotional wellness is wide-ranging and deeply significant for entrepreneurs. Chronic stress, burnout, emotional weariness, and strained relationships are just a few of the numerous effects that can result from disregarding personal life in favor of professional achievement. Entrepreneurs must acknowledge the necessity of keeping a good balance to sustain not just their mental well-being but also the long-term survival of their company initiatives.

Techniques for Achieving Work-Life Balance in Entrepreneurship

Achieving a healthy work-life balance is an immense challenge for entrepreneurs, who often find themselves absorbed in the demands of running a firm (Tahir, 2024). However, keeping a balance between work and personal life is crucial for sustaining emotional well-being, encouraging creativity, and assuring long-term success. By adopting successful tactics and making purposeful lifestyle choices, entrepreneurs can handle the intricacies of their business lives while keeping their personal happiness and mental health. In this section, we will cover numerous approaches that entrepreneurs can adopt to attain work-life balance, presenting practical solutions to lessen the impact of stress and overwork.

1. Setting Clear Boundaries Between Work and Personal Life

One of the foundational elements to obtaining work-life balance is the establishment of clear boundaries between professional responsibilities and personal life. Entrepreneurs often transgress these lines, working late into the evening or on weekends, and this can lead to stress and troubled relationships. To avoid this, entrepreneurs need to set discrete periods for work and personal activities (Kelliher et al, 2019). Setting defined working hours—whether it's a typical 9-to-5 schedule or a tailored routine based on business needs—can help create a divide between work and life. Additionally, it is necessary to designate locations for work and pleasure. For entrepreneurs who work from home, building a designated workspace helps to set mental boundaries. When the workday finishes, physically leaving the workstation signifies a change to personal time, allowing the entrepreneur to separate from business worries. By building both temporal and spatial boundaries, entrepreneurs may protect their personal lives from being overwhelmed by business. Entrepreneurs can also gain from employing technology to impose boundaries. For instance, adopting "do not disturb" options on devices during non-work hours helps prevent the incursion of work-related emails and notifications into personal time. Entrepreneurs may also wish to adopt policies that express these boundaries to clients, employees, and collaborators. For example, clarifying expectations for response times outside of business hours helps stakeholders realize when the entrepreneur is unavailable, decreasing the need to be "always on."

2. Prioritizing Time Management and Delegation

Effective time management is key for establishing work-life balance. Entrepreneurs generally wear numerous hats, juggling tasks ranging from strategic decision-making to day-to-day operations. Without careful planning, the demands of these duties can overwhelm even the most seasoned business (Wolters & Brady, 2021). To avoid this, entrepreneurs can employ time management approaches that emphasize high-impact activities and reduce time spent on low-value chores. One common time management method is the Eisenhower Matrix, which encourages entrepreneurs to categorize tasks based on their urgency and relevance. By focusing on tasks that are both vital and urgent, entrepreneurs can ensure they are allocating their time to activities that help the growth of their business. Non-urgent jobs can be postponed for later, while trivial activities can be delegated or omitted outright (Rovida & Zafferri, 2022). This prioritization technique helps businesses escape the temptation of working on superfluous chores that eat into personal time. Delegation is another key component of time management. Many entrepreneurs struggle to let go of control and strive to manage every area of their firm themselves. This strategy, while acceptable in the early phases of business, is unsustainable in the long term and leads to burnout. By recruiting talented team members or outsourcing jobs to freelancers or external agencies, entrepreneurs may offload obligations and free up time for both high-level strategic work and personal pursuits. Learning to say "no" is also a key ability for entrepreneurs. Business owners frequently face offers, meetings, or projects that may look promising but eventually detract from their core focus (Aulet et al, 2018). Entrepreneurs should be judicious about where they put their time and energy, ensuring that each commitment matches with their long-term goals. Saying "no" to low-priority chores or opportunities creates space for more important work and personal time.

3. Embracing Flexibility and Work-Life Integration

While traditional work-life balance assumes a distinct divide between business and personal life, many entrepreneurs may discover that combining the two domains is more realistic. Work-life integration understands that the demands of business frequently necessitate flexibility, allowing entrepreneurs to alter their schedules based on their specific circumstances (Wei & Villwock, 2021). For example, instead of following a regular 9-to-5 pattern, entrepreneurs could work in bursts, taking pauses throughout the day to engage in personal activities such as spending time with family, exercising, or pursuing hobbies (Uviebinené, 2021). This strategy provides more freedom and helps entrepreneurs to coordinate their work hours with their personal priorities. Flexibility is particularly crucial for entrepreneurs who have small children or other caregiving duties, as it allows them to adapt to family requirements without sacrificing business efficiency. Technology plays a crucial role in fostering work-life integration. Tools such as project management software, cloud-based collaboration platforms, and video conferencing allow entrepreneurs to work remotely and run their enterprises from anywhere. This flexibility enables entrepreneurs to retain personal obligations while yet being connected to their business activities. However, good work-life integration demands discipline—entrepreneurs must overcome the urge to let work infiltrate into every part of their day, even when technology makes it easier to stay connected. In adopting flexibility, it's also crucial for entrepreneurs to routinely examine their workload and adapt their schedules as needed. Business demands fluctuate, and during peak periods of activity, it may be necessary to temporarily alter the balance towards work. However, during slower periods, entrepreneurs should prioritize self-care, personal relationships, and relaxation to recharge their vitality. The trick is to remain adaptable, realizing that balance is a dynamic, rather than a static, goal.

4. Practicing Mindfulness and Stress Management

Mindfulness and stress management strategies are key tools for sustaining emotional well-being and work-life balance. The high levels of stress that entrepreneurs endure can lead to anxiety, burnout, and emotional weariness if not effectively managed. Mindfulness activities, like as meditation, deep breathing exercises, and journaling, help entrepreneurs stay grounded and present, lessening the impact of stress on their mental and physical health (Yang et al, 2018). Mindfulness means cultivating awareness of one's thoughts, feelings, and environment without judgment. For entrepreneurs, practicing mindfulness helps create mental space to process complicated business decisions, handle failures, and manage daily challenges without becoming overwhelmed. Regular meditation, even for just a few minutes each day, has been proven to lower anxiety and improve attention, helping businesses to face issues with a clearer mind. In addition to mindfulness, stress management approaches such as physical exercise and time spent in nature can have considerable benefits for work-life balance. Physical activity releases endorphins, the body's natural stress relievers, and helps to alleviate the physical strain that builds up from long hours of labor. Entrepreneurs should prioritize regular exercise, whether it's a daily workout, yoga, or even a brief walk, to promote both physical and mental wellness. Time spent outdoors, away from the continual stimulus of company operations, can help encourage relaxation and mental clarity. Entrepreneurs who make time for leisure activities that they enjoy, such as hiking, gardening, or engaging in creative hobbies, find a stronger sense of fulfillment and emotional resiliency. These hobbies provide a much-needed vacation from work, helping to recharge energy levels and prevent burnout.

5. Seeking Support Networks and Mentorship

Another great strategy for establishing work-life balance is building a strong support network. Entrepreneurship can be solitary, especially for solo business owners who lack the camaraderie of a team. Developing a network of peers, mentors, and advisers may give entrepreneurs both emotional support and practical business assistance, helping them manage problems more efficiently. Peer support organizations, such as entrepreneur forums or mastermind groups, allow business owners to connect with others who understand the particular stresses of entrepreneurship (Bahrami et al, 2022). These groups give a venue for sharing experiences, discussing challenges, and exchanging ideas, all of which help ease the sense of isolation that many entrepreneurs face. Regular check-ins with peers can help generate accountability for preserving work-life balance, as entrepreneurs encourage one another to prioritize self-care and set boundaries. Mentorship is another excellent resource for entrepreneurs searching for balance. Experienced mentors who have traveled the business journey can offer insight into how to handle the competing demands of work and personal life (Haider & Dasti, 2022). They can discuss techniques for time management, delegating, and stress relief, drawing from their own experiences. A mentor can also provide perspective, helping entrepreneurs avoid common mistakes like overcommitting or ignoring personal connections. In addition to professional networks, personal support from family and friends plays a crucial role in achieving work-life balance. Entrepreneurs should talk freely with their loved ones about the problems they confront and the need for assistance. By building solid relationships and making time for family and social activities, entrepreneurs can establish a meaningful personal life that balances the demands of their business.

6. Focusing on Long-Term Sustainability and Self-Care

A vital part of attaining work-life balance is the focus on long-term sustainability. Entrepreneurship is a marathon, not a sprint, and entrepreneurs who push themselves too hard in the near term risk burning out before attaining their long-term goals. To guarantee sustained success, entrepreneurs must embrace a mindset that prioritizes sustainability and self-care. Self-care involves prioritizing one's physical, emotional, and mental wellness (El-Osta et al, 2019). Entrepreneurs should make self-care activities, such as regular exercise, healthy diet, proper sleep, and relaxation, non-negotiable aspects of their routine. Taking time for self-care not only boosts personal wellness but also improves company performance by enhancing focus, creativity, and resilience. Additionally, entrepreneurs should create sustainable work habits by avoiding overwork and making time for regular breaks. The Pomodoro Technique, for instance, encourages entrepreneurs to work in focused spurts, followed by brief pauses. This strategy minimizes mental tiredness and promotes productivity, allowing for a greater balance between work and personal time. By taking a long-term view, entrepreneurs can avoid the trap of overwork and focus on developing a firm that resonates with their personal values and lifestyle. This method provides a sense of fulfillment and purpose, lowering the danger of burnout and emotional tiredness.

In conclusion, finding work-life balance in entrepreneurship is a complicated task that demands purposeful effort, discipline, and self-awareness. By setting limits, managing time effectively, embracing flexibility, practicing mindfulness, seeking help, and prioritizing self-care, entrepreneurs may develop a balanced lifestyle that supports both personal well-being and company success.

The Role of Emotional Intelligence in Managing Stress and Preventing Burnout

Emotional intelligence (EI) is a vital aspect of the ability of entrepreneurs to manage stress, prevent burnout, and maintain emotional well-being while navigating the complexity of running a business (Molero Jurado et al, 2021). Often defined as the ability to detect, comprehend, control, and affect emotions in oneself and others, emotional intelligence plays a vital part in how individuals cope with the emotional problems inherent in business. High emotional intelligence equips entrepreneurs with the ability to handle stress more effectively, respond to failures with fortitude, and maintain healthy interpersonal relationships, all of which are vital to attaining long-term success and avoiding burnout.

1. Understanding Emotional Intelligence in Entrepreneurship

Emotional intelligence comprises several components that are particularly significant to entrepreneurship: self-awareness, self-regulation, motivation, empathy, and social skills (Ingram et al, 2019). Each of these components adds to how an entrepreneur handles stress, maintains balance, and establishes successful business connections.

- Self-awareness refers to the ability to recognize one's own emotions, strengths, shortcomings, and stress triggers. Self-aware entrepreneurs can notice early indicators of stress and emotional weariness, allowing them to make proactive efforts to treat these feelings before they develop into burnout. By recognizing their emotional condition, people are better positioned to make thoughtful, well-calibrated decisions, even in high-pressure situations.
- Self-regulation entails managing one's emotions in a healthy and useful manner. Entrepreneurs with good self-regulation abilities can maintain cool under stress, avoiding impulsive emotions that could lead to bad decision-making. For instance, in moments of crisis or frustration, emotion-

ally intelligent entrepreneurs are able to remain calm, analyze critically, and avoid letting negative emotions take over.
- Motivation within the context of emotional intelligence pertains to the inner drive to pursue goals with energy and tenacity. Entrepreneurs often experience failures, uncertainties, and challenges in their business travels. Emotional intelligence helps them keep focused on their long-term objective without becoming frustrated by temporary failures. This intrinsic motivation helps buffer against feelings of stress and tiredness, keeping entrepreneurs linked with their personal and professional purpose.
- Empathy allows entrepreneurs to comprehend the feelings and views of others, whether they are employees, clients, or business partners (Bacq & Alt, 2018). This emotional understanding assists in creating solid connections, fostering a supportive work environment, and resolving problems in a manner that decreases interpersonal stress. In emotionally intelligent leaders, empathy also contributes to the formation of a positive company culture, which can reduce overall stress levels in the workplace.
- Social skills, the final component of emotional intelligence, encompass communication, conflict resolution, and relationship management. Entrepreneurs with good social skills are adept at managing conversations, negotiating successfully, and cooperating with others, all of which serve to decrease stress and tension in professional relationships. Moreover, pleasant social connections give entrepreneurs the support networks they need to cope with commercial challenges.

2. Managing Stress Through Self-Awareness and Self-Regulation

One of the most significant parts of emotional intelligence in handling stress is self-awareness. Entrepreneurs who are attuned to their emotions can detect stress causes early on and take preventive actions before they spiral into unmanageable worry or burnout. Stress frequently builds up gradually, starting with tiny disappointments or pressures that increase over time. By being aware of these early signs—such as irritation, difficulty concentrating, or physical symptoms like tension headaches—entrepreneurs can intervene before their stress reaches intolerable levels (Mertens et al, 2022). Once stress is identified, self-regulation becomes vital. Emotionally savvy entrepreneurs do not conceal their emotions but rather manage them in ways that are profitable and healthful. Techniques such as deep breathing exercises, mindfulness meditation, and reflective writing can help entrepreneurs process their emotions and recover emotional balance during stressful times. For instance, practicing mindfulness helps entrepreneurs stay anchored in the current moment, minimizing the anxiety that comes from worrying about the future or ruminating on past mistakes (Miller & Verhaeghen, 2022). These self-regulation skills minimize emotional overload and help entrepreneurs respond to stress with greater clarity and tranquility. Emotional intelligence also helps entrepreneurs build efficient coping techniques. Instead of reacting impulsively to difficult situations—such as lashing out in irritation or making hasty decisions—emotionally savvy persons take a step back to examine their alternatives. This controlled response decreases the risk of making actions that worsen stress or produce further problems. Moreover, self-regulation enables entrepreneurs to maintain a healthy work-life balance by defining emotional boundaries, ensuring that work-related stress does not flow over into their personal lives.

3. The Role of Motivation in Overcoming Challenges

Entrepreneurship is inherently tough, and the road to success is often marked by failures, setbacks, and barriers. Without emotional intelligence, entrepreneurs may get disheartened when faced with these difficulties, leading to heightened stress and burnout. However, emotionally competent entrepreneurs use motivation as a cushion against misfortune. They are driven by a deep sense of purpose and a passion for their profession, which helps them persevere in the face of obstacles (Vermote et al, 2020). Motivation, as a component of emotional intelligence, also assists entrepreneurs in sustaining optimism and resilience. Rather than viewing setbacks as failures, emotionally intelligent persons perceive them as chances for growth and learning. This mindset not only decreases stress but also encourages entrepreneurs to approach problem-solving with creativity and passion. By remaining motivated and focused on long-term goals, entrepreneurs can prevent stress from overwhelming them, even during periods of extreme pressure (Goetz & Schork, 2018). In addition to personal drive, emotionally savvy entrepreneurs often inspire and motivate their colleagues. By creating an environment where employees feel valued and supported, leaders may reduce workplace stress and build a good, productive attitude. When employees are motivated and engaged, the entrepreneur benefits from a more resilient team that can jointly weather business crises, thus decreasing the weight of stress on the individual entrepreneur.

4. Empathy and Social Support as Stress Buffers

Empathy, a core feature of emotional intelligence, plays a significant role in managing stress through relationship-building and social support. Entrepreneurs with excellent empathy abilities are able to grasp the emotional needs and worries of those around them. This understanding is crucial in reducing conflicts and tensions within teams, with clients, and with business partners, all of which can contribute to stress (Kothgassner et al, 2019). By cultivating open communication and empathy-driven interactions, emotionally intelligent entrepreneurs may build a workplace culture where employees feel confident sharing their worries and emotions. This sense of psychological safety not only increases team cohesion but also lessens the overall emotional burden on the entrepreneur. When entrepreneurs are empathic leaders, they are more likely to obtain emotional support from their team during hard times, which can help buffer the harmful impacts of stress. Empathy also extends beyond professional interactions to encompass personal connections (Fuller et al, 2021). Entrepreneurs with high emotional intelligence frequently establish strong personal support networks, including family, friends, mentors, and colleagues. These relationships provide emotional sustenance during periods of high stress, allowing a platform for the entrepreneur to discuss their experiences, seek advice, and gain perspective. The availability of supporting relationships is a vital aspect in preventing burnout, as it helps entrepreneurs feel connected, understood, and valued both within and outside of their company pursuits.

5. Preventing Burnout Through Emotional Intelligence

Burnout, characterized by emotional tiredness, cynicism, and a sense of diminishing personal success, is a typical concern for entrepreneurs who struggle to handle the high demands of their profession (Puertas Molero, 2019). Emotional intelligence serves as a protective factor against burnout by giving entrepreneurs the tools they need to manage stress efficiently and maintain a healthy work-life balance. One of the major factors in burnout is extended exposure to stress without effective coping skills. Emotionally competent entrepreneurs realize when they are approaching the limits of their emotional and physical capabilities. They are able to step back, analyze their workload, and take preemptive measures to reduce stress. This can involve delegating tasks, taking breaks, or obtaining professional help such as therapy or coaching. Emotionally intelligent persons are better able to manage the emotional highs and lows that come with entrepreneurship (Molero Jurado et al, 2021). Instead of internalizing failure or becoming overwhelmed by setbacks, they keep a sense of perspective and emotional resilience. This ability to bounce back from adversities is crucial in minimizing the emotional weariness that leads to burnout. Emotional intelligence supports self-care, which is vital for minimizing burnout. Entrepreneurs with strong emotional intelligence emphasize their well-being, realizing that their mental and physical health is crucial to the success of their firm. They are more likely to engage in regular self-care routines such as exercise, relaxation, hobbies, and spending time with loved ones. These activities help to replenish emotional energy and provide a buffer against the chronic stress that can lead to burnout.

6. Developing Emotional Intelligence for Long-Term Success

While some entrepreneurs may inherently possess a high level of emotional intelligence, it is a skill that can be developed and refined over time. Entrepreneurs who invest in enhancing their emotional intelligence will gain not only from reduced stress and burnout but also from greater leadership qualities and more meaningful relationships. There are various ways entrepreneurs can focus on enhancing their emotional intelligence (Nightingale et al, 2018). Self-awareness can be cultivated through techniques such as journaling, mindfulness, and receiving input from trusted colleagues and mentors. Self-regulation can be enhanced by adopting stress management practices such as meditation, cognitive-behavioral tactics, and time management tools. Empathy and social skills can be fostered by carefully listening to others, practicing open communication, and engaging in empathy-building exercises such as role-playing or perspective-taking. Finally, motivation may be boosted by creating clear, relevant goals and constantly reflecting on the entrepreneur's personal and professional principles. By purposefully increasing their emotional intelligence, entrepreneurs may establish a more balanced, meaningful, and sustainable approach to their business. Not only will they be better equipped to handle stress and minimize burnout, but they will also be more successful leaders who can encourage and support others on their entrepreneurial journey.

In conclusion, emotional intelligence is a significant tool for entrepreneurs, enabling them to manage stress, avoid burnout, and keep a healthy balance between work and personal life. By building self-awareness, self-regulation, motivation, empathy, and social skills, entrepreneurs can build the emotional resilience needed to survive in the challenging environment of entrepreneurship. As emotional intelligence becomes more recognized as a vital aspect of entrepreneurial success, entrepreneurs who invest in developing these talents will be better positioned to achieve long-term health and commercial growth.

Sustainable Practices for Long-Term Emotional Wellbeing

Entrepreneurship is a challenging profession that typically entails juggling high levels of responsibility, uncertainty, and labor pressure. While short-term strategies for reducing stress and increasing work-life balance are crucial, entrepreneurs must also adopt sustainable practices that encourage long-term emotional well-being (Alam, 2022). Sustainable emotional well-being comprises the constant cultivation of habits and tactics that help entrepreneurs manage stress, prevent burnout, and maintain a healthy balance between their personal and professional lives over time. Sustainable emotional wellness is not a destination but a process. It involves ongoing effort, self-reflection, and modifications to guarantee that entrepreneurs can face the demands of entrepreneurship without sacrificing their health and happiness.

By adopting methods that support their emotional, mental, and physical health, entrepreneurs may succeed both in their professional and personal lives in the long term.

1. Prioritizing Self-Care as a Daily Habit

Self-care is a vital ingredient for establishing long-term emotional well-being, although it is often ignored by entrepreneurs due to their busy schedules and constant concentration on their business (Riegel et al, 2021). Sustainable self-care requires making a purposeful effort to add activities that promote relaxation, renewal, and mental clarity into the daily routine. These activities can include physical activity, appropriate sleep, healthy food, and mindfulness techniques like meditation and yoga.

- Physical Exercise: Regular physical activity is one of the most effective strategies to manage stress and promote emotional health. Exercise releases endorphins, the body's natural mood boosters, which assist to counteract feelings of anxiety and despair. Entrepreneurs should prioritize exercise not only for its physical benefits but also as a tool to improve cognitive function, stimulate creativity, and enhance their general attitude. Even a daily 30-minute stroll can greatly reduce stress and boost mental clarity (Kell, 2024).
- Adequate Sleep: Sleep is crucial for emotional well-being, and its value cannot be emphasized. Entrepreneurs who persistently sacrifice sleep to fulfill business needs generally experience cognitive deficits, psychological instability, and heightened stress levels. In the long term, sleep deprivation can lead to burnout and decreased productivity. To retain emotional wellness, entrepreneurs must commit to getting 7-8 hours of excellent sleep each night and adopt a healthy sleep regimen that involves winding down before bed and minimizing distractions.
- Healthy Eating: Nutrition plays a significant impact in emotional and mental wellness (Hosker et al, 2019). A well-balanced diet rich in vitamins, minerals, and healthy fats enhances brain function, reduces anxiety, and helps entrepreneurs regulate their energy levels throughout the day. Entrepreneurs should attempt to avoid processed foods and excessive coffee, which can lead to energy dips and emotional changes. Instead, they can focus on ingesting complete foods, fruits, vegetables, and plenty of water to maintain stable energy and emotional equilibrium.
- Mindfulness Practices: Mindfulness meditation, yoga, and other relaxation techniques help entrepreneurs stay grounded and manage stress more efficiently (Singh, 2021). Mindfulness activities encourage the brain to focus on the present moment, lowering anxiety about the future and ruminating over previous events. Regular mindfulness exercises can raise self-awareness, improve emotional regulation, and foster a sense of serenity amid the pressures of entrepreneurship. For lasting emotional well-being, entrepreneurs should incorporate mindfulness into their daily routines, even if it's just for a few minutes each day.

2. Setting Clear Boundaries Between Work and Personal Life

One of the biggest issues entrepreneurs confront is the dissolving of boundaries between their business and personal life. Due to the repetitive nature of their work, entrepreneurs may find it difficult to switch off from corporate operations, leading to a constant sense of being "on duty." Over time, this lack of separation may damage emotional well-being, as the demands of work encroach on time meant for rest, relaxation, and personal relationships. Establishing and maintaining clear boundaries between work and personal life is vital for long-term mental stability (Kelliher et al, 2019). This involves conscious planning and discipline, as well as the capacity to recognize when work is absorbing too much personal time.

- Creating a Work Schedule: Entrepreneurs should design an organized work schedule that delineates particular hours for work and non-work activities. This structure helps to prevent work from spilling into evenings, weekends, and family time. Adhering to a work schedule also boosts focus during business hours and promotes relaxation and healing during personal time. Entrepreneurs should be deliberate about setting aside time for hobbies, family, and interacting with others, as these activities provide emotional sustenance and help preserve a feeling of balance.
- Setting Technology Boundaries: Technology, while a valuable tool for running a business, can also be a cause of stress. Entrepreneurs often feel the need to be continuously connected to their phones, emails, and social media, which can lead to information overload and fatigue. To maintain mental well-being, entrepreneurs should establish boundaries with technology, such as designating tech-free zones or hours, notably during family meals, relaxation moments, and bedtime. Turning off notifications and placing limits on work-related communication after a certain hour helps create the essential mental space for relaxation and emotional recuperation.
- Delegation and Outsourcing: Entrepreneurs typically take on too many duties, resulting in feelings of overwhelm. One sustainable technique for preserving mental well-being is learning to delegate tasks and outsource work when necessary. Delegation helps entrepreneurs focus on high-priority activities while entrusting others with duties that are not central to their competence. This not only minimizes the workload but also offers entrepreneurs more time for self-care and personal interests. Entrepreneurs could learn to trust their staff, seek out freelancers, or outsource administrative jobs to create a more manageable workload.

3. Developing a Strong Support System

A solid support system is a critical aspect of establishing long-term mental wellness. Entrepreneurs who have a network of supporting relationships—both personal and professional—are better suited to handle the stress and pressures of running a business (Bisschoff et al, 2019). This network gives emotional affirmation, practical guidance, and support, helping entrepreneurs retain perspective and stay motivated during difficult times.

- Personal Relationships: Family, friends, and close personal ties are crucial sources of emotional support. Entrepreneurs should prioritize developing these relationships by constantly communicating with loved ones and sharing their experiences, both positive and negative. These personal ties offer a secure area to vent feelings, get perspective, and receive encouragement. Entrepreneurs should also set aside time for social activities, which can help them recharge emotionally and build a sense of belonging outside of their corporate identity.
- Mentorship and Peer Support: In addition to personal relationships, entrepreneurs can benefit from professional support systems, such as mentors, peer teams, and networking communities. Having a mentor—someone who has faced the obstacles of entrepreneurship and can offer guidance—provides vital emotional and practical support. Peer groups, such as entrepreneurial mastermind groups or industry associations, create a sense of camaraderie and shared knowledge. Engaging

with colleagues who encounter similar obstacles promotes emotional resilience and helps entrepreneurs feel less alienated.
- Seeking Professional Help: Emotional well-being should not be considered an afterthought. Entrepreneurs who endure persistent stress or signs of burnout may benefit from getting professional support, like as therapy or coaching. Mental health practitioners can give coping skills, assist entrepreneurs process their emotions, and provide ways to manage stress more successfully. Regularly checking in with a therapist or coach can be a vital aspect of a long-term emotional well-being plan.

4. Adopting a Growth Mindset for Resilience

A growth mindset—the concept that abilities and intelligence can be increased through hard effort, study, and perseverance—may greatly contribute to long-term mental well-being (Baker et al, 2021). Entrepreneurs with a growth mentality regard problems, failures, and losses as chances for progress rather than as insurmountable hurdles. This approach develops resilience and helps entrepreneurs remain optimistic even in the face of hardship.

- Embracing Failures as Learning Opportunities: Instead of becoming frustrated by failure, entrepreneurs with a growth mindset assess what went wrong and uncover lessons that may be applied to future attempts. This technique lowers feelings of dissatisfaction and inadequacy, which are major triggers for emotional stress. By embracing failure as a normal part of the business path, entrepreneurs can preserve their emotional well-being and continue to pursue their goals with fresh intensity.
- Focusing on Continuous Improvement: A growth mindset pushes entrepreneurs to focus on continual development rather than perfection. This lessens the pressure to achieve unreasonable expectations, which often leads to stress and burnout. Entrepreneurs who embrace a growth mindset enjoy achievement, no matter how modest, and know that success is developed over time via persistent work and learning.
- Practicing Gratitude and Positivity: Gratitude and optimism are strong practices that can help long-term emotional well-being. Entrepreneurs may integrate thankfulness into their daily routine by taking time to reflect on positive elements of their lives and their business, especially during hard times. Gratitude helps shift focus away from stressors and fosters a more happy and balanced mindset. By appreciating little accomplishments, expressing thanks for their team, and focusing on what they have done, entrepreneurs can maintain a positive mindset that buffers against emotional tiredness.

5. Creating a Purpose-Driven Business

Entrepreneurs who develop purpose-driven businesses—businesses that are connected with their personal values and contribute positively to society—are more likely to achieve long-term emotional happiness and fulfillment (Losana & Gallardo, 2019). Purpose-driven business creates a greater sense of meaning and motivation, which can help entrepreneurs traverse difficult moments with perseverance and optimism.

- Aligning firm with Personal principles: Entrepreneurs should take the time to think about their personal principles and how these values might be integrated into their firm. A values-driven strategy not only gives emotional happiness but also promotes motivation and personal fulfillment. When entrepreneurs are enthusiastic about the cause behind their jobs, they are more likely to find joy in their everyday responsibilities, especially in the face of challenges.
- Contributing to a Greater Good: Many entrepreneurs get emotional joy by building enterprises that make a good impact on society, whether through ethical methods, sustainable products, or philanthropic initiatives. Contributing to the larger good creates a sense of purpose that transcends beyond financial achievement, leading to long-term mental well-being. Entrepreneurs who feel connected to a bigger mission are better able to handle stress and retain resilience because they appreciate the broader value of their work.

CONCLUSION

The journey of entrepreneurship is typically depicted as one of tireless desire, ambition, and invention, yet under the surface lies the reality of great demands that can jeopardize the very emotional and mental welfare of entrepreneurs. As this chapter has discussed, maintaining a balance between work and personal life is not only crucial for personal fulfillment but also for sustained professional success. For too long, the discourse surrounding entrepreneurship has exalted the notion of overwork and personal sacrifice, arguing that such trade-offs are a necessary price for obtaining success. However, this perspective is rapidly being challenged as the adverse repercussions of an imbalanced lifestyle—burnout, chronic stress, mental health disorders—become more generally recognized. At the center of this conversation is the concept that emotional well-being is not a luxury but a requirement for entrepreneurs. Emotional well-being creates the foundation for resilience, creativity, effective decision-making, and long-term success, all of which are crucial in navigating the unpredictable and demanding world of entrepreneurship. By preserving emotional health through a balanced approach to work and life, entrepreneurs can better manage the psychological demands of their businesses, helping them to stay focused, adaptive, and motivated in the face of obstacles. Neglecting this balance can lead to a range of bad results, from decreased cognitive capabilities to strained relationships and physical health difficulties, which in turn diminish the entrepreneur's capacity to continue their business efforts over time. The conclusion of this chapter underlines the need for a paradigm shift in how work-life balance is seen and implemented in the business realm. Rather than perceiving it as a trade-off between personal satisfaction and professional success, entrepreneurs must acknowledge that attaining balance is crucial to their long-term survival and growth. It is about incorporating emotional well-being into the fundamental fabric of their business plans, ensuring that personal care is as prioritized as business development. Entrepreneurs who use this strategy are not only more likely to achieve financial success but also to sustain their ventures in a way that supports both personal and professional fulfillment.

In conclusion, the pursuit of work-life balance and emotional well-being is not only an individual responsibility but a strategic requirement for entrepreneurs. A well-balanced approach to life and work increases not just the personal health and happiness of the entrepreneur but also contributes to the long-term profitability of their firm. Entrepreneurs who prioritize their emotional well-being through sustainable practices are better positioned to face the inherent obstacles of business with resilience, inventiveness, and clarity. Moreover, by setting an example for their teams and fostering pleasant, balanced work environments, they contribute to a broader cultural shift that emphasizes the importance of mental health and emotional fulfillment in professional achievement. Ultimately, success in entrepreneurship should not be evaluated merely by financial or market achievements but by the capacity to live a meaningful, balanced life alongside professional activities. Entrepreneurs who learn to integrate their jobs with their personal lives harmonically and sustainably are more likely to experience not only commercial success but also a meaningful, emotionally healthy life. This holistic approach to entrepreneurship is not only desirable but required in today's fast-paced, high-stress corporate world, where the pressures of work can easily eclipse the delights of personal fulfillment. By adopting a mindset that regards emotional wellness as a fundamental component of success, entrepreneurs can establish firms that are not only financially sustainable but also thoroughly connected with their own beliefs and long-term satisfaction.

REFERENCES

Aggarwal, I., & Woolley, A. W. (2019). Team creativity, cognition, and cognitive style diversity. *Management Science*, 65(4), 1586–1599. DOI: 10.1287/mnsc.2017.3001

Alam, A. (2022). Investigating sustainable education and positive psychology interventions in schools towards achievement of sustainable happiness and wellbeing for 21st century pedagogy and curriculum. *ECS Transactions*, 107(1), 19481–19494. DOI: 10.1149/10701.19481ecst

. Ariyasinghe, S. K. (2021). Conceptualizing the Effects of Non-Secular Mindfulness Interventions in Overcoming the Challenges Related To Work-Life Imbalance.

Aulet, B., Hargadon, A., Pittaway, L., Brush, C., & Alpi, S. (2018). What I have learned about teaching entrepreneurship: Perspectives of five master educators. In *Annals of entrepreneurship education and pedagogy–2018* (pp. 2–26). Edward Elgar Publishing. DOI: 10.4337/9781788114950.00009

Bacq, S., & Alt, E. (2018). Feeling capable and valued: A prosocial perspective on the link between empathy and social entrepreneurial intentions. *Journal of Business Venturing*, 33(3), 333–350. DOI: 10.1016/j.jbusvent.2018.01.004

Bahrami, P., Nosratabadi, S., Palouzian, K., & Hegedűs, S. (2022). Modeling the impact of mentoring on women's work-life balance: A grounded theory approach. *Administrative Sciences*, 13(1), 6. DOI: 10.3390/admsci13010006

Baker, F. R., Baker, K. L., & Burrell, J. (2021). Introducing the skills-based model of personal resilience: Drawing on content and process factors to build resilience in the workplace. *Journal of Occupational and Organizational Psychology*, 94(2), 458–481. DOI: 10.1111/joop.12340

Baker, R., Puzi, N. F. H. M., Saudi, N. S. M., Zahari, H. M., Sallehudin, H., Zainol, N. A. M., & Selamat, M. N. (2024). The Influenced of Work-life Balance on Emotional Intelligence, Depression, Anxiety, and Stress. *Kurdish Studies*, 12(1), 43–57.

Balven, R., Fenters, V., Siegel, D. S., & Waldman, D. (2018). Academic entrepreneurship: The roles of identity, motivation, championing, education, work-life balance, and organizational justice. *The Academy of Management Perspectives*, 32(1), 21–42. DOI: 10.5465/amp.2016.0127

Becker, W. J., Belkin, L. Y., Tuskey, S. E., & Conroy, S. A. (2022). Surviving remotely: How job control and loneliness during a forced shift to remote work impacted employee work behaviors and well-being. *Human Resource Management*, 61(4), 449–464. DOI: 10.1002/hrm.22102

Bisschoff, M., Koen, V., & Ryke, E. H. (2019). Strategies for work–family balance in a South African context. *Community Work & Family*, 22(3), 319–337. DOI: 10.1080/13668803.2018.1473337

Chatrakul Na Ayudhya, U., Prouska, R., & Beauregard, T. A. (2019). The impact of global economic crisis and austerity on quality of working life and work-life balance: A capabilities perspective. *European Management Review*, 16(4), 847–862. DOI: 10.1111/emre.12128

Dodd, S., Anderson, A., & Jack, S. (2023). "Let them not make me a stone"—Repositioning entrepreneurship. *Journal of Small Business Management*, 61(4), 1842–1870. DOI: 10.1080/00472778.2020.1867734

El-Osta, A., Webber, D., Gnani, S., Banarsee, R., Mummery, D., Majeed, A., & Smith, P. (2019). The self-care matrix: a unifying framework for self-Care.-Selfcare Journal. SelfCare Journal.

Fuller, M., Kamans, E., van Vuuren, M., Wolfensberger, M., & de Jong, M. D. (2021). Conceptualizing empathy competence: A professional communication perspective. *Journal of Business and Technical Communication*, 35(3), 333–368. DOI: 10.1177/10506519211001125

Gabay-Mariani, L., & Boissin, J. P. (2021). Commitment profiles of nascent entrepreneurs: Insights from an empirical taxonomy among French student entrepreneurs. *International Journal of Entrepreneurial Behaviour & Research*, 27(5), 1214–1240. DOI: 10.1108/IJEBR-09-2020-0652

Goetz, L. H., & Schork, N. J. (2018). Personalized medicine: Motivation, challenges, and progress. *Fertility and Sterility*, 109(6), 952–963. DOI: 10.1016/j.fertnstert.2018.05.006 PMID: 29935653

Guercini, S., & Cova, B. (2018). Unconventional entrepreneurship. *Journal of Business Research*, 92, 385–391. DOI: 10.1016/j.jbusres.2018.06.021

Haider, Z., & Dasti, R. (2022). Mentoring, research self-efficacy, work–life balance and psychological well-being of doctoral program students. *International Journal of Mentoring and Coaching in Education*, 11(2), 170–182. DOI: 10.1108/IJMCE-07-2020-0036

Hallonsten, O. (2023). We're All Entrepreneurs Now. In *Empty Innovation: Causes and Consequences of Society's Obsession with Entrepreneurship and Growth* (pp. 47–59). Springer International Publishing. DOI: 10.1007/978-3-031-31479-7_4

Hernandez, R., Bassett, S. M., Boughton, S. W., Schuette, S. A., Shiu, E. W., & Moskowitz, J. T. (2018). Psychological well-being and physical health: Associations, mechanisms, and future directions. *Emotion Review*, 10(1), 18–29. DOI: 10.1177/1754073917697824 PMID: 36650890

Hess, F. M. (Ed.). (2006). *Educational entrepreneurship: Realities, challenges, possibilities*. Harvard Education Press.

Hosker, D. K., Elkins, R. M., & Potter, M. P. (2019). Promoting mental health and wellness in youth through physical activity, nutrition, and sleep. *Child and Adolescent Psychiatric Clinics of North America*, 28(2), 171–193. DOI: 10.1016/j.chc.2018.11.010 PMID: 30832951

Hwang, J. H., & Jung, H. S. (2021). The effects of work characteristics related to work–life imbalance on presenteeism among female workers in the health and social work sectors: Mediation analysis of psychological and physical health problems. *International Journal of Environmental Research and Public Health*, 18(12), 6218. DOI: 10.3390/ijerph18126218 PMID: 34201286

Ingram, A., Peake, W. O., Stewart, W., & Watson, W. (2019). Emotional intelligence and venture performance. *Journal of Small Business Management*, 57(3), 780–800. DOI: 10.1111/jsbm.12333

Jiménez-Ortiz, J. L., Islas-Valle, R. M., Jiménez-Ortiz, J. D., Pérez-Lizarraga, E., Hernández-García, M. E., & González-Salazar, F. (2019). Emotional exhaustion, burnout, and perceived stress in dental students. *The Journal of International Medical Research*, 47(9), 4251–4259. DOI: 10.1177/0300060519859145 PMID: 31311371

Kell, S. (2024). University Students' Perceptions of a 30-Minute Break during Class: A Realistic Practice for Wellness? *Teaching & Learning Inquiry*, 12, 12. DOI: 10.20343/teachlearninqu.12.17

Kelliher, C., Richardson, J., & Boiarintseva, G. (2019). All of work? All of life? Reconceptualising work-life balance for the 21st century. *Human Resource Management Journal*, 29(2), 97–112. DOI: 10.1111/1748-8583.12215

Khalil, R., Godde, B., & Karim, A. A. (2019). The link between creativity, cognition, and creative drives and underlying neural mechanisms. *Frontiers in Neural Circuits*, 13, 18. DOI: 10.3389/fncir.2019.00018 PMID: 30967763

Kothgassner, O. D., Goreis, A., Kafka, J. X., Kaufmann, M., Atteneder, K., Beutl, L., Hennig-Fast, K., Hlavacs, H., & Felnhofer, A. (2019). Virtual social support buffers stress response: An experimental comparison of real-life and virtual support prior to a social stressor. *Journal of Behavior Therapy and Experimental Psychiatry*, 63, 57–65. DOI: 10.1016/j.jbtep.2018.11.003 PMID: 30454876

Kumar, A., Mandal, M., & Yadav, U. S. (2022). Motivation and challenges in career choice and well being of women entrepreneurs; experiences of small businesses of Lucknow, Uttar Pradesh. *Journal of Positive School Psychology*, •••, 10890–10906.

Losana, Á. A., & Gallardo, C. F. (2019). Building Purpose-Driven Organizations. The Routledge Handbook of Positive Communication: Contributions of an Emerging Community of Research on Communication for Happiness and Social Change.

Lubua, F. (2019). *From Innovation to Academic Entrepreneurship in Computer-Assisted Language Learning (CALL)*. Ohio University.

. Lucas, W., Shroyer, E., Noel, G., & Schwartz, B. (2000). The wrong kind of lean: Over-commitment and under-represented skills on technology teams.

McFarland, D. C., & Hlubocky, F. (2021). Therapeutic strategies to tackle burnout and emotional exhaustion in frontline medical staff: Narrative review. *Psychology Research and Behavior Management*, 14, 1429–1436. DOI: 10.2147/PRBM.S256228 PMID: 34552358

Mertens, E. C., Deković, M., Van Londen, M., & Reitz, E. (2022). Parallel changes in positive youth development and self-awareness: The role of emotional self-regulation, self-esteem, and self-reflection. *Prevention Science*, 23(4), 502–512. DOI: 10.1007/s11121-022-01345-9 PMID: 35088219

Miller, J. T., & Verhaeghen, P. (2022). Mind full of kindness: Self-awareness, self-regulation, and self-transcendence as vehicles for compassion. *BMC Psychology*, 10(1), 188. DOI: 10.1186/s40359-022-00888-4 PMID: 35906630

Miller, P. J., & Cho, G. E. (2018). *Self-esteem in time and place: How American families imagine, enact, and personalize a cultural ideal*. Oxford University Press.

Molero Jurado, M. D. M., Pérez-Fuentes, M. D. C., Martos Martínez, Á., Barragán Martín, A. B., Simón Márquez, M. D. M., & Gázquez Linares, J. J. (2021). Emotional intelligence as a mediator in the relationship between academic performance and burnout in high school students. *PLoS One*, 16(6), e0253552. DOI: 10.1371/journal.pone.0253552 PMID: 34166434

Monk, N. (2023). The Efficacy of an Automated Reminder System for Employee Clock-in and Clock-out Times. *J Curr Trends Comp Sci Res*, 2(3), 251–254. DOI: 10.33140/JCTCSR.02.03.06

Mukherjee, T. (2022). Performance, Discrimination, and Work–Life Interface: Perspectives in Workplace Health and Well-being. In *Handbook of Health and Well-Being: Challenges, Strategies and Future Trends* (pp. 295–321). Springer Nature Singapore. DOI: 10.1007/978-981-16-8263-6_13

Nahkamäki, R. (2018). Living in the blurry zone: a study of the wellbeing and work-life balance of Finnish SME entrepreneurs (Master's thesis).

Nightingale, S., Spiby, H., Sheen, K., & Slade, P. (2018). The impact of emotional intelligence in health care professionals on caring behaviour towards patients in clinical and long-term care settings: Findings from an integrative review. *International Journal of Nursing Studies*, 80, 106–117. DOI: 10.1016/j.ijnurstu.2018.01.006 PMID: 29407344

Ola, O. O., John, W. O., Simeon, O. A., & Mutiu, O. A. (2019). Impact of work life balance on the social life of workers living in Lagos metropolitan borders. [ACDMHR]. *Annals of Contemporary Developments in Management & HR*, 1(2), 50–59. DOI: 10.33166/ACDMHR.2019.02.006

Puertas Molero, P., Zurita Ortega, F., Ubago Jiménez, J. L., & González Valero, G. (2019). Influence of emotional intelligence and burnout syndrome on teachers well-being: A systematic review. *Social Sciences (Basel, Switzerland)*, 8(6), 185. DOI: 10.3390/socsci8060185

. Rao, R. K., & Sharma, U. (2018). Issues in work life balance and its impact on employees: a literature review.

Riegel, B., Dunbar, S. B., Fitzsimons, D., Freedland, K. E., Lee, C. S., Middleton, S., Stromberg, A., Vellone, E., Webber, D. E., & Jaarsma, T. (2021). Self-care research: Where are we now? Where are we going? *International Journal of Nursing Studies*, 116, 103402. DOI: 10.1016/j.ijnurstu.2019.103402 PMID: 31630807

Rovida, E., & Zafferri, G. (2022). *The importance of soft skills in engineering and engineering education.* Springer. DOI: 10.1007/978-3-030-77249-9

Sexton, J. B., & Adair, K. C. (2019). Forty-five good things: A prospective pilot study of the Three Good Things well-being intervention in the USA for healthcare worker emotional exhaustion, depression, work–life balance and happiness. *BMJ Open*, 9(3), e022695. DOI: 10.1136/bmjopen-2018-022695 PMID: 30898795

Shapero, B. G., Farabaugh, A., Terechina, O., DeCross, S., Cheung, J. C., Fava, M., & Holt, D. J. (2019). Understanding the effects of emotional reactivity on depression and suicidal thoughts and behaviors: Moderating effects of childhood adversity and resilience. *Journal of Affective Disorders*, 245, 419–427. DOI: 10.1016/j.jad.2018.11.033 PMID: 30423470

Singh, A. (2021). Anantshayi technique of meditation: An empirical evidence of strategic decision making by entrepreneurs and business managers. *International Journal of Indian Culture and Business Management*, 24(2), 189–213. DOI: 10.1504/IJICBM.2021.118897

Stephan, U. (2018). Entrepreneurs' mental health and well-being: A review and research agenda. *The Academy of Management Perspectives*, 32(3), 290–322. DOI: 10.5465/amp.2017.0001

Tahir, R. (2024). Work–life balance: Is an entrepreneurial career the solution? *Journal of Entrepreneurship in Emerging Economies*, 16(4), 845–867. DOI: 10.1108/JEEE-03-2022-0077

Uviebinené, E. (2021). The Reset: Ideas to Change How We Work and Live. Hachette UK.

Vermote, B., Aelterman, N., Beyers, W., Aper, L., Buysschaert, F., & Vansteenkiste, M. (2020). The role of teachers' motivation and mindsets in predicting a (de) motivating teaching style in higher education: A circumplex approach. *Motivation and Emotion*, 44(2), 270–294. DOI: 10.1007/s11031-020-09827-5

Wei, J. L., & Villwock, J. A. (2021). Balance versus integration: Work-life considerations. *Otolaryngologic Clinics of North America*, 54(4), 823–837. DOI: 10.1016/j.otc.2021.05.007 PMID: 34215359

Wolters, C. A., & Brady, A. C. (2021). College students' time management: A self-regulated learning perspective. *Educational Psychology Review*, 33(4), 1319–1351. DOI: 10.1007/s10648-020-09519-z

Yang, E., Schamber, E., Meyer, R. M., & Gold, J. I. (2018). Happier healers: Randomized controlled trial of mobile mindfulness for stress management. *Journal of Alternative and Complementary Medicine (New York, N.Y.)*, 24(5), 505–513. DOI: 10.1089/acm.2015.0301 PMID: 29420050

Yester, M. (2019). Work-life balance, burnout, and physician wellness. *The Health Care Manager*, 38(3), 239–246. DOI: 10.1097/HCM.0000000000000277 PMID: 31261191

Chapter 4
Career Resilience and the Limitations of Quiet-Quitting in Mike Judge's Office Space

Kelvin Ke Jinde
Xi'an Jiaotong-Liverpool University, China

ABSTRACT

This article examines the limitations of quiet-quitting in the American cult comedy Office Space (dir. Mike Judge 1999). It argues that the representations of workers in the film suggest that workers who quietly-quit may run the risk of marginalization and ostracization in the workplace as such actions can affect the performances and morale of fellow colleagues. The significance of this article lies in showing how Office Space functions not only as an allegory of workers' dissatisfaction in a toxic workplace. It also functions as a cautionary tale regarding the limitations of quiet-quitting as a long-term strategy to cope with work dissatisfaction. Lastly, the analysis offers a humanities approach and contribution to the thinking of a more healthy and productive work environment by analyzing the representations and limitations of quiet-quitting in cinema.

INTRODUCTION

Cinematic representations of labor, the working class, and the tensions that naturally exist between workers and management remain popular in cinema (Greene, 2010). Movies like *The Company Men*, *The Big Short* and many others reflect a continuing desire amongst filmmakers to make films that critique the effects of corporatism, bureaucracy, and neoliberalism. But while Greene argues that we should read films politically and "to actively engage in cinema, and all cultural discourses, as forms and forums of political debate and ideological struggle" (Greene, 2010, Conclusion, para. 13), the focus here shifts away from ideological debates and towards emphasizing the importance of developing human capital,

DOI: 10.4018/979-8-3693-3673-1.ch004

which is "the knowledge, skills, and health that people accumulate throughout their lives, enabling them to realize their potential as productive members of society" (World Bank Group, 2019).

Office Space is one such film that allows us to see how important human capital development is in relation to work or career dissatisfaction. Importantly, the film also shows us that it is far better for workers to think productively rather than pessimistically about career development. In this manner, *Office Space* offers us an entry to see how pessimism often leads nowhere and that positive actions are required in order to bring about positive outcomes. *Office Space* is a Hollywood comedy that pokes fun at the monotony and absurdities of office life in a tech company during the nineties. Written and directed by Mike Judge, creator of *Beavis and Butthead* and *Idiocracy*, *Office Space* is a movie that offers a vision of white-collar work that feels like a "life sentence...that crushes the spirit" (Ebert, 1999 para 12). The film specifically details the frustrations that come with "encounters with annoying colleagues, lurking bosses, broken printers...flair" while celebrating the "desire to burn it all down" (Kring-Schreifels, 2019 para 6).

Peter Gibbons (played by Ron Livingston) is the main protagonist of the film. His problem, however, is that he hates his job. To cope with his depression and dread, Peter regularly attends therapy. One day, he asks to be hypnotized. But a mistake during the session leaves Peter in a state of blissful apathy. After that, we see Peter enacting a series of passive-aggressive actions in the workplace. Indeed, Peter's actions can even be seen as being part of a soft or quiet rebellion in the workplace. These actions include arriving late for work, dressing casually for work, and talking back to his managers. Peter even stops pretending that he has a lot of work to do during office hours and openly plays games on his workstation. At the same time, we see this newly formed Peter embarking on a new relationship with Joanna (played by Jennifer Aniston). Indeed, we are given a glimpse of a different Peter which is bold, assertive, and optimistic.

But Peter's bliss at work is soon interrupted by the appearance of external consultants who are planning the next round of layoffs in the company. Frustrated, Peter then asks his friends Michael Bolton and Samir Nagheenanajar to work with him to devise a plan to embezzle money from Initech by hacking their company's computer system. Unbeknownst to them, the virus goes haywire, causing substantial financial losses for Initech. But a fire mysteriously breaks out and razes the office's building to the ground, thus erasing all evidence of their crime. The film concludes with Peter deciding that he is happier working outdoors as a construction worker. But while the film seems to end on a happy note, we nonetheless have to ask ourselves whether Peter's decision to down tools or quietly-quit earlier in the film a good strategy? Could he have chosen another path? Importantly, what are the benefits and risks of using quiet-quitting as a coping mechanism and strategy for career development?

Methodology

The following is a textual analysis of *Office Space* and its representations concerning the worker, the workplace, and job dissatisfaction. But it is also a character study that examines the usefulness of quiet-quitting as a strategy to cope with work dissatisfaction. The analysis draws from and intersects studies and research relating to film studies, cultural studies, career management and human development. The aim is to examine the extent to which the protagonist's use of quiet-quitting help with work problems and dissatisfaction. The significance of this article lies in showing how *Office Space* functions not only as an allegory of workers' dissatisfaction in a toxic workplace. It also functions as a cautionary tale on the importance of adopting the right strategy to cope with work dissatisfaction or problems.

LITERATURE REVIEW

Quiet-quitting is a key theme in the film. But themes like burnout, psychological boredom with doing bullshit jobs, the lack of meaning with doing such jobs, frustrations with red-tape and bureaucracy, technostress, toxic managers and annoying colleagues are also important topics in the film. But while people rightly focus on the office-related issues in the movie, what is often missed is that the problem facing the protagonist is deciding the kind of life that will make him happy as a person. In this sense, *Office Space* is not just a subversive take on white-collar jobs or a critique of tech companies. It is also a coming-of-age story about a young man who has to decide for himself the kind of life he wants to lead as a person.

Burnout

Peter Gibbons is clearly suffering burnout from his job. Burnout "is a conceptualized syndrome as resulting from chronic workplace stress that has not been successfully managed. It is characterized by three dimensions: (a) feelings of energy depletion or exhaustion; (b) increased mental distance from one's job, or feelings of negativism or cynicism related to one's job; (c) reduced professional efficacy (WHO, 2019, para 2). Maslach and Leiter (2016) and Maslach et al. (2001) write that factors affecting job burnout result from any mismatch or imbalance between the person and the following six contexts: (a) workload, (b) control, (c) reward, (d) community, (e) fairness, and (e) values (Maslach et al., 2009, p. 414). Effects of employee burnout include absenteeism, turnover, and inadequate job performance and "is also associated with headaches, type 2 diabetes, cardiovascular problems, insomnia, depression, and anxiety" (Lubbadeh, 2020, p.12).

> Peter Gibbons: So I was sitting in my cubicle today, and I realized, ever since I started working, every single day of my life has been worse than the day before it. So that means that every single day that you see me, that's the worst day of my life.
> Dr. Swanson: What about today? Is today the worst day of your life?
> Peter Gibbons: Yeah.

The opening scenes of the film perfectly capture Peter's anxiety, dread, and pessimism about his life. Indeed, the way the scene is shot shows the stress, noise, and irritation that comes with having to deal with the long drives to work every day. This is then followed with showing Peter's daily grind at the office where he has to deal with demanding customers, annoying colleagues, and his managers reminding him about the importance of adhering to administrative procedures. To be sure Peter is clearly frustrated with the work culture of his company. But, being the nice person that he is, Peter hides his irritations and frustrations and does not lash out at his colleagues or friends. But it is obvious that it is only a matter of time before he breaks down emotionally or psychologically. But while it would be tempting to blame his bosses or colleagues, what particularly fuels Peter's hatred toward his job is the realization that he is fundamentally doing a job that is "bullshit".

Bullshit Jobs

What is a bullshit job? According to anthropologist David Graber, a bullshit job "is a form of paid employment that is so completely pointless, unnecessary, or pernicious that even the employee cannot justify its existence even though, as part of the conditions of employment, the employee feels obliged to pretend that this is not the case" (Graber, 2019, pp.9-10). Indeed, David Graber points out that the phenomenon where white-collar services jobs are increasingly expanding means that more people are doing work that is essentially bureaucratic, dull, and pointless. This creates a sense of alienation, which is a feeling where one feels "a surrender of control through separation from an essential attribute of the self, and, more specifically, separation of an actor or agent from the conditions of meaningful agency" (Horowitz, n.d., para 2).

David Graber's taxonomy of bullshit jobs, of which there are five categories, allows us to contextualize the position and pain of Peter's bullshit job as a software programmer at Initech. The five categories are flunkies, goons, box tickers, taskmasters, and duct-tapers. Flunkies are jobs that primarily exist to make someone else look or feel important, e.g., servants, assistants, etc. Goons involve a certain level of aggressiveness, e.g., PR specialists, lobbyists, telemarketers, corporate lawyers, etc. Box tickers (jobs that exist only to enable an organization to claim it is doing something, e.g., form fillers or paper pushers). Taskmasters are middle management jobs that redistribute or even create useless tasks for others, e.g., project managers, consultants, coaches, and middle management positions.

The fifth type of bullshit job is duct-tapers, which is what Peter is at Initech. Duct tapers are bullshit jobs that exist only because of a glitch or a fault. They exist to solve problems that "ought not exist in the first place" (Graber, 2019, p.40). In this sense, Peter's job is primarily a duct-taper because his job is primarily focused on updating bank software for the Y2K switch. The following exchange with Joanna (his girlfriend) explains Peter's loathing of his job.

Peter Gibbons: I sit in a cubicle and I update bank software for the 2000 switch.

Joanna: What's that?

Peter Gibbons: Well, see, they wrote all this bank software, and, uh, to save space, they used two digits for the date instead of four. So, like, 98 instead of 1998? Uh, so I go through these thousands of lines of code and, uh... it doesn't really matter. I uh, I don't like my job, and, uh, I don't think I'm gonna go anymore.

Joanna: You're just not gonna go?

Peter Gibbons: Yeah.

Joanna: Won't you get fired?

Peter Gibbons: I don't know, but I really don't like it, and, uh, I'm not gonna go.

Joanna: So you're gonna quit?

Peter Gibbons: Nuh-uh. Not really. Uh... I'm just gonna stop going.

Joanna: When did you decide all that?

Peter Gibbons: About an hour ago.

Peter's aversion to his job is also articulated by him during a talk with the company's external consultants, the Bobs.

Peter Gibbons: The thing is, Bob, it's not that I'm lazy, it's that I just don't care.

Bob Porter: Don't... don't care?

Peter Gibbons: It's a problem of motivation, all right? Now if I work my ass off and Initech ships a few extra units, I don't see another dime, so

where's the motivation? And here's something else, Bob: I have eight different bosses right now.
Bob Slydell: I beg your pardon?
Peter Gibbons: Eight bosses.
Bob Slydell: Eight?
Peter Gibbons: Eight, Bob. So that means that when I make a mistake, I have eight different people coming by to tell me about it. That's my only real motivation is not to be hassled, that and the fear of losing my job. But you know, Bob, that will only make someone work just hard enough not to get fired.

These dialogues give us a sense of what Peter hates about his job and how they make him feel as a person. But they also capture a sense of his despair over the meaninglessness of his job. Indeed, Peter feels demotivated by his job. His situation reminds us that intrinsic motivations matter as much as extrinsic motivations.

Lacking Incentives

Motivation is an important factor when it comes to jobs and careers. According to Deci and Ryan's self-determination theory, people are not only motivated by external rewards but also internally motivated to grow, be it in terms of skills, knowledge, or achievements. According to Cherry, "[s]elf-determination theory suggests that people can become self-determined when their needs for competence, connection, and autonomy are fulfilled" (Cherry, 2022, para 5). Importantly, Ryan and Deci (2000) suggest that self-determined people are motivated by intrinsic rewards, driven by enjoyment, interest, or satisfaction, and feel in control of their actions and behaviours. Peter is particularly demoralized by the bureaucratic and parsimonious culture at Initech. Now, it is true that when we first see Peter, he has already checked out from work. But just because Peter is introduced to us in this manner, it does not mean that he is naturally lazy. That is because for Peter to become a computer programmer, he most likely was not only a really hard-working student in university or college. He was also likely a passionate student of the subject.

It can even be inferred that Peter was not always the nonchalant worker that we see him at the start of the film. By extension, we can even infer that his nonchalance developed over time as he became more and more disillusioned with his time at Initech. In fact, we do get a glimpse of a different Peter, especially when he leads Michael and Samir in their plan to steal from Initech. While his actions are obviously illegal, and he should be condemned from a normative perspective, from a motivational perspective, it is here where we get to see a different side to Peter: motivated, excited, and, more importantly, engaged. Importantly, even though Peter is working with Michael and Samir, he is the one who actually installs the virus into the computer system. This is important because it highlights the point that when he has something challenging and meaningful to do, Peter becomes an entirely different person. Indeed, Bob Sydell was right when he said that the main problem facing Peter in the office is that he needs to be challenged more as an employee.

Lacking Meaning

Peter's problem with his job is that he feels that his job lacks meaning. That is because his job involves cleaning up after other people's mistakes. Or more specifically, it is about helping his company to correct the mistakes made with their cost-saving tactics, which then backfired on them. But why does it matter if his job is meaningless? After all, Peter is still paid for his efforts. The reason is because, as Marx astutely observed, alienation is that condition or state of being of the modern worker. Alienation thus underpins the psychological violence inherent in bullshit jobs. In turn, this condition causes Peter to resent his job and his life as a whole. Now, it is true that some people may not care whether their work has meaning or not, so long as they are paid for their labor. But it is clear that Peter cares and does feel that "meaning and dignity are absent" in his life (Soren & Ryff, 2023, p.12). In this sense, we can certainly say that Peter's job fits the description of a bullshit job. But why is doing a bullshit job so dreadful to the worker?

According to Harry Frankfurt, the American philosopher, bullshit, as a concept, fundamentally refers to "indifference to how things really are" (Frankfurt, 2008, p.34). Unlike lying or saying an untruth, to bullshit is to be indifferent to truth. That is, lying means a deliberate withholding of truth and saying an untruth is to say something is true even though one is not fully informed or mistook something for the truth. But bullshitting is to deliberately not care whether what one is saying is true or not. In this sense, bullshitting is about being indifferent to truth. More importantly, what this suggests is that a bullshit job is thus underpinned by this sense of indifference; not so much about truth or falsity; but an indifference or not caring whether one's work has meaning or any productive outcomes or not. To a certain extent, a bullshit job is really just doing something for the sake of doing something and is not a job that is imbued with tasks or activities that lead to any positive or productive outcomes.

So, if we extend Frankfurt's notion that bullshit is defined by indifference and extend it to Graber's argument that bullshit jobs cause psychological violence to people, it then becomes clear why Peter hates his job. But we can also look at why Peter hates his job from another perspective. That is, how consequential will it be for the company or the job at hand if Peter or his position were to disappear from his company? Will it bring the business of Initech to a halt? How sad or even happy would his colleagues be if he or his job were to disappear the next day? Seen from this perspective, it becomes a bit clearer as to why Peter hates his job. That is because no one will really mourn the loss of his job and position. In other words, he is not important at all in the workplace.

Toxic and Bureaucratic Management

Peter also works in a toxic work environment in terms of bad management. According to Donald Sull et al. (2022), a toxic workplace has five attributes. They are disrespectful, non-inclusive, unethical, cutthroat, and abusive. And since company culture is primarily driven by its leaders and managers, good or bad culture can be traced back to its leaders as well. Indeed, we do not see any of Initech's top executives in the movie. But Lumbergh, representing upper management, often displays passive aggression and bullying behaviors. This can be seen in how Lumbergh constantly harasses Peter about his TPS reports or how he keeps requesting Peter to work on weekends. Indeed, similar traits can also be seen in other managers at Initech. Toxic leaders "can be described as toxic when they manipulate and influence others through malicious and unsusceptible tactics. By doing so, toxic leaders reduce motivation and performance of followers" (Kurtulmus, 2020, p.4). One example of toxic leadership occurs when Bob Sydell tells Michael Bolton, the programmer, not the singer, that he loves Michael Bolton, the singer. Although Michael (the software programmer) is not a fan of the singer, he, in fear of a possible retrenchment, tells Bob Sydell that he is very much a fan. Importantly, the Bobs do not seem to realize that people in the office are fearful of them because they know that the company is going through a retrenchment exercise. Indeed, the Bobs do not even pretend to reassure or support fellow colleagues in that process.

So, funny as the scenes with the Bobs may be, instances like this revealed not only a passive-aggressive culture tolerated at Initech. It also reveals toxic leadership. Other examples include many scenes in which we see Lumbergh lurking around the office with a coffee mug and inspecting what everyone is busy doing at work. It seems that everyone is busy with work except him. With poor leadership, this naturally creates a morale and motivation problem for the company. As a result, it is not surprising to see Peter and many of his colleagues at Initech quietly-quit. Indeed, quiet-quitting is typically triggered by "five organizational failures." They are "(a) failure to deliver on promises, (b) inability to Prioritize Workplace Culture, (c) lack of focus on employee well-being, (d) failing to address diversity and inclusion, and (e) failing to create meaningful work opportunities" (Thalmus Mahand and Cam Caldwell, 2023 pp.12- 13). These triggers are obviously evidenced in various scenes in the movie between Peter and his managers. But on top of being in a bureaucratic organization as well as self-serving and toxic managers, Peter also has to deal with a certain amount of technostress. Ironically, despite working in a tech firm, Peter and his colleagues seem to have to deal with various small technical glitches and faults. And while the movie does not dwell too much on this aspect of the movie, the frustration and stress that the characters exhibit towards the presence and use of technology and technical devices in the office brings up the issue of technostress and the loss of a certain amount of agency and autonomy to such systems and technical devices.

Technological Stress and Losing Agency and Autonomy

Technological stress is another motif in the film. While bureaucracy can erode or limit agency and autonomy, technology or rather technocratic processes can make a person feel that they exist to serve the purposes of machines rather than the other way around. Amna Shifia Nisafani et al's (2020) writes that technostress is the "result of direct interaction between IT artefacts and human beings" (p. 243). Stress comes about from user-experience and the disorientating effects of having to learn new technologies as well as having to accommodate technological requirements. Ask anyone who has ever been asked or demanded by their managers to use the latest gadget or devices because it is the latest new thing in the market, and they will tell you that there is always a certain level of unease and anxiety about learning to use such devices properly and efficiently. Indeed, sometimes, by virtue of the fact that such technologies are new, they can even be more cumbersome and problematic for new users than older technologies. Now, this is not to say that older technologies are better than new technologies. But the same principle applies, which is that just because something is new does not mean that it is better than older technologies. On a human and personal level, an emphasis on technical devices and technology can make a person feel that they are not as important as IT artefacts That is, technical considerations trump personal considerations.

As a corollary to that, it is understandable as to why Peter feels demoralized and demotivated in the workplace. That is because he feels that he is not only doing tedious and repetitive work. He has also lost a certain amount of agency and autonomy to the technical devices and technologies of his workplace. From a personal perspective, technostress is not so much stress about using machines and technology. Rather it stems from a feeling that one is being replaced by technology. Indeed, this fear is not unwarranted. Machines and technology are increasingly disrupting jobs. Updates from the World Economic Forum and the future of jobs show the inevitable disruption of jobs and the workplace (The Future of

Jobs Report 2023). Indeed, the report suggests that "44% of workers' skills will be disrupted in the next five years" (para 16).

As technology begins to determine and control how people work and live, it is only natural that people feel angry about such a situation. But feeling angry about technology is not so much about the use of technology in the workplace per se. Rather, it is about a sense of being human. Importantly, anger stems from feeling that one's dignity is not being respected. This anger over the loss of one's autonomy, agency, and dignity figures very strongly whenever we see Peter or any of his friends face technical problems either with their computers or with the company's printer. This anger is particularly expressed in the now iconic scene in the movie where Peter, Michael, and Samir "'murder" the company's printer with a baseball bat. Indeed, by killing the printer and what it represents, the trio are, in a symbolic manner, re-claiming a sense of power over their office environment. Specifically, smashing the printer to pieces represents smashing the rational and bureaucratic strictures and structures of the office to pieces. But venting their anger on the company's printer is more than just about technical devices and technical processes. It is also about venting their anger on the kind of place Initech is and the kind of people companies like Initech are making them to be; compliant, fearful, and homogenous. But, in light of all these factors, be it issues with toxic leadership, micromanagers or with feelings of burnout, meaninglessness, and technostress, how useful is quiet-quitting as a strategy to cope with such problems?

DISCUSSION AND FINDINGS

Choosing Quiet-Quitting

The term quiet-quitting first surfaced on TikTok in 2022 when an engineer, Zaid Khan, posted a video documenting his thoughts about hustle culture. But it was Brian Creely, a Gen-X career coach and employment influencer, who used the phrase to talk about the phenomenon of employees "coasting" at work. Conceptually, quiet-quitting refers to a phenomenon where workers do "not go above and beyond at work and just meet their job description" (Harter, 2023, para 2). Amongst other reasons, the most common one is that quiet-quitters feel tired and "burnout" from their work (Galanis et al., 2023). Indeed, quiet-quitting refers to the behavior of an employee who, while still physically present at work, mentally disengages or "checks out" and only performs the bare minimum at work. Quiet-quitters typically lack enthusiasm, motivation, or interest in their job, leading them to prioritize minimal effort and disengagement over active participation or commitment to their role and the organization. Some argue that quiet-quitting is a bad thing, such as Arianna Huffington, who asserts that quiet quitting is "a step toward quitting on life" (Huffington, 2022, para 2). However, others argue that it helps emotionally and psychically tired employees "in a multitude of ways, particularly in terms of having the confidence to implement boundaries" (Chambers in Stokes, 2022, para 8). So, what are the benefits of being a quiet-quitter?

Advantages of Quiet-Quitting

Firstly, disengaging emotionally and mentally helps employees shield themselves from negativity while preserving their mental and emotional well-being in the short term. Secondly, quiet-quitting allows individuals to redirect their focus and energy away from work-related stresses and demands. By investing only the minimum effort required, employees free up time and mental space to prioritize personal life, hobbies, and interests. This may be particularly appealing to those who feel their work lacks personal fulfillment or alignment with their passions, finding solace in dedicating more time to activities outside the workplace. Third, quiet-quitting enables employees to reduce their emotional investment in their jobs, lessening the potential impact of workplace challenges on their overall well-being. Detaching from emotional aspects, such as office politics or interpersonal conflicts, may create a perception of increased emotional resilience in the short term. This reduced emotional investment could offer a sense of liberation and emotional relief as the employee becomes less affected by the fluctuations of the work environment.

Disadvantages of Quiet-Quitting

But quiet-quitting has its cons as well. Firstly, engaging in a prolonged pattern of quiet-quitting often results in career stagnation. The individual's lack of visibility and minimal effort may lead to missed opportunities for skill development, promotions, and career advancements, hindering their professional growth over time. Secondly, consistent quiet-quitting can inflict damage on an individual's professional reputation. Colleagues and supervisors may perceive them as lacking commitment, reliability, and motivation, impacting their standing within the organization and potentially affecting future career prospects.

Third, the persistent practice of quiet-quitting can lead to a decline in overall job satisfaction for the worker. Over time, a worker may experience even more unhappiness and discontent at work, largely because quiet-quitting does not allow one to showcase their ability or increase other people's confidence in their ability. Fourthly, individuals practicing quiet-quitting will naturally miss out on opportunities for skill development. By only focusing on the bare minimum, quiet quitters limit their exposure to new challenges and responsibilities and their ability to acquire new skills crucial for professional development.

Fifth, quiet-quitting often results in strained relationships with colleagues and supervisors, which in turn can impact future references and recommendations for future employment. Six, opportunities for career advancement are often tied to demonstrated commitment and proactive contributions. Individuals practicing quiet-quitting miss out on such opportunities, diminishing their chances of being considered for leadership roles or projects that could enhance their professional profile. Seven, quiet-quitting will cause employers to view disengaged employees as expendable during restructuring or downsizing efforts, increasing the vulnerability of the individual to potential layoffs or downsizing.

Lastly, the long-term practice of quiet-quitting can have a significant negative impact on mental health. The persistent disengagement, dissatisfaction, and lack of purpose at work will only contribute to stress, anxiety, and potentially depression, affecting the individual's overall well-being beyond the workplace. That is because quiet-quitting is basically a mode of being that is premised on being indifferent to one's work. By being indifferent (i.e., uninterested, apathetic, unsympathetic, and cold), one is basically removing oneself from seeing the joys and ecstasies that can be found in life. To be sure, this is not to say that one agrees with Arianna Huffington's point that one is basically quitting on life when one quiet-quits (Huffington 2022).

But quiet-quitting can foster a mindset that makes a person more insular and selfish, both of which can lead one to become marginalized and ostracized in the workplace. A clear example of how quiet-quitting can backfire on employees is the story of Milton Waddams in the movie. Portrayed as a low-level, meek, and marginalized employee, Milton is often ignored and mistreated by his colleagues. This is especially true in his interactions with Lumbergh, where they show the dehumanizing treatment that low-level employees endure in the corporate culture depicted in the film. The most notable aspect of their relationship revolves around Milton's red Swingline stapler, which Lumbergh confiscates and takes without permission. This seemingly trivial act is symbolic of how Milton, and by extension, his colleagues at Initech, treat him. Milton's turning point occurs when he discovers that he will be moved to the basement, an isolated and neglected workspace. This event pushes Milton to set the office building on fire, even though it is not explicitly shown in the film.

While Milton's actions may be extreme, they reflect a shift from passive acceptance to active resistance, showcasing his evolution from a downtrodden employee to a symbol of rebellion against the dehumanizing corporate culture. But it is precisely because he chose to quit quietly, to do the bare minimum, and not to go the extra mile at work that everyone in the office, while not exactly shunning him, does not really respect him as a colleague and a professional. This is clearly evidenced by the fact that no one even bothered to tell him that he was fired years ago or that they are planning to stop his paychecks after finding out that he is still working at Initech. However, Milton cannot claim to be totally blameless. By taking the quiet-quitting route, Milton signals to everyone that it is best to leave him alone and that they should not trust him to go the extra mile for them.

So, while Milton's situation is certainly tragic, his tragedy is largely a consequence of his not participating and contributing to his professional development and advancement. By isolating himself from the group, Milton inevitably hobbles his chances to connect with people, people who may be able to help him in his career. Milton shows the case that we cannot mindlessly engage in quiet-quitting, not if we want to advance in our careers. Indeed, there are other strategies we can adopt to better our careers. Work dissatisfaction or career setups are part and parcel of being in the workforce. To feel angry or frustrated is natural. But there are two ways to deal with frustration. The first is to engage in destructive or self-destructive actions. The second is to be more productive in dealing with such frustrations. The first step is to find the cause of our work dissatisfaction and then to take appropriate steps to address it. Now, of course, different people face different situations.

So, we will only address what seems to bother Peter Gibbons in the movie. Fundamentally, Peter Gibbons is bored of his job which requires him to do tedious and uninspiring work. Furthermore, he is repulsed by the bureaucratic and micromanaging nature of his bosses. But his work dissatisfaction is compounded by his personal dissatisfaction; being single and not in any meaningful relationship with anyone. As a result, Peter's ennui in the film can be divided into two areas; professional and personal. In terms of personal, it is not necessarily the focus here to dwell on what or how Peter should lead his personal or romantic life. But it is clear from his actions in the movie, in relation to his interactions with Joanna, one will do well to be assertive or bold enough to take a chance and strike up a conversation with someone you think might be suitable as a partner. Indeed, Peter does take his chances and even manages to be in a romantic relationship with Joanna. Hence, in this arena. Petr shows that it does pay off if one is bolder and more assertive.

But in terms of professional development, there are strategies one can adopt and use to better one's chances in the workplace. Alexander Serenko (2024, p.35) offers some insights and recommendations about quiet-quitting For employees, one will do better if one were to maximize one's efficiency by identifying "the major business processes and practices and find ways to improve or even reengineer them to maximize their efficiency". Employees should also find ways to manage stress and avoid burnouts by realizing that "it is their responsibility to arrange a productive, stress-free, working environment, to draw a line between work and home and to seek formal or informal mental help if needed". At the same time, Serenko recommends that human capital managers (a) formalize, promote and invest in knowledge sharing activities, (b) urgently capture the knowledge of employees identified as quiet quitters and "find ways to identify their unique knowledge and find ways to retain it", (c) conduct a knowledge audit (Handa et al., 2019), (d) attract and retain high performing employees, (e) introduce burnout management programs and introduce high-quality performance management practices (Gabriel and Aguinis 2022), (f) promote interpersonal and informational exchanges "between organizational decision-makers (i.e. managers) and their subordinates (i.e. workers) (Bies, 2015)", (g) review employee contracts to ensure that worker are fairly compensated. At the same time, on a national policy level, Serenko suggests that policymakers should proactively prevent further depletion of national human capital by promoting work-life balance (Crompton and Lyonette, 2006), provide government-funded employee mental health support ((Dewa et al., 2007; Chopra, 2009), and support innovation that facilitates employee efficiency.

CONCLUSION

The Greek philosopher Epictetus writes that when we grow up, we need to "put aside childish things." From this perspective, we can treat *Office Space* as a bildungsroman or as a coming-of-age story about the maturation of a young man as he becomes a working professional. Indeed, like a bildungsroman which charts the "individual growth, upbringing, and formation of the personality of a human subject" (Graham, 2019, p.5), *Office Space* also charts the maturation of Peter Gibbons becoming much more assertive and confident as a person. Like a coming-of-age story, Peter Gibbons learns at the end that he is actually not as helpless or without options as he initially thought. In fact, it is shown that he realizes that he actually possesses a certain amount of agency in his life to change his life. Indeed, Peter is taken seriously and even considered "a straight-shooter with upper management written all over him" only after he meets with the two Bobs and tells them that bad management ails the company.

The ending of the movie shows Peter radically changing his life by becoming a construction worker. To be sure, being a construction worker is not exactly what Peter wants to do in life. But what is important is that is Peter chose to reject fatalism. Instead, he chose to exercise his agency and options in life. While critics argue that the ending of *Office Space* can be seen as an ideological cop-out or retreat from showing radical change, it is argued here that this focus ignores the fact that Peter's action shows that he does have a choice to turn his life around or at least to make positive changes. Importantly, we see Peter take ownership of his decision to be a construction worker at the end. Now, while it is safe to say that being a construction worker is not exactly what Peter Gibbons had in mind as being his ideal occupation, we nonetheless see that he is happy doing the job.

In an interview with TODAY, Ron Livingston suggests that Peter is actually "a kind of a journeyman searcher…he was kind of willing to sort of jettison this thing, and I'm gonna try this thing, and I'm gonna jettison this and that, and I'm gonna be a master criminal….maybe a construction worker…so I'm sure he probably made a fifty to a hundred of those transitions before maybe settling into some boring thing that he actually enjoys doing" (TODAY 00:04:00 - 00:04:25). But Ron Livingston also suggests that the reason why *Office Space* continues to be popular with viewers is that "on a fundamental level (the movie) is a guy who is miserable and who by the end of the movie gives himself permission to quit the thing that's making him miserable and do the thing that makes him happy" (TODAY 00:03:30 - 00:04:00). Indeed, while some may argue that Peter Gibbons is not exactly doing his ideal job, it is argued here that this perspective ignores the bigger point which is that he has grown from being a timid and uninspired person to become a more assertive and assured person by the end of the film. To be sure,

Peter Gibbons has more room to grow and mature as a person. But at least we see him leaving his old life behind and daring to try new things in his life.

Importantly, Peter's story tells us that while quiet-quitting can be used to resist and disrupt the operations and work dynamics of a company, quiet-quitting can also prove detrimental to the user in terms of career stagnation, a damaged professional reputation, and increased job insecurity. Indeed, his story alerts us to fact that we will do better to adopt more proactive approaches, such as networking, exploring new career opportunities, skills development, or simply giving feedback to our employers so that our working environment and relationships can be improved over time. But his story also tells us that we have all the power to change our lives by simply changing our jobs or careers. The final scene of the film seems to reaffirm the above by showing Peter Gibbons as a construction worker. As he puts it, "This isn't so bad, huh? Makin' bucks, gettin' exercise, workin' outside." Indeed, the film's ending suggests that workers are not without agency and that it is important to think carefully about career development and take steps that will allow us to flourish professionally.

REFERENCES

Bersin, J. (2023, April 10). Don't let quiet quitting harm your career: Josh Bersin. MIT Sloan Management Review. https://sloanreview.mit.edu/article/dont-let-quiet- quitting-harm-your-career/

Bies, R. J. (2015). Interactional justice: Looking backward, looking forward. In Cropanzano, R. S., & Ambrose, M. L. (Eds.), *The Oxford Handbook of Justice in the Workplace* (pp. 89–107). Oxford University Press.

Cherry, K. (2022, November 8). How does self-determination theory explain motivation?.

Chopra, P. (2009). Mental health and the workplace: Issues for developing countries. *International Journal of Mental Health Systems*, 3(1), 1–9. DOI: 10.1186/1752-4458-3-4 PMID: 19232117

Crompton, R., & Lyonette, C. (2006). Work-life 'balance' in Europe. *Acta Sociologica*, 49(4), 379–393. DOI: 10.1177/0001699306071680

Dewa, C. S., McDaid, D., & Ettner, S. L. (2007). An international perspective on worker mental health problems: Who bears the burden and how are costs addressed? *Canadian Journal of Psychiatry*, 52(6), 346–356. DOI: 10.1177/070674370705200603 PMID: 17696020

Ebert, R. (1999). Office Space Movie Review & Film Summary (1999): Roger Ebert. movie review & film summary (1999) | Roger Ebert. https://www.rogerebert.com/reviews/office-space-1999

Frankfurt, H. G. (2005). *On bullshit*. Princeton University Press. DOI: 10.1515/9781400826537

Gabriel, K. P., & Aguinis, H. (2022). How to prevent and combat employee burnout and create healthier workplaces during crises and beyond. *Business Horizons*, 65(2), 183–192. DOI: 10.1016/j.bushor.2021.02.037

Galanis, P., Katsiroumpa, A., Vraka, I., Siskou, O., Konstantakopoulou, O., Katsoulas, T., & Graeber, D. (2019). *Bullshit jobs - the rise of pointless work, and what we can do about it*. Penguin Books Ltd.

Graham, S. (2019). *A history of the bildungsroman*. Cambridge University Press. DOI: 10.1017/9781316479926

Greene, D. (2014). *The American worker on film: A critical history, 1909-1999*. McFarland.

Handa, P., Pagani, J., & Bedford, D. (2019). *Knowledge Assets and Knowledge Audits*. Emerald. DOI: 10.1108/9781789737714

Harter, J. (2023, November 6). Is quiet quitting real? Gallup.com. https://www.gallup.com/workplace/398306/quiet-quitting-real.aspx

Horowitz, A. (n.d.). Asher Horowitz: Department of political science: Faculty of liberal arts and professional studies: York University. Asher Horowitz | Department of Political Science | Faculty of Liberal Arts and Professional Studies | York University. https://www.yorku.ca/horowitz/courses/lectures/35_marx_alienation.html

Huffington, A. (2022, August 16). Arianna Huffington on linkedin: #joyfuljoining #work #culture: 753 comments. Arianna Huffington on LinkedIn: #joyfuljoining #work #culture I 753 comments. https://www.linkedin.com/posts/ariannahuffington_joyfuljoining-work-culture-activity6965397668625805312wsOR/?utm_source=share&utm_medium=member_de sktop

Kring-Schreifels, J. (2019) Follow the path of least resistance: An oral history of 'office space', The Ringer. Available at: https://www.theringer.com/movies/2019/2/19/18228673/office-space-oral-history (Accessed: 30 August 2024).

Kurtulmuş, B. E. (2020). Toxic leadership and workplace bullying: The role of followers and possible coping strategies. The Palgrave Handbook of Workplace Well-Being, 1–20. DOI: 10.1007/978-3-030-02470-3_24-1

Lee, J., Lim, J. J., & Heath, R. L. (2017). Coping with workplace bullying through naver: Effects of LMX relational concerns and cultural differences. *International Journal of Business Communication*, 58(1), 79–105. DOI: 10.1177/2329488417735649

Lubbadeh, T. (2020). Job burnout: A general literature review. *International Review of Management and Marketing*, 10(3), 7–15. DOI: 10.32479/irmm.9398

Lufkin, B. (2022, February 25). Office space turns 20: How the film changed The way we work. BBC News. https://www.bbc.com/worklife/article/20190205-office-space-turns-20-how-the-film-changed-work

Mahand, T., & Caldwell, C. (2023). Quiet quitting – causes and opportunities. *Business and Management Research*, 12(1), 9. DOI: 10.5430/bmr.v12n1p9

Maslach, C. Leiter, M. P., & Schaufeli, W. (2009). Measuring burnout. The Oxford Handbook of Organizational Well Being, 86–108. DOI: 10.1093/oxfordhb/9780199211913.003.0005

Maslach, C., & Leiter, M. P. (2016). Burnout. Stress: Concepts, Cognition, Emotion, and Behavior, 351–357. DOI: 10.1016/B978-0-12-800951-2.00044-3

Maslach, C., Schaufeli, W. B., & Leiter, M. P. (2001). Job burnout. *Annual Review of Psychology*, 52(1), 397–422. DOI: 10.1146/annurev.psych.52.1.397 PMID: 11148311

Rechstshaffen, M. (2022, February 19). "office space": Thr's 1999 review. The Hollywood Reporter. https://www.hollywoodreporter.com/movies/movie-news/office-space-review-1999-movie-1086336/#!

Ryan, R. M., & Deci, E. L. (2000). Self-determination theory and the facilitation of intrinsic motivation, social development, and well-being. *The American Psychologist*, 55(1), 68–78. DOI: 10.1037/0003-066X.55.1.68 PMID: 11392867

Serenko, A. (2024). The human capital management perspective on quiet quitting: Recommendations for employees, managers, and national policymakers. *Journal of Knowledge Management*, 28(1), 27–43. DOI: 10.1108/JKM-10-2022-0792

Soren, A., & Ryff, C. D. (2023). Meaningful work, well-being, and health: Enacting a eudaimonic vision. *International Journal of Environmental Research and Public Health*, 20(16), 6570. DOI: 10.3390/ijerph20166570 PMID: 37623156

Stokes, V. (2022, August 29). Is "quiet quitting" really good for your health? what experts think. Healthline. http://www.healthline.com/health-news/is-quiet-quitting-really-good-for-your-health-what-experts-think#Quiet-quitting-and-health

Sull, D., Sull, C., Cipolli, W., & Brighenti, C. (2022). Why every leader needs to worry about toxic culture. *MIT Sloan Management Review*.

Team, T. I. (2020.). Free rider problem: Explanation, causes, and solutions. Investopedia. https://www.investopedia.com/terms/f/free_rider_problem.asp Why quiet quitting is a bigger problem than you think. Why quiet quitting is a bigger problem than you think. | Randstad Australia. (2023, November 17). https://www.randstad.com.au/hr-news/talent-management/why-quiet-quitting-a-bigger-problem-you-think/

World Bank Group. (2019, January 31). *About the Human Capital Project*. World Bank. https://www.worldbank.org/en/publication/human-capital/brief/about-hcp#:~:text=What%20is%20Human%20Capital%20and,as%20productive%20membe rs%20of%20society.

World Health Organization. (2019). Burn-out an "Occupational phenomenon": International Classification of Diseases. World Health Organization. https://www.who.int/news/item/28-05-2019-burn-out-an-occupational-phenomenon-international-classification-of-diseases

YouTube. (2018, October 23). "Office Space" star Ron Livingston reveals movie joke he still feels "a little bad about" | today. YouTube. https://www.youtube.com/watch?v=SNyVsCeI6pA

Chapter 5
Combating Mental Health Stigma With Artificial Intelligence:
Improving Societal Understanding

Samantha Elaine Loies
Polygence, USA

ABSTRACT

Mental health stigma remains a significant barrier to individuals seeking help and achieving optimal treatment outcomes. The pervasive nature of stigma is known to exacerbate mental health issues and deter individuals from accessing much-needed support. This research project aims to investigate the role of artificial intelligence (AI) in combating mental health stigma and improving societal understanding of mental health disorders. We will explore how AI-driven tools like chatbots, natural language processing, and social media analysis can enhance public awareness, dispel misconceptions, and foster empathy toward individuals with mental health challenges. It begins with a literature review on the current state of mental health stigma, the factors contributing to its perpetuation, and the use of AI in mental health care. The chapter identifies AI-driven interventions that hold promise for addressing mental health stigma, such as public health campaigns and targeted social media content. It analyzes these AI interventions to assess their effectiveness and potential for adoption.

INTRODUCTION

Mental health stigma remains a significant barrier to individuals seeking help and achieving optimal treatment outcomes. The antagonistic nature of stigma worsens mental health issues and deters individuals from accessing much-needed support. The goal is to investigate the role of artificial intelligence (AI) in combating mental health stigma and improving societal understanding of mental health disorders. Recently, there has been a growing interest in utilizing AI-driven tools to address mental health challenges and reduce the stigma. One of the key areas of focus is the development of AI-powered chatbots. These chatbots can serve as virtual mental health assistants, offering a safe and confidential space for individuals to express their feelings and mental health symptoms. These chatbots can converse with users by leveraging natural

DOI: 10.4018/979-8-3693-3673-1.ch005

Copyright ©2025, IGI Global. Copying or distributing in print or electronic forms without written permission of IGI Global is prohibited.

language processing capabilities, providing empathetic responses and valuable insights. Such interactions can empower individuals to seek help without the fear of judgment. Additionally, AI-driven social media analysis plays a crucial role in understanding the dynamics of mental health discussions online. Social media platforms have become a prominent arena where discussions and misinformation about mental health flourish. AI algorithms can analyze user preferences, search histories, and interactions to deliver personalized content that addresses specific mental health concerns. This customization ensures that individuals receive relevant and reliable information, leading to a better-informed public with a greater understanding of mental health disorders. AI can also be applied to promote empathy and compassion towards individuals with mental health challenges. AI tools can gauge public attitudes toward mental health and identify moments where empathy is lacking. Subsequently, AI can help design interventions that cultivate empathy by highlighting the positive outcomes of seeking help. This approach humanizes mental health issues, reducing stigma by fostering a sense of solidarity and understanding among the public. However, while AI presents promising solutions, it also raises ethical considerations. Privacy concerns regarding user data collection and the need for security measures in mental health AI applications must be addressed to ensure user trust and confidentiality. Furthermore, AI-driven tools must be continuously updated and validated to maintain accuracy and avoid perpetuating biases or stigmatizing content. As well as this, it raises the concern of human-to-computer interactions. One may feel unable to trust an AI-powered chatbot and would rather confide in an actual human when communicating about mental health topics. Those unfamiliar with and uneducated on artificial intelligence and chatbots may have concerns and fear around not only the topic, but retaining enough trust in the chatbot itself. The research aims to harness the potential of artificial intelligence in combating mental health stigma and fostering greater societal understanding. By leveraging AI-driven tools, such as chatbots, natural language processing, and social media analysis, we can enhance public awareness, dispel misconceptions, and promote empathy toward individuals facing mental health challenges. The successful integration of AI into mental health advocacy can facilitate a shift in how society perceives and supports those dealing with mental health disorders. Nonetheless, it is crucial to approach the application of AI with an ethical framework to ensure its responsible use and maximize its potential for positive change.

After comprehensive readings through different research papers, discoveries have been found about how AI chatbots are being explored for psychiatric treatment, offering potential benefits and concerns. They mimic human-like behaviors, participating in evolving dialogues with users. According to Vaidyam (2019), early chatbots like ELIZA fostered emotional attachments despite their limited understanding. They're used in suicide prevention and therapy, catering to those uncomfortable disclosing to humans. However, research on their effectiveness and usage still needs to be improved. Concerns arise about inappropriate responses and potential harm due to excessive attachment. Improving AI methods to understand and respond appropriately is vital, and ethical and responsible use must be ensured in mental health settings. In another reading, technology is being used to address the shortage of mental health workers. Chatbots offer various interaction modalities: written language, spoken language, visual language, or combinations. According to Alrazaq (2019), most chatbots (70%) are stand-alone software, but web-based chatbots are more suitable for privacy and accessibility reasons. Rule-based chatbots are more straightforward and less error-prone, while AI chatbots allow more interactive control. Current chatbots mainly focus on depression and autism, as these conditions are prevalent worldwide, and chatbots have shown effectiveness in improving social skills for autism patients. While AI chatbots show promise in meeting the increasing demand for mental health care during the shadow pandemic, they often overlook three crucial therapeutic aspects of in-person outpatient mental healthcare. In-person care can offer personalized support and encouragement, addressing these unique needs. Empathic communication in clinical encounters involves attending to complex non-verbal cues, which is challenging for chatbots. The embodied nature of in-person interactions allows for better understanding and connection between patients and healthcare providers. In-person clinics provide social connections and indirect social benefits beyond a clinical checklist. Therefore, being part of a supportive community can positively impact a person's mental well-being. While valuable tools, AI chatbots may not fully replace the empathetic care and human connection needed to address the diverse needs of individuals with mental health challenges.

After analyzing the works of Michel Foucault, Foucault's work emphasized the interplay between power and knowledge in psychiatric practices. He critiqued the medicalization of madness, leading to the marginalization of individuals in mental distress. He viewed madness as a socially constructed concept shaped by historical and cultural contexts. Foucault criticized psychiatric power's use of diagnosis, classification, surveillance, and confinement, comparing asylums to prisons. He advocated for better-qualified staff to care for patients. He also questioned the reliability of people's ability to identify individuals based on criteria of illness and insanity correctly. Overall, Foucault's perspective sheds light on the complexities and implications of power dynamics in psychiatric systems and highlights the need for critical examination and reform in mental health practices. This can be applied to AI, as confinement is not an intelligent route when dealing with mental health topics and treating symptoms. In a rule-based chatbot, specific symptoms that a human may be portraying must go under a particular category or label, feeding into the idea of confinement in mental health spaces. In "History of Madness," Foucault's analysis of the treatment of madness spans different historical periods, highlighting the shifting perceptions and control mechanisms surrounding mental illness. According to Foucault (2013), in the classical period, madness was seen as divine inspiration but later associated with sin and isolation during the rise of Christianity. The 17th century saw the establishment of asylums for once again confining and disciplining the mad. Psychiatry emerged in the 18th and 19th centuries, medicalizing madness and granting psychiatrists authority over the lives of the mentally ill. In the 20th century, the asylum system declined with deinstitutionalization and community-based care, raising concerns about new forms of exclusion and control.

The significance of caring for mental health stigma is underscored, elucidating its negative impact on individuals and society. The chapter delves into the remarkable advancements of AI, illustrating its progress and potential applications in the mental health field. This section highlights how AI can revolutionize mental health care, offering innovative solutions to address various challenges and improve overall well-being. As the chapter unfolds, it proceeds with a comprehensive literature review, analyzing an array of scholarly papers and books researched by the author. The review encompasses a wealth of valuable insights and findings from the academic community, shedding light on different perspectives, concerns, and outcomes related to integrating AI into mental health care. Throughout this chapter, the reader is invited on a journey through the intersection of mental health, AI, and stigma, drawing connections between the significance of reducing stigma, the potential of AI in mental health care, and the existing body of research that informs and shapes these crucial discussions. By combining these diverse themes, the chapter aims to foster a deeper understanding and appreciation of the subject matter while paving the way for future progress and advancements in mental health care and stigma reduction.

In an era where technological innovations are reshaping the contours of human existence, the intersection of mental health and artificial intelligence (AI) stands as a compelling and dynamic frontier. This research paper embarks on a journey to explore the multifaceted and ever-evolving landscape where mental health care and AI technologies converge. At the heart of this exploration lies the aspiration to comprehend the transformative potential of AI, particularly in the form of chatbots, in shaping the future of mental health support. The quest to unravel the nexus between mental health and AI is driven by the recognition that mental health remains one of the most pressing global challenges of our time. The burden of mental health disorders, from anxiety and depression to severe conditions like schizophrenia, weighs heavily on individuals, communities, and societies. Yet, despite the growing demand for mental health care, access to appropriate services remains a persistent challenge. This dichotomy of burgeoning need and limited accessibility prompts a crucial question: Can artificial intelligence play a pivotal role in addressing the gaps in mental health support?

It is essential to set the stage by defining the pivotal elements of this exploration: mental health and artificial intelligence. Mental health is a vital facet of human well-being, and its significance extends far beyond individual experiences. At its core, it encompasses emotional, psychological, and social well-being, impacting how individuals think, feel, and interact with the world around them. It is the foundation upon which the architecture of our lives, relationships, and aspirations is built. Thus, the vitality of mental health extends well into the domains of public health, social cohesion, and human development. However, the landscape of mental health is a complex tapestry marked by both resilience and vulnerability. On one hand, individuals exhibit remarkable adaptive capacities, even in the face of adversity. On the other hand, the world of mental health is scarred by the persistence of stigmatization, insufficient resources, and the inability to provide timely support to those in need. The statistics offer a stark reminder of the magnitude of the challenge: According to Hartl (2001), mental health conditions account for approximately 10% of the global disease burden, and approximately one in four individuals will experience a mental health condition at some point in their lives. The pervasive impact of mental health extends to a range of conditions, from common disorders such as anxiety and depression to severe and enduring conditions like bipolar disorder or schizophrenia. For individuals grappling with mental health challenges, the journey can be fraught with obstacles. Stigmatization, discrimination, and the reluctance to seek help often act as barriers to accessing necessary care. Additionally, the scarcity of mental health professionals in many parts of the world exacerbates the difficulty of obtaining timely and appropriate support.

In the wake of the digital age, artificial intelligence emerges as a defining force with the capacity to disrupt and revolutionize multiple sectors of human life. AI, the science of creating intelligent machines capable of performing tasks that typically require human intelligence, is expanding its reach into every facet of existence, including healthcare. In healthcare, AI is a transformative tool that can enhance diagnostic accuracy, streamline treatment, and facilitate personalized care. Within this broader landscape of AI's influence on healthcare, mental health emerges as a significant application sphere. The innovative application of AI technologies, particularly chatbots, demonstrates immense potential to address the chronic gaps in mental health care. AI-driven chatbots represent a new paradigm in mental health support, offering immediacy, accessibility, and potential scalability. These digital companions have the capacity to engage with individuals, offering non-judgmental support, information, and even interventions 24/7.

The transformative potential of AI-driven chatbots in mental health lies in their ability to complement traditional care. These technologies can act as an initial point of contact, providing immediate support and guidance. They can offer a safe space for individuals to seek help and explore resources, particularly in distress or uncertainty. Moreover, chatbots can potentially reduce the burden on overburdened mental health professionals, allowing them to focus on more complex and specialized cases.

At the heart of this research lies the central thesis: the convergence of mental health and AI, particularly through the application of chatbots, represents a pioneering and transformative domain that offers a pathway toward more accessible, user-centered, and ethically driven mental health support.

We will delve into the evolving landscape of AI in mental health, exploring the role of chatbots in providing support, the diversity of user perceptions, and the ethical considerations that shape their application. Additionally, our research will transcend the boundaries of time and delve into the historical insights offered by Michel Foucault's work, providing a historical context that casts a revealing light on contemporary discussions about the influence of power structures in treating individuals with psychological disorders. The significance of this research extends beyond the boundaries of academic inquiry. It resonates with the lived experiences of individuals needing mental health support, who may find solace and assistance through AI-driven technologies. Moreover, it holds the potential to guide policymakers, practitioners, and technology developers in shaping the future of mental health support that is both accessible and user-centered.

Mental health issues, such as depression, schizophrenia, and anxiety, affect millions of individuals worldwide. Integrating artificial intelligence methods into mental health care has led to the development of chatbots and conversational agents designed to offer therapeutic support. These AI-driven agents are becoming increasingly popular and effective tools in psychiatric treatment. This paper reviews the landscape of chatbots and conversational agents in the context of mental health, exploring their potential benefits, limitations, and ethical considerations. Mental health conditions pose a significant global challenge, with millions of individuals affected by disorders like depression, schizophrenia, and anxiety. The traditional one-on-one approach to mental health care faces several challenges, including a shortage of mental health professionals and the stigma associated with seeking help. To address these issues, artificial intelligence (AI) has emerged as a potential solution by developing chatbots and conversational agents capable of engaging individuals in therapeutic conversations. These AI-driven agents aim to provide a more accessible and personalized approach to mental health support. The concept of using chatbots for therapeutic purposes is not new. According to Vaidyam (2019), in the 1960s, ELIZA, one of the earliest chatbots, was designed to act as a psychotherapist. Despite its limited ability to understand the content of conversations, many users believed ELIZA to be intelligent enough to comprehend their thoughts and even formed emotional attachments to it. This early example highlights the human tendency to connect with AI entities in a therapeutic context. Chatbots have found applications in various aspects of mental health care, including suicide prevention and cognitive-behavioral therapy. One notable advantage of chatbots is their potential to help individuals who are uncomfortable disclosing their feelings to a human being. For instance, veterans, often reluctant to open up after military service, were more likely to share their experiences with a chatbot when it was presented as a virtual therapist rather than as a human-controlled entity, thus offering increased access to care. While chatbots hold significant potential, the efficacy of these systems and their impact on patients remain topics of ongoing research. For example, according to Vaidyam (2019), individuals with major depressive disorder rated the therapeutic alliance with a conversational agent significantly higher than with a clinician. However, concerns have been raised regarding the appropriateness and limitations of chatbot responses. Some built-in chatbots on smartphones are limited in their ability to address mental health problems, often providing generic responses such as "Maybe the weather is affecting you" when presented with user distress. Chatbots in mental health interact with users through various modalities. Users can communicate via written language, spoken language, or a combination of both, while chatbots may respond through a combination of written, spoken, and visual languages. Alrazaq (2019) found that most chatbots (70%) are implemented as stand-alone software despite the advantages of web-based chatbots regarding accessibility and privacy. Stand-alone chatbots require users to install specific applications on their devices, potentially limiting their reach. Chatbots in mental health can be classified into rule-based and AI-driven categories. Rule-based chatbots are relatively simple to develop and maintain as they rely on predetermined responses. Users interact with rule-based chatbots using predefined keywords and phrases. In contrast, AI-driven chatbots employ machine learning and natural language processing techniques to generate responses based on the context of the conversation. The use of chatbots in mental health predominantly focuses on conditions such as depression and autism. This emphasis aligns with the high prevalence of depression and anxiety worldwide and the reported effectiveness of chatbots in improving social skills for individuals with autism. The ability of chatbots to engage in conversations specifically tailored to these conditions has been a driving force behind their adoption. Recent research has explored the potential of AI chatbots in predicting mental health symptoms. Traditional methods often rely on self-reporting through questionnaires, which biases and inhibitions can influence. AI chatbots have demonstrated the ability to predict depression symptoms with a relatively high accuracy. According to Duvvuri (2022), in some cases, machine learning models have achieved a 73% accuracy rate in predicting seven key depression symptoms. While AI chatbots hold promise for addressing the growing demand for mental health care, they cannot fully replace human interactions. Several therapeutic aspects of in-person outpatient mental healthcare are challenging to replicate through chatbot alternatives. These include the motivational and self-advocacy support that individuals with mental illness often require, the importance of non-verbal cues in empathic communication, and the indirect social benefits provided by in-person clinics that extend beyond clinical checklists. In summary, the integration of chatbots and conversational agents into the field of mental health offers a promising avenue for providing accessible and personalized support to individuals with mental health conditions. These AI-driven tools have shown efficacy in various applications, from suicide prevention to cognitive-behavioral therapy. However, the landscape of mental health chatbots is still evolving, with ongoing research needed to understand their true therapeutic impact and limitations. It is essential to strike a balance between the advantages of AI-driven chatbots and the unique benefits of in-person mental healthcare to provide comprehensive and inclusive support to individuals facing mental health challenges. As mental health services continue to face unprecedented demand, the role of AI chatbots in the larger context of mental health care remains a topic of significant interest and research.

Michel Foucault was a prominent French philosopher and social theorist known for his influential works on power, knowledge, and the relationship between individuals and society. His contributions to the field of psychology and the understanding of mental illness have left a lasting impact on the way we perceive and treat mental health conditions. In this discussion, we will explore Foucault's ideas regarding mental illness and psychology in depth. Michel Foucault's work in mental illness and psychology is deeply rooted in his broader philosophical framework, characterized by critically examining the structures of power, knowledge, and social institutions. His exploration of the treatment of mental illness and the development of psychology as a discipline reflects his commitment to exposing the ways in which society controls and shapes human behavior, particularly in the context of mental health.

Foucault's examination of mental illness begins with his analysis of the birth of the modern asylum in the 18th and 19th centuries. He contends that the emergence of the asylum was not solely driven by a benevolent concern for the mentally ill but was, in fact, a response to broader societal changes, including industrialization and urbanization. The asylum, according to Foucault, was a mechanism to manage those individuals who did not fit into the emerging norms of rationality and productivity. This marked a significant shift from earlier practices of confinement, where the mentally ill were often hidden from public view to the asylum system, which sought to manage and control those who did not conform to societal norms. The asylum, Foucault argues, played a role in developing the disciplinary society, where individuals were subjected to various surveillance and control.

Foucault also delves into the relationship between psychiatry and power. He suggests that the emergence of psychiatry as a medical discipline and the categorization of mental illnesses were intertwined with the exercise of power. Psychiatry, according to Foucault, offered a new way to define, categorize, and control individuals whose behavior was deemed deviant or abnormal. Psychiatry, he argues, introduced the notion of mental illness as a category that could be used to pathologize and label individuals. This had significant implications for the power dynamics within society, as those who were labeled as mentally ill often found themselves subject to institutionalization, treatment, and confinement, all under the authority of medical experts. Foucault (1973) introduced the concept of the "clinical gaze" to describe the way in which psychiatrists and medical professionals examine and diagnose mental illness (p.115). The clinical gaze, he argued, allowed for the medicalization of deviant behavior and the construction of a new type of knowledge about the mind. It transformed the mentally ill into objects of medical scrutiny, and this shift in perception further solidified the power dynamics between those who were diagnosed and those who were diagnosed.

Foucault's work in "The Birth of the Clinic" (1963) and "Madness and Civilization" (1961) also highlights the role of discursive practices in forming knowledge about mental illness. He suggests that the language used to describe and categorize mental disorders is not neutral but is, in fact, a product of the broader societal norms and values. The discourse surrounding mental illness, therefore, serves as a tool of power and control, as it determines what is considered normal and what is considered abnormal. One of Foucault's central arguments is that the management of mental illness is closely tied to the normalization of individuals within society. The concept of normalization refers to the process by which society defines and enforces standards of behavior, and those who deviate from these norms are labeled as abnormal or mentally ill. In the context of mental health, this normalization involves both medical and societal practices that aim to bring individuals back into conformity with accepted standards. Foucault argues that this normalization often takes place through various forms of social control, including confinement in institutions and the administration of psychiatric treatments.

Foucault's famous concept of the panopticon is another key element in his analysis of mental illness and psychology. He borrowed the term from the design of a prison where a central watchtower allows guards to observe all inmates without the inmates knowing when they are being watched. Foucault argued that the same principles of surveillance and control found in the panopticon were at play within the institutions that managed mental illness. In this context, mental health institutions, as well as broader societal structures, subjected individuals with mental illness to constant surveillance. The awareness of being watched and evaluated contributed to their submission to societal norms and the power of psychiatrists and other authorities.

Foucault's work also acknowledges the potential for resistance and liberation within the context of mental illness. He argues that individuals with mental illness can challenge and resist the power structures that seek to control them. This resistance may take various forms, including the refusal to conform to psychiatric diagnoses and the assertion of their own agency and identity. Moreover, Foucault's work has inspired movements and critiques within psychology and psychiatry that call for a more patient-centered and humanistic approach to mental health care. These movements emphasize the importance of listening to the experiences and perspectives of individuals with mental illness and challenging the medicalization and stigmatization of their conditions. Michel Foucault's exploration of mental illness and psychology offers a profound critique of the ways in which society has historically treated and pathologized those with deviant behavior. He highlights the close relationship between power, knowledge, and the medicalization of mental illness, arguing that the treatment of mental illness is often intertwined with broader societal norms and control mechanisms.

Foucault's work challenges us to consider the implications of these power dynamics and to seek more humane and patient-centered approaches to mental health. While his analysis is not without controversy, it has undeniably influenced the fields of psychology and psychiatry, prompting critical reflections on the treatment of mental illness and the power structures that shape our understanding of the mind.

Michel Foucault's monumental work, "History of Madness," represents a pivotal and provocative exploration of the history, perception, and treatment of madness in Western society. This book not only examines the shifting attitudes toward madness but also serves as a foundational text for Foucault's later works in the fields of philosophy, psychology, and social theory. We will delve into the central themes and ideas presented in "History of Madness," dissecting Foucault's critique of the societal treatment of the insane, the construction of reason, and the profound implications of his historical analysis. Michel Foucault's "History of Madness" emerged during a period of intellectual and social upheaval in France. Influenced by existentialism, structuralism, and the broader historical context of post-war Europe, Foucault embarked on an ambitious project to trace the historical trajectory of madness. His goal was not merely to describe how societies have perceived and treated the mad over time but to question the very foundations of reason and the societal structures that both define and confine madness. At the heart of "History of Madness" is an interrogation of the concept of madness itself. Foucault argues that the definition of madness is fluid and that societies have variously defined and redefined madness to suit their cultural, political, and social needs. He asserts that madness has no inherent, universal essence but is shaped by discourse and power. Foucault's deconstruction of madness as a shifting, context-dependent construct challenges conventional notions of mental illness. He argues that it is not the mad themselves but society that determines who is considered mad and what madness means at any given point in history. This understanding forms the cornerstone of his analysis.

Foucault traces the history of the treatment of the mad, which he conceptualizes as a confinement process. He identifies a significant turning point in the seventeenth century called the Great Confinement. During this period, the management of madness shifted from religious institutions to secular institutions, including asylums and hospitals. This transition marked a profound change in the treatment of the mad. Rather than being perceived as possessed by demons or in need of spiritual redemption, the mad were now viewed as individuals whose irrationality required scientific observation and medical intervention. Foucault's critique of this transformation revolves around the idea that confinement led to the exclusion and isolation of the mad from society. The confinement of the mad symbolized society's desire to contain and control what it considered irrational. Foucault's "History of Madness" also examines the development of modern psychiatry as a discipline intimately connected with the confinement of the mad. He argues that psychiatry emerged as a means of classifying, categorizing, and understanding the irrational. In doing so, psychiatry acted as an instrument of social control, defining the boundaries of sanity and normalcy. Foucault suggests that the rise of psychiatry was not a benevolent development but a tool of power. Psychiatric institutions, in his view, reinforced social norms and sanctioned the marginalization of the insane. Psychiatry, with its medical and scientific authority, contributed to the exclusion and subjugation of the mad within society.

A central theme in "History of Madness" is the concept of reason. Foucault argues that reason is not a universal, unchanging principle but a product of historical context. He contends that the Enlightenment, often celebrated for championing reasons, was instrumental in redefining and marginalizing madness. In Foucault's view, reason, as defined by Enlightenment thinkers, became a normative standard, and anything outside of that standard was labeled as unreason or madness. The Enlightenment, emphasizing rationality, marked a shift in the perception of madness. The mad were no longer seen as possessing a different kind of reason, as in earlier periods, but as wholly irrational and dangerous. Foucault's analysis reveals the extent to which societal structures were designed to exclude and control the mad. Asylums, or "hospitals for the insane," represented institutions of confinement where the mad were isolated from the rest of society. These institutions, Foucault argues, were intended to cleanse society of the irrational and maintain social order. Foucault's critique of these structures highlights the impact of societal norms and institutions on the lives of individuals considered mad. He exposes the dehumanizing and oppressive conditions within asylums and the use of confinement as a mechanism of social control. One of the more intriguing aspects of "History of Madness" is Foucault's exploration of the connection between madness and artistic creativity. He argues that, historically, the mad and the artist were perceived similarly, as both were seen to possess a certain irrationality or "divine madness." Foucault suggests that the artistic genius and the madman share a boundary where reason dissolves and creativity flourishes. However, he also recognizes that this connection has been ambivalently received by society. The artistic genius is celebrated, while the mad are often confined and silenced. This paradox highlights the arbitrary nature of societal judgments about who is labeled as mad and who is celebrated as creative. Foucault's "History of Madness" has had a profound and enduring impact on philosophy, psychology, and sociology. It laid the groundwork for his later works, which continued to explore the dynamics of power, knowledge, and societal control. His ideas have contributed to developing critical theories that challenge dominant discourses and question the construction of normalcy and deviance. Michel Foucault's "History of Madness" is a profound and thought-provoking work that challenges conventional notions of madness, reason, and societal norms. His deconstruction of the concept of madness and his critique of the institutional confinement of the mad shed light on the shifting historical dynamics of power and knowledge. Foucault's analysis continues to be a source of inspiration for those seeking to understand the complex interplay of reason, unreason, and the treatment of the mad in society. "History of Madness" remains a testament to the enduring relevance of critical theory in understanding the human condition and the forces that shape our perceptions of madness and sanity.

Michel Foucault's "The Birth of the Clinic" (French: "Naissance de la clinique") (1963) is a pivotal work in the field of medical history and the philosophy of medicine. This book delves into the history of clinical medicine, unveiling the profound shifts in medical practice, knowledge, and power during the transition from the 18th to the 19th century in France. In this essay, we will explore the central themes, concepts, and arguments presented in "The Birth of the Clinic," shedding light on Foucault's critique of the historical development of clinical medicine and its implications for our understanding of knowledge and power in the medical field. "The Birth of the Clinic" represents the second installment in Michel Foucault's historical and philosophical analysis of the development of medical knowledge and practices. In this work, he follows the evolution of clinical medicine in France, highlighting the transformation from the traditional, individualized, and experiential approach of the 18th century to a more structured, scientific, and systematic model in the 19th century. Foucault's exploration not only exposes the historical context but also elucidates the interplay of knowledge, power, and medical institutions during this critical period. One of the central themes of "The Birth of the Clinic" is the concept of the "clinical gaze."

Foucault introduces this idea as the way in which medical practitioners observe and assess patients. He argues that the clinical gaze underwent a significant transformation during the period under examination. In the 18th century, the gaze was more personal, experiential, and individualized, with physicians relying on their sensory perceptions to diagnose and treat patients. However, in the 19th century, the clinical gaze became more objectified and standardized. It shifted from a subjective and intuitive assessment of patients to a more systematic and scientific observation. Medical practitioners increasingly relied on objective signs, such as visible symptoms, to diagnose diseases. This transition is not merely an evolution in medical technique but has profound implications for how medical knowledge is constructed and the power dynamics at play. Foucault's analysis of the clinical gaze serves as a gateway to understanding the broader epistemological shifts in medicine. He suggests that the epistemology of medicine, the way in which medical knowledge is produced and validated, underwent a radical transformation. In the 18th century, medical knowledge was largely rooted in clinical experience, the individual expertise of physicians, and an understanding of the patient's unique history. With the rise of scientific medicine, knowledge became more detached from the individual physician's experience and centered on objective, quantifiable data. Medical knowledge increasingly relied on laboratory tests, diagnostic instruments, and standardized observations. This transformation transitioned from a subjective, experiential understanding of health and disease to a more objective, empirical, and measurable approach. "The Birth of the Clinic" also underscores the changing dynamics of power within the medical field, particularly in the context of hospitals. Foucault argues that the 19th-century hospital played a central role in reconfiguring medical power. Hospitals became sites where standardized observation and diagnosis were practiced and where medical authority was exercised. The hospital, Foucault contends, was the perfect embodiment of the new clinical gaze and the objectification of medical knowledge. In the 18th century, hospitals were often viewed with suspicion, associated with the poor, the marginalized, and contagious diseases. Physicians primarily practiced in patients' homes, and hospital care was often considered a last resort. However, by the 19th century, hospitals became hubs of medical education and research, symbolizing the transformation of medical power and knowledge. The hospital setting facilitated the standardization of clinical practice and the dissemination of new medical knowledge. Foucault's exploration of the historical development of clinical medicine highlights the contingency of medical knowledge. He asserts that how medicine is practiced and understood is not a linear or inevitable progression but is shaped by historical and cultural factors. The shift from an experiential, individualized approach to a scientific, standardized medicine model was not preordained but contingent on specific historical circumstances. This emphasis on historical contingency challenges the notion of progress in medicine. Foucault's analysis suggests that what is considered progress in medicine is often influenced by the prevailing social, political, and cultural forces. This critical perspective invites reflection on the limitations of medical knowledge and the need for historical awareness in contemporary medical practice. Another key aspect of Foucault's analysis is transforming the medical subject and the object of medicine. In the 18th century, the medical subject was the individual physician who applied their unique clinical judgment to diagnose and treat patients. The object of medicine was the patient as a singular, subjective entity with a specific medical history. However, in the 19th century, the subject of medicine became more collective with the emergence of medical schools and scientific communities. The object of medicine shifted to the standardized, observable symptoms of patients. This transformation led to a shift in the role of the physician, who now played a more interpretive and organizational role in applying standardized medical knowledge. Foucault's analysis of the birth of the clinic and the transformation of clinical medicine has important implications for contemporary medical practice and the understanding of medical knowledge.

It challenges the prevailing idea that medical knowledge is objective, universal, and ahistorical. Instead, Foucault's work underscores the contingent nature of medical knowledge and the impact of historical, social, and cultural factors on medical practice. Furthermore, Foucault's exploration of the clinical gaze and the transformation of the medical subject invites reflection on the relationship between physician and patient in contemporary medicine. It raises questions about the role of standardization and objectivity in diagnosis and treatment, as well as the potential for more personalized and experiential approaches to medical practice. Michel Foucault's "The Birth of the Clinic" provides a profound and critical analysis of the historical transformation of clinical medicine in the transition from the 18th to the 19th century. His examination of the clinical gaze, the epistemology of medicine, and the shifting dynamics of medical power challenge conventional notions of medical progress and objectivity. Foucault's work underscores the contingent and historical nature of medical knowledge, inviting reflection on its implications for contemporary medical practice. "The Birth of the Clinic" remains a foundational text in the philosophy of medicine, offering insights into the historical development of clinical medicine and the complex interplay of knowledge and power in healthcare.

In this section, we will detail the methodology employed in analyzing literature and scholarly articles for the research paper, providing insights into the processes used to gather, evaluate, and integrate this content effectively. The first step in designing the methodology for analyzing literature and scholarly articles is establishing clear research objectives. The research objectives define the scope and purpose of the analysis. In this case, the research aims to explore the role of chatbots in mental health, the impact of Michel Foucault's works on the understanding of mental illness and psychology, and the historical context of mental health treatment. These objectives guide the entire methodology. The foundation of the analysis process lies in identifying, selecting, and retrieving relevant literature and scholarly articles. The selection process is characterized by systematic and strategic steps, the first being database search. Extensive searches were conducted in established academic databases to locate scholarly articles and literature pertinent to the research objectives. The search queries incorporated targeted keywords and phrases such as "chatbots in mental health," "Michel Foucault and mental illness," "history of mental health treatment," and variations of these terms. To ensure the inclusion of high-quality, pertinent sources, explicit inclusion and exclusion criteria were employed. The criteria encompassed publication date, source credibility, research methodology, and language proficiency. Peer-reviewed scholarly articles and Foucault's works directly relevant to the research objectives were prioritized. Critical reading and notetaking are essential components of the analysis process. The depth of analysis is shaped by the degree to which the content is examined critically. Active reading techniques were employed to immerse in the content of scholarly articles and Foucault's works. These techniques encompassed the annotation of text, highlighting key concepts and arguments, and the generation of margin notes. By actively engaging with the material, the aim was to comprehend the primary arguments, supporting evidence, and the broader implications presented within the content. A systematic approach to notetaking was adopted to capture and organize key insights. Digital note-taking tools, including spreadsheets and reference management software, facilitated the organization of notes. A summary of the main points, significant quotations, and key findings per the research objectives accompanied each source. Information extraction was central to the analysis, focusing on isolating data and insights directly related to the research objectives: The scholarly articles and Foucault's literature were scrutinized for key concepts, theories, and theoretical frameworks relevant to the research objectives. Emphasis was placed on the identification of concepts such as "chatbot efficacy in mental health support," "Foucauldian discourse analysis in mental health," and "historical evolution of psychiatric practices." Where applicable, empirical findings, data, and statistical information were extracted from scholarly articles. These elements were assessed for their capacity to provide substantive support for the research. Extracted data included statistics on the effectiveness of chatbots in mental health interventions and statistical trends in the historical treatment of mental illness. Quotations from scholarly articles and references cited in the literature played a crucial role in supporting arguments and augmenting the credibility of the analysis. Pertinent quotations were marked for potential direct citation in the research paper, and references provided avenues for additional source exploration. Thematic analysis and synthesis served as pivotal processes to derive structure and coherence from the gathered information: Thematic categorization was executed to group insights, data, and theories into cohesive themes. Each theme corresponds to a specific aspect of the research objectives. For instance, when investigating the role of chatbots in mental health, themes such as "effectiveness of chatbots," "user perceptions," and "ethical considerations" emerged. The synthesis stage entailed the interweaving of insights and findings from scholarly articles and Foucault's literature to craft a coherent narrative. The synthesis aimed to build a comprehensive understanding of the research topic, highlighting the relationships between concepts and theories supporting the research objectives. Comparative analysis was integral to the methodology. It involved contrasting and comparing perspectives from different sources. This approach uncovered areas of agreement and disagreement among the analyzed content. The comparative analysis added depth and nuance to the research findings. Depending on the research objectives, the analysis process might involve the development of a conceptual framework or the integration of existing theories: In cases where a conceptual framework was deemed beneficial, it was constructed based on the insights extracted from the literature. This framework provided a structural foundation for the research paper, facilitating a systematic exploration of the research topics. Integrating existing theories, particularly those expounded by Michel Foucault, was carried out to illuminate connections between Foucault's concepts and the understanding of mental health and psychology. These integrations were instrumental in elucidating the influence of Foucault's work on the research domain. Data validation and peer review were incorporated to bolster the reliability and validity of the analysis. Triangulation techniques were employed to corroborate findings by cross-referencing data from multiple sources. The triangulation approach contributed to the validation of research findings and the identification of consistent trends. Ethical considerations governed the analysis process to ensure the ethical use of scholarly articles and literature. To understand the connections between Michel Foucault's work and the contemporary research on chatbots in mental health, it is essential to explore Foucault's contributions to the understanding of mental illness and the methods applied in scholarly articles to examine chatbots' role in mental health support. Michel Foucault made significant contributions to mental health and psychology through his historical and philosophical analyses. Foucault's method often involved examining how power and knowledge intersected in society. His works, particularly "Madness and Civilization" and "Birth of the Clinic," challenged traditional approaches to mental illness and offered fresh insights into the social construction of mental health. Foucault's "Birth of the Clinic" delves into the history of medical practices and the development of clinical medicine. He discusses the transformation of clinical practices and how these transformations influenced the understanding of mental illness. Foucault's examination of the clinic as a site of knowledge production sheds light on the historical context of mental health treatment and the changing conceptions of psychological disorders. Foucault's theories on power and control are crucial to understanding the dynamics of mental health institutions and the conceptualization of mental illness. His concepts of "biopower" and "disciplinary power" offer a lens through which to examine how societies have managed and controlled individuals with mental health conditions. Many studies assess the effectiveness of chatbots in delivering mental health support.

Researchers employ quantitative and qualitative methods to measure the impact of chatbot interventions on individuals with mental health conditions. Understanding user perceptions is a critical aspect of these studies. Researchers collect data on how individuals with mental health concerns perceive and interact with chatbots. This information helps tailor chatbot interventions to user preferences. Scholars explore the ethical dimensions of integrating chatbots into mental health care. This includes discussions on privacy, confidentiality, and the potential risks of relying on artificial intelligence in sensitive contexts. Some scholarly papers draw on Michel Foucault's theories to provide a conceptual framework for understanding mental health. Researchers utilize Foucauldian discourse analysis to examine how mental illness has been constructed and categorized within society. This approach offers a historical perspective on the language and narratives surrounding mental health. Foucault's concepts of power and control are integrated into analyzing mental health practices. Scholars explore how power structures influence mental health institutions and the treatment of individuals with psychological disorders. Using Foucault's critique of traditional medical and psychiatric practices, researchers challenge conventional approaches to mental health care. They question the stigmatization of mental illness and the impact of institutionalization. The intersection of Michel Foucault's work and research on chatbots in mental health is marked by several key points. Foucault's historical analyses in "Madness and Civilization" and "Birth of the Clinic" provide a historical context for understanding the development of mental health treatment. Researchers draw on these historical insights to contextualize the contemporary use of chatbots in mental health support. The Foucauldian concept of discourse analysis is utilized in scholarly papers to investigate the language and narratives surrounding mental health. This approach is aligned with examining how chatbots contribute to constructing new discourses in mental health care. Foucault's theories on power and control find resonance in discussions on the role of chatbots in mental health. Researchers scrutinize how power structures influence the design and implementation of chatbot interventions and raise questions about control and agency in mental health support. The ethical considerations highlighted in both Foucault's work and studies on chatbots in mental health underscore the importance of privacy, confidentiality, and ethical practices in mental health care. Scholars are attentive to the ethical dimensions of integrating technology into sensitive healthcare contexts. In conclusion, the analysis of Michel Foucault's contributions to the understanding of mental illness and the examination of chatbots in mental health support provides a multifaceted perspective on the evolving landscape of mental health care. The synthesis of Foucault's historical and contemporary research insights underscores the significance of historical context, discourse analysis, power dynamics, and ethical considerations in mental health. The intersection of Foucault's work and modern research sheds light on how past ideas continue to influence the present and shape the future of mental health care. This synergy offers valuable insights for researchers, practitioners, and policymakers working in the domain of mental health support. The central research question guiding this study delves into the intersection of mental health and artificial intelligence (AI), focusing on the impact of AI technologies, including chatbots, on the mental health landscape. This discussion section will interpret the results in the context of the research question, explore the implications of our findings, and address the limitations encountered during the research process. Additionally, we will outline potential areas for further research in this evolving domain. The results of my comprehensive analysis of the intersection between mental health and AI, as well as Michel Foucault's contributions to this field, shed light on various dimensions of this critical topic. My analysis revealed a growing body of research exploring the efficacy of chatbots in providing mental health support. Chatbots offer immediate, 24/7 access to mental health information, resources, and interventions. They serve as virtual companions, providing non-judgmental listening and guidance to needy individuals. This role of chatbots in mental health is aligned with the increasing demand for accessible and convenient mental health services. The findings suggest that chatbots can address some mental health treatment gaps. By providing an avenue for individuals to seek support and information discreetly, chatbots can serve as early interventions for those who might otherwise hesitate to seek professional help. However, it is important to note that while chatbots can benefit certain individuals, they should not be viewed as a replacement for professional mental health care. Understanding user perceptions and experiences with chatbots in the mental health context is crucial. The analysis illuminated the diverse range of user perspectives. Some individuals reported positive experiences, citing the non-judgmental nature of chatbots and the convenience of accessing support at any time. Others expressed skepticism and concerns regarding the effectiveness and trustworthiness of chatbot interventions. These differing user perceptions highlight the need for personalized and user-centered interventions. Designing chatbots that adapt to individual preferences, offer empathetic responses, and respect privacy is essential to improving user engagement and satisfaction. Future research should focus on tailoring chatbots to cater to the needs and expectations of diverse user groups. Integrating AI technologies into mental health support introduces ethical considerations that demand careful attention. Privacy, confidentiality, data security, and responsible data use emerged as key concerns. Our analysis emphasized the importance of establishing ethical frameworks and guidelines for the development and deployment of AI-driven mental health interventions. The findings underscore the critical role of ethics in shaping the responsible use of AI in mental health. Researchers, practitioners, and policymakers must collaborate to ensure that AI technologies prioritize the highest standards of ethical practice. This includes safeguarding user data, obtaining informed consent, and maintaining transparency in the functioning of AI-driven mental health systems. The analysis extended to the impact of Michel Foucault's theories on mental health. Foucault's historical analyses and concepts, such as "biopower" and "disciplinary power," provided a framework for understanding the dynamics of mental health institutions, the construction of discourses surrounding mental illness, and the power structures that influence the treatment of individuals with psychological disorders. Foucault's work demonstrated the enduring relevance of historical context and power dynamics in shaping contemporary mental health practices. His critique of traditional approaches to mental illness, particularly the stigmatization and institutionalization of individuals with mental health conditions, echoes the ethical considerations raised by the integration of AI technologies into mental health care. The implications of my findings are far-reaching and influence various aspects of mental health and AI landscape. The effectiveness of chatbots in delivering mental health support suggests a promising avenue for improving access to mental health care. Chatbots can offer immediate support, especially during crises, potentially reducing the burden on overburdened mental health professionals. The implications are significant for addressing the accessibility and scalability of mental health services. The diversity of user perceptions emphasizes the importance of user-centered design in developing AI-driven mental health interventions. Adapting chatbots to user preferences, personalities, and cultural backgrounds can enhance user engagement and satisfaction. Personalization of interventions can increase the likelihood of positive user experiences. The ethical considerations underscore the need for stringent data security and responsible data use in AI-driven mental health support. Developing ethical guidelines and standards is essential to ensure that user data is protected and that individuals can trust the confidentiality of their interactions with AI systems. This has implications for data governance and the responsible use of AI technologies. The influence of Michel Foucault's work highlights the importance of historical context and power dynamics in understanding mental health practices. The implications are relevant for practitioners and policymakers as they consider the historical baggage that shapes the mental health field. Recognizing the impact of power structures on mental health institutions can lead to more equitable and patient-centered care. The implications of our findings also point to several avenues for further research: Further research should delve into the long-term effectiveness of chatbots in mental health. Large-scale, longitudinal studies can provide valuable insights into the sustained impact of chatbot interventions on mental health outcomes. Research that explores the nuances of user perceptions across diverse demographic groups can contribute to more inclusive and culturally sensitive AI-driven mental health support. Developing comprehensive ethical frameworks and guidelines for AI-driven mental health interventions should be a priority. Research in this area can inform the creation of industry standards that prioritize user privacy and ethical use of data. Future studies can delve into user-centered design principles for AI-driven mental health interventions, including the personalization of chatbots and the incorporation of cultural competence. Research addressing disparities in access to AI-driven mental health support is critical. Ensuring these technologies are accessible to all, regardless of socioeconomic status, location, or other demographic factors, is a pressing concern. While this research offers valuable insights, it is not without limitations. One limitation lies in the availability of empirical data on the long-term effectiveness of chatbots in mental health. More rigorous research, including controlled experiments and large-scale, longitudinal studies, is needed to establish the enduring impact of chatbot interventions. Another limitation relates to the diversity of user perceptions. Our analysis highlighted the variability in user experiences. Still, more in-depth research is needed to understand the specific factors influencing these perceptions, such as cultural backgrounds and individual needs. Ethical considerations are also an ongoing concern. Research focusing on developing ethical frameworks and guidelines is essential to shape the responsible use of AI technologies in mental health. The research provides a comprehensive examination of the intersection of mental health and artificial intelligence. The findings underscore the potential of AI technologies, including chatbots, to enhance mental health support, emphasizing user-centered design and ethical considerations.

In the culmination of this research journey, we have navigated the complex and dynamic terrain where mental health and artificial intelligence (AI) intersect. This conclusion section serves as a compass to guide us through the key landmarks we've encountered, restate our central thesis, and emphasize the profound significance of our research in shaping the future of mental health care. The research unveiled the burgeoning influence of AI, particularly in the form of chatbots, as a disruptive force in mental health. AI's ability to offer immediate and scalable support has ignited optimism for addressing the longstanding gaps in mental health service delivery. User perceptions of AI interventions in mental health exhibit a spectrum of experiences. From those who view chatbots as empathetic allies to those who harbor skepticism, the user landscape is rich and complex. This diversity underscores the importance of designing AI interventions that cater to individual preferences and cultural backgrounds. The ethical dimensions of AI applications in mental health are paramount. Safeguarding user privacy, ensuring data security, and adhering to ethical data practices are integral components of integrating AI technologies responsibly into mental health care. Michel Foucault's historical insights and theories, such as biopower and disciplinary power, have proven to be a beacon in understanding the historical context of mental health practices. His critical analysis of power structures in mental health institutions resonates with contemporary discussions about the influence of power in the treatment of individuals with psychological disorders. Our findings hold significant implications for the future of mental health care. They highlight the potential for enhancing support, offering user-centered interventions, and setting ethical standards for AI in mental health. Moreover, Foucault's historical insights provide a lens through which to reexamine mental health practices with an eye toward equity and patient-centered care. The central thesis of this research posits that the convergence of mental health and artificial intelligence, with an emphasis on AI technologies such as chatbots, has the potential to revolutionize accessibility, user experience, and ethical considerations within the field of mental health care. This thesis encapsulates the essence of our exploration, underlining the transformative capacity of this convergence. The significance of our research extends far beyond academic inquiry. It radiates across the landscape of mental health practice, policy, and the lives of individuals in search of solace and support. Several facets of this research carry profound significance: The significance of our research lies in its potential to make mental health support more accessible to a wider population. The immediacy and scalability of AI-driven technologies, such as chatbots, can bridge existing treatment gaps, potentially reaching those who might otherwise remain underserved. Recognizing the diverse and nuanced user perceptions emphasizes the significance of user-centered care. Designing AI interventions that respect individual preferences, cultural backgrounds, and personal needs holds the potential to enhance user engagement and satisfaction. It signifies a shift toward more personalized and tailored care.

The ethical considerations surrounding AI in mental health are of profound significance. Ensuring responsible data use, protecting user privacy, and upholding ethical standards are moral imperatives. This research underscores the importance of establishing comprehensive ethical frameworks and guidelines to shape the responsible use of AI technologies in mental health care.

Michel Foucault's enduring influence in our research highlights the impact of history and power dynamics in shaping contemporary mental health practices. Recognizing this influence is essential for fostering equitable, patient-centered care and reshaping mental health practices in light of power dynamics. At its core, the research signifies the innovation and progress unfolding at the intersection of mental health and AI. Embracing technology and historical perspectives, we lay the groundwork for a future in which mental health care is more accessible, personalized, and ethically responsible.

In closing, the confluence of mental health and artificial intelligence is a realm ripe with potential. It beckons us to reimagine mental health support, pushing the boundaries of accessibility and personalization. It urges us to address ethical considerations, ensuring the privacy and dignity of those seeking assistance. It invites us to examine history and power, acknowledging their influence on modern mental health practices. As we venture further into this intersection, let us proceed with vigilance, empathy, and responsibility. This research stands as a guiding light, illuminating the path to a future where mental health care is not only accessible to all but is also attuned to individual needs and cultural diversity. In the era of mental health and artificial intelligence, our journey continues. It is a journey marked by innovation, empathy, and responsibility. It is a journey with the potential to transform mental health care for the better. As we move forward, may our steps be guided by the insights and considerations shared in this research, forging a brighter, more inclusive future for mental health support.

REFERENCES

Abd-Alrazaq, A. A., Alajlani, M., Alalwan, A. A., Bewick, B. M., Gardner, P., & Househ, M. A. (2019). *An overview of the features of Chatbots in Mental Health: A scoping review.* International journal of medical informatics. https://pubmed.ncbi.nlm.nih.gov/31622850/

Duvvuri, V., Guan, Q., Daddala, S., Harris, M., & Kaushik, S. (2022, January 1). *Predicting depression symptoms from discord chat messaging using AI Medical Chatbots: Proceedings of the 2022 6th International Conference on Machine Learning and soft computing.* ACM Other conferences. https://dl.acm.org/doi/abs/10.1145/3523150.3523168

Foucault, M. (2008). *Madness and civilization: A history of insanity in the age of reason.* Routledge.

Foucault, M. (2013). *History of madness.* Taylor and Francis. DOI: 10.4324/9780203642603

Foucault, M., & Sheridan, A. M. (1973). *The Birth of the Clinic: An Archaeology of Medical Perception.* Routledge.

Hartl, G. (2001). *The World Health Report 2001: Mental disorders affect One in four people.* World Health Organization. https://www.who.int/news/item/28-09-2001-the-world-health-report-2001-mental-disorders-affect-one-in-four-people

Vaidyam, A. N., Wisniewski, H., Halamka, J. D., Kashavan, M. S., & Torous, J. B. (2019, July). *Chatbots and conversational agents in Mental Health: A review of the Psychiatric Landscape.* Canadian journal of psychiatry. Revue canadienne de psychiatrie. https://www.ncbi.nlm.nih.gov/pmc/articles/PMC6610568/

Chapter 6
Cultivating Emotional Intelligence:
A Catalyst for Entrepreneurial Success

Deepak Kumar Sahoo
Biju Patnaik University of Technology, Rourkela, India

Anish Kumar
https://orcid.org/0000-0002-8047-4227
O.P. Jindal Global University, India

Ajay Chandel
https://orcid.org/0000-0002-4585-6406
Lovely Professional University, India

Hewawasam P. G. D. Wijethilak
https://orcid.org/0009-0006-9611-5735
University of Colombo, Sri Lanka

ABSTRACT

This chapter explores the vital role of emotional intelligence (EI) in entrepreneurship, highlighting its significance in leadership, team dynamics, customer relations, and overall business success. As the business landscape evolves, particularly with the rise of artificial intelligence (AI), the integration of EI becomes increasingly crucial. The chapter addresses key components of emotional intelligence, the challenges entrepreneurs face in developing these skills, and the measurable impacts on employee performance, engagement, and customer satisfaction. It also discusses future trends that emphasize the synergy between EI and AI, including enhanced collaboration, personalized training, and a focus on employee well-being. Ultimately, fostering emotional intelligence is essential for entrepreneurs seeking to navigate complexities, drive innovation, and cultivate resilient organizations in a rapidly changing environment.

DOI: 10.4018/979-8-3693-3673-1.ch006

Copyright ©2025, IGI Global. Copying or distributing in print or electronic forms without written permission of IGI Global is prohibited.

INTRODUCTION: EMOTIONAL INTELLIGENCE AND ENTREPRENEURSHIP

Emotional intelligence, the newest found measure defining success in entrepreneurial activities in modern day business, is considered rather important. According to Daniel Goleman, a psychologist who defined emotional intelligence, "it is the ability to monitor and manage emotions, including emotional regression, and the ability to motivate oneself and others in social situations.". While innovation, strategic planning, and financial acumen are some of the usual factors taken into account for entrepreneurial success, navigating human emotions has now been recognized as equally important in the careers of entrepreneurs (Alkaabi et al., 2023). The perturbations, uncertainties, and turmoil of managing human feelings boil down to managing a team or crisis situations, customers or investors; entrepreneurship is indeed turbulent and uncertain. In these scenarios, emotional intelligence really comes in to play where entrepreneurs stay humble and grounded to make better decisions and forge stronger relationships.

Entrepreneurial landscape is inherently demanding, with constant change, high levels of uncertainty, and intense competition. Through the tough situation, it is proved that emotive intelligent entrepreneurs will be better equipped to handle stress and maintain an optimistic attitude despite having faced failure. Self-awareness is but just one of the numerous core constituents of EI, which enable the entrepreneur to know his emotional triggers and biases so that problems can be approached with a clear and rational mindset (Al-Tekreeti et al., 2024). That is why entrepreneurs stand better chances of developing emotional resilience, something very fundamental in matters of high-stakes decisions where stress and failure seem to feature in most cases. Besides, EI empowers entrepreneurs to react flexibly to all the circumstances and people, resulting in greater levels of productivity and engagement at the workplace.

Emotional intelligence is also significant for the relationships factor of entrepreneurship. An entrepreneur has to interact with different stakeholders: employees, investors, customers, and business partners, and their relationships with those people have to be managed. With an element called empathy, EI is defined; this would enable entrepreneurs to understand the emotional needs and concerns of these stakeholders, thus enabling a greater communication and building relationship with them (Andiani et al., 2020). Attunement to other people's emotions would help entrepreneurs create a work culture that is based on trust and collaboration as well as a mutual respect for each other. This could also improve team morale and ultimately spur organizational performance. Actually, high emotional intelligence entrepreneurs can more simply solve all the conflicts arising at each stage, effectively control team dynamics, and inspire loyalty among employees, which is critical for keeping the best professionals working (Bayram et al., 2023).

Customer relations, therefore, refer to touching an entrepreneur's heart or emotional sense with the customers. Entrepreneurs who have a connection and are able to respond with customers' emotional cues are more likely to evoke long-term loyalty and trust. In a consumer-experience age, more emotionally intelligent entrepreneurs can create such brands that resonate with their values and emotions to ultimately drive business success.

This is because emotional intelligence works as a powerful driver to foster entrepreneurial success. Such a kind of intelligence does not only enable entrepreneurs to have control over their own emotions but enables them to understand and influence the feelings of others, leading to more concrete relationships and innovation and forging sustainable businesses (Chandnani, 2023). The more dynamic entrepreneurial landscape will continue to transform, so too will the demand for higher levels of emotional intelligence; therefore, it is one skill that entrepreneurship professionals will need to develop in order to thrive and be sustainable in this competitive business arena.

CORE COMPONENTS OF EMOTIONAL INTELLIGENCE

Emotional intelligence (EI) is widely broken down into five core components, with each playing an extremely vital role in the entrepreneur's functioning to manage emotions and relationships. These include self-awareness, self-regulation, motivation, empathy, and social skills, which give a framework to learn how to tap into emotional capabilities to drive the success of a business.

1. Self-Awareness

Self-awareness constitutes the basis from which everything else is conceptualized within the context of emotional intelligence. It means the ability to identify and know what one feels, including their power over thinking and expression. In the case of entrepreneurs, emotional triggers, stress points, and biases which may obscure judgment or influence a decision are points of insight (Deb et al., 2023). A high degree of self-awareness allows entrepreneurs to judge themselves honestly in terms of strength and weaknesses so that they can control their responses in situations with high tension. It further allows self-regulation of emotions, thus helping them maintain the emotional balance, which helps them make lucid decisions even in turbulent business settings. Entrepreneurs that are more self-aware are more likely to make strategic decisions fit in with their long-term vision and values.

2. Self-Regulation

Self-Regulation or controlling one's emotions is closely related to being self-aware. This implies being able to maintain emotional calmness and composure and not behave impulsively. In business challenges, entrepreneurs face problems that are bound to happen, including financial failure, product failure, and interpersonal problems. Good entrepreneurs master the art of self-regulation and respond calmly constructively, think clearly when frustration or anxiety is sorely tempting them (Durnali et al., 2023). This allows them to be professional, and work environment that should respect rational resolution of problems rather than emotional outbursts. In addition, self-regulation increases credibility because stable leaders will not react emotionally-which means such a leader will be perceived as more trustworthy and reliable.

3. Motivation

Another indispensable part of emotional intelligence is intrinsic motivation. Intrinsic motivation involves achieving passion, resilience, and persisting in achieving goals even when obstacles exist. Entrepreneurs often go through long periods of uncertainty, financial stress, and even loss; thus, something must drive them to continue their business ventures. More than rewards that are external to the organization-advantaging profit-entrepreneurs guided by emotional intelligence are motivated by more meaningful goals such as self-fulfillment and a sense of purpose (Fedorova et al., 2024). This type of self-motivation allows them not only to be focused and determined but also to encourage their teams to be loyal to the vision of the business. Entrepreneurs with high motivation are always more creative as they continually seek new and innovative ways to develop and expand their businesses.

4. Empathy

Empathy is defined as an understanding and sharing of feelings. In the entrepreneurial context, empathy allows leaders to connect with their teams, customers, and partners in a much deeper way. Being attuned to people's emotional needs and concerns allows entrepreneurs to build more meaningful relationships, foster collaboration, and enhance team dynamics. It also plays a very critical role in customer relations (Karimi & Ataei, 2023). An entrepreneur's understanding of the emotional drivers of consumer behavior helps one position products, services, and messaging in ways that resonate with their clients. Empathy helps an entrepreneur build trust, loyalty, and a sense of belonging-tracks most important to long-term success.

5. Social Skills

Social skills, the last emotional intelligence component, are the ability to navigate social situations, build one's network, and influence others. Social skills for entrepreneurs are very essential in how they operate and manage employees, investors, customers, and partners. Well-groomed entrepreneurs with proper social skills can ensure effective communication, negotiation, conflict resolution, and team building; they inspire and lead their teams, give a pleasurable work culture, and assure partnerships that ensure business growth (Mishra & Singh, 2024). Persuasion and influence abilities also form part of social skills, such as in securing funding, closing deals, or getting the customer on side with a suggestion. Basically, social skills enable entrepreneurs to leverage their emotional intelligence to achieve business through effective interpersonal interaction.

Through this development of these core components of emotional intelligence, entrepreneurs enhance their capacities for leading people, for building better teams, and for creating businesses in order to keep the sail smooth even during the toughest times (Nooraie et al., 2023).

EMOTIONAL INTELLIGENCE AND ENTREPRENEURIAL LEADERSHIP

Entrepreneurial leadership is not only a matter of business acumen and strategic vision; it has to do with relating with people or with people management skill, inspiring teams, and with creating an environment that encourages growth and innovation. Emotional intelligence (EI) is significant to effective leadership since it enables entrepreneurs to do better with interpersonal dynamics, improve decision-making ability, and develop coping skills when stressors are at their most high (Oktalia et al., 2018). Therefore, emotional intelligence gives strong reasons for leaders with the potential of inspiring trust, driving motivation, and generally building a positive organization culture-the three elements that entrepreneurs need to ensure any type of entrepreneurial venture thrives.

Entrepreneurial leadership is the ability to soundly make decisions in uncertainty and quickly changing environments. The emotional intelligence, especially self-awareness and self-regulation, would guide entrepreneurs into keeping things in perspective and rational thinking as they experience the process of uncertainty. "Knowing their emotional reactions to uncertainty, for example being anxious or frustrated, helps leaders avoid reactive decision-making so that they can face issues with clarity and composure.". It brings emotional balance to the decisions, which then enhances the quality of their decision-making (Pathak & Muralidharan, 2024). It also serves as an excellent example to the team they are leading because a resilient and calm leader would definitely not be easily swayed when in the midst of pressure. Thereby, emotionally intelligent leaders better assess the emotional state of their workforce or team members, which enables them to offer support when necessary and keep employees focused and motivated during tough times.

The third core component of emotional intelligence is empathy, which is very relevant for an entrepreneurial leader because it provides the capacity to remain in touch with the needs, concerns, and motivations of team members. In an entrepreneurial venture, an individual deals with numerous groups of people for example, employees, partners, and clients. An empathetic leader can resonate with a different person by tailoring communication in a unique way and tailoring the leadership style to understand the needs of a person, thereby making sure that everyone feels heard and valued. This brings about a culture of trust and collaboration; hence, it enhances team cohesion and innovation. Empathy also allows leaders to address conflicts effectively, as they engage any disagreement with an understanding of each party's emotional standpoint thus making negotiation and resolution easier (Pirsoul et al., 2023).

Inspiring and motivating others is another important role in entrepreneurial leadership, and it has much to do with emotional intelligence. An emotionally intelligent entrepreneur is typically one who better understands what drives his team members and how to access these motivations in inspiring better performance (Prib, 2023). Whether it be through aligning his team members with a shared vision, encouraging his team members during tough times, or offering some form of personal recognition, the emotionally intelligent leader knows what it takes to motivate his teams toward achieving collective goals. This ability to build an emotional relationship with other people develops higher team morale since people's emotional needs are being satisfied and enhances productivity since workers find themselves more attached to the work when emotionally helped (Quintillán & Legazkue, 2019).

It is such a quality that an entrepreneurial leader requires in order to lead. It allows entrepreneurs to work through human relationships complexity, find trust, and collaboration within the team, all with leading strength and a compassionate heart. Beyond just reaching leadership effectiveness, the development of emotional intelligence among entrepreneurs will help develop a more robust and innovative business culture, one that will thrive over adversity (Raza et al., 2023).

Building Stronger Teams Through Emotional Intelligence

Emotional intelligence plays a very crucial role in new entrepreneurial venture success, mainly in allowing leaders to achieve tighter, more cohesive teams. One of the game-changers in today's competitive fast-paced business environment is having a communicating and working toward completing one goal, but most importantly, maturing to handle conflict well in the team. Emotional intelligence enables entrepreneurs to acquire skills on how to create the environment that makes them connect with employees at a deep level, understanding what gets them motivated and creating an atmosphere of trust, empathy, and open communication (Singh & Kovid, 2023).

First and foremost, emotional intelligence enhances the ability to communicate. Highly self-aware and socially skilled entrepreneurs clearly and constructively express their thoughts and feelings, inspiring their followers. In addition, they will listen more attentively to their employees and can perceive the slightest verbal and non-verbal signals (Sultan et al., 2023). It is this awareness and attachment to the emotional undertones of communications that make emotionally intelligent leaders address issues before they inflate into huge problems. In the process, emotionally intelligent leaders encourage open communication and foster teamwork and problem-solving (Tee et al., 2014).

Conflict will always be unavoidable in any team, but intervention in conflict either makes or breaks the dynamics of a team. Another element of managing conflict is to develop rather than ruin the relationships. Adequate emotional intelligence endows with great leadership qualities, allowing a disagreement to be turned into an opportunity to understand the feelings and see the perspectives of others (Sutiyatno, 2023). This way, they're in a better position to mediate and resolve such conflicts with suggestions that might satisfy everyone involved and continue harmonious coexistence within the team. Through modeling emotionally intelligent behavior during conflicts, entrepreneurs can influence others in the organization to do the same. This helps to create an atmosphere where differences are considered paths to growth rather than points of argument.

Another core element that solves the puzzle called team building is empathy-the ability to share feelings with others. An empathetic entrepreneur will have more knowledge of personal or professional problems that the members of the team may be facing and, therefore, will be better able to respond to individual needs in a supportive workplace environment where employees are truly valued and appreciated, fostering morale and loyalty (Tunio et al., 2023). When the team feels their leader cares about their well-being, they can be invested in the success of the business and do their best work. Empathy is also a source of success in building diverse teams because it makes the leaders appreciate different points of view and experiences, which takes creativity and innovation up several notches.

Emotional intelligence also works with motivating and engaging teams. Inspirational leadership will be actualized by leaders who can understand the emotional driving forces of employees. For instance, an entrepreneur who is aware that an employee thrives upon recognition and personal development has perfected his approach as an inspiration in regard to such opportunities. In this respect, emotionally intelligent entrepreneurs can align their leadership style with the emotional needs of the team to create a sense of purpose and shared vision, hence improving team cohesion and productivity (Tunio et al., 2023).

Trust is one of the most imperative elements in building solid teams through emotional intelligence. Authentic and transparent leaders with emotional integrity build trust with the team, and this makes effectiveness in teamwork feasible. The employee will be much more likely to take risks, share ideas, and work freely when they know that they are appreciated, their emotions respected, and experience the safety of their psychological selves, which ultimately amounts to greater creativity and innovative capacity and team performance (Worokinasih et al., 2021).

Emotional intelligence will enable the building of more robust and resilient teams. The emotionally intelligent leader creates an environment of better communications, conflicts of less emotional weight, leads to motivation of employees, and builds trust. Therefore, a workplace of collaboration and innovation that caters to enhancing the inventive capabilities of the workforce is established. For an entrepreneur that derives power from his/her team and that this team can contribute to the strength of the business venture, emotional intelligence becomes a helpful pursuit and one that proves to be much needed (Yitshaki, 2012).

Emotional Intelligence in the Uncertainty and Risk of Entrepreneurship

Entrepreneurship is characterized by uncertainty and risk because of business environments characterized by volatility, unpredictability, and rapid change. The number of obstacles that entrepreneurs encounter is countless, including fluctuations in markets, changes in consumer needs, financial instability, and potential attacks from competitors. Emotional intelligence in such a situation is crucial, valued for its ability to help the entrepreneur manage his or her emotions, make thoughtful decisions, and maintain resilience (Yusoff et al., 2023). Using emotional intelligence will enable entrepreneurs to embrace uncertainty and risk with greater clarity, composure, and flexibility in a way to deal with all the changes and obstacles that come with it, thus widening the success-probability tentacles.

One of the first ways emotional intelligence helps entrepreneurs in dealing with uncertainty is by raising self-awareness. High self-aware entrepreneurs develop better sense regarding how stress, fear, and anxiety may impact their thought process while deciding. This allows them a chance to pause, reflect on what has just happened, and, before approaching the same situation, do so rationally and logically, thus averting impulse or irrational decisions. Self-aware entrepreneurs will then know when to be vulnerable enough to own up to where they could lack and to listen to advice from others, thus making it completer and more balanced in handling risks. Self-awareness is also what will enable the entrepreneur to stay focused on long-term goals even when all hell breaks loose around him or her (Zhang et al., 2023).

The second variable in navigating uncertainty is self-regulation, that is the other component of emotional intelligence. It refers to managing one's emotional reaction to events and, therefore, staying calm in the face of adversity. It comes in handy when running an unpredictable business as that entrepreneur with this quality can control his emotions such that he does not fall prey to panic or frustration when making judgments. They should be in the position of strategizing on how to react to the shock. Entrepreneurs are not required to react instinctively over responses to new, demanding situations. They have emotional control that makes them more flexible and adaptable in an environment where the change is the only certainty (Zhao & Sang, 2023).

Risk Motivation, the other central component of emotional intelligence, becomes a great motivator when put into a high-risk situation. Intrinsic motivation, of course, means being a self-motivated entrepreneur in the sense that his purpose and passion make him do it and not merely for an external reward (Alkaabi et al., 2023). This inner motivation keeps them going and determined, and if one fails or there is uncertainty, an emotionally intelligent entrepreneur goes ahead motivated with the goal to be successful and to learn from it. This resiliency becomes crucial in riding out the storms of unexpected challenges and remaining committed to the entrepreneurial vision, regardless of what happens outside.

Empathy also plays another huge role in dealing with uncertainty and risk-particularly, team dynamics and stakeholder relationships. An empathetic entrepreneur is also more likely to grasp, better comprehensively, the fears, worries, and drivers that shape the concerns of his or her team members in any period of uncertainty. By recognizing these emotions and offering support, empathetic leaders establish trust and psychological safety that motivates their teams to stay more active and focused. It binds a team together but also helps solve complex problems creatively because employees feel at ease in sharing ideas with one another and taking calculated risks. On the other hand, empathy helps entrepreneurs manage relationships that are easy with investors, customers, and partners; thus, it is helpful in communicating freely in difficult times (Al-Tekreeti et al., 2024).

Social Skills-This includes ability to build strong relationships, the capability to influence others, and coping with ambiguity in an entrepreneurial context. In situations where entrepreneurship is bound up with uncertainty, strength in social skills will be instrumental in marshaling support from stakeholders since, for example, it may allow them to gain confidence among investors, find new partners, or boost team morale (Andiani et al., 2020). Communication, negotiation, and conflict resolution skills are very useful when there is a need for building consensus and when that is essential, especially in uncertain conditions requiring the preservation of valuable networks, in pursuit of survival and growth.

Emotional intelligence gives entrepreneurs a level of defense and flexibility in the midst of the complexities and vagaries of entrepreneurship. With self-awareness, self-regulation, motivation, empathy, and social skills, an emotionally intelligent entrepreneur can manage his emotional responses, stay sharp and on target, and stimulate others toward a cause as well as take calculated risks. This enhances his chances for survival and converts many that seem to be uncertainties into opportunities (Bayram et al., 2023).

Emotional Intelligence and Customer Relations

Emotional intelligence is important in customer relationship building, an essential part of entrepreneurial success. The highly emotionally intelligent entrepreneur will better understand the emotional needs and concerns of his customers. In a highly competitive marketplace, customer loyalty is what makes or breaks the business, and emotional intelligence can act as a great differentiator wherein entrepreneurs create more personalized empathetic and responsive customer experiences (Chandnani, 2023).

Empathy: One of the primary dimensions of emotional intelligence in customer relationships - being able to be in other people's shoes and understanding how they feel. Empathy means that an entrepreneur, from the perspective of his customer, will be able to see situations in terms of the emotional drivers, motivations, and pain points. Entrepreneur is at a greater advantage if he can start predicting what the customer could be craving next (Deb et al., 2023). This understanding at a deeper level allows entrepreneurs to further develop their products, services, or ways of communicating based on insights into customers. Demonstration of empathy will enhance authenticity and meaning in interactions and go a long way to building trust and loyalty. For example, a sympathetic entrepreneur will easily redeem the concern or frustration of a customer and, thereby, convert a potential experience into a positive one by showing real care in the process of resolving the issue (Durnali et al., 2023).

Self-awareness is another very critical component of emotional intelligence that bears an impact on customer relations. Entrepreneurs with high self-awareness recognize their own feelings and how these can rub off to lead to certain results while interacting with customers (Fedorova et al., 2024). This allows entrepreneurs to manage their emotional responses when confronted by challenging circumstances such as addressing complaints or dealing with customers disadvantageously positioned. Self-awareness allows an entrepreneur to remain composed, professional, and solution-focused when confronted by emotionally charged or confrontational issues. It also enables them to measure how their words and behavior may be received by customers, thus allowing effective clear, considerate, and respectful communication.

Association with Self-Awareness Self-regulation further increases an entrepreneur's ability to deal with tense customer interactions by having a strong association with self-awareness. This attributes control over frustration, anger, or impatience to the entrepreneur. The entrepreneur may then diffuse tension-sapped situations, answer customers wisely and objectively, and thus maintain a positive relationship with customers (Karimi & Ataei, 2023). Self-regulation enables the entrepreneur to answer both negative and positive customer feedback that can be useful in learning from them and bringing necessary changes. Through this, with emotional stability, business people are in a position to develop a customer-focused culture where issues revolve around service excellence and problem resolution.

Communication skills also lie in the areas enhanced by emotional intelligence, especially in developing effective customer relations. The business person with such a high emotional intelligence can listen extensively and pick on the overt and slight emotional cuings and body language that may come to show a customer's emotions or worry. This affords the entrepreneur an attentive ear to which they can direct problems better and respond in a manner that hits a chord with the emotional level of the customer. In addition to that, emotionally aware entrepreneurs can change their style of communication to be in line with the customer's needs, such as when reassurance is needed, explanations are required, or a listening ear has to be made empathetically. Such customized interactions lead to customers who are satisfied and leave a positive impression of the brand (Mishra & Singh, 2024).

It also assists with conflict resolution, a staple of customer relationships. Conflicts or misunderstandings could pop up, and the entrepreneur will be able to deal with this by being sensitive and diplomatic, given good emotional intelligence. The entrepreneur, having stayed calm, empathetic, and solution-oriented, successfully de-escalates tensions and turns bad experiences into opportunities for demonstrating commitment to customer satisfaction (Nooraie et al., 2023). Emotionally intelligent entrepreneurs can take responsibility over mistakes, offer genuine apologies, and seek mutually beneficial solutions rather than retaining a defensive stance. Such behavior will not only solve the issue at hand but also foster customer trust and loyalty in the long run.

Emotional intelligence enables entrepreneurs to fill this demand by developing authentic relationships between customers and the entrepreneurship and working towards providing customized experiences that meet the pertinent emotional needs of their customers. This, in return, not only helps in retaining a customer but also generates good reputation for the business, thereby ensuring the long-term success (Oktalia et al., 2018).

Building and maintaining strong customer relationships requires emotional intelligence. Empathy, self-awareness, self-regulation, and effective communication allow emotionally intelligent entrepreneurs to create experiences that have a positive impact on customers for longer. Being aware of one's own emotions and managing those of others helps to earn their trust through resolving conflicts with dignity and being different in the market arena. For these reasons, emotional intelligence has become one of the major drivers of customer loyalty and satisfaction besides business growth (Pathak & Muralidharan, 2024).

Enhancing Creativity and Innovation Through Emotional Intelligence

Creativity and innovation are aspects of being entrepreneurial, as they create business opportunities that can help companies differentiate themselves in a competitive market, solve complex problems, and continually evolve. Emotional intelligence, therefore, becomes a fundamental element in environments that involve creativity and innovation. Entrepreneurs who foster emotional intelligence can manage better, encouraging open communication and building an ethos to promote risk taking and out-of-the-box thinking. Emotional intelligence unlocks the creative potential of teams; hence, for entrepreneurs, a factor that drives innovation in their organizations (Pirsoul et al., 2023).

In an attempt to reflect on how emotional intelligence builds creativity, emotional intelligence aids in creating a positive emotional environment. Emotions like stress, fear, or anxiety often block creativity and make it hard to think freely and chart new ideas. High emotional intelligence entrepreneurs are always keen to be aware of such emotional blockers and create safe and supportive atmospheres wherein team members feel free to express their ideas and no one worries about being pounded for mistakes (Prib, 2023). Emotional security is another area that the smartly emotionally intelligent leaders create so that their teams feel liberated to experiment with innovative ideas and explore novel concepts and ways of thinking that step beyond the traditional way of thinking-both of which are fatal to innovation.

Another realm of emotional intelligence that further enlists creativity and innovation is empathy. An empathic entrepreneur might realize the perspective of not just his team members but also customers. Such deep comprehension helps them see problems through different lenses that lead to much more innovative solutions, truly meeting the needs of their target market. Empathetic leaders also do a better job at creating an inclusive work environment by valuing and integrating diverse viewpoints into the creative process. In that process, because those different backgrounds bring something unique to the table, thought diversity often is found there (Quintillán & Legazkue, 2019). Self-awareness is another core element of emotional intelligence, through which entrepreneurs come to understand how their own emotions influence their creative processes. Entrepreneurial self-awareness may enable such entrepreneurs to pinpoint conditions during which they are most creative and try to replicate those conditions, for instance, by controlling the amount of stress they experience, by creating a stimulating work environment, or by tapping into their internal motivations. Self-awareness also allows entrepreneurs to become conscious of what stage of mind they are stuck at or blinders that enclose their creative thinking, thus giving them a way to get out of those and have a wholly open-minded view (Raza et al., 2023).

Self-regulation, or the ability to control one's emotional response, is just as crucial for innovation to thrive. Entrepreneurs who are better regulators of their emotions would not get frustrated easily with setbacks or challenges that can happen in the creative process. Unlike emotions that hinder the growth of entrepreneurs, emotionally intelligent entrepreneurs remain stalwart and focused since they perceive challenges as opportunities for growth. Emotional resilience inspires teams to keep experimenting with solutions when adversity presents itself. This further creates a culture where failure becomes something that leads to success; it is what fuels creative exploration (Singh & Kovid, 2023).

Emotional intelligence also enhances the strength of communication, which is crucial for collaborative innovation. Strong social skills characterize the kind of entrepreneurs who create free-flowing and transparent communication among people in a team in developing ideas from one another. They can deliver constructive motivational feedback instead of discouraging members within the team. This, therefore, makes them provide an avenue for a culture of trust in which risk-taking creative methods by team members will be supported (Sultan et al., 2023). Further, emotionally intelligent leaders will know how to work around group dynamics to ensure that all voices are heard and the best ideas are brought to the surface.oeving with emotional intelligence enhances the ability of an entrepreneur to inspire and motivate their teams. Because, emotionally intelligent leaders would know what makes people tick- emotionally: autonomy, purpose, recognition. With these emotional drivers in place, it will be easy to have the style of leadership to that which will create an environment that empowers team members to find creativity and contribute to the innovative efforts of the organization. For example, entrepreneurs can enhance motivation and inspire continuing innovations towards change by allowing freedom for many team members to try new ideas and ensuring recognition for the creative effort (Sutiyatno, 2023). Entrepreneurs can better unlock the creative potential of their teams through a positive emotional climate, encouraging diverse perspectives, developing emotional resilience, and maintaining open communication. More innovative solutions, products, and services will be developed, driving long-term success in business. Emotional intelligence finally creates an entrepreneurial culture where creativity thrives and results naturally in innovation.

TOOLS AND TECHNIQUES TO DEVELOP EMOTIONAL INTELLIGENCE

EI is not an innate property, but a skill that develops with conscious practice and appropriate instruments. Developing emotional intelligence has become crucial for entrepreneurs in so far as it helps them develop their leadership, improve the dynamics of their teams, contribute to innovation, and understand the fast-moving nature of enterprise (Tee et al., 2014). Considering these aspects of self-awareness, self-regulation, empathy, and social skills can better equip entrepreneurs with emotional competencies for entrepreneurial success. Here are some effective tools and techniques to help cultivate emotional intelligence.

1. Mindfulness and Self-Reflection

Mindfulness is an excellent practice that allows the entrepreneur to develop self-awareness by bringing their attention to the present moment without judgment. A person who observes his thoughts and emotions, using mindfulness meditation, gets better feedback from his internal experiences about how they shape his behavior. Mindfulness practice makes entrepreneurs aware of emotional triggers and patterns; hence, they can eventually be more intentional in how they respond in troubling situations. By this high self-awareness of responding to emotions, an entrepreneur will better regulate his emotions and maintain focus even under stress (Tunio et al., 2023).

Journaling is one of the reflective tools, providing a systematic approach by which one investigates their feelings, thoughts, and responses to situations of day-to-day life. Journaling allows the entrepreneur to examine his or her response in light of emotions to diverse business problems, to observe recurring themes, as well as fields for improvement. By frequent reflection on themselves, entrepreneurs learn better what they are emotionally strong at and what needs to develop. This further develops their EQ, perpetually (Worokinasih et al., 2021).

2. Emotional Regulation Techniques

Another crucial skill that needs to be developed to function effectively within high-pressure entrepreneurial environments is self-emotion regulation. Of effective approaches to emotional regulation, cognitive reappraisal is the one which is considered central. This reappraisal technique is done when negative or stressful circumstances are presented in a much more positive or constructive perspective. Through this technique, entrepreneurs might alter their outlook and perception of a challenge, so they do not get fixated on the setback but see opportunities for improvement (Yitshaki, 2012).

Another excellent resource is deep breathing techniques or progressive muscle relaxation, which can bring about fast relief and calm the nervous system quickly. In tense moments or with heightened emotional arousal, slow, deep breathing will help lower heart rates and give entrepreneurs time to gather themselves. Such techniques prove especially useful for the period of the difficult conversation when conditions are high pressured on decision-making and conflict between the teams needs to be resolved (Yusoff et al., 2023).

3. Empathy Development

Empathy, which is the ability to understand and share another person's feelings, is very essential for an entrepreneur looking to build more effective relationships with his or her employees, customers, and partners. Listening actively aids empathy and is also one of the most effective tools applied. Such listening is characterized by full concentration on the other person, not interrupting them, giving feedback, and showing real interest in their perspective (Zhang et al., 2023). Practicing active listening will allow an entrepreneur to feel, as well as understand, the emotions, concerns, and motivations of others and respond accordingly-emotionally attuned and supportively.

This is made possible through another process of empathy building: perspective-taking-the process in which entrepreneurs consciously try to walk a mile in other people's shoes and see things from their point of view. It can be something done during day-to-day interaction by asking oneself, "How would I feel if this happened?" or "What might this person need or expect of me?" It becomes more ingrained over time, forcing entrepreneurs to become more empathetic and responsive to the emotions of those they care about (Zhao & Sang, 2023).

4. Improving Social Skills Through Networking and Collaboration

The ability to develop social skills, such as communication, conflict resolution, and relationship management, falls under emotional intelligence. Business entrepreneurs can improve on these by actively looking for times where they can network and collaborate. Engaging in professional networks, attending industry events, or joining entrepreneurial groups puts an individual into practice when building connections and navigating through various forms of social dynamics. It also serves as valuable feedback as to how well the individual's communication style is coming off, therefore helping business entrepreneurs improve their approach to communication (Alkaabi et al., 2023).

They can actually practice collaborative leadership within their own teams: they encourage open debate, facilitate inclusion in decision-making, and create an atmosphere where all voices are heard. This develops team cohesion not just within themselves but also sharpens social skills by learning how to tolerate opinions, mediate conflicts, and how to derive a shared purpose (Al-Tekreeti et al., 2024).

5. Receiving Feedback and Coaching

Feedback is an important tool that would help develop emotional intelligence since it is a means of one developing external insights into one's emotional behavior and its impact on others. Entrepreneurs can get feedback from one's team, mentors, or other peer colleagues so as to understand how they are regarded in distinct emotional situations. Feedback reveals blind spots-areas that may be unknowingly subjected to emotional reactions that have indirectly influenced decisions, relationships, and morale among the team (Andiani et al., 2020).

Engagement with a professional coach or mentor that may assist in the emotional intelligence building process can also be very beneficial. Coaches can help the entrepreneurs in personalized exercises and role-plays, as well as hold them accountable for progress. Targeted guidance can accelerate emotional growth and get entrepreneurs to work on actual specific emotional challenges in their leadership (Bayram et al., 2023).

6. Building Emotional Resilience

A resilient emotional self enables entrepreneurs to cope with events such as failure and frustration. Indeed, entrepreneurs who experience frequent failures and setbacks require building their resilience to bounce back from adversity. One of the ways to build resilience is through a growth mindset-that is, that abilities and intelligence can be developed through hard work and learning (Chandnani, 2023). Converting failures and obstacles into sources of growth and not insurmountable threats helps entrepreneurs take an optimistic view of events, which promotes emotional resilience.

The practice of gratitude is another effective way of building up resilience. In this respect, the entrepreneurs should periodically revisit their experience as they gain their experience over a period of time from their business venture and celebrate the good things that befall them through their entrepreneurial journey. The feelings of gratitude keep them in the right perspective when faced with challenging situations, and the experience helps them to be motivated and energized even in the face of some insurmountable challenges (Deb et al., 2023).

Emotional intelligence is slowly developed through experience and self-learning about themselves. Incorporation of tools like mindfulness, emotional regulation techniques, active listening and feedback makes one's emotional intelligence much higher. Besides improving their leadership qualities, such skills help develop better relationships, create innovation, and make them equipped to handle the uncertainties and risks involved in entrepreneurship. Essentially, emotional intelligence becomes a foundation to entrepreneurial success, as it begins to shape in which way entrepreneurs relate to others, whom they choose to collaborate with, and the decisions they make and manage through their businesses (Durnali et al., 2023).

Challenges in Developing Emotional Intelligence

Developing emotional intelligence is incredibly rewarding for entrepreneurs but also very difficult. The possibility that emotional intelligence can enhance leadership, decision-making, and many others' relationships may be exceptional; however, its development process is often confronted with other barriers. Such barriers emanate from deep-seated habits, psychological personal characteristics, and business-related external pressures outside. Understanding and overcoming such barriers are important to entrepreneurs who intend to develop their emotional intelligence (Fedorova et al., 2024).

1. Overcoming the Barriers to Self-Awareness

One of the most basic challenges in creating emotional intelligence is in the process of building self-awareness. Most entrepreneurs, especially those who are conditioned to make rapid decisions, would not be aware of their emotional triggers and how emotions may be affecting their actions. Continuous thinking about business would inevitably impede reflection on oneself and therefore, little time evaluating one's emotional self (Karimi & Ataei, 2023). Moreover, the emotional blind spots concerning the characteristics that make up his behavior are hard to accept by people. Unless they result in feedback from others or intentional practice of self-reflection, these blind spots remain unnoticed until it becomes more challenging to develop deeper self-awareness.

Furthermore, customs or social standards will restrain reflection on oneself, especially for those cultures where thought is considered inferior to doing. The entrepreneur views reflection as an action of vulnerability or fragility and is unwilling to delve into practices that facilitate emotional reflection. Winning these battles requires an openness to stepping aside, reflecting on personal actions, and openness to criticism that results in change (Mishra & Singh, 2024).

2. Controlling Emotional Control in Such Toughest Moments

The other important area through which entrepreneurs need to develop emotional intelligence is the regulation of emotions when things start getting tough. Risks, uncertainties, and occasional failures inherent in the process of entrepreneurship evoke frustration, anxiety, or fear. It is really very challenging to keep one's cool about them when things go wrong. Of all the areas of emotional intelligence, one finds this quite challenging. Since such crises can spell business doom, entrepreneurs will find it hard to remain focused and calm at such crisis junctions (Nooraie et al., 2023).

It gets complicated when the entrepreneur is a team leader. In stressful situations, unchecked emotions do not only cloud judgment but also affect the relationships and dynamics of the team members. Stressed entrepreneurs who cannot control their emotions may unconsciously transfer stress to the teams, thereby reducing their morale and productivity. Emotional regulation calls for patience and practice, but in the frantic world of an entrepreneur, there is very little time to slow down and consciously manage emotions (Oktalia et al., 2018).

3. Balancing Empathy with Decision-Making

One of the most important aspects of emotional intelligence is empathy-teaching an entrepreneur how to connect with his employees, customers, and partners. There is also a bit of a problem there, in balancing the role of empathy against objectivity. Excessive sensitivity can sometimes prevent an entrepreneur from making the necessary and tough decisions that adversely affect other people's lives. The entrepreneur might find it difficult to fire a low-performing employee or cut ties with a long-standing business partner, even though this is what is generally required for the success of the business (Pathak & Muralidharan, 2024).

Over-empathy also makes entrepreneurs overloaded in taking others' emotions or problems unto themselves, resulting in over burnout. One should learn to carry out empathy and create a sense of understanding and relationship while creating clear boundaries and making choices that help align with the business's strategy. Therefore, achieving such a balance requires a delicacy of emotional intelligence and leadership principles.

4. Breaking Old Behavioral Patterns

For most entrepreneurs, emotional intelligence development also means breaking old patterns of behavior that have been instilled very deep over the years. For instance, some might react defensively to criticism, or the feelings can be suppressed. In some cases, direct confrontation may even be avoided altogether. All these require conscious effort to wire emotional responses in a different manner, which in turn consumes time and even hurts emotionally. In fact, these entrepreneurs, who have anchored their firms on swift decisioning and behavior-driven action, will have a difficult time leading into an emotionally astute and reflective management style (Pirsoul et al., 2023).

What makes this particularly challenging is that developing emotional intelligence often requires someone to step out of their comfort zone. For example, the entrepreneur-the control freak may rebel at the idea of accepting mistakes or showing vulnerabilities; others may not learn to task their team members emotionally, particularly if they have always done everything themselves.

5. Coping with External Influences and Demands

Entrepreneurs are exposed to too many external pressures and expectations that will not allow them to focus on developing emotional intelligence. Stakeholders, customers, or investors expect entrepreneurs in these high-stakes environments to produce results immediately, with little allowance for emotional reflection or growth (Prib, 2023). There is always pressure to perform, meet deadlines, and drive profit, so it becomes challenging for entrepreneurs to prioritize their emotional well-being or invest in EI skills. Therefore, emotional intelligence may be treated as a postscript; it may be something to attend to when time allows itself, which might surely delay development.

Moreover, some industries or entrepreneurial cultures undervalue emotional intelligence by preferring toughness, assertiveness, and decisiveness. Entrepreneurs in that environment may feel compelled to suppress their emotions or avoid any emotional growth just to fit the industrial mold, which makes the development of emotional intelligence even more challenging (Quintillán & Legazkue, 2019).

6. Giving and Acting on Feedback

However, although feedback is one of the weapons many people use to improve emotional intelligence, feedback is often hard to take and do something about as an entrepreneur. The employees are less likely to give honest feedback with a boss in a leadership position for fear of reprisal or to keep harmony. Entrepreneurs are often faced with the inability to gather candid insights from those within their team or peers that may help in improving their emotional intelligence (Raza et al., 2023).

Listening to any feedback which may readily be available to an entrepreneur is also very hard because they feel an impulsive need to defend themselves. Emotional behavior criticism becomes very personal, and entrepreneurs struggle with taking this to be an opportunity for growth, not as the attack on their character. This is a very critical but sensitive area of development in emotional maturity in seeking, accepting, and acting on feedback (Singh & Kovid, 2023).

Building up emotional intelligence as an entrepreneur requires intrinsic and extrinsic challenges. It's demanding work, from developing self-awareness and appropriate control over emotions during pressure to empathizing and understanding when to use it in the weighing scales of decision-making, until such a time that old habits have to be unlearned. All this takes persistent effort, practice, and resilience in the face of difficulty. But the returns are enormous-better leadership, better relationships, and longer-term success as an entrepreneur (Sultan et al., 2023).

MEASURING THE EFFECT OF EMOTIONAL INTELLIGENCE TO BUSINESS PERFORMANCE

Emotional intelligence has lately received increased recognition as an important determinant of business performance. However, the contribution is almost impossible to quantify. Such complexities arise from the fact that emotional intelligence is multifaceted, and it may manifest in many different ways in an organization. Yet, several metrics and methodologies can be used to measure the effect of emotional intelligence on business results. This awareness can guide entrepreneurs and leaders in making the right decisions concerning developing emotional intelligence within their teams and organization (Sutiyatno, 2023).

1. Performance and Productivity of Employees

One of the most direct measures in assessing influence is through employee performance and productivity-related metrics. Organizations may carry out performance appraisals that include EI-related competencies such as teamwork, conflict resolution, and communication skills. Through the assessment of these competencies against traditional performance metrics such as sales figures, project completion rates, and quality of work, businesses can determine the influence of emotional intelligence on an employee's overall effectiveness.

Research has proven that employees with high levels of emotional intelligence perform better, along with other effective abilities in problem-solving, creativity, and collaboration, which in return lead to higher productivity. KPIs can be measured before and after emotional intelligence training programs to understand the impact on performance results (Tee et al., 2014).

2. Employee Engagement and Satisfaction

To a great extent, emotional intelligence has a direct correlation to employee engagement and job satisfaction. Highly engaged employees are usually more committed to work as compared to other employees, demonstrate much more motivation and, usually, are positive contributors to the organizational culture. The impact of EI can be measured through employee engagement surveys assessing multiple dimensions like emotional climate, trust in leadership, and workplace relationships in an organization (Worokinasih et al., 2021).

Surveys that seek questions on the perceptions of the emotional intelligence of their leaders, their personal feelings at work, or levels of motivation can help determine if it is possible to identify any correlation between emotional intelligence and any form of engagement. Increases in engagement scores following some form of emotional intelligence training or initiative might be interpreted as a sign of a positive organizational climate and employee satisfaction.

3. Team Dynamics and Collaboration

With emotionally intelligent members in a team, this means the attainment of effective teamwork and cooperation becomes more feasible. The interaction between the teammates can be gauged towards gaining an insight into how emotional intelligence would affect teamwork and cooperation. This can be done by carrying out 360-degree feedback assessments that bring out comments from the team members regarding their interactions and patterns of communication and conflict resolution (Yitshaki, 2012).

By metrics, for instance, cohesion in a team, trust levels and the effectiveness of managing conflict then, one would be able to analyze whether there has been a positive change before and after the emotional intelligence development initiatives. Improved outcome in these metrics may therefore mean that enhanced emotional intelligence leads to better collaboration and teamwork performance, resulting in overall business performance.

4. Customer Satisfaction and Retention

Internal influence does not stop at the customers. Entrepreneurs and leaders can measure customer satisfaction and retention through metrics, thereby determining how emotional intelligence influences the customer experience. Some key indicators include customer feedback, Net Promoter Scores, and rates of customer retention (Yusoff et al., 2023).

Emotionally intelligent workers typically tend to understand customer needs more and respond appropriately to their concerns while offering excellent service. Organizations may measure the impact of emotional intelligence on customer experiences and loyalty by comparing customer satisfaction metrics before and after undertaking an emotional intelligence training for customers interacting with their customer-facing employees.

5. Leadership Effectiveness

Emotional intelligence is specifically important for good leadership. While organizations can measure the impact of EI on leadership, though after an assessment, it can portray the leadership, decision-making style, and team management as compared to each other. Surveys and assessments measuring emotional intelligence among leaders can portray how their emotional competencies influence inspirational, motivational, and connective relations with teams (Zhang et al., 2023).

Feedback from the team members and direct reports should also be used in evaluating leadership effectiveness, thus giving insights on how emotionally intelligent leadership leads to success in the organization. A positive relationship between emotional intelligence and effective leadership might be indicated through increased ratings in leadership effectiveness after the training.

6. Financial Performance

At the end of the day, every business is measured by its bottom line. While correlations may not be all that straightforward to make between emotional intelligence and financial outcomes, however, the measurements can be made in terms of metrics and be analyzed over time in the data. Organizations can compare financial metrics, such as revenue growth, profitability, and cost reduction, alongside those of the implementation of emotional intelligence initiatives.

Longitudinal studies on the financial performance of organizations prior to and after the implementation of emotional intelligence training are truly golden in terms of value and quality of evidence. Success in such organizations often translates to a betterment in employee engagement and consequently, to higher customer satisfaction through greater levels of emotional intelligence, showing positive impact on financial performance (Zhao & Sang, 2023).

Measuring the impact of emotional intelligence in business success involves looking into the areas of employee performance and engagement, team dynamics, customer satisfaction, leadership effectiveness, and financial metrics. These are the value areas used in assessment tools and methodologies that can generate organization-driven insights that can be used to understand the contributions of emotional intelligence toward overall success. With increasing awareness of the importance of emotional intelligence, investments in its development will likely reap well for the individual members of the organization and the business in general. Ultimately, an entrepreneurial environment that commits itself to developing emotional intelligence will be more resilient, adaptable, and hence more successful (Alkaabi et al., 2023).

FUTURE TRENDS: EMOTIONAL INTELLIGENCE AND ENTREPRENEURSHIP IN AN AI AGE

As AI is changing the business landscape, its intersection with EI remains a challenge for and an opportunity for entrepreneurs. As AI is rapidly changing the face of business and how it interacts with customers and manages internal dynamics, the already-worked rules are being rewritten. In this very evolving environment, emotional intelligence henceforth remains alive to entrepreneurial success. Emotional intelligence provides a counterbalance to the otherwise impersonal nature of technology. Some of the trends and key changes related to the future of emotional intelligence in entrepreneurship with AI (Al-Tekreeti et al., 2024).

1. Enhanced Human-Machine Collaboration

The most striking trend is the integration of more AI tools, which can supersede human capabilities. Entrepreneur adoption of AI for data analysis, decision-making, and routine tasks will increase the demand for emotional intelligence. This synergy will require sensitivity toward the interpretation of data generated by AI systems and applying it appropriately through empathetic engagement in those decision-making processes (Andiani et al., 2020). A successful entrepreneur would have to make judicious use of insights from AI without losing that subjective touch while ensuring emotional bonding with the teams and the customers being served.

Moreover, AI can be very useful in providing useful support in emotive cue detection in customer interactions through the aid of sentiment analysis and natural language processing. Entrepreneurs who will be able to adequately blend AI capability with emotional intelligence will do better in improving the experiences of customers and relationships.

2. Emotional Intelligence Training Powered by AI

With the expanding knowledge of emotional intelligence, people are looking to apply AI techniques in EI training programs. AI-based learning platforms can customize a learning process based on reviewing individual profiles of emotions and accordingly defining content to address deficient aspects related to emotional competencies. For example, virtual AI-powered coaching programs can present real-time adaptive learning paths for entrepreneurs and employees in key areas such as self-regulation, empathy, and communication skills (Bayram et al., 2023).

Such AI-enriched training programs make emotional intelligence development more accessible, scalable, and effective, especially for geographically dispersed teams. With AI assisting in EI training, the business can develop a culture of emotional intelligence that will align well with technological advancements of the future.

3. Employee Well-being and Mental Health

This eventually leads to discussions about the aspect of employee wellbeing and mental health as AI grows in the workplace. Indeed, with automation increasingly doing routine jobs, employees may feel anxious about losing their jobs or changing arrangements in the workplace. Entrepreneurs who focus on emotional intelligence will be better able to assist their teams through such transitions. Some of these items include identifying signs of anxiety, promoting openness, and creating an atmosphere of psychological safety (Chandnani, 2023).

The AI systems can enable monitoring of employees' well-being through engagement data to provide insight into their morale. This information can cause entrepreneurs to take responsible measures in ensuring that their business is supporting mental well-being, which serves to further prove that emotional intelligence is essential for ensuring a healthy work environment.

4. Customer-Centric AI Solutions

As more businesses come to employ AI in customer interactions-assume chatbots and virtual assistants, for example-it dawns on the brains behind these technologies: emotional intelligence should be put into these technologies. Entrepreneurs are going to make sure AI solutions are efficient, but they will also learn to understand human emotions and respond accordingly. Such a trend has facilitated the development of emotionally intelligent AI systems that can read customer moods and adjust accordingly (Deb et al., 2023).

Emotionally aware AI solutions are to be the focus of entrepreneurs when they ensure high customer satisfaction and loyalty. The businesses will attract customers by using AI capabilities and human emotional insight together to create a personalized and empathetic customer experience, making it unique among businesses in the competitive market.

5. Diversity and Inclusion through Emotional Intelligence

In the era of AI, diversity and inclusion are what matters the most. With the absence of bias in the workplace, entrepreneurs are now learning the importance of emotional intelligence in making inclusive workplaces where diverse voices are seen and valued. AI will help identify biases in hiring processes and interactions at work to enable organizations to correct the wrongs. But it is emotional intelligence that will make leaders and employees practice inclusion (Durnali et al., 2023).

Future trends will likely involve training employees and arming them with emotional intelligence in their new role as a champion of diversity and inclusion. When equitable environments are the target of the organization, the actual sustenance of understanding, empathy, and cooperation in diverse groups is made up of these emotional intelligences.

6. Resilience in the Face of Change

Entrepreneurial resilience will be insufficient in terms of increasing the velocity of technological change; new competencies by entrepreneurs will be needed. Emotional intelligence will be the ultimate competitor; through it, a person is able to face uncertainty and pull through on new challenges and maintain an optimistic outlook. Entrepreneurs who develop their emotional quotient will better be able to lead their organization through the disruptions caused by AI and other technologies (Fedorova et al., 2024).

Emotional intelligence will thus play a role in leadership development programs that make future leaders even better prepared for the kinds of complexities seen in a business environment quickly evolving under the pressures of emerging technologies. Improved emotional resilience will enable entrepreneurs to remain flexible, creative, and on course toward long-term success even as technology continuously advances under the pressures it creates (Kari.mi & Ataei, 2023)

The future of entrepreneurship in the age of AI will thus be informed all the more by emotional intelligence. Once businesses have settled into the nuances of AI, they will wake up and realize that it is, in fact, emotional intelligence that will be most pivotal in creating human connections, providing a positive customer experience, and protecting employee welfare (Mishra & Singh, 2024). This would therefore mean the entrepreneur embracing that symbiotic relationship between emotional intelligence and AI would not only be positioning themselves for success but also creating robust, resilient inclusive organizations that could thrive in any future landscape. Eventually, this nexus of emotional intelligence and technology shall redefine the future of entrepreneurship when outlining the cumulative value of human emotional competencies in a digital world.

CONCLUSION

In summary, entrepreneurs need to develop emotional intelligence that will allow them to navigate through the complexities of modern-day business environments. Since emotional intelligence is the key to leadership, team dynamics, and customer relationship, among other factors determining organizational success, its importance cannot be oversimplified. The challenges in the development of emotional intelligence—overcoming barriers to self-awareness, responding to emotions under stress, and merging the role of empathy with the role of making decisions—are areas where conscious and intentional practice is necessary. In light of the rising tide of artificial intelligence, interaction between emotional intelligence and technology comes to assume the critical role in it. These entrepreneurs, through embracing this synergy of their practice and that of their organizations, will find that fostering emotional competencies elevates not only their personal journey toward leadership but also pushes innovation, resiliency, and employee engagement within their respective organizations. Emotional intelligence, therefore, shall build a culture in the workplace of humanity and empathy in support of sustainable success in an increasingly shifting marketplace. As the business landscape continues to evolve and accelerate, emotional intelligence will prove to be an even more valuable strength to sustain and leverage for better use; it will allow leaders to thrive in uncertainty and positively transform their organizations and customers in meaningful and lasting ways.

REFERENCES

Al-Tekreeti, T., Al Khasawneh, M., & Dandis, A. O. (2024). Factors affecting entrepreneurial intentions among students in higher education institutions. *International Journal of Educational Management*, 38(1), 115–135. DOI: 10.1108/IJEM-09-2023-0470

Alkaabi, H. S., Aajeel, B. N., & Rahman, M. M. A. (2023). The impact of strategy implementation practices on entrepreneurial orientation through emotional intelligence/an applied study at the University of Information and Communication Technology–Baghdad. *International Journal of Professional Business Review: Int.J. Prof. Bus. Rev.*, 8(12), 1.

Andiani, A., Rizani, D., Khoirunnisa, R., & Khairunnisak, K. (2020). The important role of emotional intelligence to face competitive business. *Iptek Journal of Proceedings Series*, 0(1), 58. DOI: 10.12962/j23546026.y2020i1.7984

Bayram, G. E., Shah, S. H. A., & Tunio, M. N. (Eds.). (2023). *Women's Empowerment Within the Tourism Industry*. IGI Global. DOI: 10.4018/978-1-6684-8417-3

Chandnani, S. (2023). Role of emotional intelligence in sales success. *Tjjpt*, 44(4), 6325–6332. DOI: 10.52783/tjjpt.v44.i4.2175

Deb, S., Nafi, S., Mallik, N., & Valeri, M. (2023). Mediating effect of emotional intelligence on the relationship between employee job satisfaction and firm performance of small business. *European Business Review*, 35(5), 624–651. DOI: 10.1108/EBR-12-2022-0249

Durnali, M., Orakci, Ş., & Khalili, T. (2023). Fostering creative thinking skills to burst the effect of emotional intelligence on entrepreneurial skills. *Thinking Skills and Creativity*, 47, 101200. DOI: 10.1016/j.tsc.2022.101200

Fedorova, Y., Pilková, A., Mikuš, J., Holienka, M., & Momot, D. (2024). *Measuring the emotional intelligence of entrepreneurs*. Publikacja/Publication. DOI: 10.18690/um.epf.5.2024.7

Karimi, H., & Ataei, P. (2023). The effect of entrepreneurship ecosystem on the entrepreneurial skills of agriculture students: The mediating role of social intelligence and emotional intelligence (The case of University of Zabol, Iran). *Current Psychology (New Brunswick, N.J.)*, 42(27), 23250–23264. DOI: 10.1007/s12144-022-03479-z PMID: 35854700

Mishra, A., & Singh, P. (2024). Effect of emotional intelligence and cognitive flexibility on entrepreneurial intention: Mediating role of entrepreneurial self-efficacy. *Journal of Entrepreneurship in Emerging Economies*, 16(3), 551–575. DOI: 10.1108/JEEE-05-2022-0142

Nooraie, F., Salehi, M., & Enayati, T. (2023). The effect of emotional and organizational intelligence on academic entrepreneurship. *Educational Researcher*, 18(73).

Oktalia, D., Irianto, A., & Sentosa, S. (2018). The influence of emotional intelligence and persistence on the income of small-scale peyek snack entrepreneurs in Padang. *Proceedings of the PICEEBA-2018*. https://doi.org/DOI: 10.2991/piceeba-18.2018.87

Pathak, S., & Muralidharan, E. (2024). Contextualizing emotional intelligence for commercial and social entrepreneurship. *Small Business Economics*, 62(2), 667–686. DOI: 10.1007/s11187-023-00775-1

Pirsoul, T., Parmentier, M., Sovet, L., & Nils, F. (2023). Emotional intelligence and career-related outcomes: A meta-analysis. *Human Resource Management Review*, 33(3), 100967. DOI: 10.1016/j.hrmr.2023.100967

Prib, H., & Bobko, O. (2023). Psychological characteristics of entrepreneurs working in stress-related conditions. *Scientific Bulletin of Mukachevo State University Series. Pedagogy and Psychology*, 9(2). Advance online publication. DOI: 10.52534/msu-pp2.2023.57

Quintillán, I., & Legazkue, I. (2019). Emotional intelligence and venture internationalization during economic recession. *International Journal of Entrepreneurial Behaviour & Research*, 26(2), 246–265. DOI: 10.1108/IJEBR-08-2018-0521

Raza, S. A., Tunio, M. N., Ali, M., & Puah, C. H. (Eds.). (2023). *Entrepreneurship and Green Finance Practices: Avenues for Sustainable Business Start-ups in Asia*. Emerald Publishing Limited. DOI: 10.1108/9781804556788

Singh, N., & Kovid, R. K. (2023). *Women entrepreneur's emotional intelligence and firm performance: Mediating role of networking competencies*. FIIB Business Review., DOI: 10.1177/23197145231184307

Sultan, M. F., Tunio, M. N., Aziz, A., & Shaikh, S. K. (2023). Social innovation and social entrepreneurship in the wake of COVID-19: A perspective from the developing side of the world. In *Frugal Innovation and Social Transitions in the Digital Era* (pp. 113–118). IGI Global.

Sutiyatno, S. (2023). The role of emotional, spiritual, and social intelligence on entrepreneurship intention of informatics and computer students: Self-leadership as a mediating variable. *Journal of Economics. Finance and Management Studies*, 6(4), 1482–1491. DOI: 10.47191/jefms/v6-i4-10

Tee, S., Chin, S., Raman, K., Yeow, J., & Eze, U. (2014). The contributing roles of emotional intelligence and spiritual intelligence in entrepreneurial innovation and creativity. *World Journal of Management*, 5(2), 66–77. DOI: 10.21102/wjm.2014.09.52.06

Tunio, M. K., Hamid, A. B. A., Latiff, A. S. A., & Hafeez, M. (2023). Unlocking organizational sustainability: The role of talent management through the lens of the AMO Theory. *Pakistan Journal of Humanities and Social Sciences*, 11(3), 3530–3547. DOI: 10.52131/pjhss.2023.1103.0634

Tunio, M. N., Shaikh, E., Katper, N. K., & Brahmi, M. (2023). Nascent entrepreneurs and challenges in the digital market in developing countries. *International Journal of Public Sector Performance Management*, 12(1-2), 140–153. DOI: 10.1504/IJPSPM.2023.132244

Worokinasih, S., Nuzula, N., Damayanti, C., Fauziah, S., & Syarifah, I. (2021). Is emotional intelligence matter in youth entrepreneur? *Proceedings of AEBMR-K*, 210928(012). Advance online publication. DOI: 10.2991/aebmr.k.210928.012

Yitshaki, R. (2012). How do entrepreneurs' emotional intelligence and transformational leadership orientation impact new ventures' growth? *Journal of Small Business and Entrepreneurship*, 25(3), 357–374. DOI: 10.1080/08276331.2012.10593578

Yusoff, Y., Anwar, I. F., Rahayu, S. B., Lajin, N. F. M., & Ridzwan, M. (2023). A review on integrating emotional intelligence with artificial intelligence in social media marketing among entrepreneurs. [JOCSSES]. *Journal of Contemporary Social Science and Education Studies*, 3(2), 44–50.

Zhang, H., Zhou, X., Nielsen, M. S., & Klyver, K. (2023). The role of stereotype threat, anxiety, and emotional intelligence in women's opportunity evaluation. *Entrepreneurship Theory and Practice*, 47(5), 1699–1730. DOI: 10.1177/10422587221096905

Zhao, Y., & Sang, B. (2023). The role of emotional quotients and adversity quotients in career success. *Frontiers in Psychology*, 14, 1128773. DOI: 10.3389/fpsyg.2023.1128773 PMID: 36844276

Chapter 7
Developing a Mindfulness-Based Intervention for Entrepreneurial Stress Reduction

Aayushi Pandey
https://orcid.org/0000-0001-7584-0520
Lovely Professional University, India

Shashank Mittal
O.P. Jindal Global University, India

Xuan-Hoa Nghiem
https://orcid.org/0000-0003-2292-0257
Vietnam National University, Hanoi, Vietnam

ABSTRACT

This chapter explores developing and implementing mindfulness-based interventions (MBIs) tailored for entrepreneurs to reduce stress and enhance well-being. Recognizing the unique challenges faced by entrepreneurs, the chapter examines the theoretical foundations of mindfulness and its relevance to entrepreneurship. It outlines practical strategies for creating effective MBIs, including considerations for diverse populations and the integration of technology. The chapter also discusses the importance of measuring the effectiveness of these interventions and addresses potential challenges, such as participant resistance and sustainability of practices. By highlighting future directions for research, practice, and policy, this chapter aims to contribute to a deeper understanding of how mindfulness can transform entrepreneurial experiences, foster resilience and promote a healthier entrepreneurial ecosystem.

DOI: 10.4018/979-8-3693-3673-1.ch007

Copyright ©2025, IGI Global. Copying or distributing in print or electronic forms without written permission of IGI Global is prohibited.

INTRODUCTION

Entrepreneurship is often described as innovative, full of possibility and great reward, but it is equally associated with high levels of stress and pressure. Entrepreneurs frequently walk through challenges faced with financial instability and market competition as well as having to deal with running a business (Molek-Winiarska & Żołnierczyk-Zreda,2018). All these pressures can have negative impacts on both mental and physical health, creating impaired well-being and critical or creative thinking skills. It is, therefore, essential to seek constructive stress-reducing measures that can ensure the sustenance of entrepreneurial success as well as overall well-being.

Recent concern has been given to mindfulness techniques because of recent studies on reducing stress and attaining better psychological well-being. Mindfulness was defined by Kabat-Zinn as "paying attention in the present moment to whatever is happening or developing in the present moment, without judgment." Mindfulness helps one become aware of as well as accept their thoughts, emotions, and bodily sensations (Mulla et al.,2017). It has been proven that mindfulness lowers stress, emotional regulation, and also builds up resilience. Considering the distinct nature of stress that entrepreneurs have to deal with, a pragmatic methodology for improving wellbeing and productivity will be brought about by mindfulness.

Therefore, the point of intersection between mindfulness and entrepreneurship can be stated as an interesting area to study. A chronic state of stress in entrepreneurs increases the chances of burnout and subsequent loss of motivation. Mindfulness thus allows entrepreneurs to build coping that reduces their stress levels but also builds a higher quality of clarity and focus (Charoensukmongkol,2019). This practice encourages letting go amidst the chaos of entrepreneurial life in order to reflect on experience, make informed decisions, and undergo an even more balanced approach to work-life.

This chapter will develop a mindfulness-based intervention specially tailored to entrepreneurs who want to reduce stress and improve their well-being. It will be evidence-based and grounded in the philosophy of mindfulness. By focusing on entrepreneurs' stressors and the benefits of mindfulness, this chapter will provide a comprehensive framework for developing an effective MBI (Zhang et al., 2021; Charoensukmongkol, 2019).

The development of such an intervention requires great consideration of the contextual background of entrepreneurship. Entrepreneurship involves high demands, with no single downtime to spare for engaging in classical mindfulness practices (Sharma & Rush,2014; Bazarko et al.,2013). For that reason, the MBI must be broad enough to enable the entrepreneur to take up mindfulness exercises considering his time and schedule. This will provide the best possibility of consistent practice while having the widest accessibility for the intervention.

In this regard, through assessment tools and methodologies, the mindfulness-based intervention would be evaluated to ensure that its impact on stress reduction and overall well-being can indeed be measured according to participant feedback, self-report measures of stress, and objective assessments of entrepreneurial performance. With this as a clear framework for evaluating the intervention, the chapter would provide some valuable insights in the practical application of mindfulness in entrepreneurship.

This implies as the entrepreneurs' needs expand, finding effective ways of managing stress is even more important. Mindfulness appears to be a kind of intervention which would enable entrepreneurs to manage issues with good levels of resilience and clarity (Schmidt,2016). Through the development of a mindfulness-based intervention with application for this population, this chapter contributes to an emerging body of research and practice aimed at fostering entrepreneurship well-being. By equipping entrepreneurs with stress-management techniques, we will promote a living system of sustainable entrepreneurial capitalism.

UNDERSTANDING MINDFULNESS

Mindfulness comes from ancient contemplative traditions, most notably Buddhism, but now predominantly utilized in contemporary psychology and wellness activities. In loosest terms, mindfulness is being purposefully and non-judgmentally aware of the present moment. By this practice, one is requested to be alert about his thoughts, feelings, and sensations in his body without reacting or letting himself get overtaken by them (Khong, 2009). Deep awareness is the chief propeller of mindfulness that makes individuals take a balanced view of their experiences, thereby developing healthy mental well-being and emotional strength (Zhang et al., 2021).

The concept of mindfulness lies in four major primary components: attention, acceptance, awareness, and non-judgment. Attention is the capacity for being present with your breath, body feelings, and surroundings. Focusing allows the grounding of the mind, since it tends to drift toward past regrets or anxiety about the future. Acceptance is non-action with respect to one's thoughts and feelings, letting them simply arise without judgment or efforts to either change or suppress them (Mulla et al.,2017; Bazarko et al.,2013). This acceptance breeds compassion toward oneself and prevents some of the inner turmoil that usually faces stress. Awareness is an extension of attention that teaches the individual to realize that his or her thoughts and feelings are transitory states, not real things. Finally, the concept of non-judgment encourages individuals to view their experiences without categorizing them as good or bad and thus tend to become more objective and forgiving (Rupprecht et al.,2019).

Scientific studies have established the fact that mindfulness, among other psychological improvements, can aid in reducing stress and regulating emotional states (Garland et al.,2015). It is established that mindful practice lowers even cortisol levels, the stress hormone, hence improving conditions associated with emotional stability and general mental well-being. Another fact that mindfulness may help in obtaining is how to actually focus, be more creative, and solve problems, which clearly makes it an excellent advantage for entrepreneurs in solving complex tasks under pressure and making the most critical decisions. Calm and clarity will result from mindfulness, meaning that people will work more purposefully and with more direction toward what they are doing, which automatically improves performance and satisfaction in general.

From only its application in a clinical setting, in the last couple of years, the mindfulness practice has proven to transcend the clinical arena into education, health, and corporate sectors. These mind-based interventions, MBSR and MBCT have been developed to help the individuals cultivate mindfulness in a structured format (Baer, 2019). These interventions often combine mindfulness practices, such as meditation, mindful breathing, and body scan exercises, which can easily be tailored to fit the goals and situations of participants. For this reason, MBIs are a popular effective stress management and mental health intervention to both enhance and maintain their well-being.

Mindfulness brings the very much needed tool in entrepreneurship-a customized particular approach used to confront the specific stressors and challenges of business owners (Zhang et al., 2021). The lives of most entrepreneurs are usually marked by uncertainty and stress, which may induce anxiety and burnout. However, introducing mindfulness practice into daily routines may develop coping strategies that foster resilience and make dealing with difficulties easier, clearer, and more graceful (Molek-Winiarska &

Żołnierczyk-Zreda,2018). Mindfulness contributes not only to the entrepreneur but to their organizations by fostering a culture that emphasizes well-being, collaboration, and innovation.

In a nutshell, mindfulness is the most powerful tool encouraging people to be aware and accepting and non-judgmental about being present in this moment. Its psychological benefits in stress reduction and emotional regulation make it an important tool for use by such individuals, especially entrepreneurs, against the specific pressures of running a business. Embracing mindfulness promotes resilience, improves the capability of making better decisions, and hence overall well-being for entrepreneurs.

THE INTERSECTION OF MINDFULNESS AND ENTREPRENEURSHIP

Entrepreneurs' landscapes always remain undecided, uncertain and dynamic. Multiple and diverse stressors confront entrepreneurs in the forms of financial pressure, competition, and demands of management of a team among other things that might greatly affect the emotional and psychological well-being of entrepreneurs (Hosseininia et al.,2024). The feeling of such challenges during the innovative and growth stages of building a business increases the level of stress, can cause burnout, and even reduce their general well-being (Mulla et al.,2017). In this regard, mindfulness becomes a vital resource helping entrepreneurs navigate the complexities of their journey towards developing personal resilience alongside professional success.

One of the most significant advantages of mindfulness for entrepreneurs is its role in improving emotion regulation. Entrepreneurship involves much roller coaster emotion - from the excitement of something new to the anxiety of setbacks. Mindfulness practice would encourage the individual to pay attention to emotional responses rather than judging them, thereby allowing insights into the reaction and more intentional choice. Such an awareness increases the level of seriousness of an entrepreneur when dealing with problems. It provides the basis for them to react less impulsively due to the pressures associated with stress or anxiety (Engel et al.,2021). Through emotional intelligence, mindfulness equips entrepreneurs to lead authentically and empathetically, enhancing the work environment's positive nature.

In addition, mindfulness improves concentration and attention-critical skills for a business entrepreneur who is likely to have many conflicting priorities. Training the mind in mindfulness practice helps to ground it in the moment, reduces mind wandering, and improves attention. These advantages of focus also translate to benefits for the entrepreneurial business in that the decisions generally have to be made under pressure and in situations where little information is available (Bazarko et al.,2013; Hosseininia et al.,2024). Examples include mindfulness techniques such as mindful breathing or mini-meditation sessions that people can work into daily routines for improving cognitive function and renewing how one approaches tasks through enhanced problem-solving skills and creativity.

Such practice of mindfulness itself contributes to a better work-life balance and is meaningful to sustainable entrepreneurial success. Although entrepreneurs are likely not going to draw strict lines between their personal and professional lives, the lack of distinction might cause them to burnout and a decrease in their mental health. With mindfulness, one gets the motivation to take care of himself (Hosseininia et al.,2024). Thus, reminders abound in order to take breaks and find a balance. By integrating mindfulness into actual operations, entrepreneurs can gain healthier routines, reduce stress factors, and feel a space for reflection and rejuvenation. It ensures the benefits derived in terms of personal well-being but infuses a wellness culture within their organization with effects on team dynamics and productivity (Rupprecht et al.,2019).

Second, mindfulness can be a source of innovation and creativity-an essential basis for entrepreneurship. It tends to promote interest in what one undergoes. Its ability to provide the space with which the exploration is done non-judgmentally allows entrepreneurs to come out of their binding patterns of thought and brainstorm novel ideas. Such freedom leads to innovative solutions and business strategies, creating an opportunity for entrepreneurship to adapt to a competitive landscape (Seabrook et al.,2020).

With the growth in recognition and acceptance of the intersection between mindfulness and entrepreneurship, many entrepreneurs and organizations are embracing mindfulness-based interventions in the very fabric of their professional development. Such programs integrate mindfulness practices into the workplace, equipping the entrepreneur with this most valuable stress management tool while fostering a culture of well-being that will make a difference in collaboration, creativity, and general organizational success (Louise et al.,2018). Mindfulness can help create an environment and culture that nurtures individual growth and group or collective development.

Generally, combining mindfulness and entrepreneurship provides a golden opportunity to satisfy some of the entrepreneurs' specific needs. Mindfulness promotes good emotional regulation, focuses the mind, enhances work-life balance, and encourages creativity-an excellent guide to help the entrepreneur navigate better stress management. Entrepreneurs who embrace mindfulness practice its benefits not only towards themselves but also towards the thriving and resilient entrepreneurial ecosystem that can adapt to the complexities of an ever-changing business landscape (Louise et al.,2018; Terzimehić et al.,2019).

DEVELOPING A MINDFULNESS-BASED INTERVENTION (MBI)

Creating a well-designed mindfulness-based intervention targeted towards entrepreneurship brings a reflective approach to entrepreneurs' specific concerns, combined with mindfulness's fundamental concepts (Dark-Freudeman et al.,2022; Saunders & Kober,2020). Several initial steps in this process involve identifying who the intervention will reach, establishing a clear framework for the intervention, including core mindfulness practices within it, and being responsive to the context of entrepreneurship.

Understanding the Target Audience

The first step towards the design of an MBI would be to conduct a thorough scrutiny of the target group: entrepreneurs and leaders. In this process, their particular stressors are identified such as financial insecurity, lack of time, and the pressure of continuously innovating. Surveys, interviews, or focus groups could be adopted to ascertain their experiences about the incidences of stress and possible deterrents in practicing mindfulness-based practices. These unique dynamics offer insight into designing an intervention that is relevant yet connected to entrepreneurs' everyday realities (Dark-Freudeman et al.,2022).

Establishing a Clear Framework

A clear model is an absolute need in forming the structure and content of the MBI. It should define the intended outcome of the intervention, which includes reducing stress, enhancing emotional regulation, and increasing resilience (Emery & Flora, 2020). It should further specify the MBI design, including the course length, for example eight weeks, frequency of sessions, for example, once a week or bi-weekly, and the basic mode of delivery, for example, face-to-face workshops and modules or internet-based or delivery modality.

Defining key goals and a framework allows participants to have an outline of mindfulness practice well in advance, and it also allows monitoring of progress while undergoing the intervention.

Incorporating Essential Mindfulness Practices

Any MBI has core mindfulness practices built into the program, grounded in evidence and in keeping with the underlying principles of mindfulness itself (Crane & Hecht, 2018). Some key items to avoid forgetting include:

1. Mindful Breathing: Very simple yet profoundly potent, mindful breathing exercises can permit participants to find a stable place to anchor their attention and develop a sense of calm. 4-7-8 breathing patterns, for example, can be used to help a person relax and focus.
2. Body Scan: The body scan practice encourages participants to cultivate awareness of bodily sensations, more deeply rooting in the present moment. This exercise may be particularly well-suited to entrepreneurs, who frequently experience bodily tension that stems from stressful situations.
3. Mindful Movement: Including gentle movement practices, such as yoga or tai chi, can add potency to the MBI by fostering one's physical well-being and thus enabling participants to 'live' mindfulness in everyday life.
4. Meditation: Guided themes of meditation can be used with regard to compassion, gratitude, and acceptance and aimed at helping the participants develop a non-judgmental attitude toward their experiences. Meditation can be customized in the entrepreneurship context by encouraging the participants to reflect on the challenges and aspirations in their business.
5. Mindful Journaling: Journal prompts that require reflection on daily experiences, thoughts and emotions in relation to the entrepreneurship will further facilitate the mindfulness practice among individuals. They can write in detail about their feelings in and about entrepreneurship, plan for personal and professional life.

Ensuring Adaptability to the Entrepreneurial Context

Entrepreneurship is known to be an environment that is constantly changing. Similarly, the MBI should be flexible enough to support the timetables and schedule of participants. This can include providing shorter, bite-sized mindfulness practices that entrepreneurs can easily fit into their busy days, as well as self-directed practice resources. Further, incorporating technology, such as mobile apps or online platforms, can facilitate the accessibility of guided mindfulness exercises and community support, so entrepreneurs can interact with the MBI at their convenience.

Building a Supportive Community

Building community among participants is also one way of increasing the effectiveness of this MBI (Emery & Flora, 2020). It can be achieved through group discussions, peer support, and related experiences in mindfulness practice. The participants' responsibility and encouragement are attested to the safety of the space as they set themselves on their mindfulness practice journey.

In summary, the mindfulness-based intervention for entrepreneurs requires a holistic approach in acknowledging their unique challenges but integrating the core mindfulness practices. If the target audience is understood, if the framework is clear, including the essential mindfulness exercises, there is room for flexibility, and there is community support, then the MBI can be more effectively promoted toward stress reduction and an improved feeling of well-being in the entrepreneur population. An efficiently designed MBI can empower entrepreneurs to lead their journeys in much better ways with more resilience, clarity, and purpose.

Implementation Strategies

Implementing an MBI for entrepreneurs would involve a careful planning and implementation strategy to ensure the engagement of participants for the intervention learned (Saunders & Kober, 2020; Emerson et al.,2020). The following section provides an overview of some of the strategic practices in implementation; these include participant recruitment, training facilitators, design of program logistics, technology utilization, promotion of ongoing practice, and effectiveness.

1. Participant Recruitment

It will require effective recruitment in order to attract diverse groups of entrepreneurs, who will benefit from the MBI. To reach the potential participants, organizations should make use of several channels including:

- Networking Events: Attend or host entrepreneurial meetups, workshops, and conferences to connect with potential participants and introduce them to the concept of mindfulness.
- Social Media and Websites and Online Forums: Advantages and logistics of MBI, through social media. Sites, and online forums targeting entrepreneurs.
- Networking with Business Organizations: Reach out to the members of local chambers of commerce, entrepreneurship centers, and business incubators for promoting the program among its members.
- Incubation Incentive: Offering incentives like discounts, scholarship, and free introductory session to remove financial barriers.

Advantages of MBI—Learning to cope with stress, learning ways of sustaining greater focused attention, and developing creativity can motivate entrepreneurs to take part in the program.

2. Training Facilitators

An MBI success depends on the facilitators doing the sessions. It is very important that these facilitators have a good background in mindfulness and experience with entrepreneurs. Best approaches to training facilitators are:

- Mindfulness Training Programs: Accreditation for facilitators to undergo MBSR or MBCT mindfulness training programs for them to acquire specific skills and knowledge needed.
- Entrepreneurial Contextualization: An understanding by the facilitators of the peculiar problems of entrepreneurs, therefore their facilitation skills will enable them to help lead the participants in mindfulness exercises and discussions in terms of dealing with some stressors and scenarios pertinent to the participants.
- Continuous Development: Provide continuous professional development via activities such as workshop or retreat related to mindfulness and entrepreneurship. This puts the facilitators in a position to keep up with current best practice and new research and its applications.

3. Designing Program Logistics

The MBI's logistics should be carefully designed to make it accessible and engaging for participants. The highest considerations are:

- Session Modality: In-person, online, or hybrid? In-person treatment may encourage closer community relationships, while sessions can be taken online for more flexibility.
- Durations of sessions and durations of the program: Consider the hectic schedules of attending participants and choose the most convenient times for the program sessions. For example, an eight-week program with weekly sessions of 60 to 90 minutes strikes a balance between thoroughness and accessibility.
- Curriculum Development: Create a comprehensive curriculum that states the topics to be covered during each session, practices, and what to learn. Ensure that each session builds upon the previous one to achieve progressive enhancement of mindfulness skills.

4. Utilizing Technology

Technology can be a powerful tool in enhancing the presentation and accessibility of the MBI. Strategies for implementation:

- Online Learning Platforms: Utilize any interactive sessions using Zoom or Microsoft Teams, which can facilitate discussion, breakout groups, and guided practice.
- Mindfulness Apps: Recommend or make available mindfulness apps that offer guided meditations, breathing practices, and mindfulness reminders to help participants in their everyday lives.
- Community Forums: Develop online forums or chat groups where participants can connect and continue relationships, experience, and support one another beyond the formal sessions. The community may be an influential facilitator for commitment and accountability

5. Promoting Ongoing Practice

Continued practice outside formal MBI sessions is crucial to ensure long-term positive effects. Efforts to promote continued practice include

- Daily Mindfulness Challenges—Introduce your participants to daily or weekly challenges that encourage them to undertake mindfulness exercises, such as mindful eating, walking, or gratitude journaling.
- Resource Sharing - Provide participants with resources such as guided meditations, articles, or book recommendations that they could read independently.
- Follow-Up Sessions- Schedule the follow-up sessions or booster workshops periodically to help participants reconnect, share experiences, and hone their mindfulness exercises.

6. Evaluating Effectiveness

Evaluation strategies, including participant outcomes and the program's effectiveness in assessing the impacts of the MBI, would be pertinent. Some of the approaches are as follows:

- Pre- and Post-Assessment Survey: Useful validated instruments to ascertain the decrease in stress levels, emotional regulation, improved concentration, and overall welfare during the pre-test and its post-test variant.
- Qualitative Feedback: Interview and focus groups of participants to provide participant feedback that can be brought forth in the understanding of experiences, problems, and perceived benefits of MBI.
- Longitudinal Studies: Conduct follow-up assessments at set intervals after a particular period, say, three months and six months following the intervention, to measure the sustainability of mindfulness practices and their effect on entrepreneurial stress.

Accordingly, a mindfulness-based intervention for entrepreneurs will be successfully implemented through strategic participant recruitment, effective facilitator training, thoughtful program logistics, the use of technology, the encouragement of ongoing practice, and robust evaluation strategies. For each of these, the MBI can effectively promote stress reduction, improvement in well-being, and empowerment of entrepreneurs to thrive in their professional endeavors.

MEASURING EFFECTIVENESS

Measuring the effectiveness of the MBI to an entrepreneur is critical to better understanding the impact of this intervention on the well-being, stress levels, and overall performance of the participants (Novak & Honan, 2019). Employing a combination of quantitative and qualitative assessment methods would give program developers comprehensive insights into how well the MBI would meet its objectives and how participants would experience and assimilate mindfulness practices into their everyday lives. This section identifies critical strategies for measuring the effectiveness of the intervention (Kauffman et al.,2015).

1. Pre- and Post-Assessment Surveys

The primary mechanism of measuring effectiveness is a pre- and post-assessment survey. This would measure many different aspects of how well the participants' well-being, stress, emotional regulation, and levels of mindfulness are affected before and after the treatment. Considerations for this method are:

- Standardized Instruments: Use standardized scales and measures of constructs for perceived stress, mindfulness, emotional quotient, and overall well-being. The most common instruments utilized include the Perceived Stress Scale, the Mindful Attention Awareness Scale, and the Emotional Quotient Inventory.
- Baseline Data Collection: The baseline survey is conducted before the onset of the MBI. This sets a baseline for data to be used as a reference point during the intervention to assess changes.
- Follow-Up Assessments: Administer the same questionnaires shortly after the intervention and then later (at three months and six months) to track changes and assess the degree to which mindfulness exercises are sustained.

2. Qualitative Feedback

Though quantifiable measures are helpful, gathering qualitative feedback will also be essential to understanding the participants' self-reports about their experiences and perceptions of the MBI. This might be achieved in the following ways:

- Interviews and Focus Groups: These can either be one-to-one interviews or focus group discussions in which the participants are interviewed to explore their thoughts, feelings, and insights about the intervention. The qualitative approach will allow for a better understanding of the benefits or challenges that participants would experience, which may not have been captured through surveys.
- Reflection Journals: Distribute reflection journals to program participants that can be utilized during the program's duration. In these journals, participants can record thoughts, feelings, or experiences concerning their mindfulness practices. These journals may be helpful to qualitative data sources regarding participants' journeys through the program, including changes in mindset or behavior because of the MBI.

3. Behavioral Observations

Behavioral observations may also provide insight into how participants apply mindfulness practices within their entrepreneurial contexts (Gomes et al.,2018). Important strategies include:

- Self-Reported Change in Behavior: Add end-assessment surveys that will ask participants to comment on some behavioral changes they experienced in their lives and the workplace after attending the MBI. For instance, they can comment on patient levels, make better decisions, and communicate with the rest of the team members.
- Peer Feedback: A peer feedback element could be added to the design wherein the participants receive feedback from peers, colleagues, or team members regarding changes in their behavior and interactions since they received the intervention. This is an exogenous source of information that will be used to evaluate the effect of mindfulness exercises.

4. Longitudinal Studies

Systematic longitudinal studies shall be conducted to assess the effectiveness of the MBI over a long period and quantify the changes the participants brought about. The following shall be considered for conducting this type of study:

- Long-Term Follow-Up Measurements: Establish follow-up measurements at three months, six months, and one-year post-intervention to measure the continuation of mindfulness practices in daily life and their effects on well-being and stress levels.
- Performance Metrics Measurement: For instance, entrepreneurs might measure specific performance metrics, such as business growth, employee satisfaction, and overall productivity, to establish the relationship of mindfulness practice with objective business outcomes over time.

5. Program Improvement Feedback

The MBI shall be continually improved through feedback regarding the structure and content of the program delivery. Strategies are also as follows:

- Participant Satisfaction Surveys: These shall focus on assessing participants' perceptions of relevance, effectiveness, and areas for improvement regarding the intervention. Questions can focus on usefulness in specific practices, session formats, and overall participant experience.
- Facilitator Insights: B ring in facilitators to have a debriefing discussion after MBI to procure their insights about engagement with participants, challenges faced, and the opportunities to improve the future editions.

Measuring mindfulness-based intervention's effectiveness in entrepreneurs requires multiple approaches combining quantitative assessments, qualitative feedback, behavioral observation, and longitudinal studies. Such diversified approaches to evaluation help a program developer gain in-depth knowledge about how the MBI impacts the participants' well-being and their ability to tackle stress effectively. Through continuous evaluation, developmental steps can be undertaken iteratively so that the MBI does not dwindle and remains relevant and valuable to the entrepreneur navigating the complexity of his professional journey.

CHALLENGES AND CONSIDERATIONS

Implementation and development of a program such as an MBI for entrepreneurs go hand-in-hand with numerous opportunities. However, the possibility of specific challenges and considerations that arise during the development process cannot be discounted (Alberti et al.,2019; Lim et al.,2018). The challenge can allow developers and facilitators to anticipate what obstacles may arise along the way, change their strategies, and build a more effective intervention. Some key challenges and considerations regarding MBIs for entrepreneurs are discussed below:

1. Counter Mindfulness Practice

Preparing an MBI for an entrepreneur is not without many challenges, particularly in being countered by the individual into resisting mindfulness practice. Most entrepreneurs work under one form of pressure that tends to take care to focus on the urgent and the productive and hence are skeptical of the mindfulness culture. Others may feel that mindfulness practices are merely a luxury they do not need (Molek-Winiarska & Żołnierczyk-Zreda,2018; Kauffman et al.,2022). There is a need to overcome this resistance by communicating the practical benefits of mindfulness. These include better concentration, improved decision-making ability, and less stress. Use testimonies, research findings, and relatable anecdotes that show mindfulness's positive effect on entrepreneurial success. An effort to instill mindfulness practices in everyday life, such as a short breathing exercise or mindful walking, may alleviate concerns about time commitment.

2. Variability in Experiences

A second point is individuals' diversity and susceptibility to mindfulness exercises. Since every founder originates from a different context, lifestyle, personality, and even different kinds of challenges in life, these differences may influence how they engage in the activity and benefit from it. One participant might instantly benefit from the mindfulness exercises, while another may find it hard to relate or even feel uncomfortable during the exercises and sessions (Gabriel et al.,2019). To address this, facilitators should make an environment friendly to open dialogue where participants feel free to share their personal experiences without fear of judgment. Offering alternative options for mindfulness practice and allowing the participants to make a choice that resonates best with them can help increase individual participation and ownership.

3. Continuing Practice After Intervention

The other important aspect is continuing mindfulness even after the end of the MBI. Participants are likely highly motivated during the intervention, but how could everyday entrepreneurial life stack up as a challenge to maintain mindfulness practices for such a prolonged duration? To provide the necessary resources to keep people engaged, it is essential to offer strategies that suggest continued practice-availability of resources, guided meditation, apps, and follow-up sessions or booster workshops. Further, a community of participants may lead to accountability and help each other continue their mindfulness beyond the program.

4. Handling Different Needs and Context

Different entrepreneurs' businesses, as well as the operation context, have different kinds of needs and stressors. A single standardized approach to mindfulness would probably perform less effectively than a varied approach in addressing participants' various needs. The MBI needs to be adapted to situations in which entrepreneurs work (Blank et al.,2019). This could involve industry-specific case studies, scenarios, and discussions to allow participants to link the learning materials to their practical, everyday realities. Feedback from participants during the program can also enable facilitators to modify practices and content to better respond to participants' needs and expectations.

5. Determining Effectiveness and Impact

Determining the effectiveness of the MBI is problematic in its own right. Given that mindfulness experiences are subjective, such an intervention's results can hardly be measured. Participants might say that their well-being has changed; however, these changes are not automatically a cause that translates into business metrics. With a more robust evaluation framework that combines quantitative and qualitative approaches, a better chance exists of fully understanding the impact of the MBI. It should also be mentioned that the effects of mindfulness may only appear after a specific time, and its evaluation would thus have to follow a long-term perspective.

6. Training and Competence of Facilitators

Success with an MBI depends on facilitation experience and training, especially their foundation in mindfulness practice and work experience with entrepreneurs. Some approaches to handling resistance, keeping the clients engaged, and creating a favorable atmosphere for learning must also be included in facilitator training. Facilitators also need ongoing professional development opportunities to hone their skills further and stay current with best practices in mindfulness and entrepreneurship (Bach-Mortensen et al., 2018).

The following considerations and potential issues emerge in developing and implementing a mindfulness-based intervention among entrepreneurs; however, if these are recognized and engaged, these can be incorporated to strengthen the program. Probably the most important reason for this is that it can help create an open, adaptable, and supportive environment to conduct entrepreneurship programs. This factor will help entrepreneurs face their particular problems and utilize the transformative power of mindfulness in their personal and professional lives. Overcoming these challenges will enable the participants to build resilience, improve their well-being, and succeed in their entrepreneurial ventures.

Future Recommendations

As the entrepreneurship landscape continues to unfold, so must processes supporting well-being and resilience among entrepreneurs. The increasing focus on mindfulness-based interventions holds much promise for boosting both individual and organizational performance. This section outlines potential future directions for research, practice, and policy related to MBIs tailored for entrepreneurs.

1. Extending the Research on Multiple Populations

Future research should entail the extension of knowledge on how MBIs can be tailored to different entrepreneurial populations' diverse needs. Stressors and challenges unique to technology startups, social enterprises, or creative industries tend to influence how entrepreneurs engage in mindfulness practices. These studies can point researchers to best practices and optimize interventions to make them more relevant and impactful. Additionally, such research will help develop a more culturally sensitive program by understanding how cultural background, gender, and age impact receptiveness to mindfulness.

2. Technology Integration and Digital Tools

Technology-based integration represents another direction for enhancing access and engagement with MBIs. Digital platforms and apps will be more accommodating to fit with the entrepreneurial lifestyle. Future interventions can exploit virtual or augmented reality and gamification to create experiences that entrepreneurs familiar with these technologies are more likely to relate to. Online support communities or peer groups can also be designed to provide a kind of peer interaction and support to encourage continued practice after an intervention. Further research into these digital tools can be incorporated into the development of MBIs to investigate their effectiveness in improving mindfulness outcomes further.

3. Longitudinal Studies on Impact and Sustainability

A longitudinal study will help understand the temporal effect of MBIs on entrepreneurs. Participant tracking over more extended periods will determine whether mindfulness practice affects resilience, well-being, and business performance over time. Such studies may also shed more light on why mindfulness practices seem sustainable and under what conditions they are likely to be sustained in the context of the continually changing business requirements. An understanding of such long-term results can become critical for interventions toward fine-tuning intervention models and identifying the most salient elements of support.

4. Thematic Focus on Organization Integration

Since employee wellness is gaining ever more significance, fostering MBIs as an integral part of organizational culture and structure appears to be one of the promising areas. Such future efforts may explore the possibility of organizations incorporating mindfulness practices into business values and work models to create a comfortable environment for entrepreneurs and employees. This is where designing training programs for specific needs, introducing regular mindfulness workshops, or creating specific workplace mindfulness spaces can help. Research into the effects of organizationally integrated MBIs on workplace culture, teaming dynamics, and general productivity will be an excellent input resource for entrepreneurs and organizational leaders.

5. Joint Work With Commercial and Mental Health Professionals

Consequently, the prospects for MBIs should also draw attention to collaboration between business practitioners and mental health professionals. Collaboration between these professionals will help them generate more holistic interventions that resonate with the complexity of entrepreneurial stress. Mental health professionals can offer insights on psychological resilience and coping mechanisms, while business experts can bring industry-specific issues and needs to the discussion. With such an interdisciplinary approach, MBIs could be better designed and delivered to create a more holistic support system for entrepreneurs.

6. Policy Implications and Advocacy

Ultimately, a policy change that will work proactively on the benefits of mental health and well-being in entrepreneurship is an important future direction. Policymakers can be of great importance in stimulating consciousness regarding mindfulness and well-being as crucial components of entrepreneurial success.

To this end, policymakers might establish pathways through which access to mindfulness training and support for mental health may be provided to entrepreneurs through support structures, financial funding for MBIs, and other resources. In this sense, MBIs might be developed at a higher level, for instance, as part of national entrepreneurship programs or as part of public health initiatives, and the potential policy implications of doing so are what could be researched further in the future.

Mindfulness-based interventions for entrepreneurial stress reduction have a very bright future ahead. The field will grow by extending the research to diverse populations, leveraging the support of technology and long-term studies, integrating organizational practices, fostering interdisciplinary collaboration, and advocating supportive policies. This will help not only individual well-being but also the overall resilience and thriving entrepreneurial ecosystem.

CONCLUSION

In today's world, when speed and uncertainty are the words of the day, there is always a huge need to pay attention to an entrepreneur's psychology. The stressors related to building and maintaining a venture have heavy repercussions on entrepreneurs' stress, burnout, and overall welfare. Mindfulness-based interventions present a compelling approach to overcoming these challenges by providing tools that allow entrepreneurs to handle stress, be emotionally resilient, and have healthier work-life balances.

In this chapter, we viewed the theoretical underpinning of mindfulness, the intersection of mindfulness and entrepreneurship, and the process involved in developing and implementing effective MBIs specifically tailored to the needs of entrepreneurs. MBIs empower entrepreneurs to develop a presence, awareness, and method of managing emotions that make their minds better responsive and focused as opposed to resultant stress and reactivity in operating around challenges.

Incorporating these thoughts into the future would focus on issues and challenges that will continue to be pressing in the development and delivery of MBIs. These include resistance to mindfulness practice, sustainability of mindfulness habits, and tailoring interventions to varied contexts. Finally, technology will further facilitate increased use; longitudinal research will establish the long-term effects of mindfulness, and cross-modal business and mental health professionals can further ascertain what impact mindfulness is being portrayed on entrepreneurial wellbeing.

In the long run, mindfulness would benefit individual entrepreneurs, transform organizational cultures, and contribute to more resilient entrepreneurship ecosystems. Mindfulness promotes mental well-being and provides a friendly environment in which entrepreneurs may flourish and deliver innovation, creativity, and sustainable business practices.

The possibilities for mindfulness-based interventions influencing entrepreneurial stress reduction are numerous and multifaceted. Thus, with further exploration, innovation, and implementation of these practices, we can set the stage for healthier, more resilient entrepreneurs who will have fewer problems navigating the complexities of the modern business world. Thus, this path of striving for mindfulness in entrepreneurship is not just one of securing individual benefit or service to the greater entrepreneurial community but working towards its consciousness with mindfulness that enhances a culture of mental wellness, resilience, and sustainable success.

REFERENCES

Alberti, S., Gladfelter, A., & Mittag, T. (2019). Considerations and challenges in studying liquid-liquid phase separation and biomolecular condensates. *Cell*, 176(3), 419–434. DOI: 10.1016/j.cell.2018.12.035 PMID: 30682370

Bach-Mortensen, A. M., Lange, B. C., & Montgomery, P. (2018). Barriers and facilitators to implementing evidence-based interventions among third sector organisations: A systematic review. *Implementation Science : IS*, 13(1), 1–19. DOI: 10.1186/s13012-018-0789-7 PMID: 30060744

Baer, R. (2019). Assessment of mindfulness by self-report. *Current Opinion in Psychology*, 28, 42–48. DOI: 10.1016/j.copsyc.2018.10.015 PMID: 30423507

Bazarko, D., Cate, R. A., Azocar, F., & Kreitzer, M. J. (2013). The impact of an innovative mindfulness-based stress reduction program on the health and well-being of nurses employed in a corporate setting. *Journal of Workplace Behavioral Health*, 28(2), 107–133. DOI: 10.1080/15555240.2013.779518 PMID: 23667348

Blank, R., Barnett, A. L., Cairney, J., Green, D., Kirby, A., Polatajko, H., Rosenblum, S., Smits-Engelsman, B., Sugden, D., Wilson, P., & Vinçon, S. (2019). International clinical practice recommendations on the definition, diagnosis, assessment, intervention, and psychosocial aspects of developmental coordination disorder. *Developmental Medicine and Child Neurology*, 61(3), 242–285. DOI: 10.1111/dmcn.14132 PMID: 30671947

Charoensukmongkol, P. (2019). Contributions of mindfulness to improvisational behavior and consequences on business performance and stress of entrepreneurs during economic downturn. *Organizational Management Journal*, 16(4), 209–219. DOI: 10.1080/15416518.2019.1661820

Crane, R. S., & Hecht, F. M. (2018). Intervention integrity in mindfulness-based research. *Mindfulness*, 9(5), 1370–1380. DOI: 10.1007/s12671-018-0886-3 PMID: 30294386

Dark-Freudeman, A., Jones, C., & Terry, C. (2022). Mindfulness, anxiety, and perceived stress in university students: Comparing a mindfulness-based intervention (MBI) against active and traditional control conditions. *Journal of American College Health*, 70(7), 2116–2125. DOI: 10.1080/07448481.2020.1845180 PMID: 33400631

Emerson, L. M., De Diaz, N. N., Sherwood, A., Waters, A., & Farrell, L. (2020). Mindfulness interventions in schools: Integrity and feasibility of implementation. *International Journal of Behavioral Development*, 44(1), 62–75. DOI: 10.1177/0165025419866906

Emery, M., & Flora, C. (2020). Spiraling-up: Mapping community transformation with community capitals framework. In *50 Years of Community Development Vol I* (pp. 163-179). Routledge.

Engel, Y., Noordijk, S., Spoelder, A., & van Gelderen, M. (2021). Self-compassion when coping with venture obstacles: Loving-kindness meditation and entrepreneurial fear of failure. *Entrepreneurship Theory and Practice*, 45(2), 263–290. DOI: 10.1177/1042258719890991

Gabriel, A. S., Podsakoff, N. P., Beal, D. J., Scott, B. A., Sonnentag, S., Trougakos, J. P., & Butts, M. M. (2019). Experience sampling methods: A discussion of critical trends and considerations for scholarly advancement. *Organizational Research Methods*, 22(4), 969–1006. DOI: 10.1177/1094428118802626

Garland, E. L., Farb, N. A., Goldin, P. R., & Fredrickson, B. L. (2015). The mindfulness-to-meaning theory: Extensions, applications, and challenges at the attention–appraisal–emotion interface. *Psychological Inquiry*, 26(4), 377–387. DOI: 10.1080/1047840X.2015.1092493 PMID: 27087765

Gomes, H. S., Maia, Â., & Farrington, D. P. (2018). Measuring offending: Self-reports, official records, systematic observation and experimentation. *Crime Psychology Review*, 4(1), 26–44. DOI: 10.1080/23744006.2018.1475455

Hosseininia, G., Aliabadi, V., Karimi, H., & Ataei, P. (2024). The interaction between exploratory behaviours and entrepreneurial opportunity recognition by agriculture students: The mediating role of strategic learning and mindfulness. *Innovations in Education and Teaching International*, 61(4), 649–664. DOI: 10.1080/14703297.2023.2192511

Kauffman, J. M., & Badar, J. (Eds.). (2022). *Navigating students' mental health in the wake of COVID-19: Using public health crises to inform research and practice*. Taylor & Francis. DOI: 10.4324/9781003264033

Khong, B. S. L. (2009). Expanding the understanding of mindfulness: Seeing the tree and the forest. *The Humanistic Psychologist*, 37(2), 117–136. DOI: 10.1080/08873260902892006

Lim, C., Kim, K. J., & Maglio, P. P. (2018). Smart cities with big data: Reference models, challenges, and considerations. *Cities (London, England)*, 82, 86–99. DOI: 10.1016/j.cities.2018.04.011

Louise, S., Fitzpatrick, M., Strauss, C., Rossell, S. L., & Thomas, N. (2018). Mindfulness- and acceptance-based interventions for psychosis: Our current understanding and a meta-analysis. *Schizophrenia Research*, 192, 57–63. DOI: 10.1016/j.schres.2017.05.023 PMID: 28545945

Molek-Winiarska, D., & Żołnierczyk-Zreda, D. (2018). Application of mindfulness-based stress reduction to a stress management intervention in a study of a mining sector company. *International Journal of Occupational Safety and Ergonomics*, 24(4), 546–556. DOI: 10.1080/10803548.2018.1452843 PMID: 29578373

Mulla, Z. R., Govindaraj, K., Polisetti, S. R., George, E., & More, N. R. S. (2017). Mindfulness-based stress reduction for executives: Results from a field experiment. *Business Perspectives and Research*, 5(2), 113–123. DOI: 10.1177/2278533717692906

Novak, I., & Honan, I. (2019). Effectiveness of paediatric occupational therapy for children with disabilities: A systematic review. *Australian Occupational Therapy Journal*, 66(3), 258–273. DOI: 10.1111/1440-1630.12573 PMID: 30968419

Rupprecht, S., Koole, W., Chaskalson, M., Tamdjidi, C., & West, M. (2019). Running too far ahead? Towards a broader understanding of mindfulness in organisations. *Current Opinion in Psychology*, 28, 32–36. DOI: 10.1016/j.copsyc.2018.10.007 PMID: 30390478

Saunders, D., & Kober, H. (2020). Mindfulness-based intervention development for children and adolescents. *Mindfulness*, 11(8), 1868–1883. DOI: 10.1007/s12671-020-01360-3 PMID: 33584870

Saunders, D., & Kober, H. (2020). Mindfulness-based intervention development for children and adolescents. *Mindfulness*, 11(8), 1868–1883. DOI: 10.1007/s12671-020-01360-3 PMID: 33584870

Schmidt, A. T. (2016). The ethics and politics of mindfulness-based interventions. *Journal of Medical Ethics*, 42(7), 450–454. DOI: 10.1136/medethics-2015-102942 PMID: 27099360

Seabrook, E., Kelly, R., Foley, F., Theiler, S., Thomas, N., Wadley, G., & Nedeljkovic, M. (2020). Understanding how virtual reality can support mindfulness practice: Mixed methods study. *Journal of Medical Internet Research*, 22(3), e16106. DOI: 10.2196/16106 PMID: 32186519

Sharma, M., & Rush, S. E. (2014). Mindfulness-based stress reduction as a stress management intervention for healthy individuals: A systematic review. *Journal of Evidence-Based Complementary & Alternative Medicine*, 19(4), 271–286. DOI: 10.1177/2156587214543143 PMID: 25053754

Terzimehić, N., Häuslschmid, R., Hussmann, H., & Schraefel, M. C. (2019, May). A review & analysis of mindfulness research in HCI: Framing current lines of research and future opportunities. In *Proceedings of the 2019 CHI conference on human factors in computing systems* (pp. 1-13). DOI: 10.1145/3290605.3300687

Zhang, D., Lee, E. K., Mak, E. C., Ho, C. Y., & Wong, S. Y. (2021). Mindfulness-based interventions: An overall review. *British Medical Bulletin*, 138(1), 41–57. DOI: 10.1093/bmb/ldab005 PMID: 33884400

Chapter 8
Does Entrepreneurial Leadership Influence Employees' Emotional Wellbeing During Crisis?

Swati Sisodia
GD Goenka University, India

Sumaira Jan
Humanities, Social Sciences & Management, National Institute of Technology, Srinagar, India

ABSTRACT

Despite the uncertainty in today's competitive business environment, the current study investigates the implicit influence of Entrepreneurial Leadership on workers' emotional well-being in MSME's from the unorganized restaurant sector. The employees of Delhi/NCR based MSME's unorganized restaurant sector are the target population for this research. The study's main goal is to add to the literature on Indian MSMEs unorganized restaurant sector, which is a mostly neglected and under-researched group. The study provides a deeper understanding of the impact of entrepreneurial leadership on emotional wellbeing. This research has discovered that crises can provide opportunities for enterprises to become more robust, to be more proactive, to learn from their mistakes, to engage in building social networks and strengthen the interpersonal relationships so as to improve the overall emotional wellbeing of the employees working in MSMEs.

INTRODUCTION

Crisis had a negative impact on all the sectors in Indian economy, pushing many micro, small medium enterprises (MSMEs) to scale back their operations. MSMEs began to experience the financial strain generated directly by extended curfews & lockdowns (Eggers, 2020). Many organizations are battling to maintain 'service continuity,' while others are simply 'hibernating,' or even closing down operations, having huge repercussions for employee's and their wellbeing (Bartik, et al., 2020). Emotional wellbeing has been identified as a critical problem for employees, businesses, and society as a whole (REBA,

DOI: 10.4018/979-8-3693-3673-1.ch008

2019). Employee emotional wellbeing is associated with a multitude of performance indicators, including efficiency, turnover, creativity, job satisfaction, anxiety, optimism & work–life balance (Almohtaseb et al., 2021). Social distancing, self-isolation, loneliness, fear of losing job, instability, and increasing uncertainty had an adverse impact on employee's emotional quotient.

Employee response to leadership in terms of motivation and satisfaction, which are critical characteristics of employee's wellbeing, has been the subject matter of research nowadays. Recently, a more agile and adaptive entrepreneurial approach has arisen, derived from the junction of strategic and entrepreneurial mind-set, that is better suited for operating and sustaining business in an uncertain & volatile environment. Entrepreneurial leaders are seen by their followers as forward-thinker, self-assured, and courageous, and they instill confidence and conviction in their employees through a spill over effect (Chesbrough, 2020). The goal of entrepreneurial leadership (EL) aspires to foster creative and inventive thinking as well as the development of well-considered delicate tactics to maximize available resources and maintain employee's resilience at the time of adversity/crisis (Ahmed, Zhao, & Faraz, 2020). Few studies have shown that employee attitudes and behaviours are influenced by organizational confidence in leadership, affecting both individual wellbeing & company outcomes (Bilal et al., 2021).

Entrepreneurial leadership (EL) and employee's emotional wellbeing have become an acute element that organizations gravitate to deal with economic constraints posed by the crisis. Furthermore, the pandemic has resulted in long-term emotional stress and a disordered psychological condition among workers, which could have significant consequences for the long-term sustainability of MSMEs. The majority of research conducted in the past on COVID-19 focuses on coping with stress/anxiety, work life balance, flexible working hours, adaptability to change, positive attitude, and optimism. Lee, & You, (2020), state that loss of interest & anxiety, restlessness, fear of losing job all result in disturbed emotional wellbeing of employees. Emotional distress and anxiety appear as an outcome of constant/instant stressful situation caused by COVID-19 pandemic (Banu, & Suresh, 2020).

Strident criticism contributes to emotional discomfort and work burnout, whereas authentic leader can increase employees' well-being by making proactive interventions and improving working safety and satisfaction. Entrepreneurial Leadership is focused towards nurturing a supportive, diverse and purposeful corporate climate that fosters positive attitude and promotes interpersonal and organizational sustainability. Various studies have discovered significant correlation between autonomy, self-esteem, ego, and self-actualization (Xian, Li & Huang, 2020).

In crisis like COVID-19, Entrepreneurial Leadership is viewed as a booster for improved organizational commitment and can serve as an expediter, motivator and absorber against stress (Kumar, & Ayedee, 2021). Under the Conservation of Resource Theory, each uncertainty is unfavourable for an individual's well-being. According to the theory, every unpredictable situation is destructive for an individual's overall wellbeing. It is worth investigating the relationship and impact of entrepreneurial leadership on the emotional wellbeing of employees particularly working in MSMEs. In this regard, our research objectives are influenced by the current pandemic and previous work on entrepreneurial leadership and emotional wellbeing of employee in a developing country like India.

Restaurant ownership saw huge challenges during the COVID pandemic. Additionally, it is a difficult business because it has to constantly develop to satisfy the changing tastes and preferences of customers. It is one of India's leading service-based businesses, accounting for roughly 3% of the country's GDP. According to the Federation of Hotels and Restaurant Associations of India (FHRAI), India's overall structure for the hospitality industry, the organized sector has 53,000 hotels and 7 million restaurants, while the unorganized sector has 23 million eateries. According to FHRAI projections, India's hospitality

& tourism sector is facing a serious crisis, with 70 per cent of all hospitality establishments likely to close without government intervention. Keeping in view the importance and relevance of this sector, we aim to examine the impact of entrepreneurial leadership of such restaurant entrepreneurs who are part of MSMEs on the emotional well-being of their employees.

Despite the uncertainty of COVID-19, the current study investigates the implicit influence of EL on workers' emotional well-being in MSMEs (Unorganized restaurants). The employees of Indian MSMEs (Unorganized restaurants) are the target population for this research. The aim and scope of this study is to explore the key factors conducive to emotional wellbeing during COVID-19 crisis and to examine the relationship and impact of entrepreneurial leadership on emotional wellbeing of an individual working in MSMEs. By examining these relationships, we might comprehend the situational variables that promote emotional wellbeing. The study's main goal is to add to the literature on Indian MSMEs specifically unorganized restaurant sector, which is a mostly neglected and under-researched group.

LITERATURE REVIEW

The COVID-19 outbreak has spread across the globe, severely impacting the national/global economy. The COVID-19 pandemic, as well as the associated lockdown precautions, pose major hazards to people's emotional well-being around the world. Because of which employee's wellbeing and mental health become the topmost precedence to overcome this crisis situation for every organization. Several studies conducted in the past reveal that COVID-19 pandemic had a significant impact on emotional health of employees (Pappa et al., 2020). The unprecedented COVID-19 crisis has posed a huge challenge for Micro Small Medium Enterprises (MSMEs) in terms of devising survival strategies. To combat the pandemic scenario of COVID-19 and improve emotional well-being & organizational sustainability, MSMEs must adopt new techniques and demand more accountability in their leadership style (Hamouche, 2020). COVID-19 has compelled both researchers and academicians to focus on change-oriented, self-starting and future-focused behaviour as a result of the dynamic structure of current organizations.

According to studies, small-medium enterprises and start-ups are at a significant probability of insolvency during the COVID-19 crisis due to their early phases and limited scope as well as their survival credibility (Rashid & Ratten, 2021). The COVID 19 pandemic has posed a challenge to traditional entrepreneurial operations, and it has had an impact on learning mechanisms in an evolving business environment. However, in a dynamic and unpredictable work environment, it's more important than ever for business leaders to urge their followers to abandon the antiquated way of job performance and use their zeal to become proactive in their actions (Frishammar et al., 2019).

Entrepreneurial Leadership (EL) is concerned with individual traits namely vision, identifying and exploiting opportunities, self-confidence, problem-solving, risk-taking capacity, reliant, proactive and decision-making etc. EL becomes more relevant when business is facing crisis/challenges. It requires quick response by taking decisive actions. Clarity, assertiveness, and positive reinforcement should all be considered at the time of decision-making. Leadership has been shown to have a substantial impact on both individual well-being & organizational sustainability when it comes to strategic climate (Shinbrot et al., 2019). AI Saidi (2020) further suggested that effective leadership ensure coordination, transparent communication and team spirit. Nonetheless, the role of effective leadership in pandemic management cannot be overstated. Businesses are likely to face unfathomable disruptions during a crisis. Hence, the primary objective of the leader would be to rebuild, recover, and embrace crisis mode. As a result, employees may be exposed to the greatest risk in a variety of ways. They might not be able to deal with the complexity & distress at the workplace. For this, employees need to have emotional, psychological, interpersonal empowerment & managerial support. Delegating leadership responsibilities are more effective during crisis. It will build team autonomy, increase level of agreeableness and empower decision making amongst the employees (Berjaoui & Karami-Akkary, 2019).

Mani & Mishra (2020) study affirmed that during difficult times, employee's morale is low, and they feel insecure in the organization as the economy suffers. In such hard times leaders' support, motivation and encouragement can help them in building strong employee engagement. Transformational leadership style goes beyond rewarding desirable performance by cognitively training & encouraging followers to go beyond their own individual interests for achieving collective goal.

Constructive feedback and recognition of work are critical during COVID-19. The pandemic created ambiguity amongst the employees due to job loss and disturbed work-life balance. McGuinness (2020) stated that to be an effective leader one needs to possess skills such as positive accountability, foresightedness, empathy (put people first), and decisive adaptability. Further, he added that all these skills will help the leader in dealing with employees' stress level, job insecurity, and engagement, promote commitment, and anticipate the barriers and environmental situations. The way leaders manage difficult situations, particularly during a pandemic, distinguishes them. As a result, leaders must control emotions, analyze information quickly, prioritize demands, and avoid reacting impetuously. The COVID-19 crisis management literature provides strategic direction & decision-making to maintain psychological, emotional financial, social, mental and corporate welfare/wellbeing (Van Bavel et al., 2020).

The service industry (hospitality & tourism), which includes hotels, restaurants, and bars, was worse hit by the crisis (Nicola et al., 2020). Because there are so many social connections and gatherings in the foodservice industry, it was susceptible to health emergencies like pandemics (Yang et al., 2020). Owing to the lockdown and reduced seating capacity, several locations were closed down, and customers were avoiding themselves to visit the public places due to the fear of COVID19 (Kim & Lee, 2020). According to Severson & YaffeBellany, in 2020, half of the restaurants would collapse; consequently, developing a strategy that supports & maintain client demand is essential (Sigala, 2020). As COVID-19 became more severe, it had a detrimental effect on restaurant businesses' liquidity and operational hazards due to a dramatic drop in client demand (Ozili & Arun, 2020). Even after lifting the restrictions customers' footfall or recovery was fairly sluggish (Gursoy & Chi, 2020). Customers were avoiding public places and were becoming deeply concerned about sanitation and safety, putting restaurant owners in a difficult position (Ozili & Arun, 2020). Thus, restaurant owners have also had to rethink and restructure their operating costs and capital investments (Baig, et al., 2020). Restaurant entrepreneurs faced challenges at both ends, customers as well as employees. From the customers' perspective, the first biggest challenge was to maintain social distancing, sustaining operative hygiene and frequent sanitization, the next biggest challenge was to manage customer behaviour. COVID19 has profoundly altered consumer behaviour and sparked various new restaurant sector trends such as contactless experience, digital payments, cloud kitchens, digital marketing, and immunity booster food options.

Employees in restaurants frequently face emotional stimuli, and they are required to regulate their emotions as part of their basic responsibilities, which can contribute to psychological distress, anxiety, emotional exhaustion, reduced level of self-esteem, & life dissatisfaction (Chen, & Eyoun, 2021; Satici et al., 2020). According to studies in the hospitality sector, employee emotional stress can lead to lower work satisfaction, efficiency, and organizational commitment, as well as greater intention to quit (Rathi, & Lee, 2016; Labrague, & Santos, 2020). The psychological contract theory is commonly utilized to investigate the reasons for job insecurity among workers (Keim et al., 2014). This theory outlines the expectations of the employee-employer association beyond the legal contract and helps ensure that employees receive fair compensation and benefits while also reducing job instability by giving them a sense of power. In addition, some of the factors such as duplication/ burdensome work, destructive criticism, unhealthy work environment, negative competition, distrust, lack of confidence, demotivation, and lack of social relationships were shown as a predictor of low emotional wellbeing (Dandotiya, & Aggarwal, 2022; Kumar et al., 2021; Shah et al., 2021; Rezvani et al., 2021). Thus, making it imperative to study the impact of effective leadership on the emotional well-being of such employees.

Research Gap

The potentially destructive aspect of the COVID-19 pandemic is certain to have a negative influence on emotional stability because autonomy and a degree of stability over one's surrounding and overall life circumstance are significant aspects of emotional well-being (Tripathy, & Bisoyi, 2021). This has shifted the focus of researchers and practitioners to study in-depth regarding latent variables such as entrepreneurial leadership, coping with stress, life satisfaction, and positive attitude. The Entrepreneurial Leadership gains more relevance during a crisis scenario. Despite the increased emphasis on entrepreneurial leadership in organizations, and leadership domains during crisis, very few academicians and researchers have attempted to study the relationship between entrepreneurial leadership & predictors of employee emotional wellbeing. This study seeks to fill the gap by constructing a questionnaire to analyze the relationship between the two. We suggest a study which will decipher the impact of entrepreneurial leadership on emotional wellbeing among employees working in MSMEs. Considering the fact that no such study for MSME employees was seen during the review of literature, this study becomes more imperative and need of the hour.

Research Framework and Hypothesis Development

Leader-member exchange theory emphasizes building a strong social relationship among employees. Entrepreneurial leader focuses on the quality and strength of the relationship with the followers thereby resulting in improved employee's wellbeing, commitment, efficiency, performance, loyalty, and reduce turnover. Solomon (2020) found that following the first mortality and persistent social media coverage of a pandemic, the general public's anxiety increased. According to some researchers, sensation of danger and vulnerable to crisis, could be the signal of disturbing individual wellbeing (Brooks et al., 2020. The post-COVID-19 pandemic has a negative impact on employees' emotional wellbeing, productivity, confidence, etc. and induces fear of losing their job, social change, and life goals. Thereby, increasing the role of entrepreneurial leadership during crisis situations. A leader's role can be diverse & can motivate an employee to be emotionally stable, build a positive attitude, aid in stress management etc. Previous research has revealed that leadership style has an impact on employee emotional understanding and mental health, with good supervisor evaluations increasing employee psychological, emotional & mental well-being by over 50% (Ghafoor, et al., 2011). Ethical leaders can increase employees' well-being by initiating decisive initiatives and enhancing working safety, adaptive environment and satisfaction whereas hard-line criticism and aggressive supervision behaviour contribute to work burnout and emotional distress (Lee, & You, 2020).

Entrepreneurial leaders are credited with making a welcoming, inclusive, and engaging work environment that promotes good attitudes, and enhances organizational commitment and individual and organizational growth (Pan, & Lin, 2022). Professionals can also address their basic social requirements for connection and belongingness by participating in a worthy, productive leader-follower interchange, which is helpful to their emotional stability (Wang, et al., 2021; Shipman, Burrell, & Mac Pherson, 2021). Numerous studies have discovered evidence of a connection between autonomy, self-confidence, optimism, satisfaction and self-esteem (Pathak, & Joshi, 2021). When confronted with problems, optimistic people are better at regulating their negative emotions/feelings and are much more adaptable and receptive to new experiences (Sun, et al., 2021). In the current situation, where MSMEs are on the point of slamming their operations, optimism can inspire people to think of innovative methods to conquer the issue, giving them a sense of satisfaction and success that will improve their overall life satisfaction (Pathak, & Joshi, 2021).

Moreover, entrepreneurial leadership is also concerned about compensation and reward management. According to Conservation of Resources Theory, in addition to being influencers signaling possible developmental prospects (Seltzer, & Numerof, 1988). Previous studies have highlighted the indirect positive association between entrepreneurial leaders and emotional wellbeing. In addition, several other authors have revealed that mood disorder, stress, depression, dissatisfaction, and financial instability are negatively associated with emotional wellbeing (Hansson, et al., 2022; Guidetti, et al., 2021; Sahni, 2020).

Based on this, the present study proposes the following model of impact of entrepreneurial leadership on dimensions of emotional wellbeing in figure 1:

Figure 1. Proposed model depicting relationship between entrepreneurial leadership and dimensions of emotional wellbeing

The model proposes that entrepreneurial leadership significantly impacts coping with stress, adaptability to change, positive attitude, emotional understanding, life satisfaction, optimism, self-esteem and emotional control among employees working in unorganized restaurant sector in Delhi/NCR region. All these variables represent emotional wellbeing in the current study.

Table 1. The proposed hypotheses are given below:

S.No.	Proposed Hypotheses
1	Entrepreneurial leadership has a significant impact on coping with stress among employees working in micro, small and medium sized enterprises.
2	EL has a significant impact on adaptability to change among MSME employees.
3	EL has a significant impact on positive attitude among MSME employees.
4	EL has a significant impact on emotional understanding among MSME employees.
5	EL has a significant impact on life satisfaction among MSME employees.
6	EL has a significant impact on optimism among MSME employees.
7	EL has a significant impact on self-esteem among MSME employees.
8	EL has a significant impact on emotional control among MSME employees.

Based on the aforementioned viewpoints on emotional wellbeing, it would be interesting to investigate the presence and effect of entrepreneurial leadership on emotional dimensions of employees working in MSMEs. This study is applicable and can attain more prominence in the rapidly changing business environment.

DATA AND METHODOLOGY

Research Objectives

The main objective of this research is to determine the impact of EL on various dimensions of emotional wellbeing among employees working in unorganized restaurant sector (MSME's) in Delhi/NCR region. We will firstly unveil major dimensions of emotional well-being existing among employees working in MSMEs in Delhi/NCR from the literature review and then determine the influence of entrepreneurial leadership on each of these dimensions. And in the end, an empirical model will be put forward based on the final results of the study.

Data

This research is based on quantitative approach and uses Structural Equation Modelling (SEM) to check the proposed hypotheses. The sample was taken from micro, small and medium-sized unorganized restaurant employees in the Delhi/NCR area using a judgmental sampling technique. The data collection took place from October 2020 to April 2021 and involved seeking responses from 369 employees of MSME's from the geographical area of Delhi/NCR. They were asked variety of questions on various aspects of emotional wellbeing and entrepreneurial leadership including coping with stress (COP, 4 items), adaptability to change (AC, 4 items), positive attitude (PA, 4 items), emotional understanding (EU, 4 items), life satisfaction (LS, 4 items), optimism (OPT, 5 items), self-esteem (SE, 4 items), emotional control (EC, 4 items) and entrepreneurial leadership (EL, 7 items). Sample size was derived using Krejcie & Morgan's sample size formula. We chose Delhi/NCR region because it has the diverse demographic population (as per Indian institute of Human settlement survey, 2011) which makes our study more generalized, and hence applicable to other regional employees from MSME's. The dependent variables in this study include emotional wellbeing aspects of coping with stress (COP), adaptability to change (AC), positive attitude (PA), emotional understanding (EU), life satisfaction (LS), optimism (OPT), self-esteem (SE), emotional control (EC) and the independent variable is entrepreneurial leadership (EL). The scale was developed by the authors on the constructs retrieved from the literature.

Data Analysis and Interpretation

In analyzing data, the first step involved screening data for missing values and normality. No missing values were found. For normality checking, skewness, kurtosis and Kolmogorov and Smirnov's test were used. Results are given in Table 1.

Table 2. Normality checking

Variable	Standard Deviation	Skewness	Kurtosis	Kolmogorov-Smirnov Test Statistic Sig.	
COP	.88663	-.607	.030	.654	.000
AC	1.05494	.299	-.991	-.39	.000
PA	.56006	-1.597	3.244	.024	.000
EU	.76446	-.796	.324	-1.336	.000
LS	1.19071	.200	-1.190	-.566	.000
OPT	.88878	-1.334	1.570	1.678	.000
SE	.94281	-.837	-.209	-.842	.000
EC	.81603	-1.574	2.645	.245	.000
EL	.88421	-1.233	1.017	.75	.000
KMO Measure of Sampling Adequacy				.898	
Bartlett's Test of Sphericity		Approx. Chi-Square		7186.624	
		Sig.		.000	

Bollen (1989) suggests that for data to be normal, the values of skewness and kurtosis should be in the range of ± 2.0 and ± 3.0 respectively. All values are in the suggested range. Kolmogorov and Smirnov test presents that data is not normal. Considering the fact that this test is sensitive towards sample size of 300 and more (Ghasemi & Zahedias, 2012) and normality already established by skewness and kurtosis, we assume that data is normal. KMO value is good showcasing adequacy of data as per Kaiser (1974).

Next the instrument which comprised of questions on entrepreneurial leadership and various dimensions of emotional wellbeing (Coping with stress, Adaptability to change, Positive attitude, Emotional understanding, Life satisfaction, Optimism, Self-esteem and Emotional control) was checked for its validity and reliability. For this, values of Composite reliability (CR), average variance extracted (AVE), maximum shared variance (MSV) and average shared variance (ASV) were taken into consideration. The values are presented below in Table 2. All values are in prescribed limits: CR (more than 0.7), AVE (more than 0.5) and MSV and ASV values (lower than AVE) as per Hair, et al (2010). The results reveal that the scale is robust, valid and reliable.

Table 3. Reliability and validity testing

Variable	CR	AVE	MSV	ASV
EL	.858	.715	.211	.327
COP	.877	.543	.271	.236
AC	.836	.640	.433	.320
PA	.913	.731	.256	.277
EU	.920	.672	.239	.411
LS	.856	.629	.154	.132
OPT	.847	.671	.253	.334
SE	.832	.560	.523	.597
EC	.707	.561	.256	.421

Next Exploratory factor analysis was done using SPSS V.21 to determine if the various items load on their corresponding variables. The results show that all items precisely load on their corresponding factors. EFA results are given in table 3. After EFA, CFA was performed to determine if every factor loaded, represents its corresponding aspect. The analysis revealed that all the factors typically representing their corresponding aspects. CFA model diagnostics are given in table 3 below. All values including chi-square (less than 2), CFI (more than 0.95), TLI (more than 0.95) and RMSEA (less than 0.05) represent good model fit as per Schermelleh-Engel et al., 2003.

Table 4. Factor loadings with coefficient of determination (R^2) values

Variable name	Code	Loading	R^2
Coping with stress	COP1	.781	.7
	COP2	.716	
	COP3	.838	
	COP4	.552	
Adaptability to change	AC1	.840	.98
	AC2	.861	
	AC3	.857	
	AC4	.829	
Positive attitude	PA1	.778	.29
	PA2	.687	
	PA3	.486	
	PA4	.656	
Emotional understanding	EU1	.700	.5
	EU2	.715	
	EU3	.686	
	EU4	.683	

continued on following page

Table 4. Continued

Variable name	Code	Loading	R²
Life satisfaction	LS1	.880	.55
	LS2	.884	
	LS3	.864	
	LS4	.754	
Optimism	OPT1	.743	.68
	OPT2	.747	
	OPT3	.755	
	OPT4	.818	
	OPT5	.757	
Self esteem	SE1	.819	.82
	SE2	.834	
	SE3	.826	
	SE4	.751	
Emotional Control	EC1	.780	.72
	EC2	.776	
	EC3	.775	
	EC4	.719	
Entrepreneurial Leadership	EL1	.809	
	EL2	.841	
	EL3	.814	
	EL4	.828	
	EL5	.732	
	EL6	.577	
	EL7	.796	
Model fit diagnostics			
CMin		933.532	
DF		704	
C-min/df		1.326	
CFI		.970	
TLI		.966	
RMSEA		.030	

After determining that the instrument used by study is robust, reliable and valid, the impact of entrepreneurial leadership on each variable of emotional engagement among employees of micro, small and medium enterprises in Delhi/NCR was deciphered. The results of proposed hypotheses are given below in table 4:

Table 5. Structural equation modelling results

Impact of Entrepreneurial Leadership on various dimensions of emotional wellbeing	Estimate	S.E.	Est./S.E.	Two-Tailed P-Value	Accept/Reject Hypothesis
EL→COP	.187	.072	2.60	.005	Accept
EL→AC	.261	.152	1.72	.002	Accept
EL→PA	.248	.069	3.59	.001	Accept
EL→EU	.426	.154	2.76	.001	Accept
EL→LS	.227	.058	3.91	.006	Accept
EL→OPT	.567	.261	2.17	.001	Accept
EL→SE	.477	.087	5.48	.001	Accept
EL→EC	.253	.151	1.67	.003	Accept

The results show that entrepreneurial leadership significantly impacts all of the dimensions of emotional wellbeing. This leads us to the acceptance of all the proposed hypotheses.

RESULTS AND DISCUSSION

Study statistics reveal that the scale used is robust, valid, reliable and hence can be used for future research as well. The results indicate that entrepreneurial leadership significantly impacts dimensions of emotional wellbeing (coping with stress, adaptability to change, positive attitude, emotional understanding, life satisfaction, optimism, self-esteem, emotional control) among employees of micro, small and medium sized unorganized restaurants in Delhi/NCR region. The coefficient of determination was found to be maximum in adaptability to change (.98), followed by self-esteem (.82), emotional control (.72), coping with stress (.7) and optimism (.68). The lowest value was found in the case of positive attitude (.29).

The small and medium restaurants are always on the lookout for change, reacting to it and seizing opportunities. So as to increase emotional resilience the entrepreneurial leader must always promote and motivate its employee's behaviour (namely, innovation, flexible in adapting change etc.). Leaders play a significant role in motivating its employees, by providing constructive feedback so as to create a positive work environment.

Motivated employees are future-oriented, build positive attitudes, change-oriented, self-confident, high esteem and capable in managing their stress level especially during crisis situations. Moreover, positive attitude ($r^2 = .2$) is at least contributing dimension of emotional wellbeing. The studies conducted in the past revealed that an effective entrepreneurial leadership can moderate workplace uncertainties by portraying himself as a mentor and freely investigating and exploiting opportunities in the business environment. Effective EL will encourage workers to participate in decision-making and inspire the employees to work together with a common intent to solve problems, provide a nurturing environment where work uncertainty is not seen as a barrier but rather as a chance to thrive in the organization. Because of its distinct traits and properties, entrepreneurial leadership has proven to be fruitful, as it has greatly aided people in working efficiently and obtaining their emotional wellbeing. The findings of the hypothesis test revealed that transformational/entrepreneurial climate leadership and emotional well-being have a favorable and substantial association. This also demonstrates that the hypothesis proposed at the start of the investigation can be accepted. Further findings of the study reveal that a lack of appropriate, transparent, and succinct information related significantly to higher emotional distress and avoidance behaviours. Restaurant entrepreneurs must cut fixed expenses or move from fixed to variable costs, and implement severe cost control measures whenever possible, which may include closing certain stores, lowering employee compensation, downsizing, and dismissals of employees.

The final model based on hypotheses results with R^2 values is given below in figure 2. The model depicts that EL has a significant impact on emotional wellbeing of MSME employees in the unorganized restaurant sector.

Figure 2. Final model depicting significant relationships between entrepreneurial leadership and dimensions of emotional wellbeing in terms of coefficient of determination

Implication

Restaurants are capital-intensive enterprises. They were closed for six months, resulting in adverse cash flow, increasing fiscal deficits, and massive loss of jobs. Restaurant operators are struggling with persistence in the face of this unusual situation. Several billion restaurants have closed their doors and may never reopen. This predicament necessitates government relief policies and actions to save these MSMEs. For at least a year, the government may cogitate deferring statutory dues namely GST, advanced tax payments, and pollution control permission costs incurred by restaurant owners. This strategy might allow enterprises to save some working capital for more pressing expenses such as paying salaries and wages, as well as paying small potential suppliers. The government can also provide "unemployment pay cover" for personnel in this industry who have abandoned their jobs as a result of the crisis. It is critical to provide social welfare plans for workers who have been laid off in this industry. All this will aid in maintaining their emotional well-being.

From a practical standpoint, it is clear that those who are still employed have more negative emotional, psychological and behavioural effects, such as elevated psychological morbidity, family abuse, low self-esteem, and alcohol use, than those who are furloughed. Secondly, due to a variety of unexpected employment circumstances, people employed during the crisis were severely harmed. Most working staff, for example, were obliged to swiftly adjust to a brand-new service delivery system focused on takeaway and delivery modes due to social distancing regulations and the compelled shutdown of in-house eating. Furthermore, working personnel faced a higher risk of COVID-19 contamination, whereas detained and laid-off workers did not. As a result of this research, businesses that continue to operate or reopen while the pandemic is still underway must contemplate the strains and pressures placed on personnel. Employed personnel, for example, were not entitled to unemployment benefits despite a changed service delivery structure and higher exposure. As a result, restaurant entrepreneurs must spend the effort to emphasize their staff' well-being by implementing risk-mitigation techniques that will reduce their physical, emotional and financial distress. Restaurant operators, for instance, might partly furlough their workers and then vary shifts so that everyone gets some work as well as some time off. Furthermore, employers could notify their employees about accessible resources and helplines, such as the "National Suicide Prevention Lifeline and the Substance Abuse and Mental Health Services Administration (SAMHSA) National Helpline", which provide unhindered support in crises for individuals experiencing aggravated emotional wellbeing and/or substance use concerns. Finally, employers could advise their employees on healthy stress coping strategies, such as taking care of one's physical and mental health, frequently socializing and taking time to unwind.

Moreover, managers/leaders should be liberal with frontline workers' shift patterns during the crisis. For future crises, leaders must design customized sick leave programs so that employees demonstrate high-level employee commitment without distressing about financial insecurity. There should be clear & transparent communication between changing benefits & policies to employees. Restaurant owners may also make cross-training a routine culture after the pandemic to ensure that personnel have diverse skill sets. The acquired skill set will indeed enhance the sense of emotional control and understanding in the workplace. Furthermore, mindfulness training can be conducted to assist mitigate the favourable connection between emotional wellbeing and job commitment among frontline personnel. Workshops on meditation & yoga can be assimilated into employee wellness initiatives. Restaurants might probably subscribe to mindfulness applications for their employees to assist them to handle the stress and anxiety that comes with a crisis. Moreover, they can offer free counselling sessions to employees. Firms should promote a supportive culture/environment & constructive feedback mechanism to keep staff motivated, committed & satisfied.

All this makes the study of great value for the leaders, entrepreneurs, managers, policy makers and future researchers as well.

CONCLUSION

The study provides a deeper understanding of the impact of entrepreneurial leadership on emotional wellbeing. This research has discovered that crises can provide opportunities for enterprises to become more robust, to be more proactive, to learn from their mistakes, to engage in building social network and strengthen the interpersonal relationships so as to improve the overall emotional wellbeing of the employees working in MSMEs unorganized restaurant sector. The impact on emotional wellbeing of the employees working in MSMEs during COVID 19 pandemic is classified as moderate. Likely, this favourable impact on the emotional wellbeing of an employee is due to proactive entrepreneurial leadership. However, the current study also highlights that various aspects of emotional wellbeing such as positive attitude, emotional understanding, and life satisfaction are significantly impacted by COVID19 pandemic.

Coping with stress, adaptability to change, positive attitude, emotional understanding, life satisfaction, optimism, self-esteem, emotional control and entrepreneurial leadership are all part of the model presented in this study. There is a scarcity of research on the relationship between these variables, particularly in small medium enterprises. As a result, this study seeks to address this gap by exploring these links and contributing to new ways to organizational commitment through effective entrepreneurial leadership and employee's wellbeing.

To summarize, when knowledgeable populations have faith in their leaders and feel cared for as valued members of the organization, they are far less likely to experience significant levels of anxiety during pandemic conditions. EL is a form of transformational leadership style where leaders pursue innovation, risk taking ability, and seize opportunity. As a result of the findings of this study, we believe that entrepreneurial leadership is significantly capable of coping with organizational crisis & management.

Limitations and Directions for Future Researchers

There are several shortcomings in the current study that need to be addressed. When we study the linkage between entrepreneurial leadership and emotional wellbeing of employees at workplace, we do not really consider personal traits into account. Some employees, for instance, might be a little more sensitive than others. We have taken into consideration only one geographical area. We believe that a larger geographical area with more sample size will be able to give better results. This study was also constrained by time and other resources.

This study's conclusions have ramifications for theory, research, and practice. The questionnaire established in this study can be used by researchers to look into the aspects of EL that are most significant in steering individual and group follower behaviour, as well as organizations, toward entrepreneurial initiations. The questionnaire can also be used in studies aiming to evaluate the impact of EL on emotional wellbeing of employees working in women owned enterprises. Educators that want to enhance the quantity and quality of entrepreneurial leaders can use this instrument to assess their students' entrepreneurial leadership skills and enlist them in entrepreneurial leadership education and training programs that are tailored to their specific requirements. In this article, we only conducted a questionnaire survey. Future research on the refereeing roles of challenge-hindrance stressors could be conducted using experiment methods. This research should be expanded in the future to incorporate other organizational dimensions such as organizational citizenship behaviour and structural difficulties, particularly in the Indian setting, where the business environment has evolved through time and core competence has become the norm. Because this study focuses on cohort group comparisons, longitudinal studies to understand the ramifications of changes in EL style and how firms flourish would have been appropriate.

REFERENCES

Ahmed, F., Zhao, F., & Faraz, N. A. (2020). How and when does inclusive leadership curb psychological distress during a crisis? Evidence from the COVID-19 outbreak. *Frontiers in Psychology*, 11, 1898. DOI: 10.3389/fpsyg.2020.01898 PMID: 32849111

Al Saidi, A. M. O., Nur, F. A., Al-Mandhari, A. S., El Rabbat, M., Hafeez, A., & Abubakar, A. (2020). Decisive leadership is a necessity in the COVID-19 response. *Lancet*, 396(10247), 295–298. DOI: 10.1016/S0140-6736(20)31493-8 PMID: 32628904

Almohtaseb, A., Almahameed, M., Sharari, F., & Dabbouri, E. (2021). The effect of transformation leadership on government employee job satisfaction during Covid-19. *Management Science Letters*, 11(4), 1231–1244. DOI: 10.5267/j.msl.2020.11.015

Baig, A., Hall, B., Jenkins, P., Lamarre, E., & McCarthy, B. (2020). The COVID-19 recovery will be digital: A plan for the first 90 days. *McKinsey Digital, 14*.

Banu, S., & Suresh, B. (2020). COVID-19 and its impact on micro, small and medium enterprises in India. *Mukt Shabd Journal*, 9(X), 606–617.

Bartik, A. W., Bertrand, M., Cullen, Z. B., Glaeser, E. L., Luca, M., & Stanton, C. T. (2020). *How are small businesses adjusting to COVID-19? Early evidence from a survey* (No. w26989). National Bureau of Economic Research.

Berjaoui, R. R., & Karami-Akkary, R. (2020). Distributed leadership as a path to organizational commitment: The case of a Lebanese School. *Leadership and Policy in Schools*, 19(4), 610–624. DOI: 10.1080/15700763.2019.1637900

Bilal, M., Chaudhry, S., Amber, H., Shahid, M., Aslam, S., & Shahzad, K. (2021). Entrepreneurial Leadership and Employees' Proactive Behaviour: Fortifying Self Determination Theory. *Journal of Open Innovation*, 7(3), 176. DOI: 10.3390/joitmc7030176

Bollen, K. (1989). A new incremental fit index for general structural equation models. *Sociological Methods & Research*, 17(3), 303–316. DOI: 10.1177/0049124189017003004

Brooks, S. K., Webster, R. K., Smith, L. E., Woodland, L., Wessely, S., Greenberg, N., & Rubin, G. J. (2020). The psychological impact of quarantine and how to reduce it: Rapid review of the evidence. *Lancet*, 395(10227), 912–920. DOI: 10.1016/S0140-6736(20)30460-8 PMID: 32112714

Chen, H., & Eyoun, K. (2021). Do mindfulness and perceived organizational support work? Fear of COVID-19 on restaurant frontline employees' job insecurity and emotional exhaustion. *International Journal of Hospitality Management*, 94, 102850. DOI: 10.1016/j.ijhm.2020.102850 PMID: 34785844

Chesbrough, H. (2020). To recover faster from Covid-19, open up: Managerial implications from an open innovation perspective. *Industrial Marketing Management*, 88, 410–413. DOI: 10.1016/j.indmarman.2020.04.010

Dandotiya, R., & Aggarwal, A. (2022). Effects of COVID-19 on hotel industry: A case study of Delhi, India. *Revista Turismo & Desenvolvimento (Aveiro)*, 38, 35–53.

Eggers, F. (2020). Masters of disasters? Challenges and opportunities for SMEs in times of crisis. *Journal of Business Research*, 116, 199–208. DOI: 10.1016/j.jbusres.2020.05.025 PMID: 32501306

Frishammar, J., Richtnér, A., Brattström, A., Magnusson, M., & Björk, J. (2019). Opportunities and challenges in the new innovation landscape: Implications for innovation auditing and innovation management. *European Management Journal*, 37(2), 151–164. DOI: 10.1016/j.emj.2018.05.002

Ghafoor, A., Qureshi, T. M., Khan, M. A., & Hijazi, S. T. (2011). Transformational leadership, employee engagement and performance: Mediating effect of psychological ownership. *African Journal of Business Management*, 5(17), 7391–7403. DOI: 10.5897/AJBM11.126

Ghasemi, A., & Zahediasl, S. (2012). Normality Tests for Statistical Analysis: A Guide for Non-Statisticians. *International Journal of Endocrinology and Metabolism*, 10(2), 486–489. DOI: 10.5812/ijem.3505 PMID: 23843808

Guidetti, G., Cortini, M., Fantinelli, S., Di Fiore, T., & Galanti, T. (2022). Safety Management and Wellbeing during COVID-19: A Pilot Study in the Manufactory Sector. *International Journal of Environmental Research and Public Health*, 19(7), 3981. DOI: 10.3390/ijerph19073981 PMID: 35409664

Gursoy, D., & Chi, C. G. (2020). Effects of COVID-19 pandemic on hospitality industry: Review of the current situations and a research agenda. *Journal of Hospitality Marketing & Management*, 29(5), 527–529. DOI: 10.1080/19368623.2020.1788231

Hair, J., Black, W., Babin, B., & Anderson, R. (2010). *Multivariate data analysis*. Prentice-Hall.

Hamouche, S. (2020). COVID-19 and employees' mental health: Stressors, moderators and agenda for organizational actions. *Emerald Open Research*, 2(2), 15. DOI: 10.1108/EOR-02-2023-0004

Hansson, J., Landstad, B. J., Vinberg, S., Hedlund, M., & Tjulin, Å. (2022). Small business managers and Covid-19—The role of a sense of coherence and general resistance resources in coping with stressors. *PLoS One*, 17(3), e0265029. DOI: 10.1371/journal.pone.0265029 PMID: 35302995

Kaiser, H. (1974). An index of factorial simplicity. *Psychometrika*, 39(1), 31–36. DOI: 10.1007/BF02291575

Keim, A. C., Landis, R. S., Pierce, C. A., & Earnest, D. R. (2014). Why do employees worry about their jobs? A meta-analytic review of predictors of job insecurity. *Journal of Occupational Health Psychology*, 19(3), 269–290. DOI: 10.1037/a0036743 PMID: 24796228

Kim, J., & Lee, J. C. (2020). Effects of COVID-19 on preferences for private dining facilities in restaurants. *Journal of Hospitality and Tourism Management*, 45, 67–70. DOI: 10.1016/j.jhtm.2020.07.008

Krejcie, R. V., & Morgan, D. W. (1970). Determining sample size for research activities. *Educational and Psychological Measurement*, 30(3), 607–610. DOI: 10.1177/001316447003000308

Kumar, A., & Ayedee, D. (2021). Technology adoption: A solution for SMEs to overcome problems during COVID-19. *Forthcoming. Academy of Marketing Studies Journal*, 25(1).

Kumar, P., Kumar, N., Aggarwal, P., & Yeap, J. A. (2021). Working in lockdown: The relationship between COVID-19 induced work stressors, job performance, distress, and life satisfaction. *Current Psychology (New Brunswick, N.J.)*, 40(12), 6308–6323. DOI: 10.1007/s12144-021-01567-0 PMID: 33746462

Labrague, L. J., & Santos, J. D. L. (2020). Fear of COVID-19, psychological distress, work satisfaction and turnover intention among front line nurses. *Research Square*, 1–18. DOI: 10.21203/rs.3.rs-35366/v1

Lee, M., & You, M. (2020). Psychological and behavioral responses in South Korea during the early stages of coronavirus disease 2019 (COVID-19). *International Journal of Environmental Research and Public Health*, 17(9), 2977. DOI: 10.3390/ijerph17092977 PMID: 32344809

Lee, M., & You, M. (2020). Psychological and behavioral responses in South Korea during the early stages of coronavirus disease 2019 (COVID-19). *International Journal of Environmental Research and Public Health*, 17(9), 2977. DOI: 10.3390/ijerph17092977 PMID: 32344809

Luo, M., Guo, L., Yu, M., & Wang, H. (2020). The psychological and mental impact of coronavirus disease 2019 (COVID-19) on medical staff and general public—A systematic review and meta-analysis. *Psychiatry Research*, 291, 113190. DOI: 10.1016/j.psychres.2020.113190 PMID: 32563745

Mani, S., & Mishra, M. (2020). Non-monetary levers to enhance employee engagement in organizations–"GREAT" model of motivation during the Covid-19 crisis. *Strategic HR Review*, 19(4), 171–175. DOI: 10.1108/SHR-04-2020-0028

Nicola, M., Alsafi, Z., Sohrabi, C., Kerwan, A., Al-Jabir, A., Iosifidis, C., Agha, R., & Agha, R. (2020). The socio-economic implications of the coronavirus pandemic (COVID-19): A review. *International Journal of Surgery*, 78, 185–193. DOI: 10.1016/j.ijsu.2020.04.018 PMID: 32305533

Ozili, P. K., & Arun, T. (2020). Spillover of COVID-19: impact on the Global Economy. *Available atSSRN* 3562570. DOI: 10.2139/ssrn.3562570

Pan, T. H., & Lin, Y. N. (2022). Organizational Commitment Impact on Job Well-Being of SMEs Employees in Taiwan in Post-COVID-19 Era. *Education Quarterly Eeview*, 5(1). Advance online publication. DOI: 10.31014/aior.1992.05.01.407

Pappa, S., Ntella, V., Giannakas, T., Giannakoulis, V. G., Papoutsi, E., & Katsaounou, P. (2020). Prevalence of depression, anxiety, and insomnia among healthcare workers during the COVID-19 pandemic: A systematic review and meta-analysis. *Brain, Behavior, and Immunity*, 88, 901–907. DOI: 10.1016/j.bbi.2020.05.026 PMID: 32437915

Pathak, D., & Joshi, G. (2021). Impact of psychological capital and life satisfaction on organizational resilience during COVID-19: Indian tourism insights. *Current Issues in Tourism*, 24(17), 2398–2415. DOI: 10.1080/13683500.2020.1844643

Rashid, S., & Ratten, V. (2021). Entrepreneurial ecosystems during [the survival of small businesses using dynamic capabilities. *World Journal of Entrepreneurship, Management and Sustainable Development*.]. *COVID*, •••, 19.

Rathi, N., & Lee, K. (2016). Emotional exhaustion and work attitudes: Moderating effect of personality among frontline hospitality employees. *Journal of Human Resources in Hospitality & Tourism*, 15(3), 231–251. DOI: 10.1080/15332845.2016.1147935

REBA (Reward & Employee Benefits Association). (2019). *Employee Wellbeing Research 2019*. June, Reba Group.

Rezvani, M. Q., Chaudhary, N., Huseynov, R., Li, M., Sharma, A., Jafarova, R., & Huseynova, C. (2021). Impact of organizational commitment on employee productivity during [evidence from Afghanistan and India.]. *COVID*, •••, 19.

Sahni, J. (2020). Impact of COVID-19 on Employee Behavior: Stress and Coping Mechanism During WFH (Work From Home) Among Service Industry Employees. *International Journal of Operations Management*, 1(1), 35–48. DOI: 10.18775//ijom.2757-0509.2020.11.4004

Salari, N., Hosseinian-Far, A., Jalali, R., Vaisi-Raygani, A., Rasoulpoor, S., Mohammadi, M., Rasoulpoor, S., & Khaledi-Paveh, B. (2020). Prevalence of stress, anxiety, depression among the general population during the COVID-19 pandemic: A systematic review and meta-analysis. *Globalization and Health*, 16(1), 1–11. DOI: 10.1186/s12992-020-00589-w PMID: 32631403

Satici, B., Gocet-Tekin, E., Deniz, M., & Satici, S. A. (2021). Adaptation of the Fear of COVID-19 Scale: Its association with psychological distress and life satisfaction in Turkey. *International Journal of Mental Health and Addiction*, 19(6), 1980–1988. DOI: 10.1007/s11469-020-00294-0 PMID: 32395095

Schermelleh-Engel, K., Moosbrugger, H., & Muller, H. (2003). Evaluating the fit of structural equation models: Test of significance and descriptive goodness-of-fit measures. *Methods of Psychological Research Online*, 8(2), 23–74.

Seltzer, J., & Numerof, R. E. (1988). Supervisory leadership and subordinate burnout. *Academy of Management Journal*, 31(2), 439–446. DOI: 10.2307/256559

Severson, K., & Yaffe-Bellany, D. (2020, 20 March). Independent restaurants brace for the unknown. The New York Times. Retrieved from

Shah, C., Chowdhury, A., & Gupta, V. (2021). Impact of COVID-19 on tourism and hospitality students' perceptions of career opportunities and future prospects in India. *Journal of Teaching in Travel & Tourism*, 21(4), 359–379. DOI: 10.1080/15313220.2021.1924921

Shinbrot, X. A., Wilkins, K., Gretzel, U., & Bowser, G. (2019). Unlocking women's sustainability leadership potential: Perceptions of contributions and challenges for women in sustainable development. *World Development*, 119, 120–132. DOI: 10.1016/j.worlddev.2019.03.009

Shipman, K., Burrell, D. N., & Mac Pherson, A. H. (2021). An organizational analysis of how managers must understand the mental health impact of teleworking during COVID-19 on employees. *The International Journal of Organizational Analysis*.

Sigala, M. (2020). Tourism and COVID-19: Impacts and implications for advancing and resetting industry and research. *Journal of Business Research*, 117, 312–321. DOI: 10.1016/j.jbusres.2020.06.015 PMID: 32546875

Solomon, I. G. (2020). The influence of leadership based on emotional intelligence concerning the climate of an organization. *International Journal of Management Science and Business Administration*, 6(5).

. Sun, T., Zhang, W. W., Dinca, M. S., & Raza, M. (2021). Determining the impact of Covid-19 on the business norms and performance of SMEs in China. *Economic Research-Ekonomska Istraživanja*, 1-20.

Tripathy, S., & Bisoyi, T. (2021). Detrimental impact of COVID-19 pandemic on micro, small and medium enterprises in India. *Jharkhand Journal of Development and Management Studies*, 19(1), 8651–8660.

Van Bavel, J. J., Baicker, K., Boggio, P. S., Capraro, V., Cichocka, A., Cikara, M., & Willer, R. (2020). Using social and behavioural science to support COVID-19 pandemic response. *Nature Human Behaviour*, 4(5), 460–471. DOI: 10.1038/s41562-020-0884-z PMID: 32355299

Wang, W., Huang, W., Liu, X., & Hennessy, D. A. (2021). Psychological impact of mandatory COVID-19 quarantine on small business owners and self-employed in China. *Current Psychology (New Brunswick, N.J.)*, 1–13. PMID: 34155428

Xian, J., Li, B., & Huang, H. (2020). Transformational leadership and employees' thriving at work: The mediating roles of challenge-hindrance stressors. *Frontiers in Psychology*, 11, 1400. DOI: 10.3389/fpsyg.2020.01400 PMID: 32655458

Yang, Y., Liu, H., & Chen, X. (2020). COVID-19 and restaurant demand: Early effects of the pandemic and stay-at-home orders. *International Journal of Contemporary Hospitality Management*, 32(12), 3809–3834. DOI: 10.1108/IJCHM-06-2020-0504

Chapter 9
Entrepreneurial Mindfulness:
A Path to Inner Peace and Professional Fulfilment

Deepak Kumar Sahoo
Biju Patnaik University of Technology, Rourkela, India

Mohit Yadav
https://orcid.org/0000-0002-9341-2527
O.P. Jindal Global University, India

Ajay Chandel
https://orcid.org/0000-0002-4585-6406
Lovely Professional University, India

Majdi Quttainah
https://orcid.org/0000-0002-6280-1060
Kuwait University, Kuwait

ABSTRACT

This chapter explores the significance of mindfulness for entrepreneurs, emphasizing its role in fostering inner peace and professional fulfilment. It examines the connection between mindfulness practices and enhanced focus, reduced stress, and improved emotional resilience. By integrating mindfulness into their daily routines, entrepreneurs can cultivate a deeper sense of purpose, strengthen interpersonal relationships, and achieve a healthier work-life balance. The chapter also addresses challenges entrepreneurs face in practicing mindfulness, such as time constraints and skepticism, while highlighting future trends, including technological integration and personalized approaches. Ultimately, mindfulness emerges as a transformative tool that empowers entrepreneurs to navigate the complexities of their journeys with greater clarity and satisfaction.

DOI: 10.4018/979-8-3693-3673-1.ch009

INTRODUCTION TO ENTREPRENEURIAL MINDFULNESS

Entrepreneurship has been ridden by increasingly complex demands to be innovative, finding solutions amidst uncertainty and intense pressure. Amidst these raging demands for responsibilities and deadlines and the need to take decisions rapidly, mindfulness has emerged as a growing tool for personal and professional development for many entrepreneurs. Mindfulness is defined as full presence and awareness applied to the entrepreneurial journey. Mindfulness provokes a higher understanding of thought, emotion, and action processes to bring about clarity and focus in their lives that arise through emotional intelligence (Alshebami et al., 2023).

Mindfulness is the process of deliberate attention given to thoughts and feelings without judgment, which could greatly transform the lives of entrepreneurs. It helps in understanding the emotional turbulence, or the excitement of a new venture that usually seems to accompany entrepreneurship (Anh & Pham, 2022). The inclusion of mindfulness in the daily life of entrepreneurs enhances the sense of self-awareness in them so they react more sensibly to problems rather than impulsively reacting to them. This can result in a more effective way of decision making and relation building between them and their colleagues, clients, or stakeholders.

Mindfulness research demonstrates that it helps to greatly reduce stress and enhance the mental resilience of an individual. It thus happens that for an entrepreneur, who is more likely to be engrossed with high stress levels and uncertainty, this benefit becomes particularly valuable. Mindfulness practice forms the core basic tool with which one could regulate the emotional rollercoaster of entrepreneurship with which a person engaged in entrepreneurship would like to go through. They have not only created inner peace in a mind but also some essential cognitive functions that are needed for entrepreneurial success, such as creativity and problem-solving ability (Aránega et al., 2023).

Besides personal practices, entrepreneurial mindfulness can shape organizational culture. By instigating a mindful work culture, entrepreneurs will create more collaborative, innovative teams. Mindfulness can become a social activity-an activity done collectively-and reduces stigma around mental health. It makes entrepreneurial practice a facilitator for healthier working environments that make profits by giving importance to well-being in their service.

As we dive deeper into the concept of entrepreneurial mindfulness, it is important to note that it's holistic. This does not mean mental and emotional well-being; it opens up for somebody a deeper connection with his purpose and values. Many entrepreneurs are driven by a passionate love for their ideas and a need to try and create difference (Aripin et al., 2024). Mindfulness allows them to reconnect with those motivations, making sure that their entrepreneurial endeavors are propelled by something more than just financial success but through meaningful contributions to society.

Mindfulness is no longer just a trend at the entrepreneurial journey but a needed evolution for peace and professional fulfillment. It is then that business entrepreneurs, who have embraced the practice, are better prepared to navigate the demands of the roles they will be fulfilling, leading to more reflective decisions, higher levels of resilience, and, ultimately, a more satisfying entrepreneurial experience. Entrepreneurial mindfulness is a process of self-actualization and development that leads not only to business success but personal greatness as well.

THE CONNECTION BETWEEN MINDFULNESS AND ENTREPRENEURSHIP

Enhancing Creativity and Innovation

Mindfulness enhances a creative and inventive state of affairs, all elements that result in the eventual triumph of entrepreneurial pursuit. Through mindfulness training, mental space remains uncluttered because the entrepreneurs are encouraged to be more immersed in the activity by removing fear as well as judgment when thinking of new ideas (Cai et al., 2023). Being mindful, entrepreneurs open their minds to curiosity and experimentation, thereby giving way to the discovery of unique opportunities and the conjuring of innovative solutions that will otherwise remain unnoticed.

Improving Decision-Making and Risk Management

Entrepreneurship is essentially a space where decision making is made in uncertainty with a lot on the line. Mindfulness can equip the entrepreneur with insight that gives quite a clear and composed approach to decisions. If an entrepreneur took some time to step back and reflect, taking a much longer and more careful view of his choices, not only of the positive outcomes but also the risks, then this approach will lead to better risk management of challenges by entrepreneurs as they walk through doors with more well-balanced things in view (Dhammika & Sewwandi, 2023). Mindfulness, in this sense, helps to develop emotional intelligence wherein the entrepreneur can understand situations well enough to respond appropriately for more informed and effective decision-making.

Building Emotional Resilience

Entrepreneurs should expect that their entrepreneurial journey would be beset with ups and downs; hence, the need to be emotionally resilient. Mindfulness develops an entrepreneur's sense of resilience by educating them to acknowledge and process their emotions, without feeling overwhelmed. Setbacks or failure become opportunities for growth rather than feelings of overwhelming frustrations when held by a constructive perspective of the mindful entrepreneur. However, this ability to spring back will be beneficial not only for personal well-being but also for building a healthier organizational culture where resilience becomes a common value among individuals (Gelderen et al., 2019).

Fostering Stronger Relationships

Mindfulness does more than benefit its practitioners; it forms the basis for more potent relationships in an entrepreneurial ecosystem. Mindfulness with active listening and empathy thereby shapes the nature of communication between entrepreneurs and their teams and stakeholders. The mindful entrepreneur, therefore, is more aware of people's needs and perspectives, creating stronger relations and collaborations (Gordon & Schaller, 2014). This relational quality of mindfulness can therefore give way to a more cohesive team and supportive networks, conducive to the success of the entrepreneurial venture.

Aligning Purpose and Values

Entrepreneurship is founded largely upon a desire to do something impactful, and mindfulness will remind the entrepreneur to reconnect to a core set of values and purpose. When the daily operations of working on a small business become lost in the fray-and forgotten-is the real reason for the entrepreneurial pursuit. Mindfulness helps entrepreneurs to be self-reflection, hence scrutinizing and harmonizing their business activities with what makes them ticks. The harmonization of entrepreneurship business practices leads to satisfaction and authenticity in running such a business (Hassannezhad et al., 2020).

There are so many multidimensional connections between mindfulness and entrepreneurship, anything from creativity to building relationships, decision making, emotional resilience, and alignment with purpose. Being more mindful through embracing it brings on the possibility of entrepreneurs having a more holistic approach to their work; they'll be more likely to be more effective because they are going to be better entrepreneurs for all these reasons and also being more enriching and a fulfilling entrepreneurial experience (Hosseininia et al., 2024). So, mindfulness acts as a guiding principle in helping them thrive personally and professionally by embracing the complexity that's associated with their journey.

BENEFITS OF MINDFULNESS FOR ENTREPRENEURS

Enhancing Focus and Concentration

Improvement in the area of concentration and focus is one of the most important benefits of mindfulness to entrepreneurs. In an era filled with distractions-from constantly receiving notifications from devices to demands placed on multitasking-keeping attention on critical tasks can be difficult. Mindfulness practices, such as meditation and mindful breathing, train the brain to focus on the present moment. Such an increased attention span enables entrepreneurs to solve difficult problems with calmness and concentration, thereby enhancing productivity and quality (Indrianti et al., 2024).

Reducing Stress and Anxiety

Entrepreneurship presents a doubtlessly stressful and anxiety-provoking activity in many relationships, with doubt and burdening responsibility. Mindfulness serves as an effective antidote, calming and clearing the mind. The ability to encourage others to be aware of their thoughts and feelings without judgment helps entrepreneurs deal better with the stress related to activity. Doing mindfulness meditation reduces the level of cortisol in a person along with overall well-being improvement, so entrepreneurs can face their battles from a calm, composed, and more peaceful perspective of mind (Iram et al., 2022).

Promoting Emotional Resilience

Entrepreneurs usually face rejections, failures, and other unseen things so emotional resilience forms is very crucial. Mindfulness fosters such resiliencies through which entrepreneurs can process their emotions and responses constructively. A mindful entrepreneur is not wholly overwhelmed by negative sentiments but possesses time to reflect on experiences and learn. This ability to recover and bounce back also makes them more resilient mentally but very encouraging to look at things optimistically by promoting a positive growth mindset that perceives difficulties as means of learning (Karali, 2023).

Enhancing Creativity and Problem-Solving

Mindfulness also promotes the thinking behind creativity and problem-solving. When businesspeople are mindful, they are more prone to think outside of the box and from different perspectives when different solutions are needed. Mindfulness therefore provides potential for innovative solutions and creative breakthroughs that result in a business standing out better among its competitors. It also encourages divergent thinking, meaning that entrepreneurs would generate a wider spread of ideas and alternatives in deciding on complex options.

Improving Interpersonal Relationships

Strong entrepreneurship relationships absolutely require mindfulness in building these connections. Mindful entrepreneurs are more present during conversations, leading to active listening and empathetic participation. Such a sense of awareness translates to perfect communication and collaborative relationships with team members, clients, and partners. Building up a supportive relationship based on trust and respect because of mindfulness makes for a more synchronized and effective workplace (Kelly & Dorian, 2017).

Increasing Job Satisfaction and Fulfillment

Mindfulness integrated into an entrepreneurial pathway can have a significant impact on job satisfaction as well as overall life satisfaction. Mindfulness is the awareness for oneself of being in alignment with personal values that are how entrepreneurs connect to their passions and motivations. Such an alignment provides a sense of purpose yet increases commitment to the work. The more entrepreneurship is fun and meaningful, the stronger the possibility of long-term satisfaction and a much deeper sense of attainment (Kim et al., 2022).

By bringing mindfulness into the daily routine of entrepreneurs, focus will be improved, stress reduced, emotional resilience developed, creativity boosted, and personal and professional relationships will grow stronger, and job satisfaction as well. In that respect, entrepreneurs can easily and more effectively pass through their journey by cultivating a mindful approach to work through integration of practices like mindfulness into their daily routines. In doing so, they improve their own wellbeing while building a healthier and more innovative entrepreneurial ecosystem by contributing to one.

MINDFULNESS PRACTICES FOR ENTREPRENEURS

Meditation Techniques

One of the most effective mindfulness practices available for entrepreneurs is meditation. Since meditation comes in a multitude of forms, it can also fit into any schedule. Because of this, meditation can be done by anyone. One very popular technique using guided meditation is when an entrepreneur listens to recordings that take him or her through visualization and breath work. This tends to clear the mind and reduce stress, so one will be clearer and focused (Liu et al., 2022). Another good technique is transcendental meditation in which a mantra is silently repeated. It facilitates deep relaxation and awareness. Keeping as little time of the day as just 10-15 minutes to meditate brings a great difference in maintaining the mental balance and productivity of an entrepreneur.

Mindful Breathing

Mindful breathing is a simple and powerful practice which can easily be fit into the routine. The beauty of this practice for entrepreneurs is that it can be conducted anywhere, at any time. One learns to focus on the breath-that is, on taking slow, deep, cued inhalations and exhalations. People get grounded in the present moment, and this alone quiets the mind; and, of course, it brings peace and clarity. Even minutes of mindful breathing before a meeting or in a stressful moment can enhance focus and composure in a snap (Moder et al., 2023).

Body Scan

The body scan is one of the mindfulness techniques that entails focusing on various parts of the body so that there is relaxation and heightened awareness. Entrepreneurs can practice this technique lying down or sitting comfortably with their eyes closed, mentally scanning themselves from head to toe. In these various areas of focus, they may be able to discover and release constriction that results in relaxation (Overall, 2020). For entrepreneurs who have experienced a long stretch at work, this exercise might even be more rejuvenating, as it allows them to reconnect with their body while flushing away the stress they have built up during the day.

Mindful Walking

Introducing movement to mindfulness practices may make the activity feel more fulfilling and positive for the body. Mindful walking is walking slowly and deliberately, paying attention to every step and the feeling in the body. Entrepreneurs might take short walks during breaks to train their minds on their surroundings and the rhythm of their breath. This will not only call for physical activity but also a break in time spent gazing at screens, creating mental rejuvenation. In addition to the above, one can also go for reflective walks that add to the experience. Natural environments have been shown to reduce stress and enhance well-being (Ozcan et al., 2023).

Journaling

Another wonderful mindful practice is journaling. Self-reflection and clarity can motivate entrepreneurs. Their ability to write down thoughts and feelings about experiences helps them gain insight into their emotional states and patterns of thought. This practice further motivates gratitude and the reflective side of positive thinking, which helps them cultivate a sense of abundance rather than scarcity. Journaling is a way that sets the intention and acts of goal setting for entrepreneurs, keeping them aligned with values and purpose in life (Plana-Farran et al., 2022).

Mindfulness in Daily Tasks

A more practical approach toward developing awareness would be to integrate mindfulness into all the daily activities. Whether it's a meeting, email exchanges, or even a routine as simple as eating or cleaning, an entrepreneur can enhance his ability to focus when he is fully present in the activity. This requires strict involvement in what is going on, elimination of distractions, and being fully engaged in the experience. With mindfulness integration in the daily tasks, entrepreneurs will experience their overall productivity and satisfaction improved, making routine activities as opportunities for being mindful.

Mindfulness practices are easy to adapt to and very accessible, thus ideal for entrepreneurs in search of greater well-being and performance. Techniques such as meditation, mindful breathing, body scanning, mindful walking, journaling, and how to apply mindfulness in everyday life can all help entrepreneurs build a sustainable practice which further fosters inner peace and professional fulfillment (Ratanavanich & Charoensukmongkol, 2024). The benefits do not stop with the individual entrepreneur but also have an impact within the health of the entrepreneurial ecosystem.

CULTIVATING A MINDFUL WORK ENVIRONMENT

Creating a Culture of Mindfulness

A mindful work environment should begin with creating a culture that encourages and supports mindfulness practices for all employees. This starts with leadership; when leaders demonstrate mindfulness behaviors-through breaks in meditation, active listening, and openness to communication-they in turn set positive examples for the entire organization. Leaders can also organize mindfulness workshops and training for the employees to be introduced to the mindset; thus, such cultures are normalized within the workplace (Raza et al., 2023). By including mindfulness in the organizational culture, the firms create an environment where employees feel cared about, not only in their personal life but also in their professional development.

Encouraging Open Communication

Open communication is the heart of any mindful work setting. Encouraging employees to speak their minds and hearts, maintaining a culture of mutual trust and cooperation, gives birth to respect and an open process for ideas and concerns. Even mindful practices of communication, such as listening actively and giving non-judgmental feedback, can help create a safe space from which sharing of ideas and concerns is encouraged. Regular check-ins and team meetings - as well as one-on-ones - can actually be designed to prioritize mindfulness, letting the team members share their experiences and insights freely. This not only enhances interpersonal relationships but also the cohesion and collaboration of teams (Sultan et al., 2023).

Designating Mindfulness Spaces

There is also the physical work environment, which can contribute to the ability of employees to practice mindfulness. Designing mindfulness spaces in the form of quiet rooms or meditation spaces or nature-inspired zones could be considered for retreats from the everyday hustle and bustle of work life. They can provide comfortable seating, calming decor, and even furnish guides such as recorded meditation or literature on mindfulness. It is within these spaces that organizations provide employees with the opportunity to take mindful breaks, recharge, and return to their tasks refreshed and laser focused (Tunio et al., 2023).

Incorporating Mindfulness into Meetings

Meetings often become frazzled and less productive, which leads to disengagement and frustration. Organizations can start by ensuring practices such as starting the meeting with a moment of silence or a brief mindfulness exercise foster the mindful atmosphere at meetings. By encouraging the participants to set intentions about the meeting, this will help produce a focused and collaborative environment. Another practice that encourages inclusiveness such as allowing every single person to have his or her chance to share thoughts without interruption further promotes mindfulness in group settings (Uslay & Erdoğan, 2014).

Promote Work-Life Balance

A healthy work environment cares for the well-being of employees, and this means promoting a healthy work-life balance. Assisting the employees in using regular breaks, setting boundaries around work hours, and using vacation time helps prevent burnout and overall healthiness. Flexible work arrangement, such as remote options or adjusted schedules, will also contribute to the mindfulness aspect of work (Yang et al., 2021). This can only be achieved by exemplifying a commitment toward work-life balance, which could portray in an organization that cares about the psychological well-being of employees and respects their private lives. In that way, organization will show mindfulness culture that actually promotes productivity and wellness.

Providing Mindfulness Resources

Organizations can plant further a mindful working environment by offering materials to help employees practice mindfulness. Some materials would be in the form of mindfulness apps, workshops, or seminars led by mindfulness experienced professionals. Other educational material such as literature in books or articles about mindfulness can also give a fair chance at the staff's freedom to be educated on the subject. Resources that encourage mindfulness are an investment in employee well-being because they reflect an organization's commitment towards its employees and open channels towards possibilities of personal development (Ye et al., 2024).

For this reason, intentional effort and commitment from leadership and employees are necessary in creating a mindful work environment (Alshebami et al., 2023). A culture of mindfulness in an organization, open communication, and developing mindfulness spaces can help foster mindfulness. Mindfulness in meetings, work-life balance, and provision of resources contribute significantly to this holistic approach in enhancing individual well-being while making the workforce engaged, productive, and innovative for organizational success.

CHALLENGES TO PRACTICING MINDFULNESS AS AN ENTREPRENEUR

Time Constraints

The biggest challenges one faces in order to be mindful have been observed as time. With that in hand, so many are the responsibilities linked with being an entrepreneur-from managing teams to keeping up with the clients' demands-it can be quite challenging to find even a few minutes in the day to be mindful. The mere thought that mindfulness requires hours of uninterrupted time upholds most entrepreneurs from adding it to their busy schedules (Anh & Pham, 2022). A challenge of entrepreneurship, it's fast paced and so often these reflective times and self-care get written off to the side as less important than completing urgent business-oriented pursuits. This might be mitigated if it's realized that mindfulness does not have to be done in long quantities.

Skepticism and Misconceptions

Entrepreneurs think they are skeptical of mindfulness, wondering if it is just a fad and if it truly doesn't contribute to personal growth and development in the workplace. The primary myth associated with mindfulness is that it refers only to relaxation or that it provides very little real benefits; therefore, the skepticism runs rampant. Such skepticism may run deep in high-pressure environments where results are weighed against well-being. A method to conquer such a hurdle would be education on how mindfulness has been useful and exposure through the experiences of fellow entrepreneurs who have practiced mindfulness (Aránega et al., 2023).

High Stress Levels

The intrinsically high stress level of entrepreneurship can thus become a paradox in the head of the entrepreneur: he very well knows he should practice mindfulness in order to release the critical level of stress, but he just cannot be productive in practicing the mindfulness behavior. Whence, when an entrepreneur feels excessive stress, he will likely instinctively react to the situation rather than taking a step back in order to practice mindfulness - such as working more hours or trying to multitask (Aripin et al., 2024). This way, this very cycle makes the entrepreneur usually burnt out and less productive, overall. Break the pattern by giving mindfulness a conscious status as a preventative measure against stress instead of an afterthought.

Lack of Support and Resources

Most businessmen, especially those in the startup environment and small organizations, will obviously lack institutional support for mindfulness practices. Without any established structures of organization that may help promote and encourage mindfulness, one may not be able to inculcate and adhere to such practices (Cai et al., 2023). Thirdly, limited accessible resources like mindfulness classes or seminars may hinder the sustainability of mindful practice. Again, entrepreneur ventures may seek external resources or communities that believe in mindfulness practice, thereby creating a community of like-minded people who can have feedback and accountability.

Personal Resistance

Mindfulness requires one to become vulnerable and acknowledge his or herself, which is somewhat uncomfortable with some entrepreneurs. Being confronted by negative emotions and thoughts normally goes against the natural reluctance of a mindfulness practice. An entrepreneur might think that admitting stress or even asking for help would portray a person as fragile or less capable in their minds. That reluctance leads some to resist the full embrace of mindfulness, missing opportunities that arise from practicing the approach. To overcome this, an attitude of openness and adaptability must be developed; one must embrace vulnerability as a source of strength to the heightened resilience and growth (Dhammika & Sewwandi, 2023).

Balancing Mindfulness with Performance Expectations

Within a pressure-cooker environment, the pressure to meet performance expectations contradicts mindfulness. Entrepreneurs can feel guilty about taking time for mindfulness activities mainly when deadlines are to be met or targets achieved. This can create some inner conflict, and then there begins a vicious cycle of neglect for self-care to get more productive. Entrepreneurs need to shift their minds toward seeing mindfulness as an opportunity for better performance instead of something that might take away the latter. The tug-of-war competing demands that drive entrepreneurs first to see mindfulness as an investment in their well-being and effectiveness should help them balance better.

While the benefits of mindfulness to entrepreneurs are significant, several challenges stand in their way. Most of these include time pressures, an aversion to change, stress, lack of support, and pressure to perform as well as resistance to change. The path to successfully incorporating mindfulness into entrepreneurial careers will depend on the recognition of these challenges as well as actively seeking strategies to counteract them. By paying due emphasis on mindfulness as one of the significant aspects of one's well-being, entrepreneurs can enhance their efficiency, strength, and satisfaction levels in their professional worlds (Gelderen et al., 2019).

MINDFULNESS AND PROFESSIONAL FULFILLMENT

Understanding Professional Fulfilment

Professional fulfillment can be very well described as that feeling of satisfaction and meaning attached to one's work. For entrepreneurs, this feeling generally comes from how their business endeavors align with personal values, passions, and set goals. However, the hurried life of being an entrepreneur tends to overwhelm the sense of fulfillment sometimes, giving rise to feelings of burnout, disconnection, and frustration. Mindfulness acts as a potent antidote by allowing entrepreneurs to reawaken to the purposeful agenda and rediscover meaning in professional lives (Gordon & Schaller, 2014).

Reconnecting with Purpose and Values

Reconnecting to purposes and values is the most impactful way in which mindfulness contributes to professional satisfaction. Through practices such as meditation and self-reflection, entrepreneurs are made to become clearer about what matters most to them. This clarity makes them align their business practices with their core values, and this creates feelings of authenticity in whatever one does (Hassannezhad et al., 2020). Business owners who are led by a sense of purpose would find their work more fulfilling and challenging because the purpose behind it is very much associated with their values and aspirations.

Fostering a Growth Mindset

Having a growth mindset is perhaps one of the most important attributes that mindfulness can cultivate toward professionalism fulfillment. From being fearful of what might go wrong to fear of failing, mindfulness motivates entrepreneurs to be curious and open to challenges as learning opportunities. It also equips business owners with resilience and adaptability, making them face challenges with hope and optimism. As they learn by experience, this journey can itself be regarded as growth, leading to an overall increase in their fulfillment and satisfaction (Hosseininia et al., 2024).

Enhancing Well-Being and Reducing Burnout

It is now evident that there is a relationship between mindfulness and one's well-being, but for entrepreneurs, it takes on a more important dimension. One of the ways mindfulness helps entrepreneurs is by creating lower stress and anxiety levels that contribute to improved mental-emotional states. Wellness benefits avoid the ever-increasing tendency towards burnout in entrepreneurs. The better a person's mental health through mindfulness, the greater will be quality of life, alongside producing more sustainable work patterns, with greater professionalism over time (Indrianti et al., 2024).

Strengthening Relationships and Community

The quality of relationships is often in sync with professional fulfillment as such. Mindfulness brings about stronger connections between people through empathy and active listening, among others. This can help entrepreneurs get an intuitive sense of the needs and feelings of team members, clients, and stakeholders (Iram et al., 2022). More substantial meaningful interactions and even a deep feeling of belonging within the entrepreneurial community can be realized this way. With increased depth in relationships, entrepreneurs find increased satisfaction in a collaborative effort, hence overall fulfillment.

Encouraging Balance and Harmony

This balance in the work and life of a person creates long-term professional fulfillment: A mindful entrepreneur will learn how to be aware of his needs and limitations and establish limits and priorities for himself that will work better towards creating a healthier boundary in regard to his own care. The same energy set into that seems to contribute to his better well-being will be positively influencing his effectiveness at work. The fullness felt in personal life translates well into a fruitful relationship between the personal and business realms (Karali, 2023).

Mindfulness, therefore, is much needed in the entrepreneurial journey towards professional fulfillment. Mindfulness is transformative for entrepreneurs because it connects them with purpose, fosters a growth mindset, enhances well-being, strengthens relationships, and encourages balance in life (Kelly & Dorian, 2017). In this regard, embracing mindfulness practices by entrepreneurs unlocks deeper fulfillment and meaning at work, which serves them well personally and professionally. In this world so often bound by start-ups, where illusion is a common result, mindfulness offers a guiding light to enlightenment on the path to success and fulfillment.

FUTURE TRENDS IN MINDFULNESS FOR ENTREPRENEURS

Increased Integration of Technology

It is exactly the increased integration of technology that will increase mindfulness practices for entrepreneurs. Apps and mindfulness platforms are designed with guided meditations, tools for stress management, and community support. These technologies are improved and developed with users' needs in mind, with certain attributes of accessibility and functionality. Future trends may also encompass virtual reality experiences that could afford the complete immersion of entrepreneurs into mindfulness practice in a unique way through which they can disentangle themselves from work pressures. This makes it easier for entrepreneurs to include mindfulness in their day-to-day operations and blend it into their lives (Kim et al., 2022).

Workplace Mindfulness Programs

The growing need for organizations to recognize the importance of mental health and wellness with regards to productivity and the well-being of employees as a whole will lead workplaces to implement these mindfulness programs. In corporations, the idea of having structured mindfulness programs can be incorporated through weekly meditation sessions, workshops, and wellness retreats in a workplace that instills a mindful culture in its employees (Liu et al., 2022). Not only do these programs contribute positively to individual well-being but also to the richness of team dynamics, ultimately resulting in a more engaged and productive workforce.

Emphasis on Personalization

This is an upcoming tendency towards personal mindfulness models in the near future. Due to increased awareness of individual needs and preferences, mindfulness practices will become more tailored to manage distinct lifestyles and working environments. One of these options may be preferred: short mindfulness breaks, specific meditation styles, or mindfulness techniques applied in daily tasks (Moder et al., 2023). Thus, entrepreneurs will be able to devise their own personalized mindfulness routine that focuses on their goals in personal and professional terms.

Mindfulness as a Leadership Competency

Mindfulness is likely to become one of the critical competencies in effective leadership in entrepreneurship, wherein emotional intelligence and resilience become increasingly important for the organization. They will thus be better equipped to respond to and transform challenges into a positive work atmosphere by training and empathizing with their teams-an area of training for the future entrepreneurial leaders: mindfulness techniques that would enable them to connect more meaningfully with their teams, worry less, and think more carefully. Focusing in on mindfulness will help the individual leader but also contribute to healthier organizational cultures (Overall, 2020).

Research and Evidence-Based Practices

Further investigations into the benefits of mindfulness will likely encourage even more entrepreneurs into practicing innovation in this field. The more evidence that is gathered about how mindfulness influences productivity, creativity, and well-being, the greater the number of entrepreneurs embracing its benefits will be. All these will eventually lead to developing new mindfulness practices and interventions targeting specifically the entrepreneurs, and it will become all the more important for the entrepreneurs to incorporate mindfulness into their professional travels (Ozcan et al., 2023).

Global and Cultural Perspectives

As mindfulness will be gaining more acceptance in every part of the world, future trends will thus be more inclusive of its cultural and global scope. Entrepreneurship, with people coming from different cultures, will offer diversity in perspective to the practice of mindfulness, and thereby hybrid approaches that include other cultural traditions will come to the forefront (Plana-Farran et al., 2022). The global perspective of mindfulness will add the mindfulness movement with a great sense of inclusiveness and encourage an all-round perspective on well-being in the entrepreneurial context.

Focus on Sustainable Practices

As more people become aware of concerns on the environment and social life, future trends of mindfulness for entrepreneurs may focus increasingly on sustainability. Consequentially, mindful entrepreneurs will look for ways that fit in with ethical business performance and concern for the welfare of people. This is likely to appear in mindful decision-making that takes into account the broader impact of their actions on the environment and society at large. By linking the two concepts of mindfulness and sustainability, entrepreneurs will then be able to develop a sense of purpose furthering their fulfillment as well as being fair to their values.

The future of mindfulness for entrepreneurs, in other words, will indeed be exciting as there is increased integration into technology, corporate initiatives, personalized approaches, and the most important one- the development of leadership competency (Ratanavanich & Charoensukmongkol, 2024). As the more researched evidence emerges on the benefits of mindfulness, the latter will become increasingly vital to defining entrepreneurial business landscapes. How the entrepreneur moves along this path of embracing these trends fosters a more mindful approach at work for their betterment regarding well-being, creativity, and professional fulfillment in an ever-evolving business world.

CONCLUSION

Mindfulness can be viewed as a critical practice for the entrepreneur's personal self-welfare and for professional satisfaction in the face of increasing complexity and demands within the entrepreneurial environment. The development of mindfulness will help the entrepreneur rediscover a sense of purpose, decrease levels of stress, and develop resilience such that a good quality work experience will be evident. Mindfulness, integration into one's daily endeavors and the support from mindful work environments serve to open the gateway to sustainable success. Because of such trends in the future, growth in technology, practices tailored to individualism and focus on workplace mindfulness programs will better empower entrepreneurs to acknowledge mindfulness as a critical component of their journeys. Through mindfulness, entrepreneurs not only improve their lives but also contribute to a healthier and more innovative entrepreneurial ecosystem that enables future generations to thrive in a balanced and fulfilling manner. Mindfulness, then, will be the beacon guiding them through all those challenges and opportunities ahead toward a much more conscious and impactful entrepreneurial experience.

REFERENCE

Alshebami, A. S., Alholiby, M. S., Elshaer, I. A., Sobaih, A. E. E., & Al Marri, S. H. (2023). Examining the relationship between green mindfulness, spiritual intelligence, and environmental self-identity: Unveiling the path to green entrepreneurial intention. *Administrative Sciences*, 13(10), 226. DOI: 10.3390/admsci13100226

Anh, B., & Pham, M. (2022). The role of mindfulness and perceived social support in promoting students' social entrepreneurial intention. *Entrepreneurial Business and Economics Review*, 10(1), 145–160. DOI: 10.15678/EBER.2022.100110

Aránega, A. Y., Castaño Sánchez, R., & Ribeiro-Navarrete, S. (2023). Techniques to strengthen entrepreneurship: Is mindfulness a useful concept for resilience development? *Journal of Enterprising Communities: People and Places in the Global Economy*.

Aripin, Z., Sikki, N., & Fatmasari, R. R. (2024, January). An in-depth exploration of empirical research on entrepreneurial mindfulness: A systematic literature review to explore nuances, findings, and challenges. *Journal of Jabar Economic Society Networking Forum*, 1(2), 1–15.

Cai, B., Chen, Y., & Ayub, A. (2023). "Quiet the mind, and the soul will speak"! Exploring the boundary effects of green mindfulness and spiritual intelligence on university students' green entrepreneurial intention–behavior link. *Sustainability (Basel)*, 15(5), 3895. DOI: 10.3390/su15053895

Dhammika, B. B. K., & Sewwandi, D. (2023). Role of mindfulness in entrepreneurial success: A review. *Editorial Board*, 4(01), 98–117.

Gelderen, M., Kibler, E., Kautonen, T., Muñoz, P., & Wincent, J. (2019). Mindfulness and taking action to start a new business. *Journal of Small Business Management*, 57(sup2), 489-506. https://doi.org/DOI: 10.1111/jsbm.12499

Gordon, J., & Schaller, T. (2014). The role of mindfulness in entrepreneurial market analysis. *Journal of Research in Marketing and Entrepreneurship*, 16(1), 7–25. DOI: 10.1108/JRME-02-2013-0005

Hassannezhad, Z., Zali, M., Faghih, N., Hejazi, R., & Mobini, A. (2020). A process model of entrepreneurial alertness among technopreneurs. *International Business Research*, 13(3), 96. DOI: 10.5539/ibr.v13n3p96

Hosseininia, G., Aliabadi, V., Karimi, H., & Ataei, P. (2024). The interaction between exploratory behaviours and entrepreneurial opportunity recognition by agriculture students: The mediating role of strategic learning and mindfulness. *Innovations in Education and Teaching International*, 61(4), 649–664. DOI: 10.1080/14703297.2023.2192511

Indrianti, Y., Abdinagoro, S. B., & Rahim, R. K. (2024). A resilient startup leader's personal journey: The role of entrepreneurial mindfulness and ambidextrous leadership through scaling-up performance capacity. *Heliyon*, 10(14), e34285. DOI: 10.1016/j.heliyon.2024.e34285 PMID: 39113945

Iram, T., Bilal, A., Ahmad, Z., & Latif, S. (2022). Does financial mindfulness make a difference? A nexus of financial literacy and behavioural biases in women entrepreneurs. *IIM Kozhikode Society & Management Review*, 12(1), 7–21. DOI: 10.1177/22779752221097194

Karali, N., Mastrokoukou, S., & Livas, C. (2023). Mindful minds and entrepreneurial spirits in higher education: A scoping review. *Frontiers in Education*, 8, 1291845. Advance online publication. DOI: 10.3389/feduc.2023.1291845

Kelly, L., & Dorian, M. (2017). Doing well and good: An exploration of the role of mindfulness in the entrepreneurial opportunity recognition and evaluation process. *New England Journal of Entrepreneurship*, 20(2), 26–36. DOI: 10.1108/NEJE-20-02-2017-B002

Kim, J., Lee, M., & Lee, J. (2022). The effects of entrepreneurs' optimism and mindfulness on psychological well-being. *International Academy of Global Business and Trade*, 18(4), 123–137. DOI: 10.20294/jgbt.2022.18.4.123

Liu, X., Wu, X., Wang, Q., & Zhou, Z. (2022). Entrepreneurial mindfulness and organizational resilience of Chinese SMEs during the COVID-19 pandemic: The role of entrepreneurial resilience. *Frontiers in Psychology*, 13, 992161. Advance online publication. DOI: 10.3389/fpsyg.2022.992161 PMID: 36275221

Moder, S., Jehle, E., Furtner, M., & Kraus, S. (2023). Short-term mindfulness meditation training improves antecedents of opportunity recognition. *Journal of Business Venturing Insights*, 19, e00381. DOI: 10.1016/j.jbvi.2023.e00381

Overall, J. (2020). Mental health among entrepreneurs: The benefits of consciousness. *International Journal of Entrepreneurship and Economic Issues*, 4(1), 70–74. DOI: 10.32674/ijeei.v4i1.20

Ozcan, N. A., Sahin, S., & Cankir, B. (2023). The validity and reliability of thriving scale in academic context: Mindfulness, GPA, and entrepreneurial intention among university students. *Current Psychology (New Brunswick, N.J.)*, 42(7), 5200–5211. DOI: 10.1007/s12144-021-01590-1

Plana-Farran, M., Blanch, Á., & Solé, S. (2022). The role of mindfulness in business administration (B.A.) university students' career prospects and concerns about the future. *International Journal of Environmental Research and Public Health*, 19(3), 1376. DOI: 10.3390/ijerph19031376 PMID: 35162407

Ratanavanich, M., & Charoensukmongkol, P. (2024). The interaction effect of goal orientation and mindfulness of entrepreneurs on firm innovation capability and its impact on firm performance. *VINE Journal of Information and Knowledge Management Systems, (ahead-of-print)*.

Raza, S. A., Tunio, M. N., Ali, M., & Puah, C. H. (Eds.). (2023). *Entrepreneurship and Green Finance Practices: Avenues for Sustainable Business Start-ups in Asia*. Emerald Publishing Limited. DOI: 10.1108/9781804556788

Sultan, M. F., Tunio, M. N., Aziz, A., & Shaikh, S. K. (2023). Social innovation and social entrepreneurship in the wake of COVID-19: A perspective from the developing side of the world. In *Frugal Innovation and Social Transitions in the Digital Era* (pp. 113–118). IGI Global.

Tunio, M. N., Shaikh, E., Katper, N. K., & Brahmi, M. (2023). Nascent entrepreneurs and challenges in the digital market in developing countries. *International Journal of Public Sector Performance Management*, 12(1-2), 140–153. DOI: 10.1504/IJPSPM.2023.132244

Uslay, C., & Erdoğan, E. (2014). The mediating role of mindful entrepreneurial marketing (MEM) between production and consumption. *Journal of Research in Marketing and Entrepreneurship*, 16(1), 47–62. DOI: 10.1108/JRME-11-2013-0034

Yang, H., Zhang, L., Wu, Y., & Shi, H. (2021). Benefits and costs of happy entrepreneurs: The dual effect of entrepreneurial identity on entrepreneurs' subjective well-being. *Frontiers in Psychology*, 12, 767164. Advance online publication. DOI: 10.3389/fpsyg.2021.767164 PMID: 34777177

Ye, D., Liu, M. J., Luo, J., & Yannopoulou, N. (2024). How to achieve swift resilience: The role of digital innovation-enabled mindfulness. *Information Systems Frontiers*, 26(2), 551–573. DOI: 10.1007/s10796-021-10225-6

Chapter 10
Evaluating the Impact of Wellness Programs on Entrepreneurial Burnout

Thi Minh Ngoc Luu
https://orcid.org/0000-0002-5972-7752
International School, Vietnam National University, Hanoi, Vietnam

Sandeep Kumar Singh
https://orcid.org/0000-0002-1741-7254
O.P. Jindal Global University, India

Shivani Dhand
https://orcid.org/0000-0002-4809-1365
Lovely Professional University, India

ABSTRACT

This chapter explores the critical impact of wellness programs on entrepreneurial burnout, emphasizing their role in promoting resilience and sustainable business practices. As entrepreneurs face unique pressures that contribute to stress and burnout, effective wellness initiatives become essential for enhancing overall well-being. This study evaluates various types of wellness programs, innovative digital solutions, and their long-term effects on entrepreneurial sustainability. Additionally, it addresses the challenges of implementing these programs and highlights the need for supportive policies and community involvement. Future trends indicate a shift towards personalized, technology-driven wellness solutions that foster holistic health. By prioritizing wellness, entrepreneurs can cultivate healthier work environments, ultimately leading to increased productivity and business success.

INTRODUCTION

Entrepreneurship is often envisioned and celebrated as a path to independence, innovation, and personal satisfaction. However, this arena of life has been less discussed and almost unexplored burnout in entrepreneurship. Entrepreneurs are generally stereotyped as those who have the magic of being

DOI: 10.4018/979-8-3693-3673-1.ch010

Copyright ©2025, IGI Global. Copying or distributing in print or electronic forms without written permission of IGI Global is prohibited.

successful, ambitious, and conventionally thriving. In reality, most entrepreneurs encounter excessive mental, emotional, and physical pressures. This builds in pressure to perform, and coupled with the inherent uncertainty of business ventures, can cumulate into a level of stress that leads to burnout. Entrepreneurial burnout is defined as chronic stress, emotional exhaustion, and absence of detachment from one's job (Smith, 2024). It is not a reaction to long working hours but a result of factors that are unique to entrepreneurial experience.

Entrepreneurs face pressures far different from those encountered by the traditional employee. Their experience is not shared in the same way that responsibilities are shared within conventional jobs. Conventional jobs share the responsibilities, quite often at the control of a larger organizational structure, whereas a lone entrepreneur is burdened with the success and failure of his or her venture. Business in the early stages, uncertainty over market conditions, and continuous need to innovate contribute to this high-stakes environment. With most entrepreneurs, the stakes feel profoundly personal-most have invested not only their finances but very crucial identity within their business (Shanafelt et al.,2017). Thus, in a moment of this pressure, it becomes devastating and tends to degenerate into burnout unless well managed. Contrary to most corporate burnout, when characterized by overwork and an absence of control, most entrepreneurial burnout is driven off to an extent by the immense emotional investments and personal risks entrepreneurs take (Rothenberger,2017).

Once entrepreneurial burnout manifests, effects will fall on the individual and the businesses that he or she is responsible for leading. A burned-out entrepreneur may lose creative drive, become indecisive, and turn cynical about work. All these psychological and mental issues may result in a reduced level of effectiveness in leadership that will eventually result in decreased productivity levels and finally lead to business failure (Bazarko et al., M. J. (2013). This is particularly concerning as startups and small firms depend on their founders' passion and vision to grow and survive. In this aspect, entrepreneurial burnout affects the entrepreneur's well-being and undermines the sustainability of his or her venture.

Several socioeconomic and cultural conditions are cited to have culminated in the reflection of entrepreneurial burnout. One such factor is the cult of hustle culture, which encourages unwarranted hard work and sacrifice in the name of success. It creates an unhealthy working culture among entrepreneurs and adds to other pressure factors. Media and the so-called high-profile success stories do not consider the aspects of self-care, balance, and mental health. For entrepreneurs, the burden of remaining "on top of their game" and looking like invincible heroes forces them to stretch even further, ignore signals that they may be tired, and wait until they are consumed with exhaustion (Goldberg et al.,1996). Rapid technological changes, globalization, and associated factors raise the threat levels against entrepreneurs by increasing competition and forcing it to become more difficult for entrepreneurs to take a step back and leave behind their businesses, thereby making the stress even higher.

As the population of entrepreneurs increases, it is evident that their mental health needs to be tended to. Entrepreneurial communities and society, in general, need to address burnout among entrepreneurs as an individual problem and a systemic one (Wach et al.,2021). Only a proper understanding of its roots will help develop wellness programs that support entrepreneurs in maintaining wellness and productivity.

UNDERSTANDING CAUSES OF ENTREPRENEURIAL BURNOUT

Entrepreneurial burnout is a multi-dimensional disease that stems from a combination of various personal, environmental, and psychological stressors. It's the unique nature of the entrepreneurial venture, high risks, and constant pressure that provides fertile ground in which to begin burnout (Omrane et al.,2018). Unlike normal career paths, entrepreneurs face a set of challenges that are exhaustible but can easily get overwhelming if not managed well. Understanding what drives entrepreneurial burnout, the first move is toward understanding the problem.

- **Financial Stress and Insecurity**

Economic insecurity appears to be most closely related to the root cause of entrepreneurial burnout. First, starting an enterprise is a capital-intensive endeavor that requires significant savings, a lot of debt, or funds through external investment to make ideas become reality. The always increasing pressure to raise incomes and to ensure profit margins can be a heavy mental strain, particularly at the early stages of the business, as it is never certain how things will go. Entrepreneurs worry about cash flow, payroll, or worse, money being taken away, which creates chronic stress. Financial stress frequently brings feelings of insecurity and disbelief, so it feeds into burnout.

- **Overwork and Lack of Boundaries**

Entrepreneurs are accustomed to longer working hours, often making work-life balance very difficult to define. Passion and drive that propel them to succeed sometimes spill over to areas where necessary boundaries should exist. Unlike employees, entrepreneurs tend to have boundaries by time but may feel available 24/7 to fix a problem, handle a client, or take advantage of a new opportunity. There is little time for recovery and only so much time before exhaustion sets in. The relentless pace without enough downtime deteriorates mental and physical well-being, which allows for burnout.

- **Isolation and Lack of Support**

Although entrepreneurship can be rewarding, it is usually a lonely journey. Entrepreneurs may work alone or with very few others, as opposed to large organizations, which have support systems. The lack of colleagues with whom to share the workload, offer one an ear regarding tricky issues, and keep up with friends during laughter and gossip leaves them isolated. Isolation is intensified when they perceive that they need to have solutions to every question and can't show signs of vulnerability. Without this infrastructure of support, entrepreneurs have to struggle with the risks of stress and uncertainty on their own. Additionally, apprehensions about appearing feeble or unsuccessful can also make entrepreneurship deter individuals from seeking assistance, even during struggles.

- **Emotional Investment and Identity Ties**

Entrepreneurs are very emotionally invested in their ventures. It often binds the entrepreneur's identity to the fate of their venture. Such investment may lead to a multiplier effect, where setbacks, failures, or losses hurt all the more. Challenges while facing small business issues make the entrepreneur almost feel as though everything is lost- personal failure mounts feelings of inadequacy and self-doubt. High pressure to succeed at all costs often places entrepreneurs over their edge, sacrificing their well-being in the bargain. While emotional attachment and identification with their business can give a sense of identity to an entrepreneur, overtime it can also blur the lines of dividing one's personal life from professional responsibilities, thereby worsening the risk of burnout.

- **Perfectionism and Fear of Failure**

Many entrepreneurs are driven by perfectionism: to be better than everyone else and never to fail. This dangerous combination of traits feeds ambition and high standards but can leave a person completely driven with no relief. Entrepreneurs tend to overburden themselves with delegating, trusting people to meet their higher standards, which makes them over-committed. Fear of failure is compounded by an even deeper fear of not impressing investors and employees or loved ones-it is something that creates constant stress and anxiety in them (Bolpagni et al.,2024). The pressure to be perfect, tempered by trials and tribulations typical of business ventures, drove entrepreneurs to psychological exhaustion.

- **Technological Overload and Constant Connectivity**

In the hyperconnected world, entrepreneurs are never turned off by technology. Due to the proliferation of smartphones, email, and social media, entrepreneurs cannot disengage from work. Constant connectivity breeds information overload and decision fatigue, which adds to burnout. They will not have time to calm their minds when they have to be accessible to customers, investors, or changing markets. Pressure to be relevant, active in social platforms and keeping track of the business's performance in real-time creates a heavy psychological burden with nearly no time to self-recover.

Understanding these core causes of entrepreneurial burnout brings up the requirement of specific interventions and wellness programs for entrepreneurs. These targeted challenges can really help entrepreneurs sustain themselves to pursue their business goals.

- **Wellness Programs in Entrepreneurship**

With more recognition given to entrepreneurial burnout, an interest in wellness programs intended to prevent and mitigate burnout is found. Traditionally implemented in corporate environments, these programs are now adapted for entrepreneurs' education in mental, physical, and emotional well-being. They help entrepreneurs manage stress, balance work and life, and be resilient (Horn et al.,2020) Entrepreneurship demands high; integrating wellness practices into everyday life is what secures that long-term success and sustainability.

Entrepreneurial wellness programs were designed to look at the challenges entrepreneurs face specifically. Unlike employees within bigger organizations, entrepreneurs do not have the structural support of HR departments or formal wellness initiatives (Jones et al.,2019). Therefore, business owners are responsible for their own wellness and that of their business. Finding resources and tools to keep them proactive and equipped to tackle stress is pretty important for them. Generally, entrepreneurial wellness programs may encompass stress management techniques, physical fitness exercises, mindfulness practices, and mental health counseling (Carnevale & Hatak,2020). In addition to preventing the backlash of burnout, wellness programs can be targeted toward enhancing productivity and creativity, and toward better decision-making based on mental and physical health.

Wellness Programs for Entrepreneurs: Similar to corporate ones, wellness programs for entrepreneurs aim at a more isolated and challenging entrepreneurial life: They may include exercise plans, nutrition coaching, regular health assessments, and many more (Sforzo et al.,2020). These programs will help entrepreneurs, who are time-constrained and normally disregard their physical health, including exercise and healthy eating habits in their daily and weekly schedules, thus increasing their energy levels and resilience (Hoert et al.,2018). Mental health support via therapy, counseling, or workshops on stress management is also important, given the high anxiety, depression, and emotional exhaustion levels among entrepreneurs (Attridge,2019). Early mental health would alleviate entrepreneurs of psychological and emotional stress associated with handling a business.

Mindfulness and meditation also became popular as wellness programs, which enable entrepreneurs to feel less stressed and be more focused (Greiser & Martini,2018). Some of these wellness activities, such as meditation, yoga, or breathing exercises, can help entrepreneurs reach a mindful state, fostering emotional regulation and stress resilience (Randerson,2020).These practices are at their best in reminding entrepreneurs to step back from the day-to-day pressures involved in running the business, giving them mental clarity and the sense that they are more in control.

Other wellness programs include peer support networks and coaching services. This is because many entrepreneurs are placed in isolated environments (Williamson et al.,2021). Such networks help entrepreneurs connect with other people experiencing the same things, promoting community and emotional support (Kuhn et al.,2021). Professional coaching, for example, informs an entrepreneur on how to integrate professional and personal life so that he or she never forgets the well-being even when focusing on business success.

Even though these wellness programs could shift the nature of the entrepreneurial experience, there is a problem. Cost and access are key limitations: many entrepreneurs lack the financial capital to invest in programs that give them full feelings of wellness. Moreover, entrepreneurship culture has naturalized overwork and hustle, discouraging individuals from practicing self-care (Nambisan & Baron,2021). Despite all this, the growing awareness of burnout and its implications on business performance has been such that more entrepreneurs are realizing the value of wellness programs as part of their long-term strategic success.

In the long run, wellness programs for entrepreneurs are essential tools that can help combat burnout and enhance business operations. Focusing on health at both physical and mental levels can help entrepreneurs maintain their energy, creativity, and resilience for success.

EVALUATING THE EFFECTIVENESS OF WELLNESS PROGRAMS

Evaluating the result of wellness programs in terms of reducing entrepreneurial burnout is essential to understand whether they are beneficial and sustainable in the long term or not. Because both professional and personal life often overlap for entrepreneurs, wellness programs must help them deal with short-term stressors but also contribute to long-term well-being and resilience (Peñalvo et al.,2021). In summary, effectiveness assessment requires different dimensions, from health improvement in every aspect - be it in mental or physical terms - to increased productivity at the business front and personal satisfaction.

Perhaps the most telling measure of wellness programs' effectiveness is looking at the change in mental health outcomes. Entrepreneurs are generally stressed, anxious, and emotionally drained, all before getting close to burnout (Pesis-Katz et al.,2020). In other words, effective wellness initiatives would show consequential changes. One would notice a reduction in the level of stress, better emotional regulation, and a more enhanced capacity to cope with problems among entrepreneurs who complete mindfulness or therapy interventions (Song & Baicker, 2019). Such developments can be monitored over time by means of surveys, self-assessment tools, and interviews, thereby throwing some light on how well the program does in addressing the mental health needs. Decreases in reported symptoms of anxiety and depression can be a good indicator of the success of a program to help mental well-being (Lattie et al.,2019).

The result that wellness programs bring about physical health is another very important aspect of evaluating the effectiveness of wellness programs. Chronic stress and burnout mainly present in physical form: chronic tiredness, poor sleep, and eventually even cardiovascular conditions (Moss,2021). Entrepreneurs who participate in wellness activities, which include measures like fitness, nutrition, or sleep management, should show remarkable health benefits in their physiology. One can measure these by improved energy levels, better sleep quality, and increased physical fitness using health assessments, wearable technology, or self-reporting tools (Becker,2019). This improvement of the body, in turn, benefits personal health and also business performance because entrepreneurs with good physical well-being are more productive and are less likely to fall victim to illness.

Another way through which one can assess the wellness programs is through business performance metrics: "If a wellness effort successfully reduces burnout, it should result in increased decision-making capabilities, creativity, and productivity.". An entrepreneur who is less mentally fatigued and less stressed may focus more on activities that matter to his business- strategic planning, problem-solving, and innovation (Kubzansky et al.,2018). Increased productivity, creativity, and business outcomes, such as revenue growth or improvement in customer satisfaction, serve as tangible evidence for the enhancement of personal well-being and business success brought by these wellness programs. The entrepreneurs can also self-evaluate these results through goal setting and tracking their performance. Still, others can evaluate them on the improvements they have made concerning their work based on positive attention from well-being practices.

Other than health and performance results, sustainability wellness becomes a long way of ensuring the sustainability of its outcomes. Programs that provide relief in the short run and fail to build sustainable habits might not help prevent burnout (Passey et al., 2018). However, an effective wellness program should integrate sustainable practices that entrepreneurs can adopt within their regular routines. Participation rates continue over time, adherence to wellness activities, and continued usage of techniques such as mindfulness, exercise, or therapy represent a few ways through which the effectiveness of wellness programs can be assessed by determining whether these policies promote lasting changes. The ease with which entrepreneurs maintain these habits in the face of ongoing business pressures and the promotion of long-term resiliency represent additional important considerations for evaluation.

Whereby, participant's feedback is utilized as part of the evaluation of wellness programs. Testimonials by entrepreneurs in terms of qualitative data like interviews and focus groups can provide deep insights into how the participants perceive the value of wellness initiatives. This is feedback on which aspects of the program are really worth it, and which require more improvement. It will also reveal cultural or individual reasons for lack of participation, such as financial constraints, busy schedules, or stigma attached to seeking help, which can all affect the program's overall effectiveness (Lowenstein et al.,2018).

Ideally, an effective wellness program would help entrepreneurs not only handle current stress and burnout but provide them with tools to prevent future ones as well. Organizations and individuals would be able to gauge how well wellness programs work toward achieving genuine, sustainable mental and physical health outcomes; business performance; long-term sustainability; and participant feedback. Further refinement of wellness programs based on rigorous evaluations will make them an even more helpful tool in promoting the well-being and success of entrepreneurs as awareness of entrepreneurial burnout grows.

Challenges in Implementing Wellness Programs for Entrepreneurs

While wellness programs can radically reduce entrepreneurial burnout, the implementation of these wellness programs comes with different challenges. Whereas other organizational employees are likely provided with different wellness resources, entrepreneurs must scout or even develop their own wellness solutions (Hameed&Irfan,2019). The stringent entrepreneurship with financial and cultural expectations creates an environment that makes it difficult for entrepreneurs to seek wellness. These challenges, therefore, pose a platform for innovative, flexible, and accessible wellness interventions tailor-made for the entrepreneurial experience.

- Time Constraints and Overcommitment

Perhaps, the biggest barrier to wellness programs is time constraints among entrepreneurs. It's quite a fact that working hours are usually hectic, with little room for self-care activities. Entrepreneurs-some who may have just started- are absorbed by tasks like product development, customer management, and fundraising. Most entrepreneurs think they cannot afford the time away from work to focus on wellness. Entrepreneurs are thrust into needing always to be "on," and they suffer from shame and even guilt whenever they cannot get away from their business (Bugaut-Heichelbech et al.,2023). This over-commitment creates stress and burnout cycles in which wellness programs can find a little toehold.

- Financial Limitations

Most entrepreneurs, particularly those in the early stages of starting a business, generally have little money. Well, at such tight cash flow, money is not invested in wellness programs, because the entrepreneurs feel they do not have any justification to allocate their hard-earned money to wellness. Many people cannot afford wellness programs like personal coaching, membership of fitness clubs, or counselors and therapists on mental health issues. Even though investing in wellness may pay off in the long run with a boost in productivity and avoidance of burnout, it is hard for entrepreneurs to justify the price tag upfront, especially when they are uncertain about their resources. Adding to this is the confusion on well-priced or cost-free resources that could be used similarly to mitigate burnout.

• Cultural Expectations and the "Hustle" Mentality

Entrepreneurial culture often glorifies overwork and "hustle," meaning that promoting wellness programs becomes a challenging task. Entrepreneurship culture often depicts the entrepreneur as "unsleeping, relentless heroes willing to do whatever it takes to make the entrepreneurial dream come true." In this context, rest, mindfulness, or self-care would only be symptomatic of weakness or lack of commitment. Many entrepreneurs internalize these cultural norms, and the fear that attending to their well-being might constitute a lack of dedication to business leads them to neglect their wellness (Dijkhuizen et al.,2018). In an entrepreneurial community where discussing mental health and self-care is generally shunned, even wellness programs meet much resistance because most entrepreneurs could not countenance doing something perceived as unproductive or indulgent.

• Isolation and Lack of Peer Support

In the final mile, entrepreneurship can be a lonely affair, and most entrepreneurs are without support networks that incite engagement with wellness programs. While corporate employees may have their wellness initiatives sponsored by their HR departments, entrepreneurs are usually left to fend for themselves in sifting through the confusions of wellness. Indeed, due to a lack of a structural support network, motivation is the only motivator for incorporating wellness into the frenetic lives of entrepreneurs. Furthermore, competition in entrepreneurship may deter individuals from interacting with people who participate in wellness activities. Moreover, if an entrepreneur does not gain a feeling of community and peer support, he will find it difficult to maintain wellness practices which intensify persistence of burnout.

• Difficulty in Sustaining Wellness Practices

Once entrepreneurs embrace wellness programs, they will certainly have difficulties in maintaining them over the long-run period. Entrepreneurship is not good ground for consistency in wellness routines because of its unpredictable and sometimes volatile nature. An entrepreneur can start out enthusiastically with a wellness program but lose interest when the demands for the business escalate. In any case, poor chances exist for sustainability of wellness programs that do not fit neatly into the lifestyle of the entrepreneur (De Freitas & Cohen,2024). For example, exhaustive or time-consuming wellness activities do not fit well in an entrepreneur's unpredictable schedule, so the activities would eventually prove frustrating and are deserted. Always under pressure to attend to their business's operations at the cost of personal well-being increases the difficulty of long-term wellness habits.

• Lack of Tailored Wellness Solutions

Most wellness programs are designed with more "ordinary" employees or corporate environments in mind and may not therefore be relevant to entrepreneurs. Entrepreneurs have specific challenges facing them, including financial instability, potential isolation, and emotional investment in their business requiring specific wellness interventions (Wagner et al., 2022). Generic wellness programs that focus only on traditional work-life balance strategies may not interest an entrepreneur who requires more flexibility and solutions tailored to this fast-paced and sometimes unpredictable lifestyle. Secondly, a lack of wellness programs relevant to entrepreneurial experience will give entrepreneurs the impression that these initiatives are not applicable or useful and will not participate at all.

- Limited Awareness and Education

The lack of awareness and education on the advantages provided by wellness programs also worsens the implementation problems. Most entrepreneurs, especially new ones, are unaware that there is a wellness-performance connection in business; therefore, they view wellness as an individual aspect that has nothing to do with one's entrepreneurial success while, in reality, it is for the maintenance of their strength, creativity, and decision-making capacity (Shir et al.,2019). Apart from this, the information relating to what one can achieve by venturing into wellness programs or even the ways of applying such wellness services within an entrepreneurial schedule is also scarce at times. This would be easily overcome when enlightening entrepreneurs on the long-term benefits of wellness programs and ways of integrating them into their entrepreneurial lifestyle.

Although there is high potential from wellness programs, time, cost, cultural, and isolation demands as well as lack of need-specific solutions have to be met and overcome. Hence the entrepreneurs will be able to handle the stresses inherent in the job they are doing while at the same time being sustainably successful by making wellness programs more accessible, affordable, and relevant with the aid of cultural change that incorporates well-being as the prime goal.

Types of Wellness Programs for Entrepreneurs

Entrepreneurship presents a range of challenges that uniquely demand wellness. Entrepreneurs face stresses and anxieties and must keep their physical and emotional well-being in top condition. Wellness programs can help entrepreneurs cope with the strain of their grueling business careers and achieve the right balance and strength. Here are some of the wellness programs tailored to the entrepreneur's needs and supporting their all-around wellness and business success (Palmer et al.,2021; Omrane et al.,2018; Sánchez-García et al.,2018).

1. Mental Health and Emotional Wellness Programs

Mental well-being is the lifeline of any entrepreneur. The stress, anxiety, or strain a person experiences dealing with uncertainty or financial risks while managing the business often comes from these individuals (Nisa et al.,2023). Entrepreneurial mental health programs focus on these kinds of issues.

- Counseling and Therapy Services: Professional mental health services provided in the form of one-to-one therapy or counseling can help the entrepreneurs learn to deal with anxiety, depression, among other emotional issues. Counseling and therapy services provide an environment where an entrepreneur can vent their emotions and develop strategies about effective coping strategies.
- Entrepreneurial support groups, whether online or offline, enable one to interact with peers who have encountered similar kinds of obstacles. There is emotional support involved, sharing advice, and a feeling of being part of a community, which can be vital for fighting isolation.
- Workshops and Webinars: Workshops and webinars on mental health provide hands-on skills, tools, and techniques for stress management, emotional competence, and resilience building.

Some topics may include techniques on stress management, work-life integration, and managing some emotional ups and downs of entrepreneurship.

2. Physical Health and Fitness Programs

Physical fitness directly affects psychological wellbeing and productivity in general. Entrepreneurial individuals who spend many hours sitting or working at their desks will benefit from programs emphasizing physical fitness. Entrepreneurial physical wellness includes:

- Structured exercise and fitness coaching: Membership in a gym, online workout classes, or work with a personal fitness coach could be beneficial for increasing one's energy and focus as well as to the entrepreneur's overall well-being. Entrepreneurs will find activities that fit into their schedule and perhaps benefit from short periods of high-intensity workouts or yoga practices that can reduce stress.
- Nutrition Counseling: Entrepreneurs are always forgetting about nutrition through poor eating habits due to their hectic schedule, which leads to poverty in health. Nutrition counseling programs provide unique meal plans while educating them on good eating habits to ensure that entrepreneurs prepare their bodies well for long working hours ahead.
- Health Monitoring Wearable Technology: Startup entrepreneurs can simply use a smartwatch or health apps to count the number of steps, monitor sleep, and track heart rate as ways to easily monitor their physical activity, sleep patterns, and heart rate. These devices keep people in check and offer them raw data regarding health.

3. Mindfulness and Meditation Programs

The rising demand among entrepreneurs who want to manage stress and increase focus in mindfulness and meditation practices enhances emotional balance, clarity, and mental resilience by encouraging people to be present and grounded (De Freitas & Cohen, 2024). Included in this category are programs:

- Guided Meditation Apps: Headspace, Calm, and Insight Timer can be an app providing guided meditations that focus on stress reduction, enhancing focus, or sleep. All these apps can help entrepreneurs practice mindfulness through shorter sessions that can fit their busy lifestyle.
- Mindfulness retreats and workshops: The mindfulness retreat will provide an opportunity for entrepreneurs to spend more time in the company of themselves; such experiences really help demarcate time for satisfying daily business demands from the scope of mental well-being. Workshops on mindfulness and meditation also provide practical tools for introducing these principles into daily life.
- Breathing exercises and stress management: short daily exercises help entrepreneurs tackle the stress in the moment, especially within high-pressure periods. Programs which teach technique such as diaphragmatic breathing or progressive muscle relaxation can significantly reduce the state of stress and level of anxiety.

4. Financial Wellness Programs

The most common cause of burnout among entrepreneurs is financial stress. It becomes hard to balance both business and personal finances, cash flow, and the uncertainty in income created by financial stress. It then affects the mental wellness of entrepreneurs. Most of the financial wellness programs targeted to help entrepreneurs include:

- Financial Planning and Budgeting Tools: Financial planning and budgeting tools are appropriately offered to the entrepreneurs by financial advisors or online platforms, which enables them to manage the financial aspects of the business and their personal lives effectively. It also provides strategies in budgeting and tax planning and cash flow management advice on managing financial stress.
- Debt Management Resources: For the entrepreneur who carries personal as well as professional debt, debt management programs teach how to reduce liabilities, consolidate loans and create payments that are sustainable. These financial coaches assist entrepreneurs in focusing on the right areas for debt repayment while they continue investing in the growth of their businesses.
- Financial Literacy Workshops: Entrepreneurship financial literacy workshops provide entrepreneurs with the vast wealth of knowledge and skills that equip them to make the right sound financial decisions. Some of the retirement planning, management of business expenses, and establishment of an emergency fund form part of the workshops.

5. Holistic Wellness Programs

Holistic wellness programs approach the view of comprehensive wellness to take into account connections between physical, mental, emotional, and spiritual health. Often, entrepreneurs find programs which include a balanced amount of both wellness strategies help promote one's overall life balance. Some holistic wellness programs may include:

- Health Coaching and Wellness: Health coaches offer personal wellness programs that include nutrition, exercise, mental health support, and lifestyle change. The health coaches will team with the entrepreneurs in coming up with appropriate wellness goals and will keep them in check of their need to maintain their wellness overtime.
- Alternative Healing Practices: This practice might be through acupuncture, chiropractic care, or massage therapy, which will give the entrepreneur relief from the pressure and rejuvenation of the body because of too long hours at work and pressure.
- Work-Life Integration Strategies: Holistic programs include some strategies through which work life integration is improved. This helps entrepreneurs have personal well-being without jeopardizing business success. Their ability to create clear boundaries, optimal use of time, and personal fulfilment besides professional success is encouraged.

6. Technology-Enabled Solutions for Wellness

Since technology has also contributed greatly towards wellness, several programs include digital platforms through which wellness becomes more accessible for entrepreneurs (Omrane et al.,2018; Sánchez-García et al.,2018). These are, in fact, technology-enabled solutions, including

- Telehealth and Virtual Therapy: Entrepreneurs can receive therapy and counseling services through telehealth, which allows them to schedule sessions in the midst of their busy lives. Virtual therapy eliminates the barriers of travel and time, making the support given more accessible.
- AI-Powered Wellness Apps: AI-powered wellness apps can offer tailored wellness programs for entrepreneurs based on personal needs. The wellness apps can depend on data from wearable devices or self-reported feedback by relying on the particular apps to suggest meditation techniques, exercise routine, or other stress management techniques to the entrepreneur.
- Online Communities and Wellness Platforms: For very busy entrepreneurs, it's priceless to have digital platforms offering wellness courses, mental health support, and helping people connect with each other. Online wellness communities provide space where entrepreneurs can hook up with other people with similar interests, such as accessing tools or seeking wellness challenges that create a sense of accountability among participants.

Tailored wellness programs for entrepreneurs range from mental well-being to physical fitness and financial wellness initiatives. These programs address unique challenges entrepreneurs face that will contribute to minimizing burnout and maximization of productivity, eventually fostering long-term success (Song & Baicker, 2019). High-tech technologies and flexibility in wellness initiatives are increasingly accessible to entrepreneurs who seek to integrate well-being into their daily routines and entrepreneurial journeys.

INNOVATIVE APPROACHES TO WELLNESS: DIGITAL AND AI-POWERED SOLUTIONS

In innovative approaches to wellness, digital and AI-powered solutions are necessary. For entrepreneurs, who run businesses at breathtaking speeds with full doses of fueling from the digital, wellness programs ought to be in pace, too, with the demands of modern business leaders (De Freitas & Cohen,2024). Though effective, it may not always fit into the demanding lifestyle of entrepreneurs through traditional wellness strategies. Some of the most outstanding flexible, accessible, and personalized digital and AI-powered wellness solutions will allow entrepreneurs to incorporate wellness practices into their daily lives in a completely non-disruptive manner without compromising the goals of the business (Bolpagni et al.,2024; Khalid et al.,2024). These cutting-edge technologies are changing how well-being is served, making it easier for entrepreneurs to preserve their mental, emotional, and physical health amidst the pressures of business.

1. AI-Powered Mental Health Support

It has transformed the delivery of mental health services with artificial intelligence to provide new sources of emotional and psychological support for entrepreneurs (Komalasari, 2024). AI-based platforms will offer specific and on-demand care for mental health to entrepreneurs at their will, whenever it arises.

- AI Chatbots and Virtual Therapists: AI chatbots like Woebot or Wysa can use NLP to provide immediate emotional support, or as a source of mental health guidance. Entrepreneurs can access them 24/7 and seek help at which time they are dealing with stress, anxiety, or depression. The AI guide can take users through CBT strategies, mindfulness exercises, or any other emotion processing-orientated exercises, giving instant support in the heat of the moment.
- Mood and Mental Status Tracking. Based on AI, Apps such as Youper or Replika allow a business owner to track their mood, stress levels, and mental status changes over time. Algorithmic-based AI analyzes trends in behavior and makes recommendations based on the individual. Entrepreneurs will be more alert to mental status changes, track them, and take early actions when faced with emotional challenges before turning into full-blown burnout.

2. Digital Fitness and Wellness Platforms

Maintaining proper physical health is crucial to entrepreneurial success; however, finding time to accommodate a fitness routine sometimes becomes an issue (Yoon et al.,2024). Digital wellness platforms use technology to devise customized fitness programs for entrepreneurs who help them achieve healthy lifestyles even during hectic schedules.

- Virtual Fitness Coaches and Apps: Websites like Future, Freeletics, and MyFitnessPal offer personalized fitness coaching and workout plans customized according to an entrepreneur's lifestyle. Digital applications giving options to exercise as an entrepreneur on a self-driven basis, or home, or in transit, or even at the office are also part of these digital tools. The workouts on these platforms are tailored according to the user's feedback, goals, and improvements toward offering a personalized and impactful approach to physical health, using AI-based recommendations.
- Wearable Fitness Trackers: Activities, heart rate, and sleep patterns are monitored through devices like Fitbit, Garmin, and Apple Watch; therefore, entrepreneurs directly receive real-time access to their health. Instant feedback and reminders from such wearables encourage entrepreneurs to engage in more movement and rest. With such fitness objectives and their progress, the traditional wellness practice of entrepreneurs could be an easy incorporation.

3. AI-powered Mindfulness and Meditation Apps

Mindfulness and meditation are proven tools in preventing stress and sharpening one's focus in the long run-which, when you think about it, is an invaluable tool for entrepreneurs. Mindfulness and meditation apps powered by AI provide the best-fit solutions for the busy entrepreneur's lifestyle and allow for mental clarity and emotional equilibrium (Chand & Sazima, 2024; Wang et al.,2024).

- Personalized Meditation Apps: This sees Calm, Headspace, and Insight Timer use AI to curate sessions for needs, stress levels, and moods. Entrepreneurs then have access to a personalized library of guided meditations, breathing exercises, and mindfulness practice customized to schedules and personal challenges. Busy professionals can complete their practices in minutes daily through these artificial intelligence-empowered platforms.
- Stress and Sleep Tracking: Most meditation apps have now synchronized with wearable devices to track stress levels and sleep patterns in order to even provide more personalized recommendations. Headspace, for example, can synchronize with an Apple Watch for guided breathing when stress levels are at an all-time high. Similarly, Calm conducts sleep stories and relaxation techniques when it receives real-time data from sleep monitors that helps entrepreneurs enhance the quality of rest and general wellbeing.

4. AI-Driven Financial Wellness Tools

Financial stress is one of the major causes of entrepreneurial burnout. The financial wellness tools and solutions powered by AI help ease this stress by offering entrepreneurs automated assistance in financial planning, budgeting, and decision-making for their businesses and personal expenditure (Bolpagni et al.,2024; Khalid et al.,2024). These can offer the real-time insights entrepreneurs need to manage their business and personal finances effectively.

- AI-Driven Finance Platforms: These are platforms like Albert or Cleo, which uses AI to offer customized personal financial advice, automatic budgeting, expense tracking, and saving. Such apps look at the small business' income and consumption patterns, business expenditures, giving real-time advice on how to manage business finances accordingly. AI-driven recommendations give entrepreneurs more room to improve financial decisions.
- Cash Flow and Risk Management Tools: Business entrepreneurs will look forward to cash flow and risk management tools provided by AI, such as QuickBooks or Xero. The AI will analyze financial data and provide this information about what may happen in the future, allowing the entrepreneur to prepare to cope with fluctuations in revenue or increases in expenditure. By automating tasks related to financial management, entrepreneurs reduce stress and focus on strategic growth of a business.

5. Virtual Wellness Communities and Support Networks

Entrepreneurship can be an isolated affair. Virtual wellness communities and support networks provide a sense of belonging and accountability as entrepreneurs connect with one another in pursuit of similar wellness goals (Khalid et al.,2024).

- Online Health Communities: Platforms such as Wellset or Mighty Networks let an entrepreneur easily enter and access a wellness-focused community where there is connectivity with peers, participation in wellness challenges, and accessing of resources. The communities give entrepreneurs access to wellness experts, group coaching, and peer support that nurtures accountability and encouragement. Online wellness workshops, fitness challenges, and mindfulness sessions enable entrepreneurs to bring about a propitious environment for their well-being.

- Peer Support Applications with AI: Circles or Wisdo are the applications that use AI to find peers aligned with the difficulty the entrepreneur faces and, therefore, creates a personal background for the support group of peers. The application utilizes AI to make deeper connections and give a space to discuss, among other things, stress, burnout, and well-being for entrepreneurs. Peer-to-peer support supports the emotional resilience and removes loneliness for entrepreneurs.

6. Telehealth and Virtual Therapy Services

This has made telehealth platforms easier to engage through, enabling entrepreneurs now to have easy access to mental health and wellness services (Szekeres & Valdes, 2022). Thus, entrepreneurs can make bookings for the sessions available in their hectic lives without traveling or sticking to time constraints through virtual therapy.

- On-Demand Therapy Platforms: Through BetterHelp, Talkspace, and Ginger, entrepreneurs can access a licensed therapist for video calls, phone calls, or message conversations. These flexible options fit entrepreneurs' schedules, enabling them to attend to mental health issues in real-time. Virtual therapy becomes a huge convenience for entrepreneurs as it pushes the agenda of mental health without compromising valuable hours of business.
- AI-Driven Mental Health Assessments: Many telehealth platforms are now integrating AI-powered mental health assessments to help therapists and entrepreneurs track their progress. Assessments will check patterns in behavior and emotional states to ultimately provide data-driven insights to tailor sessions and mental health interventions.

Digital and artificial intelligence wellness solutions are changing the way entrepreneurs make their wellness a priority. Digital and AI wellness solutions, being personal, flexible, and accessible, enable integrated wellness in an entrepreneur's life, thus contributing to fewer cases of burnout and increased productivity. As the technological landscape is rapidly changing, more opportunities will be designed for entrepreneurs to take advantage of digital wellness platforms so effectively to serve and maintain healthiness and thrive in business ventures.

Long-Term Impact of Wellness Programs on Entrepreneurial Sustainability

The effects of having wellness programs on entrepreneurial sustainability may go as far into the future as such programs can keep entrepreneurs away from stress. It is not just the relief of a short-term need to be suppressed by stress but a strategic investment in the length of business existence (Le Breton–Miller & Miller,2006). In times of uncertainty and ambiguity in ventures, the role wellness plays in helping entrepreneurs be resilient, productive, and healthy should never be underestimated. Their long-term effects spill over into individual well-being and also affect the culture in the organization, retention of employees, and ability to innovate (Ortiz-de-Mandojana & Bansal 2016). This piece discusses how long-term wellness interventions impact entrepreneurial sustainability and success.

1. Increased Productivity and Performance

Wellness programs are directly proportional to improved levels of performance among entrepreneurs and teams. Such programs create a mental, emotional, and physiological atmosphere that supports creativity and innovation (Wang et al.,2024).

- Better Concentration and Attentiveness: By engaging in higher levels of wellness, such as practicing mindfulness or fitness training, entrepreneurs will prepare themselves to work out through stress. This will allow people to sustain higher levels of concentration and attentiveness, thereby better sharpening their judgments, decisions, and problem-solving skills, further leading to better strategic planning and implementation.
- Higher Energy Levels: The physical aspect of health is the core of everything related to general energy. Those who observe healthy habits, such as exercising for a couple of hours, eating right, and resting adequately, are usually energetic during working hours. Higher energy has enabled entrepreneurs to complete tasks without burnout, enhancing performance and productivity.

2. Reduced Burnout and Turnover Rates

Such burnout is a common problem and could also endanger high rates of turnover and the loss of talented employees (Willard-Grace et al.,2019). Preventive measures in relation to potential risks associated with entrepreneurial burnout might generally be enhanced if wider wellness programs were implemented.

- Long-Term Psychological Benefits: Systematic support via mental health resources, such as counselling and peer networking, equips entrepreneurs with better ways to handle challenges without overwhelming stress. This helps an organization maintain openness related to mental health issues, thereby significantly reducing feelings of isolation and anxiety, which are two of the leading reasons for burnout.
- Worker Retention: Wellness programs indicate to the organization that it is genuinely interested in the employee's well-being. Employees will thus take pride in their engagement with such an organization and are less likely to leave it. The entrepreneur creates a stable and more experienced workforce in addition to talent retention, hence catalyzing business sustainability.

3. Promotion of a Positive Organizational Culture

Wellness programs help transform the organization's culture since they are based on teamwork, support, and respect. The organization's culture supports innovation and thus attracts the best talent.

- Team Cohesiveness and Collaboration: Wellness programs often utilize team-building activities that focus on the collaboration and communication of the employees. A team of employees who perform wellness activities together develop better interpersonal relationships, which can be integrated to develop much more effective business-oriented collaborations within the organization. The more coherent team is more likely to come up with innovative ideas and solutions for business problems, hence enhancing organizational performance.

- Attracting Talent and Building Reputation: The improvement of wellness as part of the policy of an organization enhances the reputation of the employer in the line of business. Top talents find their way into such organizations, while diverse perspectives and ideas blossom into culture characterized by a relationship of friends and mutual respect. An entrepreneur will regard the offer of wellness programs as a farsighted human resource investment with employees as a priority; hence making such a business a welcome site for all potential new employees.

4. Increased Innovation and Creativity

There is a great general rule: a healthy and well-supported workforce is often more innovative and creative. For this reason, it plays a very important role in long-term entrepreneurial success. Wellness programs that stimulate mental agility and reduce stress are pretty important to any culture of innovation.

- Encourages a Growth Mindset: Wellness programs focusing on professional development, such as workshops on creativity and innovation, foster a growth mindset among entrepreneurs and their teams. Such a mindset promotes willingness to experiment, an attitude to take risks, and adaptability-wonderfully essential elements of a sustainable entrepreneurial venture.
- Allowable Environment for Idea Formation: A wellness culture in an organization can allow the development of a safe environment to produce ideas and innovation. With wellness programs promoting brainstorming sessions, creative retreats, or innovation labs, entrepreneurs are empowered to delve into new ideas, without some form of fear holding them back from failure. This is what contributes to business growth.

5. Long Term Health and Financial Rewards

By investing in wellness programs, entrepreneurs and the organization are able to benefit from long-term returns both on health and finance (Yoon et al.,2024; Ortiz-de-Mandojana & Bansal, 2016). This is experienced through better well-being for the individual, which benefits the financial grounds of the business.

- Lower Healthcare Costs: Businesses that implement wellness programs within the organization are likely to experience lower healthcare costs from stress-related illnesses, mental health issues, and chronic disorders. Preventive care and healthy lifestyles ensure less medical expenditure by the entrepreneur and his or her employees, thus channeling these freed-up funds to other business lines.
- Improved Financial Performance: The financial performance of the organization improves because research reveals that well-developed wellness programs have led to better financial performance within the organizations. Healthy employees work more effectively and productively, generating more revenues. Again, the cost of employee turnover and health-care services is minimized, which implies the possibility of retaining the entrepreneurial business for many years.

The long-term effects of wellness programs on entrepreneurial sustainability are massive. These programs are very important to the success of sustainable business operations by helping to facilitate higher productivity, decrease burnout rates, build a supportive organizational culture, and drive innovation (Yoon et al.,2024). Moreover, giving regard to other health and financial benefits provides a strong argument for why entrepreneurs should pay attention to wellness when planning. It will be imperative to long-term survival in this fast-changing business world to invest well in the welfare of both entrepreneurs and their teams, navigating challenges, taking opportunities, and making it to success (Rucker, 2017).

POLICY AND SUPPORT FOR WELLNESS IN ENTREPRENEURSHIP

Supportive policies and frameworks for well-being within the entrepreneurial ecosystem must be established in recognition of wellness as important to sustainable entrepreneurial practices. Policymakers, business leaders, and support organizations play pivotal roles in nurturing environments conducive to health and wellness through which entrepreneurs may access resources to perform effectively (Babcock, 2021). This section discusses the various dimensions of the policy and support mechanisms that can fuel well-being in entrepreneurship, including government initiatives, organizational policies, and community support systems.

1. Government Initiatives and Policies

Wellness is influenced by many aspects of policy and mechanisms of support within the framework of government initiatives or policies.

- Incentives for Wellness Programs: Governments can offer incentives to businesses in implementing solid wellness programs. Such incentives can greatly reduce the burden on entrepreneurs, and thus they may adopt more health initiatives that could boost their employees' welfare and productivity. In this way, not only would individual businesses gain, but the general health of the working force would also improve.
- Access to Mental Health Services: The key is policies implemented by the government to increase access to mental health care, as entrepreneurs are easily victims of high levels of stress and anxiety. Such ways to extend telehealth services, subsidizing counseling services, and raise awareness about mental health can make a real difference for entrepreneurs and their teams. Of course, entrepreneurial education about mental health prepares current emerging entrepreneurs with tools to manage stress effectively.
- Policy Support for Work-Life Balance: Work-life balance can be supported through policies that include flexible work arrangements, paid family leaves, and mandatory vacation policies. This would help create a better work environment in terms of lowering burnout chances and hence long-term sustainability in entrepreneurial ventures. This policy for work-life balance challenges the government to invest in well-being to encourage entrepreneurship.

2. Organizational Policies and Practices

Such policies will provide an entrepreneurial environment within individual organizations and foster a culture of wellness that can thus resonate throughout the entrepreneurial environment.

- Comprehensive Well-being Programs: Organizations must set up and offer comprehensive well-being programs such that employees are provided for in all ways, be it physical or mental. Subsidized gym memberships, mental health days, wellness workshops, mindfulness training, and other activities for the well-being of their employees qualify this category in this regard. In this way, organizations show interest in providing a positive working place.
- Employee Assistance Programs: EAPs give employees confidential access to them when dealing with some personal or professional distress. There will be offered counseling, financial planning, and other sources of work-life balance. Through developing EAP in the organizational policies, entrepreneurs are assured that teams will be able to perform better in business and in life.
- Regular Assessments and Feedback Mechanisms: It is very important that wellness programs introduced in an organization should be evaluated to assist the organization to change as necessary, and then receive feedback from employees to establish areas of improvement and that wellness programs should be in line with the needs of the workforce. In this way, an organization can grow and evolve to suit its policies in such a way that team support thrives.

3. Community Support Systems

Apart from the individual organizations and government initiatives, wellness in entrepreneurship can also be triggered by community systems of support that partner various players toward a more encompassing approach to entrepreneur support (Ortiz-de-Mandojana & Bansal 2016).

- Networking and Mentorship Programs: The communities can offer networking events and mentorship programs which can connect entrepreneurs with more experienced professionals in the field. This network offers great business insights, emotional support, and guidance in managing the specific challenges of entrepreneurship. Wellness-based mentorship programs would certainly drive the entrepreneurs to take care of their health since they tend to put up with the pressure in running their businesses.
- Local Health and Wellness Resources. The local government and community organizations can collaborate to provide health and wellness resources for entrepreneurs through easier access to such facilities. Such departments would include holding workshops, health fairs, and more educative programs about managing stress, nutrition, and exercising the body. This would enable communities to promote entrepreneurs' responsibility over their wellbeing and develop a healthy culture for prosperity.
- Partnerships with Healthcare Providers: The collaboration between entrepreneurial organizations and healthcare providers can enhance wellness initiatives for the entrepreneurial community. When engaging with health professionals, entrepreneurs can avail themselves of available specific needs in designs workshops, screenings, and education materials. This partnership relates reliable information and support towards good health from the partners towards the entrepreneurs.

4. Awareness and Education

The general culture needs to find a new consciousness in health and wellness, which is how the importance of wellness must be raised in entrepreneurship.

- Educational Campaigns: The government, organizations, and communities can educate entrepreneurs about the benefits of wellness programs. These campaigns can focus on health-productivity relations-the health benefits translate to greater enterprise success. Therefore, education can guide stakeholders on how to motivate entrepreneurs in investing in their own personal development as a strategic priority.
- Incorporate wellness education in entrepreneurial education: One way of ensuring that the emerging entrepreneurs are well-attuned to maintaining their health well-being is through the incorporation of wellness education into entrepreneurship training programs. These would include stress management techniques, work-life balance, and self-care strategies that may be incorporated into the curricula of entrepreneurial education, in preparation for those who eventually develop businesses and encounter possible struggles on their part.

Entrepreneurs' long-term survival is well-related to his or her wellness. Therefore, it is of paramount importance to establish supportive policies and frameworks directed toward wellness in entrepreneurship. All this would be achievable if the government, organizational policies, community support systems, and educational efforts mobilized the stakeholders for supportive environments where entrepreneurs could thrive in personal and professional development (O'Neill, 2024). Hence, we invest in wellness to improve individual entrepreneurs' health and create a resilient entrepreneurial ecosystem. Wellness will be the driving force for entrepreneurship challenges and entrepreneurial opportunities as the entrepreneurial landscape continues to evolve.

FUTURE TRENDS IN WELLNESS PROGRAMS FOR ENTREPRENEURS

As more entrepreneurial activity takes place, so too do models of wellness initiatives tailored to support entrepreneurs through their journeys. The trends that are emerging today are arguably much closer to bespoke, technology-enabled, and integrative wellness, which will help entrepreneurs respond to the related challenges, hence becoming the subject of this section- several future trends likely to shape the future of wellness programs in entrepreneurship.

1. Personalization of Wellness Initiatives

Thus, the future of wellness programs will be a form of individualism, as the initiatives shall be designed and offered catering to different entrepreneurs' needs.

- Data-Driven Approach: The advancements in technology will make entrepreneurs better equipped with data analytics that can assist them in decision-making regarding better wellness. Wearable devices and health apps will inform them about better comprehension of physical activities, stress levels, and overall wellness. As entrepreneurs collect data regarding their health metrics, wellness programs could be adjusted to suit their needs based on specific objectives such as reduction of stress or improved fitness levels or mental health counseling.
- Customized Wellness Plans: Organizations are going to promote customized wellness plans that address the unique challenges of every entrepreneur. It might include personalized coaching, curated resources, and flexible options by which individuals can opt for some activity that they feel

sympathetic towards. Recognizing that the one-size-fits-all solution may not work, using such personalized approaches might help promote a higher rate of engagement and participation in wellness initiatives.

2. Integrate Technology and AI Solutions

Incorporation of technology and artificial intelligence into wellness programs is going to change how health and wellness resources are accessed by entrepreneurs.

- AI-Powered Health Platforms: AI-driven health platforms will offer entrepreneurs the best-suited, personalized wellbeing recommendation based on their habits and preferences. These could monitor the patterns of an entrepreneur's lifestyle and would, therefore, enable them to get practical advice and reminders with a corresponding set of resources to help an individual maintain a proper approach to well-being. Such automation and personalization should help promote the efficiency of wellness programs and equip entrepreneurs with health management capabilities.
- Virtual Wellbeing Communities: Virtual communities that focus on wellbeing will allow entrepreneurs to reach out to their peer groups, share experiences, and obtain support. These online forums will expand the discussions and workshops presented over the networking events with regards to wellbeing, and therefore will give entrepreneurs opportunities to approach other entrepreneurs and experts irrespective of geographical bounds. This fosters a sense of community and dispels isolation, thereby building a culture of community support.

3. Holistic View of Wellness

In the future, holistic wellness programs will focus more on the interconnected nature of physical, mental, and emotional dimensions of wellness (Wang et al.,2024).

- Mind-Body Integration. More and more wellness programs will include mindfulness, meditation, and yoga practices. When these are part of the wellbeing program in an entrepreneurial setup, it does not only help a person relax and ease stress but also greatly aids mental clarity and focus-qualities that are very important for the success of an entrepreneur. Mind-body techniques, learning how to live from a balanced perspective even in challenges, are some of the major virtue's entrepreneurs would gain from this approach.
- Work-Life Integration: Future wellness programs will work toward achieving work-life integration rather than balance. This will open flexible work environments that embrace personal commitments and self-care routines. Organizations will add policies in support of their employees to strike a healthy balance between work and life, which increases satisfaction and productivity.

4. Importance of Community and Social Ties

The future of wellness programs among entrepreneurs would be based on the significance of social networks and community support.

- Peer Support Networks: These will establish contact, experience, and advice sharing among entrepreneurs. This may be in local meetups or online forums. It can lead to collaboration and learning together. Through collective wisdom and experiences of peers, entrepreneurs will be able to reduce lonely feelings and improve their emotional wellbeing.
- CSR: As more and more organizations start adopting the value of wellness as a component in their CSR strategy, entrepreneurs will be able to contribute toward and participate in community wellness programs and partnerships with health organizations at the local level, therefore contributing to the overall wellbeing of their communities. This might endow business with better social attributes and attract socially conscious consumers and talent toward them.

5. Financial Wellness

As financial strain is one of the main causes of entrepreneurial burnout, the future wellness programs ought to comprise financial well-being as an integral aspect of the whole wellness package.

- Financial Literacy: Organizations will establish financial literacy that equips entrepreneurs with knowledge and skills needed for effective running of their financial operations. Some of the subjects to be considered for these programs are budgeting and investment strategies as well as understanding financial risks (Yoon et al.,2024). All the anxieties related to financial frustrations will be mitigated through empowering entrepreneurs with the access to financial education in making informed decisions that support them in their ventures.
- Access to Capital and Financing: These future wellness programs are also likely to provide access to resources which connect entrepreneurs with their financial advisors, funding options, and peer-to-peer lending sources. In this way, management can reduce the burden of uncertainty from financial constraints and create an environment conducive for sustainable businesses.

To be sure, the future of wellness for entrepreneurs is about transformation, influenced by the trends in personalization, technology integration, the holistic approach, community support, and financial wellness. And as entrepreneurs continue to advance through their journeys amid the continued challenges, the emerging trends shall serve as the building blocks and channels to promote health, resilience, and long-term sustainability. By embracing such trends, the entrepreneurial ecosystem will then be able to establish a culture that assumes well-being is an important feature of success, leading eventually to healthier entrepreneurs and more resilient businesses.

CONCLUSION

The pursuit of wellness programs for entrepreneurs captures the very essence of how well-being can play a critical role in building both individual success and the sustainability of entrepreneurial endeavors. More than ever now that the entrepreneurial landscape is becoming increasingly complex with its lightning-fast changes and mounting pressures, wellness initiatives become more important. Programs that work against multifaceted challenges will likely make entrepreneurs avoid burnout risk and achieve more productivity amidst a much healthier life-work balance.

Implications behind the wellness program evaluation imply that effective wellness translates into a wholesome concept that consists of physical, mental, and emotional well-being. Tailored wellness solutions are most beneficial for entrepreneurs since such solutions respond to the particularized needs of entrepreneurs, enabling proactive steps in healthy maintenance. Besides, the future of using technology and AI-powered tools to support the user through tailored resources in wellbeing is exciting, and it makes these resources more accessible and effective.

Looking forward, the trends unfolding in wellness programs - personalization, community engagement, and emphasis on financial well-being - are all the protests of a future that is more holistic and supportive for entrepreneurs. Organizations, policymakers, and communities must collaborate to develop frameworks that improve wellness while allowing entrepreneurs to push through difficulties. This collective responsibility of building a health-based culture would likely foster more robust businesses and more resilient entrepreneurial ecosystems.

Conclusion While the above argument convinces that great entrepreneurship is not just about survival of one owner, to many entrepreneurs, wellness programs would be more than just an optional add-on - they would be a critical success strategy. With wellness and that of their teams as a matter of concern for entrepreneurs, they are better equipped to face the uncertainties that mark their journey, drive innovation, and positively contribute to the economy. In this respect, recognizing the intrinsic link between health and entrepreneurial success will pave the way toward a future in which healthiness and business coexist harmoniously, ensuring a more sustainable and fulfilling entrepreneurial experience for all the time ahead.

REFERENCES

Attridge, M. (2019). A global perspective on promoting workplace mental health and the role of employee assistance programs. *American Journal of Health Promotion*, 33(4), 622–629. DOI: 10.1177/0890117119838101c PMID: 31006254

Babcock, J. (2021). The entrepreneurial characteristics of national board certified health and wellness coaches. *Coaching (Abingdon, UK)*, 14(2), 142–150. DOI: 10.1080/17521882.2020.1831562

Bazarko, D., Cate, R. A., Azocar, F., & Kreitzer, M. J. (2013). The impact of an innovative mindfulness-based stress reduction program on the health and well-being of nurses employed in a corporate setting. *Journal of Workplace Behavioral Health*, 28(2), 107–133. DOI: 10.1080/15555240.2013.779518 PMID: 23667348

Becker, G. A. (2019). *Investigating the Use of Wearable Activity Trackers to Determine Psychological Wellbeing* (Doctoral dissertation, Roosevelt University).

Bolpagni, M., Pardini, S., & Gabrielli, S. (2024). Human centered design of AI-powered Digital Therapeutics for stress prevention: Perspectives from multi-stakeholders' workshops about the SHIVA solution. *Internet Interventions : the Application of Information Technology in Mental and Behavioural Health*, 38, 100775. DOI: 10.1016/j.invent.2024.100775 PMID: 39314669

Bugaut-Heichelbech, S., Foltzer, D., & Paraschiv, C. (2023). Temporal Well-being of Entrepreneurs: An Empirical Investigation. *Revue de l'Entrepreneuriat/Review of Entrepreneurship*, 22(4), 15-41.

Carnevale, J. B., & Hatak, I. (2020). Employee adjustment and well-being in the era of COVID-19: Implications for human resource management. *Journal of Business Research*, 116, 183–187. DOI: 10.1016/j.jbusres.2020.05.037 PMID: 32501303

Chand, R., & Sazima, G. (2024). Mindful Technology. In *Mindfulness in Medicine: A Comprehensive Guide for Healthcare Professionals* (pp. 147–165). Springer Nature Switzerland. DOI: 10.1007/978-3-031-66166-2_9

De Freitas, J., & Cohen, I. G. (2024). The health risks of generative AI-based wellness apps. *Nature Medicine*, 30(5), 1–7. DOI: 10.1038/s41591-024-02943-6 PMID: 38684859

Dijkhuizen, J., Gorgievski, M., van Veldhoven, M., & Schalk, R. (2018). Well-being, personal success and business performance among entrepreneurs: A two-wave study. *Journal of Happiness Studies*, 19(8), 2187–2204. DOI: 10.1007/s10902-017-9914-6

Goldberg, R., Boss, R. W., Chan, L., Goldberg, J., Mallon, W. K., Moradzadeh, D., Goodman, E. A., & McConkie, M. L. (1996). Burnout and its correlates in emergency physicians: Four years' experience with a wellness booth. *Academic Emergency Medicine*, 3(12), 1156–1164. DOI: 10.1111/j.1553-2712.1996.tb03379.x PMID: 8959173

Greiser, C., & Martini, J. P. (2018). Unleashing the power of mindfulness in corporations. [BCG]. *The Boston Consulting Group*, 15(2), 109–122.

Hameed, I., & Irfan, Z. (2019). Entrepreneurship education: A review of challenges, characteristics and opportunities. *Entrepreneurship Education*, 2(3), 135–148. DOI: 10.1007/s41959-019-00018-z

Hoert, J., Herd, A. M., & Hambrick, M. (2018). The role of leadership support for health promotion in employee wellness program participation, perceived job stress, and health behaviors. *American Journal of Health Promotion*, 32(4), 1054–1061. DOI: 10.1177/0890117116677798 PMID: 27920214

Horn, D., Randle, N. W., & McNeil, S. R. (2020). A cross-disciplinary framework to measure workplace wellness program success. *S.A.M. Advanced Management Journal*, 85(1), 4–12.

Jones, D., Molitor, D., & Reif, J. (2019). What do workplace wellness programs do? Evidence from the Illinois workplace wellness study. *The Quarterly Journal of Economics*, 134(4), 1747–1791. DOI: 10.1093/qje/qjz023 PMID: 31564754

Khalid, U. B., Naeem, M., Stasolla, F., Syed, M. H., Abbas, M., & Coronato, A. (2024). Impact of AI-powered solutions in rehabilitation process: Recent improvements and future trends. *International Journal of General Medicine*, 17, 943–969. DOI: 10.2147/IJGM.S453903 PMID: 38495919

Komalasari, R. (2024). AI-Powered Wearables Revolutionizing Health Tracking and Personalized Wellness Management. *Timor Leste Journal of Business and Management*, 6, 42–50.

Kubzansky, L. D., Huffman, J. C., Boehm, J. K., Hernandez, R., Kim, E. S., Koga, H. K., Feig, E. H., Lloyd-Jones, D. M., Seligman, M. E. P., & Labarthe, D. R. (2018). Positive psychological well-being and cardiovascular disease: JACC health promotion series. *Journal of the American College of Cardiology*, 72(12), 1382–1396. DOI: 10.1016/j.jacc.2018.07.042 PMID: 30213332

Kuhn, K. M., Meijerink, J., & Keegan, A. (2021). Human resource management and the gig economy: Challenges and opportunities at the intersection between organizational HR decision-makers and digital labor platforms. *Research in Personnel and Human Resources Management*, 39, 1–46. DOI: 10.1108/S0742-730120210000039001

Lattie, E. G., Adkins, E. C., Winquist, N., Stiles-Shields, C., Wafford, Q. E., & Graham, A. K. (2019). Digital mental health interventions for depression, anxiety, and enhancement of psychological well-being among college students: Systematic review. *Journal of Medical Internet Research*, 21(7), e12869. DOI: 10.2196/12869 PMID: 31333198

Le Breton-Miller, I., & Miller, D. (2006). Why do some family businesses out-compete? Governance, long-term orientations, and sustainable capability. *Entrepreneurship Theory and Practice*, 30(6), 731–746. DOI: 10.1111/j.1540-6520.2006.00147.x

Lowensteyn, I., Berberian, V., Belisle, P., DaCosta, D., Joseph, L., & Grover, S. A. (2018). The measurable benefits of a workplace wellness program in Canada: Results after one year. *Journal of Occupational and Environmental Medicine*, 60(3), 211–216. DOI: 10.1097/JOM.0000000000001240 PMID: 29200188

Moss, J. (2021). *The burnout epidemic: The rise of chronic stress and how we can fix it*. Harvard Business Press.

Nambisan, S., & Baron, R. A. (2021). On the costs of digital entrepreneurship: Role conflict, stress, and venture performance in digital platform-based ecosystems. *Journal of Business Research*, 125, 520–532. DOI: 10.1016/j.jbusres.2019.06.037

Nisa, M., Srinivas, V., Rani, R., Prasad, K. D. V., & De, T. (2023). Analysing the Mental Health and Well-Being of Entrepreneurs. *Journal for ReAttach Therapy and Developmental Diversities*, 6(4s), 369–377.

O'Neill, R. (2024). By, for, with women? On the politics and potentialities of wellness entrepreneurship. *The Sociological Review*, 72(1), 3–20. DOI: 10.1177/00380261221142461

Omrane, A., Kammoun, A., & Seaman, C. (2018). Entrepreneurial burnout: Causes, consequences and way out. *FIIB Business Review*, 7(1), 28–42. DOI: 10.1177/2319714518767805

Ortiz-de-Mandojana, N., & Bansal, P. (2016). The long-term benefits of organizational resilience through sustainable business practices. *Strategic Management Journal*, 37(8), 1615–1631. DOI: 10.1002/smj.2410

Palmer, C., Kraus, S., Kailer, N., Huber, L., & Öner, Z. H. (2021). Entrepreneurial burnout: A systematic review and research map. *International Journal of Entrepreneurship and Small Business*, 43(3), 438–461. DOI: 10.1504/IJESB.2021.115883

Passey, D. G., Brown, M. C., Hammerback, K., Harris, J. R., & Hannon, P. A. (2018). Managers' support for employee wellness programs: An integrative review. *American Journal of Health Promotion*, 32(8), 1789–1799. DOI: 10.1177/0890117118764856 PMID: 29649899

Peñalvo, J. L., Sagastume, D., Mertens, E., Uzhova, I., Smith, J., Wu, J. H., Bishop, E., Onopa, J., Shi, P., Micha, R., & Mozaffarian, D. (2021). Effectiveness of workplace wellness programmes for dietary habits, overweight, and cardiometabolic health: A systematic review and meta-analysis. *The Lancet. Public Health*, 6(9), e648–e660. DOI: 10.1016/S2468-2667(21)00140-7 PMID: 34454642

Pesis-Katz, I., Smith, J. A., Norsen, L., DeVoe, J., & Singh, R. (2020). Reducing cardiovascular disease risk for employees through participation in a wellness program. *Population Health Management*, 23(3), 212–219. DOI: 10.1089/pop.2019.0106 PMID: 31513466

Randerson, A. K. (2020). Mindfulness, wellness, and spirituality in the workplace. *The Palgrave Handbook of Workplace Well-Being*, 1-22.

Rothenberger, D. A. (2017). Physician burnout and well-being: A systematic review and framework for action. *Diseases of the Colon and Rectum*, 60(6), 567–576. DOI: 10.1097/DCR.0000000000000844 PMID: 28481850

Rucker, M. R. (2017). Workplace wellness strategies for small businesses. *International Journal of Workplace Health Management*, 10(1), 55–68. DOI: 10.1108/IJWHM-07-2016-0054

Sánchez-García, J. C., Vargas-Morúa, G., & Hernández-Sánchez, B. R. (2018). Entrepreneurs' well-being: A bibliometric review. *Frontiers in Psychology*, 9, 1696. DOI: 10.3389/fpsyg.2018.01696 PMID: 30258384

Sforzo, G. A., Kaye, M. P., Harenberg, S., Costello, K., Cobus-Kuo, L., Rauff, E., Edman, J. S., Frates, E., & Moore, M. (2020). Compendium of health and wellness coaching: 2019 addendum. *American Journal of Lifestyle Medicine*, 14(2), 155–168. DOI: 10.1177/1559827619850489 PMID: 32231482

Shanafelt, T., Goh, J., & Sinsky, C. (2017). The business case for investing in physician well-being. *JAMA Internal Medicine*, 177(12), 1826–1832. DOI: 10.1001/jamainternmed.2017.4340 PMID: 28973070

Shanafelt, T. D., & Noseworthy, J. H. (2017, January). Executive leadership and physician well-being: Nine organizational strategies to promote engagement and reduce burnout. [). Elsevier.]. *Mayo Clinic Proceedings*, 92(1), 129–146. DOI: 10.1016/j.mayocp.2016.10.004 PMID: 27871627

Shir, N., Nikolaev, B. N., & Wincent, J. (2019). Entrepreneurship and well-being: The role of psychological autonomy, competence, and relatedness. *Journal of Business Venturing*, 34(5), 105875. DOI: 10.1016/j.jbusvent.2018.05.002

Smith, J. F. (2024). *Private Practice Mental Health Clinicians' Lived Experiences With Entrepreneurial Leadership, Social Learning, and Burnout Throughout the COVID-19 Global Pandemic* (Doctoral dissertation, The Chicago School of Professional Psychology).

Song, Z., & Baicker, K. (2019). Effect of a workplace wellness program on employee health and economic outcomes: A randomized clinical trial. *Journal of the American Medical Association*, 321(15), 1491–1501. DOI: 10.1001/jama.2019.3307 PMID: 30990549

Szekeres, M., & Valdes, K. (2022). Virtual health care & telehealth: Current therapy practice patterns. *Journal of Hand Therapy*, 35(1), 124–130. DOI: 10.1016/j.jht.2020.11.004 PMID: 33568266

Wach, D., Stephan, U., Weinberger, E., & Wegge, J. (2021). Entrepreneurs' stressors and well-being: A recovery perspective and diary study. *Journal of Business Venturing*, 36(5), 106016. DOI: 10.1016/j.jbusvent.2020.106016

Wagner, A., Tsarouha, E., Ög, E., Preiser, C., Rieger, M. A., & Rind, E. (2022). Work-related psychosocial demands related to work organization in small sized companies (SMEs) providing health-oriented services in Germany–a qualitative analysis. *BMC Public Health*, 22(1), 390. DOI: 10.1186/s12889-022-12700-4 PMID: 35209852

Wang, Y. C., Lu, Y., Grunwald, S., Chu, S. L., Kamble, P., & Kumar, J. (2024). An AI Approach to Support Student Mental Health: Case of Developing an AI-Powered Web-Platform with Nature-Based Mindfulness. *Journal of Hospitality & Tourism Education*, 36(3), 1–14. DOI: 10.1080/10963758.2024.2369128

Willard-Grace, R., Knox, M., Huang, B., Hammer, H., Kivlahan, C., & Grumbach, K. (2019). Burnout and health care workforce turnover. *Annals of Family Medicine*, 17(1), 36–41. DOI: 10.1370/afm.2338 PMID: 30670393

Williamson, A. J., Gish, J. J., & Stephan, U. (2021). Let's focus on solutions to entrepreneurial ill-being! Recovery interventions to enhance entrepreneurial well-being. *Entrepreneurship Theory and Practice*, 45(6), 1307–1338. DOI: 10.1177/10422587211006431

Yoon, S., Goh, H., Low, X. C., Weng, J. H., & Heaukulani, C. (2024). User perceptions and utilization of features of an AI-enabled workplace digital mental wellness platform 'mindline at work'. *BMJ Health & Care Informatics*, 31(1), e101045. DOI: 10.1136/bmjhci-2024-101045 PMID: 39153756

Chapter 11
Exploring the Relationship Between Entrepreneurial Success and Personal Well-Being

Deepak Kumar Sahoo
Biju Patnaik University of Technology, Rourkela, India

Anish Kumar
https://orcid.org/0000-0002-8047-4227
O.P. Jindal Global University, India

Ajay Chandel
https://orcid.org/0000-0002-4585-6406
Lovely Professional University, India

Rohit
https://orcid.org/0009-0004-1796-5252
Gulf Medical University, Ajman, UAE

ABSTRACT

This chapter explores the intricate relationship between entrepreneurial success and personal well-being, highlighting the interplay between ambition, mental health, and fulfilment. It examines how psychological resilience, coping mechanisms, and support systems contribute to both personal and professional outcomes for entrepreneurs. By emphasizing the significance of work-life balance and community networks, the chapter argues that well-being is integral to sustainable entrepreneurial success. Furthermore, it identifies future research directions that can deepen our understanding of this relationship, including the need for longitudinal studies and interdisciplinary approaches. Ultimately, this exploration underscores that personal fulfilment and entrepreneurial achievement are interdependent, advocating for a holistic view that nurtures both aspects to foster a thriving entrepreneurial landscape.

DOI: 10.4018/979-8-3693-3673-1.ch011

INTRODUCTION

Entrepreneurial success is widely celebrated as a badge of honour for achievement, resilience, and innovative genius but mostly against the cost of personal well-being. An entrepreneur, especially in the initial stages of building his or her venture, faces difficult challenges that have serious impacts on his or her physical, emotional, and mental well-being. Long hours, extreme stress, and the pressure to hit financial and business milestones are all aspects of a lifestyle that may be rewarding perhaps but taxing, nonetheless. There is little doubt that understanding the relationship between entrepreneurial success and personal well-being is crucial to sustaining the businesses as well as the holistic health of individuals (Binder, 2017).

Entrepreneurial passion, autonomy, and visions Entrepreneurship is primarily passionate, autonomous, and vision oriented. Pursuing entrepreneurial success, however, often involves personal health and wellness sacrifices (Çetin et al., 2022). Pursuit of funding, along with navigating the uncertainty of the market and retaining a competitive edge over other businesses, may entrench an environment for stress that accompanied the entrepreneur. Despite all this, many entrepreneurs keep pushing forward, presumably because of the assumption of securing a better life through their efforts to succeed. For others, however, the distress this inflicts becomes so pronounced that it puts at risk not only the person's personal life but also his or her business.

This chapter represents an attempt to delve into the intricate connection between entrepreneurial success and individual wellbeing. Success in entrepreneurship is defined differently, that is, profitability, expansion, and market impact, while better personal well-being entails a rather more abstract set of conditions, which include good physical health, mental stability, emotional balance, and good social relationships. An examination of these two constructs together will give one an idea of how one influences the other and how entrepreneurs strive to maintain a delicate balance between professional success and maintaining personal health (Chay, 1993).

Central to this conversation is an admission: to become successful business owners, it means not compromising on welfare but seeking deep connection. On the other hand, while striving for business success, on the additional side, there is well-being and on the subtraction side as well. Business achievements can bring satisfaction, financial revenues, and feelings of achievement-all these are additions to welfare (Chen et al., 2022). It can be noted that pressures of entrepreneurship can go up to bursting points, such as lack of business stability, fearing failure, even imbalances of work and life, and all this can easily lead to burnout and anxiety and other negative health impacts.

Not only does the well-being of entrepreneurs have specific implications for the entrepreneurial person himself or herself but also for the entrepreneurial ecosystem more generally. A healthy entrepreneur is much more likely to inspire innovations, make sound decisions, and make good value for his stakeholders; on the other hand, a well-stressed entrepreneur would most likely struggle with his ability to make creative decisions and stay successful in the longer term. Therefore, understanding how well-being can be supported and preserved during the entrepreneurial journey is crucial for fostering a healthier entrepreneurial culture (Chen & Tseng, 2021).

Limiting the negative impacts of entrepreneurship on well-being through resilience, coping mechanisms, and social support. The personal health strategies that entrepreneurs adopt to pursue business success effectively would include work-life balance, mindfulness practices, or social support from diverse networks. This book is about relating factors that contribute to success in entrepreneurship with those that help ensure personal well-being, providing insight into one route to sustainable success for entrepreneurs (Dej, 2010).

The relationship between entrepreneurial success and personal well-being is mainly explored as a dynamic interplay that needs to balance the initiative of being ambitious with self-care. With such an examination of the interface, there is hope for entrepreneurs, policymakers, and support networks to gain valuable perspectives on holistic success (Dijkhuizen, 2015).

DEFINING ENTREPRENEURIAL SUCCESS

Entrepreneurial success is somewhat of an abstract concept; definitions often vary depending on the goals of the entrepreneur, industry context, and personal aspirations. Success in entrepreneurship is often equated with gain in terms of monetary returns, revenue growth, or even market dominance (Dijkhuizen et al., 2018). Success in entrepreneurship, however, has much deeper connotations than such numbers can possibly establish. Knowing the different definitions that go with entrepreneurial success would change the way entrepreneurs approach their ventures and determine goals in terms of the ultimate evaluation of their successes.

1. Objective Measures of Entrepreneurial Success

Entrepreneurial success can be defined as a most traditional method based on objective financial measures. Among these objective financial measures are revenue growth, profitability, market share, return on investment (ROI), and business valuation. These are, in most cases, of concern for the external stakeholders: investors, business partners, and customers. They see it as a concrete manifestation of whether a venture is viable as well as with the growth potential (Dijkhuizen et al., 2017).

For example, an entrepreneur may consider his or her business successful if it achieves a certain revenue target, if operations are diversified across different markets, or has significant funding from reputable investors. Indeed, financial performance remains the critical success factor in this respect as it simply reflects how sustainable incomes, job creation, and wealth addition can be in the economy by an entrepreneur (Drnovšek et al., 2010).

However, as powerful as the financial metrics offer a concrete and universal yardstick of success, they are at the same time not always strong enough to carry the entire picture of entrepreneurial achievement. It is, for many entrepreneurs, often simply as important-if not even more so-than the hard outcome.

2. Subjective Measures of Entrepreneurial Success

While personal factors, in many ways, are more significant than financial success to entrepreneurs in defining their accomplishments, personal measurements usually include independence, satisfaction, work-life balance, and social benefits. For some entrepreneurs, the freedom to make decisions, do what is meaningful and fulfilling, and create something of value becomes more important than financial success. Success may then be defined in terms of one's ability to work independent of others, control his or her own time schedule, or create a business whose values are aligned with personal values (Gorgievski et al., 2011).

Personal satisfaction and fulfillment are highly coupled with lifestyle entrepreneurs who create a business that survives in support of their desired lifestyle and not necessarily profit-generating (Hahn et al., 2012). Thus, such entrepreneurs may consider entrepreneurial success through factors such as having fun doing what they do, enjoyment and flexibility at work, or the alignment of business goals with what they personally aspire to do.

3. Social and Impact-Driven Success

More and more, entrepreneurial success is also founded on the social and environmental impact businesses bring about. It is a new pattern for conscious capitalism and sustainability, which no longer simply talk about gains, but also positive change. Social entrepreneurs may, for instance, define success in terms of the extent to which their business solves challenges in society or contributes to environmental sustainability. Success for these entrepreneurs is measured by their positive impact on education, health, or poverty reduction, or the conservation of the environment (Karimi & Reisi, 2023).

The rise of corporate social responsibility and impact investing has stretched the definition of success to not only best practices in ethical business and contributions toward the public good but also measures such as lives improved, emissions reduced, or funds for social programs contributed. In this regard, entrepreneurial success is measured by the ability to make a difference in the world as much as metrics (Marshall et al., 2020).

4. Success as a Journey, not a Destination

Indeed, success for many entrepreneurs is more of a process than an end. For, it is growth; it is learning; it is adaptation. In that, entrepreneurial success is dynamic: a flow, which changes both the business and the entrepreneur, growing over time. What will be considered success at startup can easily be seen as not sufficient in later stages of business development. Early on, it could be launching a product; getting first-time funding or market traction may be what success is all about. Further down the line in the business, perhaps it might be with regard to the scaling of operations, international expansion, or offering new-to-the world products (Nikolaev et al., 2020).

Entrepreneurs usually rebrand success to be whatever challenges and opportunities present themselves now. Such a fluid understanding of success presupposes that entrepreneurship is an activity of constant learning, experimenting, and perseverance. The failures, pivots, and setbacks are integral elements that define an entrepreneurial experience-and that overcoming them can even be reframed as some form of success.

5. Definitions of Success Based on Multiples Dimensions

More and more, entrepreneurs are embracing a view of success that is holistic-merging professional achievement into personal well-being. For instance, this approach comes to appreciate the fact that the bottom line on the balance sheet is not the only bottom line for success; health, happiness, and a sense of purpose also represent what truly make life worth living. Entrepreneurial success, therefore, becomes achievement both on the business side and on the personal side, balance between professional ambition and personal well-being (Parasuraman et al., 1996).

In short, entrepreneurial success is an extremely individualized and contextual concept. While financial performance remains an important success marker, subjective elements encompassing the satisfactions of the entrepreneur, autonomy, social impact, and well-being are all important factors regarding how entrepreneurs define success. It is with this varied definition of success that understanding these different components may be a crucial determinant in the kind of support that is offered to the entrepreneur as he goes through his journey helping to navigate this complex interplay between the metrics of business growth and personal fulfillment (Ryff, 2019).

PERSONAL WELL-BEING IN ENTREPRENEURSHIP

Entrepreneurship is often discussed through the colors of innovation, growth, and finance, but entrepreneurship has some unique issues that one may deal with during his/her entrepreneurial career that may impact the personal well-being of an individual. Personal well-being, in a broad sense, would involve an individual's physical, mental, emotional, and social health. The concept of entrepreneurship is trying since there are numerous high demands, constant uncertainties, and intense pressures relating to the startup and running of a business. Entrepreneurship is at times appreciated through the resilience and determination of entrepreneurs but with a toll on their well-being (Sánchez-García et al., 2018).

1. The Pressures of Entrepreneurship

There are significant pressures that entrepreneurs constantly experience and which strain their personal well-being. Some of these pressures include the lack of financial security, threat of business failure, stiff competition, and the challenge to manage teams and resources. Actually, fear of loss is a primary causative factor of most common stressors. Entrepreneurs, apart from committing their money into the ventures, also time, reputation, and personal dreams. Such high risks mean that succeeding becomes a pressure that eventually leads to chronic stress, anxiety, and even burnout (Sherman et al., 2016).

Long working hours, irregular schedules and also the inability to draw a line between professional and personal life exacerbate the issue. Entrepreneurs work 24/7 as a matter of course and spend less time over those activities that matter most for winning. Such "hustle culture" they often popularize by neglecting its adverse impacts on physical as well as mental health.

2. Psychological and Mental Health Issues

Entrepreneurship is a very lonely journey. More specifically, isolation could be said to afflict entrepreneurs, especially those of the decision-making variety, who have an important responsibility in terms of providing for the sustenance and future of their people and business as a whole (Singh et al., 2023). Thus, such isolation can contribute to anxiety and depression since most entrepreneurs find themselves constantly without peers with whom they can share their experiences. Another 2019 study discovered that entrepreneurs are more likely to develop mental health conditions like depression and anxiety compared to other people because their high levels of stress with little support from others make it difficult for them to transition from one state to another.

Entrepreneurship is like a rollercoaster ride where one day is a top and the next is a bottom. Interpreting such different emotions each day can emotionally exhaust even the strong person in the world. The psychological burden of entrepreneurship may lead to burnout if left unchecked-it's a state of emotional, physical, and mental exhaustion brought on by prolonged stress.

3. Physical Health Impacts

Physical demands of entrepreneurship are also very significant. Business owners primarily ignore their physical well-being, preferring to work long hours instead of exercising, resting, and having healthy diets. Poor sleep patterns and working "around the clock" will cause physical exhaustion, lack of sleep, and a reduced immune system (Stephan, 2018). Long periods of those sources of physical stress might lead to specific health consequences, including heart disease, immunodeficiency, and chronic exhaustion.

The problem is exacerbated by a lack of regular exercise and unsound dieting habits. Most entrepreneurs spend most of their working hours sitting behind a desk or traveling for business; this often means neglecting healthy habits, which catches up and affects the general health and energy level in the long run.

4. Social Well-Being and Relationships

Another significant personal trait that entrepreneurs are very vulnerable to losing is social well-being. Quite often, entrepreneurs have to sacrifice their personal relationships and social activities to spend more time serving their ventures. Family relationships, friendships, and social engagement will be neglected in the interest of developing a business, resulting in feelings of isolation and loneliness, which is dangerous for wholesome well-being (Tisu & Vîrgă, 2022).

Pressure to maintain a profitable business also generates family strain, where an entrepreneur needs to be involved in every activity related to the business while also performing all the functions of a good spouse, father or mother, and friend. The blurring of lines between work and life raises several challenges in striking the right balance between commitments to work and personal relationships. Neglect of social well-being hurts the self-satisfaction of the entrepreneur and acts as a productivity and creativity killer in the long run.

5. Well-Being Matters to Entrepreneurial Success

Personal well-being is crucial not only to the health and happiness of the entrepreneur himself but also to entrepreneurial success. A more productive, innovative, and resilient entrepreneur faces obstacles with better approaches and methods (Tunio, 2020). This keeps entrepreneurs clear-headed mentally, emotionally stable, and physically healthy so they make better decisions, solve problems more creatively, and lead people better. A well-being approach also prevents one from burnout, ensuring that the entrepreneur will be well-staminate enough to sustain the business for the long haul.

Entrepreneurs who take good care of their well-being can be better role models for their employees, and therefore may be able to help create a healthier culture in the workplace. A balanced entrepreneur is probable to be a work-life balance supporter, mental health advocate, and creating supporting, empathetic organizational culture (Tunio et al., 2021).

6. Strategies for Enhancing Well-being

Entrepreneurs are put under great pressure; hence significant steps should be undertaken by entrepreneurs towards protection and enhancement of personal well-being. This may include defined work and personal time boundaries, mindfulness and meditation, regular physical exercise, and social support from peers, mentors, or family members. Furthermore, entrepreneurs may use techniques that encourage resilience, such as managing stress with stress management practices, and positive self-reflection to better handle all the ups and downs of their entrepreneurial journey (Wiklund et al., 2019).

Personal well-being is a significant dimension of entrepreneurial success, yet it is a one that entrepreneurs commonly sacrifice while trying to achieve business objectives. Entrepreneurs who fail on personal well-being are usually in for a fight that concerns their physical, emotional, and social well-being, not only concerning health but also in running a successful enterprise. Getting one's personal well-being right will be vital for the entrepreneurs themselves, but it will also be critical for the long-run survival and sustenance of the venture (Williamson et al., 2021).

THE INTERPLAY BETWEEN ENTREPRENEURIAL SUCCESS AND WELL-BEING

Entrepreneurial success and well-being are interrelation dynamics. They are highly complex, dynamic, and often of a bidirectional nature. Entrepreneurial success can sometimes be regarded as a source of accomplishment as well as providing a safe haven for one's personal well-being and fulfillment. Entrepreneurship can sometimes be a great challenge to a person's health, physical, mental, and emotional, especially if it is considered a point of demand that most puts onto the person (Binder, 2017). Well-being itself, however, is a basic factor in achieving and subsequent sustainability of success in business. This understanding of the play between these two factors will assist the equilibrium and safely accomplish a sustainably successful entrepreneurial journey.

1. Entrepreneurial Success as a Contributor to Well-Being

Entrepreneurial success brings great personal wellbeing for lots of reasons. Business success, financial freedom, and developing a successful venture guarantee satisfaction and happiness. The entrepreneur who attains success meets his targets, feels self-assured, has a purpose in life and gets the excitement of having created something. More specifically, financial success guarantees security, decreases anxieties pertaining to the long-term survival of a person and their business, and raises the threshold of a higher quality of life (Çetin et al., 2022).

Entrepreneurship also offers a unique chance to have freedom and control over one's professional life. As opposed to the classic employee, the entrepreneur is more often granted full decision-making authority, designing the path of the venture, and has a schedule that they would like to keep. This fact, therefore, explains why entrepreneurs may have higher job satisfaction and better mental well-being because entrepreneurs can exercise more control over their business activities for it to reflect their values and aspirations (Chay, 1993).

For most entrepreneurs, success could also be measured by what they do for others. It may be about creating jobs, developing communities, or generating social innovations; for the entrepreneur who views their business as a source through which they can make a positive contribution, there is more well-being created by knowing they have some form of positive effect. The pride that comes from being successful in such a fashion defines a significant sense of purpose and belonging (Chen et al., 2022).

2. The Negative Impacts of Entrepreneurial Success on Well-Being

Entrepreneurial success, in itself, can attribute several negative impacts on well-being. Stress, burnout, and other health problems may arise from the pursuit of business goals coupled with the heavy expectations on entrepreneurs' shoulders. The closer businesses are to actualizing their visions, the farther and farther responsibilities, pressures, and workloads are; it becomes very difficult for an entrepreneur not to carry a healthy work-life balance (Chen & Tseng, 2021).

One challenge has been the isolation that entrepreneurs feel when they succeed. The higher they go, the fewer people they may feel they can turn to for honest, impactful feedback or other forms of support. Probably fueled by fear of failing or loss of reputation, entrepreneurs may hesitate to seek help; this can leave them feeling increasingly stress-struck and anxious. The emotional burden of having all the power to decide the fates of their employees, stakeholders, and personal survival makes this loneliness worse (Dej, 2010).

More so, the pressure to continually expand the business or simply sustain success can cause entrepreneurs to forego personal wellness for their venture. Entrepreneurial heroes "endorse extended hours at work, sleep deprivation, and overall physical neglect in an attempt to cope with their businesses' rising expectations." Ultimately, this leads to nearly complete exhaustion, mental health cases, and emotional exhaustion (Dijkhuizen, 2015).

3. Well-Being as a Driver of Entrepreneurial Success

On the opposite side of the equation, entrepreneurs' well-being indeed plays a critical role in enabling them to achieve and sustain success. An entrepreneur who takes care of physical health, mental well-being, and emotional balance is more equipped to handle some of the pressures of running a business. Well-being will directly impact capabilities in decision-making, creativity, problem-solving skills, and leadership effectiveness-all of which are essential for entrepreneurial success.

Physical well-being, therefore, will also see to it that the entrepreneurs can muster enough energies to cater to all the demands of their business. Regular exercise, healthy sleep, and a healthy diet led to greater levels of productivity and resilience, thereby enabling entrepreneurs to work better through daily stressors in running a business (Dijkhuizen et al., 2018).

Heals as much for their mental and emotional wellness. Entrepreneurs who have a sense of mindfulness, managing the stress, and regulating emotions are far more likely to carry their coolness under pressure and clarity under high pressure when making a decision. Creativity and innovation are supported by mental wellness, enabling entrepreneurs to think outside the box and find new solutions for business challenges (Dijkhuizen et al., 2017). Also, emotionally resilient entrepreneurs better handle setbacks and failures which are part of the entrepreneurial journey.

Social well-being, such as keeping connections with family, friends, and peers, is yet an added factor to entrepreneurial success. A strong support system gives an emotional sense of grounding while helping suppress feelings of isolation, offers valuable advice, and encourages one during periods of increased strain. Entrepreneurs who nurture rich personal and professional relations stand a better chance of having the emotional and psychological push needed to drive and sustain ventures (Drnovšek et al., 2010).

4. Finding Balance Between Success and Well-being

Finding ways to integrate self-care into the entrepreneurial journey marks the way forward in balancing entrepreneurship's success with personal well-being. Notable proper realization by entrepreneurs that well-being is not a luxury, but a critical success factor means entrepreneurs will be expected to take on an interdependent mentality toward the relationship of personal well-being and business success rather than competing priorities (Gorgievski et al., 2011).

To set this balance, one may separate work life from the rest of the life by setting boundaries between work life and personal life. Entrepreneurs should understand how to delegate, time-manage, and prioritize the things that help sustain them, their health, and happiness. It is at times by setting realistic expectations and the ability to say no to certain opportunities that prevents one from burning out and keeping on track of the important things (Hahn et al., 2012).

A further strategy would be self-awareness and self-compassion building resilience. Entrepreneurs who are mindful, who take time regularly to disengage from activities, are encouraged, and nourish the mind and body at the same time are better suited to handle stress and maintain the high level of performance over time. advice from mentors and business networks or professional coaching also enables entrepreneurs to learn from past and useful advice can keep feet on the ground for navigating entrepreneurial endeavors' highs and lows (Karimi & Reisi, 2023).

Enterprise and personal welfare balance in a fragile equilibrium and need constant attention and effort. While success in enterprise can enhance personal welfare by means of its financial resources, autonomy, and personal accomplishment, it also brings unceasing pressure on an individual's physical and mental health. Well-being, in turn, is an extremely important factor of entrepreneurial success; they affect decisions in management, responses to unfavourable situations, and much more (Marshall et al., 2020).

Given that success and well-being stand as interconnected degrees, entrepreneurs may learn practices that can help ensure their health along with their professional goals. Strike the balance between these two variables and an entrepreneurial life that is sustainable in business growth, healthy, and fulfilling will result.

PSYCHOLOGICAL RESILIENCE AND COPING MECHANISMS

Such challenges that entrepreneurs face include high stress and adversity in the course of their journey, including uncertainty about finances, pressures of leading a team, or trying to navigate through a competitive market. Psychological resilience-the capacity to adapt to challenges and bounce back from failure-is critical to entrepreneurial success. When such resilience allows for healthy coping mechanisms, entrepreneurs handle stress, ensure their mental health, and hence sustain long-term business goals (Nikolaev et al., 2020).

1. The Importance of Psychological Resilience in Entrepreneurship

It is the ability to bounce back from adversity; while it is present, the individual grows stronger and thrives in the venture. In entrepreneurship, one needs resilience because failure or rejection and uncertainty are associated with nearly every step toward success. Markets the entrepreneur operates in are constantly changing, financial outcomes are unpredictable, and ownership brings emotional highs and lows. Resilience helps them stay focused, motivated, and optimistic even during setbacks (Parasuraman et al., 1996).

Resilient entrepreneurs better handle frustration or setbacks while learning from it instead of being overwhelmed by it. They happen to have a growth mentality that makes the challenge opportunity instead of the roadblock. This makes them see control over oneself as an ability, even when outside circumstances are no longer in their hands.

2. Building Psychological Resilience

Resilience is not a resource somehow there as a gift or innate ability. It can be built and strengthened over time, particularly in the area of entrepreneurial resilience. That is, it means viewing hardships positively-to handle setbacks as a learning experience rather than a failure-to shift the attention from what went wrong to how things could be better next time (Ryff, 2019).

Another characteristic of resilience is the sustenance of realistic optimism. Entrepreneurs must hope for their future but have their feet on the ground concerning their current reality. This balance prevents them from becoming despondent over setbacks or becoming complacent in the midst of their success. Important to building resilience is setting realistic goals and being flexible as well as acknowledging failure in order to be an integral part of the process (Sánchez-García et al., 2018).

3. Coping Mechanisms in Entrepreneurship

Entrepreneurs working in high-stress environments employ a range of coping mechanisms to cope with the psychological demands arising from their work (Sherman et al., 2016). Various such mechanisms ground these entrepreneurs and ensure that they are well over high pressure. The two broad categories under which people fall are problem-focused and emotion-focused strategies.

- Problem-focused coping is taking direct action to alter the source of stress. The entrepreneur may face financial problems, for instance, by getting new investors, perfecting their business model, or implementing upgraded marketing strategies. By doing that, entrepreneurs regain control over what happens in their lives and, therefore, reduce stress (Singh et al., 2023).
- Emotion-focused coping is the management of the response to the stressor, not the stressor itself. Techniques like mindfulness, meditation, or journaling can help entrepreneurs regulate their emotions, making them feel better when anxiety or frustration rises in their minds. Support received from fellow entrepreneurs, mentors, or family comes under emotion-focused coping, which may provide crucial 'perspective' and emotional relief.

Both coping strategies are essential; successful entrepreneurs often utilize the best combination for them based on the nature of the challenge being confronted.

4. Healthy vs. Unhealthy Coping Mechanisms

While coping mechanisms are necessary for effective stress management, entrepreneurship demands that entrepreneurs first use moderate care and caution in adopting healthy rather than improper survival strategies (Stephan, 2018). Healthy coping strategies include keeping a regular routine of exercise, the practice of mindfulness, and social support, while ensuring long-term well-being and resilience. These reduce levels of stress, enhance emotional regulation, and present mental clarity that is required for effective and sound decision-making.

On the other hand, negative coping strategies such as substance use, overwork, or evasive action diminish personal well-being and business performance. Entrepreneurs may become involved in unhealthy coping behaviors to manage stress or to block out their emotions; yet these coping strategies end in burnout, deteriorating health, and an impaired capacity to evaluate. Entrepreneurial success as well as healthful well-being require developing a sense of any undesirable coping patterns in their lives and early intervention to prevent serious long-term consequences (Tisu & Vîrgă, 2022).

5. Role of Social Support in Coping

One of the best coping strategies for entrepreneurs is that of support networks. Social support from friends, family, mentors, and professional peers provides emotional comfort, practical advice, and a sense of community. Entrepreneurs can best absorb the varying highs and lows of business ownership if they proactively keep in touch with their support network and have a place to turn for advice and guidance (Tunio, 2020).

Mentorship, for instance, is one of the important entrepreneurial resources. A mentor offers guidance from experience, insight into possible ways through which challenges might be overcome, as well as a sounding board when difficult decisions are to be made. The same applies to connecting with other entrepreneurs through networks or professional groups as avenues for accessing others' experiences and coping strategies. Social support reduces feelings of loneliness and gives the peace of mind that others have successfully conquered similar ordeals.

6. Building Individual Coping Capacity

Every entrepreneur is unique, as are their responses to stress. Personalized coping strategies-the answers to an entrepreneur's personal needs, strengths, and challenges-are also important. Regular exercise and physical activities may be used by some to relieve stress while others might benefit from writing, doing art, or music (Tunio et al., 2021).

Personalized coping strategies should also encompass self-reflection and changes in the light of changed situations. Entrepreneurship requires constant reassessment of how their coping mechanisms are performing in order to make adjustments as necessary. For instance, if his periods are those of peak workload, he shall have to manage time in order to delegate; if it is about personal stress, then he shall require more time in order to be able to emphasize his emotional self-care and mindfulness (Wiklund et al., 2019).

Psychological resilience and healthy coping strategies form the core of success as well as well-being for an entrepreneur. Developing resilience by creating healthy coping strategies along with a strong support network makes entrepreneurs more resilient towards stressors that may be faced during the entrepreneurial journey. Such practices protect not only mental but also emotional health, thereby making entrepreneurs more confident as well as clearer in the face of entrepreneurial complexities.

WORK-LIFE BALANCE AND ENTREPRENEURIAL WELL-BEING

It is indeed very challenging for most entrepreneurs to achieve and maintain a work-life balance, since the workload connected with running a business easily ignores lines between a personal life and a professional one (Williamson et al., 2021). However, work-life balance is important for maintaining long-term well-being. Entrepreneurs who are unable to sort out boundaries between work and personal time at risk more frequently of burnout, decreased productivity, and poor relationships. On the other hand, if they are able to balance things out and reach a middle path between them then their well-being increases, business performance improves and life becomes more satisfactory (Binder, 2017).

1. The Dilemma of Work-Life Balance in Entrepreneurship

Entrepreneurs are known for their commitment, passion, and relentless pursuit of business goals. Many take pride in working long hours and sometimes even sacrificing personal time to ensure their ventures grow. Relentless pursuit of business leads to short-term business success but is often a surefire drain on energy from personal health and well-being. Over-saturation of boundaries between work and personal life results in physical exhaustion, neglecting personal relationships, and insufficient time for self-care.

Challenges peculiar to entrepreneurs make work-life balance impossible. Overwhelming workload created by managing every aspect of a business, right from its finances, marketing, operations, and so on, can limit the flexibility of an entrepreneur and make it difficult for that person to maintain work-life balance. Further, pressure to succeed or fear of failure can also force entrepreneurs to devote such unwholesome amounts of time to their business at the expense of their personal lives (Çetin et al., 2022). Furthermore, since entrepreneurial ventures are naturally unpredictable-often putting in long hours and often making decisions at the last minute-any attempt at structuring work-life can be disrupted.

2. The Impact of Imbalance on Well-being

An imbalance of work and personal life can lead to far-reaching negative effects in the well-being of the entrepreneur. In the physical, long hours at work and burdensome workloads may result in fatigue, sleep deprivation, and even chronic health conditions such as stress-related disorders. Mentally and emotionally, focus on work that is extreme can lead to heightened anxiety, burnout, and feelings of isolation (Chay, 1993).

This also leads to the fact that if entrepreneurs neglect their personal and self-made life, their eventual bottoming will influence their comprehensive mental clarity, creativity, and even competency in decision-making (Chen et al., 2022). Working ceaselessly may degrade productivity and, accordingly, influence the general performance of the business. Gradually, entrepreneurial burnout appears before an entrepreneur's sight - a condition characterized by a feeling of mental exhaustion and loss of the sense of association with the job or small business he or she used to lead.

More than that, an imbalance may put a strain on interpersonal relations. Entrepreneurs may miss out in time spent with loved ones, resulting in guilt and dissatisfaction feelings. The loss of much-needed social support and meaningful personal relationships can well exacerbate stress and loneliness to decrease overall well-being.

3. Strategies to Achieve Work-Life Balance

Balancing the negative effects of work-life imbalance has to come from within; entrepreneurs consciously have to adopt strategies that include how best to manage his or her personal well-being and professional responsibilities. Balancing life means creating boundaries, effective time management, and flexibility (Chen & Tseng, 2021).

- Establishing Clear Boundaries: Entrepreneur should set clear differences between their work hours and personal time. This may include specific hours when working and non-work time, and not working on company issues during their individual time. A possible boundary setup could be having a dedicated space, such as a dedicated workspace, and communicating this to the business partners, staff members, or clients so that expectations are managed and maintained to not be constantly "on".
- Time Management and Delegation: Good time management is necessary for achieving work-life balance. Entrepreneurs can utilize calendars, to-do lists, or productivity applications to plan their work as well as personal activities. Delegation of tasks to employees, outsourcing some specific business functions, or hiring virtual assistants could also free up the time allocated to one's personal well-being. Entrepreneurs can make the most use of their time if they prioritize tasks and focus on high-impact activities (Dej, 2010).
- Creating Time for Personal Life and Self-Care: Entrepreneurship requires that entrepreneurs schedule personal time and self-care by marking regular breaks, vacations, and other personal activities on the calendars. Such breaks can revitalize energy, clarity of thought, and reduce stress levels. Some of the imperative elements of self-care include regular exercises, meditation, hobbies, and socialization with loved ones.

4. The Role of Flexibility in Work-Life Balance

The most appealing feature of entrepreneurship is flexibility, which may also be a source of creating a more balanced life. While a traditional job offers less or no opportunity to schedule time according to needs and preferences, of course, entrepreneurship gives one an opportunity to schedule time accordingly (Dijkhuizen, 2015). Flexibility may be embraced by entrepreneurs to outline everyday routines in such a way that they can accommodate business requirements as well as personal activities better, thus ensuring a healthier and more balanced lifestyle.

For example, those entrepreneurs who value time with their family can set their work engagements at times when the children are in school or out for other commitments. Once more, those who have an interest in fitness can tailor their daily work to afford time to exercise frequently or participate in other outdoor exercises. Flexibility in work would therefore help the entrepreneurs strike a pattern suitable to meet needs that may arise both personally and, in their business, hence reducing the pressure that rigid schedules present and freeing up their day for spontaneity also creativity (Dijkhuizen et al., 2018).

5. Balancing Personal and Professional Goals

Entrepreneurship and achieving a balance between work and life requires aligning personal and professional goals. Entrepreneurs treating their personal life as something of worth to the business are more likely to establish habits in place for balance. Entrepreneurship requires an approach different from one of business success and healthy living being two competing aspects. Entrepreneurs must instead find a way of securing professional goals but nurturing the personal life as well.

The holistic vision of success would include personal fulfillment, family time, physical health, and financial stability. Evaluation of personal goals besides professional goals with periodic consistency will always ensure the entrepreneurs keep well-informed about the areas they should readjust their priorities for improvement. Should an entrepreneur be wasting so much time working instead of with the people they ought to spend with, then their priorities can easily be readjusted to consciously re-allocate the time appropriately (Dijkhuizen et al., 2017).

6. Long-Term Benefits of Work-Life Balance

Work-life balance enhances well-being, but in the long run, entrepreneurial success also benefits from the pursuit of work-life balance. Entrepreneurs with a consideration for work-life balance will utilize creativity more sustainably, make even better and wiser decisions, and recover quickly from failures. Working on self-care, rest, and personal relationships will recharge their mental and emotional battery, so entrepreneurs can face business-related issues even better and with more energy (Drnovšek et al., 2010).

They will positively impact their teams and help them adopt healthier work cultures. If leaders within an organization keep well-being at the heart of things, be prepared for that to trickle down to the employees, which will create positive outcomes in morale, productivity, and turnover.

Perhaps work-life balance is the most basic element of entrepreneurial well-being. Taking strategies in creating boundaries and time management coupled with flexibility always works for the betterment of personal health and business success for entrepreneurs. The pursuit of balance is never-ending, yet entrepreneurs can be conscious of living fulfilling lives while still getting much done professionally (Gorgievski et al., 2011).

THE ROLE OF SUPPORT SYSTEMS

Generally, entrepreneurship appears to be an individualistic activity, but in reality, no entrepreneur ever succeeds alone. A support system-that could be in terms of family, friends, mentors, or professional contacts-can help in every way to ensure the well-being of the entrepreneur, thus making them more likely to succeed. Such systems offer emotional, practical, and financial assistance, helping entrepreneurs circumvent the difficulties of owning a business while ensuring they stay healthy with work-life balance and mental resilience.

1. Family and Friends Emotional Support

Entrepreneurship Journey: often quite stressful, uncertain, with ups and downs emotionally. An emotional skeleton is what family and friends add, which can anchor the entrepreneur to some extent. They provide a haven in letting out frustrations, triumphs, and encouragement in trying moments. That's crucial for mental health, but having an outlet emotionally reduces loneliness/feelings of isolation and burnout (Hahn et al., 2012).

Particularly in the families, stability and assurance may be offered much. On the other hand, entrepreneurs put so much energy and time into the business because it strains personal relationships. With the understanding of the pressures related to entrepreneurship, families may provide a way to offer support with the management of responsibilities around the house, create a balanced family life, as well as serve as a source of emotional strength. Entrepreneurs should be open with their families on business issues where the family may find an opportunity to understand and support the entrepreneur through the business life cycle (Karimi & Reisi, 2023).

2. Mentorship and Professional Advice

Mentors offer perhaps one of the most valuable sources of support for any entrepreneur. They provide the "most expert guide experience can provide." A mentor can be that sound board who helps entrepreneurs get through critical business decisions, avoid common pitfalls, and grow strategies. Beyond business advice, a mentor also gives an emotional touch as he shares stories about his own struggles and then overcoming it to become successful in his lifetime, assuring entrepreneurs that the hardship they are confronting is part of the game.

Mentorship is informal or formal, with some entrepreneurs needing industry veterans to guide them, while others find their mentorship amongst their peers; their colleagues experience sharing. The advice coming from mentors can be very valuable for the entrepreneur, helping avoid mistakes, grab opportunities, and always give him an increase in confidence on his capabilities in doing things (Marshall et al., 2020). The mentors can also broaden the network of an entrepreneur, introducing him or her to the right contacts or business partners that could eventually contribute to his well-oiled success rate.

3. Peer Networks and Entrepreneurial Communities

Entrepreneurs thrive if they form a community. Whether formal or informal, peer networks offer entrepreneurs an outlet through which to connect with others who face similar problems. They provide a platform that allows entrepreneurs to share ideas, resources, and solutions for common problems. Interaction with other peers through an industry association, entrepreneurial incubator, or online forum keeps entrepreneurs abreast of market trends and emerging business strategies as well as new technologies (Nikolaev et al., 2020).

Apart from the business practical support, entrepreneurial networks give a sense of belonging to the entrepreneurs. Entrepreneurship is a very lonely journey, especially to solo founders; hence, having a network of like-minded people helps to kill loneliness. The ability to share experience, successes, and setbacks with people who understand the entrepreneurial journey will create an environment that makes it easier for the entrepreneurs to teach each other.

4. Financial and Strategic Support

While emotional support and professional backing is considerable, financial backing usually takes the job done for an entrepreneur. Support systems can vary from investors to venture capitalists or even family and friends who believe in the entrepreneur's vision. Financial backing thereby relieves some of the stress connected with struggling with securing funding, thus allowing the entrepreneur to concentrate on business development rather than constantly worrying about cash flow (Parasuraman et al., 1996).

In addition to direct financial support, strategic support through business partnerships or alliances can be instrumental in speeding up business growth. Partnerships with other entrepreneurs or organizations will provide access to new markets and increase customer bases while opening resource channels otherwise not available. Therefore, such kinds of support bring monetary and strategic benefits, speed up business development, and ease some of the burdens endured by entrepreneurs.

5. Workplace and Team Support

It is also very vital to have the inner support that form through entrepreneur's own business. A good and reliable team enables entrepreneurs to outsource some of their responsibilities and indulge in more strategic activities rather than being involved in day-to-day functions, which may get one overwhelmed and put one in a difficult situation where one cannot cope with work activities. With a good supportive team, therefore, reduces much workload for entrepreneurs thus keeping away burnout and helps maintain healthy work-life balance (Ryff, 2019).

Giving ownership of tasks to the members of a business team and letting them take control will encourage teamwork and a more dynamic work environment. Entrepreneurs are more likely to experience continued business success for a long time into the future if they work with talented employees who are motivated and protect their own well-being. An organization that can create a welcoming work culture, where workers feel valued and connected to the business mission, increases morale and productivity among workers, which benefits the entrepreneur as well as the company.

6. The Role of Spousal Support in Entrepreneurial Success

Spousal support is very important for married entrepreneurs or people in long-term relationships. A spouse who understands the needs of entrepreneurship can be an emotional, financial, or practical source of support, and therefore might be the driving force both toward personal well-being and business success. In numerous cases, the spouse can become an informal or formal business partner: give advice, carry out specific business tasks, or insight on making some decisions (Sánchez-García et al., 2018).

Another reason why psychological closeness in the relationship between spouses may decrease stress is due to the emotional support from the partner. In addition to long hours, financial instability, and those occasional moments when the entrepreneur is uncertain about the decisions he made, the partner may be supporting and understanding, thus deflecting some of these stressors (Sherman et al., 2016). Open communication ensures that support is in place for both parties and that business complications do not strain the personal relationship.

7. Balancing Support and Independence

The balance between seeking help and independence is paramount in support systems because entrepreneurs also need to be able to operate independently and get their own personal inputs while using their support systems. Overreliance on external support can prevent one's personal growth and autonomy in decision-making for entrepreneurs. Therefore, the entrepreneur has to learn to stay resilient, problem-solve, and act efficaciously while using support networks on their part. This will ensure that they stay in control of their venture but at the same time benefit from the guidance and support of others (Singh et al., 2023).

Support systems play a significant role in entrepreneurship. Having a source of support by way of a family, mentor, peer, or investor could have a holistic effect on improving personal and business outcomes. Therefore, entrepreneurs who can develop and maintain relationships with sources of support are more likely to see their venture survive, thrive, and balance work and personal life. Being entrepreneurial can often be an isolating, stressful experience, and one needs those support systems that provide the necessary resources, advice, and emotional strength with which to navigate the complex and unpredictable world of business.

MENTAL HEALTH AND ENTREPRENEURIAL SUCCESS

For this reason, since entrepreneurship is associated with freedom, innovation, and financial independence, it still brings significant psychological and emotional difficulties. The pressure of constantly succeeding in business, uncertainty, and the assumption of many different roles impact entrepreneurs' mental health (Stephan, 2018). More and more studies point out that the connection of psychological variables with entrepreneurial success is multifaceted. Thus, though a poor mental state suppresses the performance of the businesses, the solutions in mental well-being can boost the capabilities, resilience, and overall success up.

1. The Mental Health Challenges Entrepreneurs Face

Entrepreneurs experience different mental health issues than the traditional employee. The pressure of running a business is very overwhelming, and the uncertainty of income and risky chances of failure can prove to be quite stressful. These factors lead to anxiety, depression, chronic stress, and ultimately, burnout (Tisu & Vîrgă, 2022).

Many founders, including solo founders, feel lonely. Entrepreneurship is lonely business-building; running a business can be very isolative. Entrepreneurs do not share a support system that organically goes with a larger organization. Finally, stress often relates to financial strain in establishing and growing a business, especially with personal savings or family funds being at risk.

Founder identity is another concept that contributes to mental health challenges. Most entrepreneurs anchor their personal identity and self-worth to the success of their business, making them emotionally unstable if things do not work out as planned (Tunio, 2020). For example, launching a product and it flops, missing a good investment opportunity, or experiencing an unexpected change in the market can ignite feelings of inadequacy, self-doubt, and guilt. The individual burdening emotions would thus lead to long-term issues in mental health conditions.

2. The Impact of Poor Mental Health on Entrepreneurial Success

The impact can be very serious if not dealt with since mental health issues can severely affect the mind of the entrepreneur thus causing him or her to fail in being effective. Anxiety and stress result in further poor cognitive functioning that draws out poor decisions and poor productions. Entrepreneurs who face the problem of mental health find it hard to concentrate, face low creativity, and become weaker to solve problems effectively.

Poor mental health can also strain relationships with employees, investors, and business partners. A stressed entrepreneur will not have the patience or make confused decisions to withdraw into some isolation and begin to harbor self-doubts and lose others' confidence in the business. The effectiveness of leadership declines, and it might compromise the potential for growth of the business (Tunio et al., 2021).

Burnout is also another critical issue entrepreneurs face when dealing with mental health neglect. An extended exposure to stress without proper rest or coping strategy may contribute to emotional exhaustion and detachment from the business. Entrepreneurs who experience burnout often lose interest and motivation in running the business, a situation that may ultimately end in failure of the business or even a desire to give up the venture completely.

3. Psychological Well-being as Success Factor in Entrepreneurship

The importance of mental health is therefore key to entrepreneurial success. Active management of the wellbeing of the entrepreneur will lead to sustainably keeping their business going. They are able to withstand the ups and downs of running a business through mentally building resilience. Other than that, factors such as creativity and innovation that are very necessary for growth in entrepreneurship are affected by mental health

Entrepreneurs who are prioritizing mental health also tend to make more thoughtful, strategic decisions. Better control over their emotions and a clearer mind makes entrepreneurs equipped with the capacity to have better judgments over risk and to weigh out options more thoughtfully (Williamson et al., 2021). Agility and mental malleability enable entrepreneurs to be more responsive to uncertainty and to recognize potential where others may view difficulties.

Good mental health will be associated with good leadership. Entrepreneurs who are in good mental health are likely to create a positive support environment. Where the leaders are emotionally balanced and mentally sound, they give confidence, motivation, and productivity to their workforce. Confident employees are engaged and, therefore, the overall business performs better (Wiklund et al., 2019).

4. Strategies for Maintaining Mental Health in Entrepreneurship

With the challenges attached to entrepreneurship, keeping one's mental health on course requires deliberate effort. There are several strategies that entrepreneurs can take as a means of protecting and enhancing mental well-being while they hunt for business success.

- Â Daily Self-Care Practices: Entrepreneurs should prioritize exercise, meditation, hobbies, and time spent with loved ones. Taking regular breaks, ensuring restful sleep, and performing relaxation exercises are things that can help the entrepreneur prevent burnout and maintain emotional balance (Binder, 2017).

- Building a Support Network: The entrepreneur needs to develop powerful relationships with mentors, peers, and family members who can provide guidance, perspective, and encouragement. A person surrounded by a network of like-minded fellow travelers who understand the entrepreneurial journey will help dissipate feelings of isolation and who, during bad times, can provide emotional support (Çetin et al., 2022).
- Professional Counseling: Entrepreneurship may be linked to therapy or counseling. Professionally, such a person might not always assist entrepreneurs find ways to cope with stress, anxiety, and other psychological disorders. Professional help may give stress management skills and provide an unfussy hearth in which personal problems may be ventilated or shared together with business problems.
- Setting Boundaries: Most entrepreneurs blur lines between the life of work and personal life, hence characterized by overwork and mental exhaustion (Chay, 1993). It is, therefore, in the best interest of maintaining one's mental health to set boundaries of what should be accomplished between what time, such as business hours, so that one can freshen up and have time away from work pressures.
- Time Management and Delegation: Time management reduces the feeling of the workload overloading. Those entrepreneurs that delegate and prioritize on tasks are in a better position to reduce the stress levels, suppressing the mental overload that comes with trying to do everything.
- Growth Mindset: Entrepreneurs need to instill in themselves a growth mindset where setbacks and failures are seen as ways to learn, not as personal failures. This mindset enhances resilience because people are likely to bounce back at a higher pace from challenges with new determinations (Chen et al., 2022).

5. Long-Term Benefit for Prioritizing Mental Health

Long-term benefits for investing in mental health is beyond personal wellness. An entrepreneur with good mental well-being can better maintain his creativity, innovation, and strategic thinking capacity: ability to compete within the marketplace. Good mental health also makes an entrepreneur better at problem solving; they will be bold and more confident in crises and uncertainty (Dijkhuizen et al., 2018).

Long-term business sustainability is attributed to the type of mental health afforded by the entrepreneur. More resilient entrepreneurs are then better placed to adapt to challenges associated with scaling, or problems related to relationship maintenance, which would be required for sustainability in a business venture, as well as adapting to the changing market. By managing their well-being, entrepreneurs will better lead their ventures with focus and purpose towards realizing their personal fulfilment and business success (Dijkhuizen et al., 2017).

Entrepreneurial success and mental health are hand in hand. For entrepreneurs who give value to their mental health, they are better equipped to endure the pressures of running businesses and thus will ultimately be able to sustain success. By taking care of oneself, having a good network of support around him, and seeking professional help when the time comes, an entrepreneur can safeguard his mental well-being and thus ensure that both his professional and personal lives will flourish in harmony with each other (Drnovšek et al., 2010).

BALANCING AMBITION AND PERSONAL FULFILLMENT

The drive for success is one of the most defining qualities found among entrepreneurs. Ambition drives innovation, growth, and the desire to conquer and push beyond obstacles, but at the same time, if not balanced with personal fulfillment, it can prove costly. This is perhaps why most entrepreneurs seem to be caught in the middle of having to accomplish their professional objectives while, at the same time, being happy in their personal lives (Gorgievski et al., 2011). An important balance has to be struck between, on the one hand, reaching for ambitious targets and avoiding burnout, strained relationships, and pointlessness, and, on the other, overemphasizing personal fulfillment at the expense of creativity, resilience, and long-term success.

1. The Nature of Ambition in Entrepreneurship

Ambition is part of the entrepreneurial mindset. Entrepreneurs develop a passion to innovate, disrupt industries, and build something from scratch. Such an ambition typically requires an obsessive focus on growth, expansion, and indeed most success metrics: revenue, market share, and returns for investors. And yes, many entrepreneurs are achievement-driven, always pushing boundaries and looking for the next level (Hahn et al., 2012).

While it is a primary enabler of commercial success, it can also become very myopic without balance. Ambition is okay provided it does not become "success-at-all-cost," in which personal needs and relationships are compromised for professional advancement. Entrepreneurs spend long hours at work, forget why they started their business, and compromise their health and well-being for the sake of staying in the game (Karimi & Reisi, 2023).

2. The Risks of Overemphasizing Ambition

When ambition overshadows everything else, unpleasant results arise. The most prevalent danger factor is burnout: entrepreneurs overtiring themselves mentally and physically, working too much and getting too little sleep. Burnout affects judgment, productivity, and drive to do business. Chronic stress and anxiety would relentlessly begin to destroy personal wellness along with professional performance due to the relentless pursuit of strong targets (Marshall et al., 2020).

Ambition can further become overstated and actually encroach on personal relationships. Entrepreneurs spend too much time "at work" in the business and little or no time at all with family and friends, which could then create isolation and resentment. The relationships with spouses, children, and close friends are compromised, creating a cycle whereby personal dissatisfaction spills over into professional life, compounding and making the entrepreneur feel stressed and less fulfilling (Nikolaev et al., 2020).

In extreme scenarios, the relentless pursuit of ambition makes entrepreneurs forget what they first intended to do and be in business. When it has only been about external measuring rods such as profit and fame, entrepreneurs can feel an emptiness, or existential crisis, even after attaining what they wanted. This gap between success and personal gratification may become the way to emptiness or a crisis of purpose.

3. The Meaning of Personal Satisfaction

The other significant balance to ambition is personal fulfillment. It gives meaning to one's life, it provides purpose for one's existence, and even keeps one content in both personal and professional life. Entrepreneurs who will focus on personal fulfillment are likely to know and understand clearly why they are pursuing the business goals, thus having more likelihood to sustain motivation over the long term (Parasuraman et al., 1996). At times, fulfillment is achieved through intrinsic factors such as making a positive difference, aligning your work with personal values, or developing and maintaining a sense of purpose beyond just profits.

Entrepreneurs who are satisfied with their lives are more energetic, creative and resilient for their businesses. Since this process reduces the chance of burnout and builds emotional well-being, it leads to effective decision-making and, consequently, leadership and performance of businesses. Entrepreneurs who achieve a proper balance between ambition and fulfillment are often more innovative, as they are less fuzzy in their thinking and continue to be more adaptable to change.

4. Strategies in Balancing Ambition with Personal Fulfillment

Balancing ambition with personal fulfillment requires a self-conscious effort and awareness. Several strategies can be utilized by entrepreneurs to maximize the chances of avoiding at all costs that urge for success at the expense of overall well-being and satisfaction.

- Personal Values and Purpose Will Have to be Defined: This can be in finding balance as defining personal values and purpose is the main step in seeking balance (Ryff, 2019). More so, entrepreneurs have to define what fulfilling self is in order to determine business goals and ambition personal aspiration together with ensuring ambition has purpose.
- Setting Attainable Goals and Expectations: Ambition drives growth, but properly so, it needs to be set at manageable increments. Ambitions should then be broken into smaller, achievable milestones and where the entrepreneur realizes his progress at every step. This diminished constant pressure for high-stakes success allows personal growth and reflection (Sánchez-García et al., 2018).
- Carving Out Personal Space: entrepreneurs should know the amount of free time they can allocate to families, friends, hobbies, and rest. They are able to work around boundaries that split a moment up to be devoted between work and personal life, therefore preventing overlying ambition from redefining their relationships and well-being. Other advantages include returning to work with much higher productivity and creativity.
- Passion Projects: The entrepreneur does so much work that he/she forgets other things. Some passionate and creative work helps connect him with his personal passions. These are volunteering, learning something new, or doing some kind of creative pursuit, but they serve to give them some sense of purpose other than professional ambition (Sherman et al., 2016).
- Mindfulness and Self-Reflection: Regularly reflecting on an entrepreneur's mental and emotional states can be helpful. Activities such as meditation, journaling, or just taking time to pause and assess feelings in mind attune entrepreneurs to their needs and prevent the obsessive passion for ambition.

- Beyond Money: For entrepreneurs, success can be defined in a better platform that may not be just about monetary gains but may also involve having a positive impact in the community, personal growth, or that of his or her team (Singh et al., 2023). And through their concentration on metrics converging well with the values of the entrepreneurs, the rewards shall be found in ways that are well beyond the financial achievements.

5. The Benefits of Achieving Balance

When entrepreneurs strike the right balance between ambition and personal satisfaction, both will benefit, and both their private lives and businesses get great effects. When entrepreneurs feel fulfilled, motivation is sustained over the longer term; they do not easily burn out. They are likely to enjoy the entrepreneurial journey and not only at the end where a pot of gold lies.

Balanced entrepreneurs tend to be better leaders also (Stephan, 2018). They achieve stronger relationships with employees, customers, and partners that result in a positive and collaborative work environment. This enhances the performance of teams and allows their business to grow healthily and sustainably.

Lastly, balancing personal fulfillment with ambition brings entrepreneurs more down-to-earth in perspective. They cannot be overly run by the competition or befogged in opportunities for innovation and growth. A well-rounded, fulfilled entrepreneur navigates the inevitable ups and downs of entrepreneurship better with resilience and purpose.

The balance between ambition and personal fulfillment has always been a key requirement for entrepreneurs on a path toward sustainable success. Ambition alone is what drives people to pursue set objectives and business growth, but satisfaction level in personal terms makes sure that the journey also makes sense and is worthwhile. If entrepreneurs match their ambitions to their values, make realistic goals, and create time for personal life, then they are sure of striking that balance that would serve their well-being and support their business achievements (Tisu & Vîrgă, 2022).

FUTURE RESEARCH DIRECTIONS

The study of entrepreneurial success and personal well-being is an area that is rapidly developing and offers many lines of further investigation. With the added imperatives of technology, economy, and society evolving further, understanding the nuance between these concepts becomes even more relevant. Future research may identify ways to improve entrepreneurial outcomes and overall personal fulfillment: Some of the promising areas in future research in this domain include:

1. Longitudinal Studies on Well-Being and Success

Longitudinal studies, which track entrepreneurs over time, would strengthen future research in this topic. In longitudinal studies, many aspects of how entrepreneurs' personal well-being changes over the long term are followed, and such changes are seen to affect business outcomes either positively or negatively (Williamson et al., 2021). On course following different entrepreneurs, researchers can recognize patterns and critical turning points and identify long-term impact mental health and overall well-being have on entrepreneurial success. Such a study will strengthen our understanding regarding the trajectories of entrepreneurs in their careers.

2. Diverse Entrepreneurial Contexts and Populations

Most research streams find focus on specific populations or sectors, but the context, culture, and demographics of entrepreneurs tell quite another story (Singh et al., 2023). Future research should focus on varied entrepreneurial contexts, such as social entrepreneurship, women entrepreneurs, minority-owned businesses, and startups in emerging markets. Having insight into unique challenges and coping mechanisms for these groups will provide input for support tailored to them.

3. The Impact of Technology on Well-Being

In this regard, digital tools and technologies of entrepreneurship therefore implicate both the better and the worse elements of personal well-being. Indeed, for a future research agenda it could be interesting to consider to what extent technology, including work, social media, or productivity apps (Nikolaev et al., 2020), affects the mental health and work-life balance of entrepreneurs. To what extent, for instance, might technology also improve well-being through mental health apps or online support networks?

4. Exploring the Role of Leadership Styles

Different styles of leadership can have different consequences for the well-being of the entrepreneur and an organization's health. Future research is worth probing into what specific kind of leadership approach-that is, transformational, servant, or inclusive leadership, to give two examples-has an effect on the entrepreneurial entrepreneur's and their teams' mental health outcomes (Karimi & Reisi, 2023). This in-depth knowledge on how the style of leadership impacts the culture of a workplace, worker engagement, and the satisfaction and fulfillment of an entrepreneur would reveal knowledge on effective practices leading to both personal and organizational success.

5. Mental Health Interventions and Support Mechanisms

Mental health interventions specific to entrepreneurs are now increasingly recognized as important. It would hence be valuable to research various support mechanisms that could be proposed, including peer mentorship programs, mental health workshops, or counseling services specifically offered to entrepreneurs. One could evaluate these support mechanisms to spot the best practices that should be used in supporting the mental health and well-being of entrepreneurs (Chen et al., 2022).

6. Community and Networking Role

Networking represents one of the critical roles in entrepreneurship, which might improve well-being due to support or resource availability. To better understand the differences, future studies are recommended to examine the effects that specific kinds of entrepreneurial networks—a kind of formal association or informal groups and online community—may have on individuals' well-being and business success. Better understanding how these networks function and with what effects on the mental health should lead to proper strategies for building supportive ecosystems for entrepreneurs (Çetin et al., 2022).

7. Interdisciplinary Methods of Research

Diverse fields such as psychology, sociology, economics, and management can be fetched to give a more complete insight into the relationship between entrepreneurial success and personal well-being. Since the present study was unable to tease out the interplay of social determinants, economic conditions, and psychological factors on entrepreneurial outcomes as well as on personal fulfillment (Dijkhuizen et al., 2018), further research may benefit from using interdisciplinary methods in studying the interaction of factors on entrepreneurial outcomes and personal well-being. Such a broader standpoint may be the foundation for building more encompassing models of entrepreneurship that may be able to provide a more robust representation of the intricacies surrounding entrepreneurship.

8. Measuring Success Beyond Financial Metrics

Well, while measurement of entrepreneurial success has ordinarily been based on financial metrics, such an approach gives a narrow outlook, quite panning all the other aspects of success that should not be ignored. Future research needs to consider various alternative measures of success: personal fulfillment, social impact, and, most importantly, overall quality of life. Holistic frameworks and/or approaches considering several dimensions of success can give a more comprehensive understanding of what it means to be a successful entrepreneur (Marshall et al., 2020).

9. Cross-Country and Cross-Culture Comparisons

Cultural and societal issues also influence the experiences of entrepreneurs in substantial ways. Cross-country and cross-culture comparison can gain insightful information about what consequences cultural attitudes toward entrepreneurship, work, and well-being produce in terms of personal and professional outcomes. It informs the development of a culturally sensitive support system for entrepreneurs.

The future research avenue on the interplay between entrepreneurial success and personal well-being is great with possibilities. According to these directions, scholars would help to generate deeper insights about how entrepreneurs can do well both personally and professionally. During the course of inevitable entrepreneurial landscape evolution there always will be an urgent need for research that serves to discover potent strategies toward not only successful but also sustainable well-being and resiliency in the entrepreneurial journey (Sánchez-García et al., 2018).

CONCLUSION

The relationship between entrepreneurial success and personal well-being is complex and multidimensional, and underlined is the complex interface of ambition, personal fulfillment, mental health, and support systems. As this chapter will discuss, entrepreneurial success often requires a high-wire balancing act: whereas ambition pushes entrepreneurs to pursue their goals and drive innovation, a focus on what constitutes success in external markers may carry adverse implications for personal well-being. Thus, entrepreneurs need to be oriented towards a holistic attitude toward the entrepreneurial journey.

Personal fulfillment is not just something success brings but rather an element that ought to form part of a sustainable and meaningful entrepreneurial experience.

Entrepreneurial ambitions must sit side by side with self-care, mental health, as well as relationship building. Such entrepreneurs can quickly overcome inescapable challenges and pressures to work through those because of the psychological resilience they have built up and the successful coping mechanisms available to them. Observing work-life balance and actively seeking out support systems only adds to their chances of overcoming challenges both in life and in business. This chapter highlights the importance of learning to recognize the truth that well-being and entrepreneurial success are not inversely related-that is, they are interdependent elements of an entrepreneurial experience.

Going forward, as the entrepreneurial landscape continues to change, there is a continued need for research in this field to be conducted from a critically observational angle. The subtlety with which different influences alter the relationship between success and well-being can have great insightful value for entrepreneurs, educators, policymakers, mental health professionals, and so on. Investments in research on varied contexts, leadership styles, technological impacts, and community support ensure stakeholders can design focused strategies that enable entrepreneurs to be successful but not compromise their health and wellness.

Conclusion: Entrepreneurship is a very challenging journey which, with ambition and self-reflection, offers those pursuing it the opportunity to be unique. A more conscious realization of your well-being as you journey along the path that is entrepreneurialism will find greater success not only in business but, basically in life itself. That leaves a lot of space for scrutiny and critique, but as this relationship develops further, it begins to look dramatically different, where the future success of entrepreneurial activities will be highly dependent on providing nurturing support ecosystems for entrepreneurs that focus on better mental health, work-life balance, and personal fulfillment.

REFERENCES

Binder, M. (2017). Entrepreneurial success and subjective well-being: Worries about the business explain one's well-being loss from self-employment.

Çetin, G., Altınay, L., Alrawadıeh, Z., & Ali, F. (2022). Entrepreneurial motives, entrepreneurial success and life satisfaction of refugees venturing in tourism and hospitality. *International Journal of Contemporary Hospitality Management*, 34(6), 2227–2249. DOI: 10.1108/IJCHM-11-2021-1363

Chay, Y. W. (1993). Social support, individual differences, and well-being: A study of small business entrepreneurs and employees. *Journal of Occupational and Organizational Psychology*, 66(4), 285–302. DOI: 10.1111/j.2044-8325.1993.tb00540.x

Chen, C., Zhang, J., Tian, H., & Bu, X. (2022). The impact of entrepreneurial passion on entrepreneurial success and psychological well-being: A person-centered investigation. *International Journal of Entrepreneurial Behaviour & Research*. Advance online publication. DOI: 10.1108/IJEBR-12-2021-0977

Chen, M., & Tseng, M. (2021). Creative entrepreneurs' artistic creativity and entrepreneurial alertness: The guanxi network perspective. *International Journal of Entrepreneurial Behaviour & Research*, 27(4), 1082–1102. DOI: 10.1108/IJEBR-05-2020-0306

Dej, D. (2010). Defining and measuring entrepreneurial success. In *Entrepreneurship: A Psychological Approach* (pp. 89-102).

Dijkhuizen, J. (2015). *Entrepreneurship, easier said than done: A study on success and well-being among entrepreneurs in the Netherlands*.

Dijkhuizen, J., Gorgievski, M., van Veldhoven, M., & Schalk, R. (2018). Well-being, personal success, and business performance among entrepreneurs: A two-wave study. *Journal of Happiness Studies*, 19(8), 2187–2204. DOI: 10.1007/s10902-017-9914-6

Dijkhuizen, J., Gorgievski, M., Veldhoven, M., & Schalk, R. (2017). Well-being, personal success, and business performance among entrepreneurs: A two-wave study. *Journal of Happiness Studies*, 19(8), 2187–2204. DOI: 10.1007/s10902-017-9914-6

Drnovšek, M., Örtqvist, D., & Wincent, J. (2010). The effectiveness of coping strategies used by entrepreneurs and their impact on personal well-being and venture performance. *Zbornik radova Ekonomskog fakulteta u Rijeci: časopis za ekonomsku teoriju i praksu*, 28(2), 193-220.

Gorgievski, M., Ascalon, M., & Stephan, U. (2011). Small business owners' success criteria, a values approach to personal differences. *Journal of Small Business Management*, 49(2), 207–232. DOI: 10.1111/j.1540-627X.2011.00322.x

Hahn, V. C., Frese, M., Binnewies, C., & Schmitt, A. (2012). Happy and proactive? The role of hedonic and eudaimonic well-being in business owners' personal initiative. *Entrepreneurship Theory and Practice*, 36(1), 97–114. DOI: 10.1111/j.1540-6520.2011.00490.x

Karimi, S., & Reisi, S. (2023). Satisfaction of psychological needs and entrepreneurial success: Mediating effects of well-being and work engagement (Case study: Nahavand County, Iran). *Journal of Agricultural Science and Technology*, 25(4), 847–862.

Marshall, D. R., Meek, W. R., Swab, R. G., & Markin, E. (2020). Access to resources and entrepreneurial well-being: A self-efficacy approach. *Journal of Business Research*, 120, 203–212. DOI: 10.1016/j.jbusres.2020.08.015

Nikolaev, B., Boudreaux, C. J., & Wood, M. (2020). Entrepreneurship and subjective well-being: The mediating role of psychological functioning. *Entrepreneurship Theory and Practice*, 44(3), 557–586. DOI: 10.1177/1042258719830314

Parasuraman, S., Purohit, Y. S., Godshalk, V. M., & Beutell, N. J. (1996). Work and family variables, entrepreneurial career success, and psychological well-being. *Journal of Vocational Behavior*, 48(3), 275–300. DOI: 10.1006/jvbe.1996.0025

Ryff, C. (2019). Entrepreneurship and eudaimonic well-being: Five venues for new science. *Journal of Business Venturing*, 34(4), 646–663. DOI: 10.1016/j.jbusvent.2018.09.003 PMID: 31105380

Sánchez-García, J. C., Vargas-Morúa, G., & Hernández-Sánchez, B. R. (2018). Entrepreneurs' well-being: A bibliometric review. *Frontiers in Psychology*, 9, 1696. DOI: 10.3389/fpsyg.2018.01696 PMID: 30258384

Sherman, C. L., Randall, C., & Kauanui, S. K. (2016). Are you happy yet? Entrepreneurs' subjective well-being. *Journal of Management, Spirituality & Religion*, 13(1), 7–23. DOI: 10.1080/14766086.2015.1043575

Singh, A., Krishna, S. H., Raghuwanshi, S., Sharma, J., & Bapat, V. (2023). Measuring psychological well-being of entrepreneurial success–An analytical study. *Journal for ReAttach Therapy and Developmental Diversities*, 6(4s), 338–348.

Stephan, U. (2018). Entrepreneurs' mental health and well-being: A review and research agenda. *The Academy of Management Perspectives*, 32(3), 290–322. DOI: 10.5465/amp.2017.0001

Tisu, L., & Vîrgă, D. (2022). Proactive vitality management, work–home enrichment, and performance: A two-wave cross-lagged study on entrepreneurs. *Frontiers in Psychology*, 13, 761958. Advance online publication. DOI: 10.3389/fpsyg.2022.761958 PMID: 35310274

Tunio, M. N. (2020). Academic entrepreneurship in developing countries: Contextualizing recent debate. In *Research Handbook on Entrepreneurship in Emerging Economies* (pp. 130–146). Edward Elgar Publishing. DOI: 10.4337/9781788973717.00014

Tunio, M. N., Chaudhry, I. S., Shaikh, S., Jariko, M. A., & Brahmi, M. (2021). Determinants of the sustainable entrepreneurial engagement of youth in developing country—An empirical evidence from Pakistan. *Sustainability (Basel)*, 13(14), 7764. DOI: 10.3390/su13147764

Tunio, M. N., Jariko, M. A., Børsen, T., Shaikh, S., Mushtaque, T., & Brahmi, M. (2021). How entrepreneurship sustains barriers in the entrepreneurial process—A lesson from a developing nation. *Sustainability (Basel)*, 13(20), 11419. DOI: 10.3390/su132011419

Wiklund, J., Nikolaev, B., Shir, N., Foo, M. D., & Bradley, S. (2019). Entrepreneurship and well-being: Past, present, and future. *Journal of Business Venturing*, 34(4), 579–588. DOI: 10.1016/j.jbusvent.2019.01.002

Williamson, A., Gish, J., & Stephan, U. (2021). Let's focus on solutions to entrepreneurial ill-being! Recovery interventions to enhance entrepreneurial well-being. *Entrepreneurship Theory and Practice*, 45(6), 1307–1338. DOI: 10.1177/10422587211006431

Chapter 12
How Work Environments Drive Mental Calm and Entrepreneurial Progress:
Building a Sanctuary for Success

J. S. Sathyajith
Christ University, India

K. Sudheesh
Christ University, India

ABSTRACT

This research investigates the important relationship between a healthy work environment and the mental health of entrepreneurs, particularly women. It emphasizes the importance of mental calm in achieving entrepreneurial success and identifies major aspects that influence it. The work environment has a significant impact on emotional, psychological, and total well-being. The paper highlights ways that employers can use to create a healthy work environment, such as encouraging positive connections, effective communication, and mutual respect. It emphasizes the significance of stress management, confronting harassment and abusive behavior, and incorporating social and moral ideals into corporate culture. Organizations can foster mental well-being and entrepreneurial growth by prioritizing these characteristics.

INTRODUCTION

The Precarious Perch of Entrepreneurship: Mental Calm Amidst the Hustle

In the fast-paced world of entrepreneurship maintaining mental calm is crucial for driving innovation, making strategic decisions, and sustaining long-term progress. Work environments play a pivotal role in shaping the mental well-being of entrepreneurs and directly impact their ability to thrive amidst challenges. This article explores the various ways in which work environments influence mental calm and entrepreneurial progress, offering insights into creating conducive settings for success.

The entrepreneurial journey is exhilarating, demanding, and often precarious. While the potential rewards are immense, the constant pressure to innovate, secure funding, and navigate a competitive landscape can take a toll on an entrepreneur's mental well-being. This is particularly true for female entrepreneurs, who may face additional challenges related to gender bias and a lack of access to resources.

Maintaining mental serenity in the midst of the entrepreneurial hustle is a necessity, not a luxury. A clear and concentrated mind is necessary for making informed judgments, encouraging creativity, and propelling the organization forward. This research examines the important relationship between a healthy work environment and entrepreneurs' mental well-being. It investigates the numerous aspects that contribute to mental calm in the entrepreneurial ecosystem, with a specific emphasis on techniques for empowering female entrepreneurs to thrive.

We will investigate how the organization of the workplace might either promote or drain mental well-being. By investigating the effects of elements such as healthy social relationships, effective communication, and a supportive culture, we will discover critical tactics that employers and entrepreneurs can use to foster a sense of calm and purpose in the workplace.

The article will also discuss the negative impact of stress, harassment, and a toxic work environment on mental health. We will talk about proactive steps that may be taken to reduce these concerns and establish a safe and supportive environment for entrepreneurs to thrive. Finally, we will look at the importance of social and moral norms in promoting a healthy work environment. Entrepreneurs can improve their own well-being while simultaneously creating a more sustainable and successful corporation by incorporating ethical conduct, diversity, and social responsibility into the company's basic values.

Through this investigation, we hope to provide entrepreneurs, particularly women, with the knowledge and skills they need to build a sense of mental peace in the workplace. Prioritizing well-being allows entrepreneurs to not only protect their own mental health, but also feed their innovative spirit and propel their businesses to long-term success.

Nurturing Supportive Cultures:
A supportive work culture fosters a sense of belonging and encourages open communication among team members.
Positive reinforcement and recognition of achievements contribute to a conducive atmosphere where entrepreneurs feel valued and motivated.
Encouraging Work-Life Balance:
Establishing boundaries between work and personal life promotes mental rejuvenation and prevents burnout.
Flexible work arrangements and wellness initiatives enable entrepreneurs to prioritize self-care without compromising productivity.
Fostering Collaboration and Innovation:
Collaborative workspaces stimulate creativity and problem-solving by facilitating interaction and idea exchange.
Creating spaces for brainstorming sessions and cross-functional collaboration encourages entrepreneurial teams to explore new opportunities and approaches.
Providing Resources and Support:

Access to resources such as mentorship programs, professional development opportunities, and financial support enhances entrepreneurs' confidence and resilience.

Offering psychological support services and stress management programs equips entrepreneurs with coping mechanisms to navigate challenges effectively.

Addressing Diversity and Inclusion:

Embracing diversity fosters a culture of acceptance and mutual respect, enriching the entrepreneurial ecosystem with varied perspectives and experiences.

Promoting Work Environment Wellness:

Designing ergonomic workspaces and incorporating elements of nature, such as natural light and greenery, enhances overall well-being and productivity.

Encouraging regular breaks, mindfulness practices, and physical activity supports entrepreneurs in maintaining mental clarity and focus.

Statement of Purpose

Entrepreneurship, while full of possibilities, can be a very demanding endeavor. The constant drive to develop, compete, and seek finance creates a stressful climate that can compromise the well-being of entrepreneurs, particularly women who face additional hurdles. This study addresses this essential problem by delving into the complex relationship between a good workplace and entrepreneurs' mental health.

Our primary goal is to highlight the aspects that contribute to mental tranquility in the entrepreneurial arena. We focus on tactics that help entrepreneurs, particularly women, to build a sense of calm and purpose within their work environment. This paper examines the impact of the work environment itself. We look at how healthy social ties, efficient communication, and a supportive culture can promote mental health, whereas a hostile setting can deplete it.

By identifying essential tactics for cultivating these positive elements, we hope to empower entrepreneurs to build a work atmosphere that promotes both mental health and business success.

Furthermore, we realize the negative consequences of stress, harassment, and a toxic workplace. To address this, we will go over proactive steps entrepreneurs may take to reduce these hazards and create a secure and supportive environment for themselves and their staff. Finally, we will look at the importance of social and moral norms in promoting a healthy work environment. We believe that incorporating ethical behavior, diversity, and social responsibility into a company's basic values not only promotes entrepreneurial well-being, but also leads to a more sustainable and profitable corporation.

In short, this paper seeks to be a comprehensive resource for entrepreneurs, particularly women, who want to create mental peace in their workplace. Prioritizing well-being not only protects entrepreneurs' mental health, but it also allows them to realize their full innovative potential and propels their businesses to long-term success. This, in turn, promotes a more thriving and resilient entrepreneurial ecosystem, which benefits both individuals and the whole business landscape.

Review of Literature

1. Women's Entrepreneurship and Culture: Gender Role Expectations and Identities, Societal Culture, and the Entrepreneurial Environment

Women's entrepreneurship is critical to economic progress, but the role of culture in these businesses is uncertain. This study presents a framework to investigate this gap. It examines how cultural expectations, societal values, and the business environment affect women entrepreneurs differently depending on their region and background. Understanding this dynamic allows us to better help women in business around the world. (Amanda Bullough, Ulrike Guelich, Tatiana S. Manolova & Leon Schjoedt, 09 January 2021)

2. The Effect of Entrepreneurial Mindset, Work Environment on Employees' Work Performance

This study investigates the relationship between an employee's entrepreneurial mindset and job effectiveness. It claims that traditional hiring practices based on education and experience are insufficient. According to the survey, people with an entrepreneurial spirit are more motivated and contribute more to the success of their companies. A supportive work environment that promotes creativity and innovation helps to create this mindset. The study intends to look into how these factors affect employee performance and make recommendations for improving training and workplace culture. (Abun et al., 2022)

3. The Relationship Between Entrepreneurial Intent, Gender and Personality

This study investigates how personality factors influence women's entrepreneurial inclinations. Women entrepreneurs are critical to economic progress. However, women are underrepresented in the sector. Existing study has focused on male entrepreneurs, leaving a gap in knowing what motivates women. This study addresses this issue by evaluating the psychological qualities of prospective female entrepreneurs and comparing them to aspiring male entrepreneurs and non-entrepreneurs of both genders. It searches for gendered disparities in personality traits that could explain why fewer women pursue business. (Mackenzie R. Zisser, Sheri L. Johnson, PhD, Michael A. Freeman, MD, and Paige J. Staudenmaier, 2019)

4. Analyzing the Mental Health and Well-Being of Entrepreneurs

This essay examines the mental health problems that entrepreneurs encounter. Entrepreneurship, despite its reputation for success, may be stressful and lonely owing to reasons such as unpredictability, pressure, and long hours. This can result in mental health problems such as anxiety, depression, and exhaustion. The research tries to understand these problems and uncover the coping mechanisms that entrepreneurs utilize to maintain their well-being. (M Nisa, Prof Ved Srinivas, Dr Ridhi, Kdv PRASAD, April 2023).

5. Emotional Skills for Entrepreneurial Success

This study contends that entrepreneurship education and policy frequently fail because they overlook the emotional challenges that entrepreneurs encounter. While these programs emphasize skills and information, they do not prepare entrepreneurs to deal with stress, uncertainty, and other emotional challenges. According to the author, emotional intelligence training and the development of support systems could assist entrepreneurs traverse these challenges and increase their chances of success. (Maha Aly, David B. Audretsch & Heike Grimm, 13 July 2021)

Objectives:

1. Recognize the impact of cultural factors on women's entrepreneurship
2. Investigate the link between an entrepreneurial mindset, work environment, and employee performance
3. Identify personality traits that influence women's entrepreneurial intentions
4. Analyze entrepreneurs' mental health challenges
5. Assess the impact of emotional skills on entrepreneurial success

Research Questions:
- What impact do cultural expectations and societal norms have on women entrepreneurs' success rates across areas and cultures?
- What is the correlation between employees' entrepreneurial mindset, supportive work environment, and job success in diverse industries?
- What psychological features distinguish female entrepreneurs from male entrepreneurs and non-entrepreneurs? How do these traits impact women's entrepreneurial intentions?
- What are the common mental health difficulties experienced by entrepreneurs, and how do they cope with the demands of entrepreneurship?
- What impact does emotional intelligence have on entrepreneurial success? What tactics can entrepreneurs use to strengthen their emotional skills?

Analysis:
- Qualitative Content Analysis: Extracting themes, patterns, insights from textual data for interpretation
- Comparative Analysis: Identifying similarities, differences, and trends across different research studies
- Quantitative Statistical Analysis: Analyzing numerical data to establish relationships between variables statistically
- Thematic Analysis: Identifying recurring themes or topics within qualitative data sets
- Case Study Analysis: Examining specific instances to draw broader conclusions or insights
- Meta-Analysis: Synthesizing findings from multiple studies to draw overarching conclusions

Models:

1. Grounded Theory Model: To develop a theory grounded in the data, particularly useful for exploring new phenomena or understanding complex interactions within the literature
2. Framework Analysis: To systematically organize and analyze qualitative data by applying a pre-existing framework or creating a new framework based on the literature's themes and concepts
3. Regression Analysis: To examine relationships between variables quantitatively, particularly useful for exploring the impact of entrepreneurial mindset, work environment, and personality traits on job performance or entrepreneurial success
4. Social Cognitive Career Theory (SCCT): To understand how cultural factors, personality traits, and environmental influences shape individuals' career choices and entrepreneurial intentions, particularly relevant for exploring women's entrepreneurship
5. Cognitive-Behavioral Model: To examine the interplay between thoughts, behaviors, and emotions related to stress, harassment, and well-being in entrepreneurship, particularly useful for understanding coping mechanisms and interventions

6. Entrepreneurial Ecosystem Framework: To analyze the broader context in which entrepreneurs operate, including cultural, social, economic, and policy factors, and their impact on entrepreneurial outcomes and mental well-being
7. Job Demands-Resources (JD-R) Model: To examine the balance between job demands (e.g., stress, harassment) and job resources (e.g., supportive work environment, coping strategies) in influencing job performance and mental well-being in entrepreneurship

Findings:
- Cultural expectations and societal values significantly influence the experiences and success rates of women entrepreneurs, with variations observed across different regions and cultural contexts.
- Employees with an entrepreneurial mindset tend to demonstrate higher job performance, particularly in environments that foster creativity and innovation through supportive work cultures.
- Certain personality traits, such as openness to experience, resilience, and risk-taking propensity, differentiate women entrepreneurs from their male counterparts and non-entrepreneurs, influencing their entrepreneurial intentions and behaviors.
- Entrepreneurship poses significant mental health challenges, including stress, anxiety, depression, and burnout, which are exacerbated by factors such as uncertainty, pressure, and long working hours.
- Coping mechanisms used by entrepreneurs to maintain their mental well-being include seeking social support, practicing self-care strategies, and developing resilience to navigate the demands of entrepreneurship effectively.
- Emotional intelligence plays a crucial role in entrepreneurial success, enabling entrepreneurs to effectively manage stress, uncertainty, and interpersonal relationships, thereby enhancing their ability to innovate and adapt in dynamic business environments.

Suggestions:
- Promote Cultural Sensitivity: Encourage organizations to recognize and respect cultural diversity and provide training programs to educate entrepreneurs and employees about cultural differences and how they can impact women's entrepreneurship.
- Foster Entrepreneurial Mindset: Create a work environment that encourages and rewards innovation, creativity, and risk-taking, and provide training and development programs to cultivate an entrepreneurial mindset among employees.
- Support Women's Entrepreneurship: Develop policies and initiatives aimed at addressing the unique challenges faced by women entrepreneurs, such as access to funding, networks, and mentorship opportunities, to promote gender equality in entrepreneurship.
- Prioritize Mental Health Awareness: Increase awareness about mental health issues in entrepreneurship, reduce stigma, and provide resources and support services to help entrepreneurs cope with stress, anxiety, and other mental health challenges.
- Promote Emotional Intelligence Training: Incorporate emotional intelligence training into entrepreneurship education programs and provide resources for entrepreneurs to develop their emotional skills, such as self-awareness, self-regulation, empathy, and social skills.

- Create Supportive Work Environments: Implement policies and practices that promote a positive work culture, such as flexible work arrangements, employee assistance programs, and initiatives to prevent harassment and discrimination.
- Invest in Research and Policy: Support research initiatives and policy development aimed at better understanding the factors influencing women's entrepreneurship, employee performance, mental health challenges, and the role of emotional skills in entrepreneurial success.

CONCLUSION

This study emphasizes the crucial relevance of creating a healthy work environment for supporting the mental well-being of entrepreneurs, particularly women, as they navigate the hurdles of entrepreneurship successfully. This study emphasizes the importance of mental quiet despite the hustle and bustle of business ventures, emphasizing the need to create supporting ecosystems that nourish emotional, psychological, and total well-being. The findings highlight the importance of cultural influences, work environment, personality traits, and emotional abilities in determining entrepreneurial experiences and outcomes. Cultural expectations and societal beliefs heavily impact women's entrepreneurship, whereas an entrepreneurial attitude and a supportive work environment improve employee performance and job happiness. Furthermore, the study emphasizes the mental health issues that entrepreneurs confront, as well as the necessity of coping skills and emotional intelligence in promoting well-being.

Moving forward, organizations, policymakers, and stakeholders must implement targeted interventions and initiatives to promote cultural sensitivity, cultivate an entrepreneurial mindset, support women's entrepreneurship, prioritize mental health awareness, promote emotional intelligence training, create supportive work environments, and invest in research and policy development. Organizations can protect entrepreneurs' mental health while also unleashing their full potential for innovation and success by addressing these factors and creating conducive settings that promote well-being. Finally, creating a supportive environment for female entrepreneurs benefits not only people but also adds to a more thriving and resilient entrepreneurial landscape, which drives economic growth and societal well-being.

Recommendations

- Prioritize diversity and inclusion initiatives to promote female entrepreneurs and employees from varied backgrounds. Mentorship programs, networking opportunities, and inclusive policies that address entry and progression hurdles are all examples of such initiatives.
- Provide Mental Health Support Services: Companies should offer counseling, workshops, and employee assistance programs to help entrepreneurs and workers manage stress, anxiety, and other mental health issues.
- Encourage work-life balance by creating flexible work arrangements, fostering time management skills, and discouraging overworking. This can assist entrepreneurs and employees both avoid burnout and improve their general well-being.
- Offer Emotional Intelligence Training: Develop skills like self-awareness, self-regulation, empathy, and relationship management through courses and seminars. These abilities are essential for managing the emotional hurdles of entrepreneurship and developing strong professional relationships.

- Foster a supportive work environment by encouraging open communication, giving chances for feedback and recognition, and resolving harassment and discrimination quickly and efficiently.
- Invest in research and policy development to better understand the needs and problems of female entrepreneurs and employees. Implement evidence-based interventions to promote their success.
- Facilitate networking and community building opportunities for female entrepreneurs to interact with peers, mentors, and industry experts. Building supportive networks may give invaluable resources, advice, and emotional support as you navigate the entrepreneurial journey.

REFERENCES

Almestica, M. (2012). *Work-life balance issues and mentoring strategies for women in the contract management profession.*

Applewhite, P. A. (2017). Examining the role of emotional intelligence in the work and life balance of foster care workers. Walden Dissertations and Doctoral Studies. 3517.

Badu, E., O'Brien, A. P., Mitchell, R., & Rubin, M. (2020). Workplace stress and resilience in the Australian nursing workforce: A comprehensive integrative review. *International Journal of Mental Health Nursing*, 29(1), 5–34.

Chaidi, I., Papoutsi, C., Drigas, A., & Skianis, C. (2022). *Women: E-Entrepreneurship and Emotional Intelligence.* Technium Social Sciences Journal.

Cukier, W., Saunders, V., & Stewart, S. (2022). Social Entrepreneurship and Addressing SDGs through Women's Empowerment: A Case Study of She-EO. In *World Scientific Encyclopedia of Business Sustainability, Ethics and Entrepreneurship* (pp. 83-111). World Scientific.

Haddock-Millar, J., & Tom, E. (2019). *Coaching and mentoring for work-life balance.* Taylor and Francis.

Kamberidou, I. (2020). "Distinguished" women entrepreneurs in the digital economy and the multitasking whirlpool. *Journal of Innovation and Entrepreneurship*, 9(3).

Kulkarni, A., & Mishra, M. (2022). Aspects of women's leadership in the organisation: Systematic literature review. *SA Journal of Human Resource Management*, 9(1), 9–32.

Owens, J., Kottwitz, C., & Tiedt, J. (2018). Strategies to attain faculty work-life balance. *Building Healthy Academic Communities Journal*, 2(2), 58–73.

Palmer, N. J., Davies, J., & Viney, C. (2023). Research Environment, Culture, Capacity, Capabilities and Connectivity. In *Business and Management Doctorates World-Wide: Developing the Next Generation* (pp.125-151). Emerald Publishing.

Tetterton, M. (2020). *Exploring the Challenges of Work Life Balance of Female Leadership: A Qualitative Case Study.*

Chapter 13
Leadership Behavior That Promotes Psychological Wellness at Work

Hemlata Parmar
https://orcid.org/0009-0009-1438-5427
Manipal University Jaipur, India

Utsav Krishan Murari
https://orcid.org/0009-0007-1606-6775
Sharda University, India

ABSTRACT

In contemporary organizational environments, the role of leadership extends beyond traditional managerial functions to encompass the holistic well-being of employees. It explores the critical behaviors exhibited by leaders that contribute to enhancing workplace well-being. Leadership behavior profoundly influences employees' psychological, emotional, and social health, which affects organizational outcomes such as productivity, job satisfaction, and retention. Leadership behavior that supports workplace well-being is integral to creating a thriving and sustainable organizational environment. By prioritizing empathetic communication, work-life balance, recognition, development, inclusivity, and stress management, leaders can significantly enhance the well-being of their employees, resulting in a more motivated and productive workforce. This study identifies critical leadership behaviors that support workplace well-being and examines their impact through a comprehensive review of existing literature and empirical research.

INTRODUCTION

Organizations have long recognized that employee health and well-being are significant concerns, and it is widely recognized that various factors can contribute to this (Cooper & Cartwright, 1994). Much research is available regarding the impact of leadership, management style, and behavior on employee health and well-being. Nevertheless, it is frequently challenging to determine the specific patterns and behaviors leaders and managers must exhibit to establish cultures and climates that promote positive health and well-being in the workplace. (Cameron et al., 2011). This desk-top review evaluates the evidence

DOI: 10.4018/979-8-3693-3673-1.ch013

Copyright ©2025, IGI Global. Copying or distributing in print or electronic forms without written permission of IGI Global is prohibited.

base within the confines of the commission for the NHS Northwest Leadership Academy. The primary objective is to concentrate on the leadership and management behaviors that are likely to positively or negatively impact on the health and well-being of employees in the workplace.

Policies and Procedures That Show How Serious We Are About Our Employees' Health and Safety

A healthy, productive, and long-lasting workplace is the result of an organization's commitment to its employees' physical and mental wellness. (Gilbreath & Benson, 2004). Leaders can show they care about their employees' well-being as a whole by creating and following effective rules and procedures. (Podsakoff, MacKenzie, & Podsakoff, 2009) To illustrate this dedication, below are important actions to take and examples:

1. Establish Clear Policies and Procedures
   - **Health and Safety Policies**: Develop comprehensive health and safety policies that comply with local regulations and industry standards. Ensure these policies cover workplace ergonomics, emergency procedures, and occupational health risks.
     o **Example**: Implement regular safety audits and risk assessments, and ensure that all employees have access to personal protective equipment (PPE) where necessary. (Neal & Griffin, 2006).
   - **Mental Health and Wellbeing Policy**: Create a mental health policy that promotes awareness, reduces stigma, and provides support for employees experiencing mental health issues.
     o **Example**: Offer mental health days, provide access to counseling services, and conduct mental health awareness training for all staff. (Schwartz & Porath, 2014).

2. Promote Work-Life Balance
   - **Flexible Working Arrangements**: To assist workers manage their time better, companies should institute policies that encourage things like flexible scheduling, remote work, and task sharing.
     o **Example**: Implement a "core hours" policy where employees can choose to start and end their workday within a flexible time frame, as long as they are available during core hours for meetings and collaboration. (Kelloway & Barling, 2010).
   - **Leave Policies**: Ensure that leave policies, including vacation, sick leave, parental leave, and bereavement leave, are generous and supportive of employees' needs.
     o **Example**: Provide additional paid leave for employees facing personal or family emergencies, and ensure that all leave requests are handled with empathy and understanding.

3. Implement Wellness Programs
   - **Physical Wellness**: Encourage a healthy lifestyle by launching programs like wellness challenges, on-site workout centers, and gym membership subsidies. (Salas, Cooke, & Rosen, 2008).
     o **Example**: Organize company-wide wellness challenges like step-count competitions, and offer incentives for participation and achievement.
   - **Nutritional Support**: Provide access to healthy food options and nutritional education.

- o **Example**: Stock break rooms with healthy snacks and beverages, and offer workshops on nutrition and healthy eating habits.
- **Mental Health Support**: Offer programs that support mental well-being, such as mindfulness sessions, stress management workshops, and access to professional counseling. (Cameron et al., 2011).
  - o **Example**: Collaborate with mental health experts to offer mindfulness classes and therapy at your location.

4. Promote an Inclusive Workplace
   - **Open Communication**: Ensure your staff know they are heard and appreciated by encouraging open communication and frequent feedback. (Grawitch et al., 2006).
     - o **Example**: Conduct regular one-on-one meetings between employees and managers to discuss workload, concerns, and career development.
   - **Recognition Programs**: Implement programs that recognize and reward employees' efforts and achievements. (Judge & Kammeyer-Mueller, 2012).
     - o **Example**: Create an "Employee of the Month" program and celebrate employees' accomplishments in company newsletters and meetings.
   - **Inclusive Culture**: Promote a culture of inclusivity and diversity, ensuring that all employees feel respected and valued.
     - o **Example**: Form diversity and inclusion committees to address issues, promote awareness, and organize events celebrating diverse cultures and perspectives.

5. Monitor and Evaluate
   - **Regular Surveys**: Gather input and find improvement areas by conducting frequent surveys on employee satisfaction and well-being. (Mills et al., 2013).
     - o **Example**: Use anonymous surveys to assess employee satisfaction with existing well-being programs and solicit suggestions for new initiatives.
   - **Performance Metrics**: Monitoring KPIs like employee engagement, turnover, and absenteeism can provide light on the state of health and wellness in the workplace.
     - o **Example**: Analyze data from health and wellness programs to evaluate their effectiveness and make data-driven decisions for future initiatives.
   - **Continuous Improvement**: Use the feedback and data collected to improve policies and programs continuously. (Gilbreath & Benson, 2004).
     - o **Example**: Hold quarterly review meetings with HR and management teams to discuss survey results and implement changes based on employee feedback.

A systematic strategy that incorporates proactive procedures and supportive policies into the business culture is necessary to demonstrate commitment to employee health and well-being. (Cameron et al., 2011; Grawitch et al., 2006). An employer may build a healthy workplace that cares about its people by setting clear policies, encouraging a work-life balance, introducing wellness programs, creating a friendly atmosphere, and constantly checking in to see how things are going. (Judge & Kammeyer-Mueller, 2012; Mills et al., 2013).

Multiple Approaches for Leaders to Promote Health and Wellness in Their Employees

Companies must prioritize the health and wellness of their employees more than ever before as businesses throughout the globe reopen and employees return to the office. (Schwartz & Porath, 2014). Leaders must maintain a focus on the health and safety of their team members considering the COVID-19 pandemic's emphasis on the requirement of providing a safe and healthy work environment. (Neal & Griffin, 2006).

1. **Employees' Growth and Development Should Be Prioritized**

Bring your best work to the office and help your coworkers realize their full potential. (Gilbreath & Benson, 2004). Staff members will know you care about them when you put money into their professional growth. Encourage them to keep talking about their year-end objectives and how you can be a part of their success. (Kelloway & Barling, 2010). Design challenging tasks with specific goals in mind, and provide them with opportunities for training, coaching, mentorship, and networking to help them climb the corporate ladder. (Podsakoff et al., 2009).

2. **Utilize "Day Breaks"**

"Day breaks," as I like to call them, should be implemented by every firm. One of my clients is in the business of introducing day breaks to companies with office workers. Here, members of the day-break team gather off-site to instruct workers in stress-reduction techniques including chair yoga, stretching, nutrition hacks, and sleep sessions. (Cameron et al., 2011) The day when workers and employers alike can finally say "well" instead of "sick!" is almost here!

3. **Improve the Quality of Your Conversations**

Improve the standard of your talks by speaking more slowly and with more humanity. Raise your level of empathy and develop an insatiable curiosity for the people around you. (Judge & Kammeyer-Mueller, 2012). Every day, people face and overcome the challenges that life throws at them. Having your feelings acknowledged and validated goes a long way. (Mills et al., 2013). Simply bearing witness to the lived experiences of your people and creating space for their voices is one of the greatest gifts of leadership.

4. **Keep Your Preferences for How you Work at Heart**

Those returning to the workforce must prioritize workforce planning. (Kelloway & Barling, 2010). While some of your coworkers may thrive in an office setting, others may be more extroverted and prefer to work alone. It is critical to be aware of different styles. (Schwartz & Porath, 2014). Additionally, you shouldn't assume that extra meetings are necessary simply because individuals are in an office environment. It can be helpful to promote breaks, invest in ergonomics, and make healthy dietary choices. (Podsakoff et al., 2009).

5. **Be an Example of Good Habits**

A leader's first responsibility is to set a good example by not only avoiding but actively discourage bad habits. (Cameron et al., 2011). Building a high-performance culture that values result over effort is an important part of this. So is encouraging healthy habits. Insisting that workers take personal responsibility for their own and others' well-being while simultaneously encouraging an atmosphere of competence and self-direction is equally crucial. (Grawitch et al., 2006).

6. **Inquire Further by Listening Carefully**

No longer are those who departed the office among those who have returned. Everyone has had their own unique experience. The epidemic has had a profound effect on some people, while appearing to have had little to no effect on others. (Schwartz & Porath, 2014). Find out what happened and how you might assist them in getting back to work by asking them questions. (Judge & Kammeyer-Mueller, 2012).

7. **Schedule Monthly Individual Meetings**

Each leader can set up a monthly one-on-one meeting with their direct subordinates to discuss any health issues they may be experiencing. (Neal & Griffin, 2006). A leader's ability to pay attention and read nonverbal signs is crucial. (Podsakoff et al., 2009).

8. **Be Trusting and Open-Minded**

Keep in mind that "business as usual" will not be resumed. The world and everyone's lives have been irrevocably altered as individuals make their way back to the office. (Gilbreath & Benson, 2004). To thrive in today's modern workplace, leaders must be able to roll with the punches, learn to be more adaptable, and trust their subordinates more than ever before. (Kelloway & Barling, 2010).

9. **Stay Survived**

Loss of everyday touchpoints that build culture and promote confidence in the manager-employee relationship is a common consequence of working remotely. (Cameron et al., 2011). Managers should make more time for one-on-one catchups that aren't dependent on performance or productivity alone; they should be more of an opportunity to catch up and demonstrate concern, rather than a check-in (Mills et al., 2013).

10. **Ensure Your Team Works Together**

Individualism became the norm. That resulted in adaptability and independence. The result was a mingling of priorities as well. (Schwartz & Porath, 2014). Unite your team in pursuit of common goals. People tend to underestimate how easy this is. How can we define shared success? How can we cooperate to reach our goals? A person's health and well-being benefit when they view their team as a resource for help and answers. (Neal & Griffin, 2006).

11. **Develop a Pattern for Interaction**

The crisis that compelled us to operate differently was so sudden that most of the staff is coping with PTSD symptoms. (Gilbreath & Benson, 2004). When we return to the office, the capacity to embrace face-to-face work depends on our ability to collaborate. We are doomed to failure if we ignore the importance of our meetings and collaboration and instead expect people to return to our old ways of doing things. Podsakoff et al., 2009).

12. Provide Extended Vacation Days

Many people will have to include commute time into their daily routines once they return to the job, cutting into time that could have been spent on health and wellness. (Kelloway & Barling, 2010). According to studies, sabbaticals are the most effective paid leave to prevent burnout. Companies are increasingly recognizing the value of long-term vacations, which allow employees to return to work with a renewed sense of appreciation and a high level of performance. (Cameron et al., 2011).

13. Present a Mixed-Mode Approach

One strategy that can promote health is to provide a hybrid model in which employees have the option to work remotely one day a week. (Judge & Kammeyer-Mueller, 2012). After that, during quarterly check-ins, inquire about how individuals cope with returning. With this, you can take the team's vitals at any time. (Judge & Kammeyer-Mueller, 2012).

14. Make Sure You Can Communicate With Each Other

When we were all telecommuting, we were all in the same boat. Returning to the office brings us all back to reality, but we must remember that reestablishing that work-life balance is no easy feat for any one of us. (Mills et al., 2013). Inquire about ways to ease the change. Motivate your staff to teach each other what has worked best for them. Trust is built via open communication. (Neal & Griffin, 2006).

15. Hang Out Alone in Nature

Meeting with employees one-on-one weekly, if feasible, has my full backing. (Gilbreath & Benson, 2004). Switch up the time and place of your meetings as employees return to work. Get out and enjoy the sunshine and fresh air; the weather is becoming warmer. A physically and mentally soothing setting will be created by the change of scenery and the fresh air. (Podsakoff et al., 2009).

16. Assist Team Members to Achieve Their Maximum Potential

Like a good sports coach, successful business executives must ensure that their "players" have every opportunity to succeed. (Kelloway & Barling, 2010). Which work arrangement—in-office, hybrid, or remote—will yield the best results for the individual? Asking people what they want is just part of it. Pay attention to how their part impacts the team, organization, and business. (Cameron et al., 2011).

17. Be an Instance Through Embracing Our Frailty

When building a solid work environment that prioritizes health and well-being, leaders must lead by example. (Cameron et al., 2011). This necessitates displaying some sensitivity, which in turn necessitates demonstrating the need to take pauses, manage stress, make time for exercise, etc. Great techniques include team walks and stress-reduction exercises. Everyone can lead more balanced lives if health and wellness are seen as the norm. (Mills et al., 2013).

18. **Do a 5-Minute "Brain Break" Two Time's Day**

By guiding a brief "brain break" twice a day, leaders may promote their teams' emotional and physical health. (Podsakoff et al., 2009). A mental vacation can help you relax, get more done, re-energize, have more fun, and improve your social skills. To assist teams recharge before returning to the workplace, even ten minutes a day spent playing a short game or going outside can make a big difference. (Judge & Kammeyer-Mueller, 2012).

19. **Showcase Making Time for Wellness a Priority**

As a leader, you can set a great example by taking frequent breaks, making time for yourself a priority, and discussing the things that help you stay healthy. (Neal & Griffin, 2006). This will encourage your team to do the same. Health and wellness programs and benefits are great, but leaders need to set a good example by prioritizing their health so their people will follow suit. (Kelloway & Barling, 2010).

Table 1. Pros and cons of supportive leadership on employee well-being and organizational performance

Pros	Cons
Increased Employee Engagement	**Dependency on Leadership**
A more engaged and dedicated workforce is the result of employees who feel appreciated and respected. (Cameron et al., 2011).	Employees may become overly dependent on good leaders, causing issues if the leader leaves or is unavailable. (Schwartz & Porath, 2014).
Enhanced Productivity	**Potential for Overemphasis on Well-being**
Supportive leadership leads to more efficient and effective work processes, boosting productivity. (Kelloway & Barling, 2010).	Excessive focus on well-being might detract from achieving business goals and performance targets. (Grawitch et al., 2006).
Higher Job Satisfaction	**Possible Resentment Among Peers**
Employees report higher job satisfaction, reducing turnover rates and increasing loyalty. (Podsakoff et al., 2009).	Good leadership behavior towards certain individuals may lead to perceptions of favoritism, causing resentment among peers. (Neal & Griffin, 2006).
Improved Organizational Culture	**Resource Intensive**
Promotes a positive culture, fostering collaboration, innovation, and a sense of community. (Cameron et al., 2011).	Implementing and maintaining good leadership practices can be resource-intensive, requiring time, effort, and financial investment. (Gilbreath & Benson, 2004).
Better Employee Well-being	**Risk of Burnout for Leaders**
Better emotional and physical health is a result of leaders who put their employees' needs first, which in turn reduces stress and burnout. (Schwartz & Porath, 2014).	Leaders who focus excessively on their teams' needs may face burnout themselves, impacting their effectiveness. (Kelloway & Barling, 2010).

continued on following page

Table 1. Continued

Pros	Cons
Increased Innovation and Creativity	**Challenges in Maintaining Consistency**
Creates an environment where employees feel empowered to think creatively and take risks, leading to innovation. (Grawitch et al., 2006).	Maintaining consistently good leadership behavior can be challenging, especially in large organizations with diverse teams (Neal & Griffin, 2006).

Result Analysis

Analyzing leadership behaviors that support workplace wellbeing involves examining the impact of specific leadership actions on employee health, satisfaction, and productivity. Key findings from studies and practical implementations include:

1. **Improved Employee Engagement**: An engaged workforce is the result of leaders who put an emphasis on wellness. A more engaged and dedicated workforce is the result of an environment where employees feel valued and supported. (Cameron et al., 2011).
2. **Enhanced Productivity**: Well-being-focused leadership correlates with increased productivity. Mentally and physically healthy employees perform better and are more efficient in their roles. (Kelloway & Barling, 2010)
3. **Reduced Absenteeism and Turnover**: Leadership that prioritizes employees' health and happiness leads to reduced absenteeism and employee churn. Workers are more inclined to remain with a company that cares about them as people. (Podsakoff et al., 2009).
4. **Better Mental Health**: Leadership behaviors such as empathetic communication and support for mental health resources result in improved mental health outcomes for employees. This includes reduced stress, anxiety, and depression. (Neal & Griffin, 2006).
5. **Positive Organizational Culture**: A positive organizational culture is fostered when leaders demonstrate behaviors that promote well-being. When workers feel like they belong, they are more likely to work together and develop new ideas. (Gilbreath & Benson, 2004).

Outcomes

Based on the result analysis, the following key outcomes are observed:

1. **Increased Job Satisfaction**: Employees report higher job satisfaction when leaders prioritize their well-being. This leads to a more positive work environment and greater job fulfillment. (Schwartz & Porath, 2014).
2. **Higher Retention Rates**: Organizations with supportive leadership retain more employees. This reduces recruitment costs and ensures continuity and stability within teams. (Cameron et al., 2011).
3. **Enhanced Employee Loyalty**: Workers are more loyal to companies and managers that show they care about them as individuals. This devotion manifests as more active participation in the organization's civic life. (Kelloway & Barling, 2010).

4. **Strengthened Team Cohesion**: Leadership behaviors that support well-being foster more robust team dynamics. Employees are more likely to collaborate and support each other, enhancing team performance. • (Podsakoff et al., 2009).
5. **Improved Health and Well-being Metrics**: Organizations see measurable improvements in health and well-being metrics, such as lower stress levels, fewer sick days, and higher participation in wellness programs. (Neal & Griffin, 2006).

CONCLUSION

The analysis and outcomes of leadership behaviors that support workplace well-being highlight leaders' critical role in fostering a healthy, productive, and positive work environment. Key conclusions drawn from this analysis include:

1. **Leadership Commitment is Essential**: Effective support for employee well-being requires committed leadership that prioritizes and invests in well-being initiatives. This commitment must be evident in policies, actions, and everyday interactions. (Cameron et al., 2011).
2. **Holistic Approach to Well-being**: All four aspects of health—mental, emotional, financial, and physical—must be considered to implement a comprehensive strategy for well-being. To provide all-encompassing assistance to staff, (Grawitch et al., 2006). leaders should take a thorough approach.
3. **Empathy and Communication**: Empathetic communication is a cornerstone of well-being-focused leadership. Leaders who actively listen and respond to employee needs foster trust and create a supportive work environment. (Neal & Griffin, 2006).
4. **Continuous Improvement**: Well-being initiatives must be continuously monitored and improved based on employee feedback and evolving needs. Leaders should proactively adapt and enhance well-being programs to ensure their effectiveness. (Podsakoff et al., 2009).
5. **Setting an Example**: Leaders should act in a way that promotes wellness that they would like to see their staff emulate. This involves taking breaks, reaching out for help when needed, and balancing your work and personal lives. (Kelloway & Barling, 2010).
6. **Culture of Well-being**: Integrating well-being into the culture of an organization ensures that it will transform into an essential component of the values and practices of the business. This culture is largely shaped and maintained by the leaders who exist within it. (Schwartz & Porath, 2014).

In conclusion, leadership practices that promote worker well-being in the workplace significantly benefit both the individuals and the enterprises that employ them. By prioritising well-being, leaders can establish a thriving workplace environment in which workers are healthy, engaged, and motivated to contribute to the firm's success. As businesses become more aware of the inherent connection between the well-being of their employees and their overall performance, the future of leadership will pay more attention to these behaviors.

REFERENCES

Allen, D. G., Shore, L. M., & Griffeth, R. W. (2010). The role of perceived organizational support and supportive human resource practices in the turnover process. *Journal of Management*, 29(1), 99–118. DOI: 10.1177/014920630302900107

Cameron, K. S., Mora, C., Leutscher, T., & Calarco, M. (2011). Effects of positive practices on organizational effectiveness. *The Journal of Applied Behavioral Science*, 47(3), 266–308. DOI: 10.1177/0021886310395514

Cooper, C. L., & Cartwright, S. (1994). Healthy mind; healthy organization—A proactive approach to occupational stress. *Human Relations*, 47(4), 455–471. DOI: 10.1177/001872679404700405

Gilbreath, B., & Benson, P. G. (2004). The contribution of supervisor behaviour to employee psychological well-being. *Work and Stress*, 18(3), 255–266. DOI: 10.1080/02678370412331317499

Grawitch, M. J., Gottschalk, M., & Munz, D. C. (2006). The path to a healthy workplace: A critical review linking healthy workplace practices, employee well-being, and organizational improvements. *Consulting Psychology Journal*, 58(3), 129–147. DOI: 10.1037/1065-9293.58.3.129

Judge, T. A., & Kammeyer-Mueller, J. D. (2012). Job attitudes. *Annual Review of Psychology*, 63(1), 341–367. DOI: 10.1146/annurev-psych-120710-100511 PMID: 22129457

Kelloway, E. K., & Barling, J. (2010). Leadership development as an intervention in occupational health psychology. *Work and Stress*, 24(3), 260–279. DOI: 10.1080/02678373.2010.518441

Mills, M. J., Fleck, C. R., & Kozikowski, A. (2013). Positive psychology at work: A conceptual review, state-of-practice assessment, and a look ahead. *The Journal of Positive Psychology*, 8(2), 153–164. DOI: 10.1080/17439760.2013.776622

Neal, A., & Griffin, M. A. (2006). A study of the lagged relationships among safety climate, safety motivation, safety behavior, and accidents at the individual and group levels. *The Journal of Applied Psychology*, 91(4), 946–953. DOI: 10.1037/0021-9010.91.4.946 PMID: 16834517

Osborne, S., & Hammoud, M. S. (2017). Effective employee engagement in the workplace. *International Journal of Applied Management and Technology*, 16(1), 50–67. DOI: 10.5590/IJAMT.2017.16.1.04

Page, K. M., & Vella-Brodrick, D. A. (2009). The 'what,' 'why' and 'how' of employee well-being: A new model. *Social Indicators Research*, 90(3), 441–458. DOI: 10.1007/s11205-008-9270-3

Podsakoff, P. M., MacKenzie, S. B., & Podsakoff, N. P. (2009). Recommendations for creating better concept definitions in the organizational, behavioral, and social sciences. *Organizational Research Methods*, 15(2), 192–207.

Salas, E., Cooke, N. J., & Rosen, M. A. (2008). On teams, teamwork, and team performance: Discoveries and developments. *Human Factors*, 50(3), 540–547. DOI: 10.1518/001872008X288457 PMID: 18689065

Schwartz, T., & Porath, C. (2014). Why you hate work. *Harvard Business Review*, 92(6), 58–66.

Chapter 14
Mindful Entrepreneurship:
Nurturing Mental Well-Being in Business

S. C. Vetrivel
https://orcid.org/0000-0003-3050-8211
Kongu Engineering College, India

P. Vidhyapriya
Kongu Engineering College, India

V. P. Arun
JKKN College of Engineering and Technology, India

ABSTRACT

The landscape of entrepreneurship is dynamic and demanding, often characterized by intense competition, uncertainty, and relentless challenges. In this context, the concept of mindful entrepreneurship emerges as a holistic approach that emphasizes the integration of mindfulness practices into the entrepreneurial journey. This chapter explores the intersection of entrepreneurship and mental well-being, shedding light on the significance of fostering a balanced and resilient mindset for sustainable business success. Mindful entrepreneurship encompasses various practices derived from mindfulness traditions, such as meditation, self-awareness, and cognitive reframing. By incorporating these practices into the entrepreneurial mindset, individuals can cultivate emotional intelligence, stress resilience, and heightened focus. This not only enhances personal well-being but also positively influences organizational culture and performance.

1. INTRODUCTION

In the fast-paced world of entrepreneurship, the pursuit of success often comes at a cost—mental well-being. The relentless demands of running a business, coupled with the constant pressure to innovate and excel, can take a toll on even the most resilient individuals. Yet, amidst the chaos and challenges, there exists a powerful tool that entrepreneurs can harness to not only survive but thrive: mindfulness. The chapter is a guide crafted to illuminate the transformative potential of mindfulness within the entrepreneurial landscape. In this book, we explore how cultivating mindfulness can fortify the entrepreneurial spirit, enhance decision-making, and foster sustainable success 1. (Alvarez & Sinde-Cantorna, 2014).

DOI: 10.4018/979-8-3693-3673-1.ch014

Through a blend of research-backed insights, practical strategies, and real-world examples, we invite entrepreneurs to embark on a journey of self-discovery and empowerment—a journey that prioritizes not just business achievements, but also the holistic well-being of the entrepreneurial mind.

1.1. The Importance of Mental Well-Being in Entrepreneurship

The importance of mental well-being in entrepreneurship cannot be overstated, as it directly impacts not only the success of the business but also the overall quality of life for the entrepreneur. Starting and running a business is inherently stressful, involving numerous challenges, uncertainties, and setbacks along the way. Without proper attention to mental well-being, entrepreneurs are more susceptible to burnout, anxiety, depression, and other mental health issues. Firstly, mental well-being is crucial for maintaining optimal cognitive functioning and decision-making abilities. Entrepreneurs often face high-pressure situations that require quick and effective decision-making (Annink et al., 2016; Byrnes & Taylor, 2015). When mental well-being is compromised, cognitive functions such as problem-solving, creativity, and judgment may be impaired, leading to suboptimal decisions that can negatively impact the business. Moreover, mental well-being plays a significant role in managing stress. The entrepreneurial journey is filled with ups and downs, and stress is an inevitable part of the process. However, chronic stress can have detrimental effects on both physical and mental health, leading to burnout and exhaustion. By prioritizing mental well-being, entrepreneurs can develop resilience and coping mechanisms to better manage stress and navigate the challenges of entrepreneurship. Furthermore, mental well-being is closely linked to productivity and performance. A healthy mind is more focused, motivated, and productive, enabling entrepreneurs to work efficiently and effectively towards their goals. Conversely, mental health issues such as anxiety and depression can hinder productivity, creativity, and overall performance, ultimately hindering the success of the business. Additionally, maintaining mental well-being is essential for fostering positive relationships and effective communication. Successful entrepreneurship often relies on collaboration, networking, and building strong relationships with customers, partners, and employees (Cardon & Patel, 2015). A healthy state of mind enables entrepreneurs to communicate more effectively, empathize with others, and build trust, thereby enhancing interpersonal relationships and the overall success of the business. Finally, prioritizing mental well-being is essential for achieving sustainable success and fulfillment in entrepreneurship. While financial success may be one aspect of entrepreneurship, true fulfillment comes from a sense of purpose, passion, and well-being. By nurturing their mental well-being, entrepreneurs can create a healthier work-life balance, sustain their motivation and drive, and cultivate a sense of fulfillment and satisfaction in their entrepreneurial endeavors.

2. UNDERSTANDING MINDFULNESS

2.1. Definition and Principles of Mindfulness

Mindfulness, rooted in ancient contemplative traditions but increasingly recognized in modern psychological and medical practices, is fundamentally about paying attention to the present moment with openness, curiosity, and non-judgment. At its core, mindfulness involves cultivating awareness of one's thoughts, emotions, bodily sensations, and surrounding environment without getting caught up in them or reacting impulsively. This heightened awareness allows individuals to respond to life's challenges with clarity and wisdom rather than being driven by habitual patterns or automatic reactions (Cardon et al., 2009; Carree & Verheul, 2012). The principles of mindfulness encompass several key elements: present moment awareness, which involves intentionally directing attention to the here and now rather than dwelling on the past or worrying about the future; acceptance and non-judgment, which entail acknowledging thoughts and feelings without labeling them as good or bad, right or wrong; compassion and kindness, towards oneself and others, fostering a sense of connection and empathy; and finally, a gentle curiosity, encouraging an attitude of openness and exploration towards one's inner experiences and the world around them. By embodying these principles, individuals can cultivate a deeper sense of self-awareness, emotional resilience, and inner peace, thereby transforming their relationship with themselves and the world they inhabit.

2.2. Benefits of Mindfulness in Entrepreneurship

Mindfulness offers a plethora of benefits to entrepreneurs, enabling them to navigate the complex and often turbulent waters of business with greater clarity, resilience, and effectiveness. Firstly, mindfulness cultivates heightened self-awareness, allowing entrepreneurs to recognize and understand their thoughts, emotions, and reactions more objectively. This self-awareness serves as a powerful tool for managing stress, as entrepreneurs become better equipped to identify early signs of burnout or overwhelm and take proactive steps to address them. Moreover, mindfulness fosters a more focused and present mindset, enhancing entrepreneurs' ability to concentrate on tasks at hand without being distracted by worries about the future or regrets about the past. This heightened focus not only improves productivity but also facilitates better decision-making, as entrepreneurs are able to weigh options more carefully and discern the most appropriate course of action (Clark et al., 2008). Additionally, mindfulness nurtures emotional intelligence, empowering entrepreneurs to navigate interpersonal dynamics with greater empathy, resilience, and authenticity. By fostering positive relationships with stakeholders, employees, and customers, entrepreneurs can build trust, inspire loyalty, and foster collaboration, ultimately driving the success and sustainability of their ventures. Furthermore, mindfulness cultivates creativity and innovation by fostering a curious and open-minded approach to problem-solving, enabling entrepreneurs to uncover novel solutions and seize opportunities that may have otherwise gone unnoticed. Overall, the integration of mindfulness practices into entrepreneurship not only enhances individual well-being but also promotes the growth, resilience, and long-term success of businesses in an ever-evolving marketplace.

2.3. Practical Techniques for Cultivating Mindfulness

- **Mindful Breathing**: This technique involves focusing your attention on your breath. Find a comfortable seated position, close your eyes, and take deep, slow breaths. Notice the sensation of the breath entering and leaving your body. When your mind wanders, gently bring your attention back to your breath without judgment.
- **Body Scan**: In this practice, you systematically bring awareness to different parts of your body, starting from your toes and moving up to your head. Notice any sensations, tension, or relaxation in each part of your body as you scan through it. This helps you develop awareness of physical sensations and promotes relaxation.

- **Mindful Walking**: Instead of walking on autopilot, bring mindfulness to your daily walks. Pay attention to the sensation of your feet touching the ground, the movement of your body, and the sights and sounds around you. Engage all your senses fully in the experience of walking.
- **Mindful Eating**: Transform mealtime into a mindfulness practice by bringing full awareness to the experience of eating. Notice the colors, textures, and flavors of your food. Chew slowly and savor each bite without rushing. Pay attention to feelings of hunger and fullness.
- **Mindful Meditation**: Set aside dedicated time for seated meditation. Find a quiet, comfortable space and sit with your spine erect. Close your eyes and focus your attention on your breath, a specific object, or a mantra. When thoughts arise, acknowledge them without judgment and gently return your focus to your chosen anchor.
- **Mindful Listening**: Practice active listening in your interactions with others. Focus your attention completely on the speaker without interrupting or forming responses in your mind. Notice not only the words being spoken but also the speaker's tone, body language, and emotions.
- **Gratitude Practice**: Cultivate mindfulness by expressing gratitude for the present moment and the blessings in your life. Regularly take time to reflect on the things you're grateful for, whether big or small. This practice helps shift your focus away from negativity and fosters a sense of contentment and abundance.
- **Mindful Journaling**: Set aside time each day to write down your thoughts, feelings, and observations without judgment. Use your journal as a tool for self-reflection and exploration. Notice patterns in your thinking and emotions and cultivate a sense of curiosity and openness.
- **Mindful Technology Use**: Develop awareness of how you interact with technology throughout the day. Take breaks from screens, and practice mindful usage of devices by focusing on one task at a time. Notice how technology affects your mood and attention and make intentional choices about when and how you engage with it.
- **Loving-Kindness Meditation**: This practice involves directing well-wishes towards yourself and others. Sit quietly and silently repeat phrases such as "May I be happy, may I be healthy, may I be at peace." Extend these wishes to loved ones, acquaintances, and even those with whom you have difficulty, cultivating compassion and connection.

3. THE ENTREPRENEURIAL MINDSET

3.1. Characteristics of Successful Entrepreneurs

Successful entrepreneurs often share certain characteristics that contribute to their achievements. These characteristics help them navigate the challenges of building and growing a business while capitalizing on opportunities for innovation and growth. Here are some key traits commonly associated with successful entrepreneurs:

- **Visionary Thinking**: Successful entrepreneurs have a clear vision of what they want to achieve with their business. They can anticipate trends, identify opportunities, and articulate a compelling long-term vision for their company.

- **Passion and Persistence**: Passion is what drives entrepreneurs to pursue their goals despite challenges and setbacks. Successful entrepreneurs are persistent in the face of adversity, continuously working towards their objectives with enthusiasm and determination.
- **Risk-taking and Resilience**: Entrepreneurship inherently involves risk-taking, and successful entrepreneurs are willing to take calculated risks to pursue their vision. They understand that failure is part of the journey and are resilient enough to bounce back from setbacks, learning from their experiences and adapting their approach as needed.
- **Innovative Thinking**: Successful entrepreneurs are often innovators who challenge the status quo and introduce new ideas, products, or services to the market. They possess a creative mindset, constantly seeking ways to improve and differentiate their offerings from competitors.
- **Adaptability and Flexibility**: The business landscape is constantly evolving, and successful entrepreneurs are adaptable to change. They are open-minded, willing to embrace new technologies, market shifts, and consumer preferences, adjusting their strategies accordingly to stay relevant and competitive.
- **Strong Work Ethic**: Entrepreneurship requires hard work, dedication, and a willingness to put in the time and effort needed to succeed. Successful entrepreneurs are often described as "workaholics" who are deeply committed to their ventures, often working long hours to achieve their goals.
- **Effective Communication and Leadership Skills**: Successful entrepreneurs possess strong communication skills, enabling them to convey their vision effectively to employees, investors, customers, and other stakeholders. They are also effective leaders who can inspire and motivate others to work towards a common goal.
- **Resourcefulness and Problem-solving Skills**: Entrepreneurs frequently encounter challenges and obstacles along the way, and successful ones are resourceful problem-solvers. They can think creatively, find innovative solutions to complex problems, and leverage their networks and resources effectively.
- **Financial Savvy**: Understanding the financial aspects of business is crucial for success in entrepreneurship. Successful entrepreneurs have a good grasp of financial management, budgeting, cash flow, and investment strategies, enabling them to make sound financial decisions for their ventures.
- **Customer Focus**: Successful entrepreneurs prioritize customer satisfaction and understand the importance of building strong relationships with their clientele. They listen to customer feedback, adapt their products or services based on customer needs, and strive to deliver exceptional value to their target market.

3.2. Common Mental Challenges Faced by Entrepreneurs

Entrepreneurs frequently encounter a myriad of mental challenges that can significantly impact their well-being and ability to succeed. One of the most prevalent issues is the burden of immense responsibility. Founders often shoulder the weight of decision-making, financial risks, and the overall success of their ventures, leading to high levels of stress and pressure. Moreover, the unpredictable nature of entrepreneurship introduces uncertainty, causing anxiety about the future and fear of failure (Cocker et al., 2013; Dormann & Griffin, 2015). This fear can be paralyzing, hindering innovation and decision-making. Additionally, the relentless pursuit of success can lead to burnout, as entrepreneurs pour endless hours into their businesses, neglecting their mental and physical health in the process. Moreover, isolation is another common challenge, as entrepreneurs often work long hours alone, lacking the support and camaraderie found in traditional work environments. This isolation can exacerbate feelings of loneliness and contribute to mental health issues such as depression and anxiety. Overall, navigating these mental challenges is essential for entrepreneurs to cultivate resilience, maintain well-being, and sustain long-term success in their ventures.

3.3. How Mindfulness can Enhance the Entrepreneurial Mindset

Mindfulness can profoundly enhance the entrepreneurial mindset by cultivating a state of present-moment awareness, clarity, and resilience. Firstly, mindfulness enables entrepreneurs to sharpen their focus on the tasks at hand, allowing them to fully engage with the present moment without being overwhelmed by past failures or future anxieties. By practicing mindfulness, entrepreneurs can develop a heightened awareness of their thoughts, emotions, and bodily sensations, enabling them to make more informed decisions and react more skillfully to challenges as they arise (Drnovšek et al., 2010). Moreover, mindfulness fosters an attitude of non-judgmental acceptance, which is essential for navigating the uncertainties inherent in entrepreneurship. Instead of getting caught up in self-criticism or dwelling on setbacks, mindful entrepreneurs learn to acknowledge their experiences without attaching undue significance to them, thereby freeing up mental energy to focus on solutions and opportunities for growth (Dufouil, 2014). Additionally, mindfulness enhances emotional intelligence, a key component of the entrepreneurial mindset. By cultivating self-awareness and empathy through mindfulness practices, entrepreneurs can better understand their own motivations and those of others, leading to more effective communication, collaboration, and leadership within their teams and networks. Furthermore, mindfulness promotes adaptability and resilience in the face of adversity. By learning to observe their thoughts and emotions without getting swept away by them, entrepreneurs can better cope with stress, uncertainty, and failure, bouncing back more quickly and creatively from setbacks.

4. MANAGING STRESS AND BURNOUT

4.1. Recognizing Signs of Stress and Burnout

Recognizing signs of stress and burnout is paramount for entrepreneurs striving to cultivate mental well-being in their business ventures. Stress, often regarded as a normal part of entrepreneurial life, can escalate into burnout when left unmanaged. Understanding the subtle cues that signify escalating stress levels is crucial. Physiological manifestations such as headaches, fatigue, and sleep disturbances can serve as early indicators. Additionally, cognitive symptoms like difficulty concentrating, indecisiveness, and memory lapses may emerge, hindering entrepreneurial effectiveness (Eatough et al., 2016). Emotional signs including irritability, anxiety, and a sense of overwhelm may also surface, impacting both personal well-being and business performance. Entrepreneurs must also recognize behavioral changes indicative of mounting stress and burnout. Increased reliance on coping mechanisms like alcohol or substance abuse, changes in eating habits, and social withdrawal are common behavioral manifestations. Furthermore, neglect of personal care, diminished productivity, and persistent procrastination can signify the erosion of mental well-being. Recognizing these behavioral shifts enables entrepreneurs to intervene early, preventing the progression from stress to burnout. Moreover, entrepreneurs must remain attuned to interpersonal signs of stress and burnout, both within themselves and among their team members (Iyengar & Lepper, 2000). Decreased communication, conflicts, and withdrawal from collaborative efforts may denote underlying stressors impacting team dynamics. Recognizing these relational disruptions prompts entrepreneurs to foster open dialogue, prioritize team cohesion, and implement supportive measures to mitigate burnout risk.

4.2. Strategies for Stress Management

Managing stress and preventing burnout are crucial aspects of maintaining mental well-being, especially for entrepreneurs who often face high-pressure situations and demanding work environments. Incorporating strategies for stress management into the entrepreneurial journey is essential for sustaining productivity, creativity, and overall success. By integrating these strategies into their daily routines, entrepreneurs can effectively manage stress, prevent burnout, and nurture their mental well-being while navigating the challenges of building and growing a successful business (Iyengar & Lepper, 2000). Mindful entrepreneurship emphasizes the importance of prioritizing mental health and adopting practices that promote resilience, creativity, and overall fulfillment in both work and life. Here are some effective strategies for managing stress and nurturing mental well-being in the context of mindful entrepreneurship:

- **Mindfulness and Meditation:** Practicing mindfulness and meditation can help entrepreneurs cultivate awareness of their thoughts, emotions, and bodily sensations. Mindfulness techniques, such as deep breathing exercises and body scans, can promote relaxation and reduce stress levels. Regular meditation sessions, even if brief, can provide entrepreneurs with a sense of calm and clarity amidst the chaos of running a business.
- **Time Management:** Effective time management is crucial for reducing stress and maintaining work-life balance. Entrepreneurs can use various time management techniques, such as prioritizing tasks, setting realistic deadlines, and delegating responsibilities to team members. By managing their time efficiently, entrepreneurs can minimize stressors related to feeling overwhelmed or overworked.
- **Healthy Lifestyle Choices:** Adopting a healthy lifestyle is fundamental for managing stress and promoting overall well-being. This includes prioritizing regular exercise, eating a balanced diet, staying hydrated, and getting an adequate amount of sleep. Engaging in physical activity releases endorphins, which are natural stress relievers, while nutritious food and sufficient rest support cognitive function and resilience against stress.
- **Setting Boundaries:** Establishing clear boundaries between work and personal life is essential for preventing burnout. Entrepreneurs can set specific work hours, designate "off" times for responding to emails and calls, and create dedicated spaces for relaxation and leisure activities. By respecting these boundaries, entrepreneurs can recharge and avoid the detrimental effects of constant work-related stress.
- **Seeking Social Support:** Building a strong support network of friends, family members, mentors, and fellow entrepreneurs can provide invaluable emotional support during challenging times. Having someone to talk to, share experiences with, and seek advice from can help entrepreneurs cope with stress and gain perspective on their situations. Additionally, participating in networking events and joining professional communities can foster a sense of belonging and camaraderie.

- **Practicing Self-Compassion:** Entrepreneurs often hold themselves to high standards and may experience self-criticism when faced with setbacks or failures. Practicing self-compassion involves treating oneself with kindness and understanding, especially during difficult times. By cultivating self-compassion, entrepreneurs can develop resilience in the face of adversity and bounce back from challenges with greater ease.
- **Mindful Communication:** Effective communication is essential for managing stress in interpersonal relationships, both within the business and with external stakeholders. Practicing mindful communication involves active listening, expressing oneself clearly and respectfully, and being mindful of nonverbal cues (Kadowaki et al., 2016). By fostering open and empathetic communication channels, entrepreneurs can reduce misunderstandings and conflicts that contribute to stress.
- **Taking Breaks and Downtime:** Building regular breaks and downtime into one's schedule is essential for preventing burnout and maintaining mental well-being. Whether it's taking short breaks throughout the workday, scheduling regular vacations, or engaging in hobbies and leisure activities, allowing oneself time to rest and recharge is crucial for long-term sustainability as an entrepreneur.

4.3. Implementing Mindfulness Practices to Prevent Burnout

Implementing mindfulness practices is an essential strategy for preventing burnout and nurturing mental well-being in the realm of entrepreneurship. In the high-stakes environment of business, where stress and pressure are constant companions, cultivating mindfulness can serve as a powerful antidote (Lechmann & Schnabel, 2014; Li et al., 2014). Mindfulness involves paying attention to the present moment non-judgmentally, acknowledging thoughts, feelings, and bodily sensations without getting caught up in them. By incorporating mindfulness practices into their daily routines, entrepreneurs can effectively manage stress and reduce the risk of burnout. One key aspect of implementing mindfulness practices is establishing a regular meditation routine. This could involve dedicating a few minutes each day to sit quietly and focus on the breath or engage in guided meditation sessions. Through consistent practice, entrepreneurs can develop greater awareness of their thoughts and emotions, allowing them to respond to challenges with clarity and composure rather than reacting impulsively. Moreover, meditation can help cultivate resilience, enabling entrepreneurs to bounce back from setbacks and navigate uncertainty more effectively. Another important mindfulness practice for preventing burnout is cultivating self-compassion. Entrepreneurs often hold themselves to high standards and may be prone to self-criticism when things don't go as planned (Loewe et al., 2015). By practicing self-compassion, entrepreneurs learn to treat themselves with kindness and understanding, recognizing that failure and mistakes are inevitable parts of the journey. This mindset shift can alleviate the pressure to constantly perform and reduce the negative impact of setbacks on mental well-being. In addition to formal meditation and self-compassion practices, integrating mindfulness into everyday activities can further support mental well-being. Simple practices such as mindful eating, walking, or even taking short breaks to breathe deeply can help entrepreneurs stay grounded and present amidst the hustle and bustle of business life (Luchman & González-Morales, 2013). By bringing mindfulness into various aspects of their day, entrepreneurs can create moments of pause and rejuvenation, preventing stress from accumulating and leading to burnout. Furthermore, fostering a culture of mindfulness within the business environment can benefit not only individual entrepreneurs but also their teams. Encouraging employees to participate in mindfulness training or incorporating mindfulness practices into team meetings can promote a supportive and resilient organizational culture.

By prioritizing mental well-being and emphasizing the importance of self-care, entrepreneurs can create a healthier work environment where individuals thrive and burnout is less likely to occur.

5. BUILDING RESILIENCE

5.1. The Importance of Resilience in Entrepreneurship

Building resilience is a critical aspect of entrepreneurship, as it serves as a cornerstone for navigating the turbulent and unpredictable nature of the business landscape. Resilience, in the context of entrepreneurship, refers to the ability to bounce back from setbacks, adapt to changes, and persevere in the face of challenges. It encompasses mental toughness, flexibility, and a positive mindset, all of which are essential traits for entrepreneurs striving to succeed in a competitive environment (Sevä et al., 2016). One of the key reasons why resilience is so important in entrepreneurship is the inherent uncertainty that comes with starting and running a business. Entrepreneurs often face numerous obstacles and setbacks, including financial difficulties, market fluctuations, and unexpected hurdles. In such situations, resilience allows entrepreneurs to maintain their composure, think creatively, and find innovative solutions to overcome obstacles. Rather than being paralyzed by adversity, resilient entrepreneurs view challenges as opportunities for growth and learning.

Moreover, building resilience can help entrepreneurs cope with the inevitable failures and rejections that come with entrepreneurship. Failure is an inherent part of the entrepreneurial journey, and those who lack resilience may be discouraged by setbacks and give up on their endeavors prematurely (Reymen et al., 2015). However, resilient entrepreneurs are able to bounce back from failure, learn from their mistakes, and use them as stepping stones toward future success. By maintaining a resilient mindset, entrepreneurs can cultivate perseverance and determination, which are essential qualities for long-term sustainability in business. In addition to navigating external challenges, resilience also plays a crucial role in safeguarding entrepreneurs' mental well-being. The entrepreneurial journey can be mentally taxing, with high levels of stress, anxiety, and pressure to perform. Without resilience, entrepreneurs may succumb to burnout or experience negative effects on their mental health (Roche et al., 2014). However, resilient entrepreneurs are better equipped to manage stress, maintain a healthy work-life balance, and seek support when needed. By prioritizing their mental well-being and building resilience, entrepreneurs can sustain their passion and enthusiasm for their ventures while minimizing the risk of experiencing mental health issues. Furthermore, resilience is essential for fostering innovation and adaptability in entrepreneurship. In today's rapidly evolving business landscape, the ability to pivot and embrace change is crucial for staying competitive. Resilient entrepreneurs are not afraid to experiment, take calculated risks, and adapt their strategies based on evolving market dynamics. They possess the resilience to weather uncertainty and embrace change as an opportunity for growth and innovation. By fostering a culture of resilience within their organizations, entrepreneurs can empower their teams to embrace change, experiment with new ideas, and drive innovation forward.

5.2. Developing Resilience Through Mindfulness

Developing resilience through mindfulness is a fundamental aspect of building resilience in the context of mindful entrepreneurship. Mindfulness practices offer a powerful toolkit for entrepreneurs to cultivate mental well-being amidst the challenges and uncertainties inherent in the business landscape. At its core, mindfulness involves paying deliberate attention to the present moment without judgment, fostering a deep awareness of one's thoughts, feelings, and sensations (Rocca et al., 2002). This heightened awareness enables entrepreneurs to navigate setbacks, failures, and stressors with greater equanimity and clarity. One key way mindfulness enhances resilience is by promoting emotional regulation. Through mindfulness practices such as meditation, entrepreneurs learn to observe their emotions without becoming overwhelmed by them. This allows for a more balanced response to stressful situations, reducing the likelihood of being consumed by negative emotions like fear or frustration. By developing this emotional resilience, entrepreneurs can maintain a steady focus on their goals and adapt more effectively to changing circumstances.

Moreover, mindfulness cultivates a sense of perspective, enabling entrepreneurs to see challenges as opportunities for growth rather than insurmountable obstacles. By adopting a non-judgmental attitude towards their experiences, entrepreneurs can approach setbacks with curiosity and openness, seeking valuable lessons and insights that can inform their future decisions. This mindset shifts fosters resilience by empowering entrepreneurs to reframe adversity as a natural part of the entrepreneurial journey, rather than a reflection of personal failure. Additionally, mindfulness fosters greater self-awareness, which is essential for recognizing and addressing the early signs of burnout or overwhelm (Ryan & Deci, 2001). By regularly checking in with themselves through mindfulness practices, entrepreneurs can identify when they need to step back, recharge, or seek support. This proactive approach to self-care not only safeguards mental well-being but also sustains long-term resilience, ensuring entrepreneurs can weather the inevitable highs and lows of business ownership without sacrificing their health or happiness.

6. EMOTIONAL INTELLIGENCE IN BUSINESS

6.1. Understanding Emotional Intelligence (EQ)

Understanding emotional intelligence is crucial in the context of business resilience and mindful entrepreneurship as it forms the cornerstone of effective leadership, communication, and decision-making within organizations. Emotional intelligence encompasses the ability to recognize, understand, and manage one's own emotions, as well as the capacity to perceive and influence the emotions of others. In the realm of business, this skill set is indispensable for fostering healthy work environments, building strong relationships, and navigating challenges with resilience. At its core, emotional intelligence enables entrepreneurs and business leaders to cultivate self-awareness, which is the foundation of effective leadership. By understanding their own emotions, strengths, and weaknesses, entrepreneurs can make informed decisions, manage stress effectively, and maintain a positive outlook even in the face of adversity. Moreover, self-awareness allows leaders to recognize and regulate their emotions, preventing impulsive reactions that could hinder productivity or damage relationships. In addition to self-awareness, emotional intelligence involves empathy, the ability to understand and resonate with the emotions of others (Ryff, 2017). Empathetic leaders are better equipped to build trust, foster collaboration, and inspire loyalty among team members. By empathizing with their employees' perspectives and experiences, entrepreneurs can create a supportive work environment where individuals feel valued and understood, thus enhancing morale and motivation. Furthermore, emotional intelligence plays a crucial role in effective communication, a cornerstone of successful entrepreneurship. Entrepreneurs with high emotional intelligence can express themselves clearly and assertively while also being attentive to the emotions and reactions of their audience. This skill is particularly valuable in negotiations, conflict resolution, and customer interactions, where the ability to understand and respond to the emotions of others can mean the difference between success and failure (Saarni et al., 2008). In the context of business resilience, emotional intelligence enables entrepreneurs to adapt to change, overcome setbacks, and persevere in the face of challenges. By maintaining a balanced emotional state and leveraging their resilience, entrepreneurs can bounce back from failures, learn from mistakes, and continue to innovate and grow their businesses.

6.2. Enhancing EQ Through Mindfulness Practices

Enhancing Emotional Intelligence (EQ) through mindfulness practices holds significant importance in fostering resilience and promoting mental well-being within the realm of mindful entrepreneurship. Emotional Intelligence, a critical component of successful leadership and business management, encompasses the ability to recognize, understand, and manage one's own emotions, as well as those of others. By integrating mindfulness practices into the entrepreneurial journey, individuals can develop a deeper awareness of their emotions, thoughts, and reactions, thereby enhancing their EQ and ultimately fortifying their resilience in the face of challenges. Mindfulness, characterized by non-judgmental awareness of the present moment, serves as a powerful tool for cultivating emotional intelligence (Stephan, 2018). Through mindfulness practices such as meditation, deep breathing exercises, and body scans, entrepreneurs can sharpen their self-awareness and emotional regulation skills. By learning to observe their thoughts and feelings without attachment or judgment, individuals can gain insight into their emotional patterns and triggers, enabling them to respond to situations with greater clarity and composure.

Moreover, mindfulness practices facilitate improved interpersonal skills, a cornerstone of emotional intelligence in business settings. By honing their ability to empathize and communicate effectively with others, entrepreneurs can foster stronger relationships with employees, clients, and stakeholders. Mindful listening, for instance, involves being fully present and attentive during interactions, allowing individuals to better understand the needs and perspectives of others. This heightened sense of empathy not only fosters positive relationships but also enhances collaboration and teamwork within the business environment. Furthermore, mindfulness practices can help entrepreneurs navigate the inevitable stressors and setbacks inherent in the entrepreneurial journey (Taris et al., 2008). By cultivating a mindset of acceptance and resilience, individuals can approach challenges with greater equanimity and adaptability. Mindfulness-based stress reduction techniques, such as mindful breathing and progressive muscle relaxation, provide entrepreneurs with practical tools for managing stress and maintaining emotional balance amidst uncertainty and adversity.

6.3. Applying Emotional Intelligence in Decision-Making and Leadership

Emotional intelligence (EI) plays a pivotal role in decision-making and leadership within the context of business resilience and mindful entrepreneurship. In essence, EI refers to the ability to recognize, understand, and manage one's own emotions, as well as the emotions of others. In the dynamic landscape of business, where uncertainty and challenges are commonplace, leveraging EI becomes indispensable for navigating through turbulent times while fostering a resilient and sustainable enterprise. In decision-making, individuals with high EI possess the capacity to effectively evaluate situations by considering not only rational factors but also emotional nuances. They acknowledge the impact of emotions on their thought processes and weigh them appropriately in their assessments (Thompson et al., 1992). By doing so, they can make more holistic and empathetic decisions that resonate with stakeholders and engender trust. Moreover, EI enables leaders to navigate conflicts and crises with composure, as they can regulate their own emotions and diffuse tense situations constructively, fostering a harmonious work environment conducive to innovation and productivity. Furthermore, in the realm of leadership, EI serves as a cornerstone for effective interpersonal relationships and inspiring teamwork. Leaders who exhibit high EI are adept at empathizing with their team members' perspectives and concerns, thereby fostering a culture of inclusion and psychological safety. By understanding the emotional needs and motivations of their employees, EI-driven leaders can tailor their communication and management styles to cultivate a supportive and empowering workplace environment. This, in turn, leads to higher levels of employee engagement, loyalty, and resilience in the face of challenges. Within the framework of business resilience, the application of EI extends beyond individual decision-making and leadership to organizational culture and strategy. Emotionally intelligent organizations prioritize the well-being and mental health of their employees, recognizing that resilient businesses are built upon a foundation of emotionally healthy and motivated individuals. By promoting practices such as mindfulness, self-care, and empathetic leadership, these organizations nurture a resilient workforce capable of adapting to change and thriving amidst adversity. In the context of mindful entrepreneurship, EI serves as a guiding principle for ethical and sustainable business practices. Mindful entrepreneurs leverage their emotional intelligence to cultivate a deeper understanding of their customers' needs and values, fostering authentic connections and loyalty. Moreover, they prioritize social responsibility and environmental sustainability, recognizing the interconnectedness of business success with societal well-being. By integrating EI into their entrepreneurial endeavors, mindful leaders can create businesses that not only thrive economically but also contribute positively to the broader community and environment.

7. CULTIVATING CREATIVITY AND INNOVATION

7.1. The Link Between Mindfulness and Creativity

The link between mindfulness and creativity within the framework of cultivating creativity and innovation, particularly in the context of mindful entrepreneurship, is profound and multifaceted. Mindfulness, rooted in the practice of being present and aware of one's thoughts, feelings, and surroundings without judgment, fosters a mental state conducive to creativity. By cultivating mindfulness, entrepreneurs can tap into their innate creativity and innovative capacities, thereby enhancing their ability to generate novel ideas, solutions, and strategies within the realm of business (Thurik et al., 2016). One key aspect of mindfulness that contributes to creativity is its ability to quiet the incessant chatter of the mind and create space for insights and inspiration to emerge. In the fast-paced and often chaotic world of entrepreneurship, where constant multitasking and decision-making are the norm, this ability to quiet the mind can be invaluable. By practicing mindfulness techniques such as meditation, deep breathing, or mindful movement, entrepreneurs can train their minds to focus, which allows them to access deeper levels of creativity. Furthermore, mindfulness promotes a mindset characterized by openness, curiosity, and non-attachment—qualities essential for creativity and innovation. When individuals approach challenges with a beginner's mind, free from preconceived notions or rigid thinking patterns, they are more likely to uncover unconventional solutions and perspectives. Moreover, by cultivating non-attachment to outcomes, entrepreneurs can embrace experimentation and risk-taking, essential elements of the creative process. Additionally, mindfulness enhances self-awareness and emotional intelligence, enabling entrepreneurs to better understand their own thought processes, emotions, and motivations. This self-awareness not only fosters personal growth and well-being but also provides valuable insights into one's creative strengths and areas for development. By recognizing and leveraging their unique talents and perspectives, entrepreneurs can fuel their creative endeavors and differentiate themselves in the competitive business landscape. Moreover, mindfulness practices promote a deeper connection with the present moment and the world around us, which can inspire creativity through increased observation, appreciation, and empathy. By immersing themselves fully in their experiences and interactions, entrepreneurs can gain valuable insights into consumer needs, market trends, and societal shifts, thereby informing their creative ideation and innovation efforts.

7.2. Techniques for Sparking Creativity

Cultivating creativity and innovation while nurturing mental well-being in business is crucial for entrepreneurial success (Tobias et al., 2013). By implementing these techniques, entrepreneurs can cultivate a creative and innovative environment while nurturing the mental well-being of their team members, ultimately driving business success. The following are some techniques to spark creativity within this framework:

- **Mindfulness Practices**: Incorporating mindfulness techniques such as meditation, deep breathing exercises, or mindfulness walks can help entrepreneurs quiet their minds and focus attention. Mindfulness allows individuals to become more aware of their thoughts and emotions, providing clarity and space for creative ideas to emerge.
- **Diverse Perspectives and Collaborative Environment**: Encourage diversity within your team and create an inclusive environment where individuals feel comfortable expressing their ideas (Torp et al., 2012). Collaborative brainstorming sessions or interdisciplinary collaborations can lead to innovative solutions by combining different perspectives and expertise.
- **Embrace Failure and Iteration**: Foster a culture that views failure as a learning opportunity rather than a setback. Encourage experimentation and iteration, where ideas are tested, refined, and adapted based on feedback. Embracing failure reduces fear of taking risks and promotes a growth mindset conducive to creativity and innovation.
- **Continuous Learning and Exploration**: Encourage lifelong learning and curiosity within your organization. Provide resources for employees to attend workshops, conferences, or pursue further

education. Encourage exploration outside of the business domain, as insights from diverse fields can inspire creative solutions to business challenges.
- **Create Space for Creativity**: Designate physical or virtual spaces within the workplace that foster creativity and innovation. These spaces should be conducive to collaboration, equipped with tools for ideation (whiteboards, sticky notes, etc.), and free from distractions. Flexible work environments that allow for autonomy and self-expression can also stimulate creativity.
- **Challenge Assumptions and Conventional Thinking**: Encourage employees to question assumptions and challenge conventional wisdom (Torp et al., 2017). Encourage divergent thinking by exploring multiple perspectives and considering unconventional solutions to problems. This can lead to breakthrough innovations that disrupt traditional practices and industries.
- **Cross-Pollination of Ideas**: Facilitate interactions between individuals from different departments or industries to promote cross-pollination of ideas. Host interdisciplinary workshops, networking events, or industry meetups to facilitate knowledge sharing and idea exchange. Exposure to diverse perspectives can spark new insights and innovative solutions.
- **Storytelling and Visualization**: Encourage storytelling as a means of communicating ideas and fostering creativity within the organization. Use visualization techniques such as storyboarding or mind mapping to translate abstract concepts into tangible representations. Storytelling can inspire empathy, engage emotions, and stimulate creative thinking.
- **Encourage Playfulness and Playful Thinking**: Create opportunities for playfulness and spontaneous creativity within the workplace. Incorporate playful activities such as team-building games, improvisation exercises, or design challenges to stimulate imagination and foster a sense of fun. Playfulness can lower inhibitions and unlock creative potential.
- **Support Work-Life Balance and Mental Well-being**: Recognize the importance of work-life balance and mental well-being in fostering creativity and innovation. Encourage employees to prioritize self-care, set boundaries, and maintain healthy habits. Provide resources such as counseling services, wellness programs, or flexible work arrangements to support mental well-being.

7.3. Fostering Innovation Within the Business Through Mindfulness

Fostering innovation within a business through mindfulness is a multifaceted approach that intertwines the principles of mindfulness with the dynamics of creativity and innovation. At its core, mindfulness cultivates a heightened awareness of the present moment, encouraging individuals to engage fully with their surroundings, thoughts, and emotions without judgment. This heightened awareness serves as a foundation for fostering creativity and innovation within a business context. One key aspect of fostering innovation through mindfulness is the cultivation of a conducive environment that prioritizes mental well-being (Totterdell et al., 2006). By promoting practices such as meditation, deep breathing exercises, and mindful movement, businesses can empower employees to manage stress effectively, enhance their focus, and tap into their creative potential. Creating dedicated spaces for mindfulness practices within the workplace, such as meditation rooms or quiet zones, further reinforces the organization's commitment to supporting employees' mental well-being. Mindfulness also plays a crucial role in enhancing cognitive flexibility and divergent thinking, both of which are essential for generating innovative ideas. Through mindfulness practices, individuals learn to observe their thoughts without clinging to them, allowing for a more fluid and adaptive mindset. This increased cognitive flexibility enables employees to approach challenges from multiple perspectives, leading to the emergence of novel solutions and innovative approaches to problem-solving. Furthermore, mindfulness fosters a culture of open-mindedness and collaboration within the organization. By encouraging individuals to approach interactions with curiosity and empathy, mindfulness cultivates an environment where diverse ideas are welcomed and valued. This inclusive culture not only promotes creativity but also fosters a sense of psychological safety, empowering employees to take risks and explore unconventional ideas without fear of judgment. In addition to enhancing individual creativity, mindfulness can also facilitate collective innovation within teams and across departments (Tranfield et al., 2003). Mindful communication practices, such as active listening and non-judgmental feedback, promote constructive dialogue and facilitate the exchange of ideas. By creating opportunities for employees to engage in collaborative problem-solving and brainstorming sessions, businesses can harness the collective intelligence of their teams to drive innovation and drive the organization forward.

8. NAVIGATING UNCERTAINTY AND FAILURE

8.1. Embracing Uncertainty as Part of the Entrepreneurial Journey

Navigating uncertainty is an inherent aspect of the entrepreneurial journey, often characterized by a myriad of challenges and unforeseen obstacles. Within the framework of mindful entrepreneurship, embracing uncertainty becomes a vital component in nurturing mental well-being while steering through the tumultuous waters of business ventures. Rather than viewing uncertainty as a deterrent or a source of anxiety, entrepreneurs can adopt a mindset that perceives it as an opportunity for growth and innovation. This shift in perspective enables individuals to approach uncertainties with resilience and adaptability, essential qualities for success in the dynamic landscape of entrepreneurship (Ugwu et al., 2016). Embracing uncertainty entails acknowledging the inherent unpredictability of the business environment and understanding that failure and setbacks are not indicative of personal shortcomings but rather valuable learning experiences. By reframing failures as opportunities for reflection and improvement, entrepreneurs can cultivate a sense of mindfulness that fosters self-awareness and emotional equilibrium. This mindfulness allows individuals to navigate uncertainty with grace and composure, mitigating the negative effects of stress and anxiety on mental well-being. Moreover, embracing uncertainty encourages entrepreneurs to adopt a flexible and iterative approach to problem-solving and decision-making. Rather than striving for rigid control over every aspect of their ventures, mindful entrepreneurs are willing to experiment, iterate, and pivot in response to changing circumstances. This adaptive mindset not only fosters innovation and creativity but also promotes a sense of empowerment and agency in the face of uncertainty. Furthermore, embracing uncertainty as part of the entrepreneurial journey fosters a culture of openness and vulnerability within the business community. By sharing their experiences of failure and uncertainty, entrepreneurs can create a supportive ecosystem where individuals feel comfortable seeking guidance and support from their peers. This sense of camaraderie and solidarity not only strengthens mental well-being but also cultivates resilience and collective growth.

8.2. Overcoming Fear of Failure

Navigating uncertainty and embracing failure are inherent challenges in the entrepreneurial journey, yet they often evoke a profound fear of failure within individuals. This fear can be paralyzing, hindering progress and stifling innovation. However, overcoming this fear is essential for fostering a mindset conducive to mindful entrepreneurship and nurturing mental well-being in business. One effective strategy for overcoming the fear of failure is to reframe it as an opportunity for growth and learning (Wendsche & Lohmann-Haislah, 2017) (Wiklund et al., 2016). Instead of viewing failure as a reflection of personal inadequacy, entrepreneurs can perceive it as a natural part of the learning process. By embracing failure as a teacher, individuals can extract valuable lessons from their setbacks, enabling them to refine their strategies and improve their approach in future endeavors. This shift in perspective empowers entrepreneurs to approach challenges with resilience and optimism, recognizing that each setback brings them one step closer to success. Moreover, practicing mindfulness can play a pivotal role in overcoming the fear of failure and navigating uncertainty with grace. Mindfulness cultivates present-moment awareness and non-judgmental acceptance, allowing entrepreneurs to acknowledge their fears without being consumed by them. By staying grounded in the present moment, individuals can avoid getting swept away by catastrophic thinking about the future and instead focus on taking proactive steps to address challenges as they arise. Mindfulness practices such as meditation, deep breathing, and body scans can help entrepreneurs develop the inner resources needed to cope with uncertainty and adversity with equanimity. Furthermore, fostering a supportive community of fellow entrepreneurs can provide invaluable encouragement and perspective in times of uncertainty. By surrounding themselves with like-minded individuals who understand the highs and lows of the entrepreneurial journey, individuals can gain reassurance that they are not alone in facing challenges. Sharing experiences, seeking advice, and offering support within this community can help entrepreneurs overcome feelings of isolation and self-doubt, empowering them to persevere in the face of adversity.

8.3. Leveraging Mindfulness to Bounce Back From Setbacks

In the dynamic landscape of entrepreneurship, where uncertainty and failure are inevitable companions, leveraging mindfulness can serve as a potent tool for navigating setbacks and fostering mental well-being. By embracing mindfulness, entrepreneurs cultivate a heightened awareness of their thoughts, emotions, and reactions, enabling them to respond to challenges with clarity and resilience. When confronted with setbacks, rather than succumbing to despair or becoming overwhelmed by the uncertainty, mindful entrepreneurs are equipped to acknowledge their feelings without judgment and observe their circumstances with a sense of curiosity and openness (Williams & Shepherd, 2016). This mindful approach allows for a more constructive perspective, enabling entrepreneurs to extract valuable lessons from setbacks and adapt their strategies accordingly. Moreover, mindfulness empowers entrepreneurs to maintain a balanced perspective amidst the inevitable ups and downs of business, fostering a sense of inner peace and well-being essential for sustained success in the entrepreneurial journey.

9. FOSTERING POSITIVE RELATIONSHIPS

9.1. Importance of Interpersonal Relationships in Business

Fostering positive interpersonal relationships in business is paramount to the success of any venture, and it lies at the heart of mindful entrepreneurship, where the focus extends beyond mere profit to encompass the well-being of all involved. In today's fast-paced and competitive business landscape, the significance of cultivating strong connections cannot be overstated. These relationships serve as the bedrock upon which trust, collaboration, and mutual support are built, fostering an environment conducive to innovation and growth. At the core of successful business interactions are interpersonal skills, which enable entrepreneurs to effectively communicate, negotiate, and empathize with others (Wincent & Örtqvist, 2009). By prioritizing these skills, entrepreneurs can forge meaningful connections with clients, employees, and stakeholders alike, fostering a sense of belonging and loyalty within the business community. Moreover, investing time and effort into nurturing these relationships can yield long-term benefits, such as increased customer satisfaction, enhanced employee engagement, and a broader network of opportunities. In addition to driving business success, interpersonal relationships play a pivotal role in nurturing mental well-being in entrepreneurship. The inherent challenges and uncertainties of running a business can take a toll on one's mental health, making it essential to cultivate a support system of trusted individuals who can offer guidance, encouragement, and perspective. Through open communication and a culture of empathy, entrepreneurs can create a safe space where mental health is prioritized and stigma is reduced, fostering resilience and adaptability in the face of adversity.

9.2. Communicating Mindfully

Communicating mindfully is a foundational element in fostering positive relationships within the realm of mindful entrepreneurship, nurturing mental well-being in business. Mindful communication involves being fully present, attentive, and empathetic in our interactions with others. It requires a conscious effort to listen deeply, without judgment or preconceived notions, and to respond thoughtfully rather than reactively (Wincent et al., 2008) (Wirback et al., 2014). By practicing mindful communication, entrepreneurs can cultivate stronger connections with their colleagues, clients, and stakeholders, leading to more collaborative and harmonious working environments. One key aspect of communicating mindfully is maintaining open and transparent dialogue. This involves being honest and authentic in our communication, sharing our thoughts and feelings openly while also being respectful of others' perspectives. By fostering an environment of trust and transparency, entrepreneurs can build stronger relationships based on mutual respect and understanding. Additionally, mindful communication involves being mindful of the impact of our words and actions on others. This means choosing our words carefully, speaking with kindness and compassion, and being aware of the emotions and reactions of those we are communicating with. Furthermore, mindful entrepreneurs recognize the importance of active listening in effective communication. This means not only hearing what others are saying but also understanding their perspectives and feelings. By practicing active listening, entrepreneurs can demonstrate empathy and validation, which are crucial for building positive relationships.

9.3. Building Strong Networks and Partnerships

Building strong networks and partnerships is a cornerstone of fostering positive relationships within mindful entrepreneurship, essential for nurturing mental well-being in business. These networks encompass a diverse array of connections, from mentors and peers to clients and collaborators. By actively cultivating these relationships, entrepreneurs can create a supportive ecosystem that not only bolsters their business endeavors but also promotes personal growth and resilience. Effective networking involves not only seeking opportunities for mutual benefit but also offering support and guidance to others within the community. Collaboration and partnership not only expand one's reach and resources but also foster a sense of belonging and camaraderie, crucial for maintaining mental well-being amidst the challenges of entrepreneurship. Moreover, strong networks provide avenues for sharing experiences, insights, and best practices, enriching the entrepreneurial journey with collective wisdom and camaraderie. By prioritizing the development of meaningful connections and partnerships, mindful entrepreneurs can cultivate a thriving support system that sustains both their professional success and mental well-being.

10. SUSTAINABLE SUCCESS AND WELL-BEING

10.1. Redefining Success Beyond Financial Metrics

In the contemporary landscape of business, there's a growing recognition that success extends far beyond mere financial gain. Instead, a paradigm shift towards Sustainable Success and Well-being is gaining traction, acknowledging the interconnectedness between business prosperity, environmental sustainability, and societal well-being. This redefinition of success prioritizes holistic measures that encompass not just economic growth but also social impact and environmental stewardship. Within this framework, Mindful Entrepreneurship emerges as a guiding principle, emphasizing the importance of nurturing mental well-being in business practices. Mindfulness in entrepreneurship involves cultivating awareness, compassion, and resilience in the face of challenges. It encourages entrepreneurs to prioritize their mental health alongside their business goals, recognizing that personal well-being is fundamental to sustainable success. In adopting Mindful Entrepreneurship, businesses prioritize practices that promote mental well-being among employees, such as flexible work arrangements, access to mental health resources, and fostering a supportive organizational culture. Furthermore, they integrate mindfulness techniques into decision-making processes, encouraging thoughtful reflection and ethical considerations. By embracing Sustainable Success and Well-being through Mindful Entrepreneurship, businesses not only contribute to a healthier bottom line but also foster a more compassionate and sustainable world. This approach aligns business objectives with broader societal goals, creating value not only for shareholders but also for employees, communities, and the planet. Ultimately, it's a holistic vision of success that prioritizes harmony between prosperity and well-being, both within and beyond the business realm.

10.2. Balancing Work and Personal Life

Balancing work and personal life is a fundamental aspect of sustainable success and well-being in mindful entrepreneurship. In today's fast-paced business world, entrepreneurs often find themselves consumed by the demands of their ventures, neglecting their personal lives and mental well-being in the process. However, prioritizing work-life balance is essential not only for maintaining one's health and relationships but also for sustaining long-term success in business. Mindful entrepreneurs recognize the importance of nurturing their mental well-being alongside their business pursuits. They understand that achieving sustainable success requires a holistic approach that encompasses both professional and personal fulfillment. By cultivating mindfulness practices such as meditation, self-reflection, and stress management techniques, entrepreneurs can develop resilience in the face of challenges and maintain a healthy perspective on their work and life.

10.3. Long-Term Strategies for Maintaining Mental Well-Being While Growing a Successful Business

Maintaining mental well-being while growing a successful business requires a strategic and holistic approach rooted in sustainable practices. Sustainable success and well-being in entrepreneurship emphasize the importance of nurturing mental health alongside business growth. One long-term strategy involves prioritizing self-care rituals that promote balance and resilience. This may include regular exercise, mindfulness practices such as meditation or yoga, and setting boundaries to protect personal time and space for relaxation. Additionally, fostering a supportive work culture that values open communication, empathy, and work-life integration can significantly contribute to the mental well-being of both entrepreneurs and their teams. Furthermore, incorporating mindfulness into business practices can enhance mental clarity, decision-making, and creativity. Mindful entrepreneurship involves cultivating awareness of thoughts, emotions, and behaviors in the entrepreneurial journey. Integrating mindfulness techniques into daily routines, such as mindful breathing exercises or reflective journaling, can help entrepreneurs manage stress, stay focused, and foster a positive mindset amidst challenges.

11. CONCLUSION

Maintaining mental well-being while growing a successful business requires a strategic and holistic approach rooted in sustainable practices. Sustainable success and well-being in entrepreneurship emphasize the importance of nurturing mental health alongside business growth. One long-term strategy involves prioritizing self-care rituals that promote balance and resilience. This may include regular exercise, mindfulness practices such as meditation or yoga, and setting boundaries to protect personal time and space for relaxation. Additionally, fostering a supportive work culture that values open communication, empathy, and work-life integration can significantly contribute to the mental well-being of both entrepreneurs and their teams. Furthermore, incorporating mindfulness into business practices can enhance mental clarity, decision-making, and creativity. Mindful entrepreneurship involves cultivating awareness of thoughts, emotions, and behaviors in the entrepreneurial journey. Integrating mindfulness techniques into daily routines, such as mindful breathing exercises or reflective journaling, can help entrepreneurs manage stress, stay focused, and foster a positive mindset amidst challenges. Moreover, fostering a sense of purpose beyond profit can provide intrinsic motivation and fulfillment, contributing to long-term mental well-being. Aligning business goals with values, social responsibility, and environmental sustainability can create a sense of meaning and connection, enhancing overall satisfaction and resilience in the face of adversity.

REFERENCES

Alvarez, G., & Sinde-Cantorna, A. I. (2014). Self-employment and job satisfaction: An empirical analysis. *International Journal of Manpower*, 35(5), 688–702. DOI: 10.1108/IJM-11-2012-0169

Annink, A., Gorgievski, M., & Den Dulk, L. (2016). Financial hardship and well-being: A cross-national comparison among the European self-employed. *European Journal of Work and Organizational Psychology*, 25(5), 645–657. DOI: 10.1080/1359432X.2016.1150263

. Arlington, VA: American Psychiatric Publishing

Byrnes, R. T., & Taylor, S. N. (2015). Voluntary transition of the CEO: Owner CEOs' sense of self before, during and after transition. *Frontiers in Psychology*, 6, 1633. DOI: 10.3389/fpsyg.2015.01633 PMID: 26579018

Cardon, M. S., & Patel, P. C. (2015). Is stress worth it? Stress-related health and wealth trade-offs for entrepreneurs. *Applied Psychology*, 64(2), 379–420. DOI: 10.1111/apps.12021

Cardon, M. S., Wincent, J., Singh, J., & Drnovsek, M. (2009). The nature and experience of entrepreneurial passion. *Academy of Management Review*, 34(3), 511–532. DOI: 10.5465/amr.2009.40633190

Carree, M. A., & Verheul, I. (2012). What makes entrepreneurs happy? Determinants of satisfaction among founders. *Journal of Happiness Studies*, 13(2), 371–387. DOI: 10.1007/s10902-011-9269-3

Clark, A., Colombier, N., & Masclet, D. (2008). Never the same after the first time: The satisfaction of the second-generation self-employed. *International Journal of Manpower*, 29(7), 591–609. DOI: 10.1108/01437720810908910

Cocker, F., Martin, A., Scott, J., Venn, A., & Sanderson, K. (2013). Psychological distress, related work attendance, and productivity loss in small-to-medium enterprise owner/managers. *International Journal of Environmental Research and Public Health*, 10(10), 5062–5082. DOI: 10.3390/ijerph10105062 PMID: 24132134

Dormann, C., & Griffin, M. A. (2015). Optimal time lags in panel studies. *Psychological Methods*, 20(4), 489–505. DOI: 10.1037/met0000041 PMID: 26322999

Drnovšek, M., Örtqvist, D., & Wincent, J. (2010). The effectiveness of coping strategies used by entrepreneurs and their impact on personal well-being and venture performance. *Proceedings of Rijeka Faculty of Economics*, 28(2), 193–220.

Dufouil, C., Pereira, E., Chêne, G., Glymour, M. M., Alpérovitch, A., Saubusse, E., Risse-Fleury, M., Heuls, B., Salord, J.-C., Brieu, M.-A., & Forette, F. (2014). Older age at retirement is associated with decreased risk of dementia. *European Journal of Epidemiology*, 29(5), 353–361. DOI: 10.1007/s10654-014-9906-3 PMID: 24791704

Eatough, E., Shockley, K., & Yu, P. (2016). A review of ambulatory health data collection methods for employee experience sampling research. *Applied Psychology*, 65(2), 322–354. DOI: 10.1111/apps.12068

. ing styles

Iyengar, S. S., & Lepper, M. R. (2000). When choice is demotivating: Can one desire too much of a good thing? *Journal of Personality and Social Psychology*, 79(6), 995–1005. DOI: 10.1037/0022-3514.79.6.995 PMID: 11138768

Johansson Sevä, I., Larsson, D., & Strandh, M. (2016). The prevalence, characteristics and well-being of "necessity" self-employed and "latent" entrepreneurs: Findings from Sweden. *International Journal of Entrepreneurship and Small Business*, 28(1), 58–77. DOI: 10.1504/IJESB.2016.075682

Kadowaki, H., Kayano, T., Tobinaga, T., Tsusumi, A., Watari, M., & Makita, K. (2016). Analysis of factors associated with hesitation to restart farming after depopulation of animals due to 2010 foot-and-mouth disease epidemic in Japan. *The Journal of Veterinary Medical Science*, 78(8), 1251–1259. DOI: 10.1292/jvms.15-0559 PMID: 27149890

Kallioniemi, M. K., Simola, A., Kaseva, J., & Kymäläinen, H.-R. (2016). Stress and burnout among Finnish dairy farmers. *Journal of Agromedicine*, 21(3), 259–268. DOI: 10.1080/1059924X.2016.1178611 PMID: 27081893

Lechmann, D. S. J., & Schnabel, C. (2014). Absence from work of the self-employed: A comparison with paid employees. *Kyklos*, 67(3), 368–390. DOI: 10.1111/kykl.12059

Li, W.-D., Fay, D., Frese, M., Harms, P. D., & Gao, X. Y. (2014). Reciprocal relationship between proactive personality and work characteristics: A latent change score approach. *The Journal of Applied Psychology*, 99(5), 948–965. DOI: 10.1037/a0036169 PMID: 24635530

Loewe, N., Araya-Castillo, L., Thieme, C., & Batista-Foguet, J. M. (2015). Self-employment as a moderator between work and life satisfaction. *Academia (Caracas)*, 28(2), 213–226. DOI: 10.1108/ARLA-10-2014-0165

Luchman, J. N., & González-Morales, M. G. (2013). Demands, control, and support: A meta-analytic review of work characteristics interrelationships. *Journal of Occupational Health Psychology*, 18(1), 37–52. DOI: 10.1037/a0030541 PMID: 23339747

. of entrepreneurs: A Malaysian survey. International

Reymen, I. M. M. J., Andries, P., Berends, H., Mauer, R., Stephan, U., & Van Burg, E. (2015). Understanding dynamics of strategic decision making in venture creation: A process study of effectuation and causation. *Strategic Entrepreneurship Journal*, 9(4), 351–379. DOI: 10.1002/sej.1201

Rocca, S., Sagiv, L., Schwartz, S. H., & Knafo, A. (2002). The Big Five personality factors and personal values. *Personality and Social Psychology Bulletin*, 28(6), 789–801. DOI: 10.1177/0146167202289008

Roche, M., Haar, J. M., & Luthans, F. (2014). The role of mindfulness and psychological capital on the wellbeing of leaders. *Journal of Occupational Health Psychology*, 19(4), 476–489. DOI: 10.1037/a0037183 PMID: 24933594

Roche, M., Haar, J. M., & Luthans, F. (2014). The role of mindfulness and psychological capital on the wellbeing of leaders. *Journal of Occupational Health Psychology*, 19(4), 476–489. DOI: 10.1037/a0037183 PMID: 24933594

Ryan, R. M., & Deci, E. L. (2001). On happiness and human potentials: A review of research on hedonic and eudaimonic well-being. *Annual Review of Psychology*, 52(1), 141–166. DOI: 10.1146/annurev.psych.52.1.141 PMID: 11148302

Ryff, C. D. (2017). Eudaimonic well-being, inequality, and health: Recent findings and future directions. *International Review of Economics*, 64(2), 159–178. DOI: 10.1007/s12232-017-0277-4 PMID: 29057014

Saarni, S. I., Saarni, E. S., & Saarni, H. (2008). Quality of life, work ability, and self-employment: A population survey of entrepreneurs, farmers, and salary earners. *Occupational and Environmental Medicine*, 65(2), 98–103. DOI: 10.1136/oem.2007.033423 PMID: 17666452

Stephan, U. (2018). Entrepreneurs' Mental Health and Well-Being: A Review and Research Agenda. *The Academy of Management Perspectives*, 32(3), 290–322. DOI: 10.5465/amp.2017.0001

Taris, T. W., Geurts, S. A. E., Schaufeli, W. B., Blonk, R. W. B., & Lagerveld, S. E. (2008). All day and all of the night: The relative contribution of two dimensions of workaholism to well-being in self-employed workers. *Work and Stress*, 22(2), 153–165. DOI: 10.1080/02678370701758074

Thompson, C. A., Kopelman, R. E., & Schriesheim, C. A. (1992). Putting all one's eggs in the same basket: A comparison of commitment and satisfaction among self- and organizationally employed men. *The Journal of Applied Psychology*, 77(5), 738–743. DOI: 10.1037/0021-9010.77.5.738

Thurik, R., Khedhaouria, A., Torr'es, O., & Verheul, I. (2016). ADHD symptoms and entrepreneurial orientation of small firm owners. *Applied Psychology*, 65(3), 568–586. DOI: 10.1111/apps.12062

Tobias, J. M., Mair, J., & Barbosa-Leiker, C. (2013). Toward a theory of transformative entrepreneuring: Poverty reduction and conflict resolution in Rwanda's entrepreneurial coffee sector. *Journal of Business Venturing*, 28(6), 728–742. DOI: 10.1016/j.jbusvent.2013.03.003

Torp, S., Nielsen, R. A., Gudbergsson, S. B., & Dahl, A. A. (2012). Worksite adjustments and work ability among employed cancer survivors. *Supportive Care in Cancer*, 20(9), 2149–2156. DOI: 10.1007/s00520-011-1325-3 PMID: 22086407

Torp, S., Syse, J., Paraponaris, A., & Gudbergsson, S. (2017). Return to work among self-employed cancer survivors. *Journal of Cancer Survivorship: Research and Practice*, 11(2), 189–200. DOI: 10.1007/s11764-016-0578-8 PMID: 27837444

Totterdell, P., Wood, S., & Wall, T. (2006). An intraindividual test of the demands-control model: A weekly diary study of psychological strain in portfolio workers. *Journal of Occupational and Organizational Psychology*, 79(1), 63–84. DOI: 10.1348/096317905X52616

Tranfield, D., Denyer, D., & Smart, P. (2003). Towards a methodology for developing evidence-informed management knowledge by means of systematic review. *British Journal of Management*, 14(3), 207–222. DOI: 10.1111/1467-8551.00375

Ugwu, D. I., Orjiakor, C. T., Enwereuzor, I. K., Onyedibe, C. C., & Ugwu, L. I. (2016). Business-life balance and well-being: Exploring the lived experiences of women in a low-to-middle income country. *International Journal of Qualitative Studies on Health and Well-being*, 11(1), 30492. Advance online publication. DOI: 10.3402/qhw.v11.30492 PMID: 27080016

Wendsche, J., & Lohmann-Haislah, A. (2017). A meta-analysis on antecedents and outcomes of detachment from work. *Frontiers in Psychology*, 7, 2072. DOI: 10.3389/fpsyg.2016.02072 PMID: 28133454

Wiklund, J., Patzelt, H., & Dimov, D. (2016). Entrepreneurship and psychological disorders: How ADHD can be productively harnessed. *Journal of Business Venturing Insights*, 6, 14–20. DOI: 10.1016/j.jbvi.2016.07.001

Williams, T. A., & Shepherd, D. A. (2016). Victim entrepreneurs doing well by doing good: Venture creation and well-being in the aftermath of a resource shock. *Journal of Business Venturing*, 31(4), 365–387. DOI: 10.1016/j.jbusvent.2016.04.002

Wincent, J., & Örtqvist, D. (2009). A comprehensive model of entrepreneur role stress antecedents and consequences. *Journal of Business and Psychology*, 24(2), 225–243. DOI: 10.1007/s10869-009-9102-8

Wincent, J., Örtqvist, D., & Drnovsek, M. (2008). The entrepreneur's role stressors and proclivity for a venture withdrawal. *Scandinavian Journal of Management*, 24(3), 232–246. DOI: 10.1016/j.scaman.2008.04.001

Wirback, T., Möller, J., Larsson, J.-O., Galanti, M. R., & Engström, K. (2014). Social factors in childhood and risk of depressive symptoms among adolescents—A longitudinal study in Stockholm, Sweden. *International Journal for Equity in Health*, 13(1), 96–107. DOI: 10.1186/s12939-014-0096-0 PMID: 25384415

Chapter 15
National and Regional Economic Growth and Development Fostered by Entrepreneurship Ecosystems

José G. Vargas-Hernandez
https://orcid.org/0000-0003-0938-4197
Tecnològico Nacional de Mèxico, ITS Fresnillo, Mexico

ABSTRACT

This study aims to analyze the national and regional economic growth and development fostered by entrepreneurship ecosystems. Based on the assumption that entrepreneurship ecosystems theoretical framing has a specific configuration to be applied in national and regional socioeconomic ecosystems for economic growth and development assuming that there is only one to optimize value objectives on terms of economic value and entrepreneurship configuration. The method employed is the descriptive leading to the meta-analytical reflection based on the conceptual, theoretical, and empirical research literature. It is concluded that entrepreneurship ecosystems are powerful means to foster national and

INTRODUCTION

The state of conceptual, theoretical, and empirical studies of entrepreneurial ecosystem research and development, focusing on the elements and causal relationships linked to outcomes aimed to a comprehensive understanding of the contextual nature and its contribution to entrepreneurship and economic development policy (Webster & Watson, 2002). Research on entrepreneurial ecosystems program is conceptual, theoretical, and empirically evolving in a complex socio-economic system despite the existent gaps, leading to the design and implement of a transdisciplinary entrepreneurship research program.

Research is interested in the entrepreneurship activity generation of objective value and on the entrepreneurial activity emerging and influencing changes in regional socioeconomic order of the community. The priority of each objective value approaches the balance between human subjectivity of economic, social, natural environment and technological, there is a risk of missing the complex connections between the entrepreneurship inputs and evolutions of regional socio-economic systems.

DOI: 10.4018/979-8-3693-3673-1.ch015

The entrepreneurial ecosystem research is framed by the analysis of a dominant economic purpose with specific outputs and outcomes connected to economics and business, organizational strategy, value creation, competitive advantage digital affordances, productive entrepreneurship, regional economic growth, resource allocation, among other (Adner & Kapoor, 2010; Adner, 2017; Jansson et al., 2014; Autio et al. 2018; Stam, 2015; Content et al., 2020; Acs et al., 2014; Autio & Levie, 2017).

State of the art of empirical research on the interrelation between regional entrepreneurship ecosystem framework and economic development to synthesize from a complex systems perspective. Research on entrepreneurship ecosystem studies is influenced by complex systems of local actors among others, incubators, startups, accelerators, mentors, government agencies and officials, universities, research centers, co-working and maker spaces, customers, and so on in interaction with socio-economic forces such as institutions, values, norms, narratives, etc. in environments and contexts that extend beyond organizational boundaries (Roundy *et al.*, 2018; Thompson *et al.*, 2018).

The complex system perspective integrates entrepreneurship geography and economic growth. This empirical literature is divided on the effects on aggregate economic growth of entrepreneurship, geography of entrepreneurship and spatial heterogeneity. The geographical institutional and relational foundations in dynamic interactions and economic synergies between entrepreneurship actors of entrepreneurship ecosystems in localized contexts corresponds to innovation systems (Borissenko & Boschma, 2016).

Economic development and growth supported by entrepreneurship is concerned with causal evidence (Schumpeter, 1934; Leibenstein,1968; Baumol, 1990; Audretsch *et al.*, 2006; Bosma *et al.* (2018). Carree & Thurik, 2010; Fritsch, 2013). Entrepreneurship geography and economic growth empirical literature as an entrepreneurial ecosystem framework that explains spatial heterogeneity affecting the prevalence of regional entrepreneurship (Stam, 2015; Stam & Spigel, 2018; Stam & Van de Ven, 2021).

Finance in entrepreneurship ecosystems has a disproportionate position to be explored in economic geography and regional innovation systems and development, a role that has become explicit in the emerging entrepreneurship ecosystems perspective (Gjelsvik & Trippl 2018; Acs et al. 2017; Bonini & Capizzi, 2019; Isenberg, 2011). Research on financial knowledge and mechanisms supporting the aggregate level the entrepreneurship ecosystems to perform, creating jobs and increasing economic activities (Armington & Acs 2002; Benneworth, 2004; Cross, 1981; Fritsch & Mueller2004; Leendertse et al., 2021).

Research on entrepreneurship finance assumes contextual differences when stretching into economic geography and regional development (Steyaert & Katz 2004). Entrepreneurship finance needs a theoretical foundation regarding subsidy and credit in emerging economies despite that context is not relevant as entrepreneurship finance research tends to focus on universal patterns (Ucbasaran et al., 2001). Research on entrepreneurial finance in economic geography and regional development assume contextual differences (Steyaert & Katz 2004).

The development of a theoretical concept of entrepreneurial ecosystems is created by the fusion of diverse institutional, economic, social, cultural, biological, behavioral perspectives, which difficulties the definitions and measurements (Audretsch & Belitski, 2017). The concept of entrepreneurship ecosystems is dynamic acknowledging the cognitive belief systems, processes, and economic interactions. Design on experimental research simultaneously create rigorous theoretical knowledge and practical insights with reliable knowledge about changes in cognitions, behaviors, affects and performance, leading to the emergence and disappearance of entrepreneurship, and the relationship between entrepreneurship and economic and social development (Williams *et al.*, 2019).

Research tries to investigate the relationship between entrepreneurship and economic growth and development (Kritikos, 2015; Stoica et al., 2020). to build a well-functioning despite the differences in outputs of ecosystems. Research on entrepreneurial ecosystems questions what is generalizable in opposition to what is inherently bounded to local economic, social, and political contexts with policy implications of Western contexts applicable to the global south and emerging economies (Tsvetkova *et al.*, 2019; Cao & Shi, 2020). Local economic structures in agglomeration economies, clusters, and complex systems responding to local development conditions lead to create varied innovative start-ups (Capozza *et al.*, 2018).

Causal mechanisms in entrepreneurship socio-ecosystems are analyzed with the aim of linking empirical to explain entrepreneurship economies by the frameworks of Stam (2015);Stam & Van de Ven (2019); and Thurik et al., (2013). Experimentation by economic actors combining successful and failed experiments is not a subject of entrepreneurship ecosystem research. Replication studies accumulate knowledge and increase confidence in findings, such as the ecosystem as moderator for economic development (Davidsson, 2004; Bruns *et al.*, 2017; Content *et al.*, 2020).

Productive entrepreneurship is the entrepreneurial activity that contributes to the economic net output and to the capacity to produce additional output. Productive entrepreneurship can be situated at the center of research agenda for an analysis of network interdependencies affecting value creation at the economy and firm levels. Productive entrepreneurship is defined as any entrepreneurial activity that has the capacity to produce and contributes to economic net output in high-growth firms leading to job creation targeting the economic development policy (Baumol, 1990; Stam & Bosma, 2015; Brown & Mason, 2017). The entrepreneurial output measures do not capture all the innovative economic activities.

Productive entrepreneurship is a category defined as an aggregate economic value empirically measured in monetary terms as high in growth beyond a performance threshold (Bos & Stam, 2014; Davidsson, 2004; Stam, 2015). The entrepreneurship ecosystem research approaches reorient productive entrepreneurship and economic development rather than innovation and venture creation. Entrepreneurship ecosystem activities constitute an antecedent to urban innovation reflecting the creation of urban activities related to economic development.

The spread of academic and scientific research institutions in the last century is considered the root of rapid economic and demographic growth with changes in consumption and lifestyles patters with improvements in human wellbeing (Mokyr, 2002). Science is considered to remedy the sustainability crises generated by economic and population growth. Capitalization of scientific knowledge in services economy has led to transformation of academic institutions towards entrepreneurial universities during the 20th Century.

This study aims to analyze the national and regional economic growth and development fostered by entrepreneurship ecosystems, based on the assumption that entrepreneurship ecosystems theoretical framing has a specific configuration to be applied in national and regional socioeconomic ecosystems for economic growth and development assuming that there is only one to optimize value objectives on terms of economic value and entrepreneurship configuration. It begins with an analysis of institutional change, leading to entrepreneurship socio-ecosystems and its impact on national and regional economic growth and development. Finally, some conclusions are inferred.

INSTITUTIONAL CHANGE ANALYSIS

The economic approach to institutional change sustains that institutions emerge to produce collective goods, capture rents, reduce uncertainty and safeguards from opportunistic behavior of partners. Institutions change in new economic conditions fueling the market failures creating gains from collective organizations in new schemes (Akerloff, 1970; Greif, 1998; Hechter, 1987; North, 1990; Ostrom, 1990; Weingast & Marshall, 1988; Williamson, 1985; Wilson, 1980).

The institutional ideas analysis provides solutions to economic crisis such as the deflation of the 1930s which lead to the built of Swedish institutions model rearticulating labor and business ideas and interests as integral parts of the model. The institutional Swedish model encompasses the public sector institutions that ceases to benefit the economy and become drag upon it.

Institutional ideas are relevant by providing instructions to economic agents and socio-political actors. Individuals involved in the entrepreneurship ecosystems embody intentions, behaviors, attitudes, etc., not aligned with the institutional, economic, social, and cultural context including entrepreneurship actors and agents. Entrepreneurial intention considers factors among others are the environmental and economic growth in the region or country concerned (Lee & Peterson, 2000; Cohen & Winn, 2007; Del Giudice et al., 2017; Sharif et al., 2021).

Economic conditions changed during the 1980s disturbed the institutional equilibrium after labor encroached upon the interests of business that defected, constructed, and developed a new set of institutional ideas and institutions leading to new equilibrium to be defined and implemented in function of changing the structural conditions. Changing attitudes through entrepreneurship and start-up education in developing economic regions may reflect the necessity which may not be equated with more dynamic economies (Van Stel & Storey, 2004; O'Connor, 2013; Acs et al., 2008b; Isenberg & Brown, 2014; Mazzucato, 2014; Colombelli et al., 2016).

The regional entrepreneurship ecosystem explains the changes in regional communities and taking market economics. The regional entrepreneurship ecosystem focusing on productive entrepreneurship is concerned with the socioeconomic systems depleted and declining communities through increasing the scales and introducing modern technologies, productive entrepreneurial ventures, etc. The value effect of entrepreneurship is assessed in relation to ecosystem and socioeconomic change in the trajectory of communities.

The regional socioeconomic stability is determined by regional economics and market activities extending beyond the regional socioeconomic activities. The regional entrepreneurship ecosystem has an impact on the regional economic stability. Whether creation of disruption of balance or equilibrium, entrepreneurship activities in a region provides the market dynamics of economy inducing stability from disruption or moving disruption to instability. Entrepreneurship ecosystems theoretical framing has a specific configuration to be applied in regional socioeconomic ecosystems assuming that there is only one to optimize value objectives on terms of economic value and entrepreneurship configuration.

The design of institutional structures in periods of institutional structural transformation and change are subject to the relevance of the diverse interests of economic agents and socio-political actors. Change of ecosystem represents a stability analysis of the socioeconomic structure. The primary functions in productive socioeconomic function and entrepreneurship change functions are in systemic combination. Among the entrepreneurship agents and actors create financial, economic, social, commercial, etc. ventures to sustain and change the dynamics of the organizational entrepreneurship ecosystem.

Entrepreneurship ecosystems have developed macro-dynamics focus coupled with entrepreneurship ecosystems ascending as the prevailing metaphor for forces located influencing the connections between the ecosystem's elements and outcomes. This approach aims to explain the entrepreneurship ecosystems factors, among others, institutional culture and regulations, market structure and so on, and economic performance (Content *et al.*, 2020; Hechavarría & Ingram, 2019; Iacobucci & Perugini, 2021; Mikic *et al.*, 2020; Nicotra *et al.*, 2018; Szerb *et al.*, 2019; Xie *et al.*, 2021). The macro-dynamics focus on entrepreneurial ecosystem research generates insights for economic development, but the practical implications are unclear for entrepreneurship as unstated theory (Hannigan *et al.*, 2021).

Social diverse entrepreneurship actors are reactive and proactive driving autogenic change while keeping socioeconomic activities. Social diversity is a critical indicator of socioeconomic activity. Social diversity is a mix of human representations into the regional socioeconomic system and entrepreneurship change as an internal pressure across the various levels of economic activities responding to external pressures of change of composed configuration, structure, and functions.

Knowledge management (KM) and intellectual capital (IC) perspectives are adopted by research to confirm the cultural levels of the humane orientation (HO) with economic development as the moderating variable on the relationship between culture and humane entrepreneurships. Environmentally sustainable and social orientation perspectives are crucial for the emergence of human entrepreneurship ecosystems (HEEs) aimed at supporting the economic, social, and ecological environment (Canestrino *et al.* 2023).

A regional entrepreneurship ecosystems alternative framing within a regional socioeconomic system comprises responsible economic actions in an endogenous change agent for socioeconomic structure and function composition shifts aimed to value creation outcomes in many dimensions. Structural institutional change is indetermined to subsequent institutional forms.

Formal institutions are an element for economic action and the productive use of resources affecting entrepreneurship ecosystem and its welfare consequences (Granovetter, 1992; Acemoglu et al., 2005; Baumol, 1990). The interacting economic organizations involved in entrepreneurship ecosystems provide resources and support to individual entrepreneurs at place.

Institutional analyses examine economic and political change processes of new economic institutions (American Journal of Sociology, 1996; Campbell & Pedersen, 1996; Guthrie, 1999; Li, Tsui, & Weldon, 1999; Lin, forthcoming; Min, 1995; Oi & Walder, 1999; Orru, Biggart, & Hamilton, 1997]. Institutions with strong opposing forces on the change process follow a spiral trajectory without contradicting the impact of exogenous forces in institutional change such as the ideological paradigms in times of economic and political crisis. The agenda of institutional change and replacement depends on the dynamic convergence of economic and political conditions such as legitimacy crisis and market failures, etc. which enable new policies.

ENTREPRENEURSHIP SOCIO-ECOSYSTEMS

Entrepreneurship is a term that attracts the attention from managerial and economic researchers (Zhao *et al.*, 2014; Nicotra *et al.*, 2018; Usai *et al.*, 2018). An entrepreneur is a job creator to promote economic growth aimed to improve the lives of population (Acs et al., 2016; Acs, *et al.*, (2018). The primary objective of entrepreneurship is based on the increased economic value creation. Entrepreneurship ecosystems are concerned with how entrepreneurs and firms survive, grow, prosper, and shape the economic activities of regional entrepreneurship ecosystems (Audretsch & Belitski, 2021).

Conceptualization of entrepreneurship ecosystems does not result from individual behaviors but from economic, social, and cultural forces (Van de Ven, 1993) placed within a network of interdependent actors within a geographical territory to support the creation and development of innovative organization projects beyond the network structure of firms (Nicotra et al., 2018). Entrepreneurship ecosystem is defined as the set of interdependent factors and actors fostering entrepreneurship aiming to create economic wealth and prosperity in a territory (Stam, 2015; Prahalad, 2005).

The entrepreneurship ecosystem is formed by the required elements to sustain entrepreneurial activities aimed to generate economic wealth and prosperity in a specific territory (Prahalad, 2005). Entrepreneurial ecosystem activities affect the economy, society, organizations, firms, and individuals (Prahalad, 2005). Entrepreneurship is a mechanism in the community of a regional entrepreneurial ecosystem framing across disciplines for the regional analysis to move the socioeconomic orders.

Entrepreneurship ecosystem engages with institutional, economic, social, physical natural environments, knowledge, technological, etc. over time to balance the regional socioeconomic order of the community. These elements of entrepreneurship ecosystem engage are not individually divisible determinants and do not emphasize any specific aspect.

The entrepreneurial ecosystem objectifies the economic patterns of new venturing and prioritizing the new value-added ventures and productive entrepreneurship, incorporating performance measures, competitiveness, etc. (Stam, 2015; Wurth *et al.*,2021; Spigel & Harrison, 2018; Stangler & Bell-Masterson, 2015; Sitaridis & Kitsios, 2020). The entrepreneurship ecosystem has an output the productive entrepreneurship which contributes to the economic output leading to aggregate value creation (Baumol, 1990).

Entrepreneurship ecosystems framework place priority on the creation of entrepreneurship activities and the regional entrepreneurship ecosystem framework places priority on influencing stability of the regional socioeconomic community.

Innovation and entrepreneurship are entwined with economic growth and development (Acs, et al., 2017). Entrepreneurship has an intrinsic relationship with economic growth and development (Acs, 2006). Productive entrepreneurship has positive effects on economic growth and job creation (Criscuolo *et al.*, 2014; Haltiwanger *et al.*, 2013; Stam *et al.*, 2011; Wong *et al.*, 2005). Research using GEM data reveals that entrepreneurship opportunities have a significant positive effect on economic growth and development.

A shift from productive entrepreneurship to social entrepreneurship recognize the effects on wider economic development (Harms & Groen, 2017; Thompson et al., 2018; Shepherd & Patzelt, 2020). Productive entrepreneurship includes innovative start-ups and entrepreneurial workforce to foster economic productivity (Stam, 2015). Performance of an entrepreneurship economy is more dependent on startups and innovative firms than on economies of scale (Audretsch & Thurik, 2001; Thurik *et al.*, 2013).

An entrepreneurial socio-ecosystem is a complex set of interactions between individuals, groups, and institutions within the socio-economic, informational, and institutional context (Audretsch & Belitski, 2016). Entrepreneurship in complex economic systems is a driver of economic development (Schumpeter, 1934). The entrepreneurial ecosystem elements and outputs have positive correlations between each other which confirms the systemic nature of the complex systems in entrepreneurship economies. The elements of entrepreneurship economies are interdependent in complex systems (Aghion *et al.*, 2009; Simon, 1962). Physical infrastructure, traditional transportation and digital infrastructure are contextual elements that enable economic interaction and entrepreneurship (Audretsch *et al.*, 2015).

Entrepreneurship ecosystem is linked to digital technologies in extensive research with implications for the economic, social, and cultural development environments.

The complex systems approach build on conceptual complications on the evolution of entrepreneurship economies (Arthur, 2013; Hidalgo & Hausmann, 2009; Ostrom, 2010; Simon, 1962; Feld & Hathaway, 2020; Roundy *et al.*, 2018; Stam & Van de Ven, 2021). Entrepreneurship creates and responds to uncertainty conditions that alter the dominant socioeconomic activities within the ecosystem boundary.

Measurement development is needed to determine and quantify the elements and qualify entrepreneurship economies. Measurements of complex entrepreneurship socio-ecosystems do not always separate economic inputs and outputs in which economic agents at the micro level interact and experiment with each other to form an evolving economic system aimed to create social wealth (Beinhocker, 2006). The entrepreneurship ecosystem activity influences advancing or retarding wealth and living standards of socioeconomic development.

Specific entrepreneurship measures are combined with general measures of regional culture and trust in societies where individuals trust each other in economic and investments interactions and trust between organizations in cooperation projects (Zak & Knack, 2001). Synthesis and integration of large quantity of data are instruments to measure the changing nature, elements, outputs, and outcomes of regional economies (Stam, 2015). Harmonized dataset must be composed to measure the quality of elements of entrepreneurship economies.

Entrepreneurship ecosystem environments are focused on the broader contexts of entrepreneurial activities which have smaller economic impacts (Gnyawali & Fogel, 1994; Van de Ven, 1993; Welter, *et al.*, 2017). Economic agency and institutions in regional economy participate in constantly developing technological innovation, institutional and organizational arrangements (Arthur, 2013). The organizational size is related with the growth of the physical and digital infrastructure entrepreneurship ecosystem essential for socioeconomic interactions among the stakeholders, actors, and agents (Audretsch *et al.*, 2015).

Entrepreneurial ecosystems literature has not provided a framework for economic policy because the lack of credible and accurate metrics. Structural economic policy requires annual data in the context of evolving crises with frequent monitoring.

ECONOMIC GROWTH AND DEVELOPMENT

Entrepreneurial ecosystems address issues affecting stability, economic growth, and the well-being of firms. The entrepreneurship ecosystems are linked to economic growth (Acs *et al.*, 2018; Lafuente *et al.*, 2016; Lafuente *et al.*, 2019). Entrepreneurship is an economic and social phenomenon of power to propel the economic growth (Valliere & Peterson, 2009)

The term of entrepreneurship ecosystem is applied to growth and development of regional socioeconomic communities influencing the evolution of socioeconomic systems and how sustain, expand, and diminish the habitats. The entrepreneurship ecosystems are a place-based composite structural unit to include a bundle of institutions, economics, social arrangements, physical environment, knowledge, technology and entrepreneurship in specific time and place. Each of these elements contributes to the regional socioeconomic order.

Entrepreneurship-driven economic development is the means for creating economic development defined as the structural changes to the economy and its institutional and social fabric beyond the productivity growth and gross domestic product, and dimensions of employment, well-being, inequality, etc. (Acemoglu, 2012). The regional entrepreneurship ecosystem enables change mechanisms within the regional socioeconomic ecosystem. Traditional economic development concepts of entrepreneurship ecosystems emphasize the need for resource accumulation and dynamic capabilities focusing on innovation and strategy of the entrepreneurship ability of firms to growth sensing and seizing opportunities (Teece, 2014; 2007).

Theoretical development on entrepreneurship ecosystems as a conceptual framework is a growing field in relation to change and stability of regional socioeconomic ecosystems. Purpose, function, and effects of entrepreneurship ecosystem research influencing the regional economies is informed by the transfer concepts of forest ecology. Entrepreneurship ecosystem is an alternate framework of an ecological view of entrepreneurship applied to regional economies (Cronin et al., 2021). Adopting an entrepreneurship ecosystem view engages with ecological approaches adapting methods to improve capabilities and abilities that have entrepreneurship and evolutionary impacts on specific socioeconomic communities.

Regional entrepreneurship ecosystem framing is an alternative research approach to operationalize other different models and necessary tools to analyze entrepreneurship ecologies, and the dynamics change of socioeconomic systems instead of focusing on productive entrepreneurship as a concept of value creation (Stam, 2015; Wurth *et al.*, 2021).

Regional entrepreneurship has implications with the autogenic change as a socioeconomic response in terms of entrepreneurship behaviors to reshape structures, composition, and functions at regional socioeconomic community. The principles of the entrepreneurship ecosystems stem from the economic functions from an objective perspective of entrepreneurial activities. The different perspectives on the entrepreneurship functions in an economy contrasts the disruptive behavior of Schumpeter (1976) to the one oriented toward achievement of the balance and equilibrium of the economic systems which encompasses the consequences of Schumpeterian entrepreneurship (Kirzner, 2009).

New ventures and entrepreneurship activities in a socio-economic ecosystem seizes emerging new opportunities through knowledge spill-over and by responding to experienced and perceived external changes and disruptions to the region. Human capital has effects on entrepreneurial ecosystem in emerging economies. Countries in emerging economies proceed from requirement – based entrepreneurship towards creating opportunity-based firms (Santos *et al.*, 2021).

An entrepreneurship ecosystem framework can combine the approaches of economic growth and entrepreneurship geography for long-term economic development. Entrepreneurship is an input variable in the economic growth approach and output variable in the entrepreneurship geography. Economic geography criticizes the approach to national systems of innovation, however noting that entrepreneurship is a localized phenomenon (Cooke *et al.*, 1997; Stam, 2007; Dahl & Sorenson, 2009; Feldman *et al.*, 2005; Feldman, 2014; Gertler, 2010; Welter, 2011). Economic geography resolves the paradox between local and regional change, investment, and development. Established firms in the entrepreneurship ecosystem are the bedrock of regional and local economy, often driven by growth-oriented start-up processes and growing firms.

Output and outcome of entrepreneurship ecosystems are related to change of places of socioeconomic arrangements. The specific entrepreneurship systems supporting and sustaining socioeconomic activities are affected by the entrepreneurial activity and less concerned with the systems science and systems theory.

There are different frameworks of entrepreneurial ecosystems based on the elements of the entrepreneurship geography and economic growth. Vedula & Kim, (2019) propose five elements and six Isenberg & Onyemah, (2016), seven, Radosevic & Yoruk, (2013) and fourteen elements integrated in a framework by Acs *et al.* (2014). Economic growth led to knowledge investments, growth in demand and congestion of physical environment. Economic growth and entrepreneurship affect the inputs of entrepreneurship geography such as serial entrepreneurs becoming venture capitalists and creating networks.

The entrepreneurial ecosystem has moderating effects on the relation between economic growth and entrepreneurship outputs at regional level. Regional economies can be quantified and qualified with an entrepreneurship ecosystem approach. Activities and actors in entrepreneurial ecosystems have priority for management and governance with objective measures of regional economic, social, and environmental performance. The entrepreneurship ecosystem approach is an inclusive means of regional and human interactions framing the analysis through increasing entrepreneurship activities pursuing objective economic and value measures.

Using a composed harmonized dataset to measure the quality of elements of the entrepreneurship economies. Regions with low gross regional product (GRP) may have high entrepreneurial output. The Entrepreneurial Ecosystem Index measures the quality of entrepreneurship economies. However, the Entrepreneurial Ecosystem Index captures the quality of entrepreneurship economies better than the gross regional product (GRP).

The added value in theory-based metrics measure the quality of regional entrepreneurship ecosystems and captures the ecosystem dimensions beyond the level of regional economic development. The concept of the regional entrepreneurship ecosystem concept is related to changing mechanisms of a holistic ecology different to dominant models focusing on entrepreneurial activities in economics, social and environmental outcomes. An alternate focus is on the entrepreneurship ecosystem activities instead of the holistic concept of regional stability and the changing socioeconomic structure. The regional entrepreneurship ecosystem reframes a holistic balance of socioeconomic regions in which entrepreneurship is a functional initiative-taking and reactive element that changes the socioeconomic system.

Reflecting on the entrepreneurial activities in a socioeconomic ecosystem influencing regional stability. The entrepreneurship ecosystems have effects on economic growth depending on the context, opportunities, entrepreneurship growth-oriented types leading the economic growth instead of necessity and self-employed entrepreneurship (Bosma *et al.*, 2018, 2011; Fritsch, 2013; Stam et al., 2011; Stam & Van Stel, 2011).

Regional entrepreneurship ecosystem is a mechanism of change to influence entrepreneurial activities on structural changes in the elements contributing to the socioeconomic community. The economics of communities in wealth production, distribution and utility have different profiles in regional entrepreneurial ecosystems.

Significant trade-off between context-specific data and availability of regional harmonized data enables comparisons between regions. Entrepreneurial economies element is interdependent in network analyses aiming to reveal that entrepreneurship economies are interdependent systems. The indicator network engagement informs on the prevalence of public-private leadership in the context organizations involved in collaborative innovation projects, which require improvements to measure leadership in the quality of entrepreneurship economies and the prevalence of regional public-private partnerships (Olberding, 2002).

The entrepreneurship ecosystem approach includes the metrics to improve regional entrepreneurship economies and provide lens for public policymaking. Policymaking requires a set of specific cluster, innovation and entrepreneurship policy prescriptions and instruments to promote start-ups programs and foster scale-ups to counter the economic path-dependency nature in entrepreneurship ecosystems (Van Stel & Storey, 2004; Fritsch & Storey, 2014; Brown & Mason, 2014). Collecting richer data can improve the metrics. Entrepreneurial ecosystem metrics facilitate a collective learning process combined with dialogue to improve regional economies. Entrepreneurship ecosystems metrics are essential input for ex-post policy evaluation and can be combined with qualitative insights which enable to monitor the improvements in productivity and economic growth.

Productive entrepreneurship and innovation-driven have an impact on competitiveness, job creation and economic development (Wennekers *et al.*, 2005). Increasing self-employment improves economic resilience and flexibility. Networks of entrepreneurs' relationships make decisions on the start and growth business based on economic and social factors (Sorenson, 2018).

The entrepreneurship system analysis based on an economic cycle; financing entrepreneurship growth is in the wake of a mega-event (Spilling, 1996). Entrepreneurship ecosystem has a cumulative self-perpetuating effect on future entrepreneurship though a process of entrepreneurship recycling in economies acting as catalyst for entrepreneurial practices and activities (Mason & Harrison, 2006). The entrepreneurial re-cycling process involves the transfer of entrepreneurial knowledge and learning within ecosystems leading to individuals becoming dealmakers, advisors, directors, mentors, and serial entrepreneurs with a role within economies as venturing tending to confer positive spillovers (Parker, 2013).

CONCLUSIONS

The analysis on national and regional economic growth and development fostered by entrepreneurship ecosystems concludes that entrepreneurship ecosystems are powerful means to foster national and regional economic growth and development. Entrepreneurial ecosystem is a regional economic development strategy based on creating supportive environments aimed at fostering innovative start-ups. Entrepreneurial ecosystems and top management strategies research are more concerned with the diverse types of economic, social, cultural, and political environments supporting growth entrepreneurship within a regional territory.

There are interdependencies between the elements of entrepreneurial economies as complex systems. Development of methodology to qualify provides an insight of the interdependence of elements into the quality of entrepreneurship economies in relation to the outputs. The entrepreneurial ecosystem has moderating effects on the relation between economic growth and entrepreneurship output at regional level. Entrepreneurship output is an indicator of emergent elements and property of entrepreneurship economies using metrics and multiple data sources to determine the outputs at regional level in the form of innovative unicorns and new firms.

Local and regional entrepreneurship ecosystem research analyses the implications and trajectories by prioritizing value objective by the effect of entrepreneurship behaviors on a socioeconomic community. Blockbuster entrepreneurship in embryonic entrepreneurship ecosystems has rare occurrences, low levels of embeddedness and traction in local economies, shaped by market access, local human capital, access to capital ventures and stock markets, etc.

The quality of entrepreneurship economies can be analyzed and determined with a synthesis of elements of entrepreneurship ecosystem metrics into an entrepreneurship ecosystem index to entrepreneurship outputs. The quality of entrepreneurship economies can be measured with external validity to show the ranking of regions and variation ranges. The quality of entrepreneurial economies can be determined by composed entrepreneurial ecosystems index and the analyses related to entrepreneurship outputs.

REFERENCES

A., Naudé, W., Goedhuys, M. (Eds.). *Entrepreneurship, Innovation, and Economic Development*. Oxford University Press, Oxford.

Acemoglu, D., Johnson, S., Robinson, J.A. (2005). Institutions as a fundamental cause of long-run growth. *Handb. Econ. Growth*. 385–472. .DOI: 10.1016/S1574-0684(05)01006-3

Acs, Z., Åstebro, T., Audretsch, D., & Robinson, D. T. (2016). Public policy to promote entrepreneurship: A call to arms. *Small Business Economics*, 47(1), 35–51. DOI: 10.1007/s11187-016-9712-2

Acs, Z., Stam, E., Audretsch, D., & O'Connor, A. (2017). The Lineages of the Entrepreneurial Ecosystem Approach. *Small Business Economics*, 49(1), 1–10. DOI: 10.1007/s11187-017-9864-8

Acs, Z. J. (2006). How is entrepreneurship good for economic growth? *Innovations*, 1(1), 97–106.

Acs, Z.J., Autio, E., Szerb, L., (2014). National systems of entrepreneurship: measurement issues and policy implications. *Res. Policy* 43, 476–494. https://doi.org/. respol.2013.08.016.DOI: 10.1016/j

Acs, Z. J., Desai, S., & Klapper, L. F. (2008b). What does Bentrepreneurship^ data really show? *Small Business Economics*, 31(3), 265–281. DOI: 10.1007/s11187-008-9137-7

Ács, Z. J., Szerb, L., Autio, E., & Lloyd, A. A. (2017). *The Global Entrepreneurship Index*. The Global Entrepreneurship and Development Institute. DOI: 10.1007/978-3-319-63844-7_3

Acs, Z. J., Szerb, L., Lafuente, E., & Lloyd, A. (2018). *Global Entrepreneurship Index*. The Global Entrepreneurship and Development. Institute. (Original work published 2018), DOI: 10.1007/978-3-030-03279

Adner, R. (2017). Ecosystem as Structure: An Actionable Construct for Strategy. *Journal of Management*, 43(1), 39–58. DOI: 10.1177/0149206316678451

Adner, R., & Kapoor, R. (2010). Value creation in innovation ecosystems: How the structure of technological interdependence affects firm performance in new technology generations. *Strategic Management Journal*, 31(3), 306–333. DOI: 10.1002/smj.821

Aghion, P., David, P. A., & Foray, D. (2009). Science, technology, and innovation for economic growth: Linking policy research and practice in "STIG systems.". *Research Policy*, 38(4), 681–693 DOI: 10.1016/j.respol.2009.01.016

Akerloff, G. A. (1970). The market for lemons: Quality uncertainty and the market mechanism. *The Quarterly Journal of Economics*, 84(3), 485–500. DOI: 10.2307/1879431

American Journal of Sociology. (1996). *Symposium on market transition*. 101: 908-1096.

Armington, C., & Acs, Z. (2002). The Determinants of Regional Variation in New Firm Formation. *Regional Studies*, 36(1), 33–45. DOI: 10.1080/00343400120099843

Arthur, W. B. (2013). *Complexity economics: A different framework for economic thought*, SFI Working Paper 2013-04-012.

Arthur, W. B. (2013). *Complexity Economics*. Oxford University Press.

Audretsch, D. B., & Belitski, D. B. (2017). Entrepreneurial ecosystems in cities: Establishing the framework conditions. *The Journal of Technology Transfer*, 42(5), 1030–1051. DOI: 10.1007/s10961-016-9473-8

Audretsch, D. B., & Belitski, M. (2016). Entrepreneurial Ecosystems in Cities: Establishing the Framework Conditions. *The Journal of Technology Transfer*, 42(5), 1030–1051. DOI: 10.1007/s10961-016-9473-8

Audretsch, D. B., Heger, D., & Veith, T. (2015). Infrastructure and entrepreneurship. *Small Business Economics*, 44(2), 219–230. DOI: 10.1007/s11187-014-9600-6

Audretsch, D. B., Keilbach, M. C., & Lehmann, E. E. (2006). *Entrepreneurship and Economic Growth*. Oxford University Press. DOI: 10.1093/acprof:oso/9780195183511.001.0001

Audretsch, D. B., & Thurik, R. (2001). What's new about the new economy? Sources of growth in the managed and entrepreneurial economies. *Industrial and Corporate Change*, 10(1), 267–315. . 1. 267 https://doi.org/.DOI: 10. 1093/ icc/10

Autio, E., & Levie, J. (2017). *Management of entrepreneurial ecosystems*. The Wiley Handbook of Entrepreneurship, 43, 423–449. DOI: 10.1002/9781118970812.ch19

Autio, E., Nambisan, S., Thomas, L. D., & Wright, M. (2018). Digital affordances, spatial affordances, and the genesis of entrepreneurial ecosystems. *Strategic Entrepreneurship Journal*, 12(1), 72–95. DOI: 10.1002/sej.1266

Baumol, W. J. (1990). Entrepreneurship: Productive, unproductive, and destructive. *Journal of Political Economy*, 98(5, Part 1), 893–921. DOI: 10.1086/261712

Baumol, W. J. (1990). Entrepreneurship: Productive, unproductive, and destructive. *Journal of Political Economy*, 98(5, Part 1), 893–921. DOI: 10.1086/261712

Beinhocker, E. D. (2006). *The origin of wealth: Evolution, complexity, and the radical remaking of economics*. Random House Business.

Benneworth, P. (2004). In What Sense Regional Development? Entrepreneurship, Underdevelopment and Strong Tradition in the Periphery. *Entrepreneurship and Regional Development*, 16(6), 439–458. DOI: 10.1080/0898562042000249786

Bonini, S., & Capizzi, V. (2019). The Role of Venture Capital in the Emerging Entrepreneurial-Finance Ecosystem: Future Threats and Opportunities. *Venture Capital*, 21(2-3), 137–175. DOI: 10.1080/13691066.2019.1608697

Bonini, S., & Capizzi, V. (2019). The Role of Venture Capital in the Emerging Entrepreneurial Finance Ecosystem: Future Threats and Opportunities. *Venture Capital*, 21(2-3), 137–175. DOI: 10.1080/13691066.2019.1608697

Borissenko, Y., & Boschma, R. (2016). A critical review of entrepreneurial ecosystems: towards a future research agenda, No 1630. Section of Economic Geography: Utrecht University.

Bos, J. W. B., & Stam, E. (2014). Gazelles and industry growth: A study of young high- growth firms in the Netherlands. *Industrial and Corporate Change*, 23(1), 145–169. DOI: 10.1093/icc/dtt050

Bosma, N., Content, J., Sanders, M., & Stam, E. (2018). Institutions, entrepreneurship, and economic growth in Europe. *Small Business Economics*, 51(2), 483–499. DOI: 10.1007/s11187-018-0012-x

Bosma, N., Stam, E., & Schutjens, V. (2011). Creative destruction and regional productivity growth: Evidence from the Dutch manufacturing and services industries. *Small Business Economics*, 36(4), 401–418. DOI: 10.1007/s11187-009-9257-8

Brown, R., & Mason, C. (2014). Inside the high-tech black box: A critique of technology entrepreneurship policy. *Technovation*, 34(12), 773–784. DOI: 10.1016/j.technovation.2014.07.013

Brown, R., & Mason, C. (2017). Looking inside the spiky bits: A critical review and conceptualization of entrepreneurial ecosystems. *Small Business Economics*, 49(1), 11–30. DOI: 10.1007/s11187-017-9865-7

Bruns, K., Bosma, N., Sanders, M., & Schramm, M. (2017). Searching for the existence of entrepreneurial ecosystems: A regional cross-section growth regression approach. *Small Business Economics*, 49(1), 31–54. DOI: 10.1007/s11187-017-9866-6

Campbell, J., & Pederson, O. (2001). Conclusion: The second movement in institutional analysis. In Campbell, J., & Pederson, O. (Eds.), *The Rise of Neoliberalism and Institutional Analysis: 249–282*. Princeton University Press. DOI: 10.1515/9780691188225-014

Canestrino, R., Magliocca, P., Ćwiklicki, M., & Pawełek, B. (2023). Toward the emergence of "humane" entrepreneurial ecosystems. Evidence from different cultural contexts. *Journal of Intellectual Capital*, 24(1), 177–204. DOI: 10.1108/JIC-07-2021-0200

Cao, Z., & Shi, X. (2020). A systematic literature review of entrepreneurial ecosystems in advanced and emerging economies. *Small Business Economics*, 51(2). Advance online publication. DOI: 10.1007/s11187-020-00326-y

Capozza, C., Salomone, S., & Somma, E. (2018). Local industrial structure, agglomeration economies and the creation of innovative start-ups: Evidence from the Italian case.

Carree, M. A., & Thurik, A. R. (2010). *The impact of entrepreneurship on economic growth. Handbook of Entrepreneurship Research*. Springer., DOI: 10.1007/978-1-4419-1191-9_20

Cohen, B., & Winn, M. I. (2007). Market imperfections, opportunity and sustainable entrepreneurship. *Journal of Business Venturing*, 22(1), 29–49. DOI: 10.1016/j.jbusvent.2004.12.001

Colombelli, A., Krafft, J., & Vivarelli, M. (2016). To be born is not enough: The key role of innovative start-ups. *Small Business Economics*, 47(2), 1–15. DOI: 10.1007/s11187-016-9716-y

Content, J., Bosma, N., Jordaan, J., & Sanders, M. (2020). Entrepreneurial ecosystems, entrepreneurial activity, and economic growth: New evidence from European regions. *Regional Studies*, 54(8), 1007–1019. . 2019. 1680827DOI: 10. 1080/ 00343404

Cooke, P., Uranga, M. G., & Etxebarria, G. (1997). Regional innovation systems: Institutional and organisational dimensions. *Research Policy*, 26(4), 475–491. DOI: 10.1016/S0048-7333(97)00025-5

Criscuolo, C., Gal, P. N., & Menon, C. (2014). The dynamics of employment growth. OECD *Sci.Technol. Ind. Policy Pap*, 96. Advance online publication. DOI: 10.1787/23074957

Cronin, M. A., Stouten, J., & van Knippenberg, D. (2021). The Theory Crisis in Management Research: Solving the Right Problem. *Academy of Management Review*, 0294(4), 667–683. Advance online publication. DOI: 10.5465/amr.2019.0294

Cross, M. (1981). *New Firm Formation and Regional Development*. Gower Publishing Company.

Dahl, M. S., & Sorenson, O. (2009). The embedded entrepreneur. *European Management Review*, 6(3), 172–181. DOI: 10.1057/emr.2009.14

Davidsson, P. (2004). *Researching entrepreneurship*. Springer.

Del Giudice, M., Carayannis, E. G., & Maggioni, V. (2017). Global knowledge intensive enterprises and international technology transfer: Emerging perspectives from a quadruple helix environment. *The Journal of Technology Transfer*, 42(2), 229–235. DOI: 10.1007/s10961-016-9496-1

Entrepreneurship & Regional Development, 30(7–8), 749–775. https://doi.org/. 2018. 14570DOI: 10.1080/08985 626

Feld, B., & Hathaway, I. (2020). *The Startup Community Way: Evolving an Entrepreneurial Ecosystem*. Wiley.

Feldman, M., Francis, J., & Bercovitz, J. (2005). Creating a cluster while building a firm: Entrepreneurs and the formation of industrial clusters. *Regional Studies*, 39(1), 129–141. DOI: 10.1080/0034340052000320888

Feldman, M. P. (2014). The character of innovative places: Entrepreneurial strategy, economic development, and prosperity. *Small Business Economics*, 43(1), 9–20. DOI: 10.1007/s11187-014-9574-4

Fritsch, M. (2013). New business formation and regional development: A survey and assessment of the evidence. *Foundations and Trends in Entrepreneurship*, 9(3), 249–364. Advance online publication. DOI: 10.1561/0300000043

Fritsch, M., & Mueller, P. (2004). Effects of new Business Formation on Regional Development Over Time. *Regional Studies*, 38(8), 961–975. DOI: 10.1080/0034340042000280965

Fritsch, M., & Storey, D. J. (2014). Entrepreneurship in a regional context: Historical roots, recent developments, and future challenges. *Regional Studies*, 48(6), 939–954. DOI: 10.1080/00343404.2014.892574

Gampbell, J. T., & Pedersen, O. K. (Eds.). (1996). *Legacies of change: Transformations of postcommunist European economies*. New York: de Gruyter.

Genoa. InBates, R., Greif, A., Levi, M., Rosenthal, J. L., & Weingast, B. (Eds.), *Analytical Narratives: 23–63*. Princeton University Press.

Gertler, M. S. (2010). Rules of the game: The place of institutions in regional economic change. *Regional Studies*, 44(1), 1–15. DOI: 10.1080/00343400903389979

Gjelsvik, M., & Trippl, M. (2018). Financial Organisations: An Overlooked Element in Regional Innovation Systems. In Isaksen, A., Martin, R., & Trippl, M. (Eds.), *New Avenues for Regional Innovation Systems–Theoretical Advances, Empirical Cases and Policy Lessons* (pp. 107–125). Springer International Publishing. DOI: 10.1007/978-3-319-71661-9_6

Granovetter, M. (1992). Economic institutions as social constructions: A framework for analysis. *Acta Sociologica*, 35(1), 3–11. DOI: 10.1177/000169939203500101

Greif, A. (1998) Self-enforcing political systems and economic growth: Late medieval

Guthrie, D. (1999). *Dragon in a three-piece suit: The emergence of capitalism in China*. Princeton University Press. DOI: 10.1515/9781400823383

Haltiwanger, J., Jarmin, R. S., & Miranda, J. (2013). Who creates jobs? Small versus large versus young. *The Review of Economics and Statistics*, 95(2), 347–361. Advance online publication. DOI: 10.1162/REST_a_00288

Hannigan, T. R., Briggs, A. R., Valadao, R., Seidel, M. D. L., & Jennings, P. D. (2021). A new tool for policymakers: Mapping cultural possibilities in an emerging AI entrepreneurial ecosystem. *Research Policy*. Advance online publication. DOI: 10.1016/j.respol.2021.104315

Harms, R., & Groen, A. (2017). Loosen up? Cultural tightness and national entrepreneurial activity Technological. *Technological Forecasting and Social Change*, 121, 196–204. DOI: 10.1016/j.techfore.2016.04.013

Hechavarría, D. M., & Ingram, A. E. (2019). Entrepreneurial ecosystem conditions and gendered national-level entrepreneurial activity: A 14-year panel study of GEM. *Small Business Economics*, 53(2), 431–458. DOI: 10.1007/s11187-018-9994-7

Hechter, M. (1987). *Principles of Group Solidarity*. University of California Press.

Hidalgo, C. A., Balland, P.-A., Boschma, R., Delgado, M., Feldman, M. P., Frenken, K., & Zhu, S. (2018). The principle of relatedness. In Morales, A. J., Gershenson, C., Braha, D., Minai, A. A., & Bar-Yam, Y. (Eds.), *Unifying themes in complex systems* (Vol. IX). Springer. DOI: 10.1007/978-3-319-96661-8_46

Iacobucci, D., & Perugini, F. (2021). Entrepreneurial ecosystems and economic resilience at local level. *Entrepreneurship and Regional Development*, 33(9-10), 689–716. Advance online publication. DOI: 10.1080/08985626.2021.1888318

Isenberg, D. (2011). *The Entrepreneurship Ecosystem Strategy as a New Paradigm for Economic Policy: Principles for Cultivating Entrepreneurship*. Presentation at the Institute of International and European Affairs.

Isenberg, D., & Brown, R. (2014) For a booming economy, bet on high-growth firms, Not Small Businesses. Babson Entrepreneurship Ecosystem Project. Retrieved from http://blogs.hbr.org/2014/02/for-a-booming-economy-bet-on-high-growth-firms-not-small-businesses/

Isenberg, D., & Onyemah, V. (2016). Fostering scaleup ecosystems for regional economic growth (innovations case narrative: Manizales-Mas and Scale Up Milwaukee. *Innov. Technol. Governance. Innovations: Technology, Governance, Globalization*, 11(1-2), 60–79. DOI: 10.1162/inov_a_00248

Jansson, N., Ahokangas, P., Iivari, M., Perälä-Heape, M., & Salo, S. (2014). The competitive advantage of an ecosystemic business model: The case of OuluHealth. *Interdisciplinary Studies Journal*, 3(4), 282–295.

Kirzner, I. M. (2009). The alert and creative entrepreneur: A clarification. *Small Business Economics*, 32(2), 145–152. DOI: 10.1007/s11187-008-9153-7

Kritikos, A. S. (2015). *Entrepreneurship and Economic Growth. International Encyclopedia of the Social & Behavioral Sciences* (2nd ed., Vol. 7). Elsevier.

Lafuente, E., Acs, Z. J., Sanders, M., & Szerb, L. (2019). The global technology frontier: Productivity growth and the relevance of Kirznerian and Schumpeterian entrepreneurship. *Small Business Economics*, 55(1), 153–178. DOI: 10.1007/s11187-019-00140-1

Lafuente, E., Szerb, L., & Acs, Z. J. (2016). Country level efficiency and national systems of entrepreneurship: A data envelopment analysis approach. *The Journal of Technology Transfer*, 41(6), 1260–1283. DOI: 10.1007/s10961-015-9440-9

Lee, S. M., & Peterson, S. J. (2000). Culture, entrepreneurial orientation, and global competitiveness. *Journal of World Business*, 35(4), 401–416. DOI: 10.1016/S1090-9516(00)00045-6

Leendertse, J., Schrijvers, M., & Stam, E. (2021). Measure Twice, Cut Once: Entrepreneurial Ecosystem Metrics. *Research Policy*, 104336. Advance online publication. DOI: 10.1016/j.respol.2021.104336

Leibenstein, H. (1968). Entrepreneurship and development. *The American Economic Review*, 58, 72–83.

Li, J. T., Tsui, A. S., & Weldon, E. (Eds.). (2000). *Management and organizations in the Chinese context*. St. Martin's Press. DOI: 10.1057/9780230511590

Lin, Y.-M. (2004). *Between politics and markets: Firms, competition, and institutional change in post-Mao China*. Cambridge University Press.

Mason, C. M., & Harrison, R. T. (2006). After the exit: Acquisitions, entrepreneurial recycling, and regional economic development. *Regional Studies*, 40(1), 55–73. DOI: 10.1080/00343400500450059

Mazzucato, M. (2014) Start-up myths and obsessions, *The Economist*, February 3 rd 2014. https://www.economist.com/blogs/schumpeter/2014/02/invitation-mariana-mazzucato

Mikic, M., Horvatinovic, T., & Kovac, I. (2020). Climbing up the regional intellectual capital tree: An EU entrepreneurial ecosystem analysis. *Journal of Intellectual Capital*. Advance online publication. DOI: 10.1108/JIC-07-2020-0258

Min, C. (1995). *Asian management systems: Chinese, Japanese, and Korean styles of business*. Routledge.

Mokyr, J. (2002). *The Gifts of Athena: Historical Origins of the Knowledge Economy*. Princeton University Press.

Nicotra, M., Romano, M., Del Giudice, M., & Schillaci, C. E. (2018). The causal relation between entrepreneurial ecosystem and productive entrepreneurship: A measurement framework. *The Journal of Technology Transfer*, 43(3), 640–673. DOI: 10.1007/s10961-017-9628-2

North, D. (1990). *Institutions, Institutional Change and Economic Performance*. Cambridge University. DOI: 10.1017/CBO9780511808678

O'Connor, A. (2013). A conceptual framework for entrepreneurship education policy: Meeting government and economic purposes. *Journal of Business Venturing*, 28(4), 546–563. DOI: 10.1016/j.jbusvent.2012.07.003

Oi, J. C., & Walder, A. G. (Eds.). (1999). *Property rights and economic reform in China*. Stanford University Press. DOI: 10.1515/9780804764193

Olberding, J. C. (2002). Does regionalism beget regionalism? the relationship between norms and regional partnerships for economic development. *Public Administration Review*, 62(4), 480–491. DOI: 10.1111/0033-3352.00201

Orru, M., Biggart, N. W., & Hamilton, G. G. (1997). *The economic organization of East Asian capitalism*. Sage.

Ostrom, E. (1990). *Governing the Commons*. Cambridge University Press. DOI: 10.1017/CBO9780511807763

Ostrom, E. (2010). Beyond markets and states: Polycentric governance of complex economic systems. *The American Economic Review*, 100(3), 641–672. DOI: 10.1257/aer.100.3.641

Parker, S. C. (2013). Do serial entrepreneurs run successively better-performing businesses? *Journal of Business Venturing*, 28(5), 652–666. DOI: 10.1016/j.jbusvent.2012.08.001

Prahalad, C. K. (2005). *The Fortune at the Bottom of the Pyramid: Eradicating Poverty through Profits*. Pearson Education.

Radosevic, S. & Yoruk, E. (2013). Entrepreneurial propensity of innovation systems: theory, methodology and evidence. *Res. Policy* 42, 1015–1038. https://doi.org/. respol.2013.01.011.DOI: 10.1016/j

Roundy, P. T., Bradshaw, M., & Brockman, B. K. (2018). The emergence of entrepreneurial ecosystems: A complex adaptive systems approach. *Journal of Business Research*, 86(1), 1–10. . jbusres.2018. 01. 032DOI: 10.1016/ j

Santos, L. L., Borini, F. M., & Pereira, R. M. (2021). Bricolage as a path towards organizational innovativeness in times of market and technological turbulence. *Journal of Entrepreneurship in Emerging Economies*, 13(2), 282–299. DOI: 10.1108/JEEE-02-2020-0039

Schumpeter, J. A. (1934). *The Theory of Economic Development*. Harvard Univ. Press.

Schumpeter, J. A. (1976), Capitalism, socialism, and democracy. *George Allen & Unwin* Ltd [1943].

Sharif, K., Kassim, N., Faisal, M. N., & Zain, M. (2021). Impact of skill on bi-dimensional trust within small-to-medium sized enterprises upstream relationships. *EuroMed Journal of Business*, 16(1), 39–68. DOI: 10.1108/EMJB-03-2020-0020

Shepherd, D. A., & Patzelt, H. (2020). A call for research on the scaling of organizations and the scaling of social impact. *Entrepreneurship Theory and Practice*, 61(3), 104225872095059.

Simon, H. A. (1962). The architecture of complexity. *Proceedings of the American Philosophical Society*, 106, 467–482.

Sitaridis, I., & Kitsios, F. (2020). Competitiveness analysis and evaluation of entrepreneurial ecosystems: A multi-criteria approach. *Annals of Operations Research*, 294(1), 377–399. DOI: 10.1007/s10479-019-03404-x

Sorenson, O. (2018). Social networks and the geography of entrepreneurship. *Small Business Economics*, 51(3), 527–537. DOI: 10.1007/s11187-018-0076-7

Spigel, B., & Harrison, R. (2018). Toward a process theory of entrepreneurial ecosystems. *Strategic Entrepreneurship Journal*, 12(1), 151–168. DOI: 10.1002/sej.1268

Spilling, O. (1996). The Entrepreneurial System: On Entrepreneurship in the Context of a Mega-Event. *Journal of Business Research*, 36(1), 91–103. DOI: 10.1016/0148-2963(95)00166-2

Stam, E. (2007). Why butterflies don't leave: Locational behavior of entrepreneurial firms. *Economic Geography*, 83(1), 27–50. DOI: 10.1111/j.1944-8287.2007.tb00332.x

Stam, E. (2015). Entrepreneurial ecosystems and regional policy: A sympathetic critique. *European Planning Studies*, 23(9), 1759–1769. . 2015. 1061484DOI: 10. 1080/ 09654313

Stam, E., & Bosma, N. (2015). Local policies for high-growth firms. In Audretsch, D. B., Link, A., & Walshok, A. (Eds.), *The Oxford handbook of local competitiveness*. Oxford University Press.

Stam, E., Hartog, C., Van Stel, A., & Thurik, R. (2011). Ambitious entrepreneurship and macro-economic growth. Minniti, M. (Ed.). *The Dynamics of Entrepreneurship. Evidence from the Global Entrepreneurship Monitor Data*. Oxford University Press, Oxford, pp. 231–249.

Stam, E., & Spigel, B. (2018). Entrepreneurial ecosystems. Blackburn, R., De Clerq, C., Heinonen, J. (Eds.). *The SAGE Handbook of Small Business and Entrepreneurship*. DOI: 10.4135/9781473984080.n21

Stam, E., & Van de Ven, A. (2021). Entrepreneurial Ecosystem Elements. *Small Business Economics*, 56(2), 809–832. DOI: 10.1007/s11187-019-00270-6

Stam, E., & Van de Ven, A. H. (2019). Entrepreneurial ecosystem elements. *Small Business Economics*. Advance online publication. DOI: 10.1007/s11187-019-00270-6

Stam, E., Van Stel, A. (2011). Types of Entrepreneurship and Economic Growth. Szirmai,

Stangler, D., & Bell-Masterson, J. (2015). Measuring an entrepreneurial ecosystem. Kauffman foundation. Retrieved from https://www.kauffman.org/wpcontent/uploads/ 2019/12/measuring_an_entrepreneurial_ecosystem.pdf

Steyaert, C., & Katz, J. (2004). Reclaiming the Space of Entrepreneurship in Society: Geographical, Discursive and Social Dimensions. *Entrepreneurship and Regional Development*, 16(3), 179–196. DOI: 10.1080/0898562042000197135

Stoica, O., Roman, A., & Rusu, V. D. (2020). The Nexus between entrepreneurship and economic growth: A comparative analysis on groups of countries. *Sustainability (Basel)*, 12(3), 1186. DOI: 10.3390/su12031186

Szerb, L., Lafuente, E., Horváth, K., & Páger, B. (2019). The relevance of quantity and quality entrepreneurship for regional performance: The moderating role of the entrepreneurial ecosystem. *Regional Studies*, 53(9), 1308–1320. DOI: 10.1080/00343404.2018.1510481

Teece, D. J. (2007). Explicating dynamic capabilities: The nature and microfoundations of (sustainable) enterprise performance. *Strategic Management Journal*, 28(13), 1319–1350. DOI: 10.1002/smj.640

Teece, D. J. (2014). The foundations of enterprise performance: Dynamic and ordinary capabilities in an (economic) theory of firms. *The Academy of Management Perspectives*, 28(4), 328–352. DOI: 10.5465/amp.2013.0116

Thompson, T. A., Purdy, J. M., & Ventresca, M. J. (2018). How entrepreneurial ecosystems take form: Evidence from social impact initiatives in Seattle. *Strategic Entrepreneurship, 12(1).Journal*, 12(1), 96–116. DOI: 10.1002/sej.1285

Thurik, A. R., Stam, E., & Audretsch, D. B. (2013). The rise of the entrepreneurial economy and the future of dynamic capitalism. *Technovation*, 33(8-9), 302–310. . technovation.2013.07. 003DOI: 10. 1016/ j

Tsvetkova, A., Pugh, R., & Schmutzler, J. (2019). Beyond global hubs: Broadening the application of systems approaches. *Local Economy*, 34(8), 755–766. DOI: 10.1177/0269094219897535

Ucbasaran, D., Westhead, P., & Wright, M. (2001). The Focus of Entrepreneurial Research: Contextual and Process Issues. *Entrepreneurship Theory and Practice*, 25(4), 57–80. DOI: 10.1177/104225870102500405

Usai, A., Scuotto, V., Murray, A., Fiano, F., & Dezi, L. (2018). Do entrepreneurial knowledge and innovative attitude overcome 'imperfections' in the innovation process? Insights from SMEs in the UK and Italy. *Journal of Knowledge Management*, 22(8), 1637–1654. DOI: 10.1108/JKM-01-2018-0035

Valliere, D., & Peterson, R. (2009). Entrepreneurship and economic growth: Evidence from emerging and developed countries. *Entrepreneurship and Regional Development*, 21(5–6), 459–480. DOI: 10.1080/08985620802332723

Van de Ven, A. H. (1993). The development of an infrastructure for entrepreneurship. *Journal of Business Venturing*, 8(3), 211–230. DOI: 10.1016/0883-9026(93)90028-4

Van Stel, A., & Storey, D. (2004). The link between firm births and job creation: Is there a Upas tree effect? *Regional Studies*, 38(8), 893–909. DOI: 10.1080/0034340042000280929

Vedula, S., & Kim, P. H. (2019). Gimme shelter or fade away: The impact of regional entrepreneurial ecosystem quality on venture survival. *Industrial and Corporate Change*, 28(4), 827–854. DOI: 10.1093/icc/dtz032

Webster, J., & Watson, R. T. (2002). Analyzing the past to prepare for the future: Writing a literature review. *Management Information Systems Quarterly*, 26(2), xiii–xxiii.

Weingast, B., & Marshall, W. (1988). The industrial organization of Congress; or, why legislatures, like firms, are not organized as markets. *Journal of Political Economy*, 1(1), 132–163. DOI: 10.1086/261528

Welter, F. (2011). Contextualizing entrepreneurship—Conceptual challenges and ways forward. *Entrepreneurship Theory and Practice*, 35(1), 165–184. DOI: 10.1111/j.1540-6520.2010.00427.x

Wennekers, S., van Wennekers, A., Thurik, R., & Reynolds, P. (2005). Nascent entrepreneurship and the level of economic development. [Crossref. ISI.]. *Small Business Economics*, 24(3), 293–309. DOI: 10.1007/s11187-005-1994-8

Williams, D. W., Wood, M. S., Mitchell, J. R., & Urbig, D. (2019). Applying experimental methods to advance entrepreneurship research: On the need for and publication of experiments. *Journal of Business Venturing*, 34(2), 215–223. . jbusvent. 2018. 12. 003DOI: 10. 1016/ j

Williamson, O. (1975). *Markets and Hierarchies*. Free.

Wilson, J. Q. (1980). The politics of regulation. In Wilson, J. Q. (Ed.), *The Politics of Regulation: 357–394*. Basic Books.

Wong, P. K., Ho, Y. P., & Autio, E. (2005). Entrepreneurship, innovation, and economic growth: Evidence from GEM data. [Crossref. ISI.]. *Small Business Economics*, 24(3), 335–350. DOI: 10.1007/s11187-005-2000-1

Wurth, B., Stam, E., & Spigel, B. (2021). Toward an Entrepreneurial Ecosystem Research Program. *Entrepreneurship Theory and Practice*. Advance online publication. DOI: 10.1177/1042258721998948

Xie, Z., Wang, X., Xie, L., & Duan, K. (2021). Entrepreneurial ecosystem and the quality and quantity of regional entrepreneurship: A configurational approach. *Journal of Business Research*, 128, 499–509. DOI: 10.1016/j.jbusres.2021.02.015

Zak, P. J., & Knack, S. (2001). Trust and growth, *Economic Journal,* vol. Ill, 295-321)

Zhao, J., Qi, Z., & De Pablos, P. O. (2014). Enhancing enterprise training performance: Perspectives from knowledge transfer and integration. *Computers in Human Behavior*, 30, 567–573. DOI: 10.1016/j.chb.2013.06.041

Chapter 16
Navigating Entrepreneurial Stress:
Effective Techniques for Reducing Burnout Risk

Xuan-Hoa Nghiem
https://orcid.org/0000-0003-2292-0257
Vietnam National University, Hanoi, Vietnam

Shashank Mittal
O.P. Jindal Global University, India

Shivani Dhand
https://orcid.org/0000-0002-4809-1365
Lovely Professional University, India

ABSTRACT

This chapter explores effective strategies for managing stress and preventing burnout among entrepreneurs. Given the unique challenges faced in entrepreneurship, understanding the factors contributing to stress is essential. The discussion includes various stress management techniques, such as mindfulness practices, organizational support, and technological tools that enhance productivity and well-being. Future trends, including the integration of artificial intelligence and a focus on holistic wellness, highlight the evolving landscape of stress management. By prioritizing mental health, entrepreneurs can foster resilience, improve work-life balance, and create supportive environments for themselves and their teams. This chapter aims to equip entrepreneurs with actionable insights to navigate their entrepreneurial journey while safeguarding their mental health.

INTRODUCTION

Entrepreneurship is often described as the path of freedom, innovativeness, and personal realization. Reality, however, easily veers off course from the prevailing glamour. First, entrepreneurs face some unique stresses (Kuruppu,2024). For example, such fears include uncertainty regarding finance, high

DOI: 10.4018/979-8-3693-3673-1.ch016

hours of work, stiff competition, and the persistent pressure to succeed in ventures. All these risks merge to constitute an upsetting setting that can easily deteriorate the mental, emotional, and psychosomatic state of an individual. Entrepreneurial stress, if not in control, leads to burnout-the state of emotional, physical, and mental exhaustion. That happens to large business owners and startup founders. Burnout directly affects personal health and can potentially jeopardize business performance, innovation capacity, and long-term sustainability (White and Gupta, 2020; Lee et al., 2023; Wang et al., 2023).

Entrepreneurial work tends to be characterized by high levels of autonomy, decision-making pressure, as well as responsibility over the business and employees. Entrepreneurship often blurs the boundaries between professional and personal life and entrepreneurs cannot automatically "switch off" the work at predetermined times like traditional employees. The constant pressure to adapt to fluctuating markets, more crucially, manage financial uncertainty, and meet the expectations of investors or clients will heighten stress. At that point, managing stress becomes more than a private health issue but a strategic business imperative. Business owners who neglect proper mental health care can give way to some loss in decision-making, creativity, and leadership capabilities, very tools needed for running a good venture.

Burnout is the syndrome of chronic stress, and it's becoming increasingly relevant to the entrepreneurial environment. As research further brings out, entrepreneurs are particularly vulnerable to burnout due to the risky or demanding nature of the work they carry out. Unlike employees working in organizations that are large in size and can afford a support system, most entrepreneurs work individually without a team or network to share the burden of responsibility with (Satow, 2012). This in itself provides a significant reason to feel inadequate, frustrated, and finally exhausted due to burnout. The symptoms from exhaustion and cynicism to a sense of isolation and reduced performance have devastating effects on both the bottom line of the individual and the organisation.

With this increased awareness of these problems, entrepreneurs must recognize the importance of proactive stress management and burnout prevention. Successful stress management techniques contribute to improved personal well-being and business performance. The development of active resilience, emotional intelligence, and healthy work-life integration means that the long-term outcome for entrepreneurs will be better. The current chapter covers various stress management practices that would be highly valuable for entrepreneurs, such as mindfulness, time management, and practices related to physical well-being. In fact, it dwells on aspects of organizational support systems, technological tools, and social networks in risk reduction of burnout.

This chapter is an attempt to provide meaningful insights into sustaining personal wellness along with venture sustainability as the root causes of entrepreneurial stress and burnout along with offering practical solutions towards addressing them. Entrepreneurial endeavors that focus on mental health and stress reduction may help the entrepreneur succeed in their professional and personal life.

THE CONCEPT OF ENTREPRENEURIAL STRESS

Entrepreneurial stress is unique and growing from the very different experience entrepreneurs do in building a business compared to most jobs. Most entrepreneurship challenges require diving into multiple roles, making high-stakes decisions, and facing uncertainty all the time; it isn't like what most people experience when preparing for a job. Start-up pressures can bring extreme mental, emotional, and, at times, even physical strain to entrepreneurs, driving many of them to chronic stress (Gorgievski & Stephan,2016).

The uncertainty of the entrepreneurial venture process has been one of the key contributors to entrepreneurial stress. The entrepreneur fights multiple battles from accessing funding and then finding ways to manage cash flow to dealing with competition in the marketplace and managing consumers' expectations. More often than not, entrepreneurs are faced with situations that are totally out of their control. This is partly due to uncertainty: a company's prosperity or failure may depend on whether these numerous factors change, from changes in economic landscapes to shifts in regulatory policies to changes in consumer tastes, most of which no one can predict with any certainty (Rauch et al.,2018). For start-ups, the pressure mounts even further. The deadlines to begin generating returns can be ruinous on top of personal finances, reputation, and relationships.

A second major stressor of entrepreneurship is workload. Entrepreneurs are known to work for longer hours than employees. This implies that their work and personal lives overlap so that the individual can never recognize which is which. Since entrepreneurs normally work for a long to sustain their business, a lack of work-life balance raises stress. Increased frequencies of being unable to take downtime and physically disconnecting from work can lead to mental and physical exhaustion, further mounting stress levels.

Entrepreneurial stress also stems from decision-making. The entrepreneur is largely in charge of his business, and decisions related to hiring, product development, and market strategies can often have lasting implications (Nambisan & Baron,2021). This constant decision-making, often under time pressure and without the luxury of big data, can induce a type of mental fatigue and lead to a paralyzing inability to decide. Self-doubt and fear of failure can also be added contributors to stress for entrepreneurs, especially those with less experience or resources.

External pressures are only one part of a culture of entrepreneurial stress. There are also some internal factors which lead to entrepreneurial stress. Many entrepreneurs do not have many alternate motivations because of their deep personal investment in their business, which makes it awkward to separate their identity from the venture's success (Wach,2021). This usually leads to perfectionism where entrepreneurs have set themselves and their ventures to impossible standards and become self-critical if they are unable to live up to those expectations. Continued fear of inability to meet these expectations leads to an overwhelming amount of self-criticism and inability to delegate tasks leading to more stress. They can also be isolated, because it appears that they run the business alone and without the support of a big team to share the burden and responsibilities of business operations.

Entrepreneurial stress, although exceedingly common, is in no way inevitable. Identifying sources and effects of the same gives an entrepreneur his/her first step toward lessening the blow of the same. Realizing the stressors specific to a journey makes entrepreneurs begin to implement strategies that would help manage their workload, maintain a healthier work-life balance, and prevent what prolonged stress can take emotionally.

THE BURNOUT PHENOMENON IN ENTREPRENEURSHIP

What is Burnout? Signs and Symptoms

Burnout is the mental status experienced when an individual becomes emotionally, mentally, and physically drained due to a prolonged period of exposure to high levels of stress, such as in the cases of entrepreneurship where individuals are exposed to very high pressure. The condition is not like regular fatigue since its impact is experienced in all aspects of life, and usually people have feelings of depersonalization, reduced control, and mental exhaustion. Burnout is dangerous for entrepreneurs because their personal well-being is intricately bound to that of the business (Omrane et al.,2018). Typically, burnout presents in the form of symptoms including continuous exhaustion, chronic feelings of restlessness and irritation, decreased ability to concentrate, and increased feelings of being emotionally distant from work. A highly entrepreneurial person suffering burnout may feel that they cannot work hard enough, no matter how hard they try, leading into the cycle of being overwhelmed with work and stress.

The emotional impact is just as deep. They may start to start despising their business and the zeal and enthusiasm that initially characterized their actions (Palmer et al.,2021). Doubt their competencies, or even lose the value in what they are doing, adding to feelings of inadequacy. Other signs may include insomnia and headaches as well as a weakening immune system, which makes daily activity more challenging (Čigarská & Birknerová, 2021). Left unchecked, over time, burnout can lead to severe effects such as depression and anxiety and other mental health issues.

The Burnout Cycle: How Stress Begets Burnout

For the most part, the process by which stress escalates into burnout is cyclical. Entrepreneurs are energized and motivated by their goals at first, but accumulating stress from extra hours, uncertainty, and the pressure of running a business leach away this energy. When stress is chronic, the entrepreneur becomes caught in a state of emotional exhaustion to the point that even the most minute tasks seem overwhelming. The impact tends to be accompanied by depersonalization where business owners become estranged from their enterprise, and a negative attitude could be developed towards it (Obschonka et al.,2023).

At this point, entrepreneurs become physically drained to the extent that they also lose touch with the business they once so enthusiastically built. Failure or inadequacy is the conclusion if observable progress cannot be achieved with ever-present stressors. This introduces a vicious cycle where the entrepreneur will do everything in their power to break the deadlock of burnout, and once again, this will drain them more, creating yet another vicious cycle (Čigarská & Birknerová,2021). If such a cycle is not interrupted by interference, severe personal and professional outcomes may arise, eventually leading to the collapse of the business venture.

Emotional, Physical, and Cognitive Effects of Burnout

Burnout costs are thus multi-faceted, touching on personal and business issues. Entrepreneurship burns one out at the emotional level: frustration, resentment, and disillusion may haunt them. They begin considering their venture a burden rather than an opportunity for leveraging business ventures to wealth and innovation. It can contribute to poor judgment and lack of motivation to innovate or take calculated risks (Palmer et al.,2021). This can also cause stress relations with employees, co-founders, and investors because an entrepreneur may eventually become less communicative or over-critical.

In literal terms, it can greatly affect the physical system. For example, entrepreneurs may experience chronic fatigue, insomnia, or some other illness such as hypertension and gastrointestinal complaints. When physical well-being is compromised, it would be difficult to manage the daily functions of the business, which again becomes a cause of stress and further leads to low productivity. Severe prolonged effects may result in serious health issues like cardiovascular diseases (Khammissa et al.,2022).

Burnout intellectually handicaps one's critical thinking and creativity—two major skills which entrepreneurs depend on to solve problems and innovate. Psychologically, they may become confused, forget their memory, and lose focus, making it quite difficult for them to process information or make rational business decisions (Khammissa et al.,2022). Entrepreneurs might fall prey to indecisiveness or even hasty decisions simply because of getting rid of the pressure. The degradation in cognitive performance degrades the quality of leadership and strategic direction, which can have long-term negative consequences for the business.

Why Entrepreneurs are Particularly Vulnerable to Burnout

Entrepreneurship is, by nature, often extremely personal and personal so that entrepreneurs invest much emotional, financial, and physical energy into their venture. As soon as the lines of work and personal life become indistinct, it becomes rather difficult for an entrepreneur to actually step back and recharge. Entrepreneurial culture tends to glorify more than usual, hard work, and uncompromising hustle in a manner that even glorifies this thought: only sacrifice can lead a person towards success. This is where entrepreneurs hear warning signs too late or in most cases, even ignore them (Obschonka et al.,2023).

Lastly, most entrepreneurs spend their time alone in the first years of their business and often have no support apparatus in place, as workers in the larger organization might. The absence of a mentor, peers, or even stable team to share responsibilities with may then lead to isolation, which will make it more challenging to handle stressful conditions and prevent eventual burnout (Khammissa et al.,2022).

In conclusion, burnout is one of those prevalent problems in the entrepreneurial world that, if not arrested in time, can seriously retard personal and business success. Understanding the stages of burnout and recognizing its symptoms early on can help entrepreneurs take proactive steps against its damaging effects.

RISK FACTORS CONTRIBUTING TO ENTREPRENEURIAL BURNOUT

Entrepreneurial burnout is not an independent syndrome but is, instead, the consequence of several interacting risk factors. Stress resulting from entrepreneurship and personal-environmental factors can lead entrepreneurs toward mental and physical exhaustion (Obschonka et al.,2023). Knowledge of these risk factors is essential to mitigating burnout and ensuring sustainable business practices. The following sections summarize some of the largest contributors to entrepreneurial burnout.

Personality Traits and Perfectionism

The personality traits of entrepreneurs are some that probably predispose them to burnout. For example, perfectionism is one of the strongest personality features among entrepreneurs: they often set very high standards for themselves and their business environments (Wach et al.,2021). The propensity to try to be the best is undoubtedly a good quality; however, perfectionists are usually unable to delegate tasks, and in order not to let others make mistakes, they micromanage, convinced that nobody else can do it better. This endless pressure to control every other detail in the business leads to overwork and no ability to set priorities, which eventually causes chronic stress.

Entrepreneurship with high ambition may reach a level where he or she does not even know how to slow down or take a break despite their necessity. Pressure to attain success rapidly will require one to work longer hours with less than adequate time for rest and recoupment. In these conditions, the likelihood of burnout becomes significantly higher. Other desirable traits include resilience and flexibility, as entrepreneurship involves emergent and unstructured activity (Čigarská & Birknerová, 2021). Under such circumstances, it is difficult for people with lower emotional resiliency to cope with the negative aspects, which hastens the process of burnout.

Organizational and Industry Pressures

The risk of burnout was critically determined by the external environment in which the entrepreneur works. For instance, industries of tech start-up or high growth sectors require a short while for scaling, a constant innovation, and high competition. In such fast-paced industries, the entrepreneurs are compelled to be abreast of industry trends, use advances in technology, and be better than others. Under such conditions, an environment such as this easily predisposes people to burnout without respite (White and Gupta, 2020).

This may be significant in smaller or early-stage businesses. Entrepreneurs often run "one-man bands" whereby one entrepreneur plays all the roles, and these can include positions such as CEO, accountant, and customer service. Working under such conditions leads to very heavy workloads and isolation (Torrès et al.,2022). In addition, entrepreneurs seldom have formal structures nor clear frameworks upon which operations are carried out; therefore, they are sure to make decisions time and again without having information to inform the decisions being made. Such high numbers of decisions can lead to decision fatigue, yet another major factor of burnout.

Work-Life Imbalance

Work-life imbalance is one of the most prevalent risk factors for entrepreneurial burnout. Most entrepreneurs only put so much time and energy into their business, which is usually drawn from their personal lives (Irfan et al.,2023). Traditional employees are likely to have more defined lines between work and home; however, entrepreneurs find that they fall under similar living and working conditions. They can work at untimely hours, plus nights and weekends, and even when they're not actively working on the job, their minds don't turn off and disengage from business things. Not having downtime with an inability to disconnect prevents them from replenishing their energy reserves, hence resulting in chronic fatigue.

Additionally, this pressure to keep performing and scaling the business results in lacking personal relationships, hobbies, and self-care. Eventually, this lack of a balanced life brings dissatisfaction and depletes an entrepreneur's energy (Yester, 2019) The whole life can be felt to have been turned into an investment for work, which gradually leads to worse stress. When there is no chance to rest or for creativity or interaction with people, the psychological burden can grow too heavy to bear.

Isolation and Lack of Support Systems

Entrepreneurship generally turns into a lonely affair, especially for those involved in small-scale businesses or new ventures lacking adequate support staff. Indeed, entrepreneurs have to bear the entire burden of success or failure of the business on their own shoulders, which can lead to feelings of isolation (Neneh, 2024). It leaves the entrepreneur with no systems such as managers, departments of human resources, or any mentor who will have them look to guidance and feedback from; the latter only adds to the burden of lack of reliability.

Entrepreneurs are also less likely to seek assistance from other entrepreneurs because they fear admitting to stress or burnout may be perceived as weakness. Lack of stress expressions continually accumulate with no venue for relief. When neither mentorship nor teamwork exists, complexity in such issues leaves the entrepreneur to struggle alone through problems that most likely translate to mental and emotional exhaustion.

Financial and Economic Pressures

One of the big stressors for most entrepreneurs is financial, especially for those who are new to their ventures. It is the uncertainty of a revenue stream, pressure to find funding, and that payroll or operating expense needs to be met-the list goes on and on. Entrepreneurs frequently place on themselves the burden of keeping the business afloat, employees happy and paid, and investors satisfied, so there is an immense level of stress (Irfan et al.,2023).

These financial burdens are compounded by instability in the economy, changes in markets, and the dynamic nature of consumers (Khalatur et al.,2021). For example, an entrepreneur may have to make crucial decisions to adapt to economic times, such as cost-cutting measures or readjusting business policies, which could heighten stressors. The threat of failure cannot be alleviated when one's finances are not secure. Again, this would exacerbate anxiety and emotional stress.

Unrealistic Expectations and High Pressure to Succeed

The internal expectations are usually too difficult for entrepreneurs to meet. Societies glamorize entrepreneurship; the expectation is that prosperous entrepreneurs who deliver high productivity and exceptional value to the market do so through lots of hustle, risk-taking, and continuous innovation of products and processes. Social pressure does have a way of limiting confessions among entrepreneurs when they may be experiencing bottlenecks in their businesses or need to reduce their operations (Ronnie & Philip,2021). A lot of entrepreneurs are also too positive about themselves, with hope against hope that they will never go wrong. This has placed them in much denial wherein they do not look forward to assistance and refuse to delegate as this would most probably lead to exhaustion at all costs.

In addition, investors, stakeholders, and customers may raise high expectations on entrepreneurs for instant growth and continuous improvement. The need to meet these expectations, coupled with a constant fear of disappointing others, greatly enhances stress. Moreover, pressure to deliver instantly without the luxury of much time to ponder or recharge could leave entrepreneurs to their maximum limits, increasing burnout risk (Muenks et al.,2018).

Entrepreneurial burnout, then, is a function of personal traits, environmental pressures, and the demanding nature of business ownership. Without knowing the risk factors for burnout, no entrepreneur can protect well-being or sustain a business over time (Morrish,2019). The key message here is to recognize these risk factors early on so that entrepreneurs can proactively prevent these and thus implement strategies to manage stress loads more effectively.

EFFECTIVE STRESS MANAGEMENT TECHNIQUES

Entrepreneurs need to achieve an equilibrium between personal well-being and business success (Patro & Kumar, 2019). Efficient stress management can protect one from entrepreneur burnout, increase productivity, and promote better mental health for entrepreneurs. Some of the effective techniques for entrepreneurs that reduce the level of entrepreneurial stress are as mentioned below.

Prioritizing Work-Life Balance

To avoid burnout and sustain entrepreneurship in the long run, an entrepreneur has to achieve a healthy work-life balance. For most entrepreneurs, work and personal life become one, but separation is much needed (Patro & Kumar, 2019). Experts have clearly said that scheduling regular breaks, setting defined working hours can help not get into the overwork cycle that becomes constant. Even a short break for a vacation or an entire day for a business can be refreshing, thereby ensuring that returns are better made in terms of decisions and productivity.

Besides out-of-work life, personal relationships and activities may keep entrepreneurs vital for the time being and give their lives a sense of purpose. One can spend quality time with family or pursue their hobbies on sports or yoga, which is convenient and healthy. An entrepreneur with work hours and free time will be able to recharge and not feel overworked and get ready for burnout.

Time Management and Delegation

Among the skills that reduce entrepreneurial stress is effectively managing time. Getting overwhelmed is very easy simply because many entrepreneurs are handling numerous tasks in a single day (Holman et al.,2018). Prioritizing what is urgent and important reduces the mental load and makes workload easier to deal with. For instance, to-do lists, calendars, and project management software can help entrepreneurs keep things on track since they focus on the critical tasks that are done without overwhelming them.

Delegation of authority is one of the critical aspects of time management. Many entrepreneurs become victims of doing everything themselves, thinking only they know better than to do the job right. This brings undue stress and, at times, burnout (Niffin et al.,2021). Freeing one's time to think and formulate decisions on high-level thinking by delegating to employees or even hiring someone to pay the bills, do accounting, marketing, or administration is a plus. Letting other people handle certain tasks frees you up to focus on other activities and empowers the team for a collaborative environment.

Mindfulness and Relaxation Skills

Mindfulness and relaxation techniques can manage stress very amply and improve mental clarity. Meditation, deep breathing exercise, and mindfulness can help entrepreneurs remain grounded, reduce anxiety, and effectively work under highly stressful situations by giving them a chance to hunker down (Luberto et al.,2020). Mindfulness encourages an individual to focus on the present moment instead of getting drowned in the numerous tasks ahead, which increases mental resilience and better emotional regulation (Neneh, 2024).

Other relaxation techniques, such as yoga and progressive muscle relaxation, would help entrepreneurs to unwind physically and mentally. Engaging in such practices within a regular schedule helps entrepreneurs take control of their level of stress. Even a few minutes each day spent in deep breathing exercises can help relieve stress and improve concentration.

Developing a Support Network

A very effective means through which entrepreneurial stress can be managed even better is through a strong support network (Boon & Biron, 2016). Entrepreneurs experience much isolation, especially at the initial stages of any business. Isolation tends to increase stress and feelings of burnout. Entrepreneur connections with mentors or business coaches can offer valuable advice, feedback, and emotional support. Through sharing experiences and challenges, entrepreneurs can learn new insights, strategies for coping with stress, and the feeling that one is not alone in their journey.

Another important factor is a positive work culture. The entrepreneur should communicate with the team transparently, and cooperation and criticism must be promoted. A facilitative team can divide the workload, introduce new concepts, and provide emotional support to the entrepreneur (Neneh, 2024). Consequently, stress levels can be reduced on the entrepreneur's side. Having a supportive and understanding network while navigating life as an entrepreneur is often highly necessary.

Physical Health and Exercise

Another significant relationship is the direct connection between physical health and mental well-being; exercise is certainly one of the best ways to manage stress. Exercise releases endorphins, a natural mood lift, and reduces the production of hormones that cause stress, like cortisol (Oaten & Cheng, 2007). This includes running, yoga, or even a walk at work to improve energy levels, focus, or stress relief.

Healthy nutrition, appropriate sleep, and minimal intake of caffeine or alcohol are also factors of physical fitness. Because stress tends to weigh them down even more and productivity is impaired when a person's physical well-being is unhealthy, entrepreneurs have to learn to get into a healthy balance so that their business goes well (Luberto et al.,2020). A good entrepreneur treats his or her physical well-being as they treat the business-that is, optimal well-being results in greater performance and sounder decision-making.

Setting Realistic Expectations and Boundaries

One of the most common causes of entrepreneurial burnout is having inflated expectations of what it takes to be successful. For one, entrepreneurs often set themselves and their business ventures quite high ceilings, with such expectations forming an adhesive nonstop feeling that stress may accompany. Entrepreneurs should set realistic, achievable goals and be aware that a successful business takes time to establish (Ronnie & Philip, 2021).

Even entrepreneurs have to learn how to establish boundaries with clients, investors, and even themselves. This involves laying down limits on working hours, setting clear expectations on the part of stakeholders, and knowing what to say "no" when necessary. Boundaries help avoid overcommitment and allow entrepreneurs to maintain a work-life balance.

Professional Help and Counselling

Entrepreneurs suffering from overused stress or burnout may require professional assistance. Counselling, therapy, or coaching will provide entrepreneurs with more means of keeping their stress levels reduced and conquering a number of buried emotional or psychological issues. Cognitive-behavioral therapy (CBT), as well as other types of therapies, are likely to help change distorted thought patterns and coping techniques, as well as anxiety(Martin, 2013).

Entrepreneurially focused counselling or coaching can be very helpful based on the topic. It deals with entrepreneurial challenges that business owners only encounter. Such professionals can offer insight on how to better manage the journey of entrepreneurship while keeping one's well-being intact.

Developing Resilience and Emotional Intelligence

Resilience is one of the most essential attributes for entrepreneurs to develop dynamic adjustment and bounce back responses in respect of obstacles and setbacks. Thus, entrepreneurs should focus on developing resilient personalities in the sense of learning not to treat challenges as a source of threat but rather as opportunities for growth (Neneh, 2024). Cultivation of a learning mentality from failure and flexibility can reduce the emotional consequences of obstacles and keep entrepreneurs motivated.

Another great factor to consider is emotional intelligence (EI), or EI if you like, in stress management. The more the entrepreneur mastered EI, the better he was at understanding himself and others and managing his emotions and feelings and those of others. In fact, this is quite useful in situations when there are greater needs for empathy and self-awareness leading to better communication and conflict resolution (Holman et al.,2018).

Effective stress management strategies are used by entrepreneurs in an effective attempt to face the inevitable difficulties of a business. Indeed, while better time management, mindfulness, physical health, and building a strong support network may keep burnout at bay, they are a barrier to long-term success. Good health ensures that one is well as he or she lays the basis for a thriving business.

BUILDING RESILIENCE: PREVENTING BURNOUT BEFORE IT HAPPENS

One of the factors in resilience is the ability to regain strength while trying to recover from setbacks or challenges, adaptation, and maintaining a secure state of mental soundness even under highly stressed circumstances (Mahmoud & Rothenberger, 2019). For entrepreneurs, resilience building is very important in constructing the impetus of preventing burnout before it happens. All the uncertainties, pressure, and risks that go with entrepreneurship-built resilience as a means of having the mental and emotional capacity to face an eldritch circumstance without collapsing into exhaustion and overwhelm (Paiva-Schwanz et al.,2022). Encouraging the production of resilience from an early stage will mean that entrepreneurs can prevent burnout and be equipped with the correct mindset that may lead to sustainable growth and success.

Cultivating a Growth Mindset

Adopting a growth mindset is undoubtedly one of the key strategies for developing resilience. For entrepreneurs with a growth mindset, the challenges and failures are viewed as learning and development opportunities, not threats to their success. This lessens the level of the emotional toll that setbacks could take; entrepreneurs begin to learn how to regard every obstacle as a stepping stone towards betterment (Muenks et al.,2018). It not only strengthens the elasticity of resilience but also creates innovation and creativity, which are the nucleus of entrepreneurship.

Growing in one's mindset is practicing reframing one's notion of negatives to experience something rather than dwelling on mistakes(Aguilar, 2018). The habit of asking, "What can I learn from this experience?" will help an entrepreneur build mental resilience and keep them focused on long-term growth instead of short-term setbacks. This mindset keeps the entrepreneurs motivated and optimistic even in adverse situations.

Developing Emotional Awareness and Regulation

Resilience is also a characteristic of emotional awareness and control. An entrepreneur that has emotional awareness controls stress better; because they are attuned to whether they can handle so much at any one time and would take all the necessary steps to control his levels before it gets out of hand. This ability to understand what triggers your emotions, manage a response to stressors, and navigate through difficult situations in life is EI (Mahmoud & Rothenberger, 2019).

Therefore, to develop emotional awareness, entrepreneurs can practice mindfulness and introspection by checking themselves out frequently on the level of their emotional state. Journaling or any form of meditation is a great technique to help an entrepreneur refine their perception of what is causing them stress (Neneh, 2024). After emotional awareness is created, entrepreneurs should learn to regulate their emotions by having healthier coping behaviours like deep breathing, exercise, or talking to others about how they feel. Being able to deal and administer control over emotions results in lower tendencies of burnout since no stress will have accumulated over time.

Building a Strong Support System

Entrepreneurship can be a rather isolated experience, but resilience is often strengthened through support from others. Building a strong network of mentors, peers, and advisors helps to provide entrepreneurs with precious insight, encouragement, and emotional support during difficult moments (Mahmoud & Rothenberger,2019). Having a supportive system reduces feelings of isolation and gives entrepreneurs a place to air struggles, to brainstorm solutions, and to receive feedback.

The bottom line for entrepreneurs is having relations with individuals who understand the competitive struggles entrepreneurs face as business owners (Khalatur et al.,2021). They often have exceptional networking opportunities when networking with other entrepreneurs or joining mastermind groups, wherein they get to relate to similar experiences and specific advice on resolving entrepreneurial stress. There is also the strong personal relationships an entrepreneur should maintain with his family and friends so that the entrepreneur can have a well-rounded support system both professionally and personally.

Setting Clear Boundaries and Managing Expectations

Probably the most effective way of preventing burnout is through the establishment of clear boundaries within work life. Entrepreneurs, in truth, tend to over-commit themselves towards their business and lead to chronic stress and exhaustion (Ksreiner et al., 2009). The ability to say "no" to non-essential things and set specific working hours limits is crucial for an entrepreneur to maintain this necessary balance and avoid overwork. This can also keep a client, investor, or employee informed of your boundaries so that their expectations are realistic in terms of time and availability, and even performance.

Besides the external limits, entrepreneurs have to set realistic expectations on themselves. Many entrepreneurs get involved in the process that makes them think they must exhaust themselves to succeed (Čigarská & Birknerová, 2021). It cannot continue for long because entrepreneurs soon get overworked and exhausted. Focus on setting achievable goals, along with setting milestones that take into account available time and resources, helps entrepreneurs recognize that growth is gradual, and setbacks are but natural to the journey, and hence unneeded stress will be reduced and resilience will increase.

Practicing Self-Care and Prioritizing Well-Being

One of the most important components of resilience is self-care. This is habitually neglected by busy entrepreneurs. Preventing burnout requires regular attention to physical, mental, and emotional well-being (Søvold et al., 2021). Very simple practices such as getting enough sleep, eating a healthy diet, and exercising regularly mean dramatically improved energy levels and reduced stress. Entrepreneurs who take care of their wellness and wellbeing will be able to tackle challenges clear-headed and concentrated to maintain control over the work (Dalphon, 2019).

Aside from health problems, mental self-care practices such as mindfulness, meditation, or therapy may also protect the entrepreneur from feelings of uncertainty linked to entrepreneurship (Luberto et al.,2020). This may bring resilience through the lessened tension, emotion management, and prevention of the 'build-up' of stress. The more frequently the entrepreneur can obtain a stream of personal care moments, the more enduring the drivers will be: motivation, creativity, and passion.

Learning to Embrace Flexibility and Adaptability

Resilience means flexibility. Ideally, an entrepreneur should be flexible in thought, eager to change direction when there is a need to do so, and able to adapt quickly to an environment that will present uncertainty (Karman, 2020). The route of the entrepreneur, therefore, is mostly zigzag; the resilience of the entrepreneurs is a higher probability that such a flexible entrepreneur will come out victorious.

This means adapting to change and for entrepreneurs to achieve the virtues of adaptability, they must be mindful of continuous learning or improvement (Shim & Lee,2019). Instead of becoming fixed in their approach, entrepreneurs must let their minds open up to new ideas, feedback, and alternative solutions (Shim & Lee,2019). This makes entrepreneurs better equipped to handle challenges and avoid the disappointment that is often ushered in by unwarranted changes. Adaptability builds resilience by allowing innovativeness and, thus, maintaining a leadership edge in a rapidly evolving market.

Continuous Learning and Skill Development

Entrepreneurs who continuously learn and develop their skills are better positioned to deal with the complexity of running a business. Continuous learning enables entrepreneurs to be in harmony with industry trends and business strategies as well as suitable personal development (Muenks et al.,2018). This proactive attitude not only strengthens resilience through increased confidence and competence but equips one with tools and skills that will enable him or her to better face more challenges.

Through attending workshops or course enrollment, mentoring, and others, continuous learning would cultivate a growth mentality and ensure that entrepreneurs always move forward from what they have learned earlier (Holman et al.,2018). It is through curiosity and adaptability that entrepreneurs could better navigate the uncertainty of business ownership and nurture their mental well-being.

Resilience for the entrepreneur is built to prevent burnout, sustain well-being, and endure long-term periods. Through emotional intelligence, setting boundaries, managing their emotions, and taking care of themselves, entrepreneurs will put together the necessary mental and emotional strength needed to navigate the entrepreneurial journey successfully. A resilient entrepreneur copes with stress and change and can achieve success without giving up on personal well-being (Shim & Lee, 2019).

THE ROLE OF ORGANIZATIONAL SUPPORT IN BURNOUT PREVENTION

Organizational support is the most influential factor in preventing burnout among entrepreneurs. It is highly important in cases where an entrepreneur is working under a bigger business structure or managing a staff of employees. An organization's developed culture, resources, and systems can significantly influence how an entrepreneur handles stress while striving to maintain a normal work-life balance (Xu & Yang, 2021). Organizational support practices help reduce the risk of burnout through well-being, teaming, and sustainable work practices (Halbesleben & Wheeler,2015). This section discusses how organizational support contributes to burnout prevention by entrepreneurs and their teams.

Fostering a Supportive Organizational Culture

A supportive organizational culture is the foundation for preventing burnout. Openness between the entrepreneur and the employee is fostered by an organization that generates a team culture where people feel collaboration, open communication, and mutual respect between oneself and others (Wu, G et al.,2018). It helps to overcome the type of isolation commonly experienced by entrepreneurs, especially when at the nascent stages of the business. A great work culture encourages openness and offers a safe space in which people can share challenges, ask for advice, and come up with solutions (Dalphon, 2019).

Then, organizational leaders will set the tone for this culture. If leaders can give examples of taking breaks, prioritizing work-life balance, and managing their stress, then messages are conveyed that well-being is important (Wu et al., 2018). This empowers entrepreneurs to respond likewise, not overworking themselves or their teams. A culture that emphasizes mental health and work-life balance acts as a buffer for burnout.

Access to Resources and Tools

The second aspect that determines whether there will not be burnout is the availability of the organizational resources and tools needed. This is where successful entrepreneurs, especially those managing teams, gain the much-needed availability of all the tools required to delegate, automate, and streamline business operations (García-Martínez et al.,2020). When entrepreneurs are thoroughly swamped with administration work and overwhelmed by the need to perform every single item individually, they develop much stress. They are on the verge of burnout quickly. Through technological tools, administrative assistance, or even mentorship programs, organizational support should help lighten the workload, enabling entrepreneurs to cope with high-priority tasks.

More resources, such as mental health support, counseling services, and wellness programs, may give entrepreneurs the capacity to manage stress effectively (Machovec,2020). Most organizations provide employee assistance programs to offer confidential support and service for mental health concerns, including stress management and other personal problems. In this regard, many organizations demonstrate care for their employees or entrepreneurs, hence reducing burnout.

Encouraging Healthy Work-Life Integration

Healthy work-life integration is important in preventing burnout, and organizations are generally key to supporting this integration. Entrepreneurs often find themselves without boundaries between their work and personal lives. They often end up with long hours, constant stress, and exhaustion to the extent that it becomes full-time employment (García-Martínez et al.,2020). Organizations can help mitigate this by encouraging flexible working arrangements, like remote work options, flexible hours, or the ability to take time off when needed.

In the workplace, an organisation that genuinely shows a preference for sleep and recovery empowers entrepreneurs to take their edge off freely without any regret for being within the norms, and employees can recharge (Dalphon,2019). Organizational policies that support work-life integration reduce stress, enhance productivity, and are good for long-term well-being.

Providing Mentorship and Guidance

Mentorship and mentoring are critical forms of organizational support that may provide sustenance against the entrepreneurial burnout scenario. Entrepreneurs, and more so new entrants into entrepreneurship, face complex problems and multiple decisions at a single point in time, and may easily become overwhelmed by these complexities (Burgess et al.,2018). Access to mentors or advisory services within an organization provides entrepreneurs with the wisdom and support they may need in dealing with critical outcomes of these challenges. A mentor can advise them in day-to-day situations, share lessons from their own experiences, and assist in the development of resilience in entrepreneurs so that they may be capable of overcoming problems and arising as potential winners in a competitive game (Ramani et al.,2024). Mentorship programs also act as an area for personal development to take place together with professional development, and entrepreneurs find encouraging room to learn and grow professionally (Lin & Reddy, 2019). This support reduces pressure in decision-making but further empowers entrepreneurs to take charge of their businesses confidently. Guiding the entrepreneurs through these relationships ensures fewer anxieties about the sustainability of business ventures but leans on long-term sustainability.

Building a Collaborative Team Environment

Entrepreneurs would feel frustrated because they have to do everything for themselves; a good team environment within an organization will ease the burden as it distributes all the roles and fosters teamwork. When there is a team that can be relied upon, then entrepreneurs can delegate some tasks, focus on high-level strategic decisions, and reduce this pressure of managing everything in the business (Ramani et al.,2024).

Helping the entrepreneurs perform well and succeed by fostering collaboration as well as teamwork. Promoting open communication, periodic feedback, and shared goals and objectives make them feel that they belong to a team responsible for their work, thus making it easier to manage stress and avoid burnout (Noguera et al.,2018). Entrepreneurs who feel that their teams support them will be more likely to sustain their enthusiasm and passion for their jobs since they are relieved of having constant pressure to meet individual performance requirements.

Promoting Career Development and Growth

The other very important way the organization can prevent burnout is through career development and growth. An entrepreneur who has opportunities for continuous learning, training, and growth is most likely to be engaged, motivated, and inspired at work. When the organizations invest in the development of their entrepreneurs, it creates a sense of value and purpose and helps reduce feelings of stagnation or burnout.

Providing the scope for growth, training in leadership or attending industry events helps a budding entrepreneur build entrepreneurial capability but keeps him grounded to long-term goals (Ramani et al.,2024). It thus is an investment in growth that brings about a sense of purpose and progress, countering the frustration and exhaustion typical of burnout.

Organizational support is one of the key factors for entrepreneur burnout. Through the encouragement of a supportive culture, providing resources, work-life balance, mentorship, and facilitating collaboration, support by organizations will result in an environment that allows entrepreneurs to survive. With the right support, entrepreneurs can fight off stress and challenges, as well as prevent burnout.

TECHNOLOGICAL TOOLS FOR MANAGING STRESS

Entrepreneurship in today's fast-paced business world is turning to technological tools that help to manage stress and enhance one's life well-being. These can significantly support different organizations of entrepreneurship where one can be able to take care of their mental well-being, keep track of tasks, or even keep in good work-life balance. This section will explore several technological solutions for managing stress effectively and minimizing the risk of burnout among entrepreneurs.

Mental Health and Mindfulness Apps

Mental health and mindfulness applications have become popular tools to manage stress. These applications provide guided meditations, mindfulness exercises, and resources for mental health, which may help entrepreneurs find better ways of coping. Headspace, Calm, and Insight Timer are applications that have structured programs for relaxation and mindfulness, which users can easily fit into their daily schedule (Burgess et al.,2018).

The frequent application of such apps would, above all, enable businesspeople to better get to know the emotions and thoughts that happen in their brains; alleviate tension; and stabilize feelings (Tereso et al.,2019). In giving a few minutes each day to practice mindfulness, businesspeople can cultivate attention and resilience, thereby gaining the energy to take up tasks and remain positive toward them.

Task and Project Management Tools

The best stress-reducing management of work and projects for entrepreneurs is when they keep themselves organized and focused; some applications like Trello, Asana, or Monday.com, which can divide projects into smaller tasks and have deadlines that break and track the progress at any time needed, help avoid massive pressure and a sense of accomplishment in completing tasks(Tereso et al.,2019).

Moreover, these tools will enable teams to work in concert, or to share the work and communicate more coherently. The clear overview of projects and tasks allows entrepreneurs to allocate their time and resources more effectively in order to reduce the risk of burnout caused by disorganization and unchecked deadlines (Heigermoser et al.,2019).

Time Management and Productivity Apps

Even entrepreneurs trying to maximize their efficiency while reducing stress, like every other category of user, require tools like Todoist, RescueTime, and Focus@Will to guide actions in prioritizing tasks, setting goals, and monitoring productivity trends. More so, identifying patterns of time-wasting habits and streamlining workflows are some of the ways that help entrepreneurs create a balanced schedule capable of giving room to breaks and downtime.

Apps can also use techniques such as the Pomodoro Technique, where people work in focused intervals followed by short breaks (Heigermoser et al.,2019). This kind of structured approach not only enhances productivity but also ensures that entrepreneurs take necessary breaks to recharge, reducing the possibilities of burnout.

Communication and Collaboration Platforms

Communication is key while trying to reduce stress in entrepreneurship, especially in handling a team. Slack, Microsoft Teams, and Zoom are some websites that enable smooth communication and cooperation and help entrepreneurs stay connected with their teams while reducing the stress of constantly attending meetings. These tools can enable instant exchange of ideas, feedback, and updated information that can further facilitate teamwork and increase efficiency (Ansell & Gash,2018).

Communication can be streamlined to ensure fewer misunderstandings and a cooperative environment. Such support networks can relieve pressure associated with running a business, and sharing workloads is eased and problems together are navigated.

Health and Fitness Tracking Devices

Health and fitness tracking devices, such as smartwatches and fitness bands, significantly help in the management of stress to ensure good physical health. The Fitbit and Apple Watch enable such an understanding by providing data on the level of physical activity, heart rate, and sleep patterns (Burgess et al.,2018). Regular exercise keeps away stress and uplifts the mood, and entrepreneurs encourage activity throughout the day.

Entrepreneurs can maintain personal health and wellness when they are capable of formulating goals and monitoring progress in fitness, which leads to exercise in daily life. Furthermore, some devices also remind the entrepreneur to take a break, breathe, or even stretch, which develops self-care habits and prevents burnout in the end.

Digital journaling and reflection tools

Digital journaling and reflection tools help entrepreneurs cope with their thoughts and feelings, provide an outlet to deal with their stress levels, and applications such as Day One, Journey, and Penzu, which users can use to record their thought and reflect the experiences of the day or track their emotional well-being over time (Marion & Fixson, 2021). This should make entrepreneurs better aware of themselves, realize what stressors are, and produce strategies for coping.

Therefore, reflecting on the experiences allows entrepreneurs to celebrate some achievements and progress, so they are motivated and resilient. Digital journaling also assists in therapeutic discharge when one states his/her feelings and drives away anxiety.

Online Support Communities and Forums

Virtual support communities and forums provide entrepreneurs with an avenue to connect with peers who face similar issues. Sites like Reddit, LinkedIn groups, and entrepreneur-specific forums offer access to valuable resources and advice as well as a feeling of community. Interacting with other people in such spaces can also reduce feelings of isolation and gives them a little more of the motivation they need when things get tough (Ansell & Gash,2018).

Through such online websites, entrepreneurs share one another's issues, seeking opinions from each other based on past experiences. This relatability with others who know how painful it is to be an entrepreneur equips people with additional coping mechanisms and newly found perspectives that increase resistance to stress.

The business owner is instead empowered to manage stress, a highly precious resource in navigating the troubles of business ownership (Chang & Benson,2022).Some are apps dedicated to mental health and mindfulness while others specialize in task management and communication; they all empower the individual to oversee one's stress and living needs. Moreover, it can help entrepreneurs reduce the risk of being burnt out and support them to find a more sustainable way toward success.

FUTURE TRENDS IN ENTREPRENEURIAL STRESS MANAGEMENT

The future of entrepreneurship is changing just like the various methods and technologies used to manage stress and avoid burnout. It means today's entrepreneur needs to understand some of these tendencies to be sure they embrace sustainable practices in their business ventures. In this section, we explore emerging trends that will significantly shape how entrepreneurs deal with stress soon.

Increased Integration of Artificial Intelligence (AI)

AI integration will soon change the way entrepreneurs relate to their mental health and productivity (Brynjolfsson & McAfee, 2017). Applications mustered by AI will give specific insights regarding any pattern seen in their behavior, hence giving those recommendations for stress management and well-being. For example, if an algorithm spots patterns in a person, like habits at work, emotional states, and productivity, it can suggest exercises in mindfulness, remind people to take a break, or even optimize working schedules.

Chatbots and other AI-based virtual assistants can also provide immediate help for mental well-being, giving the required resources and techniques to the point of maximum stress. This will enable entrepreneurs to seek help at the point where they need it most by breaking the stigma of mental health and spreading the culture of well-being.

Virtual Reality (VR) for Stress Relief

Virtual reality is emerging as an intense tool for stress relief and mental wellbeing. VR experiences transport you to calm environments with the intention of helping their users relax and be mindful in an immersive fashion. Entrepreneurs will increasingly seek out VR meditation or stress relief programs to take quick mental breaks from the pressures of running a business (Tarrant et al.,2018).

Team training or building can be held in the virtual reality setting, hence cultivating teamwork and interaction among teams that work remotely (Yin, J. et al.,2020). By creating interactive and engaging environments, VR will help improve the staff's dynamics while offering a place for stress relief.

Enhanced Focus on Employee Well-Being

Only when mental health is much better understood, will an organization's bottom line rely more and more on ensuring that the well-being of employees is addressed as a fundamental part of their success. Indeed, organizations will invest much more seriously into the development of supportive work environments which foster holistic well-being, such as work-life balance and mental health. Such a trend will call upon entrepreneurs to create more holistic well-being programs that should feature mental health resources and wellness initiatives besides flexible work arrangements (Chang & Benson,2022).

Also, companies can formulate policies such as mandatory mental health days, regular check-ins on wellness, and mental health training of their managers. In response to the onset of burnout symptoms within their teams, these measures would avoid the shortage of a productive workforce in any given company. This proactivity in well-being measures would help develop a culture that is supportive with an enabling environment to foster entrepreneurship without jeopardizing mental health.

Emphasis on Work-Life Integration

This encompasses more and more entrepreneurs and organizations adopting flexible work arrangements because the concept of work-life integration is now becoming popular. While traditional work-life balance has the tendency to separate work and personal life, there should be a higher-fluid approach that blends work and personal responsibilities in an easy and flowing manner (Burgess et al.,2018).

This will raise flexible hours of work, remote working opportunities, and ability to carry personal activities during working hours. The entrepreneur embracing work-life integration can easily manage stress, meaning all the scheduling issues can be solved according to personal and professional realms (Hensellek & Puchala,2021). In actuality, this shift can increase employee satisfaction and reduce burnout.

Development of Holistic Wellness Platforms

More holistic wellness platforms are likely to emerge in the future, integrating various resources and services into one solution. Stand-alone operational platforms may offer several services, including mental health support, fitness tracking capabilities, nutrition advice, and stress management resources, all under one roof (Casillo et al.,2024).

Giving these platforms a holistic view on well-being will enable entrepreneurs to take ownership of their mental health more proactively. This will allow its users to be monitored on both physical and emotional aspects, set goals, and access tailored resources, thus creating a much more personalistic approach in dealing with stress.

Increasing Popularity of Remote Work and Digital Nomadism

An essential conclusion of the rise of remote work and digital nomadism is that entrepreneurs increasingly need to manage stress in new ways. As individuals will focus on working flexibly, it will be an avenue to balance their responsibilities to professional life and ensure good health and well-being (Hensellek & Puchala,2021). This will reflect the creation of new resources and communities that provide support to remote workers in managing their stress better, connecting them with other people, and fostering their productivity.

A remote lifestyle for entrepreneurship will offer diverse digital resources or tools to support well-being, including virtual co-working spaces, online support groups, and workshops with a focus on mental health and productivity (Thompson,2019). This group environment may well help to counteract isolationism-one of the most criticized negatives of remote work-making them a community which helps to manage stress.

Focus on Mindfulness and Mental Health Education

As mental wellness continues to rise in public awareness, so will there be increased mindfulness and education taught in each entrepreneurship program or business school (Burgess et al.,2018). Future entrepreneurs will be better equipped to empower themselves with healthy mental practices as part of their daily functions.

Stress management and mental well-being will be regular work packages of workshops, training programs, and education tools used in curricula on entrepreneurship. Future entrepreneurs will, therefore, be equipped early with the best practices for entrepreneurial work when they face the problems of running a business without holding back their mental well-being (Khalatur et al.,2021).

Future management of entrepreneurial stress through technology, emphasizing greater well-being and flexibility at work. With the emergence of AI, VR, and wellness platforms, entrepreneurs will be armed with more innovative means that support mental health and productivity. Moreover, employee well-being and mindfulness education will be highly valued; this powers entrepreneurs to develop a healthier working environment, reducing burnout and enabling long-term success. Entrepreneurial longevity, in turn, will depend on embracing these trends.

CONCLUSION

Taking a conclusion, managing stress and preventing burnout is very important for entrepreneurs involved in business complexities. As has been explored in this chapter, entrepreneurial journey is inherently characterized by challenges that lead to the highest levels of stress and, subsequently, to burnout. What then is the nature of entrepreneurial stress? On what factors does burnout emerge? When acquainted with all the above, people can proactively hold onto their mental health and better their well-being.

With proper stress management practices ranging from mindfulness to organizational support, several entrepreneurial burnout risks can be significantly mitigated. At a similar time, the use of technological tools such as mental health apps, project management software, and communication platforms will help entrepreneurs improve efficiency, work well, and enhance overall well-being (Engel et al., 2021). These tools enable entrepreneurs to adopt healthier habits, to create more balanced work environments, and to promote the culture of mutual support among the employees of an organization.

Looking ahead, the trends in stress management for the future seem to be highly inclined toward a holistic approach to well-being, AI integration, and flexible work. Since the entrepreneurial landscape contains these very entrepreneurs, the innovations arising from these future trends would present them with new avenues in effectively managing stress (Lek et al., 2020). Entrepreneurial resilience and adaptability to job demands would thus arise as a result of embracing some of these trends while maintaining a sustainable approach to work.

At the most basic level, this involves giving careful attention to one's mental health and well-being, as this is not just a personal responsibility but also something critical to any long-term success in business. When entrepreneurs assume ownership over stress, they initiate ripples in their own lives and those of the teams and organizations they lead. A culture of well-being for entrepreneurs has the potential to make them role models for others, compelling others to pay attention to their mental health, and, in doing so, contribute to a healthier and more productive entrepreneurial ecosystem. It won't be easy; however, with all the right tools and strategies in place, entrepreneurs will be able to play out their path in resilience, confidence, and renewed purpose.

REFERENCES

Aguilar, E. (2018). *Onward: Cultivating emotional resilience in educators*. John Wiley & Sons. DOI: 10.1002/9781119441731

Ansell, C., & Gash, A. (2018). Collaborative platforms as a governance strategy. *Journal of Public Administration: Research and Theory*, 28(1), 16–32. DOI: 10.1093/jopart/mux030

Boon, C., & Biron, M. (2016). Temporal issues in person–organization fit, person–job fit and turnover: The role of leader–member exchange. *Human Relations*, 69(12), 2177–2200. DOI: 10.1177/0018726716636945 PMID: 27904171

Brynjolfsson, E., & Mcafee, A. N. D. R. E. W. (2017). Artificial intelligence, for real. *Harvard Business Review*, 1, 1–31.

Burgess, A., van Diggele, C., & Mellis, C. (2018). Mentorship in the health professions: A review. *The Clinical Teacher*, 15(3), 197–202. DOI: 10.1111/tct.12756 PMID: 29318730

Casillo, M., Cecere, L., Colace, F., Lorusso, A., & Santaniello, D. (2024). Integrating the Internet of Things (IoT) in SPA Medicine: Innovations and challenges in digital wellness. *Computers*, 13(3), 67. DOI: 10.3390/computers13030067

Chang, W. L., & Benson, V. (2022). Jigsaw teaching method for collaboration on cloud platforms. *Innovations in Education and Teaching International*, 59(1), 24–36. DOI: 10.1080/14703297.2020.1792332

) Čigarská, B. N., & Birknerová, Z. (2021). Burnout syndrome and Coping strategies: knowledge, approaches, foundations concerning its incidence among entrepreneurs. *THE POPRAD ECONOMIC AND MANAGEMENT*, 98.

Dalphon, H. (2019). Self-care techniques for social workers: Achieving an ethical harmony between work and well-being. *Journal of Human Behavior in the Social Environment*, 29(1), 85–95. DOI: 10.1080/10911359.2018.1481802

Engel, Y., Noordijk, S., Spoelder, A., & van Gelderen, M. (2021). Self-compassion when coping with venture obstacles: Loving-kindness meditation and entrepreneurial fear of failure. *Entrepreneurship Theory and Practice*, 45(2), 263–290. DOI: 10.1177/1042258719890991

García-Martínez, J. A., Rosa-Napal, F. C., Romero-Tabeayo, I., López-Calvo, S., & Fuentes-Abeledo, E. J. (2020). Digital tools and personal learning environments: An analysis in higher education. *Sustainability (Basel)*, 12(19), 8180. DOI: 10.3390/su12198180

Gorgievski, M. J., & Stephan, U. (2016). Advancing the psychology of entrepreneurship: A review of the psychological literature and an introduction. *Applied Psychology*, 65(3), 437–468. DOI: 10.1111/apps.12073

Halbesleben, J. R., & Wheeler, A. R. (2015). To invest or not? The role of coworker support and trust in daily reciprocal gain spirals of helping behavior. *Journal of Management*, 41(6), 1628–1650. DOI: 10.1177/0149206312455246

Heigermoser, D., de Soto, B. G., Abbott, E. L. S., & Chua, D. K. H. (2019). BIM-based Last Planner System tool for improving construction project management. *Automation in Construction*, 104, 246–254. DOI: 10.1016/j.autcon.2019.03.019

) Hensellek, S., & Puchala, N. (2021). The emergence of the digital nomad: A review and analysis of the opportunities and risks of digital nomadism. *The flexible workplace: Coworking and other modern workplace transformations*, 195-214.

Holman, D., Johnson, S., & O'Connor, E. (2018). Stress management interventions: Improving subjective psychological well-being in the workplace. *Handbook of well-being*, 1-13.

Irfan, M., Khalid, R. A., Kaka Khel, S. S. U. H., Maqsoom, A., & Sherani, I. K. (2023). Impact of work–life balance with the role of organizational support and job burnout on project performance. *Engineering, Construction, and Architectural Management*, 30(1), 154–171. DOI: 10.1108/ECAM-04-2021-0316

Karman, A. (2020). Flexibility, coping capacity and resilience of organizations: Between synergy and support. *Journal of Organizational Change Management*, 33(5), 883–907. DOI: 10.1108/JOCM-10-2019-0305

) Khalatur, S., Masiuk, Y., Kachula, S., Brovko, L., Karamushka, O., & Shramko, I. (2021). Entrepreneurship development management in the context of economic security. *Entrepreneurship and sustainability issues*, 9(1), 558.

Khammissa, R. A., Nemutandani, S., Feller, G., Lemmer, J., & Feller, L. (2022). Burnout phenomenon: Neurophysiological factors, clinical features, and aspects of management. *The Journal of International Medical Research*, 50(9), 03000605221106428. DOI: 10.1177/03000605221106428 PMID: 36113033

Kniffin, K. M., Narayanan, J., Anseel, F., Antonakis, J., Ashford, S. P., Bakker, A. B., Bamberger, P., Bapuji, H., Bhave, D. P., Choi, V. K., Creary, S. J., Demerouti, E., Flynn, F. J., Gelfand, M. J., Greer, L. L., Johns, G., Kesebir, S., Klein, P. G., Lee, S. Y., & Vugt, M. V. (2021). COVID-19 and the workplace: Implications, issues, and insights for future research and action. *The American Psychologist*, 76(1), 63–77. DOI: 10.1037/amp0000716 PMID: 32772537

Kreiner, G. E., Hollensbe, E. C., & Sheep, M. L. (2009). Balancing borders and bridges: Negotiating the work-home interface via boundary work tactics. *Academy of Management Journal*, 52(4), 704–730. DOI: 10.5465/amj.2009.43669916

) Kuruppu, A. (2024). Small Business Burnout: Reversing the Entrepreneurial Exit.

Lee, S. H., Patel, P. C., & Phan, P. H. (2023). Are the self-employed more stressed? New evidence on an old question. *Journal of Small Business Management*, 61(2), 513–539. DOI: 10.1080/00472778.2020.1796467

Lek, J., Vendrig, A. A., & Schaafsma, F. G. (2020). What are psychosocial risk factors for entrepreneurs to become unfit for work? A qualitative exploration. *Work (Reading, Mass.)*, 67(2), 499–506. DOI: 10.3233/WOR-203299 PMID: 33074213

Lin, J., & Reddy, R. M. (2019). Teaching, mentorship, and coaching in surgical education. *Thoracic Surgery Clinics*, 29(3), 311–320. DOI: 10.1016/j.thorsurg.2019.03.008 PMID: 31235300

Luberto, C. M., Hall, D. L., Park, E. R., Haramati, A., & Cotton, S. (2020). A perspective on the similarities and differences between mindfulness and relaxation. *Global Advances in Health and Medicine : Improving Healthcare Outcomes Worldwide*, 9, 2164956120905597. DOI: 10.1177/2164956120905597 PMID: 32076580

Machovec, G. (2020). Selected tools and services for analyzing and managing open access journal transformative agreements. *Journal of Library Administration*, 60(3), 301–307. DOI: 10.1080/01930826.2020.1727280

Mahmoud, N. N., & Rothenberger, D. (2019). From burnout to well-being: A focus on resilience. *Clinics in Colon and Rectal Surgery*, 32(06), 415–423. DOI: 10.1055/s-0039-1692710 PMID: 31686993

Marion, T. J., & Fixson, S. K. (2021). The transformation of the innovation process: How digital tools are changing work, collaboration, and organizations in new product development. *Journal of Product Innovation Management*, 38(1), 192–215. DOI: 10.1111/jpim.12547

Martin, A. (2013). (Leuphana Universität Lüneburg, Institut für Mittelstandsforschung, Hrsg.). (2013). Die Beurteilung der Arbeitsbedingungen durch Unternehmer und Arbeitnehmer, Schriften aus dem Institut für Mittelstandsforschung, No. 43, Leuphana Universität Lüneburg, Institut für Mittelstandsforschung. Verfügbar unter: https://www. econstor.eu/bitstream/10419/71296/1/739971433.pdf

Morrish, L. (2019). *Pressure vessels: The epidemic of poor mental health among higher education staff.* Higher Education Policy Institute.

Muenks, K., Wigfield, A., & Eccles, J. S. (2018). I can do this! The development and calibration of children's expectations for success and competence beliefs. *Developmental Review*, 48, 24–39. DOI: 10.1016/j.dr.2018.04.001

Nambisan, S., & Baron, R. A. (2021). On the costs of digital entrepreneurship: Role conflict, stress, and venture performance in digital platform-based ecosystems. *Journal of Business Research*, 125, 520–532. DOI: 10.1016/j.jbusres.2019.06.037

Neneh, B. N. (2024). Why peer support matters: Entrepreneurial stressors, emotional exhaustion, and growth intentions of women entrepreneurs. *Entrepreneurship Research Journal*, 14(3), 985–1019. DOI: 10.1515/erj-2021-0501

Noguera, I., Guerrero-Roldán, A. E., & Masó, R. (2018). Collaborative agile learning in online environments: Strategies for improving team regulation and project management. *Computers & Education*, 116, 110–129. DOI: 10.1016/j.compedu.2017.09.008

Oaten, M., & Cheng, K. (2007). Improvements in self-control from financial monitoring. *Journal of Economic Psychology*, 28(4), 487–501. DOI: 10.1016/j.joep.2006.11.003

Obschonka, M., Pavez, I., Kautonen, T., Kibler, E., Salmela-Aro, K., & Wincent, J. (2023). Job burnout and work engagement in entrepreneurs: How the psychological utility of entrepreneurship drives healthy engagement. *Journal of Business Venturing*, 38(2), 106272. DOI: 10.1016/j.jbusvent.2022.106272

Omrane, A., Kammoun, A., & Seaman, C. (2018). Entrepreneurial burnout: Causes, consequences and way out. *FIIB Business Review*, 7(1), 28–42. DOI: 10.1177/2319714518767805

Paiva-Salisbury, M. L., & Schwanz, K. A. (2022). Building compassion fatigue resilience: Awareness, prevention, and intervention for pre-professionals and current practitioners. *Journal of Health Service Psychology*, 48(1), 39–46. DOI: 10.1007/s42843-022-00054-9 PMID: 35136862

Palmer, C., Kraus, S., Kailer, N., Huber, L., & Öner, Z. H. (2021). Entrepreneurial burnout: A systematic review and research map. *International Journal of Entrepreneurship and Small Business*, 43(3), 438–461. DOI: 10.1504/IJESB.2021.115883

) Patro, C. S., & Kumar, K. S. (2019). Effect of workplace stress management strategies on employees' efficiency. *International journal of scientific development and research*, 4(5), 412-418.

Ramani, S., Kusurkar, R. A., Lyon-Maris, J., Pyörälä, E., Rogers, G. D., Samarasekera, D. D., Taylor, D. C. M., & Ten Cate, O. (2024). Mentorship in health professions education–an AMEE guide for mentors and mentees: AMEE Guide No. 167. *Medical Teacher*, 46(8), 999–1011. DOI: 10.1080/0142159X.2023.2273217 PMID: 37909275

Rauch, A., Fink, M., & Hatak, I. (2018). Stress processes: An essential ingredient in the entrepreneurial process. *The Academy of Management Perspectives*, 32(3), 340–357. DOI: 10.5465/amp.2016.0184

Ronnie, J. B., & Philip, B. (2021). Expectations and what people learn from failure. In *Expectations and actions* (pp. 207–237). Routledge. DOI: 10.4324/9781003150879-10

Satow, L. (2012). *Stress- und Coping-Inventar (SCI)*. Vollständige Test- und Skalendokumentation.

Shim, W., & Lee, S. W. (2019). An agile approach for managing requirements change to improve learning and adaptability. *Journal of Industrial Information Integration*, 14, 16–23. DOI: 10.1016/j.jii.2018.07.005

Søvold, L. E., Naslund, J. A., Kousoulis, A. A., Saxena, S., Qoronfleh, M. W., Grobler, C., & Münter, L. (2021). Prioritizing the mental health and well-being of healthcare workers: An urgent global public health priority. *Frontiers in Public Health*, 9, 679397. DOI: 10.3389/fpubh.2021.679397 PMID: 34026720

Tarrant, J., Viczko, J., & Cope, H. (2018). Virtual reality for anxiety reduction demonstrated by quantitative EEG: A pilot study. *Frontiers in Psychology*, 9, 1280. DOI: 10.3389/fpsyg.2018.01280 PMID: 30087642

Tereso, A., Ribeiro, P., Fernandes, G., Loureiro, I., & Ferreira, M. (2019). Project management practices in private organizations. *Project Management Journal*, 50(1), 6–22. DOI: 10.1177/8756972818810966

) Thompson, B. Y. (2019). The digital nomad lifestyle:(remote) work/leisure balance, privilege, and constructed community. *International journal of the sociology of leisure*, 2(1), 27-42.

Torrès, O., Benzari, A., Fisch, C., Mukerjee, J., Swalhi, A., & Thurik, R. (2022). Risk of burnout in French entrepreneurs during the COVID-19 crisis. *Small Business Economics*, 58(2), 1–23. DOI: 10.1007/s11187-021-00516-2 PMID: 38624594

Wach, D., Stephan, U., Weinberger, E., & Wegge, J. (2021). Entrepreneurs' stressors and well-being: A recovery perspective and diary study. *Journal of Business Venturing*, 36(5), 106016. DOI: 10.1016/j.jbusvent.2020.106016

Wach, D., Stephan, U., Weinberger, E., & Wegge, J. (2021). Entrepreneurs' stressors and well-being: A recovery perspective and diary study. *Journal of Business Venturing*, 36(5), 106016. DOI: 10.1016/j.jbusvent.2020.106016

Wang, Q., Khan, S. N., Sajjad, M., Sarki, I. H., & Yaseen, M. N. (2023). Mediating role of entrepreneurial work-related strains and work engagement among job demand– resource model and success. *Sustainability (Basel)*, 15(5), 4454. DOI: 10.3390/su15054454

White, J. V., & Gupta, V. K. (2020). *Stress and well-being in entrepreneurship: a critical review and future research agenda*. Res. Occu. Stress Well Being., DOI: 10.1108/S1479-355520200000018004

Wu, G., Wu, Y., Li, H., & Dan, C. (2018). Job burnout, work-family conflict and project performance for construction professionals: The moderating role of organizational support. *International Journal of Environmental Research and Public Health*, 15(12), 2869. DOI: 10.3390/ijerph15122869 PMID: 30558218

Xu, Z., & Yang, F. (2021). The impact of perceived organizational support on the relationship between job stress and burnout: A mediating or moderating role? *Current Psychology (New Brunswick, N.J.)*, 40(1), 402–413. DOI: 10.1007/s12144-018-9941-4

Yester, M. (2019). Work-life balance, burnout, and physician wellness. *The Health Care Manager*, 38(3), 239–246. DOI: 10.1097/HCM.0000000000000277 PMID: 31261191

Yin, J., Yuan, J., Arfaei, N., Catalano, P. J., Allen, J. G., & Spengler, J. D. (2020). Effects of biophilic indoor environment on stress and anxiety recovery: A between-subjects experiment in virtual reality. *Environment International*, 136, 105427. DOI: 10.1016/j.envint.2019.105427 PMID: 31881421

Chapter 17
Social Support Networks and Their Role in Entrepreneurial Well-Being

Shashank Mittal
O.P. Jindal Global University, India

Shivani Dhand
https://orcid.org/0000-0002-4809-1365
Lovely Professional University, India

Xuan-Hoa Nghiem
https://orcid.org/0000-0003-2292-0257
Vietnam National University, Vietnam

ABSTRACT

This chapter explores the critical role of social support networks in enhancing entrepreneurial well-being and success. It examines the types of social support, including emotional, informational, and instrumental support, and their impact on mental health, resilience, and business outcomes. The chapter discusses the evolving nature of these networks in the digital age, highlighting the influence of technology and online platforms in fostering connections among entrepreneurs. Additionally, it addresses the challenges faced in building and maintaining meaningful relationships within support networks and provides strategies for cultivating effective connections. Future trends, such as increased digitalization, AI integration, and a focus on diversity and inclusion, are also considered. By understanding and leveraging social support networks, entrepreneurs can create robust ecosystems that contribute to personal and professional growth.

INTRODUCTION

Entrepreneurship is often described as the path of freedom, innovativeness, and personal realization. Reality, however, easily veers off course from the prevailing glamour. First, entrepreneurs face some unique stresses (Kuruppu, 2024). For example, such fears include uncertainty regarding finance, high hours of work, stiff competition, and the persistent pressure to succeed in ventures. All these risks merge

DOI: 10.4018/979-8-3693-3673-1.ch017

Copyright ©2025, IGI Global. Copying or distributing in print or electronic forms without written permission of IGI Global is prohibited.

to constitute an upsetting setting that can easily deteriorate the mental, emotional, and psychosomatic state of an individual. Entrepreneurial stress, if not in control, leads to burnout-the state of emotional, physical, and mental exhaustion. That happens to large business owners and startup founders. Burnout directly affects personal health and can potentially jeopardize business performance, innovation capacity, and long-term sustainability (White & Gupta, 2020; Lee et al., 2023; Wang et al., 2023).

Entrepreneurial work tends to be characterized by high levels of autonomy, decision-making pressure, as well as responsibility over the business and employees. Entrepreneurship often blurs the boundaries between professional and personal life and entrepreneurs cannot automatically "switch off" the work at predetermined times like traditional employees. The constant pressure to adapt to fluctuating markets, more crucially, manage financial uncertainty, and meet the expectations of investors or clients will heighten stress. At that point, managing stress becomes more than a private health issue but a strategic business imperative. Business owners who neglect proper mental health care can give way to some loss in decision-making, creativity, and leadership capabilities, very tools needed for running a good venture.

Burnout is the syndrome of chronic stress, and it's becoming increasingly relevant to the entrepreneurial environment. As research further brings out, entrepreneurs are particularly vulnerable to burnout due to the risky or demanding nature of the work they carry out. Unlike employees working in organizations that are large in size and can afford a support system, most entrepreneurs work individually without a team or network to share the burden of responsibility with (Satow, 2012). This in itself provides a significant reason to feel inadequate, frustrated, and finally exhausted due to burnout. The symptoms from exhaustion and cynicism to a sense of isolation and reduced performance, have devastating effects on both the bottom line of the individual and the organization.

With this increased awareness of these problems, entrepreneurs must recognize the importance of proactive stress management and burnout prevention. Successful stress management techniques contribute to improved personal well-being and business performance. The development of active resilience, emotional intelligence, and healthy work-life integration means that the long-term outcome for entrepreneurs will be better. The current chapter covers various stress management practices that would be highly valuable for entrepreneurs, such as mindfulness, time management, and practices related to physical well-being. In fact, it dwells on aspects of organizational support systems, technological tools, and social networks in risk reduction of burnout.

This chapter is an attempt to provide meaningful insights into sustaining personal wellness along with venture sustainability as the root causes of entrepreneurial stress and burnout along with offering practical solutions towards addressing them. Entrepreneurial endeavors that focus on mental health and stress reduction may help the entrepreneur succeed in their professional and personal life.

THE CONCEPT OF ENTREPRENEURIAL STRESS

Entrepreneurial stress is unique and growing from the very different experience entrepreneurs do in building a business compared to most jobs. Most entrepreneurship challenges require diving into multiple roles, making high-stakes decisions, and facing uncertainty all the time; it isn't like what most people experience when preparing for a job. Start-up pressures can bring extreme mental, emotional, and, at times, even physical strain to entrepreneurs, driving many of them to chronic stress (Gorgievski & Stephan, 2016).

The uncertainty of the entrepreneurial venture process has been one of the key contributors to entrepreneurial stress. The entrepreneur fights multiple battles from accessing funding and then finding ways to manage cash flow to dealing with competition in the marketplace and managing consumers' expectations. More often than not, entrepreneurs are faced with situations that are totally out of their control. This is partly due to uncertainty: a company's prosperity or failure may depend on whether these numerous factors change, from changes in economic landscapes to shifts in regulatory policies to changes in consumer tastes, most of which no one can predict with any certainty (Rauch et al., 2018). For start-ups, the pressure mounts even further. The deadlines to begin generating returns can be ruinous on top of personal finances, reputation, and relationships.

A second major stressor of entrepreneurship is workload. Entrepreneurs are known to work for longer hours than employees. This implies that their work and personal lives overlap so that the individual can never recognize which is which. Since entrepreneurs normally work for a long to sustain their business, a lack of work-life balance raises stress. Increased frequencies of being unable to take downtime and physically disconnecting from work can lead to mental and physical exhaustion, further mounting stress levels.

Entrepreneurial stress also stems from decision-making. The entrepreneur is largely in charge of his business, and decisions related to hiring, product development, and market strategies can often have lasting implications (Nambisan & Baron, 2021). This constant decision-making, often under time pressure and without the luxury of big data, can induce a type of mental fatigue and lead to a paralyzing inability to decide. Self-doubt and fear of failure can also be added contributors to stress for entrepreneurs, especially those with less experience or resources.

External pressures are only one part of a culture of entrepreneurial stress. There are also some internal factors which lead to entrepreneurial stress. Many entrepreneurs do not have many alternate motivations because of their deep personal investment in their business, which makes it awkward to separate their identity from the venture's success (Wach, 2021). This usually leads to perfectionism where entrepreneurs have set themselves and their ventures to impossible standards and become self-critical if they are unable to live up to those expectations. Continued fear of inability to meet these expectations leads to an overwhelming amount of self-criticism and inability to delegate tasks leading to more stress. They can also be isolated, because it appears that they run the business alone and without the support of a big team to share the burden and responsibilities of business operations.

Entrepreneurial stress, although exceedingly common, is in no way inevitable. Identifying sources and effects of the same gives an entrepreneur his/her first step toward lessening the blow of the same. Realizing the stressors specific to a journey makes entrepreneurs begin to implement strategies that would help manage their workload, maintain a healthier work-life balance, and prevent what prolonged stress can take emotionally.

THE BURNOUT PHENOMENON IN ENTREPRENEURSHIP

What is Burnout? Signs and Symptoms

Burnout is the mental status experienced when an individual becomes emotionally, mentally, and physically drained due to a prolonged period of exposure to high levels of stress, such as in the cases of entrepreneurship where individuals are exposed to very high pressure. The condition is not like regular fatigue since its impact is experienced in all aspects of life, and usually people have feelings of depersonalization, reduced control, and mental exhaustion. Burnout is dangerous for entrepreneurs because their personal well-being is intricately bound to that of the business (Omrane et al.,2018). Typically, burnout presents in the form of symptoms including continuous exhaustion, chronic feelings of restlessness and irritation, decreased ability to concentrate, and increased feelings of being emotionally distant from work. A highly entrepreneurial person suffering burnout may feel that they cannot work hard enough, no matter how hard they try, leading into the cycle of being overwhelmed with work and stress.

The emotional impact is just as deep. They may start to start despising their business and the zeal and enthusiasm that initially characterized their actions (Palmer et al.,2021). Doubt their competencies, or even lose the value in what they are doing, adding to feelings of inadequacy. Other signs may include insomnia and headaches as well as a weakening immune system, which makes daily activity more challenging (Čigarská & Birknerová, 2021). Left unchecked, over time, burnout can lead to severe effects such as depression and anxiety and other mental health issues.

The Burnout Cycle: How Stress Begets Burnout

For the most part, the process by which stress escalates into burnout is cyclical. Entrepreneurs are energized and motivated by their goals at first, but accumulating stress from extra hours, uncertainty, and the pressure of running a business leach away this energy. When stress is chronic, the entrepreneur becomes caught in a state of emotional exhaustion to the point that even the most minute tasks seem overwhelming. The impact tends to be accompanied by depersonalization where business owners become estranged from their enterprise, and a negative attitude could be developed towards it (Obschonka et al.,2023).

At this point, entrepreneurs become physically drained to the extent that they also lose touch with the business they once so enthusiastically built. Failure or inadequacy is the conclusion if observable progress cannot be achieved with ever-present stressors. This introduces a vicious cycle where the entrepreneur will do everything in their power to break the deadlock of burnout, and once again, this will drain them more, creating yet another vicious cycle (Čigarská & Birknerová,2021). If such a cycle is not interrupted by interference, severe personal and professional outcomes may arise, eventually leading to the collapse of the business venture.

Emotional, Physical, and Cognitive Effects of Burnout

Burnout costs are thus multi-faceted, touching on personal and business issues. Entrepreneurship burns one out at the emotional level: frustration, resentment, and disillusion may haunt them. They begin considering their venture a burden rather than an opportunity for leveraging business ventures to wealth and innovation. It can contribute to poor judgment and lack of motivation to innovate or take calculated risks (Palmer et al.,2021). This can also cause stress relations with employees, co-founders, and investors because an entrepreneur may eventually become less communicative or over-critical.

In literal terms, it can greatly affect the physical system. For example, entrepreneurs may experience chronic fatigue, insomnia, or some other illness such as hypertension and gastrointestinal complaints. When physical well-being is compromised, it would be difficult to manage the daily functions of the business, which again becomes a cause of stress and further leads to low productivity. Severe prolonged effects may result in serious health issues like cardiovascular diseases (Khammissa et al.,2022).

Burnout intellectually handicaps one's critical thinking and creativity—two major skills which entrepreneurs depend on to solve problems and innovate. Psychologically, they may become confused, forget their memory, and lose focus, making it quite difficult for them to process information or make rational business decisions (Khammissa et al.,2022). Entrepreneurs might fall prey to indecisiveness or even hasty decisions simply because of getting rid of the pressure. The degradation in cognitive performance degrades the quality of leadership and strategic direction, which can have long-term negative consequences for the business.

Why Entrepreneurs are Particularly Vulnerable to Burnout

Entrepreneurship is, by nature, often extremely personal and personal so that entrepreneurs invest much emotional, financial, and physical energy into their venture. As soon as the lines of work and personal life become indistinct, it becomes rather difficult for an entrepreneur to actually step back and recharge. Entrepreneurial culture tends to glorify more than usual, hard work, and uncompromising hustle in a manner that it even glorifies this thought: only sacrifice can lead a person towards success. This is where entrepreneurs hear warning signs too late or in most cases, even ignore them (Obschonka et al.,2023).

Lastly, most entrepreneurs spend their time alone in the first years of their business and often have no support apparatus in place, as workers in the larger organization might. The absence of a mentor, peers, or even stable team to share responsibilities with may then lead to isolation, which will make it more challenging to handle stressful conditions and prevent eventual burnout (Khammissa et al.,2022).

In conclusion, burnout is one of those prevalent problems in the entrepreneurial world that, if not arrested in time, can seriously retard personal and business success. Understanding the stages of burnout and recognizing its symptoms early on can help entrepreneurs take proactive steps against its damaging effects.

RISK FACTORS CONTRIBUTING TO ENTREPRENEURIAL BURNOUT

Entrepreneurial burnout is not an independent syndrome but is, instead, the consequence of several interacting risk factors. Stress resulting from entrepreneurship and personal-environmental factors can lead entrepreneurs toward mental and physical exhaustion (Obschonka et al.,2023). Knowledge of these risk factors is essential to mitigating burnout and ensuring sustainable business practices. The following sections summarize some of the largest contributors to entrepreneurial burnout.

Personality Traits and Perfectionism

The personality traits of entrepreneurs are some that probably predispose them to burnout. For example, perfectionism is one of the strongest personality features among entrepreneurs: they often set very high standards for themselves and their business environments (Wach et al.,2021). The propensity to try to be the best is undoubtedly a good quality; however, perfectionists are usually unable to delegate tasks, and in order not to let others make mistakes, they micromanage, convinced that nobody else can do it better. This endless pressure to control every other detail in the business leads to overwork and no ability to set priorities, which eventually causes chronic stress.

Entrepreneurship with high ambition may reach a level where he or she does not even know how to slow down or take a break despite their necessity. Pressure to attain success rapidly will require one to work longer hours with less than adequate time for rest and recoupment. In these conditions, the likelihood of burnout becomes significantly higher. Other desirable traits include resilience and flexibility, as entrepreneurship involves emergent and unstructured activity (Čigarská & Birknerová, 2021). Under such circumstances, it is difficult for people with lower emotional resiliency to cope with the negative aspects which hastens the process of burnout.

Organizational and Industry Pressures

The risk of burnout was critically determined by the external environment in which the entrepreneur works. For instance, industries of tech start-up or high growth sectors require a short while for scaling, a constant innovation, and high competition. In such fast-paced industries, entrepreneurs are compelled to be abreast of industry trends, use advances in technology, and be better than others. Under such conditions, an environment such as this easily predisposes people to burnout without respite (White and Gupta, 2020).

This may be significant in smaller or early-stage businesses. Entrepreneurs often run "one-man bands" whereby one entrepreneur plays all the roles, and these can include positions such as CEO, accountant, and customer service. Working under such conditions leads to very heavy workloads and isolation (Torrès et al.,2022). In addition, entrepreneurs seldom have formal structures nor clear frameworks upon which operations are carried out; therefore, they are sure to make decisions time and again without having information to inform the decisions being made. Such high numbers of decisions can lead to decision fatigue, yet another major factor of burnout.

Work-Life Imbalance

Work-life imbalance is one of the most prevalent risk factors for entrepreneurial burnout. Most entrepreneurs only put so much time and energy in their business, which is usually drawn from their personal lives (Irfan et al.,2023). Traditional employees are likely to have more defined lines between work and home; however, entrepreneurs find that they fall under similar living and working conditions. They can work at untimely hours, plus nights and weekends, and even when they're not actively working on the job, their minds don't turn off and disengage from business things. Not having downtime with an inability to disconnect prevents them from replenishing their energy reserves, hence resulting in chronic fatigue.

Additionally, this pressure to keep performing and scaling the business results in lacking personal relationships, hobbies, and self-care. Eventually, this lack of a balanced life brings dissatisfaction and depletes an entrepreneur's energy (Yester, 2019) The whole life can be felt to have been turned into an investment for work, which gradually leads to worse stress. When there is no chance to rest or for creativity or interaction with people, the psychological burden can grow too heavy to bear.

Isolation and Lack of Support Systems

Entrepreneurship generally turns into a lonely affair, especially for those involved in small-scale businesses or new ventures lacking adequate support staff. Indeed, entrepreneurs have to bear the entire burden of the success or failure of the business on their own shoulders, which can lead to feelings of isolation (Neneh, 2024). It leaves the entrepreneur with no systems such as managers, departments of human resources, or any mentor who will have them look to guidance and feedback from; the latter only adds to the burden of lack of reliability.

Entrepreneurs are also less likely to seek assistance from other entrepreneurs because they fear admitting to stress or burnout may be perceived as weakness. Lack of stress expression continually accumulates with no venue for relief. When neither mentorship nor teamwork exists, complexity in such issues leaves the entrepreneur to struggle alone through problems that most likely translate to mental and emotional exhaustion.

Financial and Economic Pressures

One of the big stressors for most entrepreneurs is financial, especially for those who are new to their ventures. It is the uncertainty of a revenue stream, pressure to find funding, and that payroll or operating expense needs to be met-the list goes on and on. Entrepreneurs frequently place on themselves the burden of keeping the business afloat, employees happy and paid, and investors satisfied, so there is an immense level of stress (Irfan et al.,2023).

These financial burdens are compounded by instability in the economy, changes in markets, and the dynamic nature of consumers (Khalatur et al.,2021). For example, an entrepreneur may have to make crucial decisions to adapt to economic times, such as cost-cutting measures or readjusting business policies, which could heighten stressors. The threat of failure cannot be alleviated when one's finances are not secure. Again, this would exacerbate anxiety and emotional stress.

Unrealistic Expectations and High Pressure to Succeed

The internal expectations are usually too difficult for entrepreneurs to meet. Societies glamorize entrepreneurship; the expectation is that prosperous entrepreneurs who deliver high productivity and exceptional value to the market do so through lots of hustle, risk-taking, and continuous innovation of products and processes. Social pressure does have a way of limiting confessions among entrepreneurs when they may be experiencing bottlenecks in their businesses or need to reduce their operations (Ronnie & Philip,2021). A lot of entrepreneurs are also too positive about themselves, with hope against hope that they will never go wrong. This has placed them in much denial wherein they do not look forward to assistance and refuse to delegate as this would most probably lead to exhaustion at all costs.

In addition, investors, stakeholders, and customers may raise high expectations on entrepreneurs for instant growth and continuous improvement. The need to meet these expectations, coupled with a constant fear of disappointing others, greatly enhances stress. Moreover, pressure to deliver instantly without the luxury of much time to ponder or recharge could leave entrepreneurs to their maximum limits, increasing burnout risk (Muenks et al.,2018).

Entrepreneurial burnout, then, is a function of personal traits, environmental pressures, and the demanding nature of business ownership. Without knowing the risk factors for burnout, no entrepreneur can protect well-being or sustain a business over time (Morrish,2019). The key message here is to recognize these risk factors early on so that entrepreneurs can proactively prevent these and thus implement strategies to manage stress loads more effectively.

EFFECTIVE STRESS MANAGEMENT TECHNIQUES

Entrepreneurs need to achieve an equilibrium between personal well-being and business success (Patro & Kumar, 2019). Efficient stress management can protect one from entrepreneur burnout, increase productivity, and promote better mental health for entrepreneurs. Some of the effective techniques for entrepreneurs that reduce the level of entrepreneurial stress are as mentioned below.

Prioritizing Work-Life Balance

To avoid burnout and sustain entrepreneurship in the long run, an entrepreneur has to achieve a healthy work-life balance. For most entrepreneurs, work and personal life become one, but separation is much needed (Patro & Kumar, 2019). Experts have clearly said that scheduling regular breaks, setting defined working hours can help not get into the overwork cycle that becomes constant. Even a short break for a vacation or an entire day for a business can be refreshing, thereby ensuring that returns are better made in terms of decisions and productivity.

Besides out-of-work life, personal relationships and activities may keep entrepreneurs vital for the time being and give their lives a sense of purpose. One can spend quality time with family or pursue their hobbies on sports or yoga, which is convenient and healthy. An entrepreneur with work hours and free time will be able to recharge and not feel overworked and get ready for burnout.

Time Management and Delegation

Among the skills that reduce entrepreneurial stress is effectively managing time. Getting overwhelmed is very easy simply because many entrepreneurs are handling numerous tasks in a single day (Holman et al.,2018). Prioritizing what is urgent and important reduces the mental load and makes workloads easier to deal with. For instance, to-do lists, calendars, and project management software can help entrepreneurs keep things on track since they focus on the critical tasks that are done without overwhelming them.

Delegation of authority is one of the critical aspects of time management. Many entrepreneurs become victims of doing everything themselves, thinking only they know better than to do the job right. This brings undue stress and, at times, burnout (niffin et al.,2021). Freeing one's time to think and formulate decisions on high-level thinking by delegating to employees or even hiring someone to pay the bills, do accounting, marketing, or administration is a plus. Letting other people handle certain tasks frees you up to focus on other activities and empowers the team for a collaborative environment.

Mindfulness and Relaxation Skills

Mindfulness and relaxation techniques can manage stress very amply and improve mental clarity. Meditation, deep breathing exercise, and mindfulness can help entrepreneurs remain grounded, reduce anxiety, and effectively work under highly stressful situations by giving them a chance to hunker down (Luberto et al.,2020). Mindfulness encourages an individual to focus on the present moment instead of getting drowned in the numerous tasks ahead, which increases mental resilience and better emotional regulation (Neneh, 2024).

Other relaxation techniques, such as yoga and progressive muscle relaxation, would help entrepreneurs to unwind physically and mentally. Engaging in such practices within a regular schedule helps entrepreneurs take control of their level of stress. Even a few minutes each day spent in deep breathing exercises can help relieve stress and improve concentration.

Developing a Support Network

A very effective means through which entrepreneurial stress can be managed even better is through a strong support network (Boon&Biron,2016). Entrepreneurs experience much isolation, especially at the initial stages of any business. Isolation tends to increase stress and feelings of burnout. Entrepreneur connections with mentors or business coaches can offer valuable advice, feedback, and emotional support. Through sharing experiences and challenges, entrepreneurs can learn new insights, strategies for coping with stress, and the feeling that one is not alone in their journey.

Another important factor is a positive work culture. The entrepreneur should communicate with the team transparently, and cooperation and criticism must be promoted. A facilitative team can divide the workload, introduce new concepts, and provide emotional support to the entrepreneur (Neneh,2024). Consequently, stress levels can be reduced on the entrepreneur's side. Having a supportive and understanding network while navigating life as an entrepreneur is often highly necessary.

Physical Health and Exercise

Another significant relationship is the direct connection between physical health and mental well-being; exercise is certainly one of the best ways to manage stress. Exercise releases endorphins, a natural mood lift, and reduces the production of hormones that cause stress, like cortisol (Oaten & Cheng,2007). This includes running, yoga, or even a walk at work to improve energy levels, focus, or stress relief.

Healthy nutrition, appropriate sleep, and minimal intake of caffeine or alcohol are also factors of physical fitness. Because stress tends to weigh them down even more and productivity is impaired when a person's physical well-being is unhealthy, entrepreneurs have to learn to get into a healthy balance so that their business goes well (Luberto et al.,2020). A good entrepreneur treats his or her physical well-being as they treat the business-that is, optimal well-being results in greater performance and sounder decision-making.

Setting Realistic Expectations and Boundaries

One of the most common causes of entrepreneurial burnout is having inflated expectations of what it takes to be successful. For one, entrepreneurs often set themselves and their business ventures quite high ceilings, with such expectations forming an adhesive nonstop feeling that stress may accompany. Entrepreneurs should set realistic, achievable goals and be aware that a successful business takes time to establish (Ronnie & Philip, 2021).

Even entrepreneurs have to learn how to establish boundaries with clients, investors, and even themselves. This involves laying down limits on working hours, setting clear expectations on the part of stakeholders, and knowing what to say "no" when necessary. Boundaries help avoid overcommitment and allow entrepreneurs to maintain a work-life balance.

Professional Help and Counselling

Entrepreneurs suffering from overused stress or burnout may require professional assistance. Counselling, therapy, or coaching will provide entrepreneurs with more means of keeping their stress levels reduced and conquering a number of buried emotional or psychological issues. Cognitive-behavioral therapy (CBT), as well as other types of therapies, are likely to help change distorted thought patterns and coping techniques, as well as anxiety (Martin, 2013).

Entrepreneurially focused counselling or coaching can be very helpful based on the topic. It deals with entrepreneurial challenges that business owners only encounter. Such professionals can offer insight on how to better manage the journey of entrepreneurship while keeping one's well-being intact.

Developing Resilience and Emotional Intelligence

Resilience is one of the most essential attributes for entrepreneurs to develop dynamic adjustment and bounce back responses in respect of obstacles and setbacks. Thus, entrepreneurs should focus on developing resilient personalities in the sense of learning not to treat challenges as a source of threat but rather as opportunities for growth (Neneh, 2024). Cultivation of a learning mentality from failure and flexibility can reduce the emotional consequences of obstacles and keep entrepreneurs motivated.

Another great factor to consider is emotional intelligence (EI), or EI if you like, in stress management. The more the entrepreneur mastered EI, the better he was at understanding himself and others and managing his emotions and feelings and those of others. In fact, this is quite useful in situations when there are greater needs for empathy and self-awareness leading to better communication and conflict resolution (Holman et al., 2018).

Effective stress management strategies are used by entrepreneurs in an effective attempt to face the inevitable difficulties of a business. Indeed, while better time management, mindfulness, physical health, and building a strong support network may keep burnout at bay, they are a barrier to long-term success. Good health ensures that one is well as he or she lays the basis for a thriving business.

BUILDING RESILIENCE: PREVENTING BURNOUT BEFORE IT HAPPENS

One of the factors in resilience is the ability to regain strength while trying to recover from setbacks or challenges, adaptation, and maintaining a secure state of mental soundness even under highly stressed circumstances (Mahmoud & Rothenberger, 2019). For entrepreneurs, resilience building is very important in constructing the impetus of preventing burnout before it happens. All the uncertainties, pressure, and risks that go with entrepreneurship built resilience as a means of having the mental and emotional capacity to face an eldritch circumstance without collapsing into exhaustion and overwhelm (Paiva-Schwanz et al.,2022). Encouraging the production of resilience from an early stage will mean that entrepreneurs can prevent burnout and be equipped with the correct mindset that may lead to sustainable growth and success.

Cultivating a Growth Mindset

Adopting a growth mindset is undoubtedly one of the key strategies for developing resilience. For entrepreneurs with a growth mindset, the challenges and failures are viewed as learning and development opportunities, not threats to their success. This lessens the level of the emotional toll that setbacks could take; entrepreneurs begin to learn how to regard every obstacle as a steppingstone towards betterment (Muenks et al.,2018). It not only strengthens the elasticity of resilience but also creates innovation and creativity, which are the nucleus of entrepreneurship.

Growing in one's mindset is practicing reframing one's notion of negatives to experience something rather than dwelling on mistakes (Aguilar, 2018). The habit of asking, "What can I learn from this experience?" will help an entrepreneur build mental resilience and keep them focused on long-term growth instead of short-term setbacks. This mindset keeps the entrepreneurs motivated and optimistic even in adverse situations.

Developing Emotional Awareness and Regulation

Resilience is also a characteristic of emotional awareness and control. An entrepreneur that has emotional awareness controls stress better; because they are attuned to whether they can handle so much at any one time and would take all the necessary steps to control his levels before it gets out of hand. This ability to understand what triggers your emotions, manage a response to stressors, and navigate through difficult situations in life is EI (Mahmoud & Rothenberger, 2019).

Therefore, to develop emotional awareness, entrepreneurs can practice mindfulness and introspection by checking themselves out frequently on the level of their emotional state. Journaling or any form of meditation is a great technique to help an entrepreneur refine their perception of what is causing them stress (Neneh, 2024). After emotional awareness is created, entrepreneurs should learn to regulate their emotions by having healthier coping behaviours like deep breathing, exercise, or talking to others about how they feel. Being able to deal and administer control over emotions results in lower tendencies of burnout since no stress will have accumulated over time.

Building a Strong Support System

Entrepreneurship can be a rather isolated experience, but resilience is often strengthened through support from others. Building a strong network of mentors, peers, and advisors helps to provide entrepreneurs with precious insight, encouragement, and emotional support during difficult moments (Mahmoud & Rothenberger,2019). Having a supportive system reduces feelings of isolation and gives entrepreneurs a place to air struggles, to brainstorm solutions, and to receive feedback.

The bottom line for entrepreneurs is having relations with individuals who understand the competitive struggles entrepreneurs face as business owners (Khalatur et al.,2021). They often have exceptional networking opportunities when networking with other entrepreneurs or joining mastermind groups, wherein they get to relate to similar experiences and specific advice on resolving entrepreneurial stress. There are also the strong personal relationships an entrepreneur should maintain with his family and friends so that the entrepreneur can have a well-rounded support system both professionally and personally.

Setting Clear Boundaries and Managing Expectations

Probably the most effective way of preventing burnout is through the establishment of clear boundaries within work life. Entrepreneurs, in truth, tend to over-commit themselves towards their business and lead to chronic stress and exhaustion (Ksreiner et al.,2009). The ability to say "no" to non-essential things and set specific working hours limits is crucial for an entrepreneur to maintain this necessary balance and avoid overwork. This can also keep a client, investor, or employee informed of your boundaries so that their expectations are realistic in terms of time and availability, and even performance.

Besides the external limits, entrepreneurs have to set realistic expectations on themselves. Many entrepreneurs get involved in the process that makes them think they must exhaust themselves to succeed (Čigarská & Birknerová, 2021). It cannot continue for long because entrepreneurs soon get overworked and exhausted. Focus on setting achievable goals, along with setting milestones that take into account available time and resources, helps entrepreneurs recognize that growth is gradual and setbacks are but natural to the journey, and hence unneeded stress will be reduced and resilience will increase.

Practicing Self-Care and Prioritizing Well-Being

One of the most important components of resilience is self-care. This is habitually neglected in busy entrepreneurs. Preventing burnout requires regular attention to physical, mental, and emotional wellbeing (Søvold et al.,2021). Very simple practices such as getting enough sleep, eating a healthy diet, and exercising regularly mean dramatically improved energy levels and reduced stress. Entrepreneurs who take care of their wellness and wellbeing will be able to tackle challenges clear-headed and concentrated to maintain control over the work (Dalphon, 2019).

Aside from health problems, mental self-care practices such as mindfulness, meditation, or therapy may also protect the entrepreneur from feelings of uncertainty linked to entrepreneurship (Luberto et al.,2020). This may bring resilience through the lessened tension, emotion management, and prevention of the 'build-up' of stress. The more frequently the entrepreneur can obtain a stream of personal care moments, the more enduring the drivers will be: motivation, creativity, and passion.

Learning to Embrace Flexibility and Adaptability

Resilience means flexibility. Ideally, an entrepreneur should be flexible in thought, eager to change direction when there is a need to do so, and able to adapt quickly to an environment that will present uncertainty (Karman, 2020). The route of the entrepreneur, therefore, is mostly zigzag; the resilience of the entrepreneurs is a higher probability that such a flexible entrepreneur will come out victorious.

This means adapting to change and for entrepreneurs to achieve the virtues of adaptability, they must be mindful of continuous learning or improvement (Shim & Lee, 2019). Instead of becoming fixed in their approach, entrepreneurs must let their minds open up to new ideas, feedback, and alternative solutions (Shim & Lee, 2019). This makes entrepreneurs better equipped to handle challenges and avoid the disappointment that is often ushered in by unwarranted changes. Adaptability builds resilience by allowing innovativeness and, thus, maintaining a leadership edge in a rapidly evolving market.

Continuous Learning and Skill Development

Entrepreneurs who continuously learn and develop their skills are better positioned to deal with the complexity of running a business. Continuous learning enables entrepreneurs to be in harmony with industry trends and business strategies as well as suitable personal development (Muenks et al., 2018). This proactive attitude not only strengthens resilience through increased confidence and competence but equips one with tools and skills that will enable him or her to better face more challenges.

Through attending workshops or course enrollment, mentoring, and others, continuous learning would cultivate a growth mentality and ensure that entrepreneurs always move forward from what they have learned earlier (Holman et al., 2018). It is through curiosity and adaptability that entrepreneurs could better navigate the uncertainty of business ownership and nurture their mental well-being.

Resilience for the entrepreneur is built to prevent burnout, sustain well-being, and endure long-term periods. Through emotional intelligence, setting boundaries, managing their emotions, and taking care of themselves, entrepreneurs will put together the necessary mental and emotional strength needed to navigate the entrepreneurial journey successfully. A resilient entrepreneur copes with stress and change and can achieve success without giving up on personal well-being (Shim & Lee, 2019).

THE ROLE OF ORGANIZATIONAL SUPPORT IN BURNOUT PREVENTION

Organizational support is the most influential factor in preventing burnout among entrepreneurs. It is highly important in cases where an entrepreneur is working under a bigger business structure or managing a staff of employees. An organization's developed culture, resources, and systems can significantly influence how an entrepreneur handles stress while striving to maintain a normal work-life balance (Xu & Yang, 2021). Organizational support practices help reduce the risk of burnout through well-being, teaming, and sustainable work practices (Halbesleben & Wheeler, 2015). This section discusses how organizational support contributes to burnout prevention by entrepreneurs and their teams.

Fostering a Supportive Organizational Culture

A supportive organizational culture is the foundation for preventing burnout. Openness between the entrepreneur and the employee is fostered by an organization that generates a team culture where people feel collaboration, open communication, and mutual respect between oneself and others (Wu, G et al.,2018). It helps to overcome the type of isolation commonly experienced by entrepreneurs, especially when at the nascent stages of the business. A great work culture encourages openness and offers a safe space in which people can share challenges, ask for advice, and come up with solutions (Dalphon,2019).

Then, organizational leaders will set the tone for this culture. If leaders can give examples of taking breaks, prioritizing work-life balance, and managing their stress, then messages are conveyed that well-being is important (Wu, G et al.,2018). This empowers entrepreneurs to respond likewise, not overworking themselves or their teams. A culture that emphasizes mental health and work-life balance acts as a buffer for burnout.

Access to Resources and Tools

The second aspect that determines whether there will not be burnout is the availability of the organizational resources and tools needed. This is where successful entrepreneurs, especially those managing teams, gain the much-needed availability of all the tools required to delegate, automate, and streamline business operations (García-Martínez et al.,2020). When entrepreneurs are thoroughly swamped with administration work and overwhelmed by the need to perform every single item individually, they develop much stress. They are on the verge of burnout quickly. Through technological tools, administrative assistance, or even mentorship programs, organizational support should help lighten the workload, enabling entrepreneurs to cope with high-priority tasks.

More resources, such as mental health support, counseling services, and wellness programs, may give entrepreneurs the capacity to manage stress effectively (Machovec,2020). Most organizations provide employee assistance programs to offer confidential support and service for mental health concerns, including stress management and other personal problems. In this regard, many organizations demonstrate care for their employees or entrepreneurs, hence reducing burnout.

Encouraging Healthy Work-Life Integration

Healthy work-life integration is important in preventing burnout, and organizations are generally key to supporting this integration. Entrepreneurs often find themselves without boundaries between their work and personal lives. They often end up with long hours, constant stress, and exhaustion to the extent that it becomes full-time employment (García-Martínez et al.,2020). Organizations can help mitigate this by encouraging flexible working arrangements, like remote work options, flexible hours, or the ability to take time off when needed.

In the workplace, an organization that genuinely shows a preference for sleep and recovery empowers entrepreneurs to take their edge off freely without any regret for being within the norms, and employees can recharge (Dalphon,2019). Organizational policies that support work-life integration reduce stress, enhance productivity, and are good for long-term well-being.

Providing Mentorship and Guidance

Mentorship and mentoring are critical forms of organizational support that may provide sustenance against the entrepreneurial burnout scenario. Entrepreneurs, and more so new entrants into entrepreneurship, face complex problems and multiple decisions at a single point in time, and may easily become overwhelmed by these complexities (Burgess et al.,2018). Access to mentors or advisory services within an organization provides entrepreneurs with the wisdom and support they may need in dealing with critical outcomes of these challenges. A mentor can advise them in day-to-day situations, share lessons from their own experiences, and assist in the development of resilience in entrepreneurs so that they may be capable of overcoming problems and arising as potential winners in a competitive game (Ramani et al.,2024). Mentorship programs also act as an area for personal development to take place together with professional development, and entrepreneurs find encouraging room to learn and grow professionally (Lin & Reddy, 2019). This support reduces pressure in decision-making but further empowers entrepreneurs to take charge of their businesses confidently. Guiding the entrepreneurs through these relationships ensures fewer anxieties about the sustainability of business ventures but leans on long-term sustainability.

Building a Collaborative Team Environment

Entrepreneurs would feel frustrated because they have to do everything for themselves; a good team environment within an organization will ease the burden as it distributes all the roles and fosters teamwork. When there is a team that can be relied upon, then entrepreneurs can delegate some tasks, focus on high-level strategic decisions, and reduce this pressure of managing everything in the business (Ramani et al.,2024).

Helping the entrepreneurs perform well and succeed by fostering collaboration as well as teamwork. Promoting open communication, periodic feedback, and shared goals and objectives make them feel that they belong to a team responsible for their work, thus making it easier to manage stress and avoid burnout (Noguera et al.,2018). Entrepreneurs who feel that their teams support them will be more likely to sustain their enthusiasm and passion for their jobs since they are relieved of having constant pressure to meet individual performance requirements.

Promoting Career Development and Growth

The other very important way the organization can prevent burnout is through career development and growth. An entrepreneur who has opportunities for continuous learning, training, and growth is most likely to be engaged, motivated, and inspired at work. When the organizations invest in the development of their entrepreneurs, it creates a sense of value and purpose and helps reduce feelings of stagnation or burnout.

Providing the scope for growth, training in leadership or attending industry events helps a budding entrepreneur build entrepreneurial capability but keeps him grounded to long-term goals (Ramani et al.,2024). It thus is an investment in growth that brings about a sense of purpose and progress, countering the frustration and exhaustion typical of burnout.

Organizational support is one of the key factors for entrepreneur burnout. Through the encouragement of a supportive culture, providing resources, work-life balance, mentorship, and facilitating collaboration, support by organizations will result in an environment that allows entrepreneurs to survive. With the right support, entrepreneurs can fight off stress and challenges, as well as prevent burnout.

TECHNOLOGICAL TOOLS FOR MANAGING STRESS

Entrepreneurship in today's fast-paced business world is turning to technological tools that help to manage stress and enhance one's life well-being. These can significantly support different organizations of entrepreneurship where one can be able to take care of their mental well-being, keep track of tasks, or even keep in good work-life balance. This section will explore several technological solutions for managing stress effectively and minimizing the risk of burnout among entrepreneurs.

Mental Health and Mindfulness Apps

Mental health and mindfulness applications have become popular tools to manage stress. These applications provide guided meditations, mindfulness exercises, and resources for mental health, which may help entrepreneurs find better ways of coping. Headspace, Calm, and Insight Timer are applications that have structured programs for relaxation and mindfulness, which users can easily fit into their daily schedule (Burgess et al.,2018).

The frequent application of such apps would, above all, enable businesspeople to better get to know the emotions and thoughts that happen in their brains; alleviate tension; and stabilize feelings (Tereso et al.,2019). In giving a few minutes each day to practice mindfulness, businesspeople can cultivate attention and resilience, thereby gaining the energy to take up tasks and remain positive toward them.

Task and Project Management Tools

The best stress-reducing management of work and projects for entrepreneurs is when they keep themselves organized and focused; some applications like Trello, Asana, or Monday.com, which can divide projects into smaller tasks and have deadlines that break and track the progress at any time needed, help avoid massive pressure and a sense of accomplishment in completing tasks (Tereso et al.,2019).

Moreover, these tools will enable teams to work in concerts, or to share the work and communicate more coherently. The clear overview of projects and tasks allows entrepreneurs to allocate their time and resources more effectively in order to reduce the risk of burnout caused by disorganization and unchecked deadlines (Heigermoser et al.,2019).

Time Management and Productivity Apps

Time management and productivity apps: Even entrepreneurs trying to maximize their efficiency while reducing stress, like every other category of user, require tools like Todoist, RescueTime, and Focus@Will to guide actions in prioritizing tasks, setting goals, and monitoring productivity trends. More so, identifying patterns of time-wasting habits and streamlining workflows are some of the ways that help entrepreneurs create a balanced schedule capable of giving room to breaks and downtime.

Apps can also use techniques such as the Pomodoro Technique, where people work in focused intervals followed by short breaks (Heigermoser et al.,2019). This kind of structured approach not only enhances productivity but also ensures that entrepreneurs take necessary breaks to recharge, reducing the possibilities of burnout.

Communication and Collaboration Platforms

Communication is key while trying to reduce stress in entrepreneurship, especially in handling a team. Slack, Microsoft Teams, and Zoom are some websites that enable smooth communication and cooperation and help entrepreneurs stay connected with their teams while reducing the stress of constantly attending meetings. These tools can enable instant exchange of ideas, feedback, and updated information that can further facilitate teamwork and increase efficiency (Ansell & Gash,2018).

Communication can be streamlined to ensure fewer misunderstandings and a cooperative environment. Such support networks can relieve pressure associated with running a business, and sharing workloads is eased and problems together are navigated.

Health and Fitness Tracking Devices

Health and fitness tracking devices, such as smartwatches and fitness bands, significantly help in the management of stress to ensure good physical health. The Fitbit and Apple Watch enable such an understanding by providing data on the level of physical activity, heart rate, and sleep patterns (Burgess et al.,2018). Regular exercise keeps away stress and uplifts the mood, and entrepreneurs encourage activity throughout the day.

Entrepreneurs can maintain personal health and wellness when they are capable of formulating goals and monitoring progress in fitness, which leads to exercise in daily life. Furthermore, some devices also remind the entrepreneur to take a break, breathe, or even stretch, which develops self-care habits and prevents burnout in the end.

Digital Journaling and Reflection Tools

Digital journaling and reflection tools help entrepreneurs cope with their thoughts and feelings, provide an outlet to deal with their stress levels, and applications such as Day One, Journey, and Penzu, which users can use to record their thought and reflect the experiences of the day or track their emotional well-being over time (Marion & Fixson, 2021). This should make entrepreneurs better aware of themselves, realize what stressors are, and produce strategies for coping.

Therefore, reflecting on the experiences allows entrepreneurs to celebrate some achievements and progress, so they are motivated and resilient. Digital journaling also assists in therapeutic discharge when one states his/her feelings and drives away anxiety.

Online Support Communities and Forums

Virtual support communities and forums provide entrepreneurs with an avenue to connect with peers who face similar issues. Sites like Reddit, LinkedIn groups, and entrepreneur-specific forums offer access to valuable resources and advice as well as a feeling of community. Interacting with other people in such spaces can also reduce feelings of isolation and gives them a little more of the motivation they need when things get tough (Ansell & Gash,2018).

Through such online websites, entrepreneurs share one another's issues, seeking opinions from each other based on past experiences. This relatability with others who know how painful it is to be an entrepreneur equips people with additional coping mechanisms and newly found perspectives that increase resistance to stress.

The business owner is instead empowered to manage stress, a highly precious resource in navigating the troubles of business ownership (Chang & Benson,2022).Some are apps dedicated to mental health and mindfulness while others specialize in task management and communication; they all empower the individual to oversee one's stress and living needs. Moreover, it can help entrepreneurs reduce the risk of being burnt out and support them to find a more sustainable way toward success.

FUTURE TRENDS IN ENTREPRENEURIAL STRESS MANAGEMENT

The future of entrepreneurship is changing just like the various methods and technologies used to manage stress and avoid burnout. It means today's entrepreneur needs to understand some of these tendencies to be sure they embrace sustainable practices in their business ventures. In this section, we explore emerging trends that will significantly shape how entrepreneurs deal with stress soon.

Increased Integration of Artificial Intelligence (AI)

AI integration will soon change the way entrepreneurs relate to their mental health and productivity (Brynjolfsson & McAfee,2017). Applications mustered by AI will give specific insights regarding any pattern seen in their behavior, hence giving those recommendations for stress management and wellbeing. For example, if an algorithm spots patterns in a person, like habits at work, emotional states, and productivity, it can suggest exercises in mindfulness, remind people to take a break, or even optimize working schedules.

Chatbots and other AI-based virtual assistants can also provide immediate help for mental wellbeing, giving the required resources and techniques at the point of maximum stress. This will enable entrepreneurs to seek help at the point where they need it most by breaking the stigma of mental health and spreading the culture of well-being.

Virtual Reality (VR) for Stress Relief

Virtual reality is emerging as an intense tool for stress relief and mental wellbeing. VR experiences transport you to calm environments with the intention of helping their users relax and be mindful in an immersive fashion. Entrepreneurs will increasingly seek out VR meditation or stress relief programs to take quick mental breaks from the pressures of running a business (Tarrant et al.,2018).

Team training or building can be held in the virtual reality setting, hence cultivating teamwork and interaction among teams that work remotely (Yin, J. et al.,2020). By creating interactive and engaging environments, VR will help improve the staff's dynamics while offering a place for stress relief.

Enhanced Focus on Employee Well-Being

Only when mental health is much better understood, will an organization's bottom line rely more and more on ensuring that the well-being of employees is addressed as a fundamental part of their success. Indeed, organizations will invest much more seriously into the development of supportive work environments which foster holistic well-being, such as work-life balance and mental health. Such a trend will call upon entrepreneurs to create more holistic well-being programs that should feature mental health resources and wellness initiatives besides flexible work arrangements (Chang & Benson,2022).

Also, companies can formulate policies such as mandatory mental health days, regular check-ins on wellness, and mental health training of their managers. In response to the onset of burnout symptoms within their teams, these measures would avoid the shortage of a productive workforce in any given company. This proactivity in well-being measures would help develop a culture that is supportive with an enabling environment to foster entrepreneurship without jeopardizing mental health.

Emphasis on Work-Life Integration

This encompasses more and more entrepreneurs and organizations adopting flexible work arrangements because the concept of work-life integration is now becoming popular. While traditional work-life balance has the tendency to separate work and personal life, there should be a higher-fluid approach that blends work and personal responsibilities in an easy and flowing manner (Burgess et al.,2018).

This will raise flexible hours of work, remote working opportunities, and ability to carry out personal activities during working hours. The entrepreneur embracing work-life integration can easily manage stress, meaning all the scheduling issues can be solved according to personal and professional realms (Hensellek & Puchala,2021). In actuality, this shift can increase employee satisfaction and reduce burnout.

Development of Holistic Wellness Platforms

More holistic wellness platforms are likely to emerge in the future, integrating various resources and services into one solution. Stand-alone operational platforms may offer several services, including mental health support, fitness tracking capabilities, nutrition advice, and stress management resources, all under one roof (Casillo et al.,2024).

Giving these platforms a holistic view on well-being will enable entrepreneurs to take ownership of their mental health more proactively. This will allow its users to be monitored on both physical and emotional aspects, set goals, and access tailored resources, thus creating a much more personalistic approach in dealing with stress.

Increasing Popularity of Remote Work and Digital Nomadism

An essential conclusion of the rise of remote work and digital nomadism is that entrepreneurs increasingly need to manage stress in new ways. As individuals will focus on working flexibly, it will be an avenue to balance their responsibilities to professional life and ensure good health and well-being (Hensellek & Puchala,2021). This will reflect the creation of new resources and communities that provide support to remote workers in managing their stress better, connecting them with other people, and fostering their productivity.

A remote lifestyle for entrepreneurship will offer diverse digital resources or tools to support well-being, including virtual co-working spaces, online support groups, and workshops with a focus on mental health and productivity (Thompson,2019). This group environment may well help to counteract isolation -one of the most criticized negatives of remote work-making them a community which helps to manage stress.

Focus on Mindfulness and Mental Health Education

As mental wellness continues to rise in public awareness, so will there be increased mindfulness and education taught in each entrepreneurship program or business school (Burgess et al.,2018). Future entrepreneurs will be better equipped to empower themselves with healthy mental practices as part of their daily functions.

Stress management and mental well-being will be regular work packages of workshops, training programs, and education tools used in curricula on entrepreneurship. Future entrepreneurs will, therefore, be equipped early with the best practices for entrepreneurial work when they face the problems of running a business without holding back their mental well-being (Khalatur et al.,2021).

Future management of entrepreneurial stress through technology, emphasizing greater well-being and flexibility at work. With the emergence of AI, VR, and wellness platforms, entrepreneurs will be armed with more innovative means that support mental health and productivity. Moreover, employee well-being and mindfulness education will be highly valued; this powers entrepreneurs to develop a healthier working environment, reducing burnout and enabling long-term success. Entrepreneurial longevity, in turn, will depend on embracing these trends.

CONCLUSION

Taking a conclusion, managing stress and preventing burnout is very important for entrepreneurs involved in business complexities. As has been explored in this chapter, entrepreneurial journey is inherently characterized by challenges that lead to the highest levels of stress and, subsequently, to burnout. What then is the nature of entrepreneurial stress? On what factors does burnout emerge? When acquainted with all the above, people can proactively hold onto their mental health and better their well-being.

With proper stress management practices ranging from mindfulness to organizational support, several entrepreneurial burnout risks can be significantly mitigated. At a similar time, the use of technological tools such as mental health apps, project management software, and communication platforms will help entrepreneurs improve efficiency, work well, and enhance overall well-being (Engel et al.,2021). These tools enable entrepreneurs to adopt healthier habits, to create more balanced work environments, and to promote the culture of mutual support among the employees of an organization.

Looking ahead, the trends in stress management for the future seem to be highly inclined toward a holistic approach to well-being, AI integration, and flexible work. Since the entrepreneurial landscape contains these very entrepreneurs, the innovations arising from these future trends would present them with new avenues in effectively managing stress (Lek et al.,2020). Entrepreneurial resilience and adaptability to job demands would thus arise as a result of embracing some of these trends while maintaining a sustainable approach to work.

At the most basic level, this involves giving careful attention to one's mental health and well-being, as this is not just a personal responsibility but also something critical to any long-term success in business. When entrepreneurs assume ownership over stress, they initiate ripples in their own lives and those of the teams and organizations they lead. A culture of well-being for entrepreneurs has the potential to make them role models for others, compelling others to pay attention to their mental health, and, in doing so, contribute to a healthier and more productive entrepreneurial ecosystem. It won't be easy; however, with all the right tools and strategies in place, entrepreneurs will be able to play out their path in resilience, confidence, and renewed purpose.

REFERENCES

Aguilar, E. (2018). *Onward: Cultivating emotional resilience in educators*. John Wiley & Sons. DOI: 10.1002/9781119441731

Ansell, C., & Gash, A. (2018). Collaborative platforms as a governance strategy. *Journal of Public Administration: Research and Theory*, 28(1), 16–32. DOI: 10.1093/jopart/mux030

Boon, C., & Biron, M. (2016). Temporal issues in person–organization fit, person–job fit and turnover: The role of leader–member exchange. *Human Relations*, 69(12), 2177–2200. DOI: 10.1177/0018726716636945 PMID: 27904171

Brynjolfsson, E., & Mcafee, A. N. D. R. E. W. (2017). Artificial intelligence, for real. *Harvard Business Review*, 1, 1–31.

Burgess, A., van Diggele, C., & Mellis, C. (2018). Mentorship in the health professions: A review. *The Clinical Teacher*, 15(3), 197–202. DOI: 10.1111/tct.12756 PMID: 29318730

Casillo, M., Cecere, L., Colace, F., Lorusso, A., & Santaniello, D. (2024). Integrating the Internet of Things (IoT) in SPA Medicine: Innovations and challenges in digital wellness. *Computers*, 13(3), 67. DOI: 10.3390/computers13030067

Chang, W. L., & Benson, V. (2022). Jigsaw teaching method for collaboration on cloud platforms. *Innovations in Education and Teaching International*, 59(1), 24–36. DOI: 10.1080/14703297.2020.1792332

) Čigarská, B. N., & Birknerová, Z. (2021). Burnout syndrome and Coping strategies: knowledge, approaches, foundations concerning its incidence among entrepreneurs. *THE POPRAD ECONOMIC AND MANAGEMENT*, 98.

Dalphon, H. (2019). Self-care techniques for social workers: Achieving an ethical harmony between work and well-being. *Journal of Human Behavior in the Social Environment*, 29(1), 85–95. DOI: 10.1080/10911359.2018.1481802

Engel, Y., Noordijk, S., Spoelder, A., & van Gelderen, M. (2021). Self-compassion when coping with venture obstacles: Loving-kindness meditation and entrepreneurial fear of failure. *Entrepreneurship Theory and Practice*, 45(2), 263–290. DOI: 10.1177/1042258719890991

García-Martínez, J. A., Rosa-Napal, F. C., Romero-Tabeayo, I., López-Calvo, S., & Fuentes-Abeledo, E. J. (2020). Digital tools and personal learning environments: An analysis in higher education. *Sustainability (Basel)*, 12(19), 8180. DOI: 10.3390/su12198180

Gorgievski, M. J., & Stephan, U. (2016). Advancing the psychology of entrepreneurship: A review of the psychological literature and an introduction. *Applied Psychology*, 65(3), 437–468. DOI: 10.1111/apps.12073

Halbesleben, J. R., & Wheeler, A. R. (2015). To invest or not? The role of coworker support and trust in daily reciprocal gain spirals of helping behavior. *Journal of Management*, 41(6), 1628–1650. DOI: 10.1177/0149206312455246

Heigermoser, D., de Soto, B. G., Abbott, E. L. S., & Chua, D. K. H. (2019). BIM-based Last Planner System tool for improving construction project management. *Automation in Construction*, 104, 246–254. DOI: 10.1016/j.autcon.2019.03.019

) Hensellek, S., & Puchala, N. (2021). The emergence of the digital nomad: A review and analysis of the opportunities and risks of digital nomadism. *The flexible workplace: Coworking and other modern workplace transformations*, 195-214.

Holman, D., Johnson, S., & O'Connor, E. (2018). Stress management interventions: Improving subjective psychological well-being in the workplace. *Handbook of well-being*, 1-13.

Irfan, M., Khalid, R. A., Kaka Khel, S. S. U. H., Maqsoom, A., & Sherani, I. K. (2023). Impact of work–life balance with the role of organizational support and job burnout on project performance. *Engineering, Construction, and Architectural Management*, 30(1), 154–171. DOI: 10.1108/ECAM-04-2021-0316

Karman, A. (2020). Flexibility, coping capacity and resilience of organizations: Between synergy and support. *Journal of Organizational Change Management*, 33(5), 883–907. DOI: 10.1108/JOCM-10-2019-0305

) Khalatur, S., Masiuk, Y., Kachula, S., Brovko, L., Karamushka, O., & Shramko, I. (2021). Entrepreneurship development management in the context of economic security. *Entrepreneurship and sustainability issues*, 9(1), 558.

Khammissa, R. A., Nemutandani, S., Feller, G., Lemmer, J., & Feller, L. (2022). Burnout phenomenon: Neurophysiological factors, clinical features, and aspects of management. *The Journal of International Medical Research*, 50(9), 03000605221106428. DOI: 10.1177/03000605221106428 PMID: 36113033

Kniffin, K. M., Narayanan, J., Anseel, F., Antonakis, J., Ashford, S. P., Bakker, A. B., Bamberger, P., Bapuji, H., Bhave, D. P., Choi, V. K., Creary, S. J., Demerouti, E., Flynn, F. J., Gelfand, M. J., Greer, L. L., Johns, G., Kesebir, S., Klein, P. G., Lee, S. Y., & Vugt, M. V. (2021). COVID-19 and the workplace: Implications, issues, and insights for future research and action. *The American Psychologist*, 76(1), 63–77. DOI: 10.1037/amp0000716 PMID: 32772537

Kreiner, G. E., Hollensbe, E. C., & Sheep, M. L. (2009). Balancing borders and bridges: Negotiating the work-home interface via boundary work tactics. *Academy of Management Journal*, 52(4), 704–730. DOI: 10.5465/amj.2009.43669916

) Kuruppu, A. (2024). Small Business Burnout: Reversing the Entrepreneurial Exit.

Lee, S. H., Patel, P. C., & Phan, P. H. (2023). Are the self-employed more stressed? New evidence on an old question. *Journal of Small Business Management*, 61(2), 513–539. DOI: 10.1080/00472778.2020.1796467

Lek, J., Vendrig, A. A., & Schaafsma, F. G. (2020). What are psychosocial risk factors for entrepreneurs to become unfit for work? A qualitative exploration. *Work (Reading, Mass.)*, 67(2), 499–506. DOI: 10.3233/WOR-203299 PMID: 33074213

Lin, J., & Reddy, R. M. (2019). Teaching, mentorship, and coaching in surgical education. *Thoracic Surgery Clinics*, 29(3), 311–320. DOI: 10.1016/j.thorsurg.2019.03.008 PMID: 31235300

Luberto, C. M., Hall, D. L., Park, E. R., Haramati, A., & Cotton, S. (2020). A perspective on the similarities and differences between mindfulness and relaxation. *Global Advances in Health and Medicine : Improving Healthcare Outcomes Worldwide*, 9, 2164956120905597. DOI: 10.1177/2164956120905597 PMID: 32076580

Machovec, G. (2020). Selected tools and services for analyzing and managing open access journal transformative agreements. *Journal of Library Administration*, 60(3), 301–307. DOI: 10.1080/01930826.2020.1727280

Mahmoud, N. N., & Rothenberger, D. (2019). From burnout to well-being: A focus on resilience. *Clinics in Colon and Rectal Surgery*, 32(06), 415–423. DOI: 10.1055/s-0039-1692710 PMID: 31686993

Marion, T. J., & Fixson, S. K. (2021). The transformation of the innovation process: How digital tools are changing work, collaboration, and organizations in new product development. *Journal of Product Innovation Management*, 38(1), 192–215. DOI: 10.1111/jpim.12547

Martin, A. (2013). (Leuphana Universität Lüneburg, Institut für Mittelstandsforschung, Hrsg.). (2013). Die Beurteilung der Arbeitsbedingungen durch Unternehmer und Arbeitnehmer, Schriften aus dem Institut für Mittelstandsforschung, No. 43, Leuphana Universität Lüneburg, Institut für Mittelstandsforschung. Verfügbar unter: https://www. econstor.eu/bitstream/10419/71296/1/739971433.pdf

Morrish, L. (2019). *Pressure vessels: The epidemic of poor mental health among higher education staff*. Higher Education Policy Institute.

Muenks, K., Wigfield, A., & Eccles, J. S. (2018). I can do this! The development and calibration of children's expectations for success and competence beliefs. *Developmental Review*, 48, 24–39. DOI: 10.1016/j.dr.2018.04.001

Nambisan, S., & Baron, R. A. (2021). On the costs of digital entrepreneurship: Role conflict, stress, and venture performance in digital platform-based ecosystems. *Journal of Business Research*, 125, 520–532. DOI: 10.1016/j.jbusres.2019.06.037

Neneh, B. N. (2024). Why peer support matters: Entrepreneurial stressors, emotional exhaustion, and growth intentions of women entrepreneurs. *Entrepreneurship Research Journal*, 14(3), 985–1019. DOI: 10.1515/erj-2021-0501

Noguera, I., Guerrero-Roldán, A. E., & Masó, R. (2018). Collaborative agile learning in online environments: Strategies for improving team regulation and project management. *Computers & Education*, 116, 110–129. DOI: 10.1016/j.compedu.2017.09.008

Oaten, M., & Cheng, K. (2007). Improvements in self-control from financial monitoring. *Journal of Economic Psychology*, 28(4), 487–501. DOI: 10.1016/j.joep.2006.11.003

Obschonka, M., Pavez, I., Kautonen, T., Kibler, E., Salmela-Aro, K., & Wincent, J. (2023). Job burnout and work engagement in entrepreneurs: How the psychological utility of entrepreneurship drives healthy engagement. *Journal of Business Venturing*, 38(2), 106272. DOI: 10.1016/j.jbusvent.2022.106272

Omrane, A., Kammoun, A., & Seaman, C. (2018). Entrepreneurial burnout: Causes, consequences and way out. *FIIB Business Review*, 7(1), 28–42. DOI: 10.1177/2319714518767805

Paiva-Salisbury, M. L., & Schwanz, K. A. (2022). Building compassion fatigue resilience: Awareness, prevention, and intervention for pre-professionals and current practitioners. *Journal of Health Service Psychology*, 48(1), 39–46. DOI: 10.1007/s42843-022-00054-9 PMID: 35136862

Palmer, C., Kraus, S., Kailer, N., Huber, L., & Öner, Z. H. (2021). Entrepreneurial burnout: A systematic review and research map. *International Journal of Entrepreneurship and Small Business*, 43(3), 438–461. DOI: 10.1504/IJESB.2021.115883

) Patro, C. S., & Kumar, K. S. (2019). Effect of workplace stress management strategies on employees' efficiency. *International journal of scientific development and research*, 4(5), 412-418.

Ramani, S., Kusurkar, R. A., Lyon-Maris, J., Pyörälä, E., Rogers, G. D., Samarasekera, D. D., Taylor, D. C. M., & Ten Cate, O. (2024). Mentorship in health professions education–an AMEE guide for mentors and mentees: AMEE Guide No. 167. *Medical Teacher*, 46(8), 999–1011. DOI: 10.1080/0142159X.2023.2273217 PMID: 37909275

Rauch, A., Fink, M., & Hatak, I. (2018). Stress processes: An essential ingredient in the entrepreneurial process. *The Academy of Management Perspectives*, 32(3), 340–357. DOI: 10.5465/amp.2016.0184

Ronnie, J. B., & Philip, B. (2021). Expectations and what people learn from failure. In *Expectations and actions* (pp. 207–237). Routledge. DOI: 10.4324/9781003150879-10

Satow, L. (2012). *Stress- und Coping-Inventar (SCI)*. Vollständige Test- und Skalendokumentation.

Shim, W., & Lee, S. W. (2019). An agile approach for managing requirements change to improve learning and adaptability. *Journal of Industrial Information Integration*, 14, 16–23. DOI: 10.1016/j.jii.2018.07.005

Søvold, L. E., Naslund, J. A., Kousoulis, A. A., Saxena, S., Qoronfleh, M. W., Grobler, C., & Münter, L. (2021). Prioritizing the mental health and well-being of healthcare workers: An urgent global public health priority. *Frontiers in Public Health*, 9, 679397. DOI: 10.3389/fpubh.2021.679397 PMID: 34026720

Tarrant, J., Viczko, J., & Cope, H. (2018). Virtual reality for anxiety reduction demonstrated by quantitative EEG: A pilot study. *Frontiers in Psychology*, 9, 1280. DOI: 10.3389/fpsyg.2018.01280 PMID: 30087642

Tereso, A., Ribeiro, P., Fernandes, G., Loureiro, I., & Ferreira, M. (2019). Project management practices in private organizations. *Project Management Journal*, 50(1), 6–22. DOI: 10.1177/8756972818810966

) Thompson, B. Y. (2019). The digital nomad lifestyle:(remote) work/leisure balance, privilege, and constructed community. *International journal of the sociology of leisure*, 2(1), 27-42.

Torrès, O., Benzari, A., Fisch, C., Mukerjee, J., Swalhi, A., & Thurik, R. (2022). Risk of burnout in French entrepreneurs during the COVID-19 crisis. *Small Business Economics*, 58(2), 1–23. DOI: 10.1007/s11187-021-00516-2 PMID: 38624594

Wach, D., Stephan, U., Weinberger, E., & Wegge, J. (2021). Entrepreneurs' stressors and well-being: A recovery perspective and diary study. *Journal of Business Venturing*, 36(5), 106016. DOI: 10.1016/j.jbusvent.2020.106016

Wach, D., Stephan, U., Weinberger, E., & Wegge, J. (2021). Entrepreneurs' stressors and well-being: A recovery perspective and diary study. *Journal of Business Venturing*, 36(5), 106016. DOI: 10.1016/j.jbusvent.2020.106016

Wang, Q., Khan, S. N., Sajjad, M., Sarki, I. H., & Yaseen, M. N. (2023). Mediating role of entrepreneurial work-related strains and work engagement among job demand– resource model and success. *Sustainability (Basel)*, 15(5), 4454. DOI: 10.3390/su15054454

White, J. V., & Gupta, V. K. (2020). *Stress and well-being in entrepreneurship: a critical review and future research agenda*. Res. Occu. Stress Well Being., DOI: 10.1108/S1479-355520200000018004

Wu, G., Wu, Y., Li, H., & Dan, C. (2018). Job burnout, work-family conflict and project performance for construction professionals: The moderating role of organizational support. *International Journal of Environmental Research and Public Health*, 15(12), 2869. DOI: 10.3390/ijerph15122869 PMID: 30558218

Xu, Z., & Yang, F. (2021). The impact of perceived organizational support on the relationship between job stress and burnout: A mediating or moderating role? *Current Psychology (New Brunswick, N.J.)*, 40(1), 402–413. DOI: 10.1007/s12144-018-9941-4

Yester, M. (2019). Work-life balance, burnout, and physician wellness. *The Health Care Manager*, 38(3), 239–246. DOI: 10.1097/HCM.0000000000000277 PMID: 31261191

Yin, J., Yuan, J., Arfaei, N., Catalano, P. J., Allen, J. G., & Spengler, J. D. (2020). Effects of biophilic indoor environment on stress and anxiety recovery: A between-subjects experiment in virtual reality. *Environment International*, 136, 105427. DOI: 10.1016/j.envint.2019.105427 PMID: 31881421

Chapter 18
The Effectiveness of Cognitive-Behavioral Therapy for Entrepreneurial Anxiety

Hewawasam P. G. D. Wijethilak
https://orcid.org/0009-0006-9611-5735
University of Colombo, Sri Lanka

Sandeep Kumar Singh
https://orcid.org/0000-0002-1741-7254
O.P. Jindal Global University, India

Preet Kanwal
https://orcid.org/0009-0006-5114-8381
Lovely Professional University, India

ABSTRACT

Entrepreneurial anxiety is a pervasive issue that impacts the mental health and performance of business leaders, often leading to burnout, impaired decision-making, and reduced productivity. Cognitive-Behavioral Therapy (CBT) has emerged as an effective approach to managing this anxiety by helping entrepreneurs identify and reframe negative thought patterns, develop emotional resilience, and cultivate healthier coping strategies. This chapter explores how CBT techniques can be applied specifically to the challenges entrepreneurs face, such as stress, uncertainty, and isolation. It also discusses the limitations of CBT, particularly the barriers that entrepreneurs encounter in accessing and sustaining therapy. Future directions include leveraging technology to expand access to CBT, integrating mental health strategies into entrepreneurial education, and fostering a supportive entrepreneurial ecosystem that prioritizes mental well-being. By addressing these areas, CBT can continue to play a crucial role in promoting entrepreneurial success and mental health.

DOI: 10.4018/979-8-3693-3673-1.ch018

INTRODUCTION

Entrepreneurship is a field regarded by many as thrilling and rewarding. It is associated with innovation, independence, and the prospects of considerable financial benefits. At the same time, it creates considerable pressures, uncertainties, and risks that can make the lives of entrepreneurs anxious. Among the usual psychological problems that stem from the special demands created by an entrepreneur when establishing and running a business are entrepreneurial anxieties. Such demands trigger chronic stress and anxiety, mainly because of the constant need to make critical decisions, manage financial instability, compete with peers, and perpetuate personal and professional relationships. This phenomenon has recently gained much attention as it is being recognized that such entrepreneurial setup requires a healthy mental perspective toward long-term success and sustainability.

Such has been the reception of Cognitive-Behavioral Therapy (CBT)-a recognized and evidence-based treatment for psychological problems-by the world that it has become a healthy prescription for anxiety disorders. CBT views the identification and deconstruction of negative thought patterns and behavior, as well as teaching coping skills, as effective methods in managing anxiety. First, it was created to be used in the treatment of depression and generalized anxiety disorder, especially panic disorders. Now, its applications have expanded to include a huge number of psychological conditions like work-related stress and anxiety. It is quite suitable for entrepreneurs since, when dealing with perfectionism and many fears of failure combined with overthinking, they require, as a rule, shortchanges in attitudes. CBT involves changing unhelpful thought patterns and teaching real-world skills, including relaxation, and experiential behaviors, thus making it the most productive means of lowering anxiety among entrepreneurs.

Entrepreneurial anxiety cuts beyond mental health issues but instead involves major business issues. As it has been proven through research, there is a probable effect of anxiety on the thinking process, even causing burnout, which means it adversely affects the outcome and sustainability of a business idea. In general, entrepreneurs are high-achievers resulting in tremendous pressure on their performance that brings about a vicious cycle of pressure that not only hampers the entrepreneurs' psychological health but also degrades the ability to lead the business effectively. If unchecked, this cycle will lead to longer symptoms like depression and long-run health problems. Implementation of Cognitive-Behavioral Therapy in entrepreneurs will break the vicious cycle of fear by making them see the anxiety-causing thoughts in the minds, understand their irrationality and replacing with alternative healthy and constructive perspective.

The integration of CBT in the entrepreneurial landscape provides an important development because it helps entrepreneurs come out of the vicious cycle of anxiety in a proactive solution-focused way. These will be able to empower entrepreneurs to be aware of what provokes anxiety, build resilience, and obtain better mental health by focusing on both the cognitive and behavioral aspects of anxiety. Again, application in CBT is very much practical-oriented, offering entrepreneurs a set of strategies that can fit their daily routine with minimal disruption to business activities.

We will take a step by step of the effectiveness of Cognitive-Behavioral Therapy in dealing with entrepreneurial anxiety, investigating its foundation principles, some therapeutic techniques, and real-life applications. We then check its application in entrepreneurial decision making and entrepreneurial creativity, as well as overall wellbeing, and make a strong case for adding mental health activities like CBT to the entrepreneurial toolbox as a vital element of entrepreneurial success.

UNDERSTANDING ENTREPRENEURIAL ANXIETY

Causes and Contributing Factors

This demand-generating anxiety for entrepreneurial venture lies in the unique pressures of launching and running a business. Unlike a wage job, entrepreneurship harbors such high uncertainty that entrepreneurs must take crucial decisions based on partial information. Usually, financial instability is one major concern-the unpredictability of cash flows in new businesses and the risk of personal savings. Furthermore, entrepreneurs often wear hats by doing everything themselves, including handling their small change like day-to-day running, marketing, and sales-all under fewer working hours. This uncertainty of whether one's business will thrive leads to multi-tasking, consequently giving way to anxiety (Thompson et al., 2020).

External pressure to innovate and outshine the competitors adds weight to stress, including sectors that are flexible with a fast-moving need to stay ahead of trends and changed consumer wants. Consequently, this is usually achieved on tight resources. One of the major fears is the fear of failure, as most entrepreneurs tend to equate self-esteem with business performance. The consequences are not only financial but also reputation damage and dissatisfaction among investors, employees, and even family members. Stressors can be so complex and compound anxiety that it impacts personal as well as professional well-being and productivity drastically.

Impact on Deciding and Business Performance

Entrepreneurial anxiety can have a tremendous impact on decision-making processes. Under high degrees of stress, people tend to rely more on cognitive shortcuts, which can lead them into making poorly judged decisions and reacting rather than choosing out of careful judgment. Anxiety tends to blur judgment, so it's difficult for one to look at a position objectively and examine risks and opportunities. Entrepreneurs will become too scared, avoiding necessary risks that would push their business to the next level, or they will impetuously act in a bid to hurriedly solve their anxiety. These cases can hinder business growth and stability.

Anxiety also decreases creativity and innovation. Entrepreneurship requires a focused mind in a bid to strategically think and come up with creative solutions for complex problems. However, during anxiety, it becomes hard for them to even think of something new anymore. With so much pressure always on them, there's also a danger of burnout-a state of emotional exhaustion that makes the entrepreneur less productive. Burnout doesn't just affect the entrepreneur; it trickles down to the business-employees' morale becoming reduced, and overall performance suffers.

The Entrepreneurial Personality and Anxiety

Most entrepreneurs are susceptible to developing anxiety due to certain personalities. One of the biggest personality elements concerning entrepreneurs is perfectionism. Most successful entrepreneurs set exceedingly high standards of excellence for themselves and their business venture. While this aggressive pursuit of excellence may help in achieving success, it does bring in significant levels of internal pressure when not met. Fear of failure thus becomes an overhyped phenomenon because perfectionists find it difficult to accept setbacks or mistakes-the result being chronic stress and self-doubts.

The entrepreneur is typically a high achiever, performing well in fast-paced and challenging dynamic environments. Ambition is good but at a price. When pursued to perfection, the entrepreneurs will forget to care about their mental and physical health, overwork, and isolate from social support. This imbalance contributes to the vicious circle of stress and anxiety, because the entrepreneur cannot stop working and detached himself from the business for fear of losing it.

The Emotional Toll of Entrepreneurship

Entrepreneurial struggles are often more emotional because entrepreneurs can be lonely, with nobody close by who could feel how difficult it is for them to bear the pressure. This loneliness, coupled with the uncertainty in the businessman's business about how it would turn out each day, might contribute to anxiety and depression tendencies in entrepreneurs. The traditional employee, who thinks his career is defined or that he safely sits in his workplace, doesn't face these issues. Entrepreneurs always have to tread the ambiguity of uncertainty in everything they have to do, which would be emotionally wearing down.

Responsibility is another great emotional burden. Entrepreneurs bear the collective responsibility for themselves, but also for their employees, investors, and customers. This heavy responsibility creates pressure, which contributes over time to chronic anxiety and stress. Such emotional challenges create a desperate need to recognize them in due course and deal with them. It becomes essential to both preserve the entrepreneurs' mental health and the sustainability of businesses.

First, to understand the complexities of the concept of entrepreneurial anxiety, an effective response can be acquired. Once the pressures associated with being an entrepreneur are acknowledged, the individual can then take proactive steps to prevent such anxiety from negatively affecting their decision-making and creativity abilities as well as general well-being.

COGNITIVE-BEHAVIORAL THERAPY (CBT)

Core Principles of Cognitive-Behavioral Therapy (CBT)

The most popular form of psychotherapy which bases itself in the world of interaction between thought, emotion, and action is known as Cognitive-Behavioral Therapy (CBT). This form of therapy is based on the fundamental presumption that most of our thoughts have a bearing on how we feel and behave. Now that negative or irrational patterns of thought have been identified, people can be made to change the way they respond to problematic situations in life and reduce stress while raising their prospects for mental well-being. CBT is based on the assumption that most psychological disorders are the result of dysfunctional thinking and destructive lifestyle habits and attempts to modify them in a structured and coherent manner.

Cognitive restructuring is perhaps the cardinal tool of CBT: learning to recognize and replace negative thought streams. In this way, entrepreneurs may think "When my company goes bust, I am a failure" and therefore heighten their anxiety. CBT enables individuals to confront such maladaptive beliefs and replaces them with the more balanced and realistic outlooks to have, such as "However bad my business is doing, it has nothing to do with who I am as a person." Such alteration in outlook assists in curtailing emotional disturbances and triggers more adaptive ways of reacting to agonizing situations.

Behavior Modification in CBT

Behavior modification is another major component of CBT. This aspect focuses on the modification of behavior that leads to causing anxiety. For example, one common coping mechanism that sets in when people are anxious is avoidance, but usually worsens the problem in the long run. Entrepreneurs may avoid important business decisions because they fear that failure will lead to stagnation and raise the level of stress further. CBT encourages people to face their fears gradually through a process called exposure therapy that helps build up the resistance of the individual and lowers down the level of anxiety over a period.

Behavioral modification techniques can apply in the entrepreneur context, reducing habits that increase their stress levels, such as overworking or procrastinating. With CBT, entrepreneurs learn healthier behavior, like goal setting, priority, and management of time. Such practical strategies are very essential to reduce day-to-day pressures from entrepreneurship and avoid burnout. Behavioral modification through CBT is action-oriented; it looks at actual steps that will minimize anxiety and ensure improved functioning (Carpenter et al., 2018; Hofmann et al., 2014).

How CBT Addresses Anxiety

CBT works by changing both cognitive and behavioral elements of the condition. Catastrophic thinking is one of the things characterizing anxiety. In such situations where uncertainty prevails, people often imagine the worst-case scenario. Entrepreneurs, being exposed to high stakes and uncertainty, oftentimes fall into such catastrophic thinking patterns that deepen their anxiety. It will teach them to recognize when they go about catastrophic thinking and guide them in an evaluation of evidence behind their fear. In this manner, entrepreneurs shall be able to stay better with their challenges and lower their anxiety.

Besides cognitive restructuring, CBT adds to relaxation so that the person learns how to regulate the physiological symptoms of anxiety, such as a fast heart rate, muscle tension, and speedy breathing. Incorporation of techniques such as deep breathing, progressive muscle relaxation, and mindfulness could be incorporated into CBT. The reason is that these techniques help enable people to calm down their nervous system and to stay focused under pressure. These are particularly applicable to entrepreneurs who have the experience of high-pressure situations such as negotiation or critical decision-making situations.

Success of CBT in Treating Various Anxiety Disorders

CBT is one of the most effective therapies, and its reputation has stood the test of time in treating cases of anxiety disorders. These include generalized anxiety disorder, panic disorder, and social anxiety disorder. It is more suitable for practical people who need to get definite solutions to manage their anxiety. Because it is relatively short-term that lasts for 12 to 20 sessions, it generally appeals to busy entrepreneurs who do not have time to spare for long-term therapy.

A major number of studies have proven the effectiveness of CBT in relieving anxiety symptoms and after completion of therapy, often extending benefits. Relieving entrepreneurs from anxiety attacks, CBT is instrumental and builds long-term skills that benefit entrepreneurs when faced with future stressors.

Such skills include the ability to detect unhelpful patterns of thinking, be more active in their line of work by trying to solve problems, and relaxation techniques, which frees entrepreneurs into becoming capable of maintaining their mental well-being independently after therapy has ended.

Relevance of CBT in the Entrepreneurial Context

The adaptability of CBT is what makes it particularly relevant in the entrepreneurial context. Unlike other forms of therapy that focus on deep-rooted emotional issues, CBT centers on present challenges and provides actionable strategies to resolve anxiety. Entrepreneurs are benefited by the practical approach that CBT brings forward, for this approach addresses the results-oriented mindset that makes entrepreneurs and facilitates with tools that can be directly applied in their business lives. That is, such an approach helps entrepreneurs overcome both cognitive distortions and useless behaviors, thereby ultimately building mental strength, improving decision-making capabilities, and managing constant pressure and stress.

To summarize, the combination of cognitive restructuring, modification of behavior, and anxiety management techniques makes CBT highly effective therapeutic approach for entrepreneurial anxiety. CBT equips entrepreneurs with the ability to recognize and challenge negative thought patterns along with healthier behaviors, helping entrepreneurs onto the path to reduced anxiety and improved well-being (Pecino et al., 2019).

APPLYING CBT TO ENTREPRENEURIAL ANXIETY

Identifying Negative Thought Patterns

A key step in the process of applying Cognitive-Behavioral Therapy to manage entrepreneurial anxiety involves unearthing negative patterns of thought that underpin distress. Entrepreneurs, by virtue of owning a startup, face tremendous uncertainty and risk. This can often lead them to thoughts like "I'll never make it," "If I fail, my reputation is ruined," or "I am unable to handle this challenge." These cognitive distortions–overgeneralizations, catastrophic thinking, and black-and-white thinking–heighten anxiety. Thus, the anxiety in danger imperils mental health and choice-making. CBT helps entrepreneurs recognize these irrational thoughts and evaluates them objectively (Guo et al., 2022).

For instance, a businessman who has his funding proposal turned down would come to think, "This spells doom for my business." CBT would encourage him to question that by asking, "Is that really true? Have other businesses succeeded after facing setbacks?" Entrepreneurs are taught to examine the case for and against his or her negative thoughts, with the aim of transforming them into more balanced, realistic perspectives. Instead of that failure, the entrepreneur can consider it an opportunity to learn or become better. This sort of cognitive restructuring reduces anxiety and enables entrepreneurs to attack problems more lucidly and with more confidence.

Managing Decision Paralysis and Fear of Failure

The inability to make crucial business decisions because of intense fear of possible failure is probably one of the most recognizable symptoms of entrepreneurial anxiety. For instance, CBT may help an entrepreneur to break down complex decisions into steps that can be managed more easily. By focusing on solutions, which are actionable rather than paralyzed fears of what may be, entrepreneurs can take incremental steps toward a goal.

Decision-making frameworks of CBT may include helping entrepreneurs to think through the potential outcomes and recognize whether the negative outcome is really an exaggerated exaggeration.

Another area where core CBT techniques may be utilized is in the form of exposure therapy, which may successfully reduce fear of failure. Exposure therapy is considered gradual, controlled exposure to feared situations, and it is in this manner that entrepreneurs build up their resilience to anxiety. For example, an entrepreneur may begin with small, low-stakes decisions that will gradually move toward making major business decisions. Eventually, exposures reduce the emotional charge that accompanies decision-making for entrepreneurs, creating the capacity for entrepreneurs to approach challenges without much fear (Otto et al., 2019).

Implementing Behavioral Strategies for Stress Management

Behavioral strategies in CBT are helpful in managing the stress associated with entrepreneurial anxiety. Entrepreneurs often use overworking, procrastination, or avoidance of critical tasks to handle stress. CBT promotes the adoption of healthier behaviors that will help manage stress and potentially promote work-life balance. Strategies such as time management, goal setting, and prioritization assist entrepreneurs in organizing their workload better so that they can dissipate that feeling of being overwhelmed.

Another behavioral technique is planning time for continuous breaks and relaxation. An entrepreneur often forgets to self-calm, and thus burnout is the outcome. CBT introduces stress reduction activities in the daily life of a person, including physical exercise, meditation, or leisure. These behaviors minimize stress and improve cognitive ability, hence enhancing business performance (Reichl & Spinath, 2014).

One of the areas where CBT is especially effective is through mindfulness and relaxation techniques. Since entrepreneurs are often in an environment of constant high-pressure situations, this helps significantly in managing anxiety. Deep breathing, progressive muscle relaxation, and mindfulness meditation are commonly used in CBT to help a person control the physiological symptoms of anxiety. These techniques ensure entrepreneurs stay focused and do not get buckled by a major situation, like negotiating contracts or presenting to investors.

Developing Resilience and Mental Flexibility

CBT assists entrepreneurs to develop long-term resilience-that is, an extremely needed competency as entrepreneurship is unsteady. Reinforcement by means of CBT will help entrepreneurs develop adaptive thought patterns and behaviors so as to thrive in adversity and maintain mental elasticity. Moreover, CBT fosters the development of a growth mindset-in essence, challenges are perceived as learning opportunities rather than as threats to succeeding. This mentality will see to it that entrepreneurs do not quit easily but will put up with hardship times (Evriani, 2024).

Entrepreneurs are constantly faced with changing scenarios; thus, mental flexibility is very important. CBT makes entrepreneurs change their patterns of thinking and problem-solving when it becomes necessary. If some unforeseen shock eventually meets an entrepreneur in the face-a new trend in the market or even when his product fails-CBT evades limiting thinking and looks out for multiple solutions or alternative strategies to face the situation. Such adaptable thinking keeps anxiety low and enables better pivoting and responding to new situations for the entrepreneur (León et al., 2021).

Enhancing Emotional Regulation and Self-Compassion

The other important aspect of applying CBT in entrepreneurial anxiety is enhancing emotional control. Entrepreneurs are known to possess very mercurial emotions, ones that change from excitement to frustration. If not managed, this may result in emotional instability in people. CBT gives individuals techniques for identifying and controlling these feelings. As a result, entrepreneurs remain balanced in the emotions while dealing with stressful situations. For example, when the entrepreneur's escalating anxiety peaks right before delivering a crucial presentation, CBT would have the entrepreneur take some breath, label what he is experiencing, and concentrate on calming thoughts, hence reducing the immediate stress response (Rudaleva, 2018).

Thirdly, CBT provides self-compassion, which is a vital attribute when entrepreneurs happen to be their worst critics. Entrepreneurs always generate massive amounts of stress simply because their expectations tend to far outweigh the real outcome should things fail to meet those expectations. Self-blame or inadequacy can be very common feelings that entrepreneurs experience due to lack of achievement. It is here that CBT steps in-to self-compassionate thinking. It will help entrepreneurs talk to themselves more with kindness and compassion than when they are wrong. This practice mitigates the emotional impact of becoming an entrepreneur, meaning they are able to maintain good mental health in the long term (Verweij et al., 2016).

Integrating CBT into Daily Entrepreneurial Practices

It is thus relevant that entrepreneurs apply the skills of CBT in their everyday living. This can be achieved through setting a time span each day for cognitive restructuring exercises or journaling of thoughts and behaviours or through mindfulness and relaxation techniques during stressed periods. The consistency with which the entrepreneurs use the methods of CBT thereby achieves greater self-awareness and strength, helping entrepreneurs to tackle anxiety proactively, rather than reactively.

In addition, entrepreneurs also could employ CBT skills in providing supportive settings within their business environment. A caring environment of self-care and stress reduction among all employees creates a much healthier, productive work environment in which employees, inclusive of the owner, can help to improve their overall health and well-being. It is from this perspective that entrepreneurs not only benefit but thrive personally as well as professionally, hence leading to the maximization of long-term success with their venture.

Conclusion CBT provides the anxious entrepreneur with a more structured and practical approach to managing anxiety. Through unearthing and challenging negative thoughts, changing unhelpful behaviors, and building emotional resilience, this will help an entrepreneur understand and cope with the pressures of running a venture confidently and clearly.

EFFECTIVENESS OF CBT FOR ENTREPRENEURS

Addressing the Unique Stressors of Entrepreneurship

CBT could well be the best therapy for entrepreneurs as it directly faces the stresses brought on by these factors: uncertainty, financial risk, and the pressure to succeed. Entrepreneurship is defined by the uncertainty of its environmental context, where the outcome is unknown, and the expectation of failure can be imminent at any point in time. Such unpredictability may serve to foster intense anxiety in entrepreneurs, and without natural coping mechanisms, entrepreneurs are easily swamped. CBT offers the systematic approach helping entrepreneurs deal with these stressors through pragmatic tools in anxiety management, problem-solving and emotional resiliency.

Focusing on the relationship of thoughts, emotions, and behaviors, CBT helps entrepreneurs understand how their thought process is worsening their level of anxiety. For example, an entrepreneur may perhaps always be filled with the fear of the failure of the business; hence, their deliberations and confidence levels can become victims. CBT, therefore, enables such entrepreneurs to fight against those negative thoughts and replace them with constructive outlooks instead of catastrophic results. This cognitive reappraisal further brings down anxiety and improves decision-making skills under stress-a critical skill set for entrepreneurs.

Improving Emotional Regulation and Mental Resilience

An important advantage for entrepreneurs through CBT is that it facilitates emotional regulation. Entrepreneurs encounter extreme ups and downs emotionally as they navigate their way through the challenges of running a business. Indeed, without emotional management, such volatility can cause stress, burnout, and even depression. CBT teaches entrepreneurs to record and regulate their emotional reactions with practices like mindfulness and deep breathing and cognitive restructuring (Lan et al., 2021).

For instance, if something is wrong in the business, CBT reminds entrepreneurs to recognize their first emotional reaction perhaps getting frustrated or disappointed-and to cease acting on impulse. In fact, reframing these thoughts and releasing the feelings actually helps entrepreneurs respond more calmly in difficult circumstances, such as in trying situations to negotiate deals or leading teams under great pressure.

Apart from this, CBT enhances psychological resilience, which becomes an important factor for long-term entrepreneurial success. Entrepreneurs are constantly exposed to challenging situations that require them to be adaptable and resistant. CBT helps develop the growth mindset that makes entrepreneurs view setbacks as a chance to learn rather than being failures. Such psychological flexibility will enable entrepreneurs to bounce back from challenges with much confidence and have less chance of chronic anxiety or burnout (Hansen et al., 2015)

Enhancing Productivity and Decision-Making

Anxiety could blur the minds of entrepreneurs to such an extent that it would debilitate their productivity and inability to take decisive judgments leading to procrastination, indecision, or poor judgment. CBT modifies these factors by helping entrepreneurs break into sound steps to deal with such overwhelming tasks and enables them to build some strategies to deal with decision paralysis. Behavior modification tools such as prioritizing tasks and goal setting help entrepreneurs plan their work in ways that reduce stress and improve attention to their task.

CBT helps entrepreneurs avoid rigid, black-and-white views of success and failure through cognitive distortions such as all-or-nothing thinking. Entrepreneurs who would regard business outcome experience as one-sided, for example, "If I do not succeed, everything will fall apart," learn more matured views that allow more mental clarity at decision time. This would result in more rational, balanced choices, which, in turn, will have a good effect on the performance of the business.

For one, CBT action-oriented strategizing can help an entrepreneur dramatically increase the degree to which he or she takes calculated risks. Most entrepreneurs are afraid of bold decisions due to fear or probable rejection. This flexibility encourages an entrepreneur to work toward uncertainty as part of the process and toward making decisions based on reasonable assessments rather than inflated fears. This mentality enables the entrepreneur to take the initiative in the expansion of their business instead of being paralyzed through fear of anxiety.

Preventing Burnout and Promoting Work-Life Balance

Among these problems, burnout is the most prevalent since handling one's business may consume too much time, and sleepless nights may be inevitable for the passionate individual entrepreneur, compelling such an entrepreneur to neglect the self. What is interesting about this method in preventing burnout among entrepreneurs is that it helps promote good work habits and work-life balance. Techniques of time management and stress-reducing techniques help entrepreneurs place boundaries between personal and professional lives so that there won't be room for emotional exhaustion.

Again, CBT stresses the need for self-compassion - a perspective entrepreneurs could learn too: don't beat up on themselves if things aren't going well. Entrepreneurs seem to push themselves to the limit, striving for perfection and then beating themselves up when they fail to reach the ideal. As a result, feel inadequate at times, adding more to one's anxiety. CBT helps entrepreneurs develop self-compassion in light of the challenges against themselves harsh self-criticism that often fuels burnout in order to use a healthier and sustainable approach at work.

In addition, relaxation practices and mindfulness, including progressive muscle relaxation, can become ingrained in daily routines to reduce the presence of burnout even more significantly on an entrepreneur's life. Those who incorporate them into their daily routines will operate at a stress level and concentration where demands related to their business can be boiled over more effectively. These practices also make it possible to develop improved sleeping habits and maximize one's well-being as well, maximizing productivity and health over the long term.

Long-Term Benefits and Sustainability

The advantage of CBT is not only a relief of symptoms in anxiety but also long-term coping skills it provides entrepreneurs to continue using even after therapy is finished. In the case of entrepreneurs undergoing CBT, it is not just reduced present levels of anxiety but also gains provided for control over future stressors independently. Sustainability is very crucial in an entrepreneurial context because it is the realization that pressure and uncertainty are ongoing concerns.

Research shows that the skills learned through CBT, such as cognitive restructuring, managing emotions, and modifying behavior, remain applicable several months after treatment is completed. If entrepreneurs work hard to use these approaches, they usually tend to have small anxiety levels and large mental stamina, and therefore they can cope with later adversity in their business much more easily.

Practically solution-focused, CBT is therefore particularly therapeutic for this population because it resonates fully with an entrepreneurial mindset. Entrepreneurs focus on tangible results; goal setting, tracking, and implementing action strategies to satisfy objective progress resonate perfectly well with this need. It ensures that CBT reduces anxiety while empowering entrepreneurs to take proactive steps toward personal and professional development (Spigel & Harrison, 2017; Cantner et al., 2020)

Cognitive Behavioral Therapy has worked well for the special needs of entrepreneurs. It provides these entrepreneurs with tools that are to be used to manage anxiety levels, to be wise in a decision-making process, and not get into burnout. This way, the entrepreneurs can dive into the professional sphere with enhanced confidence and emotional resilience. Gains from the long-term include heightened productivity, a healthy mind, and good work-life balance, which are of immense value for entrepreneurs who wish to excel in their ventures and hold the health of minds (Cavanaugh et al., 2020).

CHALLENGES AND LIMITATIONS

Time Constraints and Commitment

The greatest limitation in the implementation of CBT for entrepreneurs has to be time commitment. There are a lot of tasks that entrepreneurs are usually swamped with, from handling business activities to dealing with financial matters. It is hard to find free time to attend therapy. In general, CBT is comprised of a scheduled series of sessions accompanied by further homework such as journaling, thought logs, or mindfulness practice. Those entrepreneurs whose schedules are always called to order might not be able to commit fully to therapy, curbing the success of treatment.

On the other hand, the fast-moving and dynamic nature of entrepreneurship can distract some entrepreneurs from considering therapy as an important business matter. Leaders of businesses may consider therapy as a low-priority issue rather than urgent business problems such as closing deals, managing staff, or acquiring capital. This time conflict will often prevent them from consistently carrying out regular sessions of CBT or practically relating to what has been learned from the therapy sessions, hence shortening long-term potential benefit.

Resistance to Vulnerability

Another stigma against discussing personal vulnerabilities impedes the functioning of CBT for entrepreneurial anxiety. Entrepreneurs are often seen as - and see themselves as, being among the most independent, resilient, and driven kind of individuals. It may therefore be difficult for entrepreneurs to admit to experiencing anxiety or emotional problems since their perception is that this is a weakness. This has the actual speaking of negative thought patterns and emotional triggers and cannot be comfortable with entrepreneurs as they portrayed confidence and control in various business activities (Anasseri, 2021; Carpenter et al., 2018; Hofmann et al., 2014).

This also acts as a barrier to the therapeutic process because most of the strength of CBT does depend upon how open the client is towards reflection and emotional processing. An entrepreneur will find it very hard to let go of his or her desperate need to be in control and to accede to the idea that having help or being vulnerable by uttering words 'I am anxious' instead of being a failure is an active step towards growth and also towards mental health enhancement.

Difficulty in Sustaining Long-Term Practice

While CBT is a practical methodology for the management of anxiety, one of its major drawbacks is the failure to maintain long-term practice of the techniques. Application of cognitive restructuring, behaviour modification, as well as emotional regulation strategies must be continuous for CBT to be successful. Hence, entrepreneurs being more aggressive and having a lot of stress due to early success in their therapy might again revert back to their old habits while being under stress. The business demands are highly stressful and quite unpredictable and bring about non-consistency in the usage of techniques related to CBT, therefore minimizing long-term effectiveness.

Moreover, people in business may be seeking short-term remedies for their anxiety thinking CBT will reduce the anxiety in the short run. However, CBT is generally a process that only through persistence ends up results in being long-lasting. This means that people are likely to quit therapy too early before they fully learn the skills of self-management of anxiety.

Limited Access to Mental Health Resources

The second limiting factor is few qualified practitioners of CBT for entrepreneurs who may live in remote locations or whose regions are characterized by fewer services in mental health settings. With CBT one of the best researched and applied types of therapy, not everyone who offers treatment has dealt with entrepreneurial challenges or understands the complexities of the entrepreneurial mindset. For instance, an inappropriate therapist who cannot modify CBT to the proper entrepreneurial context could downsize the appropriateness and impact of therapy.

Another is that therapy in general may be an unaffordable resource for some entrepreneurs, especially those just starting to build the business or are running on a shoestring budget. In-person therapy sessions can be costly, and not everyone is covered by insurance that would provide resources for mental health services. This financial burden could ward entrepreneurs from getting help they so desperately need or completing any course of CBT treatment (Evriani, 2024)

Difficulty in Addressing Deep-Rooted Issues

CBT is very effective in treating distorted cognition and anxiety disorders. However, if the entrepreneurs are suffering from deep-rooted psychological problems, CBT would not be adequate for such cases. CBT concentrates on present cognition and action targeting negative spirals and creating more adaptive responses. But a couple of entrepreneurs may suffer from deep-rooted psychological problems because of childhood experiences or trauma or long-standing emotional problems. Such issues require more intensive approaches through therapy.

CBT is time-bound and solution-oriented, yet in most cases, it doesn't tend to delve into the psychological roots of an entrepreneur's anxiety. Anxiety can be associated with deeper other emotional impairments, and psychodynamic therapy, trauma-informed therapy, or mindfulness-based cognitive therapy (MBCT) should be consulted to completely recover.

Challenges in Integrating CBT into Entrepreneurial Culture

It is the entrepreneurial culture that becomes a challenge in making the effective integration of CBT techniques happen. Entrepreneurship encourages many times hustling, grit, and more perseverance. This creates an environment where stress and anxiety can easily be normalized and even glorified. The entrepreneurs may end up pushing anxiety further rather than confronting it head on. Such a cultural bent towards hardiness and self-reliance makes it hard to fully merge the CBT approach because it makes entrepreneur stand still, reflect, and admit to how he or she feels (Ben-Itzhak et al., 2015; Irfan et al., 2021).

Besides, mental illness suffers stigma in some entrepreneurial ecosystems. Being open about the issue might make some entrepreneurs fear judgment from their peers or investors. Such entrepreneurs have a fear of stigma that keeps them away from CBT or other therapeutic options, since they fear admitting to being vulnerable will taint their reputation and business standing.

Although CBT has helped many entrepreneurs overcome entrepreneurial anxiety, its application is challenging and bounded by limitations in the face of time constraints, resistance to vulnerability, difficulty in sustaining long-term practice, limited access to mental health resources, and the need for deeper psychological intervention. Furthermore, the tempo and also stress of entrepreneurship together with cultural perceptions on resilience and self-reliance might tend to hinder an entrepreneur from embracing CBT in its entirety. Conversely, wherever applied suitably and implemented within an enabling environment, CBT remains to positively impact the anxiety levels and overall mental well-being of entrepreneurs.

FUTURE DIRECTIONS AND RECOMMENDATIONS

Integrating Technology with CBT for Entrepreneurs

With the integration of technology, future innovations might enhance the efficiency and availability of Cognitive-Behavioral Therapy for entrepreneurs. Digital mental health platforms and mobile applications may ease the availability of flexible and on-demand CBT techniques for entrepreneurs, even in far-flung places and overcoming time constraints. Guided exercises in CBT mood tracking and cognitive restructuring can provide ample opportunity for entrepreneurs to spend all their busy schedules.

Virtual therapy sessions and teletherapy can extend the reach of specialized CBT practitioners, who understand the entrepreneurial context. Entrepreneurs can thus participate in therapy through video calls or chat-based therapy without ever needing to commute to a fixed location or compromise on scheduling around it. As virtual mental health services will continue expanding, entrepreneurs will have opportunities to continue regular CBT sessions even against hectic demands of work.

Another technology-based innovation will be applying artificial intelligence to tailor specific CBT programs towards entrepreneurs. AI could analyze where specific individual areas of stress, behavioral patterns, and emotional responses are and how one could best tailor exercises or feedback in their unique problems. It may increase the effectiveness of CBT by allowing direct intervention, hitting the specific target parts in an entrepreneur's mind and emotions.

Enhancing Entrepreneurial Support Networks

Entrepreneurial communities and networks can play a larger role to demystify mental health care as a supportive environment for CBT practice. Entrepreneurial support networks, such as co-working spaces, business accelerators, and incubators, can lead mental health initiatives, for instance, CBT workshops, peer support groups, and stress management programs, which could not only allow entrepreneurs easy access to mental health resources but would also dissipate stigma around therapy taking in professional settings.

Encouraging peer support and cooperation among network members can help to alleviate some feelings of isolation that may exacerbate entrepreneurial anxiety. Entrepreneurs often feel lonely because the journey has taken them far from the comfort of what once was considered normal. Support programs from peers allow entrepreneurship leaders to openly share their challenges and experiences, which might make it easier to embrace CBT techniques within the framework of a strategy that addresses the issue of mental health. Mentorship programs that focus on mental health support could also help prevent burnout and promote the well-being of future business leaders.

Integrating CBT with Entrepreneurial Training Programs

The other area of future work is to incorporate CBT principles into entrepreneurial training and education curriculums. Only a small number of entrepreneurs have technical, or business skills combined with sufficient emotional resilience to cope with the psychological pressures involved in entrepreneurships. It would be very helpful to add CBT methods, including managing stress, controlling emotions, and reframing cognition, to entrepreneurial curriculums to better prepare entrepreneurs in being able to manage anxiety as well as other mental health issues before they become debilitating.

Entrepreneurship education programs could also introduce emotional intelligence (EI) training, which aligns well with CBT's focus on self-awareness and emotional management. It will be through formal education where entrepreneurs learn CBT strategies to improve not only their mental well-being but also their leadership skills, decision-making, and in general interpersonal abilities. Such integration may lead to the creation of a business leadership generation that might better cope with the psychological pressures associated with entrepreneurship.

Promoting Long-Term Mental Health Practices

While CBT has been typically a short-term intervention, the need for long-term mental health support should be prioritized for entrepreneurs. Future studies and treatments could focus on how to amalgamate these mental health practices with CBT in a manner that can bring a more sustainable change over time. For instance, while using CBT with mindfulness-based therapies or some kind of resilience training may offer the right kind of tools to the entrepreneur so that long-term mental health can be built at the earliest stages. With this cultivated mindfulness practice, entrepreneurs may be able to live in greater harmony and peace, hence reducing their level of stress as they stay focused amid business troubles.

It can also provide an additional booster session program for entrepreneurs who have successfully finished CBT. Booster sessions can reinforce the techniques learned so that entrepreneurs continue to apply them progressively as opposed to going back into anxiety or burnout. Follow-up sessions might also focus on new skills to handle challenges that may arise while an entrepreneur's business grows and changes, overcoming each challenge that has emerged.

Research into CBT's Effectiveness for Specific Entrepreneurial Profiles

Research in this area should be continued with efforts to increase the number of investigations into fitting different profiles into CBT. Entrepreneurs come from diverse backgrounds, and psychological needs vary as influenced by factors including industries, business stages, personal histories, and cultural contexts. For instance, the stressors for the founder of a tech startup are way more than those of a small business entrepreneur. The therapeutic approach applied in each case would therefore be different from the other. Research should take into consideration if CBT could be adapted according to the challenging needs of various entrepreneurs.

Another important consideration while using CBT in the entrepreneurial ecosystems across the globe is the cultural considerations. Entrepreneurs in diverse cultures may approach or look at issues on mental health, therapy, or expression of emotions differently. This means that the interventions with CBT that are to be taken are in appropriateness with respect to cultural values will play as the determining factor for making the therapy more accessible and hence effective for a larger population of entrepreneurs.

Encouraging Mental Health Literacy in Entrepreneurial Ecosystems

Consequently, this wide entrepreneurial ecosystem will assist entrepreneurs to realize their mental well-being by increasing their mental health literacy. Activism from various stakeholders, among them investors, business mentors, and organizations that support entrepreneurship may cause entrepreneurs to focus on the primary concern regarding their own mental health as part of a global business strategy. This can be through education and resource provision coupled with the open discussion of any mental health concerns by providing an avenue for entrepreneurs to adopt an anxiety management strategy and address psychological problems in a timely and proactive manner (Kang et al., 2019; Stam & Ven, 2019).

Owners can be nudged by investors and business partners to invest in their mental wellbeing, either through the adoption of work-life balance policies, mental health days, or provision of therapy services. Entrepreneurial success is not just about financial performance but also on the sustenance of a business leader's emotional and psychological health. We will make mental health literacy the top priority of every level of the entrepreneurial ecosystem. This way, there will be an environment of encouragement which supports entrepreneurs to take CBT and treatment of other types free from stigma and hesitation.

Entrepreneurial mental health support: Future of CBT for Entrepreneurial Anxiety in Access Expansion, Entrepreneurial Culture Integration and Long-term Maintenance Support. With technology at their beck and call, networks designed to support them, and access to nurturing a CBT-based entrepreneurial training regime, plus promoting mental health literacy, entrepreneurs can better handle anxiety. Approaches to maintaining mental well-being should shift with the entrepreneurial environment, so strategies used to ensure CBT stays as relevant as possible and adaptable to remain an effective enabler of resilience and true long-term success.

CONCLUSION

It has been observed to be a very effective intervention tool in the management of entrepreneurial anxiety, where practical tools to face specific psychological challenges related to entrepreneurship can be offered. Through making people aware and reframing negative thoughts, CBT enables entrepreneurs to regulate their emotions better, manage stress, and achieve healthy mental states. CBT provides an action-oriented and goal-directed approach, which makes it particularly suitable for entrepreneurship. Entrepreneurs are action-oriented people who rely on action plans and measurable results. Targeted strategies such as cognitive restructuring, activation, and mindfulness practice may help entrepreneurs to better the responses to the pressures and uncertainties that abound in the process of setting up and running a business.

However, although CBT has shown effectiveness in reducing symptoms of anxiety and augmenting emotional strength, its practice in entrepreneurial contexts is filled with huge challenges and limitations. Availability of time for an entrepreneurial lifestyle creates problems, with resistance to vulnerability and the challenge in maintenance of long-term practice limiting benefits from therapy. In addition, fast-paced, high-pressure environments characterizing some of these entrepreneurship environments oppose the consistent practice CBT requires. Entrepreneurs sometimes also face challenges around access to qualified mental health professionals who have a specialization in the unique needs of entrepreneurship, particularly entrepreneurs based in more rural or otherwise underserved geographies.

Accessibility through technology alone; integration of CBT-based pedagogy in entrepreneurial education; and inciting a culture of mental well-being within entrepreneurial ecosystems must be future directions. Digital platforms and virtual therapy may be promising areas by which the flexibility entrepreneurs require can be availed, while CBT incorporated into entrepreneurial training programs will prepare business leaders to handle anxiety from the word go. We can promote mental health literacy and long-term mental health practices by keeping nothing secret, so we can create an environment where entrepreneurs feel supported in seeking help without stigma or judgment.

While the entrepreneurial journey looks long and stressful, full of uncertainty with mood swings, CBT offers a real, evidenced-based management to such issues. That means entrepreneurs who undergo CBT stand a better chance of achieving improved mental health, increased emotional resilience, and ultimately, long-term success in both aspects of life. As the landscape of entrepreneurship continues to be in flux, it would be paramount that there are corresponding evolutions in mental health care, to ensure the next generation of entrepreneurs experience sustainable well-being alongside business growth.

REFERENCES

Anasseri, M. (2021). Effect of cognitive-behavioral group therapy on the anxiety and depression of war-handicapped. *Journal of Archives in Military Medicine*, 9(1). Advance online publication. DOI: 10.5812/jamm.114085

Ben-Itzhak, S., Dvash, J., Maor, M., Rosenberg, N., & Halpern, P. (2015). Sense of meaning as a predictor of burnout in emergency physicians in israel: A national survey. *Clinical and Experimental Emergency Medicine*, 2(4), 217–225. DOI: 10.15441/ceem.15.074 PMID: 27752601

Carpenter, J., Andrews, L., Witcraft, S., Powers, M., Smits, J., & Hofmann, S. (2018). Cognitive behavioral therapy for anxiety and related disorders: A meta-analysis of randomized placebo-controlled trials. *Depression and Anxiety*, 35(6), 502–514. DOI: 10.1002/da.22728 PMID: 29451967

Cavanaugh, K., Lee, H., Daum, D., Chang, S., Izzo, J., Kowalski, A., & Holladay, C. (2020). An examination of burnout predictors: Understanding the influence of job attitudes and environment. *Health Care*, 8(4), 502. DOI: 10.3390/healthcare8040502 PMID: 33233620

Evriani, T., & Fardana, N. A. (2024). How does the effectiveness of cognitive behavior therapy in reducing academic anxiety influence the academic procrastination of undergraduate students? *Buana Pendidikan Jurnal Fakultas Keguruan Dan Ilmu Pendidikan*, 20(1), 22–28. DOI: 10.36456/bp.vol20.no1.a8698

Guo, X., Guo, X., Wang, R., & Zhang, Y. (2022). Effects of perinatal cognitive behavioral therapy on delivery mode, fetal outcome, and postpartum depression and anxiety in women. *Computational and Mathematical Methods in Medicine*, 2022, 1–8. DOI: 10.1155/2022/8304405 PMID: 36199781

Hansen, A., Buitendach, J., & Kanengoni, H. (2015). Psychological capital, subjective well-being, burnout and job satisfaction amongst educators in the umlazi region in south africa. *SA Journal of Human Resource Management*, 13(1). Advance online publication. DOI: 10.4102/sajhrm.v13i1.621

Hofmann, S., Wu, J., & Boettcher, H. (2014). Effect of cognitive-behavioral therapy for anxiety disorders on quality of life: A meta-analysis. *Journal of Consulting and Clinical Psychology*, 82(3), 375–391. DOI: 10.1037/a0035491 PMID: 24447006

Irfan, M., Khalid, R., Khel, S., Maqsoom, A., & Sherani, I. (2021). Impact of work–life balance with the role of organizational support and job burnout on project performance. *Engineering, Construction, and Architectural Management*, 30(1), 154–171. DOI: 10.1108/ECAM-04-2021-0316

Kang, Q., Li, H., Cheng, Y., & Kraus, S. (2019). Entrepreneurial ecosystems: Analysing the status quo. *Knowledge Management Research and Practice*, 19(1), 8–20. DOI: 10.1080/14778238.2019.1701964

Lan, X., Liang, Y., Wu, G., & Ye, H. (2021). Relationships among job burnout, generativity concern, and subjective well-being: A moderated mediation model. *Frontiers in Psychology*, 12, 613767. Advance online publication. DOI: 10.3389/fpsyg.2021.613767 PMID: 33716877

León, J., Molero, F., Laguía, A., Mikulincer, M., & Shaver, P. (2021). Security providing leadership: A job resource to prevent employees' burnout. *International Journal of Environmental Research and Public Health*, 18(23), 12551. DOI: 10.3390/ijerph182312551 PMID: 34886276

Otto, M., Hoefsmit, N., Ruysseveldt, J., & Dam, K. (2019). Exploring proactive behaviors of employees in the prevention of burnout. *International Journal of Environmental Research and Public Health*, 16(20), 3849. DOI: 10.3390/ijerph16203849 PMID: 31614684

Pecino, V., Mañas, M., Díaz-Fúnez, P., Aguilar-Parra, J., Padilla-Góngora, D., & López-Liria, R. (2019). Organisational climate, role stress, and public employees' job satisfaction. *International Journal of Environmental Research and Public Health*, 16(10), 1792. DOI: 10.3390/ijerph16101792 PMID: 31117168

Reichl, C., & Spinath, F. (2014). Work–nonwork conflict and burnout: A meta-analysis. *Human Relations*, 67(8), 979–1005. DOI: 10.1177/0018726713509857

Rudaleva, I. (2018). Research of organizational and personal factors of professional burnout of personnel in a consulting organization. *Helix*, 8(01), 2372–2376. DOI: 10.29042/2018-2372-2376

Spigel, B., & Harrison, R. (2017). Toward a process theory of entrepreneurial ecosystems. *Strategic Entrepreneurship Journal*, 12(1), 151–168. DOI: 10.1002/sej.1268

Stam, E. and Ven, A. (2019). Entrepreneurial ecosystem elements. Small Business Economics, 56(2), 809-832. https://doi.org/ Cantner, U., Cunningham, J., Lehmann, E., & Menter, M. (2020). Entrepreneurial ecosystems: a dynamic lifecycle model. Small Business Economics, 57(1), 407-423. https://doi.org/DOI: 10.1007/s11187-019-00270-6\

Thompson, N., Gelderen, M., & Keppler, L. (2020). No need to worry? anxiety and coping in the entrepreneurship process. *Frontiers in Psychology*, 11, 398. Advance online publication. DOI: 10.3389/fpsyg.2020.00398 PMID: 32226405

Verweij, H., Heijden, F., Hooff, M., Prins, J., Lagro-Janssen, A., Ravesteijn, H., & Speckens, A. (2016). The contribution of work characteristics, home characteristics and gender to burnout in medical residents. *Advances in Health Sciences Education : Theory and Practice*, 22(4), 803–818. DOI: 10.1007/s10459-016-9710-9 PMID: 27651045

Chapter 19
The Effects of Financial Stress on Entrepreneurial Mental Health

Mohit Yadav
https://orcid.org/0000-0002-9341-2527
O.P. Jindal Global University, India

Preet Kanwal
https://orcid.org/0009-0006-5114-8381
Lovely Professional University, India

Majdi Anwar Quttainah
https://orcid.org/0000-0002-6280-1060
Kuwait University, Kuwait

ABSTRACT

This chapter explores the profound effects of financial stress on the mental health of entrepreneurs, highlighting how chronic financial pressures can impair decision-making, foster burnout, and strain personal and professional relationships. Untreated financial stress can lead to long-term mental health issues such as anxiety and depression, adversely impacting both the individual and their business. The chapter examines the role of financial literacy and support systems in mitigating stress, emphasizing the importance of proactive strategies to manage financial challenges. It also discusses the importance of resilience and coping mechanisms in protecting entrepreneurs' mental health and sustaining business performance. Ultimately, the chapter underscores the need for greater awareness and support in addressing financial stress to ensure long-term entrepreneurial success and well-being.

DOI: 10.4018/979-8-3693-3673-1.ch019

Copyright ©2025, IGI Global. Copying or distributing in print or electronic forms without written permission of IGI Global is prohibited.

INTRODUCTION: THE EFFECTS OF FINANCIAL STRESS ON ENTREPRENEURIAL MENTAL HEALTH

Entrepreneurship is often greeted as the highway to independence and financial freedom; however, it has a set of issues that stress the mental health of an entrepreneur. Among the most common and long-lasting stressors imposed on entrepreneurs lies in financial stress. This is in contrast to employment provision since, with traditional employment, the income will likely be stable and more predictable, while with entrepreneurship, finances are usually uncertain, with revenue streams fluctuating, and there is also the pressure of managing the sustainability of the business's finances. This stress bears a bearing not only on the business's viability but also greatly affects the mental health of those running such ventures.

There are many causes for financial stress in entrepreneurship, including inadequate cash flow, mounting debt, fluctuating markets, and pressure to raise funding. Most entrepreneurs invest personal savings or borrow large amounts of money to begin or launch their businesses, adding yet another layer of anxiety if the venture suffers a decline in performance or fails to generate the returns expected. This uncertainty in finances creates a chronic state of worry and stress, which develops into serious mental health issues such as anxiety, depression, and burnout over time. Because the nature of entrepreneurship often requires long hours and personal sacrifice, this, too, adds to the psychological burden. Moreover, external pressure from society and the internal pressure to create may sometimes be in conflict with the failure of not being able to address the financial needs of entrepreneurs, leading them to feel a sense of self-doubt, feeling of failure, and isolation.

The entrepreneurial environment inherently is one of risk, and with that risk goes unpredictability. Financial instability can amplify that unpredictability, and hence can impact the entrepreneur's decisions. There, financial pressure grabs the center-stage position of every entrepreneur, which makes them lose their clarity or rationality. Every entrepreneur is rendered a victim of reactive decisions, leading towards short-term solutions rather than the all-time peaceful postures of the business, further aggravating financial difficulties and resultant psychological pressure. The psychological weight associated with juggling financial stress and business operation becomes heavy enough to drive even the most seasoned entrepreneurs into emotional and cognitive exhaustion.

Beyond the business dimension, financial stress affects an entrepreneur's personal life. Most entrepreneurs find financial concerns spill over into relationship lives where social support systems affect their emotional resilience. This stress can be manifested physically, as in sleep disturbances and exhaustion, and other stress-related illnesses, which negatively affects both mental and physical health. The stigma attached to talking about financial struggles and mental health issues may also deny entrepreneurs access to such help, thereby prolonging the condition as they are left to carry on with the challenge single-handedly.

One significant aspect of long-term sustainability is to understand the deep impact financial pressure can have on mental health. Entrepreneurial and business systems will have to battle these financial pressures, but they need tools, resources, and support systems to help manage the mental health impacts. By probing into the interaction between financial pressure and entrepreneurial mental health, we realize the need for a holistic approach to entrepreneur support, which involves both financial management and mental well-being. In doing so, we promote not just healthy individuals but a far more sustainable and resilient entrepreneurial system.

Understanding Financial Stress in Entrepreneurship

The financial stress involved in entrepreneurship would be one of the most unavoidable aspects of it. In contrast to the traditional employment with predictable income, more likely, the entrepreneur faces uncertain income flows, volatile market conditions, and also has to keep looking for financing to support business operations and expansion. One definition that might be used for financial stress in entrepreneurship is the stress or pressure accompanying anxiousness as a result of money-related challenges and uncertainties. These pressures can take different forms, depending on the business's life cycle, the industry, and the entrepreneur's financial knowledge and capitals. At its heart is the relentless fear of not generating enough cash flow, not covering the cost of requirements, or sustaining profitability.

Among the most common causes of financial stress for entrepreneurs is a lack of cash flow. Early-stage startups face the predicament of how to balance costs of growth when incoming revenues are not as immense. An entrepreneur is bound to deal with many financial obligations to employees, operational costs, marketing, and/or product development. This places tremendous pressure on entrepreneurs to ever-wit their finances and look for new revenues or funding sources, which may run the risk of having to touch personal savings or a large amount of debt. Other cases may include the need to use personal savings or incur high levels of debt, which certainly worsens financial anxiety.

Debt is one of the significant contributors to financial anxiety during entrepreneurship. The early stages of most ventures depend more than the later stages on personal loans, credit cards, or other lines of credit. Debt offers a source of necessary capital to launch or grow a business but leaves a sizeable financial burden on the other side. Repayment deadlines become a cause of big stress when cash flow is not so reliable-it results in all-nighters and always keeps a person on edge. Moreover, the fear of further accumulation with no guarantee of success heightens the psychological impact as entrepreneurs often begin questioning their own decision and abilities.

Market volatility also plays an important role in making the entrepreneur face financial stress. The reasons are that most businesses are subject to market whims and fancies. Whims and fancies of the market in terms of changes in consumption behavior, competition, and broader economic issues do have a huge impact on business performance. External forces thus challenge entrepreneurs to either maintain transformation through innovation or cost-cutting measures, or strategic reorientation. These changes, however, relate to an investment in finance and risk taking, which increases the tension surrounding financial stability. Entrepreneurs, especially in highly competitive industries, are constantly pressed on to maintain an industry trend and stay ahead of the curve to compete, straining their financial resources and being chronic victims of stress.

Another source of financial pressure is the challenge of accessing capital. While very few founders could grow their venture successfully without external funding, many startups rely on it to drive growth and survival. The journey to accessing capital is, however, usually marred with a number of challenges. Entrepreneurs had to navigate through pitching to investors, tight financial expectations, and business plans, all while keeping operations going in their ventures. All these factors of uncertainty of securing investment, coupled with the fear of rejection, may eventually impose huge mental strain. This pressure is especially intense for those entrepreneurs who have invested some of their private resources in the business and now feel responsible for its success.

By understanding the sources of financial stress in entrepreneurship, it is evident that running a business is far from being simple. Entrepreneurs face the daily operations challenges but also the psychological impacts of financial uncertainty. Noting the multidimensional nature of financial stress will help entrepreneurs and other stakeholders clearly identify the required tools or support systems that can ease the impact on businesses so that they may regain sustainability coupled with maintaining their own health.

Psychological Impact of Financial Stress

Financial stress affects entrepreneurs in a wide-reaching and deep sense. The constant pressure of maintaining financial stability, with the added strain of losing so much in the event of failure, most likely leads to a myriad of mental health issues. The consequences of these impacts can therefore serve as a basis for initiatives aimed at identifying the need for mental health support and preventive services in the entrepreneurial sphere.

Anxiety and Depression

Entrepreneurs are highly prone to anxiety and depression, especially when financial stress becomes unmanageable. Because of the uncertainty of income and the tension in being able to pay salaries, cover bills, and invest in the future, chronic worry is likely to result. This chronically anxious state can then become difficult relaxing, or overthinking, with bodily manifestations such as headaches, tension, and even fatigue. Chronic anxiety causes depression, especially if an insurmountable financial strain exists. It can be hopeless, feel worthless and exhausted, further lowering levels for the proper management of the business. In extreme instances, financial strain can foster debilitating depression that has disastrous effects on personal relationships and quality of life (Sweet et al., 2013).

Burnout and Exhaustion

Entrepreneurs tend to dedicate many hours to the business, drawing on a sense of deep commitment to what they are doing and a feeling of obligation to get it right in order to succeed. Combining these pressures with financial pressures can quickly burn out. Burnout is characterized by both emotional, mental, as well as physical depletion based on ongoing stress and overwork. For entrepreneurs under financial pressure, the demands to manage everything about the business—sales and marketing, operations, and finance—may overwhelm. This results in the sensation of being "stretched too thin" or always "on edge," with no sense of exit. (Salgado, 2020).

Cognitive Overload and Decision-Making Impairments

Financial stress can also affect the cognitive state, especially in deciding aspects. Such pressure to take care of finance, alongside other responsibilities, puts immense psychological weight on the brain, minimizing the potential to focus clearly. Entrepreneurs may fail to prioritize accordingly, leading to deluded financial decisions such as cutting costs on areas directly linked to their sustainable gains or deferring the needed investment. It creates reactive decision-making behavior in the mind of the entrepreneur, including short term fixes rather than adopting long term strategies. This makes it a vicious cycle were bad decisions fuel financial problems and vice versa, causing more mental strain (Simonse et al., 2022; Khan et al., 2022).

Self-Doubt and Imposter Syndrome

Money stress can hurt an entrepreneur's ego and confidence depending on whether their set goals have not been met or slowed down in business growth. Self-perceived entrepreneurial success among entrepreneurs often becomes equated with the business's success; in case of financial difficulties, it is like personal failure. It sends the entrepreneur into self-doubt due to self-questioning abilities, decisions and prospects. Imposter syndrome is an internalized fear of being exposed as a "fraud" despite apparent accomplishments and is more commonly found among entrepreneurs who are under financial pressure. Impostor syndrome makes entrepreneurs feel that their success is undeserved or that they will inevitably fail; this brings about more emotional tension and more reluctance to take risks, which can in turn decrease financial stress (White et al., 2019).

Loneliness and Isolation

If there is financial pressure accompanying the entrepreneurial venture, it can be lonely. Not everyone supports the entrepreneurial mindset of a person being resilient, self-confident and competent, thus this removes the luxury of airing complaints or finding solace. As such, many entrepreneurs quietly suffer in isolation from their friends, family, or other professional networks. This level of isolation worsens the mental health as it makes the entrepreneur feel they have no one to really turn to for all their troubles or when depression finally hits them. The isolation and emotional exhaustion involved in a lack of support have increased the psychological distress that financial stress generates in an entrepreneur's recovery process (Miquel et al., 2022).

Long-Term Emotional Consequences

Unless controlled, the effects of stress can lead to long-term emotional consequences outside the entrepreneurial experience. Chronic stress does not just affect mental health but even has effects on physical health where people will suffer from high blood pressure, weak immunities, and cardiovascular problems. Long-term financial pressure raises the possibility of developing resultant long-term mental health disorders, including generalized anxiety disorder or clinical depression. Left unaddressed, entrepreneurs may be unable to continue their businesses or to launch other entrepreneurial efforts because the psychosocial scars from financial difficulties are permanent.

Therefore, awareness about the deep psychological pressure of financial pressure helps entrepreneurs be more proactive in preserving their mental health, both financially and emotionally. This awareness can even help the stakeholders such as investors, mentors, or business organizations develop programs and resources that reduce financial pressures on the entrepreneurs and mitigate potential mental effects.

Link Between Financial Stress and Mental Health

The link between financial stress and mental health has been studied extensively, and entrepreneurs are specifically at the risk of the relationship because of the inherent risks and uncertainties in managing a business. Financial stress not only directly affects the entrepreneur's mental wellbeing but also indirectly through this vicious cycle where stress further aggravates mental health issues, hence disabling an entrepreneur from handling financial distress effectively. The subsequent section describes how financial stress impacts other areas of mental wellbeing and how integration between financial well-being and mental well-being is pretty critical to entrepreneurship.

Disruption of Work-Life Balance

One of the most direct effects of financial stress is the erosion of work-life balance. Due to the tremendous time and energy spent in putting together and maintaining their businesses, entrepreneurs find it extremely hard to maintain work-life balance once financial stress is introduced. Chronic financial anxieties invade personal time, which makes it hard for entrepreneurs to disconnect mentally from their business. This blurring of boundaries leads to chronic stress, effects sleep patterns, increases irritability, and diminishes the enjoyment in personal time with family and friends. In the long run, inability to disconnect from work because of financial worries could eventually cause mental fatigue and erode personal relationships important for emotional support.

Impact on Sleep and Physical Health

Financial stress is another factor that leads to sleep disorders, which in turn escalates various mental health issues among entrepreneurs. When financial concerns seem to occupy the mind of the entrepreneur, it most often translates into racing thoughts or even inability to sleep well. A lack of adequate sleep will weaken cognitive functions such as memory, decision-making abilities or problem-solving abilities of entrepreneurs, which only makes it worse in coming to terms with financial and operational entrepreneurial challenges. Lack of sleep also contributes to the physical symptoms of stress, including headaches, muscle tension, and a weak immune system. Over time, these physical symptoms of financial stress can detract from health in general, making entrepreneurs more susceptible to mental health concerns such as anxiety and depression.

Strain on Personal and Professional Relationships

Financial stress impacts entrepreneurs firsthand; however, financial stress also creates a strain on their personal and professional relationships. In personal life, financial struggles may create tension in relationships with spouses, family members, or close friends due to the fact that such individuals are vicariously negatively affected by the financial struggle of an entrepreneur. Financial stress may create fights over financial issues or may result in entrepreneurs becoming emotionally unavailable, which leads to feelings of isolation and loneliness. This can also put a strain on professional relationships with the employees, investors, or partners since it affects the business from the financial side. It can be challenging for the entrepreneur to be frank and transparent, which subsequently thwarts trust and collaboration, thus giving the pressure a life within one's mind and emotions.

Cognitive Overload and Emotional Exhaustion

The pressure to solve financial problems creates cognitive overload for entrepreneurs as they become overwhelmed by choices and problems that need addressing. Financial stress forces entrepreneurs to make complex decisions when under pressure, impairing judgement in the process and leading to suboptimal outcomes ultimately. Therefore, in their brains, constantly considering financial problems dries up the cognitive resources. The entrepreneurs feel emotional exhaustion as they do not have enough zest or energy to move forward from that point. Often it results in a stage known as burnout, which is chronic physical and mental exhaustion, could take months or even years to recover. Depletion of emotional resources further makes entrepreneurs vulnerable to depression and other mental health disorders (Paul & Fancourt, 2022).

Self-Doubt and Imposter Syndrome

Financial stress triggers self-doubt and can eventually feed into the imposter syndrome, where entrepreneurs feel they are frauds and will be found out despite the success. When financial performance does not meet expectations, these business owners typically internalize the problem as failures and, therefore, have lower self-esteem. This state of self-doubt tends to open the floodgates for continuing cycles of unproductive thinking, making mental distress worse and further eroding confidence in their future decisions. With the pressure of financial stress, entrepreneurs find it extremely challenging to make prudent risk-taking decisions or seek business expansion opportunities which further exacerbates the viability of these businesses and perpetuates the psychology of incompetence (Hassan et al., 2018).

Long-Term Implications of Financial Stress on Mental Health

Left unchecked, the mental health consequences of financial stress become chronic; situations such as generalized anxiety disorder and major depressive disorders or even suicidal thoughts come to be long-term mental health issues. Financial stress leads entrepreneurs into a deep sense of hopelessness when they feel trapped with no way out of their financial struggle. There is always this looming dread of losing all the money in business or running out of money altogether, something that stands to adversely affect the psyche and mindset as well as the perception of both personal and professional futures. In extreme terms, when financial pressure persists over time, it gives way to or exacerbates emotional breakdown or major mental health crises that have to be dealt with at a professional level.

The association between financial stress and mental health is another cause that requires greater acknowledgment in the entrepreneurial system. Therefore, this specific strain is most often invited on the orders of entrepreneurs themselves, single-handedly and without the benefits or infrastructure in place that would shield them from the psychological effects. Since financial stress could be eased through more financial knowledge or counseling to mental health or through resilient building, their stress would not be harmful to their mental well-being as they carry through. Having an approach where mental health is considered alongside business support would remove the kind of financial stress but lead to healthier and sustainable entrepreneurial practices.

COPING MECHANISMS AND RESILIENCE STRATEGIES

Financial pressure is one of the areas of stress that come with entrepreneurship. Financial stress can be long-term exposure in business, and if it lasts, it can pose serious mental challenges. With such uncertainty and pressure in running a business, entrepreneurs need quite effective coping mechanisms and resilience strategies. These tools help alleviate psychological stress from financial situation, and they help entrepreneurs maintain their psychological well-being while dealing with the demands of their businesses. The following section gives a few practical approaches that entrepreneurs can take to build up resilience and sustain their mental strength by dealing with some stresses inherent in their journey.

1. Financial Planning and Budgeting

One of the most efficient ways of minimizing financial stress is through proactive planning and budgeting. A financial roadmap will allow an entrepreneur to understand his or her cash flows, predict when financial challenges might arise, and then make conscious decisions on expenses and investments. An entrepreneur will be able to provide himself or herself with a feeling of control over the financial situation by laying out a clear budget showing revenues, costs, and risks involved, thus overcoming anxiety. Regular review of financial statements and keeping emergency funds in place can also form a cushion for any external shocks facing uncertain financial times. This is facilitated through financial literacy because informed entrepreneurs in managing finances feel more confident in their actions.

2. Seeking Professional Advice

Entrepreneurs tend to do everything related to their business themselves. However, this also applies to financial management. Of course, getting professional advice from financial advisors, accountants, or mentors can help reduce stressful pressures involved in managing finances. Professionals can provide useful information on the optimization of cash flows, ways of sourcing funds, and clarity when dealing with complex financial matters. By consulting experts, entrepreneurs can, to a certain extent, alleviate the uncertainty that breeds financial stress and sort out which direction to take next. Mentorship also helps emotionally since experienced entrepreneurs can provide advice on how to weather financial storms based on their own experience, hence fostering resilience and confidence (Jiang et al., 2021).

3. Building a Support Network

Entrepreneurship is often pretty isolationist itself, particularly when it comes to financial stress. To keep the feelings of loneliness at bay, entrepreneurs must make sure they develop an engaging network of peers, mentors, friends, and family. Talking about the situation with close people can certainly provide the much-needed psychological venting and perspective. Networking with fellow entrepreneurs who know the peculiar stressors related to running a business can be very helpful, as they are most likely to provide practical tips on how to manage financial stress. Building a community relationship with investors, partners, or advisors also helps overcome the sense of isolation while facing financial hardship, making the burden less onerous (Elshaer et al., 2022).

4. Practicing Mindfulness and Stress-Reduction Techniques

Entrepreneurs can engage in mindfulness practices and stress-reducing techniques, such as meditation, deep breathing exercises, or yoga, to cope with the emotional strain of financial stress. Mindfulness allows people to be in the present and to focus on the current moment without being weighed down by pressure about the future or previous financial struggles. This can help entrepreneurs maintain emotional regulation and better take control of stressful situations with an unperturbed and clear mind. Apart from that, exercising, sleeping well, and proper dieting decrease stress levels, thus leading to improved general mental status, so the entrepreneur is kept stress-free during times of financial anxiety (Yuwono, 2023; Seraj et al., 2022; Yeh, 2020).

5. Time Management and Delegation

The most prominent cause of increasing financial stress is time management as people become overwhelmed by too much being pressed on them. The entrepreneur often has more than one role, which in turn might be too much pressure on the person to have everything under their control. Learning to prioritize and delegate their work gives entrepreneurs the psychological space to focus on very high-priority financial issues. Proper time management reduces the potential cognitive overload associated with juggling several responsibilities, creating space in the entrepreneur's life to spend enough time on financial planning and problem-solving. Delegation of work to some trusted members of the team or outsourcing non-core activities such as bookkeeping or administrative work could also help to lighten the daily load entrepreneurs face and ensure that they have time to think critically on strategic decisions and long-term financial health (Cardon & Patel, 2013).

6. Failure and Learned from Mistakes

Entrepreneurship resilience will call for a mindset that defines mishaps and setbacks as avenues for learning rather than failure per se. Of course, financial challenges form a part of the entrepreneurial journey. Due to growth mindset, even in critical moments, entrepreneurs can maintain their confidence since they know that failure is not an inevitable event but part of the entrepreneurial journey. Consequently, this situation will help reduce the psychological toll of financial stress when placed in perspective. Each financial crisis presents experiences that well would enable the entrepreneur to overcome future challenges in better skills and with greater strength. Entrepreneurs who treat failure not as a statement of worth or ability but as a temporary occasion are more resilient for getting over the trying period.

7. Manage Realistic Experiences and Expectations

Exaggerated expectations about growth prospects of businesses, returns on finances, or individual performances are things that make financial stress worse. Entrepreneurs have to set concrete, incremental goals and objectives where they can celebrate small victories and keep track of their progress over time. Reducing larger financial goals into simple steps makes the long-term challenges not so overwhelming as well as keeps motivation high. Realism also involves the aspect that setbacks financially are inevitable, and it will take much longer to be able to achieve success than you originally envisioned. Keeping a balanced perspective by adjusting goals as soon as they become unworkable can reduce most self-imposed pressure and help entrepreneurs remain focused on long-term sustainability (Hassan et al., 2018).

8. Mental Health Support and Therapy

Mental health support through therapy or counseling is a valuable coping mechanism when financial stress takes such a psychological toll. Mental health experts can provide tools for managing stress, anxiety, and depression that increase the ability of entrepreneurs to better deal with such cases of financial pressure. For instance, cognitive-behavioral therapy can improve upon negative ways of thinking when appraising financial strain, thus fostering healthier mental habits among entrepreneurs. Regular mental check-up with a counselor may also provide a safe space to voice concerns, navigate emotional challenges, and maintain strategies of continuing sound mental health (Baglow & Gair, 2018).

The whole process of dealing with financial stress would now require a combination of financial practical skills with emotional strength. They better face business ownership uncertainty since the entrepreneurs proactively take steps to cope with business ownership through financial planning, getting help, awareness, and psychological care. Resilience built through such strategies is beneficial not just for the well-being of the entrepreneur's mental health but also empowers them to lead their businesses out of economic challenges in a confident and clear manner. Comprehending the impact of mental health on entrepreneurship allows an individual to develop a road to success that is healthier and more sustainable.

ROLE OF FINANCIAL LITERACY AND SUPPORT SYSTEMS

Financial literacy and support systems are some of the most essential resources for any entrepreneur to maintain good mental health and manage financial stress. Entrepreneurs face financial challenges in diverse ways: cash flow management, raising capital in funding their operations, understanding tax laws, and determining their investments. In the absence of information regarding money and accessible help, these pressures can prove to be rather overwhelming, sending stress levels soaring and increasing the chances of psychological problems. This paper discusses the ways in which access to money and supportive networks can help buffer financial stressors and create a more plausible entrepreneurial experience (Khan et al., 2022).

1. Importance of Financial Literacy

Financial literacy will serve as the bases on which entrepreneurs base their financial decisions and make sense. It encompasses a good understanding of the essential financial principles relating to budgeting, cash flow management, tax obligations, and financial forecasting. Entrepreneurs with good financial literacy are well-equipped for planning the short-term and long-term positioning of their financial stability. In that regard, they will better estimate risks, provide resources better, and make strategic decisions for the financial well-being of the business. The ability of entrepreneurs in reading financial statements, balance sheets, and profit-and-loss reports allows them to track progress and react to issues before becoming significant financial stressors.

For most business owners, particularly those at their first venture in owning a business, the lack of financial management skills manifests itself in impulsive financial decisions, aggravating stresses and derailing their mental state. Such a small businessman or woman could face unexpected debts, fall short of funding, or experience undue tax liabilities as an end result of poor cash flow management or unclear financial implications of business decisions. A small entrepreneur operates at most in a state of anxiety and self-doubt without the proper managerial skills to direct finances (Adams et al., 2016).

2. Increasing Your Financial Literacy for Resolving Financial Stress

Entrepreneurs should invest in learning and developing skills in personal finance because financial stress management includes a very essential ingredient. The good thing is that financial literacy is one of the skills that can be learned and developed over a period. Entrepreneurs achieve knowledge of business finances by attending financial workshops or taking basic courses in accounting or financial management as well as working with financial coaches. These resources inform entrepreneurs on how to avoid common financial mistakes and allow them to devise strategies for remaining financially healthy (Jiang et al., 2021).

A good understanding of finance matters to entrepreneurs not only gives confidence in decision-making but also a sense of control over financial states. Control is very important when it comes to minimizing financial stress. Entrepreneurs who grasp the financial reality of the business are very unlikely to feel shocked, for instance, by dealing with debt, negotiating contracts, or looking for funds. Financial literacy further endows power on entrepreneurs' ability to foresee and prepare for possible financial problems, which enables them to take proactive measures to minimize uncertainty and emotional stress.

3. Access to Support Structures

Support networks represent a critical arena through which entrepreneurs would benefit in terms of alleviating financial stress. Not only will professional financial advisors and accountants form part of such a network, but also a network of mentors, peers, and mental health professionals ready to offer guidance and advice, and above all, emotional support. While reliable support networks ensure that entrepreneurs gain access to knowledge in instances where things get too hard to handle financially, they also give such entrepreneurs a community with which to turn at times when things become seriously stressing.

Financial advisors and accountants can provide entrepreneurs with comprehensive financial plans that lighten the burden of managing finances. Entrepreneurship can be managed with the guidance of professionals through the strategy on tax planning, investment, and debt management to find ways for optimal business financial health. These counselors can also assist entrepreneurs to determine the best possible means of sourcing for money, whether it is through loans, grants, or investment opportunities, thus therefore relieving some of the financial stress of raising capital.

Other than financial counselors, there are mentors as well as experienced entrepreneurs, who offer support and assistance by giving their own situations and insights of lessons learned concerning managing financial stress. These relationships mostly give an implication of brotherhood and perspective, which reduce the feeling of isolation. Mentors can give pragmatic insights into dealing with financial downturns, sources of financing, and strategic decision-making to move in step with personal or business goals. Such support also makes the entrepreneur feel not so isolated in the midst of such problems and further tests that financial failures are part of the entrepreneurial process and cannot be leveled with personal failure (Kiefl, 2024).

4. Role of Peer Networks and Entrepreneurial Communities

Entrepreneurial communities and peer networks also cushion financial stress. They allow entrepreneurs to share resources, exchange ideas, and discuss financial concerns among fellow entrepreneurs who share similar problems. Peer networks provide ample emotional support, encouraging collective collaboration on how to solve certain financial issues when one is at a loss about how to address them. They share each other's advice on how to raise funds, how to manage the cost of operations, and acquire financial services that will release the burden of the costs of doing it alone.

Online platforms, business clubs at the local level, and professional associations, too, provide entrepreneurs with opportunities to connect and share knowledge with peers while finding assistance in financial management tools and learning how to cope with economic downturns or industry-specific financial distresses. Such networks share knowledge and discuss financial 'shame' as much less of an issue; thus the entrepreneurs seek help before stress becomes a more serious mental health problem.

5. Mental Health Support in Financial Systems

Beyond financial literacy and business networks, mental health support within financial systems is recognized as a new and critical aspect of entrepreneur-facilitating support. Many financial institutions, venture capital firms, and entrepreneurial hubs are now being encouraged to realize the benefits of mental health services as part of their more general support to business owners. Financial services providers start now to provide mental health-related resources counseling or stress management programs - to entrepreneurs for the pressures of financial decision-making.

Other support programs for entrepreneurs aim at mental health work shops of how to cope with financial anxiety, prevent burn out, and how one recovers with financial setbacks. The programs teach entrepreneurs to care for themselves by showing that financial stress is normal and may be handled with adequate tools.

Financial literacy and support system is a key tool in helping entrepreneurs deal with financial stress. A well-understood knowledge of financial principles, as well as a network of advisors, mentors, and peers, reduces uncertainty and anxiety that entrepreneurs may feel regarding the management of their business. Financial literacy will empower entrepreneurs to make proper, well-informed decisions while providing the needed guidance and emotional strength to help drive through difficult financial decisions. All these resources, together, ensure that entrepreneurs are better positioned to hold a healthy mind and build resilience in order to cope up despite financial pressures for long-term accomplishment (Iram et al., 2022).

OTHER CONSEQUENCES OF UNADDRESSED FINANCIAL PRESSURE

Financial stress, if unchecked, could have deep profound long-lasting impact on the entrepreneur's mental, physical, as well as professional prosperity. While financial stress is most commonly associated with business troubles, chronic financial stress that has not been managed can spiral into an even more debilitating problem in both personal health and business performance. The chronic effect of financial stress can be somewhat different-effects on decision-making abilities, relationships, productivity, and quality of life-accrued either as a loss or as a gain. This chapter discusses the long-term consequences of untreated financial stress in entrepreneurs and the greater need for early intervention as well as proactive management.

1. Erosion of Mental Health and Risk of Burnout

The most evident and natural long-term consequence of the failure to treat financial stress properly in a contemporary entrepreneur is the devastating impact on mental health. Long-term financial stress leads to various conditions, such as anxiety and depression disorders and, in extreme cases, may eventually lead to the development of PTSD. These constant fears about financial insecurity, liquidity crises, or piling up debts also instill helplessness and trap a person either to endless chains of stress and failure. With passing time, these psychological problems gradually degrade an entrepreneur's emotional strength as they fail to deal with the day-to-day business pressures.

Burnout is the other significant threat. Usually, entrepreneurs under severe financial stress work themselves to an extent of losing rest, recreations, and personal time, sacrificing comfort for saving the business. These are unsustainable work patterns that may lead to burnout, which usually demoralizes the entrepreneur, making them less effective. Lifestyle adjustments such as reducing the scope of operations or taking time off are usually necessary to recover from burnout. Unmanaged financial stress, therefore can also push entrepreneurs to emotional and physical breaking points as it makes for a vicious cycle of worsening mental health along with deteriorating business performance.

2. Bad Decision Making and Avoidance of Risks

Financial stress significantly compromises an entrepreneur's mental ability and ability to make key decisions. When individuals face financial problems, entrepreneurs often have a form of "tunnel vision" that seeks short-term survival over long-range strategy. The entrepreneurs in such situations usually make inappropriate financial or organizational decisions, for instance: accepting insufficient loans, reducing the quality of the produced product, or hasty entry into partnerships that incidentally do not have long-term value added.

Unaddressed financial pressure also breeds risk aversion. An entrepreneur who is perennially distressed about the state of his or her finances tends to become excessively cautious and avoids investments or strategic growth opportunities necessary for business success, fearing that these decisions may worsen their financial predicament. Such a policy can really choke innovation and prevent the business from reaching its true potential. Alternatively, some entrepreneurs who try to hastily solve financial issues may embrace careless risks that worsen their position and finally end up with disastrous consequences on the business. Regardless of the above situations, poor judgment resulting from financial stress is often believed to undermine the long-term success of the business.

3. Worn Personal and Professional Relationships

Unaddressed financial stress does not only affect the entrepreneur but also family members and friends outside the business. High financial stress tends to get the better of entrepreneurs irrationally, and they might become irritated, withdrawn, or emotionally unavailable toward business partners, employees, and investors. Misunderstandings and conflict arising from dysfunction in communication destabilize the business even further. Over time, the nonaddressed tension hurts trust and teamwork, thus destructing the inner culture of a business and weakening the overall dynamics of a team.

On the personal front, financial constraints are stressful and do divert some energy away from relationships with family and friends. Many entrepreneurs find it hard to separate work life from personal life, with constant worry and anxiety spilling over into personal interactions. Financial distress further instills feelings of guilt, shame, or even inadequacy, especially if an entrepreneur cannot adequately meet personal financial obligations or cannot properly care for his or her family. This could lead to social withdrawal or conflict with loved ones, further deteriorating the individual's emotional detachment and stress.

4. Declining Physical Wellbeing

Not to be underrated are the physical effects of perpetual financial stress. Continual activation of the human's "fight or flight" response leads to the manufacture of stress hormones, most notably cortisol. Effective as these chemicals can be in smaller measures, their protracted use can devastate the human body. Entrepreneurs living under perpetual stress of financial strain are more prone to various health-related ailments resulting from stress, including high blood pressure, heart disease, and gastrointestinal disorders.

Financial stress is another underlying cause of sleep loss in entrepreneurs. Persistent anxiety about finances would not let the entrepreneur sleep and therefore lead to insomnia or low quality of sleep. It ultimately thins out the defense mechanisms and general mental strength, giving rise to mental problems such as anxiety and depression. It creates dangerous feedback where both the poor mental and the worsening body health are to affect an entrepreneur's performance in running his business.

5. Decreased Business Performance and Business Bankruptcy

Untreated financial stress can eventually lead to decreased business performance and, at worst, business bankruptcy. Entrepreneurs, being perpetually stressed, tend to disengage from the business, losing sight of their passion for their work. The result might mean lousy customer relationships, under-developed products, or poor marketing. As the business performance falls down, then the financial pressure will become a vicious cycle that could be difficult to conquer.

Financial pressure also prevents entrepreneurs from thinking in the most innovative and creative ways, which are important for business expansion. Rather than attempting to scale their business or creating opportunities in new markets, entrepreneurs become exceedingly focused on survival in the short term, thereby missing implied opportunities to expand or differentiate. Gradually, a reactive business can be bound down into an inability to compete meaningfully in the marketplace and heighten the risk of failure over time.

6. Reputation Damage on Entrepreneurs

Entrepreneurs with a large financial stress will also suffer reputational damage when they fail to meet their financial requirements, such as the failure to timely pay employees or creditors. Bad public perceptions can also originate from issues such as bankruptcy, lawsuits about bad debts and failure to perform on its promises to customers or investors. Reputation in the entrepreneurial world is of extreme importance as well. Financial instability will necessarily tarnish an entrepreneur's credibility through hardening future investments or partnerships.

This reputational damage can also haunt forever for the ability to recover or start new ventures in the future. Investors and stakeholders are often skeptical about dealing with entrepreneurs who have a history of financial mismanagement or instability. Therefore, untreated financial stress not only jeopardizes the current business but it also limits the future entrepreneurial opportunities.

The outcomes of untreated financial stress are dire, attacking everything about an entrepreneur's life: vision, mentality, and body physique, business performance, and personal relationships. A financial stress recession may cause burnout, poor decision-making, or even downfall unless checked in good time. Entrepreneurs need to detect signs of financial stress ahead of time and take some proactive step - and, in most cases, this would be financial literacy, support networks, or mental health care. Managing financial stress well can protect the health of one's mind, with the prospect of long-term business success increasing.

CONCLUSION

Financial stress has enormous, far-reaching, and very often underrated effects on entrepreneurial mental health. While economic pressures are part of the entrepreneurial dimension, without management, they have serious mental, emotional, and physical implications that not only affect the entrepreneur but also the well-being and sustainable survival of one's business. Chronic financial stress interferes with decision making and contributes to burnout and thus strains professional and personal relationships, having a ripple effect against long-term sustainability. Conversely, entrepreneurs facing financial stress can be prevented from the negative consequences by the implementation of relevant strategies of literacy in finance, supports, and resilience. In the end, entrepreneurs must take proactive approaches in dealing with financial challenges. They ought to realize that seeking mental health services when needed is very important and that sustaining a stable financial status is akin to promoting innovation. In this manner, business owners are able to manage their businesses while having their psyches also taken care of thereby achieving both personal and business prosperity in the long run.

REFERENCES

Adams, D., Meyers, S., & Beidas, R. (2016). The relationship between financial strain, perceived stress, psychological symptoms, and academic and social integration in undergraduate students. *Journal of American College Health*, 64(5), 362–370. DOI: 10.1080/07448481.2016.1154559 PMID: 26943354

Baglow, L., & Gair, S. (2018). Australian social work students: Balancing tertiary studies, paid work and poverty. *Journal of Social Work : JSW*, 19(2), 276–295. DOI: 10.1177/1468017318760776

Cardon, M., & Patel, P. (2013). Is stress worth it? stress-related health and wealth trade-offs for entrepreneurs. *Applied Psychology*, 64(2), 379–420. DOI: 10.1111/apps.12021

Elshaer, I., Azazz, A., Mahmoud, S., & Ghanem, M. (2022). Perceived risk of job instability and unethical organizational behaviour amid the covid-19 pandemic: The role of family financial pressure and distributive injustice in the tourism industry. *International Journal of Environmental Research and Public Health*, 19(5), 2886. DOI: 10.3390/ijerph19052886 PMID: 35270579

Hassan, N., Maon, S., & Kassim, E. (2018). Mental health predictors among malaysians during economic crisis: the 3fs influence.. DOI: 10.33422/8mea.2018.11.56

Hassan, N., Maon, S., & Kassim, E. (2018). Mental health predictors among malaysians during economic crisis: the 3fs influence.. DOI: 10.33422/8mea.2018.11.56

Iram, T., Bilal, A., Ahmad, Z., & Latif, S. (2022). Does financial mindfulness make a difference? a nexus of financial literacy and behavioural biases in women entrepreneurs. *Iim Kozhikode Society & Management Review*, 12(1), 7–21. DOI: 10.1177/22779752221097194

Jiang, Y., Zilioli, S., Balzarini, R., Zoppolat, G., & Slatcher, R. (2021). Education, financial stress, and trajectory of mental health during the covid-19 pandemic. DOI: 10.31234/osf.io/tvry4

Jiang, Y., Zilioli, S., Balzarini, R., Zoppolat, G., & Slatcher, R. (2021). Education, financial stress, and trajectory of mental health during the covid-19 pandemic. *Clinical Psychological Science*, 10(4), 662–674. DOI: 10.1177/21677026211049374

Khan, F., Siddiqui, M., Imtiaz, S., Shaikh, S., Tu, Y., & Wu, C. (2022). Determinants of mental and financial health during covid-19: Evidence from data of a developing country. *Frontiers in Public Health*, 10, 888741. Advance online publication. DOI: 10.3389/fpubh.2022.888741 PMID: 36117608

Kiefl, S., Fischer, S., & Schmitt, J. (2024). Self-employed and stressed out? the impact of stress and stress management on entrepreneurs' mental health and performance. *Frontiers in Psychology*, 15, 1365489. Advance online publication. DOI: 10.3389/fpsyg.2024.1365489 PMID: 38638509

Miquel, C., Domènech-Abella, J., Félez-Nóbrega, M., Cristóbal-Narváez, P., Mortier, P., Vilagut, G., & Haro, J. (2022). The mental health of employees with job loss and income loss during the covid-19 pandemic: The mediating role of perceived financial stress. *International Journal of Environmental Research and Public Health*, 19(6), 3158. DOI: 10.3390/ijerph19063158 PMID: 35328846

Paul, E., & Fancourt, D. (2022). Did financial interventions offset the impact of financial adversity on mental health during the covid-19 pandemic? a longitudinal analysis of the ucl covid-19 social study. DOI: 10.1101/2022.11.15.22282337

Salgado, S. (2020). Job insecurity, financial threat and mental health in the covid-19 context: the buffer role of perceived social support. DOI: 10.1101/2020.07.31.20165910

Seraj, A., Alzain, E., & Alshebami, A. (2022). The roles of financial literacy and overconfidence in investment decisions in saudi arabia. *Frontiers in Psychology*, 13, 1005075. Advance online publication. DOI: 10.3389/fpsyg.2022.1005075 PMID: 36248580

Simonse, O., Dijk, W., Dillen, L., & Dijk, E. (2022). The role of financial stress in mental health changes during covid-19. *Npj Mental Health Research*, 1(1), 15. Advance online publication. DOI: 10.1038/s44184-022-00016-5 PMID: 37521497

Sweet, E., Nandi, A., Adam, E., & McDade, T. (2013). The high price of debt: Household financial debt and its impact on mental and physical health. *Social Science & Medicine*, 91, 94–100. DOI: 10.1016/j.socscimed.2013.05.009 PMID: 23849243

Thayer, Z., & Gildner, T. (2020). covid-19-related financial stress associated with higher likelihood of depression among pregnant women living in the united states. *American Journal of Human Biology*, 33(3), e23508. Advance online publication. DOI: 10.1002/ajhb.23508 PMID: 32964542

White, N., Packard, K., & Kalkowski, J. (2019). Financial education and coaching: A lifestyle medicine approach to addressing financial stress. *American Journal of Lifestyle Medicine*, 13(6), 540–543. DOI: 10.1177/1559827619865439 PMID: 31662717

Yeh, T. (2020). An empirical study on how financial literacy contributes to preparation for retirement. *Journal of Pension Economics and Finance*, 21(2), 237–259. DOI: 10.1017/S1474747220000281

Yuwono, W., Susanna, , Ramadhani, D. S., Sasmita, E. W., & Sihotang, W. H. (2023). Analysis of the influence of the role of financial literacy on personal financial management. *European Journal of Business Management and Research*, 8(3), 57–61. DOI: 10.24018/ejbmr.2023.8.3.1891

Chapter 20
The Impact of Entrepreneurial Failures on Psychological Resilience

Deepak Kumar Sahoo
Biju Patnaik University of Technology, Rourkela, India

Thi M. Le
https://orcid.org/0000-0001-9720-308X
Vietnam National University, Hanoi, Vietnam

Anish Kumar
https://orcid.org/0000-0002-8047-4227
O.P. Jindal Global University, India

Ajay Chandel
https://orcid.org/0000-0002-4585-6406
Lovely Professional University, India

ABSTRACT

This chapter explores the profound impact of entrepreneurial failures on psychological resilience, highlighting how setbacks can serve as catalysts for personal growth and innovation. It examines the nature of entrepreneurial failure, the concept of psychological resilience, and the ways in which failure can foster resilience through learning and adaptation. Furthermore, the chapter discusses the psychological impacts of failure, strategies for building resilience post-failure, and the influence of cultural and societal factors. It also emphasizes the role of emotional intelligence in navigating the challenges of entrepreneurship and outlines effective psychological interventions and support systems. By recognizing the importance of mental health and resilience, this chapter underscores the need for a supportive ecosystem that empowers entrepreneurs to overcome obstacles, ultimately contributing to sustainable economic growth and a thriving entrepreneurial community.

DOI: 10.4018/979-8-3693-3673-1.ch020

INTRODUCTION

Entrepreneurial ventures are closely associated with innovativeness, riskiness, and pursuit of success. Instead, one of the most inevitable steps toward entrepreneurship is failure. Many start-ups and businesses failed to sustain themselves over the long run. Thus, failure should not be interpreted as a negative outcome but also an occasion for growth and personal development. In fact, how an entrepreneur goes about failure is the very factor of future success that forms. This bouncing back from mishaps is established in the definition of psychological resilience—a dynamic process in which individuals positively adapt to adversity (Borbolla-Albores & Reyes-Mercado, 2022). The ability to handle the tough times with psychological resilience is critical to entrepreneurship, and with the resilience, comes out harder and more adaptable with better preparation for future success.

Entrepreneurial failure could be in many forms, for example, financial loss, loss of confidence, broken professional relationships, or even personal disillusionment. It's personal for many entrepreneurs: the journey is all about a quest for success-indeed, self-identity-and therefore failure represents a meaningful emotional event. As such, the psychological and perhaps even physical consequences of such a failure can indeed be terrible, bringing feelings of inadequacy, depression, anxiety, and even burnout (Chadwick & Raver, 2018). Entrepreneurs, due to the nature of their activity, often invest their time, energy, and a total meltdown, so to speak-emotional well-being in their ventures. Failure usually takes an emotional toll on a business to such an extent that it is akin to a personal failure in that the person's self-esteem is damaged beyond the loss of business, and that emotional weight tends to wear off an entrepreneur's confidence and motivation in recovering and starting fresh.

But psychological resilience helps balance out the negative effects that may be put upon failure. Entrepreneurial resilience does not imply bouncing back; it means using failure as a strong tool that aids personal and professional growth. Entrepreneurs view failure as a part of learning, reframing setbacks as valuable lessons that inform what improvements can be done, how to pivot, or adjust in one's business strategies (Corner et al., 2017). This mindset enables them to deal with periods of vagueness and tension in a better way since it serves as the basis of the entrepreneur's adjustment to the volatile and unpredictable entrepreneurial environment.

Psychological resilience is cultivated through internal as well as external factors. On an internal level, entrepreneurs must establish the growth mentality, so they treat challenges as problems and not impossibilities. Thus, emotional regulation, self-awareness, and long-term orientation are a part of what makes up resilience. Strength on the outside also comes in the form of social support systems: mentors, peers, and family aid entrepreneurs in dealing with the emotional impact of failing. Being around a support network of trusted advisors with whom one can share problems, solicit support, and receive guidance enables an entrepreneur to bounce back even more effectively (Hoe & Janssen, 2022).

In conclusion, even as failure could be rather frightening and disenchanting for the entrepreneur, conversely, it can provide the possibility of growth and change. Psychological resilience is pertinent in how entrepreneurs react and bounce back from failure. The ability to develop resilience means that entrepreneurs not only cope with setbacks but also can transform them into steppingstones for success.

UNDERSTANDING ENTREPRENEURIAL FAILURE

Entrepreneurial failure is a fact of life which can be witnessed in the business world. Statistics show that most startup ventures do not survive their first few years of life. The high failure rates may seem ominous, but they are an intrinsic ingredient of the entrepreneurial process where market forces, competitive rivalry, financial instability, and other sources of failure can easily defeat even the best-planned venture. Understanding the multi-aspect nature of entrepreneurial failure is quite important since it provides insight into both the practical and emotional dimensions of business setbacks, even preparing entrepreneurs for the possibility of failure in developing the resilience to overcome such a setback (Lyu, 2024).

Actually, at its core, entrepreneurial failure represents a situation where a business fails to meet either financial, operational, or strategic objectives. The most common form of business failure is financial failure, usually resulting from a lack of cash flow, an inability to raise further investment, or poor financial management. Companies that take too long to gain stable income quickly exhaust their resources and go insolvent. Apart from financial failures, there are also types of operational defects that can destroy the success of a business (Ukil & Jenkins, 2022). These may include supply chain breakdowns, inability to optimize production processes, or an inability to scale up to meet growing demand. Other external factors that cause the failure of a venture may involve strategic errors, such as incorrect estimation of trends in the market, wrong target customers, or a product not formulated based on actual requirements from consumers.

However, internal factors play their part as well. Poor leadership, improper management, and weak team dynamics lead to more problems in the venture; therefore, an entrepreneur faces additional challenges in resolving the issue that starts unwinding. They may be without decisive decisions or during crises when they lack the appropriate experience and skills. They will also lose out when there is a change in the market conditions or due to technological disruption. Entrepreneurs who are too possessive about a model or a strategy and are not willing to shift or innovate could become losers in the rapidly changing marketplace.

Entrepreneurial failure, however, is beyond just practical or strategic outcome because it has implications that are emotional and psychological. A business, for most entrepreneurs, is far more than an economic investment; rather it reflects their vision, passion, and identity. As a result, when a firm goes bust, the experience feels more intimate and is bound to be an emotional weight of self-doubt and potentially depression (Yang, 2023). Feelings of guilt or shame may be intensified at the moment where one feels to have disgraced subordinates, investors, or even relatives. However, this emotional cost can be supplemented by a loss in finance, a position of status, or fear of future dangers, and therefore it is pretty difficult for an entrepreneur to recover and rebuild after such a defeat.

The complete comprehension of entrepreneurial failure demands the building up of the perception of the material as well as immaterial costs. And even though an entrepreneur's failure could be caused by the external market forces or to the internal inept management, the effect upon his mental and emotive welfare is just as important. There is a secret in the perception itself. Failure needs to be perceived, not as an everlasting setback but as part of the learning process for entrepreneurs. With such an attitude, entrepreneurs are more empowered to grow with necessary resilience required to handle failure, learn from experiences, and derive lessons into building success (Yao et al., 2021).

THE CONCEPT OF PSYCHOLOGICAL RESILIENCE

In simple words, resilience in psychology is about adapting to whatever situation or condition of adversity, stress, or failure with which one might be confronted and even thriving under it. In the entrepreneurial world, uncertainty and pressure and setbacks are part of the journey; therefore, resilience should be a trademark to keeping going and achieving long-term success. It's through resilience that entrepreneurs can maintain that control and purpose even when surrounded by extreme difficult challenges-an ability that enables transformation of failure into opportunity for growth and learning. Bouncing back is really about feeling more resilient, having more mental strength, and pushing through to come back stronger (Hedner et al., 2011).

Resilience is dynamic, not an inherent, attribute, and therefore must be built gradually. Resilience encapsulates emotional regulation, flexibility in thinking, and perseverance. Emotionally resilient entrepreneurs have learned to live through ups and downs without negative emotions seeping into and lowering their ability to continue making rational decisions. Another important feature is cognitive flexibility: the ability to see problems from more than one angle and to alter thinking in response to changing circumstances (Zhao & Wibowo, 2021). Feedback-open adaptable entrepreneurs who can pivot their business strategy in response are exemplary of this flexibility in a way that helps them ride through uncertainty and recover more quickly from setbacks.

There are several psychological theories on which the concept of resilience is based, but one such theory that can be considered here is the "growth mindset," developed by psychologist Carol Dweck. The core belief of a growth mindset is that abilities and intelligence can be developed through effort and learning (Jing et al., 2016). Entrepreneurs with a growth mindset approach failure not as a presentation of their inherent capabilities but as a basis of learning. This view enables them to keep going even when things go wrong and continually strive for excellence, even in the face of failure. The person with the fixed mindset, on the other hand, views defeat as a demonstration of their inability to do something else and thus has more trouble bouncing back and getting on with things.

Another critical component of psychological resilience is self-efficacy -the belief in their power to affect events and outcomes. An entrepreneur with high self-efficacy will believe in being capable of solving any problems, managing emotions, and bringing about goals, even when things get tough. Agency motivation will nurture a pro-action attitude toward failure, where temporary setbacks are just waiting to be solved rather than insurmountable barriers. This usually calls for the development of self-efficacy by setting achievable goals and commemorating small wins and developing mastery over one's skills (Lafuente et al., 2019).

Support systems also play a vital part in psychological resilience. Many entrepreneurs who are resilient depend on their networks of mentors, peers, family, or friends for both emotional and practical support. Such relationships provide positive reinforcement during challenging times, offer one an idea incubator, and strengthen an entrepreneur's sense of belonging and connection. According to research, high levels of support are capable of reducing the effects of psychological failure and preventing burnout.

Psychological resilience is the ability of an entrepreneur to cope with failure and adversity: it involves skills built in emotional regulation, cognitive flexibility, self-efficacy, and growth mindset (Hartmann et al., 2022). Developing these skills and utilizing social support helps entrepreneurs adequately resilient for recovery from failure but, more importantly, using failure as a powerful tool for success in the future. Resilience transforms failure into a steppingstone for the mindset where setbacks feed determination and innovation rather than discouragement and retreat.

ENTREPRENEURIAL FAILURE AS A CATALYST FOR GROWTH

Entrepreneurial failure-even though always perceived as a major setback-can be a great catalyst for growth and transformation. Failure may bring financial loss, emotional frustration, and even temporary cessation of one's enterprise; however, it also brings lessons that may powerfully lead to success in the future. As such, resilient entrepreneurs do not view failure as a dead-end road but as a critical stepping-stone toward personal and professional development. Failure can be considered an excellent opportunity for entrepreneurs to refine strategies, improve skills, and finally build a sustainable business in the long run (Lee & Wang, 2017).

Perhaps the greatest insight into failure is an understanding of the entrepreneurial process. Failure reveals the inadequacies found within business models, financial management, marketing approaches, and leadership styles, all of which may have been overlooked during the times of success. Entrepreneurs who have learned to welcome failure as an opportunity for learning will be in a better position to identify and correct such weaknesses (Sachdev, 2023). Reflective ability results in stronger decision-making ability and a more refined approach in subsequent business ventures. For example, inability to succeed in the marketplace may imply that an entrepreneur will conduct better market research and choose a product or service that is more adaptable in a subsequent endeavor. This way, failure provides the chance of honing both analytical abilities and strategic planning.

Failure also promotes emotional and psychological development, especially about resilience and perseverance. Of course, entrepreneurship will only be complete with persistence in adversity; and it is often with failure that such a trait is intensified. With every failure, the entrepreneur is bound to face challenges, harsh conditions, and has to push him or herself past his or her comfort zone. In the long run, this process lays down ground for emotional toughness and mental flexibility, which makes them better at handling future hurdles with less pain (Bullough & Renko, 2013). Success in overcoming failure also enhances one's self-understanding because entrepreneurs gain a better understanding of their strengths, weaknesses, and their limitations. This new consciousness then becomes a resource for both development and leadership.

Aside from the development aspect, failure can also spark innovation. For entrepreneurs, the drive is one of solving a problem to create value; this failure then points out the missing gaps that would attract solution innovation. Many of the most memorable breakthroughs that have transformed the innovation landscape were once failures; entrepreneurs who are forced to rethink their approach on product launch may ultimately find new ideas or previously ignored markets. For example, a business owner who has determined that a product launch failed discovers a much more promising niche for their business or even finds better technology that will transform their industry. In that regard, with failure comes the prospect of identifying new possibilities. Entrepreneurship at all times makes them stay ahead of any innovation, hence making them relevant for the long term (Bullough et al., 2014).

Failure also helps make entrepreneurs increase their credibility and trustworthiness in the eyes of investors, partners, and stakeholders. Those people who go about openly admitting their failures, look into what they learned, and showcase the ability to adapt are often considered more experienced and capable leaders. Investors are known to appreciate that a businessperson who has experienced failure is, in general, more cautious, wise, and willing to adjust in later ventures. It is often this maturity that comes as a result of failure that makes entrepreneurs more appealing investment and collaboration candidates (Duchek, 2018).

Failure is not a barrier to entrepreneurial success but an open gateway to growth, learning, and innovation. Entrepreneurs who take failure to learn become able to create more robust and responsive businesses through that insight. Entrepreneurs learn strategies, become better known to themselves, develop innovations, and eventually become in a better position to reach greater success in the future through the lessons of failures learned by their failures. Therefore, failure, accepted on one's entrepreneurial journey, becomes a catalyst for success and resiliency.

PSYCHOLOGICAL IMPACTS OF ENTREPRENEURIAL FAILURE

Consequent upon such a failure, the psychological impact on entrepreneurship is quite deep and wide: it reaches not only into an entrepreneur's professional career but, even into his/her mental and emotional life. Entrepreneurship often involves quite personal activities where one invests time, resources, energy, and passion for building a venture. In such a case, the failure of the venture can bring very negative effects leading to a multiplicity of bad feelings and psychological tasks (Shepherd & Patzelt, 2017). Unless such impacts are well managed, they may limit the recovery and reengagement abilities of the entrepreneur in future entrepreneurial activities. It is therefore necessary for the entrepreneur to understand psychological consequences of failure in navigating this challenging experience so as to build resilience for the future.

The most immediate psychological consequence of entrepreneurial failure is a deep sense of personal failure. Because of their identities and perceived self-worth being tied up with the performance of the business, entrepreneurs find it very challenging to differentiate between failing in their venture and failure of themselves. This identification culminates in the accomplishment of deep feelings of inadequacy and shame and self-doubt. Entrepreneurs question themselves, becoming skeptical about their abilities, choices and their judgment capability. Their confidence level drops drastically. In fact, the inner conflict is often compounded with external pressure from investors, family, employees, and peers that may increase feelings of guilt or disappointment (González-López et al., 2019).

The other most frequent psychological consequence of entrepreneurial failure is depression with anxiety. The emotional tensions associated with the loss of a business are bound up with problems of finance loss, professional relationship collapse, and uncertainty of the future leading to depressive disturbances. Being hopeless, losing enthusiasm for things they used to enjoy, and feeling like they have lost the fun in life because of business endeavors. Anxiety resulting from the fear of the unknown - possibly the uncertainty of what to do about the professional future or their outstanding financial liabilities. The dread of failure would give an entrepreneur tremendous fear of failures, and now that makes it hard to take more risks in their business (Liu et al., 2023).

In some cases, entrepreneurial failure may lead to burnout, especially if the entrepreneur has spent much time and energy on the business, with little recovery and support. Burnout is experienced as exhaustion, which includes both physical and emotional depletion, detachment from the task through reduced performance, and a decreased feeling of achievement. An entrepreneur who becomes burnt out is sure to feel mentally drained and have a hard time focusing on new ideas; it is therefore challenging to regain the creative spark to enable innovation. Chronic stress and burnout have negative impacts on physical health, like sleeplessness, frequent headaches, and weakening of immune systems.

Other psychosocial impacts relate to erosion of confidence-in oneself and perhaps towards others. Failure entrepreneurs may become wary of depending on other people to cooperate because they eventually expect to be disappointed. This mistrust can lead to isolation, which in turn worsens feelings of loneliness and disconnection from professional networks (Ayala & Manzano, 2014). Self-trust is also often compromised as the entrepreneur questions their ability to make sound decisions, assess risk, or otherwise implement one's vision. Loss of self-trust can indeed lead to a paralysis of action where the possibility of repeating mistakes holds entrepreneurs back from taking action.

Psychologically, the failure experienced in entrepreneurship extends beyond the individual but to their personal relationships. Financial and emotional stress can result in conflicts in families, friends, or business partners. Such entrepreneurs withdraw into themselves due to shame and guilt, followed by avoiding social lives, where loneliness, and psychological pressure from a lack of support in the coping process are maximized (Borbolla-Albores & Reyes-Mercado, 2022).

Although entrepreneurial failure indeed poses serious psychological challenges to entrepreneurs, these impacts can be overcome. Overcoming the psychological disadvantages of failure is supported by appropriate strategies such as mentoring support, mental health support, and connectivity with peer groups that assist entrepreneurs in engaging with emotions with renewed confidence to refocus confidence. Psychological recovery from failure requires a different attitude about seeing failure as not being permanently lost but only temporally failed. Entrepreneurs who can process their emotions and extract lessons from the experience often prove to be more ready to continue or resume "new" endeavors with strength and optimism.

Psychological effects of failure in entrepreneurship can range from personal failure to depression, anxiety, and burnout. Loss of self-confidence, social isolation, and the tension on personal relationships make things worse. However, acknowledging these and engaging the resilience-building skills may enable entrepreneurs to cope with the psychological weight of failure by putting things behind and coming back more positive, stronger and fuller self-awareness, more prepared for next opportunities (Chadwick & Raver, 2018).

BUILDING RESILIENCE POST-FAILURE

Building resilience in the aftermath of entrepreneurial failure is a crucial step towards healing and eventually further success. Failure is painful, yet it may serve as a wellspring of deep learning and nourishment for personal growth. The entrepreneur better able to bounce back and press on toward their goals with renewed energy after experiencing setbacks and challenges is one who develops resilience. This type of building resilience necessitates emotional, cognitive, and behavioral alteration in helping entrepreneurs not only deal with failure but recover and learn from adversity. The potential to renew activities of entrepreneurship after failure necessitates resilience after failure to maintain long-term recovery (Corner et al., 2017).

Acceptance and acknowledgment: Acknowledging the experience is the initial step in building resilience after failure. Denial and escape through running away from failure continue to prolong emotional pain and eliminates the prospect of effective learning. Entrepreneurs would fight their disappointment, frustration, or guilt feelings and attribute those as part of the process. They can come out from a defeat mentality to a development one if they accept failure as part of the entrepreneurial journey (Hoe & Janssen, 2022). Acceptance is allowing the self and others to displace the fear of judgment and is suggesting that failure does not indicate one's capability or future prospect. It's a temporary setback, not an indelible stain on inadequacy.

Reflection is another important ingredient of building resilience. Then, after failure, honest reflection of what went wrong and what one could have done differently would be helpful. It will do more than analyzing the influence of such factors as market conditions and competition but also into personal decision-making, leadership style, and business model. The greatest lesson entrepreneurs can learn is areas where they need improvement and will help them when starting their next business. Getting a lesson from failure is what shapes new skills and sensibilities into turning mistakes into opportunities. It outlines resilience in adapting these lessons to situations (Lyu, 2024).

Building a supporting structure after failing is very important as well. In most cases, most entrepreneurs suffer their failures alone; however, social support offers emotional encouragement, practical advice, and a feeling of belonging. Seeking advice from mentors, peers, or advisors who have been in similar predicaments may help and limit feelings of loneliness. Friends and family members can also provide much-needed emotional stability during times of uncertainty (Ukil & Jenkins, 2022). Surrounding oneself with positivity deters the psychological pressure of failure and creates resilience to bounce back. A good network can also motivate and encourage taking risks again, which is important in returning to entrepreneurial life.

Building a growth mindset is essential to resilience building. This is the mindset developed by psychologist Carol Dweck-that one can develop ability and intelligence through effort and learning. Entrepreneurs with this kind of mindset view failures as something that will lead them to success, seeing errors as part and parcel of the learning process. More probably, resilient entrepreneurs in the future would be one who takes risks in calculated steps. Entrepreneurs look for improvement, as well as challenges are great opportunities for development. A growth mindset allows entrepreneurs to redefine failure from being a recipe for reinvention instead of an end (Yang, 2023).

And finally, reaching realistic and achievable goals is another essential step in rebuilding resilience after failure. Ambitious entrepreneurs set goals that might be a bit too big to meet in the short term and get frustrated. Breaking these major goals into smaller steps that are easier to accomplish creates that feeling of accomplishment and builds confidence and momentum. Each small accomplishment fosters the impression that progress is possible, thus transforming discouragement into a resilient feedback mechanism. Achieving realistic goals is going to reduce the chances of burnout. The entry of the entrepreneur into a business will be paced when entrepreneurs control their self-pacing in the pursuit of achieving their goals (Yao et al., 2021).

One of the most underestimated behaviors of resilience is self-care. An entrepreneur who neglects to take proper care of their bodies and minds may not have the grit to try again once they commit a failure. In that concern, exercise, sleep, and mindfulness such as meditation can help entrepreneurs get over the stress and regain their emotional balance. Time off the business to refresh intellectually and emotionally in some way is what enables entrepreneurs to get back with renewed clarity and purpose. The element of resilience is not just persistence but in fact, such a person knows when to take rest and get back and then attempt something again (Hedner et al., 2011).

Action builds resilience after failure. While reflection and planning are a crucial part of the process, actual actions toward new prospects enable one to finally emerge as a better-off person over failure. It is the willingness to try again, even to lose, which displays a kind of resilience that leads to long-term success. Whether launching a new venture, pivoting an existing one, or venturing into a completely new industry, there is readiness to act, even fear of failure with each new attempt now a possibility for success and a chance to apply the lessons learned from past failures.

Building resilience after the failure of an entrepreneurial venture is a multi-dimensional process involving acceptance, reflection on self, support systems, development of a growth mindset, goal setting, and the like. A resolute entrepreneur is one who accepts failure as a learning experience and is willing to adapt his or her strategies to emerge more prepared to take the next step in handling more challenges that come their way. This perspective isn't about failing but succeeding through the calamities. This resilience-building habit helps entrepreneurs turn setbacks into steppingstones toward greater success and fulfillment (Zhao & Wibowo, 2021).

CULTURAL AND SOCIETAL INHIBITORS OR FACILITATORS TO ENTREPRENEURIAL RESILIENCE

Entrepreneurial resilience is certainly not based on personal character or individual experience. Much importance must be attached to the cultural and societal factors that contribute to entrepreneurial resilience. The working environment is hugely determining of how the entrepreneur perceives failure, recovers from setbacks, and finally builds up resilience in the longer run. There are differences across cultures, social norms, and community expectations in perceiving failure and resources to recover. Awareness and understanding of these cultural and social influences enhance insight into the larger context in which resilience emerges and how to help entrepreneurs within such diverse settings (Jing et al., 2016).

For example, in the Western world, especially countries like in the United States, failure is a must-not-be-avoided and even a worthy part of the process that leads to a successful end. In fact, the whole culture of Silicon Valley encourages "failing fast," which simply implies learning through trying and experimentation with minimal lag time for adjustment. Thus, failure becomes a familiar ground for learning, eventually ridding itself of stigmas in business failures (Lafuente et al., 2019). The commonality in these types of settings is that entrepreneurs are highly likely to speak out about their failures and seek peers for advice, promising to re-engage in a new venture with a community, for instance, that values perseverance.

Conversely, in other cultural contexts, failure presents a form of higher stigma-that can push the issue into a nebulous sphere. In most Asian cultures, a poor show in business means being viewed as failing personally and thus involving shame at both the individual level and social level between the family and community. An entrepreneur may fail to take risks or publicly disclose their failure because of fear of having failed and the associated social consequences, thereby reposing them in isolation and restriction of their ability to learn from each experience (Hartmann et al., 2022). Social pressure to succeed can cause too much psychological tension and therefore make it difficult for entrepreneurs to recover psychologically and professionally after some form of failure. In such settings, resilience is harder to build because cultural attitudes restrict open discussion of failure and sharing the lessons learned.

Societal-level support systems also affect entrepreneurial resilience in different ways. These include mentors, networks, and financial resources. In such institutional support systems for entrepreneurship-where for example, government has programs to facilitate the birth of new startup companies, business incubators, and venture capital networks-an entrepreneur can find support to rebound from failure to start anew. Such support systems give one an assurance that should they fail, it will not be a prevalence of failure in their entrepreneurial career. Under such conditions, entrepreneurship is likely to foster resilience because there are resources outside of themselves that they can rely on to bounce back from setbacks (Lee & Wang, 2017).

However, in poorer or less-developed areas without the necessary financial assets or entrepreneurial resources, resilience might be harder to come by. For example, entrepreneurs working within developing economies face systemic obstacles such as inadequate access to capital, weak infrastructure, and burdensome regulatory climates. Without funding, good mentorship, or good networking, entrepreneurs might be unable to bounce back when failure arises in such environments (Sachdev, 2023). More importantly, failure in such societies might hinder an individual's belief in his or her ability to recover setbacks because roles that would provide them with entrepreneurial uplifting cases are limited to those who have actually rebounded from the failure of doing business. This also creates an unyielding atmosphere because entrepreneurship must navigate the structural obstacles without outside support that encourages healing and regeneration.

Religion and spiritual beliefs also determine how entrepreneurial resilience can come into being. In certain societies, religious activities and beliefs create a framework to view failure as part of the larger divine plan, or at times it is a step toward self-actualization. For example, trusting in God's plan like in many Islamic cultures, may encourage the acceptance of failure as a test of faith and an opportunity for spiritual growth. In Buddhist philosophy, the same approach is represented in many Eastern philosophies: failure is a normal part of life (Bullough & Renko, 2013), and resilience comes through mindfulness, detachment from material outcomes, and impermanence. These cultural settings may also provide the entrepreneur with spiritual belief with which he can still maintain his focus and momentum even after experiencing failure.

Media and social constructs of entrepreneurship add another layer to resilience. In societies where epic stories of entrepreneurial heroism do not speak and believe about the struggles as much as failures that accompany it, entrepreneurs are even forced to stick by such uninhibited myths of success. It can create a false narrative of success that came easily and a general attitude about keeping failure hidden. It may be difficult for entrepreneurs in this kind of environment to develop resilience since in this environment, the societal narrative does not normalize failure or provide examples of how one might recover from it (Bullough et al., 2014). Media showcasing the successes and failures of entrepreneurs keep the perspective of entrepreneurship one-dimensional and resilient, urging individuals whose failure is part of the process and, being resilient, adjust to issues.

Cultural and societal influence on development tend to play a very crucial role in the development of entrepreneurial resilience. The cultural climate of a society may lead to the production of more resilient entrepreneurs if the culture normalizes failure, there is an institutional support structure, and open dialogue about setbacks is fostered. It may inhibit resilience if the culture stigmatizes or there is a lack of a support structure for entrepreneurs, which makes recovery and reengagement after setbacks difficult (Duchek, 2018). There are therefore so many cultural and social factors that one has to understand when creating settings that help inspire resilience in both entrepreneurs and their attitudes towards failure as a bridge to success rather than a total failure. Building such a culture which recognizes the need for learning from failure will thus empower entrepreneurs to become resilient enough for sustainable entrepreneurial success.

THE ROLE OF EMOTIONAL INTELLIGENCE IN ENTREPRENEURIAL RESILIENCE

EI is the most central element in the development of entrepreneurial resilience. This capacity Molds and prepares entrepreneurs to employ emotional intelligence in successfully dealing with obstacles and failures along their path. Emotional intelligence can be generally defined as the ability to perceive, appraise, and respond to emotion with awareness. It influences both the intellective and the non-intellective aspects of an individual's decision-making, encompasses self-awareness, and allows for the accomplishment of goal-directed behavior by gaining influence over, controlling, and/or reducing one's personal experience of emotion and that of others (Shepherd & Patzelt, 2017). It is a crucial aspect that determines how a person will react to failure, stress, and adversity. Emotional intelligence positions entrepreneurs to be more able to handle the highs and lows of emotions associated with entrepreneurship, and once failures begin to happen, they can recover faster and keep continuing on with confidence and optimism. The dynamic relationship between emotional intelligence and resilience includes emotional regulation, empathy, self-awareness, and adaptability.

The most prominent component of emotional intelligence when it comes to building a resilient model is emotional regulation. Entrepreneurs experience huge emotions that have a wonderful sense of achieving a lot or plunging into sad, desolate feelings in case of failure. Controlling these emotions will, therefore, be the key to creating psychological stability rather than bowing down to massive emotions. Successful entrepreneurs who are good at emotional regulation will most probably deal with frustration, anxiety, and disappointment when they fail. Instead of maladaptive emotions, they can foster such emotions in a healthy, positive way. This makes it possible for them to focus and make rational decisions when things are getting worse during intense moments. Their emotional regulation is the base of resilience because it enables entrepreneurs not to freeze up with fear or stress (González-López et al., 2019).

The other vital component of emotional intelligence that significantly contributes to entrepreneurial resilience is self-awareness. Self-awareness is the process of knowing and understanding one's emotional responses, strengths, weaknesses, and behavioral patterns. Good self-aware entrepreneurs are in an appropriate position to know they are emotionally ill or that the stress level is unbearable. This enables them to take control and start seeing support, taking time off, or redoing their approach towards a problem (Liu et al., 2023). Self-awareness enables the entrepreneur to reflect constructively over the failures, know the areas they must improve upon, and to not treat setbacks as failures but as a way of learning instead of being defeated. This introspection and adjustment is even more about picking up oneself from failure, a prerequisite for long-term resilience.

The ability to understand and share the feelings of others, a thing termed as empathy, works indirectly but is very essential in forming entrepreneurial resilience. Most of the activities of entrepreneurship include managing teams, partners, customers, and investors who bring along their emotions and expectations in the relationship. Entrepreneurs who have high empathy will handle such interpersonal dynamics with sensibility, leading to vigorous relationships and resource support. Whenever things get sour or become tough, empathy will help an entrepreneur in maintaining connections-both emotional and practical-that are important when times get tough. Building and maintaining a network of supportive relationships helps build resilience, that is by preventing entrepreneurship to feel isolated and gives access to means of rehabilitation from setbacks (Ayala & Manzano, 2014).

Emotional intelligence gives entrepreneurs a particular sense of adaptability and flexibility-very important parts of resilience. Entrepreneurship is uncertain most of the time. Changing circumstances require an entrepreneur to adapt in business if they are to achieve their goals. Emotionally intelligent entrepreneurs are always set to adapt to circumstances involving changing situations, embracing change and uncertainty as opportunities for growth rather than backing up with fear or any form of resistance (Borbolla-Albores & Reyes-Mercado, 2022). In that capacity, they can pivot business models, strategies, and approaches and turn setbacks into opportunities for innovation. Actually, with emotional intelligence, enterprising people can remain hopeful and positive even after the venture fails, depending on their knowledge of their emotions, which would keep them motivated and geared for successive attempts whenever original plans go awry.

Emotional intelligence further leads to the nourishment of a positive attitude, which may be crucial for resilience. Entrepreneurs with higher emotional intelligence are apt to be more optimistic in their steps and have less fixation with regard to negative possibilities. They view failure as an inconsequential setback and cling to the hope of succeeding, no matter the current setbacks they are encountering (Chadwick & Raver, 2018). This positive attitude, anchored on emotional intelligence, fosters a mindset for persistence and pushes entrepreneurs back into the fray despite even the most insurmountable odds. Positive thinking allows entrepreneurs to reinterpret failure as a learning moment-the lessons learned from mistakes will have them rising again, stronger.

A successful entrepreneur should know how to control their emotions in order to have the right decisions and act in the right way in a tough situation. Apart from controlling one's emotions, entrepreneurial failure emotionally intelligent entrepreneurs tend to understand other's emotions and motivations much better, which is hugely beneficial when one has to lead a team through a difficult time. Entrepreneurial failure will impact the business owner himself, as well as his employees and collaborators (Corner et al., 2017). Entrepreneurs with solid emotional intelligence would be able to give their teams the emotional support and guidance that motivate them in times of uncertainty. This type of emotional leadership is also very important in keeping morale and resilience at a high level within the larger organization, rather than allowing setbacks to grow into defeatism - but instead, stimulating collective problem-solving and perseverance.

At last, the person has increased self-compassion, which one needs in cases of recovery from a failure process. Hence, self-compassion means the following: it occurs when experiencing struggle, and one will be gentle with himself or herself to realize that it is a part of human life to fail and will not be so hard on himself or herself by criticizing or punishing him or herself too much for mistakes. Thus, entrepreneurs with high emotional intelligence tend to enjoy self-compassion that enable them to bounce back faster as well as less emotionally damaged after failure. Self-forgiveness, the ability to move forward without extreme self-blame, is, therefore, critical for maintaining long-run resilience (Hoe & Janssen, 2022).

Entrepreneurial resilience is built on emotional intelligence. Emotional regulation, self-awareness, empathy, adaptability, and self-compassion in the overcoming of inevitable entrepreneurial journey pitfalls and failures differentiate the entrepreneur who is emotionally intelligent from the rest. These emotional skills empower entrepreneurs to bounce back with greater resilience, and optimism and a lot of persistence and creativity are observed in the pursuit of entrepreneurial goals (Lyu, 2024). Indeed, whereas, in most other business fields, failure is often not taken seriously until it becomes lethal, in some venture fields failure is considered one of the steppingstones along the route to success, while emotional intelligence represents a critical component of entrepreneurial resilience by equipping entrepreneurs with psychological and emotional tools to convert an anticipated downturn into a growth opportunity.

PSYCHOLOGICAL INTERVENTIONS AND SUPPORT FOR ENTREPRENEURS

Entrepreneurs suffer from high levels of stress, uncertainty, and risk; thus, there is a likelihood that such entrepreneurs become particularly vulnerable to mental health challenges once failure occurs. Targeted interventions and support systems are therefore required when fostering psychological resilience and eventual success. Psychological interventions include therapies, counseling, peer support, and wellness programs to equip the entrepreneur with tools and coping mechanisms to manage failure, reduce potential stressors, and maintain healthy mental well-being. Apart from recovery, the treatments emphasize learning specific emotional and cognitive skills to manage future situations (Ukil & Jenkins, 2022).

Among all psychological therapy for entrepreneurs, **cognitive-behavioral therapy (CBT)** stands out. It seeks the identification and challenging of negative automatic thoughts connected with failure, which may sometimes include negative self-esteem often supported with feelings of guilt or apprehension that one will err once again in the future. Entrepreneurs who experience failed events may tend to internalize this failure and perceive it as a matter of personal inadequacy, rather than a challenging situation. CBT helps them make all these changes in their thought, shifting from the defeatist mindset towards growth and learning. In doing so, CBT helps them develop more rational or less negative thinking patterns, thus encouraging resilience and keeping risks of depression or anxiety within bounds. This therapeutic approach also empowers entrepreneurs with practical coping mechanisms to handle stress and emotional misery associated with failure (Yao et al., 2021).

The third useful psychological intervention for entrepreneurs is **mindfulness-based stress reduction (MBSR)**. MBSR practices such as meditation, deep breathing, and body scan training people to stay in the present and handle any form of stress in the present. Entrepreneurship can be extremely stressful since there is always a demand and deadline, and uncertainty, leading to chronic stress. Mindfulness practice allows businesspeople to be more aware of their emotional states than being controlled by their emotions, thereby increasing the capacity for greater emotional regulation (Yang, 2023). This reduces the rehashing of previous failures and fear of potential difficulties, thus allowing entrepreneurs to be lucid and focused in minds. The resilience of entrepreneurs will improve with continued mindfulness as it gradually enhances balancing, reduces burnouts, and improves on decision-making, which are very important aspects concerning entrepreneurial success.

Indeed, **peer support groups** would feel the community and shared understanding of it is crucial to be upheld by entrepreneurs when facing failure. Entrepreneurial contexts are very few who believe that it is dependent only upon their success or failure with the business. It is in this regard that the peer support groups consist of fellow entrepreneurs who understand challenges associated with entrepreneurial phases, providing a space for experience sharing, obtaining feedback, and giving emotional comfort (Hedner et al., 2011). These groups give a type of belonging and erode loneliness for entrepreneurs as they let their feelings loose with others. When the stories of success and failure are shared, participants come to empathize with other members, such that the perspective about own challenges may change, considering failure as part of the experience but not personal failing. Such interactions also enhance accountability and motivation, therefore supporting resilience even more.

Mentoring programs also become a way to assist entrepreneurs during their psychological battles. A mentor, especially the experienced entrepreneur, guides and encourages them through his or her own experiences of either success or failure. Having an experienced mentor to turn to during challenging times may offer more support to entrepreneurs and overwhelming feelings would reduce. Mentors can also help entrepreneurs gain an eye to look over the immediate setbacks. Long term goals are thus focused. The encouragement and wisdom gained from the entire mentorship would be in a big way able to make all the difference, making their resilience enhanced and they can confidently struggle through some very tough times (Zhao & Wibowo, 2021).

Workshop and training sessions on mental health and resilience can offer practical tools for entrepreneurs to work through stress and anxiety, develop emotional intelligence, and achieve better work-life balance. These sessions tend to deal with issues of stress management, time management, emotional regulation, and other strategies for maintaining mental well-being in the high-pressure setting of running a business. Training in these areas would place an entrepreneur in better positions to cope with the emotional demands of running a business. Workshops targeting psychological effects such as that of failure, imposter syndrome, or perfectionism can help entrepreneurs build resilience by normalizing these experiences and offering strategies to overcome them (Jing et al., 2016).

Workplace wellness programs: The trend of programs in the workplace as a valuable resource to promote mental wellness among entrepreneurs or small business owners is marked by giving access to professionals specializing in mental health, stress management tools, and wellness-related initiatives like yoga, fitness programs, and nutritional guidance. Wellness programs that focus on mental health provide entrepreneurs with the means to stressfully manage through proactive and preventative means (Lafuente et al., 2019). Wellness routines can be integrated into the lifestyle of entrepreneurs to reduce the risks of burnout, build psychological resilience, and remain wholesome even in unfavorably business conditions.

Other innovation at the disposal of entrepreneurs is the **online mental health platforms** and teletherapy. These have been posited as accessible and flexible avenues for entrepreneurs who require psychological guidance. With these solutions, entrepreneurs can access therapy or counseling sessions from anywhere due to busy scheduled lives. Online self-guided mental health platforms, whether it is a meditation app, mental health tracking tools, or a virtual support group, provide quicker access to stress-relieving techniques and emotional support for entrepreneurs. This can particularly be helpful for entrepreneurs who are not confident enough to visit the therapists because of the lack of time, stigma, or cost (Hartmann et al., 2022).

Another important thing to use when entrepreneurship involves building resilience is the practice of **positive psychology interventions**, which focuses more on strengths than weaknesses. For example, gratitude journaling is the practice where an individual will take time at regular intervals to reflect on those aspects of their life that he is most thankful for in their private and public lives (Lee & Wang, 2017). In doing this, it changes their focus from failures and areas of weakness and puts emphasis on what was achieved and where they have the opportunity for growth. Positive psychology interventions help entrepreneurs build optimism, enhance emotional well-being, and maintain a more hopeful outlook even in the most trying of times.

Another core intervention used with entrepreneurs is the induction of **self-compassion practice.** Self-compassion refers to the way by which one treats himself gently and compassionately in any failure rather than having self-criticism or criticism. Self-compassionate entrepreneurs would easily recover from failures because they would not pine on their mistakes and consider failure as a method for growth. Encouraging entrepreneurs to be self-compassionate in their practices through therapy and coaching can positively help them. Self-compassion would make entrepreneurs better at attributing failures and reduce the emotional impacts of shock experienced during entrepreneurial ventures (Sachdev, 2023). Psychological interventions are essential because they ensure a support system for entrepreneurs in raising resilience and creating mental well-being. From cognitive-behavioral therapy and mindfulness-based practices to peer support groups, mentoring, and positive psychology, these interventions seem to supply entrepreneurs with all the emotional ammunition they could need when bouncing back from failure and embarking on their entrepreneurial journey with renewed confidence. As more and more factors of psychological demands related to entrepreneurship are brought under scrutiny, mental health support will have to become part and parcel of entrepreneurial ecosystems so that businesses would be able to achieve long-term success and sustainability of companies while entrepreneurs' well-being is ensured (Bullough & Renko, 2013).

IMPLICATIONS

The impact of entrepreneurial failures on psychological resilience in several ways leads toward practical, managerial, social, and ethical domains for implications. It is always important to recognize such implications to create an environment where entrepreneurs can bounce back from these setbacks and develop the needed resilience for long-term success.

Practical Implications

Entrepreneurs practically must build their business framework with support systems by fostering psychological propensity. This may involve launching mentorship programs, peer support groups, and provision of mental health service providers. Training on emotional intelligence, mindfulness, and stress management should be included as part of entrepreneurial development programs (Bullough et al., 2014). Education on entrepreneurial coping mechanisms may prevent entrepreneurs from throwing in the towel when faced with failure. A culture that encourages the discussion around failure and mental health can help reduce stigma while encouraging entrepreneurs to seek the assistance they require. The better the entrepreneur is at taking an active approach to mental well-being, the more resistant he or she will be towards mental developments and therefore better decision makers and likely to produce future success.

Managerial Implication

On the psychological resilience of employees, it enhances the concept of innovation and sustainability within entrepreneurial organizations. Managers and leaders in entrepreneurial firms put work into an environment in which the fear of failure does not affect individual performance. Policies that support the well-being of workers, such as providing flexible work arrangements, wellness programs, or open communication about challenges, can give employees the empowerment to take calculated risks without fear of repercussions (Duchek, 2018). Developing managers on emotional intelligence would also enhance their ability to serve the better needs of the teams. Grooming a more adaptive and engaging workforce in psychological resilience drives organizational growth and success.

Social Implications

From a social perspective, building entrepreneurs' resilience contributes towards a better, more innovative economy. Resilient entrepreneurs are more liable to take more risks, form new businesses, produce jobs, and lead other parts of the economy. More so, every mistake or failure that they gain from can influence others to persevere and be open to change. This promotes resilient culture to the individual entrepreneurs while helping the broader entrepreneurial ecosystem (Shepherd & Patzelt, 2017). Such initiatives as local support networks, workshops, or public forums to boost resilience can be helpful to the community at large. Building and raising entrepreneurial business potentially nurtures better economic opportunities that might seem harder to realize without an open support system for entrepreneurship between the parties.

Ethical Implications

This should be treated earnestly in ethical terms. The organization and stakeholders in the entrepreneurial ecosystem have a moral obligation to foster environments that commend mental health and well-being. Therefore, entrepreneurs need to be provided with equitable access to the available resources and support systems and not be discriminated or stigmatized. Policymakers, educators, and industry leaders should champion ethical principles that place mental well-being at the heart of entrepreneurship. This is because entrepreneurs' emotional well-being ultimately defines entrepreneurship and the economy at large. What is also important is that the level of failure in society is looked upon with regard to how and in what manner failure can be portrayed as a means toward growth and innovation instead of a badge of shame or stigma (González-López et al., 2019).

The multilateral implications that understandings of the influence of entrepreneurial failures would have on psychological resilience hold very great depth and breadth. Their practical, managerial, social, and ethical dimensions need to be discussed to develop an entrepreneurial supporting ecosystem. It can lead towards more sustainable and innovative entrepreneurial ecosystems, not only for oneself but for others (Liu et al., 2023).

CONCLUSION

In conclusion, the psychological resilience implications for entrepreneurs, managers, and society arising from entrepreneurial failures form a complex issue with significant implications. Against this backdrop, the entrepreneurial landscape continues to evolve, and it is only right that this understanding of failures not as some form of setbacks but as a part of the entrepreneurial process needs to be acted upon. Knowing these failures' impact on resilience aids entrepreneurs to develop coping strategies or strategies whereby they can better handle challenges, with a mindset of looking at adversities as opportunities for improvement and innovation.

Psychological support systems are very important. In place are practical interventions such as mentorship programs, peer support groups, and mental health resources that will aid entrepreneurs in building up resilience and the effective handling of emotion when dealing with failure. Managers and leaders in organizations also constitute a necessary part of the cultural advocates towards the normalizing of discussions around mental health as well as providing support for employees in their pursuit of personal and professional growth. Emotional intelligence and open communication therefore can enhance aspects of decision-making, of team dynamics, and ultimately productivity.

Social implications further exist outside the hero stories of individual entrepreneurial resilience fostered. Such resilient entrepreneurs contribute more to both economic growth and innovation, finally benefiting not only the community but also society at large. We can raise a new generation of entrepreneurs who are not only willing to pursue their aspirations but are equipped to overcome inevitable challenges by cultivating an environment encouraging taking risks and embracing failure as part of learning.

Ethically speaking, all stakeholders of the entrepreneurial ecosystem should take a step and highlight mental health and well-being through various initiatives. This involves advocating the kind of policies that will prove supportive towards resources for mental health, decreasing stigma around failures, and inculcating a culture of resilience. When addressed through these considerations, we are in a better position to create an inclusive and supportive environment by empowering entrepreneurs to thrive.

In essence, the interplay between entrepreneurial failure and psychological resilience is an area that may prove to be very critical in need of focus for any person as such involved in the entrepreneurial ecosystem. This can best help the individual understand and address emotional and psychological dimensions in entrepreneurship that could support better paths and resilience leading to well-being for the individual but innovation and economic growth for society. Indeed, while the entrepreneurial journey is strewn with impediments, with the right tools and adequate support during failure, we are building a vibrant, resourceful entrepreneurial community capable of negotiating these very complexities of modern business.

REFERENCES

Ayala, J. C., & Manzano, G. (2014). The resilience of the entrepreneur. Influence on the success of the business. A longitudinal analysis. *Journal of Economic Psychology*, 42, 126–135. DOI: 10.1016/j.joep.2014.02.004

Borbolla-Albores, A., & Reyes-Mercado, P. (2022). Entrepreneurial failure and resilience: A continuous interplay between rigidity and flexibility. *Jurnal Manajemen Dan Kewirausahaan*, 24(1), 1–14. DOI: 10.9744/jmk.24.1.1-14

Bullough, A., & Renko, M. (2013). Entrepreneurial resilience during challenging times. *Business Horizons*, 56(3), 343–350. DOI: 10.1016/j.bushor.2013.01.001

Bullough, A., Renko, M., & Myatt, T. (2014). Danger zone entrepreneurs: The importance of resilience and self-efficacy for entrepreneurial intentions. *Entrepreneurship Theory and Practice*, 38(3), 473–499. DOI: 10.1111/etap.12006

Chadwick, I., & Raver, J. (2018). Psychological resilience and its downstream effects for business survival in nascent entrepreneurship. *Entrepreneurship Theory and Practice*, 44(2), 233–255. DOI: 10.1177/1042258718801597

Corner, P., Singh, S., & Pavlovich, K. (2017). Entrepreneurial resilience and venture failure. *International Small Business Journal*, 35(6), 687–708. DOI: 10.1177/0266242616685604

De Hoe, R., & Janssen, F. (2022). Re-creation after business failure: A conceptual model of the mediating role of psychological capital. *Frontiers in Psychology*, 13, 842590. DOI: 10.3389/fpsyg.2022.842590 PMID: 35310260

Duchek, S. (2018). Entrepreneurial resilience: A biographical analysis of successful entrepreneurs. *The International Entrepreneurship and Management Journal*, 14(2), 429–455. DOI: 10.1007/s11365-017-0467-2

González-López, M. J., Pérez-López, M. C., & Rodríguez-Ariza, L. (2019). Clearing the hurdles in the entrepreneurial race: The role of resilience in entrepreneurship education. *Academy of Management Learning & Education*, 18(3), 457–483. DOI: 10.5465/amle.2016.0377

Hartmann, S., Backmann, J., Newman, A., Brykman, K. M., & Pidduck, R. J. (2022). Psychological resilience of entrepreneurs: A review and agenda for future research. *Journal of Small Business Management*, 60(5), 1041–1079. DOI: 10.1080/00472778.2021.2024216

Hedner, T., Abouzeedan, A., & Klofsten, M. (2011). Entrepreneurial resilience. *Annals of Innovation & Entrepreneurship*, 2(1), 7986. DOI: 10.3402/aie.v2i1.6002

Hoe, R., & Janssen, F. (2022). Re-creation after business failure: A conceptual model of the mediating role of psychological capital. *Frontiers in Psychology*, 13, 842590. Advance online publication. DOI: 10.3389/fpsyg.2022.842590 PMID: 35310260

Jing, T., Dancheng, L., & Ye, Z. (2016). Study of impact on undergraduates' entrepreneurial failure based on the model of psychological resilience-knowledge acquisition. *English Language Teaching*, 9(8), 224–230. DOI: 10.5539/elt.v9n8p224

Lafuente, E., Vaillant, Y., Vendrell-Herrero, F., & Gomes, E. (2019). Bouncing back from failure: Entrepreneurial resilience and the internationalization of subsequent ventures created by serial entrepreneurs. *Applied Psychology*, 68(4), 658–694. DOI: 10.1111/apps.12175

Lee, J., & Wang, J. (2017). Developing entrepreneurial resilience: Implications for human resource development. *European Journal of Training and Development*, 41(6), 519–539. DOI: 10.1108/EJTD-12-2016-0090

Liu, X., Yuan, Y., Sun, R., Zhao, C., & Zhao, D. (2023). Influence of entrepreneurial team knowledge conflict on ambidextrous entrepreneurial learning—A dual-path perspective of entrepreneurial resilience and fear of failure. *Journal of Innovation & Knowledge*, 8(3), 100389. DOI: 10.1016/j.jik.2023.100389

Lyu, Y. (2024). Interplay of entrepreneurial failure experience, entrepreneurial resilience, and re-entrepreneurship performance: Evidence from China. *Environment and Social Psychology*, 9(3). Advance online publication. DOI: 10.54517/esp.v9i3.2069

Sachdev, N. (2023). Entrepreneurial resilience: What makes entrepreneurs start another business after failure. *Asian Journal of Economics. Business and Accounting*, 23(18), 46–58.

•Shepherd, D. A., & Patzelt, H. (2017). Researching entrepreneurial failures. In *Trailblazing in entrepreneurship: Creating new paths for understanding the field* (pp. 63-102). DOI: 10.1007/978-3-319-48701-4_3

Tunio, M. N. (2020). Academic entrepreneurship in developing countries: contextualizing recent debate. In *Research handbook on entrepreneurship in emerging economies* (pp. 130–146). Edward Elgar Publishing. DOI: 10.4337/9781788973717.00014

Tunio, M. N., Chaudhry, I. S., Shaikh, S., Jariko, M. A., & Brahmi, M. (2021). Determinants of the sustainable entrepreneurial engagement of youth in developing country—An empirical evidence from Pakistan. *Sustainability (Basel)*, 13(14), 7764. DOI: 10.3390/su13147764

Tunio, M. N., Jariko, M. A., Børsen, T., Shaikh, S., Mushtaque, T., & Brahmi, M. (2021). How entrepreneurship sustains barriers in the entrepreneurial process—A lesson from a developing nation. *Sustainability (Basel)*, 13(20), 11419. DOI: 10.3390/su132011419

Ukil, M., & Jenkins, A. (2022). Willing but fearful: Resilience and youth entrepreneurial intentions. *Journal of Small Business and Enterprise Development*, 30(1), 78–99. DOI: 10.1108/JSBED-03-2022-0154

Yang, A. (2023). Psychological resilience of entrepreneurial failure: An application of positive psychology to entrepreneurial failure repair. *Academic Journal of Management and Social Sciences*, 5(2), 17–21. DOI: 10.54097/ajmss.v5i2.06

Yao, K., Li, X., & Liang, B. (2021). Failure learning and entrepreneurial resilience: The moderating role of firms' knowledge breadth and knowledge depth. *Journal of Knowledge Management*, 25(9), 2141–2160. DOI: 10.1108/JKM-10-2020-0772

Zhao, H., & Wibowo, A. (2021). Entrepreneurship resilience: Can psychological traits of entrepreneurial intention support overcoming entrepreneurial failure? *Frontiers in Psychology*, 12, 707803. DOI: 10.3389/fpsyg.2021.707803 PMID: 34594271

Chapter 21
The Role of Emotional Intelligence in Promoting Mental Peace, Healthy Work Environments, and Emotional Well-Being Among Entrepreneurs

Tiago Manuel Horta Reis da Silva
https://orcid.org/0000-0001-5220-1718
King's College London, UK

ABSTRACT

Emotional intelligence (EI), defined as the ability to recognize, understand, and manage one's emotions and those of others, is an essential competency for entrepreneurs, influencing both their personal well-being and the health of the workplace they create. Entrepreneurship is often marked by volatility, stress, and emotional highs and lows, making EI a vital tool for navigating these challenges. This chapter explores how EI can contribute to mental peace, create healthy work environments, and foster emotional well-being among entrepreneurs. It also emphasizes the importance of EI in moving and handling procedures, a critical aspect in healthcare industries that entrepreneurs can learn from to promote physical and emotional health in their teams. Finally, the chapter ties these findings to the United Nations' Sustainable Development Goals (SDGs), particularly Goal 3 (Good Health and Well-being) and Goal 8 (Decent Work and Economic Growth), highlighting how EI interventions can support broader global well-being objectives.

DOI: 10.4018/979-8-3693-3673-1.ch021

1. INTRODUCTION

1.1 Overview of Emotional Intelligence and its Relevance in Entrepreneurship

Emotional intelligence (EI) has emerged as a critical factor in the entrepreneurial landscape, where the ability to navigate complex emotional landscapes can significantly influence success. Defined as the capacity to recognize, understand, and manage one's own emotions and those of others, EI is essential for entrepreneurs who must frequently engage with diverse stakeholders, including employees, investors, and customers (da Silva, 2022; da Silva, 2024a; Reis da Silva, 2024a). Goleman (1995) posits that EI encompasses skills such as emotional awareness, empathy, and emotional regulation, which are vital for effective leadership and interpersonal relations in business settings (Othman & Muda, 2018). The relevance of EI in entrepreneurship is underscored by its association with various positive outcomes, including enhanced leadership performance, improved mental health, and increased employee satisfaction (Rodrigues et al., 2019; Reis da Silva, 2024b; Reis da Silva, 2024c). Research indicates that entrepreneurs with high emotional intelligence are better equipped to handle the inherent uncertainties and stresses of running a business (Reis da Silva, 2024b, Reis da Silva, 2024c). For instance, Othman & Muda (2018) highlight that emotional intelligence fosters entrepreneurial behaviour among individuals, particularly in high-pressure environments (Othman & Muda, 2018). This capability allows entrepreneurs to maintain mental peace and resilience, which are crucial for sustaining creativity and productivity in their ventures. Furthermore, emotional intelligence contributes to the creation of healthy work environments, where employees feel valued and understood, thereby enhancing overall organizational performance (Liu & Li, 2013).

In the context of entrepreneurship, EI can be linked to frameworks such as integrative medicine and sustainable development, which emphasize holistic approaches to well-being. By integrating emotional intelligence into business practices, entrepreneurs can cultivate environments that prioritize mental health and emotional well-being, aligning with the principles of sustainable development (Sumathi, 2024). This cross-disciplinary perspective not only enriches the understanding of emotional intelligence but also provides actionable strategies for entrepreneurs seeking to enhance their leadership effectiveness and organizational culture.

1.2 Challenges Faced by Entrepreneurs in Maintaining Mental Peace and Well-being

The entrepreneurial journey is fraught with challenges that can adversely affect mental peace and overall well-being. Entrepreneurs often grapple with financial uncertainties, high expectations, and the emotional strain of potential failures, which can lead to stress, anxiety, and burnout (Wardana et al., 2020; da Silva, 2022; da Silva, 2024). Shepherd (2019) emphasizes that the solitary nature of entrepreneurship can exacerbate feelings of isolation, further complicating the emotional landscape that entrepreneurs must navigate (Wardana, 2018; Reis da Silva, 2024d). To counter these challenges, emotional intelligence serves as a protective buffer, enabling entrepreneurs to manage their emotions and those of their teams effectively. For instance, Liu & Li (2013) demonstrate that team leaders with high emotional intelligence foster a positive emotional climate, which in turn enhances job satisfaction among team members (Liu &

Li, 2013). This suggests that cultivating emotional intelligence not only benefits individual entrepreneurs but also contributes to the overall health of the organization.

Moreover, practices such as mindfulness and emotional regulation can empower entrepreneurs to build resilience against stressors. Sumathi (2024) notes that emotional intelligence is critical for navigating the emotional challenges inherent in entrepreneurship, particularly in high-stress situations. By fostering an emotionally intelligent workplace, entrepreneurs can create a culture that prioritizes mental well-being, ultimately leading to improved performance and satisfaction among employees.

1.3 Chapter Objectives and Approach

This chapter aims to elucidate the multifaceted role of emotional intelligence in promoting mental peace, healthy work environments, and emotional well-being among entrepreneurs. The objectives include exploring the intersection of emotional intelligence with various fields such as nursing care for older adults, integrative medicine, and the United Nations' Sustainable Development Goals (da Silva and Rodrigues, 2023; Reis da Silva, 2024a; da Silva, 2024a; da Silva, 2024b). By examining these cross-disciplinary connections, the chapter seeks to provide a comprehensive understanding of how emotional intelligence can enhance entrepreneurial success. Additionally, the chapter will offer actionable strategies for entrepreneurs to improve emotional regulation, foster resilience, and cultivate emotionally intelligent work cultures. This approach will draw on insights from research on emotional intelligence, practical examples from various disciplines, and the latest findings in the field. By highlighting the importance of emotional intelligence in promoting well-being, this chapter aims to contribute to the growing body of knowledge on the intersection of emotional intelligence and entrepreneurship.

2. EMOTIONAL INTELLIGENCE: CONCEPT AND THEORIES

2.1 Defining Emotional Intelligence

Emotional Intelligence (EI) has undergone significant evolution since its introduction by Salovey and Mayer in 1990 and its popularization by Goleman in 1995. EI is defined as the ability to recognize, understand, and manage one's own emotions as well as the emotions of others, thereby facilitating effective behaviour and relationship management (Othman & Muda, 2018; da Silva, 2022; da Silva, 2024a; Reis da Silva, 2024a). Goleman (1995) delineates EI into four primary domains: self-awareness, self-management, social awareness, and relationship management. These domains empower individuals to navigate complex emotional landscapes, which is particularly crucial in both personal and professional contexts (Rodrigues et al., 2019). In the realm of entrepreneurship, the effective management of emotions is paramount. Entrepreneurs are often faced with the dual challenge of leading teams while simultaneously addressing the emotional demands of building and sustaining a business. This makes EI an invaluable asset for achieving both personal and professional success. Research indicates that entrepreneurs who exhibit high levels of emotional intelligence are better equipped to handle the stresses associated with leadership, thereby fostering a more positive work environment (Liu & Li, 2013). The ability to manage emotions not only enhances individual performance but also contributes to the overall health of the organization, promoting resilience and adaptability in the face of challenges (Sumathi, 2024).

Moreover, the significance of EI extends beyond individual capabilities; it plays a crucial role in shaping organizational culture. By fostering an emotionally intelligent workplace, entrepreneurs can cultivate environments that prioritize mental well-being, thereby enhancing employee satisfaction and productivity (Wardana et al., 2020). The integration of emotional intelligence into business practices can lead to improved communication, collaboration, and conflict resolution, ultimately driving organizational success (Wardana, 2018).

2.2 Theoretical Models of EI

Several theoretical models have been developed to elucidate the concept of emotional intelligence. The ability model proposed by Mayer and Salovey (1997) emphasizes the cognitive processes underlying EI, including the ability to perceive, use, understand, and manage emotions (Cai et al., 2020). This model posits that emotional intelligence is fundamentally a set of skills that can be developed and refined over time, making it a dynamic construct rather than a fixed trait. In contrast, Goleman's mixed model incorporates both emotional competencies and personal and social skills necessary for effective leadership (Дрібас et al., 2020). This model highlights the importance of emotional regulation and interpersonal skills in achieving personal and organizational goals. Goleman's framework has gained widespread acceptance in both academic and practical settings, emphasizing the relevance of EI in various domains, including education, healthcare, and business (Boybanting, 2023).

Bar-On's model (2006) offers another perspective by viewing EI as a collection of interrelated emotional and social competencies that influence how individuals understand and express themselves, interact with others, and cope with daily demands (Khatri, 2018). This model underscores the multifaceted nature of emotional intelligence, suggesting that it encompasses a broad range of skills that contribute to overall effectiveness in personal and professional contexts. Despite their differences, these models share a common emphasis on the role of emotional regulation in achieving personal and interpersonal effectiveness. For entrepreneurs, understanding these frameworks provides valuable insights into how emotional intelligence can be cultivated and applied in business contexts, ultimately enhancing leadership effectiveness and organizational performance (Reynolds & O'Dwyer, 2008).

In 1977–1979, Darwin Nelson and Gary Low conducted a three-year study project that gave rise to transformative emotional intelligence (TEI). The project's goal was to comprehend how healthy, prosperous, and productive people of all ages develop holistically (Hammett et al., 2011; Hammett et al., 2018). They created person-centered learning environments, research-derived positive assessments, and practical models for coaching, mentoring, counselling, teaching, and leadership and personal excellence (Low et al., 2019; Low et al., 2021). A fundamental component of the transformational learning process, positive assessment helps individuals develop and expand their inner resources by gaining self-awareness of important emotional abilities, competences, and strategies (Nelson et al., 2013). The creation of crucial Personal, Emotional, Relational, and Life (PERL) learning domains, the significance of positive assessment as a crucial initial step in learning and development, the requirement for an integrated person-team-centered learning process, and the significance of wholesome and fruitful relationships were among the project's main conclusions (Low et al., 2019; Low et al., 2021). The main conclusions remain the foundational learning pillars of transformational emotional intelligence, highlighting the significance of positive and healthy interactions in people's lives, families, workplaces, communities, and society at large (Hammett et al., 2011; Hammett et al., 2018).

Studies have indicated that PERL behaviours, abilities, and tactics are essential for enhancing well-being, success, and optimistic outlooks on life and work (Nelson et al., 2013). These abilities support the development of inner resources, positive appraisal, stress-reduction communication, and other critical skills that productive, healthy individuals acquire (Hammett et al., 2011; Hammett et al., 2018). Established in 2004, the Institute for Emotional Intelligence (TEI) aims to exchange best practices and research findings (Low et al., 2019; Low et al., 2021). Building a dynamic, skills-based learning strategy is the main goal in order to attain personal excellence, which is now considered a necessary component of a well-being and productive individual (Nelson et al., 2013). Decades of study and practice have produced innovative educational programs that encourage equality and personal success (Low et al., 2019; Low et al., 2021). With an emphasis on attaining excellence, laying a foundation of fundamental TEI skills with positive assessment broadens consciousness, self-knowledge, and internal resources (Hammett et al., 2011; Hammett et al., 2018). The transformational theory of emotional intelligence (EI) is a concept that assists people in developing excellence from within by fusing PERL capabilities with critical and constructive thinking. It highlights how crucial it is to establish aspirational objectives, personal standards, and the capacity for critical and constructive thought. The goal of the idea is to make people resilient, healthy, and able to deal with fast change (Low et al., 2019; Low et al., 2021). The burgeoning transformational notion of emotional intelligence emerged from the collision of Eastern and Western philosophical and psychological ideas. TEI-centric evaluations and PERL skills have been implemented in academic, corporate, and organizational settings in over 80 PhD dissertations and other significant research (Hammett et al., 2011; Hammett et al., 2018). The idea highlights how crucial intelligent self-direction is in a society that is changing quickly and full of stress. The seven guiding principles and tenets of the TEI philosophy are as follows: Practical Life Philosophy, research derived theory, Person-centered learning, relationship focused, skills-based, positive change and intelligent self-direction (Nelson et al., 2013; Hammett et al., 2011; Hammett et al., 2018).

TEI philosophy, which has its roots in positive psychology and humanistic traditions, emphasizes the potential for personal growth and development throughout life (Low et al., 2019; Low et al., 2021). The writings of Seymour Epstein, John Gardner, Abraham Maslow, and Carl Rogers had an impact on it. Through the use of a five-step Emotional Learning System and fundamental affective skills, TEI's research-derived philosophy promotes growth motivation and emotional development (Nelson et al., 2013). The system's main goals are to break bad habits and cultivate thoughtful, productive thinking (Low et al., 2019; Low et al., 2021). A methodical way to acquiring the fundamental abilities and techniques of emotional intelligence is the Emotional Learning System (ELS). It entails self-evaluation, self-awareness, comprehension, education, and self-improvement. Achieving health, well-being, happiness, and success in one's life and profession requires relationship-focused learning (Hammett et al., 2011; Hammett et al., 2018). Research produced a transformational learning-development framework that includes thirteen crucial Personal, Emotional, Relational, and Life (PERL) abilities to promote self-awareness and well-rounded competences for effective career and life management. Self-worth, stress management, assertiveness, empathy, comfort, decision-making, personal leadership, drive strength, time management, and commitment ethic are among the ten PERL skill categories (Nelson et al., 2013). Experience learning is made dynamic, powerful, and engaging by the integration and interrelatedness of TEI skills (Low et al., 2019; Low et al., 2021).

In order to create self-awareness and balanced competences for career/life success, the Transformative Emotional Intelligence (TEI) framework, a transformative learning-development paradigm, focusses on thirteen critical Personal, Emotional, Relational, and Life (PERL) abilities (Nelson et al., 2013). Ten PERL skill categories are included in the framework, including drive strength, commitment ethic, self-worth, stress management, assertion, empathy, comfort, and decision making. In addition, it offers a useful learning model for positive transformation that walks people through a five-step process for learning, growing, and successfully changing. Learning how to regulate, direct, use, and model interpersonal, emotional, and relational skills—all crucial for one's health, well-being, and success in life and the workplace—is the aim of transformational emotional intelligence (EI) education (Nelson et al., 2013).

2.3 EI in Entrepreneurial Contexts: A Critical Competency for Success

Emotional Intelligence (EI) has increasingly been recognized as a pivotal factor influencing entrepreneurial success. The ability to understand and manage emotions—both one's own and those of others—enables entrepreneurs to navigate the complexities of their roles effectively (da Silva, 2022). This section will explore the critical role of EI in entrepreneurship, supported by various studies that highlight its impact on entrepreneurial behaviours, decision-making, and overall business performance.

2.3.1 The Importance of Emotional Intelligence in Entrepreneurship

Research indicates that emotional intelligence is a significant predictor of entrepreneurial success. For instance, Othman & Muda (2018) argue that EI plays a vital role in fostering entrepreneurial behaviours among individuals, particularly in university settings where students are contemplating their career paths. The ability to regulate, use, and manage emotions effectively can enhance students' attitudes towards entrepreneurship, thereby increasing their entrepreneurial intentions (Rodrigues et al., 2019). This foundational understanding of EI as a precursor to entrepreneurial behaviour underscores its importance in shaping future entrepreneurs. Moreover, Allen et al. (2020) conducted a meta-analysis comparing general mental ability and emotional intelligence in entrepreneurial settings, concluding that EI is a more significant predictor of entrepreneurial success than cognitive ability alone. This finding challenges the traditional view that cognitive skills are the primary determinants of entrepreneurial outcomes, suggesting that emotional competencies are equally, if not more, important. Entrepreneurs with high EI are better equipped to handle the emotional demands of leadership, make informed decisions, and foster a positive organizational culture.

2.3.2. Emotional Intelligence and Leadership in Entrepreneurship

Leadership is a critical component of entrepreneurship, and emotional intelligence significantly influences leadership effectiveness. Prib (2023) emphasizes that understanding relationships and managing emotional dynamics are essential for entrepreneurs operating in high-stress environments (Reis da Silva, 2024a). Entrepreneurs who can navigate their own emotions and those of their team members are more likely to create supportive work environments that foster collaboration and innovation. Furthermore, research found that entrepreneurs with high EI are more adept at conflict management and team building, which are crucial for maintaining a healthy organizational climate (Amar et al., 2014). The ability to connect with team members on an emotional level fosters trust and loyalty, essential elements for long-term business success. This emotional connection not only enhances team dynamics but also mitigates the emotional toll that business pressures can impose on both leaders and employees (da Silva, 2022; Reis da Silva, 2024a).

2.3.3 Emotional Intelligence and Decision-Making

Effective decision-making is another area where emotional intelligence plays a crucial role. Entrepreneurs often face high-stakes decisions that can significantly impact their businesses. Hmieleski and Baron (2009) found that entrepreneurs with higher levels of EI are better at making decisions in dynamic and competitive markets (Stumm et al., 2009). This ability to manage emotions allows entrepreneurs to remain calm under pressure, consider multiple perspectives, and make informed choices that align with their business goals. Moreover, emotional intelligence enables entrepreneurs to evaluate opportunities and risks more effectively. highlight that the self-perceived ability to regulate emotions is strongly related to entrepreneurial success, as it allows entrepreneurs to assess situations more accurately and respond appropriately (Ordiñana-Bellver et al., 2022). This emotional regulation is particularly important in high-pressure situations where impulsive decisions can lead to negative outcomes.

2.3.4. Emotional Intelligence and Resilience

Resilience is a critical trait for entrepreneurs, who often encounter setbacks and failures. Emotional intelligence contributes significantly to an entrepreneur's ability to bounce back from challenges. Research by Cai et al. (2018) suggests that EI is positively correlated with entrepreneurial intentions, as it helps individuals cope with the uncertainties and stresses inherent in entrepreneurship. Entrepreneurs with high EI are more likely to view failures as learning opportunities rather than insurmountable obstacles, fostering a growth mindset that is essential for long-term success.

Additionally, emotional intelligence can enhance an entrepreneur's ability to manage stress and maintain mental well-being. The ability to recognize and regulate emotions can prevent burnout and promote a healthier work-life balance, which is crucial for sustaining entrepreneurial endeavors over time. Khalid et al. (2018) found that emotional intelligence significantly influences entrepreneurial self-efficacy, which in turn impacts resilience and persistence in the face of challenges.

3. PROMOTING MENTAL PEACE THROUGH EMOTIONAL INTELLIGENCE

3.1 Stress Management and Resilience

Emotional intelligence (EI) plays a crucial role in stress management and resilience, particularly in high-pressure environments such as entrepreneurship. Entrepreneurs often face significant stressors, including financial uncertainties, market fluctuations, and interpersonal conflicts. Research indicates that individuals with high EI are better equipped to manage stress effectively, as they can recognize and regulate their emotions in response to challenging situations (Altinyelken, 2018). This ability not only helps entrepreneurs cope with immediate stressors but also fosters resilience, enabling them to bounce back from setbacks and maintain a positive outlook. Studies have shown that emotional regulation strategies, which are integral components of EI, can mitigate the negative effects of stress. For instance, Grecucci et al. (2015) found that mindfulness practices promote healthier emotional responses, allowing individuals to manage their emotions more effectively during stressful situations. By cultivating mindfulness, entrepreneurs can enhance their emotional regulation skills, leading to improved stress management and resilience. This is particularly important in entrepreneurial contexts, where the ability to adapt to changing circumstances and recover from failures is essential for long-term success.

Moreover, the relationship between EI and resilience is supported by evidence suggesting that emotionally intelligent individuals are more likely to employ adaptive coping strategies when faced with stress. Research indicates that high EI is associated with greater use of problem-solving and acceptance strategies, which are more effective than avoidance strategies in managing stress (Septiani et al., 2022). This adaptive approach not only reduces the immediate impact of stress but also contributes to overall mental well-being, allowing entrepreneurs to thrive in their endeavors.

3.2 EI and Mental Health

The connection between emotional intelligence and mental health is well-documented, with numerous studies highlighting the protective effects of EI against mental health issues such as anxiety and depression (Reis da Silva, 2024e). Individuals with high EI are better able to navigate their emotional experiences, leading to improved psychological well-being (Zarchi et al., 2020). For entrepreneurs, who often encounter high levels of stress and uncertainty, cultivating EI can serve as a buffer against mental health challenges. Research has shown that mindfulness, a key component of EI, is associated with lower levels of psychological distress. For example, a study by Sadoughi & Hesampour (2016) found that mindfulness practices significantly reduce symptoms of depression and anxiety among university students (Reis da Silva, 2024e). This suggests that integrating mindfulness into emotional intelligence training can enhance mental health outcomes for entrepreneurs, enabling them to maintain emotional balance and well-being amidst the challenges of running a business. Furthermore, the ability to regulate emotions effectively is linked to better mental health outcomes. Emotional regulation strategies, such as cognitive reappraisal and acceptance, are associated with lower levels of emotional distress and greater psychological resilience (Jakupčević et al., 2021). By developing these skills, entrepreneurs can enhance their emotional well-being, leading to improved mental health and overall life satisfaction.

3.3 Mindfulness and Integrative Medicine for Emotional Regulation

Mindfulness practices have gained recognition as effective tools for emotional regulation, particularly in the context of integrative medicine. Integrative medicine emphasizes a holistic approach to health, combining conventional medical practices with complementary therapies such as mindfulness and meditation (Kato et al., 2022). Research indicates that mindfulness can significantly enhance emotional regulation, leading to improved mental health outcomes. For instance (Zarchi et al., 2020) demonstrated that mindfulness-based training enhances emotional stability and regulation, allowing individuals to confront intrusive thoughts without becoming overwhelmed. This ability to observe emotions nonjudgmentally is crucial for entrepreneurs, who often face high-stress situations that can trigger negative emotional responses. By cultivating mindfulness, entrepreneurs can develop greater emotional awareness and regulation, leading to improved mental peace and well-being. Moreover, mindfulness practices have been shown to foster resilience by promoting adaptive coping strategies. A study by Ma and Fang (2019) found that mindfulness is associated with better emotional self-regulation, which in turn reduces psychological distress. This highlights the importance of integrating mindfulness into emotional intelligence training for entrepreneurs, as it can enhance their ability to cope with stress and maintain mental peace. In conclusion, promoting mental peace through emotional intelligence involves a multifaceted approach that includes stress management, mental health support, and mindfulness practices. By cultivating emotional intelligence, entrepreneurs can enhance their resilience, improve their emotional regulation skills, and ultimately foster a healthier work environment. This holistic approach not only benefits individual entrepreneurs but also contributes to the overall success and sustainability of their businesses.

4. THE ROLE OF EMOTIONAL INTELLIGENCE IN CREATING HEALTHY WORK ENVIRONMENTS

4.1 Fostering Emotional Support and Collaboration

A healthy work environment is characterized by emotional support, value, and connection among employees. Entrepreneurs with high emotional intelligence (EI) play a pivotal role in fostering such environments by promoting open communication, providing emotional support to their teams, and encouraging collaboration (da Silva, 2022; Reis da Silva, 2024a). The ability to recognize and understand the emotional states of team members enables leaders to offer appropriate support or interventions when needed (Koutsioumpa, 2023). For instance, entrepreneurs who practice empathy can better comprehend the emotional needs of their employees, which leads to more effective team dynamics and higher levels of job satisfaction (Gavin et al., 2017). Research indicates that emotionally supportive work cultures can significantly reduce turnover rates and enhance employee engagement. When employees feel valued and supported, they are more likely to remain committed to their organization and contribute positively to its goals (Shafiq & Rana, 2016). Furthermore, a study by Shafiq & Rana (2016) highlights that higher levels of emotional intelligence among educators correlate with increased organizational commitment, suggesting that EI can enhance the overall emotional climate within a workplace. By creating an emotionally supportive work culture, entrepreneurs can promote overall well-being within their organizations, leading to improved performance and productivity.

Moreover, fostering emotional support and collaboration can also enhance creativity and innovation within teams. When employees feel safe to express their ideas and emotions, they are more likely to engage in collaborative problem-solving and creative thinking (Kim et al, 2021). This collaborative environment not only benefits individual employees but also contributes to the organization's ability to adapt and thrive in a competitive landscape.

4.2 Building Trust and Positive Organizational Culture

Trust is a foundational element of any successful organization, and it is closely tied to emotional intelligence. Entrepreneurs who demonstrate high levels of EI are more likely to build trust within their teams by being transparent, consistent, and empathetic in their leadership (Yu et al., 2021). Trust, in turn, fosters a positive organizational culture where employees feel safe, respected, and motivated to contribute to the success of the business. Research has shown that trust among team members enhances collaboration and communication, which are essential for achieving organizational goals (Kim et al., 2014). A positive organizational culture not only promotes mental peace but also enhances emotional well-being among both entrepreneurs and employees. When individuals feel that they are working in a supportive and trusting environment, they are less likely to experience stress, burnout, or conflict (Magnini et al., 2011). For example, a study by Kim et al. (2014) found that emotional intelligence significantly influences negotiation outcomes, highlighting the importance of trust in fostering effective communication and collaboration (Kim et al., 2014). This underscores the idea that emotionally intelligent leaders can create a culture of trust that enhances overall organizational performance.

Furthermore, the relationship between emotional intelligence and trust is reciprocal; as leaders build trust through their emotional intelligence, they also encourage employees to develop their own EI skills, creating a virtuous cycle that strengthens the organizational culture (Lenka & Gupta, 2019). This dynamic not only enhances employee satisfaction but also contributes to higher levels of organizational commitment and performance.

4.3 Reducing Workplace Conflict and Enhancing Employee Well-Being

Conflict in the workplace is inevitable, but how it is managed can significantly impact the emotional well-being of both entrepreneurs and their employees. Entrepreneurs with high emotional intelligence are better equipped to manage and resolve conflicts in a way that promotes harmony and collaboration rather than division (Mónico et al., 2016). By utilizing their social skills and empathy, emotionally intelligent entrepreneurs can mediate disputes, facilitate open dialogue, and find solutions that meet the needs of all parties involved (Martino, 2023). Research indicates that effective conflict management through emotional intelligence can lead to enhanced employee well-being. For instance, a study by Lim et al. (2018) found that nurses' emotional intelligence positively influenced their organizational citizenship behaviour, which is crucial for maintaining a collaborative and supportive work environment (Christie et al., 2015). This suggests that emotionally intelligent leaders can create an emotionally safe environment where individuals feel heard and valued, ultimately reducing workplace conflict.

Moreover, the ability to manage conflicts effectively can also enhance team cohesion and collaboration. When conflicts are addressed constructively, team members are more likely to feel respected and valued, leading to improved relationships and a stronger sense of belonging within the organization (Gorji et al., 2016). This positive environment not only benefits individual employees but also contributes to the overall success and sustainability of the organisation.

5. EMOTIONAL WELL-BEING AND ENTREPRENEURIAL SUCCESS

5.1 EI and Decision-Making Under Pressure

Entrepreneurs frequently encounter high-stakes decisions that can significantly influence the success or failure of their ventures. These decisions often need to be made under pressure, with limited information and considerable emotional involvement (Reis da Silva, 2024b; Reis da Silva, 2024c). Emotional Intelligence (EI) plays a critical role in enabling entrepreneurs to remain calm, focused, and objective when making decisions in such challenging conditions. Research indicates that self-regulation, a key component of EI, helps entrepreneurs avoid impulsive decision-making driven by emotional reactions such as fear or frustration (Othman & Muda, 2018). Instead, they can approach decisions with a clear, rational mindset, which increases the likelihood of successful outcomes. For instance, Othman & Muda

(2018) highlight that individuals with high emotional intelligence are more adept at generating creative ideas and making informed decisions, which ultimately shapes their entrepreneurial characteristics and behaviours. This ability to manage emotions effectively allows entrepreneurs to evaluate risks and opportunities more accurately, leading to better decision-making processes. Furthermore, studies have shown that emotional intelligence positively correlates with entrepreneurial self-efficacy, which is crucial for navigating the uncertainties inherent in entrepreneurship (Rodrigues et al., 2019).

Moreover, the capacity to remain composed under pressure not only aids in decision-making but also influences the overall organizational climate. Entrepreneurs who demonstrate high EI can foster a culture of resilience and adaptability within their teams, encouraging employees to approach challenges with a similar mindset (Silva & Coelho, 2018). This collective emotional intelligence can lead to improved performance and innovation, as team members feel empowered to contribute their ideas and solutions without fear of negative repercussions.

5.2 Work-Life Balance and Personal Well-Being

The pursuit of entrepreneurial success often comes at the expense of personal well-being, with many entrepreneurs sacrificing their physical and emotional health in the process. Emotional Intelligence promotes a healthier work-life balance by encouraging entrepreneurs to recognize their emotional and physical limits and take proactive steps to prioritize self-care (da Silva, 2022). By practicing self-awareness and self-regulation, entrepreneurs can set boundaries, manage their workloads more effectively, and ensure that they dedicate time to personal well-being (Riyanto et al., 2020). Research has shown that individuals with high emotional intelligence are better equipped to manage stress and maintain a balanced lifestyle. For example, Silva & Coelho (2018) found that emotional intelligence significantly impacts worker attitudes, which in turn influences their ability to maintain a healthy work-life balance (Silva & Coelho, 2018). This balance is essential for sustaining long-term entrepreneurial success and avoiding burnout. Entrepreneurs who prioritize their well-being are more likely to be productive, creative, and engaged in their work, ultimately leading to better business outcomes.

Furthermore, the ability to recognize when to take a step back and recharge is crucial for preventing burnout. Emotional intelligence enables entrepreneurs to identify signs of emotional exhaustion early and take proactive measures to address them (Jiang & Park, 2012). By fostering a culture that values work-life balance, entrepreneurs can create an environment where employees feel supported in their efforts to maintain their well-being, leading to increased job satisfaction and retention.

5.3 Preventing Burnout and Maintaining Long-Term Entrepreneurial Success

Burnout is a common issue among entrepreneurs, who often work long hours under significant pressure. Emotional Intelligence can help prevent burnout by enabling entrepreneurs to recognize the signs of emotional exhaustion early and take proactive steps to address them. By practicing self-regulation, entrepreneurs can manage their stress levels, maintain emotional balance, and ensure that they do not overextend themselves (Wei et al., 2019). Research indicates that entrepreneurs with high emotional intelligence are more likely to seek support from mentors, peers, or mental health professionals when needed, further reducing the risk of burnout and promoting long-term success. For instance, Riyanto et al. (2020) emphasizes that individuals with higher emotional intelligence are better equipped to handle stress and are more inclined to reach out for help when facing challenges. This proactive approach not only mitigates the risk of burnout but also fosters a supportive network that can enhance entrepreneurial resilience.

Moreover, the ability to manage emotions effectively contributes to a more sustainable entrepreneurial journey. Entrepreneurs who cultivate their emotional intelligence are better positioned to navigate the ups and downs of business ownership, maintaining their motivation and passion for their ventures (Farhan & Rofi'ulmuiz, 2021). This emotional resilience is essential for long-term success, as it allows entrepreneurs to adapt to changing circumstances and remain focused on their goals despite setbacks.

6. INTERDISCIPLINARY CONNECTIONS: INSIGHTS FROM NURSING, INTEGRATIVE MEDICINE, AND MOVING AND HANDLING

6.1 Parallels Between Entrepreneurial Stress and Caregiving for Older Adults

The stress experienced by entrepreneurs shares significant similarities with the emotional demands faced by caregivers, particularly those involved in nursing for older adults (Cowley et al., 2023; Fitzpatrick et al., 2023; Reis da Silva, 2024f; Reis da Silva, 2024g; Reis da Silva, 2024h; Reis da Silva, 2024i). Both roles entail high levels of responsibility, emotional labor, and the necessity for resilience (da Silva, 2022; Reis da Silva, 2024a). Entrepreneurs often navigate a landscape filled with uncertainty, high expectations, and the pressure to succeed, which can lead to significant stress and emotional strain (Kildal et al., 2021; Horta Reis da Silva, 2022a; Horta Reis da Silva, 2022b; Reis da Silva, 2023a; Reis da Silva, 2023b; Reis da Silva, 2024j). Similarly, caregivers for older adults frequently encounter emotional challenges, including the burden of responsibility for the well-being of their patients, which can lead to caregiver burnout and emotional exhaustion (Moosivand, 2023; Reis da Silva, 2024k; Reis da Silva, 2024l; Reis da Silva, 2024m; Reis da Silva, 2024n).

Insights from nursing practices, such as the importance of self-care and emotional regulation, can provide valuable lessons for entrepreneurs seeking to manage their own stress and emotional well-being (da Silva, 2022; Reis da Silva and Mitchell, 2024a; Reis da Silva and Mitchell, 2024b). For instance, studies have shown that caregivers who engage in self-care practices are better equipped to handle the emotional demands of their roles, leading to improved mental health outcomes (Ramos et al., 2021; Reis da Silva, 2024e). This suggests that entrepreneurs can benefit from adopting similar self-care strategies to mitigate stress and enhance their emotional resilience. Moreover, emotional intelligence plays a crucial role in both caregiving and entrepreneurship. Caregivers with high emotional intelligence are better able to recognize and manage their own emotions, as well as those of the individuals they care for, which can lead to more effective caregiving and reduced stress (Gérain & Zech, 2021). Entrepreneurs can similarly leverage emotional intelligence to navigate the emotional complexities of their roles, fostering a supportive work environment that prioritizes mental well-being (Wojujutari et al., 2021). By recognizing the parallels between these two fields, entrepreneurs can adopt strategies from nursing to enhance their emotional resilience and overall well-being.

6.2 Integrative Medicine Approaches to Emotional Well-Being

Integrative medicine, which combines conventional and complementary therapies to promote holistic well-being, offers valuable approaches for managing emotional well-being. Techniques such as mindfulness, meditation, and stress-reduction practices can help entrepreneurs cultivate mental peace and emotional resilience (Gómez-Trinidad et al., 2021). Research indicates that mindfulness practices can significantly reduce stress and enhance emotional regulation, making them particularly beneficial for individuals in high-pressure roles such as entrepreneurship (Kaimal et al., 2021). For example, mindfulness-based interventions have been shown to improve emotional intelligence and reduce symptoms of anxiety and depression among caregivers (Utli & Aydın, 2021). By integrating these practices into their daily routines, entrepreneurs can enhance their emotional intelligence and overall well-being. The application of mindfulness not only helps in managing stress but also fosters a greater awareness of one's emotional states, enabling entrepreneurs to respond to challenges with clarity and composure (Carvalho et al., 2023).

Furthermore, integrative medicine emphasizes the importance of self-care and emotional regulation, which are essential for maintaining mental health in both caregiving and entrepreneurial contexts. By prioritizing emotional well-being through integrative practices, entrepreneurs can create a more balanced and fulfilling work-life dynamic, ultimately leading to greater success in their ventures (Vázquez et al., 2011). This holistic approach to health and well-being can serve as a valuable framework for entrepreneurs seeking to enhance their emotional resilience and overall quality of life.

6.3 Emotional Intelligence in Moving and Handling: Lessons for Entrepreneurs

Moving and handling, a critical component of nursing care, requires not only physical skill but also emotional intelligence (Horta Reis da Silva, 2022c; Horta Reis da Silva, 2022d; Reis da Silva, 2023c). Caregivers must be attuned to the emotional and physical needs of those they care for, demonstrating empathy and emotional regulation in challenging situations (Ruiz-Robledillo & Moya-Albiol, 2013; Reis da Silva, 2023c). These skills are equally important for entrepreneurs, who must navigate the emotional dynamics of their teams and clients with sensitivity and emotional awareness (da Silva, 2022).

Research has shown that emotional intelligence is essential for effective communication and relationship-building in caregiving settings (Luca et al., 2023). Caregivers who possess high emotional intelligence are better equipped to manage the emotional challenges associated with their roles, leading to improved patient outcomes and reduced stress (Lovell & Wetherell, 2016). Entrepreneurs can learn from these practices by cultivating their emotional intelligence to enhance their leadership capabilities and foster a positive work environment. Additionally, the parallels between caregiving and entrepreneurship extend to the need for effective emotional regulation during high-stress situations. Caregivers often face emotionally charged scenarios that require them to remain calm and composed while providing care (Berenbaum et al., 2020). Similarly, entrepreneurs must manage their emotions during critical business decisions, ensuring that their emotional responses do not cloud their judgment (Bru-Luna et al., 2022). By adopting the emotional regulation strategies employed by caregivers, entrepreneurs can enhance their decision-making processes and overall effectiveness in their roles.

7. THE ROLE OF EMOTIONAL INTELLIGENCE IN PROMOTING THE SUSTAINABLE DEVELOPMENT GOALS (SDGS)

7.1 Aligning EI in Entrepreneurship with SDG 3: Good Health and Well-being

Sustainable Development Goal 3 (SDG 3) focuses on promoting good health and well-being for all, which aligns closely with the objectives of Emotional Intelligence (EI) in entrepreneurship (Reis da Silva and Rodrigues, 2023; da Silva, 2024a; Reis da Silva, 2024b). Entrepreneurs who cultivate high levels of emotional intelligence contribute significantly to mental peace, emotional well-being, and the establishment of healthy work environments. By fostering an atmosphere where employees feel supported and valued, entrepreneurs can enhance the overall mental health of their teams, which is essential for achieving SDG 3 (Koutsioumpa, 2023). Research indicates that emotionally intelligent leaders are more adept at recognizing the emotional needs of their employees, which allows them to implement supportive measures that promote mental health (Koutsioumpa, 2023). For instance, Koutsioumpa (2023) emphasizes the importance of emotional intelligence in leadership, noting that leaders who exhibit high EI can create cohesive teams that prioritize well-being. This not only benefits individual employees but also contributes to a healthier organizational culture, ultimately supporting the broader goal of ensuring that individuals and communities can thrive both physically and emotionally.

Moreover, the integration of EI into entrepreneurial practices can lead to improved employee engagement and job satisfaction, which are critical components of mental well-being (Safiullah et al., 2023). By prioritizing emotional intelligence, entrepreneurs can create workplaces that not only meet the economic needs of their organizations but also support the mental health and well-being of their employees, thereby aligning with the objectives of SDG 3.

7.2 EI and Sustainable Business Practices

Emotional intelligence also plays a pivotal role in promoting sustainable business practices. Entrepreneurs with high EI are more likely to consider the long-term impact of their decisions on their employees, communities, and the environment. By fostering ethical leadership, empathy, and social responsibility, EI supports the achievement of other SDGs, such as reducing inequality and promoting sustainable economic growth (Aldawsari ,)2020). For example, emotionally intelligent leaders are better equipped to engage in ethical decision-making processes that take into account the welfare of all stakeholders involved. This approach not only enhances the reputation of the business but also builds trust and loyalty among employees and customers alike (Wardana et al., 2020). By prioritizing ethical considerations in their decision-making, entrepreneurs can contribute to sustainable practices that align with the principles of social responsibility and environmental stewardship.

Furthermore, the ability to empathize with others allows entrepreneurs to understand the broader implications of their business practices, leading to more socially responsible actions. Research by Safiullah et al. (2023) highlights the importance of emotional intelligence in servant leadership, which emphasizes the well-being of employees and the community. This servant leadership approach can significantly enhance the sustainability of business practices, as it encourages leaders to prioritize the needs of others while also achieving organizational goals.

7.3 EI, Entrepreneurship, and Community Well-Being

Entrepreneurs have the potential to impact not only their businesses but also their communities. By cultivating emotional intelligence, entrepreneurs can create businesses that prioritize the well-being of their employees and contribute to the emotional and psychological health of the broader community. This, in turn, supports the achievement of SDG 3 and other global health and well-being goals (Esen & Bulut, 2022). Research indicates that emotionally intelligent entrepreneurs are more likely to engage in community-oriented practices that enhance social cohesion and support local initiatives (Prado et al., 2022). For instance, by fostering a culture of empathy and support within their organizations, entrepreneurs can encourage their employees to participate in community service and social responsibility initiatives, thereby contributing to the overall well-being of the community (Pečiuliauskienė, 2021). This engagement not only benefits the community but also enhances the reputation and sustainability of the business.

Moreover, the emotional intelligence of entrepreneurs can influence their ability to build strong relationships with community stakeholders, including customers, suppliers, and local organizations. By prioritizing emotional connections and understanding the needs of the community, entrepreneurs can create businesses that are not only economically viable but also socially responsible (Wardana, 2018). This holistic approach to entrepreneurship aligns with the principles of sustainable development, ensuring that businesses contribute positively to the well-being of society.

8. CONCLUSION

Emotional intelligence is a critical competency for success in entrepreneurship. It influences various aspects of entrepreneurial behaviour, including leadership effectiveness, decision-making, and resilience. As research continues to highlight the importance of EI in entrepreneurial contexts, it becomes increasingly clear that fostering emotional intelligence should be a priority for aspiring entrepreneurs and educational institutions alike. By integrating emotional intelligence training into entrepreneurship education, we can better prepare future leaders to navigate the complexities of the business world and achieve sustainable success. Emotional intelligence plays a critical role in creating healthy work environments by fostering emotional support, building trust, and reducing workplace conflict. Entrepreneurs who cultivate their emotional intelligence can enhance collaboration, improve employee well-being, and ultimately drive organizational success. By prioritizing emotional intelligence in their leadership practices, entrepreneurs can create workplaces that are not only productive but also emotionally supportive and fulfilling for all employees.

Emotional intelligence is a vital component of emotional well-being and entrepreneurial success. By enhancing decision-making under pressure, promoting work-life balance, and preventing burnout, EI empowers entrepreneurs to navigate the complexities of their roles effectively. As research continues to underscore the importance of emotional intelligence in entrepreneurship, it becomes increasingly clear that fostering EI should be a priority for aspiring and established entrepreneurs alike. The interdisciplinary connections between nursing, integrative medicine, and entrepreneurship provide valuable insights into the importance of emotional intelligence and self-care. By recognizing the parallels between the emotional demands of caregiving and entrepreneurship, individuals in both fields can adopt strategies that promote emotional well-being and resilience. Integrating practices from nursing and holistic health approaches can empower entrepreneurs to navigate the challenges of their roles more effectively, ultimately leading to greater success and fulfilment.

Emotional intelligence plays a crucial role in promoting the Sustainable Development Goals, particularly SDG 3, which focuses on good health and well-being. By aligning emotional intelligence with entrepreneurial practices, entrepreneurs can enhance mental well-being, promote sustainable business practices, and contribute to the overall health of their communities. As the importance of emotional intelligence continues to gain recognition in the entrepreneurial landscape, it is essential for entrepreneurs to cultivate these skills to achieve both personal and societal success.

8.1 Summary of Key Insights

Emotional Intelligence (EI) plays a critical role in promoting mental peace, emotional well-being, and healthy work environments among entrepreneurs. By cultivating EI, entrepreneurs can effectively manage stress, prevent burnout, and foster emotionally supportive organizational cultures. These benefits not only contribute to entrepreneurial success but also align with broader global health and well-being goals, such as the Sustainable Development Goals (SDGs). Research indicates that emotionally intelligent leaders create environments that enhance employee engagement and job satisfaction, which are essential for achieving SDG 3, focused on good health and well-being (Othman & Muda, 2018; Rodrigues et al., 2019; da Silva, 2022; da Silva, 2024a; Reis da Silva, 2024a).

Moreover, the integration of EI into entrepreneurial practices can lead to improved decision-making under pressure, better work-life balance, and enhanced community well-being. Entrepreneurs who prioritize emotional intelligence are better equipped to navigate the complexities of their roles, fostering resilience and adaptability within their teams (Ciuchta et al., 2017; Wardana et al., 2020). This holistic approach to entrepreneurship not only benefits individual entrepreneurs but also contributes to the overall health of their organizations and communities.

8.2 Future Directions for EI in Entrepreneurship

As the entrepreneurial landscape continues to evolve, Emotional Intelligence will remain a key factor in ensuring the long-term well-being and success of entrepreneurs. Future research and practice should explore how EI can be further integrated into entrepreneurial training and development programs. This includes examining the effectiveness of EI training in enhancing entrepreneurial skills and fostering sustainable business practices (Ordiñana-Bellver et al., 2022; Wardana et al., 2020). Additionally, there is a need to investigate the role of emotional intelligence in promoting ethical leadership and social responsibility among entrepreneurs, as these elements are crucial for achieving the SDGs (Cai et al., 2018; Valadkhani et al., 2023).

Furthermore, interdisciplinary approaches that draw from fields such as nursing, integrative medicine, and psychology can provide valuable insights into the development of emotional intelligence in entrepreneurship. By understanding the emotional demands faced by caregivers and the holistic approaches used in integrative medicine, entrepreneurs can adopt strategies that enhance their emotional resilience and overall well-being (Allen et al., 2020; Zhang et al., 2022). This cross-disciplinary perspective can lead to innovative practices that support both individual and organizational health.

8.3 Final Thoughts on EI, Mental Peace, and Entrepreneurial Well-Being

In an increasingly fast-paced and emotionally demanding entrepreneurial world, Emotional Intelligence offers a vital pathway to mental peace, emotional resilience, and sustained success. Entrepreneurs who prioritize their emotional well-being and the well-being of their teams can create businesses that thrive not only financially but also emotionally, contributing to healthier individuals, workplaces, and communities (Khalid et al., 2018; Yan et al., 2022). As the importance of emotional intelligence continues to gain recognition in the entrepreneurial landscape, it is essential for entrepreneurs to cultivate these skills to achieve both personal and societal success.

Fostering emotional intelligence is not merely an ancillary skill for entrepreneurs; it is a fundamental competency that significantly impacts their ability to navigate challenges, build supportive work environments, and contribute positively to their communities. By embracing emotional intelligence, entrepreneurs can enhance their leadership effectiveness, promote well-being, and ultimately drive sustainable success in their ventures.

REFERENCES

Aldawsari, R. (2020). The relationship between leaders' emotional intelligence and leadership effectiveness from perspectives of leaders and faculty members at university of Hafr al Batin. , 79(79), 1-26. DOI: 10.21608/edusohag.2020.116714

Allen, J., Stevenson, R., O'Boyle, E., & Seibert, S. (2020). What matters more for entrepreneurship success? a meta-analysis comparing general mental ability and emotional intelligence in entrepreneurial settings. *Strategic Entrepreneurship Journal*, 15(3), 352–376. DOI: 10.1002/sej.1377

Amar, A., Hlupic, V., & Tamwatin, T. (2014). Effect of meditation on self-perception of leadership skills: A control group study of CEOs. *Proceedings - Academy of Management*, 2014(1), 14282. DOI: 10.5465/ambpp.2014.300

Berenbaum, R., Tziraki, C., Baum, R., Rosen, A., Reback, T., Abikhzer, J., & Ben-David, B. (2020). Focusing on emotional and social intelligence stimulation of people with dementia by playing a serious game—Proof of concept study. *Frontiers of Computer Science*, 2. Advance online publication. DOI: 10.3389/fcomp.2020.536880

Boybanting, J. (2023). Emotional intelligence and teaching performance of teachers. *International Journal of Research Publications*, 129(1). Advance online publication. DOI: 10.47119/ijrp1001291720235288

Bru-Luna, L., Vilar, M., Merino-Soto, C., Salinas-Escudero, G., & Toledano-Toledano, F. (2022). Variables impacting the quality of care provided by professional caregivers for people with mental illness: A systematic review. *Health Care*, 10(7), 1225. DOI: 10.3390/healthcare10071225

Cai, M., Humphrey, R., & Qian, S. (2020). The cross-cultural moderators of the influence of emotional intelligence on organizational citizenship behavior and counterproductive work behavior. *Human Resource Development Quarterly*, 31(2), 213–233. DOI: 10.1002/hrdq.21385

Cai, M., Humphrey, R., Qian, S., & Pollack, J. (2018). Emotional intelligence and entrepreneurial intentions: An exploratory meta-analysis. *Career Development International*, 23(5), 497–512. DOI: 10.1108/cdi-01-2018-0019

Carvalho, C., Teixeira, M., Costa, R., Cordeiro, F., & Cabral, J. (2023). The enhancing role of emotion regulation in the links between early positive memories and self-harm and suicidal ideation in adolescence. *Journal of Youth and Adolescence*, 52(8), 1738–1752. DOI: 10.1007/s10964-023-01777-8

Christie, A., Jordan, P., & Troth, A. (2015). Trust antecedents: Emotional intelligence and perceptions of others. *The International Journal of Organizational Analysis*, 23(1), 89–101. DOI: 10.1108/ijoa-07-2013-0695

Ciuchta, M., Letwin, C., Stevenson, R., McMahon, S., & Huvaj, M. (2017). Betting on the coachable entrepreneur: Signaling and social exchange in entrepreneurial pitches. *Entrepreneurship Theory and Practice*, 42(6), 860–885. DOI: 10.1177/1042258717725520

Cowley, S. A., Tzouvara, V., & Horta Reis da Silva, T. (2023). Public Health: healthy ageing and wellbeing. In Redfern's Nursing Older People. Fifth edition. Editors: Ross, Harris, Fitzpatrick and Abley. Elsevier.

da Silva, T. H. R. (2022). Emotional awareness and emotional intelligence. *British Journal of Community Nursing*, 27(12), 573–574. DOI: 10.12968/bjcn.2022.27.12.573

da Silva, T. R. (2024a). Gender Equity In Healthcare: Integrating Emotional Intelligence To Achieve The United Nations Sustainable Development Goals. *J Comm Med and Pub Health Rep*, 5(12). Advance online publication. DOI: 10.38207/JCMPHR/2024/JUL051202106

da Silva, T. R. (2024b). Advancing Gender Equity In Nursing Care For Older Adults: A Pathway To Achieving The United Nations Sustainable Development Goals. *J Comm Med and Pub Health Rep*, 5(12). Advance online publication. DOI: 10.38207/JCMPHR/2024/JUL051201105

da Silva, T. H. R., & Rodrigues, E. C. P. (2023). Body Image Related Discrimination. In Leal Filho, W., Azul, A. M., Brandli, L., Lange Salvia, A., Özuyar, P. G., & Wall, T. (Eds.), *Reduced Inequalities. Encyclopedia of the UN Sustainable Development Goals*. Springer., DOI: 10.1007/978-3-319-71060-0_61-1

Esen, Ü., & Bulut, S. (2022). Determining the effect of emotional intelligence on self-leadership. *Journal of Business Management Review*, 3(8), 563–580. DOI: 10.47153/jbmr38.3972022

Farhan, F., & Rofi'ulmuiz, M. (2021). Religiosity and emotional intelligence on Muslim student learning achievement. [IJERE]. *International Journal of Evaluation and Research in Education*, 10(2), 404. DOI: 10.11591/ijere.v10i2.20997

Fitzpatrick, J. M., Bianchi, L. A., Hayes, N., Da Silva, T., & Harris, R. (2023). Professional development and career planning for nurses working in care homes for older people: A scoping review. *International Journal of Older People Nursing*, 18, e12519. DOI: 10.1111/opn.12519

Gavin, D., Gavin, J., & Quick, J. (2017). Power struggles within the top management team: An empirical examination of follower reactions to subversive leadership. *Journal of Applied Biobehavioral Research*, 22(4). Advance online publication. DOI: 10.1111/jabr.12100

Gérain, P., & Zech, E. (2021). Are caregiving appraisal and relationship quality key mediators in informal caregiving burnout? a structural equation modelling study in Belgium and France. *Health & Social Care in the Community*, 30(5). Advance online publication. DOI: 10.1111/hsc.13684

Grecucci, A., Pisapia, N., Thero, D., Paladino, M., Venuti, P., & Job, R. (2015). Baseline and strategic effects behind mindful emotion regulation: Behavioral and physiological investigation. *PLoS One*, 10(1), e0116541. DOI: 10.1371/journal.pone.0116541

Gómez-Trinidad, M., Chimpén-López, C., Rodríguez-Santos, L., Moral, M., & Rodríguez-Mansilla, J. (2021). Resilience, emotional intelligence, and occupational performance in family members who are the caretakers of patients with dementia in spain: A cross-sectional, analytical, and descriptive study. *Journal of Clinical Medicine*, 10(18), 4262. DOI: 10.3390/jcm10184262

Gorji, A. M. H., Ranjbar, M., & Darabiniya, M. (2016). Emotional Intelligence and Job Motivation of Member Faculties in Medical Sciences Universities. *International Journal of Advances in Agricultural & Environmental Engineering*, 3(2). Advance online publication. DOI: 10.15242/ijaaee.a0516001

Hammett, R. D., Arenas, F., & Scherer, J. (2018). Facilitating full-range leadership with emotional intelligence in the USAF Squadron Officer College. The International Journal of Transformative Emotional Intelligence, 5.

Hammett, R. D., Hollon, C., & Maggard, P. (2011). Professional military education in the USAF SOS leadership course: Incorporating emotional intelligence. *The International Journal of Transformative Emotional Intelligence*, 1, 73–96. http://eitri.org/2015/11/13/professional-military-education- pme-in-the-usaf-sos-leadership-course-incorporating-emotional-intelligence/

Horta Reis Da Silva, T. (2022a). Muskuloskeletal minor injuries: assessment and treatment. In Curr, S., & Fordham-Clarke, C. (Eds.), *Clinical Skills at Glance* (1st ed., pp. 128–129). Wiley. [55]

Horta Reis Da Silva, T. (2022b). Falls - prevention, assessment and management. In Curr, S., & Fordham-Clarke, C. (Eds.), *Clinical Skills at Glance* (pp. 130–131). Wiley. [56]

Horta Reis Da Silva, T. (2022c). Moving and Handling. In Curr, S., & Fordham-Clarke, C. (Eds.), *Clinical Skills at Glance* (pp. 20–21). Wiley.

Horta Reis Da Silva, T. (2022d). Moving and Handling: turning in bed, transfer and hoisting. In Curr, S., & Fordham-Clarke, C. (Eds.), *Clinical Skills at Glance* (pp. 22–23). Wiley.

Jakupčević, K., Ercegovac, I., & Dobrota, S. (2021). Music as a tool for mood regulation: The role of absorption vs. mindfulness. *Primenjena Psihologija*, 14(2), 229–248. DOI: 10.19090/pp.2021.2.229-248

Jiang, Z., & Park, D. (2012). Career decision-making self-efficacy as a moderator in the relationships of entrepreneurial career intention with emotional intelligence and cultural intelligence. *African Journal of Business Management*, 6(30). Advance online publication. DOI: 10.5897/ajbm11.1816

Kaimal, G., Vidhukumar, K., & Padmam, M. (2021). Delinquent behaviour and emotional intelligence among inmates of juvenile homes in Kerala, India. *Kerala Journal of Psychiatry*, 34(1). Advance online publication. DOI: 10.30834/kjp.34.1.2021.230

Kato, K., Matsumoto, Y., & Hirano, Y. (2022). Effectiveness of school-based brief cognitive behavioral therapy with mindfulness in improving the mental health of adolescents in a japanese school setting: A preliminary study. *Frontiers in Psychology*, 13. Advance online publication. DOI: 10.3389/fpsyg.2022.895086

Khalid, A., Bashir, M., & Saqib, S. (2018). Collective impact of entrepreneurial self-efficacy and risk propensity on entrepreneurial intentions; mediating role of perceived social support. International Journal of Engineering & Technology, 7(3.21), 24. DOI: 10.14419/ijet.v7i3.21.17087

Khatri, S. (2018). Emotional intelligence in adolescents and its implications on their lifelong development. *International Journal of Indian Psychology*, 6(4). Advance online publication. DOI: 10.25215/0604.057

Kildal, E., Stadskleiv, K., Boysen, E., Øderud, T., Dahl, I., Seeberg, T., & Hassel, B. (2021). Increased heart rate functions as a signal of acute distress in non-communicating persons with intellectual disability. *Scientific Reports*, 11(1). Advance online publication. DOI: 10.1038/s41598-021-86023-6

Kim, K., Cundiff, N., & Choi, S. (2014). The influence of emotional intelligence on negotiation outcomes and the mediating effect of rapport: A structural equation modeling approach. *Negotiation Journal*, 30(1), 49–68. DOI: 10.1111/nejo.12045

Kim, K., Kim, J., Antonio, J., & Laws, J. (2021). Emotional intelligence, trust, and functional behavior: Longitudinal study of achievement approach to leadership emergence. *Journal of Organizational Psychology*, 21(4). Advance online publication. DOI: 10.33423/jop.v21i4.4552

Koutsioumpa, E. (2023). Contribution of emotional intelligence to efficient leadership. a narrative review. *Technium Social Sciences Journal*, 48, 204–216. DOI: 10.47577/tssj.v48i1.9529

Lenka, U., & Gupta, M. (2019). An empirical investigation of innovation process in indian pharmaceutical companies. *European Journal of Innovation Management*, 23(3), 500–523. DOI: 10.1108/ejim-03-2019-0069

Lim, S., Han, S., & Joo, Y. (2018). Effects of nurses' emotional intelligence on their organizational citizenship behavior, with mediating effects of leader trust and value congruence. *Japan Journal of Nursing Science*, 15(4), 363–374. DOI: 10.1111/jjns.12206

Liu, X., & Li, J. (2013). Effects of team leader emotional intelligence and team emotional climate on team member job satisfaction. *Nankai Business Review International*, 4(3), 180–198. DOI: 10.1108/nbri-07-2013-0023

Lovell, B., & Wetherell, M. (2016). Behaviour problems of children with asd and perceived stress in their caregivers: The moderating role of trait emotional intelligence? *Research in Autism Spectrum Disorders*, 28, 1–6. DOI: 10.1016/j.rasd.2016.05.002

Low, G. R., & Hammer, R. D. with Nelson, D. B. (2019). Transformative emotional intelligence: Achieving leadership and performance excellence. Corpus Christi, TX: Emotional Intelligence Learning Systems.

Low, G. R., & Hammett, R. D. (2021). *Transformative emotional intelligence for a positive career and life*. Emotional Intelligence Learning Systems.

Luca, R., Pollicino, P., Rifici, C., Mondo, N., Iorio, S., Cassaniti, A., & Calabrò, R. (2023). Psycho-emotional well-being in caregivers of people with acquired brain injury. An exploratory study on the human immersion model during the omicron wave. *Clinics and Practice*, 13(2), 487–496. DOI: 10.3390/clinpract13020044

Ma, Y., & Fang, S. (2019). Adolescents' mindfulness and psychological distress: The mediating role of emotion regulation. *Frontiers in Psychology*, 10. Advance online publication. DOI: 10.3389/fpsyg.2019.01358

Magnini, V., Lee, G., & Kim, P. (2011). The cascading affective consequences of exercise among hotel workers. *International Journal of Contemporary Hospitality Management*, 23(5), 624–643. DOI: 10.1108/09596111111143377

Martino, C. (2023). Organizational lay theories of intelligence and trust among minority women.. DOI: 10.14293/p2199-8442.1.sop-.prf7vg.v1

Moosivand, S. (2023). Predictors of emotional intelligence among family caregivers of cancer patients: A cross-sectional study. *Cancer Reports*, 7(1). Advance online publication. DOI: 10.1002/cnr2.1943

Mónico, L., Mellão, N., Nobre-Lima, L., Parreira, P., & Carvalho, C. (2016). Emotional intelligence and psychological capital: what is the role of workplace spirituality?. Revista Portuguesa De Enfermagem De Saúde Mental, (Spe. 3). DOI: 10.19131/rpesm.0116

Nelson, D. B., Low, G. R., Hammett, R. D., & Sen, A. (2013). *Professional coaching: A transformative and research-based model*. Emotional Intelligence Learning Systems.

Ordiñana-Bellver, D., Pérez-Campos, C., González-Serrano, M., & Valantinė, I. (2022). Emotions, skills and intra-entrepreneurship: Mapping the field and future research opportunities. *Management & Marketing*, 17(4), 577–598. DOI: 10.2478/mmcks-2022-0032

Othman, N., & Muda, T. (2018). Emotional intelligence towards entrepreneurial career choice behaviours. *Education + Training*, 60(9), 953–970. DOI: 10.1108/et-07-2017-0098

Pečiuliauskienė, P. (2021). Emotional intelligence and transformational leadership of gymnasium teachers'. Society Integration Education Proceedings of the International Scientific Conference, 2, 457-467. DOI: 10.17770/sie2021vol2.6194

Prado, J., Zárate-Torres, R., Tafur-Mendoza, A., Prada-Ospina, R., & Sarmiento, C. (2022). Impact of leadership practices on manager's pathways to goal attainment: The mediating effect of emotional intelligence. *The International Journal of Organizational Analysis*, 31(7), 2889–2902. DOI: 10.1108/ijoa-01-2022-3110

Prib, H. (2023). Psychological characteristics of entrepreneurs working in stress-related conditions. Scientific Bulletin of Mukachevo State University Series. *Pedagogy and Psychology*, 9(2). Advance online publication. DOI: 10.52534/msu-pp2.2023.57

Ramos, E., Rodríguez, M., & Castaño, Á. (2021). Resilience in in-home caregivers of older adults during the covid-19 pandemic. *Revista Latinoamericana de Bioetica*, 20(2), 91–101. DOI: 10.18359/rlbi.4813

Reis da Silva, T. H. (2023a). Ageing in place: Ageing at home and in the community. *British Journal of Community Nursing*, 28(5), 213–214. DOI: 10.12968/bjcn.2023.28.5.213

Reis da Silva, T. H. (2023b). Falls assessment and prevention in the nursing home and community. *British Journal of Community Nursing*, 28(2), 68–72. DOI: 10.12968/bjcn.2023.28.2.68

Reis da Silva, T. H. (2023c). Moving and Handling in the Community. *British Journal of Community Nursing*, 28(8), 369. DOI: 10.12968/bjcn.2023.28.8.369

Reis da Silva Tiago. (2024a) The Value of Emotional Intelligence in Midwifery: Enhancing Care and Outcomes for Mothers and Infants through Sustainable Development Goals and Leadership. Journal of Womens Healthcare & Midwifery Research. SRC/JWHMR-133. Link: https://www.onlinescientificresearch.com/articles/the-value-of-emotional-intelligence-in-midwifery-enhancing-care-and-outcomes-for-mothers-and-infants-through-sustainable-developme.pdf

Reis da Silva, T. H. (2024b). Chapter 6 – Navigating Healthcare Complexity: Integrating Business Fundamentals into Nursing Leadership. In Sedky, A. Resiliency Strategies for Long-Term Business Success. Pp. 145-168. IGI Global. DOI: 10.4018/979-8-3693-9168-6.ch006

Reis da Silva, T. H. (2024c). Chapter 11 - Integrating business essentials into Gerontological Nursing: Enhancing Care for Older Adults in Diverse Settings. In Sedky, A. Resiliency Strategies for Long-Term Business Success. Pp. 283-316. IGI Global. DOI: DOI: 10.4018/979-8-3693-9168-6.ch011

Reis da Silva, T. H. (2024d). Loneliness in older adults. *British Journal of Community Nursing*, 29(2), 60–66. DOI: 10.12968/bjcn.2024.29.2.60

Reis da Silva, T. (2024e). Can supplementing vitamin B12 improve mental health outcomes?: A literature review. *British Journal of Community Nursing*, 29(3), 137–146. DOI: 10.12968/bjcn.2024.29.3.137

Reis da Silva, T. (2024f). The Evolution of Nursing for Older Adult: A Historical Perspective. Associative J Health Sci. 3(3). AJHS. 000561. 2024. DOI: . Link: https://crimsonpublishers.com/ajhs/pdf/AJHS.000561.pdfDOI: 10.31031/AJHS.2024.03.000561

Reis da Silva. Tiago Horta (2024g). Death and Its Significance in Nursing Practice. Palliat Med Care Int J. 2024; 4(3): 555640. DOI: https://juniperpublishers.com/pmcij/pdf/PMCIJ.MS.ID.555640.pdf

Reis da Silva, T. H (2024h). Oncology and Cancer Medicine: Understanding the complexities in Older Patients. Biomed J Sci & Tech Res 55(3)-2024. DOI: DOI: 10.26717/BJSTR.2024.55.008720

Reis da Silva, Tiago Horta (2024i). "Prevalence of elder abuse: a narrative review." British journal of community nursing vol. 29,9 (2024): 442-446. doi: DOI: 10.12968/bjcn.2024.0004

Reis da Silva, T. H. (2024j). Falls prevention in older people and the role of nursing. *British Journal of Community Nursing*, 29(7), 335–339. DOI: 10.12968/bjcn.2024.0005

Reis da Silva, T. H. (2024k). Understanding body fluid balance, dehydration and intravenous fluid therapy. *Emergency Nurse*. Advance online publication. DOI: 10.7748/en.2024.e2201

Reis da Silva, T. H. (2024l). Pharmacokinetics in older people: An overview of prescribing practice. *Journal of Prescribing Practice*, 6(9), 374–381. DOI: 10.12968/jprp.2024.6.9.374

Reis da Silva, T. H. (2024m). Chronic kidney disease in older adults: Nursing implications for community nurses. *Journal of Kidney Care*, 9(4), 174–179. DOI: 10.12968/jokc.2024.9.4.174

Reis da Silva, T. H. (2024n). Loneliness in older adults. *British Journal of Community Nursing*, 29(2), 60–66. DOI: 10.12968/bjcn.2024.29.2.60

Reis da Silva, T. H., & Mitchell, A. (2024a). Integrating Digital Transformation in Nursing Education: Best Practices and Challenges in Curriculum Development. In Lytras, M., Serban, A. C., Alkhaldi, A., Malik, S., & Aldosemani, T. (Eds.), *Digital Transformation in Higher Education, Part B Cases, Examples and Good Practices*. Emerald Publishing Limited.

Reis Da Silva, T. H., & Mitchell, A. (2024b). Simulation in nursing: The importance of involving service users. *British Journal of Nursing (Mark Allen Publishing)*, 33(5), 262–265. DOI: 10.12968/bjon.2024.33.5.262

Reynolds, C., & O'Dwyer, L. (2008). Examining the relationships among emotional intelligence, coping mechanisms for stress, and leadership effectiveness for middle school principals. *Journal of School Leadership*, 18(5), 472–500. DOI: 10.1177/105268460801800501

Riyanto, P. and Sanjaya, P. (2020). Youth sports activities on emotional intelligence.. DOI: 10.2991/assehr.k.201014.088

Rodrigues, A., Jorge, F., Pires, C., & António, P. (2019). The contribution of emotional intelligence and spirituality in understanding creativity and entrepreneurial intention of higher education students. *Education + Training*, 61(7/8), 870–894. DOI: 10.1108/et-01-2018-0026

Ruiz-Robledillo, N., & Moya-Albiol, L. (2013). Self-reported health and cortisol awakening response in parents of people with Asperger syndrome: The role of trait anger and anxiety, coping and burden. *Psychology & Health*, 28(11), 1246–1264. DOI: 10.1080/08870446.2013.800517

Sadoughi, M., & Hesampour, F. (2016). The relationship between mindfulness and cognitive emotion regulation and depression among university students. *International Journal of Academic Research in Psychology*, 3(1). Advance online publication. DOI: 10.46886/ijarp/v3-i1/2378

Septiani, H., Dwidiyanti, M., & Andriany, M. (2022). The influence of mindful thought on emotional regulation in adults: A literature review. *Nurse and Health Jurnal Keperawatan*, 11(1), 70–79. DOI: 10.36720/nhjk.v11i1.359

Shafiq, M., & Rana, R. (2016). Relationship of emotional intelligence to organizational commitment of college teachers in Pakistan. *Eurasian Journal of Educational Research*, 16(62), 1–14. DOI: 10.14689/ejer.2016.62.1

Stumm, S., Chamorro-Premuzic, T., & Furnham, A. (2009). Decomposing self-estimates of intelligence: Structure and sex differences across 12 nations. *British Journal of Psychology*, 100(2), 429–442. DOI: 10.1348/000712608x357876

Utli, H., & Aydın, L. (2021). Perceptions of conscience of nursing students according to empathy levels. *International Journal of Health Services Research and Policy*, 6(2), 219–228. DOI: 10.33457/ijhsrp.916695

Valadkhani, S., Shariatpanahi, S., Atashzadeh-Shoorideh, F., & Tehrani, F. (2023). Investigating the relationship between the concepts of spiritual intelligence and entrepreneurship: a systematic review.. DOI: 10.21203/rs.3.rs-2061530/v1

Vázquez, F., Otero, P., Díaz, O., Sánchez, T., & Pomar, C. (2011). Emotional intelligence in women caregivers with depressive symptoms. *Psychological Reports*, 108(2), 369–374. DOI: 10.2466/09.13.14.pr0.108.2.369-374

Wardana, L. (2018). Implementation of co-op learning model to increase students learning achievement and their active participation in entrepreneurship subject. *Jurnal Pendidikan Bisnis Dan Manajemen*, 4(1), 40–52. DOI: 10.17977/um003v4i12018p040

Wardana, L., Purnama, C., Anam, S., & Maula, F. (2020). Attitude determinant in entrepreneurship behavior of vocational students' entrepreneurship intention. [JPEB]. *Jurnal Pendidikan Ekonomi Dan Bisnis*, 8(1), 1–13. DOI: 10.21009/jpeb.008.1.1

Wei, J., Chen, Y., Zhang, J., & Gong, Y. (2019). Research on factors affecting the entrepreneurial learning from failure: An interpretive structure model. *Frontiers in Psychology*, 10. Advance online publication. DOI: 10.3389/fpsyg.2019.01304

Wojujutari, A., Oladejo, T., Akanni, A., & Babalola, O. (2021). Spiritual intelligence, mindfulness, emotional dysregulation, depression relationship with mental well-being among persons with diabetes during covid-19 pandemic. *Journal of Diabetes and Metabolic Disorders*, 20(2), 1705–1714. DOI: 10.1007/s40200-021-00927-8

Yan, J., Huang, T., & Xiao, Y. (2022). Assessing the impact of entrepreneurial education activity on entrepreneurial intention and behavior: Role of behavioral entrepreneurial mindset. *Environmental Science and Pollution Research International*, 30(10), 26292–26307. DOI: 10.1007/s11356-022-23878-w

Yu, W., Cormican, K., Wu, Q., & Sampaio, S. (2021). In whom do we trust? critical success factors impacting intercultural communication in multicultural project teams. *International Journal of Information Systems and Project Management*, 9(3), 21–40. DOI: 10.12821/ijispm090302

Zarchi, M., Nooripour, R., Oskooei, A., & Afrooz, G. (2020). The effects of mindfulness-based training on psychological wellbeing and emotion regulation of menopausal women: A quasi-experimental study. *Journal of Research and Health*, 10(5), 295–304. DOI: 10.32598/jrh.10.5.1669.1

Zhang, H., Zhou, X., Nielsen, M., & Klyver, K. (2022). The role of stereotype threat, anxiety, and emotional intelligence in women's opportunity evaluation. *Entrepreneurship Theory and Practice*, 47(5), 1699–1730. DOI: 10.1177/10422587221096905

Дрібас, С., Makarenko, N., & Shumilina, I. (2020). Development of junior students' emotional intelligence in terms of new Ukrainian school: realities and prospects. SHS Web of Conferences, 75, 03008. DOI: 10.1051/shsconf/20207503008

Chapter 22
The Role of Mentorship in Mitigating Entrepreneurial Loneliness

Sandeep Kumar Singh
https://orcid.org/0000-0002-1741-7254
O.P. Jindal Global University, India

Preet Kanwal
https://orcid.org/0009-0006-5114-8381
Lovely Professional University, India

Thi Minh Ngoc Luu
https://orcid.org/0000-0002-5972-7752
International School, Vietnam National University, Hanoi, Vietnam

ABSTRACT

The role of mentoring in countering entrepreneurial loneliness, a commonplace problem in the business world, is analyzed in this chapter. It discusses how the entrepreneurial resilience of boosting emotional security, practical advice, and networking opportunities is provided by mentoring. The adoption of mentorship into the digital realm via virtual platforms, matching through AI, and peer-to-peer mentorship are discussed in the chapter. While discussing conflicts such as mismatched expectations and constraints in terms of time, the chapter also throws up the transformational effects that mentorship has on entrepreneurs geared towards helping them through various stages. As the entrepreneurship landscape continues to change, then creating a successful business or individual development, positive mentorship remains a crucial enabler that empowers entrepreneurs to cut across all the complexities of their ventures with confidence.

DOI: 10.4018/979-8-3693-3673-1.ch022

INTRODUCTION

Entrepreneurial loneliness is one of the most widely spread, yet least noticed challenges that entrepreneurs face when following an entrepreneurial path. Often the "glamorous" aspect of entrepreneurship connected with independence, innovation, and prosperity hides behind closed curtains true reality: periods of lonely isolation, the incredibly high levels of pressure, and scarce opportunities for emotional back-up. Entrepreneurs-those who are entrepreneurs of new firms or solo entrepreneurs-tend to feel a lonely sense of isolation, often as their role demands high-performance expectations, a feeling of constant pressure to deliver, and no real peers who understand the unique challenges they are facing in that arena. Such isolation may have profound implications on the mental health of an entrepreneur and decision-making behavior, leading to burnout or the poor performance of the business. In this regard, mentorship acts as an important resource which helps neutralize the impacts of isolation. Good mentorship provides not only professional support to entrepreneurs but also emotional and psychological support in bridging the gap created by isolation. A mentor tends to be a source of ideas and encouragement for entrepreneurs and gives them a sense of critical connectivity because of his or her experience and insight. This chapter will discuss how mentorship can play a pivotal role in mitigating entrepreneurial loneliness, building resilience, and developing the well-being of entrepreneurs.

UNDERSTANDING ENTREPRENEURIAL LONELINESS

Causes of Entrepreneurial Loneliness

Entrepreneurial loneliness arises from several factors intrinsic to the entrepreneurial journey. Among the main causes is the isolation that accompanies leadership, notably for solo founders who wear the entire weight of decision-making. Entrepreneurship can be very isolating. Others in their personal contacts likely cannot understand what they face, so there is little real support for entrepreneurs. The stress of success and the fear of failure create a mental atmosphere where many entrepreneurs feel severed from others. Entrepreneurs spend long hours building their businesses often to the detriment of contacts in their social and family lives. This serves to heighten isolation.

Psychological and Social Effects

The psychological consequences of entrepreneurial loneliness are quite big. When the isolation goes on for an extended period, stress, anxiety, and finally depression rise up. This place requires a strong mind, but if not supported properly, the emotional expense can become really high. Even self-doubt and imposter syndrome are common in entrepreneurs who think they have to appear confident from the outside while the people on the inside, who always tend to be cramped with all their inner struggles, are left alone to bear these. Socially, entrepreneurs tend to be underappreciated by their peers, which can make them feel unmoored and further isolate them from human relationships.

The Role of Isolation in Entrepreneurship

Isolation is a double-edged sword in entrepreneurship. In some respects, isolation can create creativity and innovation that can dedicate time to focus on ideals. On the other hand, deep-rooted isolation leads to bad judgments as well as reduced ability to resist stressors. Less-skilled entrepreneurs in terms of support lack resiliency in facing mishaps or constructive criticism in which vision narrows. This separation does not only have an effect on an entrepreneur's psychological well-being but can also be taken more practically to the bottom line of business results, as individuals may be less likely to seek help and to share their opinions to collaborate or take advice.

Understanding the causes and implications that can lead to entrepreneurial loneliness there is a clear connection to this cause and support and well-being for entrepreneurs to their future and success.

THE VALUE OF MENTORSHIP IN ENTREPRENEURSHIP

Emotional and Psychological Support

The most important aspect of mentorship in entrepreneurship is the emotional and psychological comfort it offers. Entrepreneurship is not easy, as most entrepreneurs go on long journeys without other people thinking along with them, facing constant pressure to live up to expectations while at the same time trying to handle their uncertainty. It's such a long journey for any entrepreneur facing constant failures and frustrations. Here, mentors act as cradles where such an entrepreneur can say out his or her fears, doubts, or frustrations. This can bring forth a huge relief from stress and anxiety, keeping the entrepreneurs focused and grounded. Since mentors have probably been there too, they give the entrepreneurs that respite by proving themselves to be empathetic and validating them for what they are going through.

Reducing Isolation Through Connection

Mentorship also acts as an antidote to that isolation which most entrepreneurs keep complaining about. Setting up a meaningful relationship with someone who is well aware of the landscape of entrepreneurship helps to counter the loneliness of leadership because giving an entrepreneur a sense of belonging is what a mentor does. More than being confident, a mentor forms part of the support network of an entrepreneur who can help expand one's circle of professional and personal relationships. This connection will help them realize that they are not alone, a fact vital in preserving mental well-being. Constant mentoring, advice, and encouragement reduce sentiments of isolation through an ongoing interaction with the mentors.

Professional Guidance and Perspective

Mentors are knowledgeable as well as experienced and thus can be of great value to entrepreneurs amidst the complexity of business. A mentor may be able to advise the entrepreneur on an assortment of matters that include how to make decisions, strategy, how to address problems together with a way of avoiding common pitfalls. This professional advice comes very handy to the novice entrepreneur as he may not possess the necessary know-how of the industry or leadership skills to deal with some of the problems. Mentors can provide the entrepreneurs with a broader perspective, allowing them to see past petty issues that face them and think more strategically. There is immense scope for help in critical business growth or crisis situations when objective and experienced input is needed to make the right decisions.

Building Entrepreneurial Confidence

Probably, one of the greatest benefits of mentoring is its ability to enhance the confidence of a businessman. Running business always requires multiple kinds of risks and hard decisions, which sometimes expose an individual to self-doubting or fear of failing, thereby making one adopt and dwell on every step carried before deciding on it. A good mentor guides an entrepreneur by relating his or her experiences while telling his or her own stories, encouraging him or her to give up nothing and helping him or her realize more about his or her strengths. Confidence realization within an entrepreneur gives him or her the boldness and the courage to take nearly any action he or she feels true. The mentors also hold the entrepreneurs responsible and advise them to surpass their limitations and continue moving on.

Fostering Long-Term Success

Lastly, mentorship simply translates into long-run success for an entrepreneur. Entrepreneurial concerns will always cut out day-to-day issues and challenges. The presence of mentors ensures that entrepreneurs will go the distance in their ventures, learn to avoid some common mistakes most people commit in them, and have the required endurance needed to sustain the running of these ventures. Mentors also provide short-term advice for entrepreneurs but more importantly help them acquire skills and mindsets that characterize them throughout their careers. By providing both emotional support and professional insight, mentors arm entrepreneurs with the tools for building businesses that have real staying power.

Entrepreneurship mentoring is beyond business advice; it involves the essential human contact and psychological support that might help counter some of the challenges of loneliness and stress on an entrepreneurial journey.

TYPES OF MENTORSHIP RELATIONSHIPS

One-on-One Mentorship

One-on-one mentorship is probably the most traditional and intimate kind of mentorship. In one-to-one mentorship, one mentor is involved with a single entrepreneur. Such a mentorship relationship is highly customized to the needs of the entrepreneur involved, because it allows for deep, focused guidance. A mentor acts as a consultant and sounding board, giving the entrepreneur specific advice in respect of his challenges, goals, or decisions. In such a close relationship, two people relate to each other like a communicative partnership wherein one would justly feel free to discuss their thoughts and vulnerabilities. One-on-one mentoring is most effective for entrepreneurs who need personal mentoring support, either to make strategic business decisions or to get reassured emotionally.

Group Mentorship and Mastermind Networks

Group mentoring enables several entrepreneurs to learn from one or more mentors at once. This usually occurs through mastermind networks or entrepreneurial peer groups. Group settings offer the opportunity for a collective environment from which entrepreneurs may share ideas, learn from peers' experiences, and receive feedback based on various perspectives. Such mentors in those settings facilitate discussions, provide collective wisdom, and nurture a feeling of community among participants. Group mentorship is effective because it acquaints the entrepreneurs with various facets of thought and expertise while at the same time making them understand that their problems are not exclusive. It also enhances networking and building relationships with fellow peers, which may be useful against loneliness and growing business opportunities.

Peer-to-Peer Mentorship

In this process, peer mentoring involves mentoring where entrepreneurs mentor their peer fellow entrepreneurs. This approach entails mutual support because the mentors utilize shared experiences and insights; peer-to-peer mentors are also subjects of similar difficulties and challenges. Benefits can be accrued by matching entrepreneurs according to similar stages or phases of the entrepreneur's journey through allowing them to exchange advice with each other, brainstorm solutions together, and hold each other accountable. Peer mentoring provides companionship in overcoming loneliness because like-minded entrepreneurs, who often face similar issues, share that relationship that is also somewhat more egalitarian in nature wherein both the people can give and take value freely.

Digital and Virtual Mentorship Platforms

In the modern age of technical advancement, digital and virtual mentorship platforms have become popular mediums in getting the mentors and the mentees connected. This opens up mentorship for entrepreneurship to anyone across borders, hence more flexibility and accessibility. Virtual mentorship is carried out through video calls, messaging, or even structured programs on specialized platforms. This is particularly useful when founders are located in far-flung locations or have busy schedules since there is no need for face-to-face meetings. Even when not physically present, virtual mentorship may still be able to build meaningful connections and offer great support; this can be achieved by scheduled check-ins and structured engagements.

Hybrid Mentorship Models

The hybrid model of mentorship incorporates individual, group mentoring, as well as virtual mentoring characteristics in coming up with more versatile and broad-based mentoring experience. For example, entrepreneurs might engage with a major mentorship program in one-to-one mentoring while participating in group sessions or log in to virtual sites for wider support. Such a multifaceted approach allows entrepreneurs to benefit from personalized advice and feedback from peers, and global expertise, all through the same mentoring framework. Hybrid models are becoming the popular option because they cater to the rich and diverse needs and preferences of modern entrepreneurs and offer a much-needed balanced mix of personal interaction and technological convenience.

Every type of mentorship relationship has different advantages, and most entrepreneurs will experience a combination of the three at some stage of their journey. Whether a one-on-one guidance or in the form of collective wisdom, these relationships play a very large role in helping mitigate entrepreneurial loneliness and fuel both personal and business growth.

MENTORSHIP AS A STRATEGY FOR BUILDING ENTREPRENEURIAL RESILIENCE

Entrepreneurial resilience is defined by the ability to emerge from adversity, somewhat reduce the blow of challenges, and stay going even in times of adversity. However, while resilience may be a crucial entrepreneurial quality, it does not develop in isolation. Rather, mentorship supports this resilience because it equips the entrepreneur with the support, perspective, and encouragement needed to contend with both the ups and downs of the journey.

Mentors help build entrepreneurial resilience by outlining their own experiences as a blueprint for dealing with obstacles. Entrepreneurs encounter many kinds of barriers that stem from real and imagined missteps of funds to strategic; it is herein where the mentor can relate how he or she has managed in the past. The stories are not only really good at providing solutions but also build self-confidence to have it through, knowing very well that experiencing setbacks is a constituent of the entrepreneur's process. A mentor's assurance during trying times further solidifies the resilient entrepreneur's ability to stand firm even when all odds are against that person.

Another way through which mentoring may promote resilience in an entrepreneur is by fostering problem-solving skills as a source of resilience. Here, the mentors may show the entrepreneur the trick of facing problematic decisions while at the same time providing alternative solutions in times of drought. This guidance enables entrepreneurs to think sharply, keep cool, and view multiple approaches before acting when crises arise. Over time, once these skills of stress management and effective problem-solving become habitual, then entrepreneurs develop a kind of toughness that enables them to bounce back right after even minor failures and continue.

Mentorship has a strong influence on another crucial area: emotional resilience. The psychological stress inherent in starting up, combined with a sense of isolation and insecurity about the capability, can be enough to wear down even the sturdiest of entrepreneurs. A mentor provides the chance for an emotional sounding board for such issues, keeping entrepreneurs from getting overwhelmed by stress, which can lead to burnout. With empathetic listening and constructive feedback, these mentors provide the emotional stability the entrepreneur may need in order to continue once the motivation wanes. This emotional toughness is crucial to ensuring long-term productivity and well-being as it allows the crossing over of emotional hills and valleys without losing proper perspective.

Mentorship also fosters a long-term perspective with pliability, qualities that even entrepreneurs sometimes forget in their haste to provide quick answers. At times they pay more attention to the present problems than to the grander view. Then, with wider experience, they may strategize and plan for the future even when crisis faces them. The other way through which mentoring empowers entrepreneurs is by focusing on flexibility and continuous learning in line with the change, to modify the strategy or pivot when necessary, bringing great strength to resilience in an ever-changing business environment.

In a very simple way, mentorship does not just keep a budding entrepreneur alive during trying times but equips the entrepreneur with the mental, emotional, and strategic tools needed to thrive. The incessant guidance, practical advice, and emotional support received from a mentor play an indispensable role in building the resilience needed to succeed at entrepreneurship. Entrepreneurs who recover quickly from setbacks and remain optimistic, confident, and tenacious approach their ventures better because of mentorship.

CREATING AN EFFECTIVE MENTORSHIP PROGRAM FOR ENTREPRENEURS

A very creative design of the mentoring program to cater to the needs of entrepreneurial ventures is very important. Purposeful interaction of mentors with mentees ought to be made more prominent in order for them to enjoy the benefit of the mentorship program. An effective mentorship program can support entrepreneurs through their most challenging times at work and prepare them with appropriate tools, knowledge, and support to help them cope with their isolation while promoting entrepreneurship. Here are some of the most important things to consider when creating an effective mentorship program for entrepreneurs.

Clear Objectives and Structure

The success of any program of mentorship depends on the definition of goals and the structure it possesses. It is important to clearly define the purpose of the program - with which of the indicators - emotional support, professional guidance, and/or skill development. A well-defined structure that will outline what to expect for mentors and mentees alike can help get both committed to the process with a clear understanding of what to expect when the program has been completed. Defining the length of time the relationship is going to last, the frequency of meetings, and the specific focus areas, such as strategy planning or leadership development, may help in structuring a productive and goal-oriented mentorship experience (Beltman & Schaeben, 2012; Yarbrough & Phillips, 2022).

Matching Mentors with Mentees

The ability of mentor-mentee pairing is quite important for the effectiveness of the program. The basis for matching need not be strictly professional; compatibility, style of communication, and shared goals can also be grounds for matching. Entrepreneurs are likely to fare better with mentors when they have an industry and business understanding, along with an interpersonal fit. Working on careful selection and matching processes, possibly through interviews or assessments, ensures that mentees can utilize the expertise of the mentor in a relationship that is founded on trust and mutual respect.

Mentor Training and Support

Experience can also guarantee that mentors have the years of experience, but not everyone is simply born to mentor. Training and resource provision for mentors can help them understand their roles better and provide effective guidance for their mentees. Such training can include strategies on communication, techniques on goal setting, and procedures for the giving of constructive feedback. Moreover, developing support systems for the mentors, such as peer networking or further professional development, will make sure that the mentors stay in the program long enough and get encouraged to complete. Support for them will allow them to have more impact while guiding and to keep on developing professionally while doing so (Baroudi & David, 2020; Bryant et al., 2015).

Setting Measurable Goals and Outcomes

Mentors and their mentees require measurable goals to judge if the mentorship program is effective or otherwise. That includes specific business milestones like revenue growth and product development or expansion in the market, and areas of personal growth like work-life balance, among others. Gains can be evaluated based on the growth towards the achievement of such goals and changes or lack thereof in the mentorship relationship. A checklist of that progress will enable the mentor and mentee to fine-tune the focus of the initiative to continue being meaningful for the entrepreneur and contribute toward his or her overall success.

Open Communication and Feedback

Open, honest communication between the mentor and mentee is the foundation of any successful mentorship program. Regular communication with both the mentor and the mentee should be done with regards to the relationship as well as progress toward goals. Periodic check-in surveys or evaluation provide regular, structured opportunities to check in for alignment and ensure that the mentee's needs are being met. Open communication creates room for flexibility that encourages flexibility in the mentorship since this allows both the mentor and the mentee to keep changing as problems become knottier and new goals arise (Stinson et al., 2016; Cree-Green et al., 2020).

Community Building

In fact, a very highly effective mentoring program goes beyond one-on-one by offering the community to entrepreneurs for support. This, of course, involves holding the right events, workshops, or networking opportunities so that relationships between the mentee and the mentor are cultivated both across industries and backgrounds. Thus, peer learning and collaboration come forth through many brainstorming sessions and shared learning experiences within this community environment. It also works well to handle isolation by providing a sense of belonging and purpose to the entrepreneurial ecosystem.

Long-Term Support and Continuity

A good mentorship program doesn't end on the attainment of an initial objective or at the end of a specified time. Long-term support and continuity are often required for entrepreneurial development, as most challenges are time-bound. The program should therefore foster the potential for continued relationships long after the formal mentorship stage and facilitate the opportunity for mentors to become mentees themselves. This development process creates a cycle of support, and through it, senior entrepreneurs are able to give back to the next generation, building resilience and collaboration within the entrepreneurial community (Goodrich, 2007;, Cheah et al., 2015).

such factors of structure clearly, following rules of matching stringently, all kinds of support provided to the entrepreneur continuously, measurable goal, open communication, building community, long time continuation, etc. can bring optimum productivity in entrepreneurial field. Additionally, it also protects entrepreneurs from suffering under the feeling of isolation and provides them with adequate business suggestions while allowing the chances of long-term success (Nate et al., 2022).

CHALLENGES AND LIMITATION OF MENTORSHIP

Although mentorship brings about many rewards for the entrepreneur, it comes with its own challenges and limitations. Therefore, both mentors and mentees have to be aware of these potential challenges to fully optimize the effectiveness of the mentorship relationship. Below are a few common challenges encountered in entrepreneurial mentoring and how they may limit the overall impact.

Mismatches of Expectations

A very common challenge in such relationships regarding mentorship is mismatches of expectations. One may expect a mentor to solve all his business problems, whereas the other is just expecting an advisory role and not all that engaged. This can lead to frustration on both sides for an ineffective mentoring experience. Mentorship and mentees have to be open with each other in terms of their expectations regarding participation, the level of involvement, the form of guidance, and outcomes (Ngalesoni, 2024).

Time Constraints and Schedules

Time is a natural constraint when it comes to mentorship as most entrepreneurs are busy, like mentors. The two parties are less likely to commit to scheduling a regular meeting or providing enough time to cultivate a meaningful relationship. This lack of consistency can bring a check to the mentee's progress and reduce the impactful potentiality of mentoring. It is suggested that mentorship programs clearly ascertain such commitments at the outset, and mentors as well as mentees have to schedule their meetings in order to ensure the long term continuance of the relationship (Shenkoya, 2023).

Lack of Industry-Specific Knowledge

It is helpful to have general business acumen, but a mentor with a lack of industry-specific knowledge may not be able to serve the targeted advice an entrepreneur needs. Sometimes, the depth of experience a mentor has will not overlap with the exact focused challenges that concern the entrepreneur's industry or business model. This could limit the specific available insights or guidance related to particular decisions. Entrepreneurs should identify mentors who have complementary industry experience or supplement the mentoring process by finding additional advisors who can fill knowledge gaps.

Over-Reliance on the Mentor

The third challenge confronting entrepreneurs is one of over-reliance on the mentor. The entrepreneur becomes completely dependent on the mentor for each and every decision or validation. While the mentor is there to provide support and guide, the final responsibility of making decisions rests with the entrepreneur. Overdependence might prevent the entrepreneur from building critical thinking and problem-solving abilities. They are likely to be highly susceptible to pressures to handle some problems without the ability to work them out on their own. To prevent this, mentors should encourage independence through training mentees how to find solutions rather than solving their problems (Osabohien, 2024).

Probability of Clash or Miscommunication

Each social contact sometimes leads to a clash or miscommunication. Misalignments in opinions, communication style, or approach towards resolution of a task also cause friction between mentors and mentees. If not addressed, disengagement ensues, culminating in the complete breakdown of a relationship in extreme cases. The lines of communication should always be open, respectful, and ready for any conflicts that might arise and might need to come up. Check-ins, especially honest ones, over time foster a productive and aligned relationship (Ejike, 2024).

Locking into Habits as Short-Term Engagement

Such mentorship relationships are often of short-term or typically defined duration. They may be either within formal program structures or by the lifecycle of the relationship itself. Short-term mentorship, although useful for insight, may not be sufficient in supporting the entrepreneur at various stages of business growth. At the end of the formal mentorship period, the entrepreneur might remain without further support or guidance. In response to the above limitations, mentoring programs should be designed to foster opportunities for long-term involvement or also to be supplemented by sufficient resources meant to facilitate transition to new mentoring relationships as the specific needs of entrepreneur's change (Thomas et al., 2005; Colvin & Ashman, 2010).

Mentor Biases and Loss of Objectivity

Through the experience that mentors have, their knowledge, and even stereotypes, they end up limiting objectivity in the recommendations they provide. Even though their insights are invaluable, the unconscious transposition of either their own preferences, risk tolerances, or experiences onto the mentee sometimes proves very limiting. This might lead to the protégé getting advice that might not apply totally in the distinctive situation or even their business environment. The entrepreneur must always be kept aware of this and must have the guidance passed through their own context and goals then seek further perspectives whenever needed (Thomas et al., 2005; DuBois et al., 2002).

Inability to Measure Success

It is impossible to measure the success or impact of mentorship. Unlike formal business strategies, value from mentorship often is of qualitative and intangible nature that includes things like emotional support, confidence building, and building resistance. While measures of revenue growth or business expansion can be directly related to mentorship, most of the benefits fall rather in the long-term or implicit context, making the program difficult to evaluate in the short run. This can lead to the undervaluation of the role that a mentor might play or failure in justifying the investment time for entrepreneurs operating with short-term results-oriented mindsets (Inzer & Crawford, 2005; Raabe & Beehr, 2003).

Finding the Right Mentor

Finding an appropriate mentor is the biggest challenge in the route-to-market for many entrepreneurs. No entrepreneur has access to networks that contain experienced mentors, and even within those networks, it is likely that someone has experience like what the entrepreneur needs. Entrepreneurs in niche industries, underrepresented groups, or emerging markets may face particular difficulty finding suitable mentors. Mentorship programs and entrepreneurial networks ought to make available diverse mentors and other relationships that might not be developed if the traditional networking mechanism were used in isolation.

Even though mentorship can indeed be an effective tool in entrepreneurship, these points underscore the importance of careful planning, effectiveness in communication, and realistic expectations to be crafted with both the mentors and the mentees in the best interest of the parties involved. Once these limitations are addressed, mentorship programs become a great structure in which to use delivering more meaningful and long-lasting support for the entrepreneur (Mouammer & Bazan, 2021; Wasim, 2023; Tshehla & Costa, 2021).

FUTURE OF MENTORSHIP IN DIGITAL AGE

The digital age is transforming how mentorship is delivered and experienced, bringing new opportunities and challenges to entrepreneurs. With the emerging technological advancements and virtual platforms, it ends the traditional face-to-face interaction of mentorship. It is more accessible, scalable, and flexible in delivery. In the next decade, digital mentorship will play a highly pivotal role in supporting entrepreneurship globally.

Virtual Mentorship Platforms

One of the more significant changes in mentoring is virtual mentoring programs, accessible online in different locations geographically, thus bringing mentors and mentees together with entrepreneurs all over the world in terms of access to expertise. This democratization will remove many of the classic barriers to accessing mentors and makes someone like a small business owner from an emerging market, or, more dire, someone from an underrepresented group, accessible to a pool of mentors which previously would not have been accessible. Virtual platforms also provide for more flexibility as there are frequent and convenient interactions possible through scheduling meetings, thus avoiding an actual need to meet in one place. It offers entrepreneurs real-time advice from mentors responding to challenges and that the possibility of receiving such feedback sooner than later.

Artificial Intelligence and Data Driven Mentorship

The future of mentorship in the digital world would take shape as AI and data analytics are integrated into the programs of mentorship. The obvious benefit of developing AI-driven platforms is the analysis of large data pools to more effectively match a mentor and mentee based on their needs, goals, and compatibility. Algorithms that are utilized to assess personality traits, professional backgrounds, and communication styles can be used in the process of creating more successful mentorship pairings while enhancing the quality of the relationship. Data-informed insights may track the development of mentoring relationships, giving individualized suggestions for areas to comment on for mentorship participants on how to improve the relationship interaction. Such data-informed methods make mentoring both focused and goal-driven and have better prospects for success.

International Networks of Mentorship

Since connecting individuals across geography becomes easy with online tools, mentorship will be more internationalized. Entrepreneurs will have access to a much wider reserve of mentors with diverse experience from various markets, cultures, and industries. International flavor will add more depth in terms of exposure to new concepts, strategies, or opportunities that may not exist locally. As global mentoring networks expand, access to knowledge will move to a whole new base as more entrepreneurs tap into international expertise to scale their businesses and enter new markets. Crossborder mentorship provides more idea exchange, culminating in global innovation and potential collaboration.

Hybrid Models of Mentorship

The potential of digital mentorship benefits but must not undermine the value of face-to-face interactions. It is expected that, in the future of mentoring, hybrid models of virtual and face-to-face meetings will occur. Online orientation may lead to meeting mentors at highly significant events, conferences, or workshops. This hybrid model combines comfort, flexibility, and accessibility of digital platforms with a closer connection that face-to-face interaction fosters. With the advancement of digital tools, virtual interactions will become more real as they use VR to build experiences like what would be in the physical world.

Peer-to-peer and group mentorship

The digital revolution also creates new peer-to-peer and group models of mentoring. These online communities or circles where entrepreneurs sit together and receive mentoring from several mentors or peers who have had similar experiences. With groups, entrepreneurs can learn as a collective unit of wisdom. Peer mentoring is indeed highly relevant in fast-paced sectors where learning from a host of people, moving through similar issues helps entrepreneurs adapt and thrive. Group mentorship, enabled through digital tools, gives entrepreneurs that network support system that dissolves isolation and creates a shared sense of community even in virtual environments (Stinson et al., 2016;, Elst et al., 2021).

On-Demand Mentorship and Micro-Mentoring

The digital economy has today significantly increased the business speed, leading to more flexible and accessible solutions in areas such as mentorship. On-demand mentorship is therefore their demand on this aspect as entrepreneurs are entitled to these short series of sessions of targeted mentorship when needed. Problems get solved or quick advice on specific problems in micro-mentoring.

END. Indeed, similar short, focused interactions may be accomplished by means of messaging applications and video calling or even voice notes-that grant real-time access to expert advice. It fits best in modern entrepreneurship faced with very time-sensitive challenges that would welcome immediate guidance.

CHALLENGES AND OPPORTUNITIES OF THE DIGITAL MENTORSHIP ERA

The virtual age certainly does hold exciting possibilities in regard to the future of mentorship, but it also offers some big challenges: it's hard to develop a strong personal relationship in a virtual setting where non-verbal cues are much reduced, and informal interactions take time to grow. The relationship may be harder to maintain once they get engaged in a relationship involving the two parties to establish mutual trust and rapport. Technology, with stable connection to the internet, is another barrier set by it for certain entrepreneurs in their own poor-resource environment.

However, opportunities are far greater than the obstacles. Digital mentoring will offer far more variability in relation to the access that entrepreneurs have in engaging with mentors under different conditions-those tailored to their individual needs and preferences. More inclusive and diverse mentorship opportunities will be fostered through digital tools so that entrepreneurs of any background can find a match for the kind of guidance they need to get ahead.

Conclusion This is even in a digital world where technology enhances the ways of mentorship delivery and experience. Digital platforms, AI-driven insights, and global networks position the entrepreneur as better placed to overcome some challenges while scaling their business to better achieve success in an increasingly connected world. Digitization is not replacing traditional mentorship, but it will expand its radius and impact in ways that will create accessibility, personalization, and effectiveness in support for the next generation of entrepreneurs.

CONCLUSION

Mentorship counters entrepreneurial loneliness by offering business guidance as well as emotional support through one's journey in building and scaling a business. As discussed in this chapter, it's that meaningfulness and value the mentorship relationship allows for addressing these typical entrepreneur challenges-high stress levels, decision fatigue, and social isolation. Whether practical advice, an ear to share new ideas, or simply reassurance when things get tough, mentoring helps entrepreneurs develop strengths in resiliency, providing a sense of connection with others in the business world.

The developing age of dignification further resounds the importance and breaks out the barriers from traditional systems to enable access to a much wider range of mentors and expertise across the globe. Such digital platforms, AI-driven mentoring to match, and peer-to-peer and group mentoring models are providing entrepreneurs with forms of support that are flexible, tailored, and diverse. Following these advantages, mentorship has now become more accessible and scalable- hence its potential availability to entrepreneurs at every stage of entrepreneurial progression.

But on the other hand, such a solution also has its downsides and constraints. There is potential conflict in expectation, time constraints, and over-reliance, which are all barriers that have to be fought for and through. Time has to be put into creating trust between entrepreneurs and mentors, and then forging forward toward expectation alignment so that business relationships can be productive and not counterproductive. Despite these headaches and pitfalls, the limitations usually succumb to the benefits as mentorship is known to nurture growth among entrepreneurs, offer emotional well-being, and ensure sustainable growth in business.

In the future, the significance of mentorship will be deeply rooted and definitely critical for entrepreneurs as the business landscape continues to grow complex and interdependent. Through both conventional and digital models of mentorship, entrepreneurs can nurture resilience, knowledge, and networks all critical to success in today's dynamic entrepreneurial environment. In that regard, mentorship will keep that essential spark going on innovation, cooperation, and personal development to succeed in today's global economy.

REFERENCES:

Baroudi, S., & David, S. (2020). Nurturing female leadership skills through peer mentoring role: A study among undergraduate students in the united arab emirates. *Higher Education Quarterly*, 74(4), 458–474. DOI: 10.1111/hequ.12249

Beltman, S., & Schaeben, M. (2012). Institution-wide peer mentoring: Benefits for mentors. *The International Journal of the First Year in Higher Education*, 3(2). Advance online publication. DOI: 10.5204/intjfyhe.v3i2.124

Bryant, A., Brody, A., Pérez, A., Shillam, C., Edelman, L., Bond, S., & Siegel, E. (2015). Development and implementation of a peer mentoring program for early career gerontological faculty. *Journal of Nursing Scholarship*, 47(3), 258–266. DOI: 10.1111/jnu.12135 PMID: 25808927

Cheah, W., Hazmi, H., Hoo, C., Chew, J., Nadira, M., & Nurva'ain, M. (2015). Peer mentoring among undergraduate medical students: Experience from universiti malaysia sarawak. *Education in Medicine Journal*, 7(1). Advance online publication. DOI: 10.5959/eimj.v7i1.331

Colvin, J., & Ashman, M. (2010). Roles, risks, and benefits of peer mentoring relationships in higher education. *Mentoring & Tutoring*, 18(2), 121–134. DOI: 10.1080/13611261003678879

Cree-Green, M., Carreau, A., Davis, S., Frohnert, B., Kaar, J., Nina, S., & Nadeau, K. (2020). Peer mentoring for professional and personal growth in academic medicine. *Journal of Investigative Medicine*, 68(6), 1128–1134. DOI: 10.1136/jim-2020-001391 PMID: 32641352

DuBois, D., Holloway, B., Valentine, J., & Cooper, H. (2002). Effectiveness of mentoring programs for youth: A meta-analytic review. *American Journal of Community Psychology*, 30(2), 157–197. DOI: 10.1023/A:1014628810714 PMID: 12002242

Ejike, O. (2024). Sustainability and project management: a dual approach for women entrepreneurs in event management. International Journal of Scholarly Research in Multidisciplinary Studies, 5(1), 024-031. DOI: 10.56781/ijsrms.2024.5.1.0036

Elst, K., Cock, D., Bangels, L., Peerlings, L., Doumen, M., Bertrand, D., & Verschueren, P. (2021). 'more than just chitchat': A qualitative study concerning the need and potential format of a peer mentor programme for patients with early rheumatoid arthritis. *RMD Open*, 7(3), e001795. DOI: 10.1136/rmdopen-2021-001795 PMID: 34611049

Goodrich, A. (2007). Peer mentoring in a high school jazz ensemble. *Journal of Research in Music Education*, 55(2), 94–114. DOI: 10.1177/002242940705500202

Inzer, L., & Crawford, C. (2005). A review of formal and informal mentoring: Processes, problems, and design. *Journal of Leadership Education*, 4(1), 31–50. DOI: 10.12806/V4/I1/TF2

Mouammer, L., & Bazan, C. (2021). Effect of mentorship on the early entrepreneurial journey of university students. *Proceedings of the Canadian Engineering Education Association (Ceea)*. DOI: 10.24908/pceea.vi0.14969

Nate, S., Grecu, V., Stavytskyy, A., & Kharlamova, G. (2022). Fostering entrepreneurial ecosystems through the stimulation and mentorship of new entrepreneurs. *Sustainability (Basel)*, 14(13), 7985. DOI: 10.3390/su14137985

Ngalesoni, O., Mwakifwamba, G., & Pandisha, H. (2024). The effectiveness of mentoring programs on empowering women entrepreneurs in tanzania: A case of babati district council. *International Journal of Entrepreneurship and Project Management*, 9(2), 1–16. DOI: 10.47604/ijepm.2366

Osabohien, R., Worgwu, H., & Al-Faryan, M. A. S. (2024). Mentorship and innovation as drivers of entrepreneurship performance in africa's largest economy. *Social Enterprise Journal*, 20(1), 76–90. DOI: 10.1108/SEJ-02-2023-0019

Raabe, B., & Beehr, T. (2003). Formal mentoring versus supervisor and coworker relationships: Differences in perceptions and impact. *Journal of Organizational Behavior*, 24(3), 271–293. DOI: 10.1002/job.193

Shenkoya, T., Hwang, K. Y., & Sung, E. H. (2023). Student startup: Understanding the role of the university in making startups profitable through university—industry collaboration. *SAGE Open*, 13(3), 21582440231198601. Advance online publication. DOI: 10.1177/21582440231198601

Stinson, J., Kohut, S., Forgeron, P., Amaria, K., Bell, M., Kaufman, M., & Spiegel, L. (2016). The ipeer2peer program: A pilot randomized controlled trial in adolescents with juvenile idiopathic arthritis. *Pediatric Rheumatology Online Journal*, 14(1), 48. Advance online publication. DOI: 10.1186/s12969-016-0108-2 PMID: 27590668

Thomas, K., Hu, C., Gewin, A., Bingham, K., & Yanchus, N. (2005). The roles of protégé race, gender, and proactive socialization attempts on peer mentoring. Advances in Developing Human Resources, Tshehla, B. and Costa, K. (2021). Exploring the relationship between mentorship and successful youth entrepreneurship at telkom, south africa. https://doi.org/DOI: 10.31730/osf.io/c5r4e

Wasim, J., Youssef, M. H., Christodoulou, I., & Reinhardt, R. (2023). The path to entrepreneurship: The role of social networks in driving entrepreneurial learning and education. *Journal of Management Education*, 48(3), 459–493. DOI: 10.1177/10525629231219235

Chapter 23
The Role of Technology in Facilitating Entrepreneurial Mental Health Support

Mohit Yadav
 https://orcid.org/0000-0002-9341-2527
O.P. Jindal Global University, India

Preet Kanwal
 https://orcid.org/0009-0006-5114-8381
Lovely Professional University, India

Rohit
 https://orcid.org/0009-0004-1796-5252
Gulf Medical University, Ajman, UAE

ABSTRACT

This chapter explores the critical role of technology in facilitating mental health support for entrepreneurs, a demographic facing unique stressors such as financial pressures and long working hours. It examines current technological solutions, including mobile applications, teletherapy platforms, and community engagement tools, that provide accessible and tailored support for mental well-being. The discussion highlights the challenges of integrating technology, such as issues of accessibility, ethical concerns, and the quality of resources, while offering best practices for effective implementation. Looking to the future, the chapter identifies potential innovations, including AI-driven personalization, virtual reality experiences, and data-driven insights, that can enhance mental health support systems. Ultimately, the chapter emphasizes the importance of fostering a resilient entrepreneurial community through thoughtful and responsible technological integration.

DOI: 10.4018/979-8-3693-3673-1.ch023

INTRODUCTION

The business scenario today is extremely fast-paced and dynamic, and any entrepreneur may face hundreds of challenges that may miserably influence his mental health. The entrepreneurial journey is fraught with uncertainty, financial pressure, and great responsibility. These stressors may manifest through mental conditions, like anxiety and depression, and burnout. Burnout and these mental conditions may have the adverse impact not just on the wellbeing of the entrepreneur but also on the success of the venture itself. The role of the mental health of the entrepreneur needs to be understood, thus holding the key to promoting resilience and sustaining business practices.

The integration of technology in the system that supports mental health has emerged as one of the key solutions as society realizes the extent of the mental health crisis, especially among high-stakes professionals such as entrepreneurs. Technology can dramatically change how entrepreneurs seek stress management tools and platforms that provide them with access to help and build supportive communities. Democratization came through the invention of mobile applications, teletherapy, wearable devices, and online support networks that de-stigmatized and made mental health care convenient for entrepreneurs to seek help.

Mobile applications have become popular because they furnish instant access to resources and support at an individual's fingertips. With mindfulness, meditation, and cognitive behavioral therapy apps, an entrepreneur can commit to self-practice aligned with one's schedule. These tools will allow entrepreneurs to strategize and develop strategies for coping with day-to-day business operations. Another critical feature is that apps offer anonymity, which can help eliminate the stigma that prevents entrepreneurs from seeking psychological support, so they are bound to be more proactive about seeking remedies to enhance their mental well-being.

Apart from mobile applications, teletherapy and online counseling have also been quite helpful in changing the landscape of psychological care. The entrepreneur is often burdened with high schedules and geographical constraints, but one can now enjoy the privilege of reaching licensed mental health professionals from their living or work venues. This will ensure that help reaches them in time without bothering associated with traveling or waiting periods, making mental health care reach them more than ever before. Virtual therapy enables entrepreneurs to have the same flexibility and choice, where entrepreneurs can afford to focus on their mental well-being alongside the complexities of a business venture.

Another potent tool monitoring your mental health comprises wearables technology. It is in this regard that many tracking devices report on physiological indicators, such as heart rate, sleep patterns, and activity levels, thereby helping entrepreneurs understand their state of mind and emotions. In the context of mental health applications, this information can aid users in knowing how their physical well-being influences their mental health and accordingly make some adjustments based on informed judgments of lifestyle and work habits. Thus, integrative approaches to mental health care stress mind-body integrity and propose a more wholesome understanding of well-being.

On the other hand, despite the optimistic views above, technology use in mental health care is accompanied by many practical problems and limitations. Issues related to data privacy, overdependence on digital tools, and a desire for human connection have to be addressed to ensure that technology is used to enhance, rather than detract from, effective mental health care. Thus, exploring the potential for technology in facilitating support for entrepreneurial mental health requires attention to the pros and cons of technology use with the end goal being a balanced approach that prioritizes well-being yet harnesses the potential of innovation.

This chapter builds on the discussion above, explores various technological solutions, focuses the light on the urgency of community support, analyzes the role of artificial intelligence and data analytics, and describes best practices for integrating technology into general mental health support for entrepreneurs. We explore how technology can be a good ally in moving the entrepreneurial community toward better mental health and well-being.

UNDERSTANDING ENTREPRENEURIAL MENTAL HEALTH

Entrepreneurial mental health addresses the psychological fitness of individuals who are undertaking the extremely challenging task of setting up and managing their own businesses. As opposed to a salaried job in which the responsibilities and expectations are primarily well defined, entrepreneurship is still a highly undefined or uncertain risk. There are several pressures that entrepreneurs experience. In terms of financial instability, having long working hours, and bearing the burden of making decisions. These factors create an environment that fosters mental health disorders, and it is therefore important to understand the challenges, more so those faced by entrepreneurs, and their implications on their well-being.

The most prevalent challenge regarding mental health that an entrepreneur faces is stress. Deadlines being over their heads, their struggle in terms of finding funds, and how growth is targeted put chronic stress under which entrepreneurs have to suffer-a contradiction for both mental and physical health. Researchers indicate that entrepreneurs experience more stress than the average person, and chronic stress can be defined through various mediums of anxiety, irritability, and short concentration span that may ultimately deteriorate one's ability to lead and innovate as an entrepreneur. Knowing the causes and consequences of stress helps implement appropriate support strategies for the entrepreneurs.

Another common mental condition of the entrepreneur is anxiety. The pressure to succeed and the fear of failure instill unease in general. An entrepreneur fears making the wrong decision and is paralyzed in his ability to take necessary risks. As entrepreneurship naturally is competitive, that anxiety is worsened as one has to constantly monitor their progress relative to others. An absence of control can lead to anxiousness, resulting in burnout, which is a state of emotional, physical, and mental exhaustion with pronounced reductions in personal well-being and business performance.

Many small business owners are lonely entrepreneurs who face almost all the challenges facing them behind closed doors, unseen by anyone.

Difficulties in mental health are usually a result of the isolation that comes with entrepreneurship. Entrepreneurs more than employees of established organizations are often without support networks and resources. A lack of close social ties can worsen feelings of stress and anxiety and thus make connections and engagement with a community of utmost importance for the entrepreneur. The burdens of loneliness can be eased through connection to a network of other entrepreneurs or from participation in peer support, which can create a sense of fellow-feeling and mutual understanding.

Another important point is the impact of work-life balance on entrepreneurship mental health. Many entrepreneurs tend to lose their personal-life segmentation, and boundaries become blurred. In pursuing business objectives, people tend to neglect their own life, themselves, and recreational activities. It can be one of the reasons that intensifies feelings of guilt and inadequacy about mental health. The first priority is work-life balance- balancing material and psychological well-being-to maintain good mental health and achieve sustainable entrepreneurship success.

Stigma also exists in the entrepreneurial community, where most entrepreneurs are afraid to report any kind of mental health-related issues or problems. Mental health issues should not be stigmatized, especially in terms of impact on entrepreneurial activities. Many entrepreneurs are often in demand to show strength and resilience in public. Cases of admitting to mental health problems may increase distrust of them or even doubts regarding their leadership. The stigma surrounding this issue can be so paralyzing that a lot of people may not open up about their mental well-being or seek help, thus entering a vicious cycle of isolation and distress. Break the negative stigma and it creates a culture of prioritizing and supporting mental health.

In essence, understanding the entrepreneurial mind requires the recognition of specific challenges and stressors that entrepreneurs face in their business activities. To this end, stress, anxiety, isolation, work-life imbalance, and stigmatization all significantly determine a person's mental wellbeing in this context. Being aware of such particular factors will, therefore, empower entrepreneurs appropriately with the right available resources and tools that would assist them in more effectively handling their mental health concerns in fostering a more supportive and resilient entrepreneurial ecosystem.

TECHNICAL METHODS OF MENTAL HEALTH SUPPORT

However, with the rapid development of technology, various new approaches in addressing mental health have been invented. Many entrepreneurs end up operating their businesses in nerve-wracking environments. New inventions have included mobile apps to teletherapy services that guide individuals on self-care and stress management or avenues for seeking professional help. Such technological solutions enable self-care and stress management and allow easy access to professional help, thus advocating for an all-rounded approach to mental health (Du, 2024; Drissi et al., 2020).

Mobile Applications

Mobile applications have dramatically transformed how one stays connected to their own mental wellbeing. Thousands of apps exist that help an individual monitor the progress of their mood, become conscious, and discover ways to overcome stressors. Apps have given entrepreneurs an immediate tool in self-care management to support themselves.

Guided meditations, stress-reduction exercises, and even mood journals give users real-time control of how one's mental health is performing. Applications such as Headspace and Calm that are genuinely quite brilliant, now offer resources that can help entrepreneurs fit mindfulness practice in between all of their busyness, build emotional resilience, and reduce anxiety.

These mood-tracking apps, including Daylio or Moodfit, will also indicate which emotions or periods appear repeatedly and thus become routine. Such apps will enable entrepreneurs to identify triggers linked to stress or anxiety and help them devise proactive measures toward managing their mental health effectively. Given that they are mobile, these applications are valuable tools for entrepreneurs who need to focus on well-being despite their stressful lifestyles.

Teletherapy and Online Counseling

There has been an amazing growth in teletherapy and online counseling services especially after the COVID-19 pandemic came. Entrepreneurially, this kind of service offers access by licensed practitioners for psychological support without necessarily undergoing the constraints of traditional in-person appointments. It also provides users with an alternative mode of making contact with their chosen therapists through video, chats, or messaging through avenues such as BetterHelp and Talkspace (Alneyadi et al., 2021).

Teletherapy will be very effective for entrepreneurs who have unpredictable schedules or lack time to care for themselves. Teletherapy will eliminate the geographical constraints and grant entrepreneurs' access to mental health specialists 24/7. Teletherapy will give entrepreneurs the power to put their mental health first, without the constraints of transportation worries and strict appointment times. This access will, therefore, not only encourage entrepreneurs to seek help but also decline the stigma attached to mental health access because it can be accessed discreetly from the comfort of one's own space.

Wearable Technology

Another exciting solution for monitoring and supporting mental health through wearable technology is the smartwatch or fitness trackers. They can provide real-time data regarding many physiological indicators: heartbeat, sleep patterns, or physical activity level. This information may be absolutely gold to entrepreneurs in terms of knowing how their physical health overlaps with their mental well-being costs (Gbollie, 2023; Musiat et al., 2014).

For instance, it was scientifically proven that poor quality sleep is related to increased feelings of anxiety and stress. Wearable sleep tracking devices can help an entrepreneur identify a pattern as possibly affecting his or her mental health, and hence promote healthier habits. Combined with a number of mental health applications, this data will provide users with the opportunity to create their own approaches to handling stress and emotional balance for better productivity and well-being.

Online Support Networks

In addition to personal uses and products, the contemporary technology has also helped in finding the online support groups that link entrepreneurs with other people facing similar challenges. Through social media, like online groups, one can get some support and share experiences, or even have companionship. Consequently, through websites like Meetup or Facebook groups devoted to the mental health of entrepreneurs, specific connections and some sense of belonging might be established among members.

Such online forums are extremely influential in reassuring and making entrepreneurs believe when in need. Interactions with peers facing similar problems help reduce the feeling of loneliness and provide motivation during difficult times. This connection can be highly instrumental to build a network of support where the pressures are relieved and alleviated to share experiences and seek relief (Su et al., 2022).

Technological innovations in mental health support provide entrepreneurs with a wide range of tools to improve themselves. From mobile applications to teletherapy, wearable technology, and even online networks of support, the technological innovation caters to the very demands that an entrepreneurial lifestyle would provide. These solutions will enable entrepreneurs to proactively take care of their mental well-being, making it easier for them to strive for resilience and lead them to successful endeavors.

COMMUNITY AND SUPPORT NETWORKS

The support network for entrepreneurs must be strong since sometimes running a business is quite lonely. Community and support networks significantly decrease the mental health problems likely to be experienced by entrepreneurs. It provides one with a sense of belonging as well as being validated; this is significant in maintaining good mental health. Many of these networks can easily be created and accessed with the use of technology. It is through them that entrepreneurs may converse with peers, mentors, and professionals who may provide them with encouragement, guidance, and support (Fernández-Bedoya, 2023; Tisu, 2023).

Online Support Groups

There are also online support groups that are one of the latest platforms through which entrepreneurs can link up with each other, thus establishing understanding. Social media forums and dedicated websites provide the entrepreneur communities that are very important either within or concerning specific industries or instances of mental health challenges. The online groups create a safe haven for people to share their experiences, seek advice, and get emotional support from like-minded individuals who understand the unique pressures of entrepreneurs.

For example, there are subreddits on Reddit, Facebook groups, and niche forums dedicated to mental health and entrepreneurship. The forums allow users to relate with one another through sharing experiences, coping mechanisms, and celebrating experiences of victory. Science has ensured how peer support reduces much distress associated with isolation and fear. Thus, entrepreneurs will have an armory of support from others who can give them constructive validation about their experiences and encourage them when help is needed.

Peer Mentoring

Peer mentoring is another form of support that an entrepreneur can receive through community support. Interaction with fellow entrepreneurs who share such similar experiences can go a long way in terms of gaining insights and encouragement. Mentor relationships can take many different forms from the formalized programs designed by business incubators to informal contacts established through networking events and online platforms.

With guidance from peer mentoring, experiences of entrepreneurship's highs and lows can be managed, their own experiences can inform discussion, and accountability can be offered. Such assistance does not only facilitate personal development but also fosters resilience over hardships. Having a mentor who understands the adventure of being an entrepreneur decreases loneliness and anxiety all over again, and seeking to have them there also reminds everyone that they should be sought at such times.

Networking Events and Workshops

I am not sure how many entrepreneurs attend networking events and workshops to network with like-minded people while gaining experience in different skills and knowledge. Some organizations organize events with a focus on mental health while entrepreneurship, sharing experience and knowledge on the subject of well-being, stress management, and work-life balance. Therefore, such gatherings allow entrepreneurs to share their stories, learn from one another, and build relationships that transcend the event.

Workshops on mental health and personal development can further be very apt at offering real tools and techniques for entrepreneurs in controlling stress and anxiety. Such events offer the exposure of expert speakers, panel discussions, and interactive sessions to equip one with strategies toward prioritizing their mental well-being in the entrepreneurial journey (Ferrazzi & Krupa, 2018).

Online Resources and Information

Apart from interpersonal support, technology has also assisted entrepreneurs in gaining access to an abundance of information and resources on mental health improvement. Entrepreneurs interested in mental health can rely on websites, podcasts, and online courses available on topics such as coping strategies, self-care practices, and managing stress.

Community resources can hence turn out as great additions to community support in order to help the entrepreneurs find out their mental illness issues and best practices to keep up good mental health. Through connecting with both community and informational resources, entrepreneurs can therefore develop a holistic system of support that addresses their mental health requirements.

Community and support systems are fundamental elements that contribute towards healthy mental conditions among entrepreneurs. All that is there for support through online support groups, peer mentorship, networking events, and accessible resources can be found in order to create an apparatus of social support that gives the entrepreneurs a chance to share experiences and to seek help whenever needed. The feelings of isolation, anxiety, and stress are only comprehensively overcome by people who connect with other individuals understanding similar challenges attached to being an entrepreneur, leading to better mental well-being and greater success in business ventures. Engaging this power of community not only strengthens personal resilience but also fortifies a culture that values the mental well-being of entrepreneurs.

AI AND DATA ANALYTICS IN MENTAL HEALTH

The introduction of AI and data analytics to the mental health support landscape may revolutionize the way resources are sought out or managed by entrepreneurs towards their mental well-being. Using vast data and complex algorithms, AI technologies can offer tailored insights, predictive analytics, and innovative tools targeting the problems entrepreneurs face. This section discusses the various applications of AI and data analytics in developing support for mental health through entrepreneurship.

Predictive Analytics

Predictive analytics happens to be one of the most promising applications of AI in mental health, thereby analyzing historical data to build patterns that can predict future outcomes. For an entrepreneur, predictive analytics may alert the early signs of possible struggles with mental health and steps for proactive intervention can be made. AI algorithms may analyze data coming in from a wearable device, self-reported mood tracking apps, or social media activity to flag concerns before they escalate.

For instance, an entrepreneur may apply a mood-tracking app to chronicle over time their mental states data. This data can then be fused with sleep patterns, exercise routines, and work trends to be analyzed by AI and offer insights into when entrepreneurs tend to increase levels of stress or anxiety. Proactive action through such proactive behavior enables entrepreneurs to take measures and seek support beforehand than during a mental health emergency, thus building their resilience and well-being.

Personalized Mental Health Interventions

AI can also facilitate the development of tailored mental health interventions more similar to the specific requirements of the entrepreneur. Considering individual data and preferences, AI-based platforms can provide particular self-practices, therapeutic exercises, or mindfulness techniques that may strike a chord with the user.

For example, through AI-powered chatbots, Woebot provides real-time support and CBT skills. The chatbots involve clients in conversations to offer individual feedback and coping tips relying on their inputs. Such interventions make mental health support more accessible and relevant to entrepreneurs that require flexible and on-demand resources that fit into busy schedules.

Enhancing Teletherapy with AI

Another interesting avenue through which the delivery of teletherapy services to entrepreneurs can be enhanced is through integration with AI. This is because AI can help therapists draw insights more directly from client data into shaping the treatment approaches tailored for a specific need. For instance, speech patterns, the sentiment of a conversation, and emotional cue can be analyzed through the use of AI algorithms in therapy sessions to give therapists a clue about the emotional state of a client.

The use of AI in teletherapy allows for the administration side, thus freeing more time for therapists to be more therapeutic and less on documentation and reporting. Automated scheduling, billing, and client progress can reduce the burden put on both therapists and clients, therefore easing the experience for entrepreneurs in search of mental health support (Achtyes et al., 2023; Gbollie, 2023; Mohr et al., 2017).

Data-Driven Insights for Organizations

For organizations that support the entrepreneur, it is critical to use data analytics so as to establish trends and issues regarding mental health within their regions. An organization can pool and analyze data regarding the mental health experiences of participants and distinguish common stressors and patterns and gaps in services. Insights from data analytics can help guide programs targeted at the mental health and well-being of entrepreneurs.

Incubators and accelerators can utilize data analytics to assess the efficiency of their mental health support delivery and accordingly take decisions using data. Organizations can build interventions specific to specific mental health challenges for their entrepreneurial community by understanding the needs of their audience and create a culture better geared toward the supportive needs of entrepreneurs (Hwang et al., 2021; Bunyi et al., 2021).

Ethical Considerations and Privacy

While the benefits of applying AI and data analytics for helping mental health care are immense, ethical considerations need to be considered and addressed, including privacy. The use of personal data in the generation of insights from AI poses questions of consent, the security of the data, and the possibility of the misuse of such sensitive data. Entrepreneurs need to be assured that their data is respected, transparent, and taken good care of, and therefore, ethical practices need to be underlined in the development and actual usage of AI.

Data integrity and anonymity of users should be protected when creating trust in AI-based mental health applications. This would go without saying that organizations and developers with ethical standards and upheld all the law required when dealing with information related to individuals while deploying the powers of AI to support mental health.

First, AI and data analytics possess transformative capabilities for transforming the nature of support towards mental health for entrepreneurs. From predictive analytics and personalized interventions to enhanced teletherapy experiences and insights driven by data for organizations, the incredible impact that these technologies can have is breathtaking. Nevertheless, responsible use of AI in mental health has to generate answers to ethical considerations and resolve a host of privacy issues. With the right support, such progress fostered by the entrepreneurial ecosystem will create a culture of well-being, resilience, and support that endows people with a desired good (Sorkin et al., 2021; Shen et al., 2022).

CHALLENGES AND LIMITATIONS OF TECHNOLOGY IN MENTAL HEALTH

The following are some of the challenges and limitations attributed to technology in mental health:
While there is much promise in how technology may better mental health support for entrepreneurs, challenges and limitations have to be addressed in this regard. Such challenges can stand as obstacles in effectively deploying and adopting technological solutions in mental health care. Knowing these challenges will ensure that technology is a facilitator and not a barrier.

Accessibility and Digital Divide

One of the major drawbacks in using the technological solution for mental health support is accessibility. Most entrepreneurs are not on par with accessing tremendous technological resources, like smartphones, high-speed internet, or advanced applications. In this manner, the problem of the digital divide excludes some people from the access of these technological solutions, especially those belonging to lower socioeconomic classes or rural areas, where there is a reduced internet connectivity.

Moreover, the effectiveness of technology in combating mental health issues depends on the digital literacy of the users. Technophobic entrepreneurs can only be able to request help from a mental health app or a teletherapy platform to which they cannot easily access because they are not familiar with it. This calls for the importance of making technological solutions user-friendly and accessible to a broad audience to vanquish these obstacles.

Quality and Credibility of Resources

Another large feature is the quality and credibility of mental health resources obtained through technology. Progress in technology in the form of available mental health applications and online platforms has led to an overwhelming number of available mental health options; however, these cannot be said to be evidence-based or developed by professionally qualified people. An entrepreneur in need of support for his or her mental health may find himself or herself with an underregulated or poorly designed application that does not actually provide information or actual strategies on how to steer one's mental health.

Lack of standardization in technology-related issues of mental health leads to confusion and such practices may result in harmful outcomes. Entrepreneurs should determine which resources are scientifically proven and reliable. That commitment will be followed by the quality and transparency shown by developers and organizations designing and marketing mental health technology.

Ethical and Privacy Issues

Use of technology in mental health is quite an important ethical and privacy concern. The gathering and evaluation of personal information may pose risks if proper safeguards are not established. Entrepreneurs may be hesitant to engage with technology if it requires them to share sensitive information about their mental health due to possible breaches of privacy or misuse of their data.

Application of AI in mental health also brings along another ethical matter that is consent, bias, and accountability. Algorithms applied in analyses of data may unconsciously carry on the biases of the data sets to produce skewed or inaccurate insights. Observing ethics while collecting data and developing AI builds trust with users and protects their rights (Alqahtani et al., 2020; Pung et al., 2018).

Potential for Over-reliance on Technology

Technology can be helpful to support the client, but dependence on technology may even undermine traditional approaches at some point. Entrepreneurs might become so reliant on apps or online resources that they forget to seek face-to-face therapy or any kind of help from a mental health practitioner. This can prove counterproductive to the treatment since human attachment and compassion are inevitable aspects of effective mental health care.

Besides, technology can complement complete mental health care rather than subrogate it. Sufficient development of holistic support for entrepreneurs will require advocating for a balanced approach that incorporates both technology-based solutions and more traditional therapeutic methods.

Limited Personalization

Even with the ongoing improvement of AI and data analytics, most technological mental health solutions are not properly personalized. A few may suggest tailored recommendations using individual-specific user data yet leave an open gap concerning how human mental health issues should be approached.

Challenges are associated specifically to entrepreneurs with their respective business ecosystems, and it is through this understanding that mental health solutions should always pay attention to such details.

Most mental health applications are also generic in scope, which makes them not very effective for a specific group of users, like entrepreneurs. Scaled provision of mental health service through tailored technology would demand an appreciation of the intricacies of issues related to this population-which is something off-the-rack technology solutions are unlikely to serve up.

As interesting avenues for enhancement in mental health support among entrepreneurs, technology promises much. However, problems and restrictions of the implementation process must be understood. Accessibility, quality, ethics, overreliance, and personalization need to be addressed for the enactment of technological solutions that meet the needs of entrepreneurs' mental health. If such challenges are considered and, in that regard, there are efforts towards sustainable ethical practice, the entrepreneurial ecosystem can tap full potential of technology towards mental wellbeing as well as resilience.

BEST PRACTICES FOR INTEGRATING TECHNOLOGY IN SUPPORT OF MENTAL HEALTH

Technology integration into the mental health support for entrepreneurs is of paramount importance if considered critically about many aspects to deliver effective and accessible services. Best practices may help organizations, developers, and entrepreneurs provide an effective supporting environment to maximize the effectiveness of technological solutions while mitigating challenges. The subsequent section portrays the key best practices for effective integration of technology into mental health support.

1. Prioritize User-Centric Design

Usability and accessibility form a showstopper for any technology-based solution for mental health. In such a scenario, it is the user-centric design principles with which the developers are supposed to be working. More intuitive and easy-to-navigate interfaces should be the principal objectives in such solutions. Through user research and usability testing, more can be drawn towards the needs and preferences of entrepreneurs, and hence, it is possible for developers to create solutions that resonate better with the target audience (Weisel et al., 2019; Anastasiadou et al., 2019; Sucharitha et al., 2020).

Further, clear instruction and accessible language together with customizing the settings are some of the features that may uplift user experience. Indeed, entrepreneurs engage and use the technology consistently. In fact, it is helpful for developers as far as they consider the feedback from users and iterate their designs to ensure that the solutions provided are effective and relevant.

2. Ensure Evidence-Based Approaches

Evidence-based practices are required to build up credibility and effectiveness of technology-based mental health resources. The developers need to ensure that the content as well as interventions in the development phase inform research and clinical guidelines by ensuring collaboration with mental health professionals. Such collaboration is bound to lead to the development of reliable applications and platforms that can provide effective coping strategies and techniques of psychotherapy (Aziz et al., 2022; Ng et al., 2019).

And thirdly, organizations should open the research process behind developing these technologies, and information issued to the users ought to be transparent about the evidence for the tools that demonstrates their relevance. This openness will create an opportunity to interact with entrepreneurs and encourage them to use the available facilities.

3. Integration with Traditional Care

This allows technology to utilize itself in supporting mental health improvement, rather than to substitute for traditional ways of therapy. With this integration of technology with conventional services, an all-encompassing support structure for entrepreneurs will be continued. For instance, the therapist may prescribe a particular application to help clients monitor their mood or to engage in mindfulness exercises between sessions.

Moreover, therapists can rely on technology to monitor student progress, gather data, and modify treatment plans. This integration will ensure a smooth experience for entrepreneurs since it will give them easy access to individualized, technology-based support while maintaining the essential human interface for efficient therapy (Pung et al., 2018; Sorkin et al., 2021).

4. Community Engagement

To expand the service and impact of mental health technology, there is a need to create a feeling of community for the users. For those entrepreneurs whose platforms include discussion forums or peer support groups, social media features allow users to interact with each other, which reduces the levels of isolation in the journey through their mental health. As these entrepreneurs share experiences, they feel as belonging and that they will open the conversation regarding mental health (Marshall et al., 2019; Roberts et al., 2021).

Organizations should actively promote community participation by conducting virtual events, webinars, and workshops that will lead to the gathering of users. It helps in the reinforcement process of seeking help, experience, and contribution in forming a supportive ecosystem for better mental health.

5. Ethical and Privacy Issues Consider

Much commitment toward ethical practices and data protection is required. The organizations and developers must protect the personal information of their users and ensure the systems fit all the rules and regulations like GDPR and HIPAA.

Data security should be managed robustly through methods such as encryption and inclusion of security authentication processes. Organizations should also be clear in their policies on how user data is collected, stored, and utilized so that their users can better understand their interactions with technology-based mental health resources.

6. Foster Continuous Education and Training

General education in technology and mental health through continuous teaching should be catered for both entrepreneurs and mental health professionals. Training sessions, workshops, and resources on the best ways of using technology should be provided to equip entrepreneurs with the tools necessary in supporting their mental health. The mental health practitioners also need training in incorporating technology into their work so that they can help the clientele integrate this information into their practices.

A culture of continuous learning will ensure that entrepreneurs and mental health professionals are abreast of the latest advancements and best practices in technology-enhanced mental health care.

Mental health support for entrepreneurs needs to be integrated with technology, thus calling for caution in the activity and putting the users at the forefront of its realization, while having evidence-based practices, ethics, and community involvement. If the organizations and the developers apply these best practices in creating effective, accessible, and supportive technological solutions then they would enhance the outcome about mental health with entrepreneurs. Technology integration would, therefore, contribute to a much healthier, resilient entrepreneurial community that helps shine practically and professionally.

FUTURE DIRECTIONS AND INNOVATIONS

The landscape of mental health support for entrepreneurs is changing rapidly, with the right technologically induced impetus and an increasingly better understanding of the specific issues these demographic faces. In moving forward, there are a number of directions and innovations that will positively impact the effectiveness of technology in providing quality mental health support. This section explores emerging developments shaping the current prospective landscape of mental health solutions for entrepreneurs.

1. Enhanced Personalization through AI

AI algorithms analyze high volumes of information-from patterns of moods and behavioral habits to contextual factors like business-related stressors-for highly customized mental health interventions.

For example, future applications might use machine learning in tailoring recommendations for mindfulness exercises, coping strategies, or therapeutic content based on real-time user feedback and interaction history. This kind of personalization will bring along more successful mental health support because solutions will resonate closer to unique experiences and challenges faced by entrepreneurs.

2. Virtual Reality (VR) and Augmented Reality (AR) Experiences

The convergence of VR and AR into mental health support provides exciting prospects to incorporate immersive experiences into therapy. Entrepreneurs can apply VR for relaxation and de-stressing in simulated environments or learn mindfulness techniques. For instance, guided meditation could take place in a tranquil virtual landscape as an effective way to escape the pressures of entrepreneurship.

In addition, AR could facilitate real-time support by superimposing mental health resources into the immediate user environment. This could include prompting users to engage in self-care or the existence of coping strategies at the point of peak stress. As these technologies advance, become cheaper, and are more easily utilized, it is likely their applications will also expand in mental health support, offering innovative, interactive ways to support well-being.

3. Integration of Biometric Data

In the future, mental health technology may also include integrating biometric data to further support mechanisms. Through wearable gadgets such as smartwatches or fitness trackers, individuals can keep track of their physiological indicators such as heart rate, sleep patterns, and intensity of physical activity. When this biometric data is combined with mental health apps, the entrepreneur will be able to know their physical health against their mental well-being.

For instance, a comparable application may explore patterns of sleep quality and exercise in order to recognize patterns of anxiety or stress build-up and will provide recommendations for improving both mental and physical well-being. This all-rounded approach will enable entrepreneurs to take initiative concerning their mental health, thus being better off.

4. Data-Driven Community Insights

Organizations gathering and analyzing information on the psychosocial experiences of entrepreneurs will make them notice trends and patterns to help inform targeted support initiatives. This data-led approach will enable organizations to tackle specifically identifiable needs within their communities more effectively.

For example, based on the reported data that a significant level of burnout among entrepreneurs is found across a specific industry group, the organization could probably develop focused workshops, resources, or even support structures for the topic. Utilize data analysis to drive community engagement and resource investment towards being able to respond more appropriately and effectively with targeted mental health support to entrepreneurs.

5. Consolidated Resource Channels and Networks of Mutual Support

Future innovations are likely to attract significant collaborative platforms that will connect entrepreneurs to one another and to mental health professionals. The opportunities for these will allow peer support networks in which entrepreneurs can share experiences, request and provide advice, as well as offer emotional support to each other.

Such collaborative settings can foster a sense of community or belonging, a feeling entrepreneur often needs to reduce those feelings of isolation they face. In addition, such a setting provides access to professional guides who may exploit both peer support and expert advice in an integrated and coherent manner.

6. Continuous Evaluation and Improvement

In tandem with technological advancement, mental health support solutions must also be assessed and improved. Organizations and developers would need to consistently review their platforms, taking comments and analyzing data to better understand areas of improvement. By using an iterative approach, stakeholders can ensure that their solutions remain relevant and effective in addressing the needs of entrepreneurs who are continually changing.

An evaluation process that may necessitate engagement with professionals in mental health can ensure that solutions align with best practices and the ethics that assure the given users with quality support.

To summarize, the future of technology in the offer of mental health support for entrepreneurs holds tremendous potential for innovation and transformation. Effective mental health landscapes would in the future be witnessed when enhancing personalization with AI, when VR and AR really become promoters of immersive experiences. Biometric data would play a part, community insights from data, collaborative sites, and continuous improvement efforts. It is with those future directions and innovation moves that stakeholders can come on a supportive ecosystem that frees the entrepreneur to focus on his mental health to pursue resilience and success, both personal and professional pursuit.

CONCLUSION

The integration of technology into mental health support systems for entrepreneurs promises a new frontier in addressing the unique challenges that this dynamic, and often demanding, demographic may face. As the entrepreneurial landscape continues to evolve, so too must our approaches to mental health care-be innovative, technology-driven solutions designed to strengthen support systems. This chapter has explored the multifaceted relationship between technology and mental health, as it shines a light on the current state, challenges, best practices, and future directions for this integration.

Entrepreneurs are a set of people under immense pressure from their financial uncertainties, long working hours, and constant demand for creativity and innovation. Such factors will really play a huge role in influencing their mental health and subsequently increase the risk of anxiety, depression, and burnout. The new doors that technology opens to entrepreneurs help them reach out to resources that otherwise may be impossible or relatively difficult to attain. For example, there are mobile apps for mindfulness practice and teletherapy sites that connect people to licensed professionals to bridge certain gaps in mental health care.

While still a developing field, technology support in mental health has many obstacles like accessibility issues, bad resources of quality, ethical dilemmas, and overdependence on it; thus, full-scale implementation is needed from the developers, organizations, and mental health professionals to be more proactive and effective, equitable, and ethical.

Best practices would include user-centric design, evidence-based approaches, engagement of the community in the process of designing and developing products, and response to privacy concerns. The influence of these technological advancements on supporting mental health could only be maximally utilized if the mental health professional groups and technology developers cooperated with one another towards developing tools that respond to the needs of entrepreneurs.

With the above in place, there will be much hope for the near future of mental health provision to entrepreneurs. Invention in tailored AI-driven interventions and immersive VR experiences and in community insights backed up by data will change the future provision of mental health services. The adaptive ecosystem will evolve in step with the ever-changing entrepreneurial environment while these technologies are continuously tested and perfected by stakeholders.

Conclusion It is not a trend but rather the necessary evolution of mental health care. As we appreciate these advances, we must be committed to creating supportiveness and giving priority to the mental health wellness of entrepreneurs, which will eventually lead to resilience and prosperity in their personal and professional lives. Rather, through the correct and proper utilization of technology, we can work together for a healthier entrepreneurial community, rich in innovation, growth, and positive outcomes of mental well-being for all.

REFERENCES:

Achtyes, E., Glenn, T., Monteith, S., Geddes, J., Whybrow, P., Martini, J., & Bauer, M. (2023). Telepsychiatry in an era of digital mental health startups. *Current Psychiatry Reports*, 25(6), 263–272. DOI: 10.1007/s11920-023-01425-9 PMID: 37166622

Alneyadi, M., Drissi, N., Almeqbaali, M., & Ouhbi, S. (2021). Biofeedback-based connected mental health interventions for anxiety: Systematic literature review. *JMIR mHealth and uHealth*, 9(4), e26038. DOI: 10.2196/26038 PMID: 33792548

Alqahtani, F., Winn, A., & Orji, R. (2020). Co-designing a mobile app to improve mental health and well-being: focus group study (preprint). DOI: 10.2196/preprints.18172

Anastasiadou, D., Folkvord, F., Serrano-Troncoso, E., & Lupiáñez-Villanueva, F. (2019). Mobile health adoption in mental health: User experience of a mobile health app for patients with an eating disorder. *JMIR mHealth and uHealth*, 7(6), e12920. DOI: 10.2196/12920 PMID: 31199329

Aziz, M., Erbad, A., Almourad, M., Altuwairiqi, M., McAlaney, J., & Ali, R. (2022). Did usage of mental health apps change during covid-19? a comparative study based on an objective recording of usage data and demographics. *Life (Chicago, Ill.)*, 12(8), 1266. DOI: 10.3390/life12081266 PMID: 36013444

Bunyi, J., Ringland, K., & Schueller, S. (2021). Accessibility and digital mental health: Considerations for more accessible and equitable mental health apps. *Frontiers in Digital Health*, 3, 742196. Advance online publication. DOI: 10.3389/fdgth.2021.742196 PMID: 34713206

Drissi, N., Ouhbi, S., Idrissi, M., Fernández-Luque, L., & Ghogho, M. (2020). Connected mental health: Systematic mapping study. *Journal of Medical Internet Research*, 22(8), e19950. DOI: 10.2196/19950 PMID: 32857055

Du, G. (2024). Empowering teenage resilience: a mobile app for personalized mental health support in the post-covid era.. DOI: 10.5121/csit.2024.140805

Fernández-Bedoya, V., Meneses-La-Riva, M. E., Suyo-Vega, J. A., & Stephanie Gago-Chávez, J. J. (2023). Mental health problems of entrepreneurs during the covid 19 health crisis: Fear, anxiety, and stress. a systematic review. *F1000 Research*, 12, 1062. DOI: 10.12688/f1000research.139581.1

Ferrazzi, P., & Krupa, T. (2018). Remoteness and its impact on the potential for mental health initiatives in criminal courts in nunavut, canada. *International Journal of Circumpolar Health*, 77(1), 1541700. DOI: 10.1080/22423982.2018.1541700 PMID: 30384817

Gbollie, E., Bantjes, J., Jarvis, L., Swandevelder, S., du Plessis, J., Shadwell, R., Davids, C., Gerber, R., Holland, N., & Hunt, X. (2023). Intention to use digital mental health solutions: A cross-sectional survey of university students attitudes and perceptions toward online therapy, mental health apps, and chatbots. *Digital Health*, 9, 20552076231216559. Advance online publication. DOI: 10.1177/20552076231216559 PMID: 38047161

Hwang, W., Ha, J., & Kim, M. (2021). Research trends on mobile mental health application for general population: A scoping review. *International Journal of Environmental Research and Public Health*, 18(5), 2459. DOI: 10.3390/ijerph18052459 PMID: 33801537

Marshall, J., Dunstan, D., & Bartik, W. (2019). The digital psychiatrist: In search of evidence-based apps for anxiety and depression. *Frontiers in Psychiatry*, 10, 831. Advance online publication. DOI: 10.3389/fpsyt.2019.00831 PMID: 31803083

Mohr, D., Lyon, A., Lattie, E., Reddy, M., & Schueller, S. (2017). Accelerating digital mental health research from early design and creation to successful implementation and sustainment. *Journal of Medical Internet Research*, 19(5), e153. DOI: 10.2196/jmir.7725 PMID: 28490417

Musiat, P., Goldstone, P., & Tarrier, N. (2014). Understanding the acceptability of e-mental health - attitudes and expectations towards computerised self-help treatments for mental health problems. *BMC Psychiatry*, 14(1), 109. Advance online publication. DOI: 10.1186/1471-244X-14-109 PMID: 24725765

Ng, M., Firth, J., Minen, M., & Torous, J. (2019). User engagement in mental health apps: A review of measurement, reporting, and validity. *Psychiatric Services (Washington, D.C.)*, 70(7), 538–544. DOI: 10.1176/appi.ps.201800519 PMID: 30914003

Pung, A., Fletcher, S., & Gunn, J. (2018). Mobile app use by primary care patients to manage their depressive symptoms: Qualitative study. *Journal of Medical Internet Research*, 20(9), e10035. DOI: 10.2196/10035 PMID: 30262449

Roberts, A., Davenport, T., Wong, T., Moon, H., Hickie, I., & LaMonica, H. (2021). Evaluating the quality and safety of health-related apps and e-tools: Adapting the mobile app rating scale and developing a quality assurance protocol. *Internet Interventions : the Application of Information Technology in Mental and Behavioural Health*, 24, 100379. DOI: 10.1016/j.invent.2021.100379 PMID: 33777705

Shen, N., Kassam, I., Chen, S., Ma, C., Wang, W., Boparai, N., Jankowicz, D., & Strudwick, G. (2022). Canadian perspectives of digital mental health supports: Findings from a national survey conducted during the covid-19 pandemic. *Digital Health*, 8, 205520762211022. DOI: 10.1177/20552076221102253 PMID: 35646379

Sorkin, D., Janio, E., Eikey, E., Schneider, M., Davis, K., Schueller, S., Stadnick, N. A., Zheng, K., Neary, M., Safani, D., & Mukamel, D. (2021). Rise in use of digital mental health tools and technologies in the united states during the covid-19 pandemic: Survey study. *Journal of Medical Internet Research*, 23(4), e26994. DOI: 10.2196/26994 PMID: 33822737

Su, Z., Cheshmehzangi, A., McDonnell, D., Chen, H., Ahmad, J., Šegalo, S., & Veiga, C. (2022). Technology-based mental health interventions for domestic violence victims amid covid-19. *International Journal of Environmental Research and Public Health*, 19(7), 4286. DOI: 10.3390/ijerph19074286 PMID: 35409967

Sucharitha, S., Manoharan, A., Dhanuraja, V., Kasi, A., & Ezhilarasan, S. (2020). Digital mental health apps for self-management of depression: A scoping exploration on awareness, attitude, and user experience among professional course students. *International Journal of Community Medicine and Public Health*, 7(9), 3594. DOI: 10.18203/2394-6040.ijcmph20203928

Tisu, L., Vîrgă, D., & Taris, T. (2023). Entrepreneurial well-being and performance: Antecedents and mediators. *Frontiers in Psychology*, 14, 1112397. Advance online publication. DOI: 10.3389/fpsyg.2023.1112397 PMID: 37928580

Weisel, K., Fuhrmann, L., Berking, M., Baumeister, H., Cuijpers, P., & Ebert, D. (2019). Standalone smartphone apps for mental health—A systematic review and meta-analysis. *NPJ Digital Medicine*, 2(1), 118. Advance online publication. DOI: 10.1038/s41746-019-0188-8 PMID: 31815193

Compilation of References

A., Naudé, W., Goedhuys, M. (Eds.). *Entrepreneurship, Innovation, and Economic Development*. Oxford University Press, Oxford.

Abbas, A., Abbas Abed Hussein Al-Janabi, A., & Al Hasnawi, H. (2017). The Effect of Hostile Work Environment on Organizational Alienation: The Mediation Role of the Relationship between the Leader and Followers. *Asian Social Science*, 13(2), 140–158. DOI: 10.5539/ass.v13n2p140

Abd-Alrazaq, A. A., Alajlani, M., Alalwan, A. A., Bewick, B. M., Gardner, P., & Househ, M. A. (2019). *An overview of the features of Chatbots in Mental Health: A scoping review*. International journal of medical informatics. https://pubmed.ncbi.nlm.nih.gov/31622850/

Acemoglu, D., Johnson, S., Robinson, J.A. (2005). Institutions as a fundamental cause of long-run growth. *Handb. Econ. Growth*. 385–472. .DOI: 10.1016/S1574-0684(05)01006-3

Achtyes, E., Glenn, T., Monteith, S., Geddes, J., Whybrow, P., Martini, J., & Bauer, M. (2023). Telepsychiatry in an era of digital mental health startups. *Current Psychiatry Reports*, 25(6), 263–272. DOI: 10.1007/s11920-023-01425-9 PMID: 37166622

Acs, Z.J., Autio, E., Szerb, L., (2014). National systems of entrepreneurship: measurement issues and policy implications. *Res. Policy* 43, 476–494. https://doi.org/. respol.2013.08.016.DOI: 10.1016/j

Acs, Z. J. (2006). How is entrepreneurship good for economic growth? *Innovations*, 1(1), 97–106.

Acs, Z. J., Desai, S., & Klapper, L. F. (2008b). What does Bentrepreneurship^ data really show? *Small Business Economics*, 31(3), 265–281. DOI: 10.1007/s11187-008-9137-7

Ács, Z. J., Szerb, L., Autio, E., & Lloyd, A. A. (2017). *The Global Entrepreneurship Index*. The Global Entrepreneurship and Development Institute. DOI: 10.1007/978-3-319-63844-7_3

Acs, Z. J., Szerb, L., Lafuente, E., & Lloyd, A. (2018). *Global Entrepreneurship Index*. The Global Entrepreneurship and Development. Institute. (Original work published 2018), DOI: 10.1007/978-3-030-03279

Acs, Z., Åstebro, T., Audretsch, D., & Robinson, D. T. (2016). Public policy to promote entrepreneurship: A call to arms. *Small Business Economics*, 47(1), 35–51. DOI: 10.1007/s11187-016-9712-2

Acs, Z., Stam, E., Audretsch, D., & O'Connor, A. (2017). The Lineages of the Entrepreneurial Ecosystem Approach. *Small Business Economics*, 49(1), 1–10. DOI: 10.1007/s11187-017-9864-8

Adams, D., Meyers, S., & Beidas, R. (2016). The relationship between financial strain, perceived stress, psychological symptoms, and academic and social integration in undergraduate students. *Journal of American College Health*, 64(5), 362–370. DOI: 10.1080/07448481.2016.1154559 PMID: 26943354

Adner, R. (2017). Ecosystem as Structure: An Actionable Construct for Strategy. *Journal of Management*, 43(1), 39–58. DOI: 10.1177/0149206316678451

Adner, R., & Kapoor, R. (2010). Value creation in innovation ecosystems: How the structure of technological interdependence affects firm performance in new technology generations. *Strategic Management Journal*, 31(3), 306–333. DOI: 10.1002/smj.821

Adula, M., Birbirsa, Z. A., & Kant, S. (2023). The effect of interpersonal, problem solving and technical training skills on performance of Ethiopia textile industry: Continuance, normative and affective commitment as mediators. *Cogent Business & Management*, 10(3), 2286672. Advance online publication. DOI: 10.1080/23311975.2023.2286672

Aggarwal, I., & Woolley, A. W. (2019). Team creativity, cognition, and cognitive style diversity. *Management Science*, 65(4), 1586–1599. DOI: 10.1287/mnsc.2017.3001

Aghion, P., David, P. A., & Foray, D. (2009). Science, technology, and innovation for economic growth: Linking policy research and practice in "STIG systems.". *Research Policy*, 38(4), 681–693. DOI: 10.1016/j.respol.2009.01.016

Aguilar, E. (2018). *Onward: Cultivating emotional resilience in educators*. John Wiley & Sons. DOI: 10.1002/9781119441731

Ahmed, F., Zhao, F., & Faraz, N. A. (2020). How and when does inclusive leadership curb psychological distress during a crisis? Evidence from the COVID-19 outbreak. *Frontiers in Psychology*, 11, 1898. DOI: 10.3389/fpsyg.2020.01898 PMID: 32849111

Akerloff, G. A. (1970). The market for lemons: Quality uncertainty and the market mechanism. *The Quarterly Journal of Economics*, 84(3), 485–500. DOI: 10.2307/1879431

Al Saidi, A. M. O., Nur, F. A., Al-Mandhari, A. S., El Rabbat, M., Hafeez, A., & Abubakar, A. (2020). Decisive leadership is a necessity in the COVID-19 response. *Lancet*, 396(10247), 295–298. DOI: 10.1016/S0140-6736(20)31493-8 PMID: 32628904

Alam, A. (2022). Investigating sustainable education and positive psychology interventions in schools towards achievement of sustainable happiness and wellbeing for 21st century pedagogy and curriculum. *ECS Transactions*, 107(1), 19481–19494. DOI: 10.1149/10701.19481ecst

Alberti, S., Gladfelter, A., & Mittag, T. (2019). Considerations and challenges in studying liquid-liquid phase separation and biomolecular condensates. *Cell*, 176(3), 419–434. DOI: 10.1016/j.cell.2018.12.035 PMID: 30682370

Aldawsari , R. (2020). The relationship between leaders' emotional intelligence and leadership effectiveness from perspectives of leaders and faculty members at university of Hafr al Batin. , 79(79), 1-26. DOI: 10.21608/edusohag.2020.116714

Alkaabi, H. S., Aajeel, B. N., & Rahman, M. M. A. (2023). The impact of strategy implementation practices on entrepreneurial orientation through emotional intelligence/an applied study at the University of Information and Communication Technology–Baghdad. *International Journal of Professional Business Review: Int.J. Prof. Bus. Rev.*, 8(12), 1.

Allen, D. G., Shore, L. M., & Griffeth, R. W. (2010). The role of perceived organizational support and supportive human resource practices in the turnover process. *Journal of Management*, 29(1), 99–118. DOI: 10.1177/014920630302900107

Allen, J., Stevenson, R., O'Boyle, E., & Seibert, S. (2020). What matters more for entrepreneurship success? a meta-analysis comparing general mental ability and emotional intelligence in entrepreneurial settings. *Strategic Entrepreneurship Journal*, 15(3), 352–376. DOI: 10.1002/sej.1377

Almestica, M. (2012). *Work-life balance issues and mentoring strategies for women in the contract management profession.*

Almohtaseb, A., Almahameed, M., Sharari, F., & Dabbouri, E. (2021). The effect of transformation leadership on government employee job satisfaction during Covid-19. *Management Science Letters*, 11(4), 1231–1244. DOI: 10.5267/j.msl.2020.11.015

Alneyadi, M., Drissi, N., Almeqbaali, M., & Ouhbi, S. (2021). Biofeedback-based connected mental health interventions for anxiety: Systematic literature review. *JMIR mHealth and uHealth*, 9(4), e26038. DOI: 10.2196/26038 PMID: 33792548

Alqahtani, F., Winn, A., & Orji, R. (2020). Co-designing a mobile app to improve mental health and well-being: focus group study (preprint). DOI: 10.2196/preprints.18172

Alshebami, A. S., Alholiby, M. S., Elshaer, I. A., Sobaih, A. E. E., & Al Marri, S. H. (2023). Examining the relationship between green mindfulness, spiritual intelligence, and environmental self-identity: Unveiling the path to green entrepreneurial intention. *Administrative Sciences*, 13(10), 226. DOI: 10.3390/admsci13100226

Al-Tekreeti, T., Al Khasawneh, M., & Dandis, A. O. (2024). Factors affecting entrepreneurial intentions among students in higher education institutions. *International Journal of Educational Management*, 38(1), 115–135. DOI: 10.1108/IJEM-09-2023-0470

Alvarez, G., & Sinde-Cantorna, A. I. (2014). Self-employment and job satisfaction: An empirical analysis. *International Journal of Manpower*, 35(5), 688–702. DOI: 10.1108/IJM-11-2012-0169

Amar, A., Hlupic, V., & Tamwatin, T. (2014). Effect of meditation on self-perception of leadership skills: A control group study of CEOs. *Proceedings - Academy of Management*, 2014(1), 14282. DOI: 10.5465/ambpp.2014.300

American Journal of Sociology. (1996). *Symposium on market transition.* 101: 908-1096.

Anasseri, M. (2021). Effect of cognitive-behavioral group therapy on the anxiety and depression of war-handicapped. *Journal of Archives in Military Medicine*, 9(1). Advance online publication. DOI: 10.5812/jamm.114085

Anastasiadou, D., Folkvord, F., Serrano-Troncoso, E., & Lupiáñez-Villanueva, F. (2019). Mobile health adoption in mental health: User experience of a mobile health app for patients with an eating disorder. *JMIR mHealth and uHealth*, 7(6), e12920. DOI: 10.2196/12920 PMID: 31199329

Andiani, A., Rizani, D., Khoirunnisa, R., & Khairunnisak, K. (2020). The important role of emotional intelligence to face competitive business. *Iptek Journal of Proceedings Series*, 0(1), 58. DOI: 10.12962/j23546026.y2020i1.7984

Anh, B., & Pham, M. (2022). The role of mindfulness and perceived social support in promoting students' social entrepreneurial intention. *Entrepreneurial Business and Economics Review*, 10(1), 145–160. DOI: 10.15678/EBER.2022.100110

Annink, A., Gorgievski, M., & Den Dulk, L. (2016). Financial hardship and well-being: A cross-national comparison among the European self-employed. *European Journal of Work and Organizational Psychology*, 25(5), 645–657. DOI: 10.1080/1359432X.2016.1150263

Ansell, C., & Gash, A. (2018). Collaborative platforms as a governance strategy. *Journal of Public Administration: Research and Theory*, 28(1), 16–32. DOI: 10.1093/jopart/mux030

Applewhite, P. A. (2017). Examining the role of emotional intelligence in the work and life balance of foster care workers. Walden Dissertations and Doctoral Studies. 3517.

Aránega, A. Y., Castaño Sánchez, R., & Ribeiro-Navarrete, S. (2023). Techniques to strengthen entrepreneurship: Is mindfulness a useful concept for resilience development? *Journal of Enterprising Communities: People and Places in the Global Economy.*

Aripin, Z., Sikki, N., & Fatmasari, R. R. (2024, January). An in-depth exploration of empirical research on entrepreneurial mindfulness: A systematic literature review to explore nuances, findings, and challenges. *Journal of Jabar Economic Society Networking Forum*, 1(2), 1–15.

Armington, C., & Acs, Z. (2002). The Determinants of Regional Variation in New Firm Formation. *Regional Studies*, 36(1), 33–45. DOI: 10.1080/00343400120099843

Arthur, W. B. (2013). *Complexity economics: A different framework for economic thought*, SFI Working Paper 2013-04-012.

Arthur, W. B. (2013). *Complexity Economics*. Oxford University Press.

Asefa, K., & Debela, K. L. "Effect of Transformational Leadership on Organizational Performance: The Mediating Role of Employee Commitment and Expert Systems (AI) Inclusion in Ethiopia," *2023 International Conference on Communication, Security and Artificial Intelligence (ICCSAI)*, Greater Noida, India, 2023, pp. 305-310, https://doi.org/DOI: 10.1109/ICCSAI59793.2023.10421269

Attridge, M. (2019). A global perspective on promoting workplace mental health and the role of employee assistance programs. *American Journal of Health Promotion*, 33(4), 622–629. DOI: 10.1177/0890117119838101c PMID: 31006254

Audretsch, D. B., & Thurik, R. (2001). What's new about the new economy? Sources of growth in the managed and entrepreneurial economies. *Industrial and Corporate Change*, 10(1), 267–315. . 1. 267 https://doi.org/.DOI: 10. 1093/ icc/10

Audretsch, D. B., & Belitski, D. B. (2017). Entrepreneurial ecosystems in cities: Establishing the framework conditions. *The Journal of Technology Transfer*, 42(5), 1030–1051. DOI: 10.1007/s10961-016-9473-8

Audretsch, D. B., Heger, D., & Veith, T. (2015). Infrastructure and entrepreneurship. *Small Business Economics*, 44(2), 219–230. DOI: 10.1007/s11187-014-9600-6

Audretsch, D. B., Keilbach, M. C., & Lehmann, E. E. (2006). *Entrepreneurship and Economic Growth*. Oxford University Press. DOI: 10.1093/acprof:oso/9780195183511.001.0001

Aulet, B., Hargadon, A., Pittaway, L., Brush, C., & Alpi, S. (2018). What I have learned about teaching entrepreneurship: Perspectives of five master educators. In *Annals of entrepreneurship education and pedagogy–2018* (pp. 2–26). Edward Elgar Publishing. DOI: 10.4337/9781788114950.00009

Autio, E., & Levie, J. (2017). *Management of entrepreneurial ecosystems*. The Wiley Handbook of Entrepreneurship, 43, 423–449. DOI: 10.1002/9781118970812.ch19

Autio, E., Nambisan, S., Thomas, L. D., & Wright, M. (2018). Digital affordances, spatial affordances, and the genesis of entrepreneurial ecosystems. *Strategic Entrepreneurship Journal*, 12(1), 72–95. DOI: 10.1002/sej.1266

Ayala, J. C., & Manzano, G. (2014). The resilience of the entrepreneur. Influence on the success of the business. A longitudinal analysis. *Journal of Economic Psychology*, 42, 126–135. DOI: 10.1016/j.joep.2014.02.004

Aziz, M., Erbad, A., Almourad, M., Altuwairiqi, M., McAlaney, J., & Ali, R. (2022). Did usage of mental health apps change during covid-19? a comparative study based on an objective recording of usage data and demographics. *Life (Chicago, Ill.)*, 12(8), 1266. DOI: 10.3390/life12081266 PMID: 36013444

Babcock, J. (2021). The entrepreneurial characteristics of national board certified health and wellness coaches. *Coaching (Abingdon, UK)*, 14(2), 142–150. DOI: 10.1080/17521882.2020.1831562

Bach-Mortensen, A. M., Lange, B. C., & Montgomery, P. (2018). Barriers and facilitators to implementing evidence-based interventions among third sector organisations: A systematic review. *Implementation Science : IS*, 13(1), 1–19. DOI: 10.1186/s13012-018-0789-7 PMID: 30060744

Bacq, S., & Alt, E. (2018). Feeling capable and valued: A prosocial perspective on the link between empathy and social entrepreneurial intentions. *Journal of Business Venturing*, 33(3), 333–350. DOI: 10.1016/j.jbusvent.2018.01.004

Badu, E., O'Brien, A. P., Mitchell, R., & Rubin, M. (2020). Workplace stress and resilience in the Australian nursing workforce: A comprehensive integrative review. *International Journal of Mental Health Nursing*, 29(1), 5–34.

Baer, R. (2019). Assessment of mindfulness by self-report. *Current Opinion in Psychology*, 28, 42–48. DOI: 10.1016/j.copsyc.2018.10.015 PMID: 30423507

Baglow, L., & Gair, S. (2018). Australian social work students: Balancing tertiary studies, paid work and poverty. *Journal of Social Work : JSW*, 19(2), 276–295. DOI: 10.1177/1468017318760776

Bahrami, P., Nosratabadi, S., Palouzian, K., & Hegedűs, S. (2022). Modeling the impact of mentoring on women's work-life balance: A grounded theory approach. *Administrative Sciences*, 13(1), 6. DOI: 10.3390/admsci13010006

Baig, A., Hall, B., Jenkins, P., Lamarre, E., & McCarthy, B. (2020). The COVID-19 recovery will be digital: A plan for the first 90 days. *McKinsey Digital, 14*.

Baker, F. R., Baker, K. L., & Burrell, J. (2021). Introducing the skills-based model of personal resilience: Drawing on content and process factors to build resilience in the workplace. *Journal of Occupational and Organizational Psychology*, 94(2), 458–481. DOI: 10.1111/joop.12340

Baker, R., Puzi, N. F. H. M., Saudi, N. S. M., Zahari, H. M., Sallehudin, H., Zainol, N. A. M., & Selamat, M. N. (2024). The Influenced of Work-life Balance on Emotional Intelligence, Depression, Anxiety, and Stress. *Kurdish Studies*, 12(1), 43–57.

Baluku, M. M., Nansubuga, F., Nantamu, S., Musanje, K., Kawooya, K., Nansamba, J., & Ruto, G. (2023). Psychological capital, entrepreneurial efficacy, alertness and agency among refugees in Uganda: Perceived behavioural control as a moderator. *Journal of Entrepreneurship and Innovation in Emerging Economies*, 23939575231194554.

Balven, R., Fenters, V., Siegel, D. S., & Waldman, D. (2018). Academic entrepreneurship: The roles of identity, motivation, championing, education, work-life balance, and organizational justice. *The Academy of Management Perspectives*, 32(1), 21–42. DOI: 10.5465/amp.2016.0127

Banu, S., & Suresh, B. (2020). COVID-19 and its impact on micro, small and medium enterprises in India. *Mukt Shabd Journal*, 9(X), 606–617.

Baroudi, S., & David, S. (2020). Nurturing female leadership skills through peer mentoring role: A study among undergraduate students in the united arab emirates. *Higher Education Quarterly*, 74(4), 458–474. DOI: 10.1111/hequ.12249

Bartik, A. W., Bertrand, M., Cullen, Z. B., Glaeser, E. L., Luca, M., & Stanton, C. T. (2020). *How are small businesses adjusting to COVID-19? Early evidence from a survey* (No. w26989). National Bureau of Economic Research.

Baumol, W. J. (1990). Entrepreneurship: Productive, unproductive, and destructive. *Journal of Political Economy*, 98(5, Part 1), 893–921. DOI: 10.1086/261712

Bayram, G. E., Shah, S. H. A., & Tunio, M. N. (Eds.). (2023). *Women's Empowerment Within the Tourism Industry*. IGI Global. DOI: 10.4018/978-1-6684-8417-3

Bazarko, D., Cate, R. A., Azocar, F., & Kreitzer, M. J. (2013). The impact of an innovative mindfulness-based stress reduction program on the health and well-being of nurses employed in a corporate setting. *Journal of Workplace Behavioral Health*, 28(2), 107–133. DOI: 10.1080/15555240.2013.779518 PMID: 23667348

Becker, G. A. (2019). *Investigating the Use of Wearable Activity Trackers to Determine Psychological Wellbeing* (Doctoral dissertation, Roosevelt University).

Becker, W. J., Belkin, L. Y., Tuskey, S. E., & Conroy, S. A. (2022). Surviving remotely: How job control and loneliness during a forced shift to remote work impacted employee work behaviors and well-being. *Human Resource Management*, 61(4), 449–464. DOI: 10.1002/hrm.22102

Beinhocker, E. D. (2006). *The origin of wealth: Evolution, complexity, and the radical remaking of economics*. Random House Business.

Beltman, S., & Schaeben, M. (2012). Institution-wide peer mentoring: Benefits for mentors. *The International Journal of the First Year in Higher Education*, 3(2). Advance online publication. DOI: 10.5204/intjfyhe.v3i2.124

Ben-Itzhak, S., Dvash, J., Maor, M., Rosenberg, N., & Halpern, P. (2015). Sense of meaning as a predictor of burnout in emergency physicians in israel: A national survey. *Clinical and Experimental Emergency Medicine*, 2(4), 217–225. DOI: 10.15441/ceem.15.074 PMID: 27752601

Benneworth, P. (2004). In What Sense Regional Development? Entrepreneurship, Underdevelopment and Strong Tradition in the Periphery. *Entrepreneurship and Regional Development*, 16(6), 439–458. DOI: 10.1080/0898562042000249786

Berenbaum, R., Tziraki, C., Baum, R., Rosen, A., Reback, T., Abikhzer, J., & Ben-David, B. (2020). Focusing on emotional and social intelligence stimulation of people with dementia by playing a serious game—Proof of concept study. *Frontiers of Computer Science*, 2. Advance online publication. DOI: 10.3389/fcomp.2020.536880

Berjaoui, R. R., & Karami-Akkary, R. (2020). Distributed leadership as a path to organizational commitment: The case of a Lebanese School. *Leadership and Policy in Schools*, 19(4), 610–624. DOI: 10.1080/15700763.2019.1637900

Bersin, J. (2023, April 10). Don't let quiet quitting harm your career: Josh Bersin. MIT Sloan Management Review. https://sloanreview.mit.edu/article/dont-let-quiet-quitting-harm-your-career/

Bies, R. J. (2015). Interactional justice: Looking backward, looking forward. In Cropanzano, R. S., & Ambrose, M. L. (Eds.), *The Oxford Handbook of Justice in the Workplace* (pp. 89–107). Oxford University Press.

Bilal, M., Chaudhry, S., Amber, H., Shahid, M., Aslam, S., & Shahzad, K. (2021). Entrepreneurial Leadership and Employees' Proactive Behaviour: Fortifying Self Determination Theory. *Journal of Open Innovation*, 7(3), 176. DOI: 10.3390/joitmc7030176

Binder, M. (2017). Entrepreneurial success and subjective well-being: Worries about the business explain one's well-being loss from self-employment.

Birhane, M., Amentie, C., Borji, B., & Kant, S. Are Ethiopian Coffee Farmers Proficient to Predict Capital Structure with Mediation of AI Based Knowledge Systems and Asset Liquidity? In *AI in Agriculture for Sustainable and Economic Management* (pp. 199-215). CRC Press. DOI: 10.1201/9781003451648-15

Bisschoff, M., Koen, V., & Ryke, E. H. (2019). Strategies for work–family balance in a South African context. *Community Work & Family*, 22(3), 319–337. DOI: 10.1080/13668803.2018.1473337

Blank, R., Barnett, A. L., Cairney, J., Green, D., Kirby, A., Polatajko, H., Rosenblum, S., Smits-Engelsman, B., Sugden, D., Wilson, P., & Vinçon, S. (2019). International clinical practice recommendations on the definition, diagnosis, assessment, intervention, and psychosocial aspects of developmental coordination disorder. *Developmental Medicine and Child Neurology*, 61(3), 242–285. DOI: 10.1111/dmcn.14132 PMID: 30671947

Bollen, K. (1989). A new incremental fit index for general structural equation models. *Sociological Methods & Research*, 17(3), 303–316. DOI: 10.1177/0049124189017003004

Bolpagni, M., Pardini, S., & Gabrielli, S. (2024). Human centered design of AI-powered Digital Therapeutics for stress prevention: Perspectives from multi-stakeholders' workshops about the SHIVA solution. *Internet Interventions : the Application of Information Technology in Mental and Behavioural Health*, 38, 100775. DOI: 10.1016/j.invent.2024.100775 PMID: 39314669

Bonini, S., & Capizzi, V. (2019). The Role of Venture Capital in the Emerging Entrepreneurial-Finance Ecosystem: Future Threats and Opportunities. *Venture Capital*, 21(2-3), 137–175. DOI: 10.1080/13691066.2019.1608697

Boon, C., & Biron, M. (2016). Temporal issues in person–organization fit, person–job fit and turnover: The role of leader–member exchange. *Human Relations*, 69(12), 2177–2200. DOI: 10.1177/0018726716636945 PMID: 27904171

Borbolla-Albores, A., & Reyes-Mercado, P. (2022). Entrepreneurial failure and resilience: A continuous interplay between rigidity and flexibility. *Jurnal Manajemen Dan Kewirausahaan*, 24(1), 1–14. DOI: 10.9744/jmk.24.1.1-14

Borissenko, Y., & Boschma, R. (2016). A critical review of entrepreneurial ecosystems: towards a future research agenda, No 1630. Section of Economic Geography: Utrecht University.

Bos, J. W. B., & Stam, E. (2014). Gazelles and industry growth: A study of young high- growth firms in the Netherlands. *Industrial and Corporate Change*, 23(1), 145–169. DOI: 10.1093/icc/dtt050

Bosma, N., Content, J., Sanders, M., & Stam, E. (2018). Institutions, entrepreneurship, and economic growth in Europe. *Small Business Economics*, 51(2), 483–499. DOI: 10.1007/s11187-018-0012-x

Bosma, N., Stam, E., & Schutjens, V. (2011). Creative destruction and regional productivity growth: Evidence from the Dutch manufacturing and services industries. *Small Business Economics*, 36(4), 401–418. DOI: 10.1007/s11187-009-9257-8

Boybanting, J. (2023). Emotional intelligence and teaching performance of teachers. *International Journal of Research Publications*, 129(1). Advance online publication. DOI: 10.47119/ijrp1001291720235288

Brieger, S. A., Sonbol, D., & De Clercq, D. (2024). Gender differences in entrepreneurs' work–family conflict and well-being during COVID-19: Moderating effects of gender-egalitarian contexts. *Journal of Small Business Management*, 62(5), 2322–2363. DOI: 10.1080/00472778.2023.2235755

Brooks, S. K., Webster, R. K., Smith, L. E., Woodland, L., Wessely, S., Greenberg, N., & Rubin, G. J. (2020). The psychological impact of quarantine and how to reduce it: Rapid review of the evidence. *Lancet*, 395(10227), 912–920. DOI: 10.1016/S0140-6736(20)30460-8 PMID: 32112714

Brown, R., & Mason, C. (2014). Inside the high-tech black box: A critique of technology entrepreneurship policy. *Technovation*, 34(12), 773–784. DOI: 10.1016/j.technovation.2014.07.013

Brown, R., & Mason, C. (2017). Looking inside the spiky bits: A critical review and conceptualization of entrepreneurial ecosystems. *Small Business Economics*, 49(1), 11–30. DOI: 10.1007/s11187-017-9865-7

Brück, T., Naudé, W., & Verwimp, P. (2013). Entrepreneurship and Violent Conflict in Developing Countries. WIDER Working Paper 2013/028. Helsinki: UNU-WIDER.

Bru-Luna, L., Vilar, M., Merino-Soto, C., Salinas-Escudero, G., & Toledano-Toledano, F. (2022). Variables impacting the quality of care provided by professional caregivers for people with mental illness: A systematic review. *Health Care*, 10(7), 1225. DOI: 10.3390/healthcare10071225

Bruns, K., Bosma, N., Sanders, M., & Schramm, M. (2017). Searching for the existence of entrepreneurial ecosystems: A regional cross-section growth regression approach. *Small Business Economics*, 49(1), 31–54. DOI: 10.1007/s11187-017-9866-6

Bryant, A., Brody, A., Pérez, A., Shillam, C., Edelman, L., Bond, S., & Siegel, E. (2015). Development and implementation of a peer mentoring program for early career gerontological faculty. *Journal of Nursing Scholarship*, 47(3), 258–266. DOI: 10.1111/jnu.12135 PMID: 25808927

Brynjolfsson, E., & Mcafee, A. N. D. R. E. W. (2017). Artificial intelligence, for real. *Harvard Business Review*, 1, 1–31.

Bugaut-Heichelbech, S., Foltzer, D., & Paraschiv, C. (2023). Temporal Well-being of Entrepreneurs: An Empirical Investigation. *Revue de l'Entrepreneuriat/Review of Entrepreneurship, 22*(4), 15-41.

Bullough, A., & Renko, M. (2013). Entrepreneurial resilience during challenging times. *Business Horizons*, 56(3), 343–350. DOI: 10.1016/j.bushor.2013.01.001

Bullough, A., Renko, M., & Myatt, T. (2014). Danger zone entrepreneurs: The importance of resilience and self-efficacy for entrepreneurial intentions. *Entrepreneurship Theory and Practice*, 38(3), 473–499. DOI: 10.1111/etap.12006

Bunyi, J., Ringland, K., & Schueller, S. (2021). Accessibility and digital mental health: Considerations for more accessible and equitable mental health apps. *Frontiers in Digital Health*, 3, 742196. Advance online publication. DOI: 10.3389/fdgth.2021.742196 PMID: 34713206

Buonomo, I., Fiorilli, C., Romano, L., & Benevene, P. (2020). The Roles of Work-Life Conflict and Gender in the Relationship between Workplace Bullying and Personal Burnout. A Study on Italian School Principals. *International Journal of Environmental Research and Public Health*, 17(23), 8745. DOI: 10.3390/ijerph17238745 PMID: 33255556

Burgess, A., van Diggele, C., & Mellis, C. (2018). Mentorship in the health professions: A review. *The Clinical Teacher*, 15(3), 197–202. DOI: 10.1111/tct.12756 PMID: 29318730

Burnes, B. (2019). The Origins of Lewin's Three-Step Model of Change. *The Journal of Applied Behavioral Science*, 56(1), 002188631989268. DOI: 10.1177/0021886319892685

Byrnes, R. T., & Taylor, S. N. (2015). Voluntary transition of the CEO: Owner CEOs' sense of self before, during and after transition. *Frontiers in Psychology*, 6, 1633. DOI: 10.3389/fpsyg.2015.01633 PMID: 26579018

Cai, B., Chen, Y., & Ayub, A. (2023). "Quiet the mind, and the soul will speak"! Exploring the boundary effects of green mindfulness and spiritual intelligence on university students' green entrepreneurial intention–behavior link. *Sustainability (Basel)*, 15(5), 3895. DOI: 10.3390/su15053895

Cai, M., Humphrey, R., & Qian, S. (2020). The cross-cultural moderators of the influence of emotional intelligence on organizational citizenship behavior and counterproductive work behavior. *Human Resource Development Quarterly*, 31(2), 213–233. DOI: 10.1002/hrdq.21385

Cai, M., Humphrey, R., Qian, S., & Pollack, J. (2018). Emotional intelligence and entrepreneurial intentions: An exploratory meta-analysis. *Career Development International*, 23(5), 497–512. DOI: 10.1108/cdi-01-2018-0019

Cameron, K. S., Mora, C., Leutscher, T., & Calarco, M. (2011). Effects of positive practices on organizational effectiveness. *The Journal of Applied Behavioral Science*, 47(3), 266–308. DOI: 10.1177/0021886310395514

Campbell, J., & Pederson, O. (2001). Conclusion: The second movement in institutional analysis. In Campbell, J., & Pederson, O. (Eds.), *The Rise of Neoliberalism and Institutional Analysis: 249–282*. Princeton University Press. DOI: 10.1515/9780691188225-014

Canestrino, R., Magliocca, P., Ćwiklicki, M., & Pawełek, B. (2023). Toward the emergence of "humane" entrepreneurial ecosystems. Evidence from different cultural contexts. *Journal of Intellectual Capital*, 24(1), 177–204. DOI: 10.1108/JIC-07-2021-0200

Cao, Z., & Shi, X. (2020). A systematic literature review of entrepreneurial ecosystems in advanced and emerging economies. *Small Business Economics*, 51(2). Advance online publication. DOI: 10.1007/s11187-020-00326-y

Capozza, C., Salomone, S., & Somma, E. (2018). Local industrial structure, agglomeration economies and the creation of innovative start-ups: Evidence from the Italian case.

Cardon, M. S., & Patel, P. C. (2015). Is stress worth it? Stress-related health and wealth trade-offs for entrepreneurs. *Applied Psychology*, 64(2), 379–420. DOI: 10.1111/apps.12021

Cardon, M. S., Wincent, J., Singh, J., & Drnovsek, M. (2009). The nature and experience of entrepreneurial passion. *Academy of Management Review*, 34(3), 511–532. DOI: 10.5465/amr.2009.40633190

Carnevale, J. B., & Hatak, I. (2020). Employee adjustment and well-being in the era of COVID-19: Implications for human resource management. *Journal of Business Research*, 116, 183–187. DOI: 10.1016/j.jbusres.2020.05.037 PMID: 32501303

Carpenter, J., Andrews, L., Witcraft, S., Powers, M., Smits, J., & Hofmann, S. (2018). Cognitive behavioral therapy for anxiety and related disorders: A meta-analysis of randomized placebo-controlled trials. *Depression and Anxiety*, 35(6), 502–514. DOI: 10.1002/da.22728 PMID: 29451967

Carree, M. A., & Thurik, A. R. (2010). *The impact of entrepreneurship on economic growth. Handbook of Entrepreneurship Research.* Springer., DOI: 10.1007/978-1-4419-1191-9_20

Carree, M. A., & Verheul, I. (2012). What makes entrepreneurs happy? Determinants of satisfaction among founders. *Journal of Happiness Studies*, 13(2), 371–387. DOI: 10.1007/s10902-011-9269-3

Carvalho, C., Teixeira, M., Costa, R., Cordeiro, F., & Cabral, J. (2023). The enhancing role of emotion regulation in the links between early positive memories and self-harm and suicidal ideation in adolescence. *Journal of Youth and Adolescence*, 52(8), 1738–1752. DOI: 10.1007/s10964-023-01777-8

Casillo, M., Cecere, L., Colace, F., Lorusso, A., & Santaniello, D. (2024). Integrating the Internet of Things (IoT) in SPA Medicine: Innovations and challenges in digital wellness. *Computers*, 13(3), 67. DOI: 10.3390/computers13030067

Cavanaugh, K., Lee, H., Daum, D., Chang, S., Izzo, J., Kowalski, A., & Holladay, C. (2020). An examination of burnout predictors: Understanding the influence of job attitudes and environment. *Health Care*, 8(4), 502. DOI: 10.3390/healthcare8040502 PMID: 33233620

Çetin, G., Altınay, L., Alrawadıeh, Z., & Ali, F. (2022). Entrepreneurial motives, entrepreneurial success and life satisfaction of refugees venturing in tourism and hospitality. *International Journal of Contemporary Hospitality Management*, 34(6), 2227–2249. DOI: 10.1108/IJCHM-11-2021-1363

Chadwick, I., & Raver, J. (2018). Psychological resilience and its downstream effects for business survival in nascent entrepreneurship. *Entrepreneurship Theory and Practice*, 44(2), 233–255. DOI: 10.1177/1042258718801597

Chaidi, I., Papoutsi, C., Drigas, A., & Skianis, C. (2022). *Women: E-Entrepreneurship and Emotional Intelligence.* Technium Social Sciences Journal.

Chandnani, S. (2023). Role of emotional intelligence in sales success. *Tjjpt*, 44(4), 6325–6332. DOI: 10.52783/tjjpt.v44.i4.2175

Chand, R., & Sazima, G. (2024). Mindful Technology. In *Mindfulness in Medicine: A Comprehensive Guide for Healthcare Professionals* (pp. 147–165). Springer Nature Switzerland. DOI: 10.1007/978-3-031-66166-2_9

Chang, W. L., & Benson, V. (2022). Jigsaw teaching method for collaboration on cloud platforms. *Innovations in Education and Teaching International*, 59(1), 24–36. DOI: 10.1080/14703297.2020.1792332

Charoensukmongkol, P. (2019). Contributions of mindfulness to improvisational behavior and consequences on business performance and stress of entrepreneurs during economic downturn. *Organizational Management Journal*, 16(4), 209–219. DOI: 10.1080/15416518.2019.1661820

Chatrakul Na Ayudhya, U., Prouska, R., & Beauregard, T. A. (2019). The impact of global economic crisis and austerity on quality of working life and work-life balance: A capabilities perspective. *European Management Review*, 16(4), 847–862. DOI: 10.1111/emre.12128

Chay, Y. W. (1993). Social support, individual differences, and well-being: A study of small business entrepreneurs and employees. *Journal of Occupational and Organizational Psychology*, 66(4), 285–302. DOI: 10.1111/j.2044-8325.1993.tb00540.x

Cheah, W., Hazmi, H., Hoo, C., Chew, J., Nadira, M., & Nurva'ain, M. (2015). Peer mentoring among undergraduate medical students: Experience from universiti malaysia sarawak. *Education in Medicine Journal*, 7(1). Advance online publication. DOI: 10.5959/eimj.v7i1.331

Chen, C., Zhang, J., Tian, H., & Bu, X. (2022). The impact of entrepreneurial passion on entrepreneurial success and psychological well-being: A person-centered investigation. *International Journal of Entrepreneurial Behaviour & Research*. Advance online publication. DOI: 10.1108/IJEBR-12-2021-0977

Chen, H., & Eyoun, K. (2021). Do mindfulness and perceived organizational support work? Fear of COVID-19 on restaurant frontline employees' job insecurity and emotional exhaustion. *International Journal of Hospitality Management*, 94, 102850. DOI: 10.1016/j.ijhm.2020.102850 PMID: 34785844

Chen, M., & Tseng, M. (2021). Creative entrepreneurs' artistic creativity and entrepreneurial alertness: The guanxi network perspective. *International Journal of Entrepreneurial Behaviour & Research*, 27(4), 1082–1102. DOI: 10.1108/IJEBR-05-2020-0306

Cherry, K. (2022, November 8). How does self-determination theory explain motivation?.

Chesbrough, H. (2020). To recover faster from Covid-19, open up: Managerial implications from an open innovation perspective. *Industrial Marketing Management*, 88, 410–413. DOI: 10.1016/j.indmarman.2020.04.010

Chopra, P. (2009). Mental health and the workplace: Issues for developing countries. *International Journal of Mental Health Systems*, 3(1), 1–9. DOI: 10.1186/1752-4458-3-4 PMID: 19232117

Christie, A., Jordan, P., & Troth, A. (2015). Trust antecedents: Emotional intelligence and perceptions of others. *The International Journal of Organizational Analysis*, 23(1), 89–101. DOI: 10.1108/ijoa-07-2013-0695

Ciuchta, M., Letwin, C., Stevenson, R., McMahon, S., & Huvaj, M. (2017). Betting on the coachable entrepreneur: Signaling and social exchange in entrepreneurial pitches. *Entrepreneurship Theory and Practice*, 42(6), 860–885. DOI: 10.1177/1042258717725520

Clark, A., Colombier, N., & Masclet, D. (2008). Never the same after the first time: The satisfaction of the second-generation self-employed. *International Journal of Manpower*, 29(7), 591–609. DOI: 10.1108/01437720810908910

Cocker, F., Martin, A., Scott, J., Venn, A., & Sanderson, K. (2013). Psychological distress, related work attendance, and productivity loss in small-to-medium enterprise owner/managers. *International Journal of Environmental Research and Public Health*, 10(10), 5062–5082. DOI: 10.3390/ijerph10105062 PMID: 24132134

Cohen, B., & Winn, M. I. (2007). Market imperfections, opportunity and sustainable entrepreneurship. *Journal of Business Venturing*, 22(1), 29–49. DOI: 10.1016/j.jbusvent.2004.12.001

Colombelli, A., Krafft, J., & Vivarelli, M. (2016). To be born is not enough: The key role of innovative start-ups. *Small Business Economics*, 47(2), 1–15. DOI: 10.1007/s11187-016-9716-y

Colvin, J., & Ashman, M. (2010). Roles, risks, and benefits of peer mentoring relationships in higher education. *Mentoring & Tutoring*, 18(2), 121–134. DOI: 10.1080/13611261003678879

Content, J., Bosma, N., Jordaan, J., & Sanders, M. (2020). Entrepreneurial ecosystems, entrepreneurial activity, and economic growth: New evidence from European regions. *Regional Studies*, 54(8), 1007–1019. . 2019. 1680827DOI: 10. 1080/ 00343404

Cooke, P., Uranga, M. G., & Etxebarria, G. (1997). Regional innovation systems: Institutional and organisational dimensions. *Research Policy*, 26(4), 475–491. DOI: 10.1016/S0048-7333(97)00025-5

Cooper, C. L., & Cartwright, S. (1994). Healthy mind; healthy organization—A proactive approach to occupational stress. *Human Relations*, 47(4), 455–471. DOI: 10.1177/001872679404700405

Corner, P., Singh, S., & Pavlovich, K. (2017). Entrepreneurial resilience and venture failure. *International Small Business Journal*, 35(6), 687–708. DOI: 10.1177/0266242616685604

Cowley, S. A., Tzouvara, V., & Horta Reis da Silva, T. (2023). Public Health: healthy ageing and well-being. In Redfern's Nursing Older People. Fifth edition. Editors: Ross, Harris, Fitzpatrick and Abley. Elsevier.

Crane, R. S., & Hecht, F. M. (2018). Intervention integrity in mindfulness-based research. *Mindfulness*, 9(5), 1370–1380. DOI: 10.1007/s12671-018-0886-3 PMID: 30294386

Cree-Green, M., Carreau, A., Davis, S., Frohnert, B., Kaar, J., Nina, S., & Nadeau, K. (2020). Peer mentoring for professional and personal growth in academic medicine. *Journal of Investigative Medicine*, 68(6), 1128–1134. DOI: 10.1136/jim-2020-001391 PMID: 32641352

Criscuolo, C., Gal, P. N., & Menon, C. (2014). The dynamics of employment growth. OECD *Sci.Technol. Ind. Policy Pap*, 96. Advance online publication. DOI: 10.1787/23074957

Crompton, R., & Lyonette, C. (2006). Work-life 'balance' in Europe. *Acta Sociologica*, 49(4), 379–393. DOI: 10.1177/0001699306071680

Cronin, M. A., Stouten, J., & van Knippenberg, D. (2021). The Theory Crisis in Management Research: Solving the Right Problem. *Academy of Management Review*, 0294(4), 667–683. Advance online publication. DOI: 10.5465/amr.2019.0294

Cross, M. (1981). *New Firm Formation and Regional Development*. Gower Publishing Company.

Cukier, W., Saunders, V., & Stewart, S. (2022). Social Entrepreneurship and Addressing SDGs through Women's Empowerment: A Case Study of She-EO. In *World Scientific Encyclopedia of Business Sustainability, Ethics and Entrepreneurship* (pp. 83-111). World Scientific.

da Silva, T. H. R. (2022). Emotional awareness and emotional intelligence. *British Journal of Community Nursing*, 27(12), 573–574. DOI: 10.12968/bjcn.2022.27.12.573

da Silva, T. H. R., & Rodrigues, E. C. P. (2023). Body Image Related Discrimination. In Leal Filho, W., Azul, A. M., Brandli, L., Lange Salvia, A., Özuyar, P. G., & Wall, T. (Eds.), *Reduced Inequalities. Encyclopedia of the UN Sustainable Development Goals*. Springer., DOI: 10.1007/978-3-319-71060-0_61-1

da Silva, T. R. (2024a). Gender Equity In Healthcare: Integrating Emotional Intelligence To Achieve The United Nations Sustainable Development Goals. *J Comm Med and Pub Health Rep*, 5(12). Advance online publication. DOI: 10.38207/JCMPHR/2024/JUL051202106 da Silva, T. R. (2024b). Advancing Gender Equity In Nursing Care For Older Adults: A Pathway To Achieving The United Nations Sustainable Development Goals. *J Comm Med and Pub Health Rep*, 5(12). Advance online publication. DOI: 10.38207/JCMPHR/2024/JUL051201105

Dahl, M. S., & Sorenson, O. (2009). The embedded entrepreneur. *European Management Review*, 6(3), 172–181. DOI: 10.1057/emr.2009.14

Dalphon, H. (2019). Self-care techniques for social workers: Achieving an ethical harmony between work and well-being. *Journal of Human Behavior in the Social Environment*, 29(1), 85–95. DOI: 10.1080/10911359.2018.1481802

Dandotiya, R., & Aggarwal, A. (2022). Effects of COVID-19 on hotel industry: A case study of Delhi, India. *Revista Turismo & Desenvolvimento (Aveiro)*, 38, 35–53.

Dark-Freudeman, A., Jones, C., & Terry, C. (2022). Mindfulness, anxiety, and perceived stress in university students: Comparing a mindfulness-based intervention (MBI) against active and traditional control conditions. *Journal of American College Health*, 70(7), 2116–2125. DOI: 10.1080/07448481.2020.1845180 PMID: 33400631

Davidsson, P. (2004). *Researching entrepreneurship*. Springer.

De Clercq, D., Kaciak, E., & Thongpapanl, N. (2022). Happy at home, successful in competition: The beneficial role of happiness and entrepreneurial orientation for women entrepreneurs. *International Journal of Entrepreneurial Behaviour & Research*, 28(6), 1463–1488. DOI: 10.1108/IJEBR-02-2021-0154

De Clercq, D., Kaciak, E., & Thongpapanl, N. (2022). Work-to-family conflict and firm performance of women entrepreneurs: Roles of work-related emotional exhaustion and competitive hostility. *International Small Business Journal*, 40(3), 364–384. DOI: 10.1177/02662426211011405

De Freitas, J., & Cohen, I. G. (2024). The health risks of generative AI-based wellness apps. *Nature Medicine*, 30(5), 1–7. DOI: 10.1038/s41591-024-02943-6 PMID: 38684859

De Hoe, R., & Janssen, F. (2022). Re-creation after business failure: A conceptual model of the mediating role of psychological capital. *Frontiers in Psychology*, 13, 842590. DOI: 10.3389/fpsyg.2022.842590 PMID: 35310260

Deb, S., Nafi, S., Mallik, N., & Valeri, M. (2023). Mediating effect of emotional intelligence on the relationship between employee job satisfaction and firm performance of small business. *European Business Review*, 35(5), 624–651. DOI: 10.1108/EBR-12-2022-0249

Dej, D. (2010). Defining and measuring entrepreneurial success. In *Entrepreneurship: A Psychological Approach* (pp. 89-102).

Del Giudice, M., Carayannis, E. G., & Maggioni, V. (2017). Global knowledge intensive enterprises and international technology transfer: Emerging perspectives from a quadruple helix environment. *The Journal of Technology Transfer*, 42(2), 229–235. DOI: 10.1007/s10961-016-9496-1

Deng, X., Gao, B., & Li, G. (2019). The Effects of Dynamic Work Environments on Entrepreneurs' Humble Leader Behaviors: Based on Uncertainty Reduction Theory. *Frontiers in Psychology*, 10, 2732. Advance online publication. DOI: 10.3389/fpsyg.2019.02732 PMID: 31920793

Dereso, C. W., Kant, S., Muthuraman, M., & Tufa, G. (2023). Effect of Point of Service on Health Department Student's Creativity in Comprehensive Universities of Ethiopia: Moderating Role of Public-Private Partnership and Mediating Role of Work Place Learning. In: Jain, S., Groppe, S., Mihindukulasooriya, N. (eds) Proceedings of the International Health Informatics Conference. Lecture Notes in Electrical Engineering, vol 990. Springer, Singapore. https://doi.org/DOI: 10.1007/978-981-19-9090-8_13

Dewa, C. S., McDaid, D., & Ettner, S. L. (2007). An international perspective on worker mental health problems: Who bears the burden and how are costs addressed? *Canadian Journal of Psychiatry*, 52(6), 346–356. DOI: 10.1177/070674370705200603 PMID: 17696020

Dhammika, B. B. K., & Sewwandi, D. (2023). Role of mindfulness in entrepreneurial success: A review. *Editorial Board*, 4(01), 98–117.

Dijkhuizen, J. (2015). *Entrepreneurship, easier said than done: A study on success and well-being among entrepreneurs in the Netherlands.*

Dijkhuizen, J., Gorgievski, M., van Veldhoven, M., & Schalk, R. (2018). Well-being, personal success and business performance among entrepreneurs: A two-wave study. *Journal of Happiness Studies*, 19(8), 2187–2204. DOI: 10.1007/s10902-017-9914-6

Dodd, S., Anderson, A., & Jack, S. (2023). "Let them not make me a stone"—Repositioning entrepreneurship. *Journal of Small Business Management*, 61(4), 1842–1870. DOI: 10.1080/00472778.2020.1867734

Dormann, C., & Griffin, M. A. (2015). Optimal time lags in panel studies. *Psychological Methods*, 20(4), 489–505. DOI: 10.1037/met0000041 PMID: 26322999

Drissi, N., Ouhbi, S., Idrissi, M., Fernández-Luque, L., & Ghogho, M. (2020). Connected mental health: Systematic mapping study. *Journal of Medical Internet Research*, 22(8), e19950. DOI: 10.2196/19950 PMID: 32857055

Drnovšek, M., Örtqvist, D., & Wincent, J. (2010). The effectiveness of coping strategies used by entrepreneurs and their impact on personal well-being and venture performance. *Zbornik radova Ekonomskog fakulteta u Rijeci: časopis za ekonomsku teoriju i praksu, 28*(2), 193-220.

Drnovšek, M., Örtqvist, D., & Wincent, J. (2010). The effectiveness of coping strategies used by entrepreneurs and their impact on personal well-being and venture performance. *Proceedings of Rijeka Faculty of Economics*, 28(2), 193–220.

Dsouza, A., & Panakaje, N. (2023). Factors Affecting Women Entrepreneurs' Success: A Study of Small and Medium-Sized Enterprises-A Review. *International Journal of Case Studies in Business* [IJCSBE]. *IT and Education*, 7(2), 51–89.

Du, G. (2024). Empowering teenage resilience: a mobile app for personalized mental health support in the post-covid era.. DOI: 10.5121/csit.2024.140805

DuBois, D., Holloway, B., Valentine, J., & Cooper, H. (2002). Effectiveness of mentoring programs for youth: A meta-analytic review. *American Journal of Community Psychology*, 30(2), 157–197. DOI: 10.1023/A:1014628810714 PMID: 12002242

Duchek, S. (2018). Entrepreneurial resilience: A biographical analysis of successful entrepreneurs. *The International Entrepreneurship and Management Journal*, 14(2), 429–455. DOI: 10.1007/s11365-017-0467-2

Dufouil, C., Pereira, E., Chêne, G., Glymour, M. M., Alpérovitch, A., Saubusse, E., Risse-Fleury, M., Heuls, B., Salord, J.-C., Brieu, M.-A., & Forette, F. (2014). Older age at retirement is associated with decreased risk of dementia. *European Journal of Epidemiology*, 29(5), 353–361. DOI: 10.1007/s10654-014-9906-3 PMID: 24791704

Durga, P., Godavarthi, D., Kant, S., & Basa, S. S. (2024). Aspect-based drug review classification through a hybrid model with ant colony optimization using deep learning. *Discov Computing*, 27(1), 19. DOI: 10.1007/s10791-024-09441-w

Durnali, M., Orakci, Ş., & Khalili, T. (2023). Fostering creative thinking skills to burst the effect of emotional intelligence on entrepreneurial skills. *Thinking Skills and Creativity*, 47, 101200. DOI: 10.1016/j.tsc.2022.101200

Duvvuri, V., Guan, Q., Daddala, S., Harris, M., & Kaushik, S. (2022, January 1). *Predicting depression symptoms from discord chat messaging using AI Medical Chatbots: Proceedings of the 2022 6th International Conference on Machine Learning and soft computing*. ACM Other conferences. https://dl.acm.org/doi/abs/10.1145/3523150.3523168

Eatough, E., Shockley, K., & Yu, P. (2016). A review of ambulatory health data collection methods for employee experience sampling research. *Applied Psychology*, 65(2), 322–354. DOI: 10.1111/apps.12068

Ebert, R. (1999). Office Space Movie Review & Film Summary (1999): Roger Ebert. movie review & film summary (1999) | Roger Ebert. https://www.rogerebert.com/reviews/office-space-1999

Eggers, F. (2020). Masters of disasters? Challenges and opportunities for SMEs in times of crisis. *Journal of Business Research*, 116, 199–208. DOI: 10.1016/j.jbusres.2020.05.025 PMID: 32501306

Ejike, O. (2024). Sustainability and project management: a dual approach for women entrepreneurs in event management. International Journal of Scholarly Research in Multidisciplinary Studies, 5(1), 024-031. DOI: 10.56781/ijsrms.2024.5.1.0036

Elshaer, I., Azazz, A., Mahmoud, S., & Ghanem, M. (2022). Perceived risk of job instability and unethical organizational behaviour amid the covid-19 pandemic: The role of family financial pressure and distributive injustice in the tourism industry. *International Journal of Environmental Research and Public Health*, 19(5), 2886. DOI: 10.3390/ijerph19052886 PMID: 35270579

Elst, K., Cock, D., Bangels, L., Peerlings, L., Doumen, M., Bertrand, D., & Verschueren, P. (2021). 'more than just chitchat': A qualitative study concerning the need and potential format of a peer mentor programme for patients with early rheumatoid arthritis. *RMD Open*, 7(3), e001795. DOI: 10.1136/rmdopen-2021-001795 PMID: 34611049

Emerson, L. M., De Diaz, N. N., Sherwood, A., Waters, A., & Farrell, L. (2020). Mindfulness interventions in schools: Integrity and feasibility of implementation. *International Journal of Behavioral Development*, 44(1), 62–75. DOI: 10.1177/0165025419866906

Emery, M., & Flora, C. (2020). Spiraling-up: Mapping community transformation with community capitals framework. In *50 Years of Community Development Vol I* (pp. 163-179). Routledge.

Engel, Y., Noordijk, S., Spoelder, A., & van Gelderen, M. (2021). Self-compassion when coping with venture obstacles: Loving-kindness meditation and entrepreneurial fear of failure. *Entrepreneurship Theory and Practice*, 45(2), 263–290. DOI: 10.1177/1042258719890991

Entrepreneurship & Regional Development, 30(7–8), 749–775. https://doi.org/. 2018. 14570DOI: 10.1080/08985 626

Esen, Ü., & Bulut, S. (2022). Determining the effect of emotional intelligence on self-leadership. *Journal of Business Management Review*, 3(8), 563–580. DOI: 10.47153/jbmr38.3972022

Evriani, T., & Fardana, N. A. (2024). How does the effectiveness of cognitive behavior therapy in reducing academic anxiety influence the academic procrastination of undergraduate students? *Buana Pendidikan Jurnal Fakultas Keguruan Dan Ilmu Pendidikan*, 20(1), 22–28. DOI: 10.36456/bp.vol20.no1.a8698

Farhan, F., & Rofi'ulmuiz, M. (2021). Religiosity and emotional intelligence on Muslim student learning achievement. [IJERE]. *International Journal of Evaluation and Research in Education*, 10(2), 404. DOI: 10.11591/ijere.v10i2.20997

Fedorova, Y., Pilková, A., Mikuš, J., Holienka, M., & Momot, D. (2024). *Measuring the emotional intelligence of entrepreneurs*. Publikacja/Publication. DOI: 10.18690/um.epf.5.2024.7

Feld, B., & Hathaway, I. (2020). *The Startup Community Way: Evolving an Entrepreneurial Ecosystem*. Wiley.

Feldman, M. P. (2014). The character of innovative places: Entrepreneurial strategy, economic development, and prosperity. *Small Business Economics*, 43(1), 9–20. DOI: 10.1007/s11187-014-9574-4

Feldman, M., Francis, J., & Bercovitz, J. (2005). Creating a cluster while building a firm: Entrepreneurs and the formation of industrial clusters. *Regional Studies*, 39(1), 129–141. DOI: 10.1080/0034340052000320888

Fernández-Bedoya, V., Meneses-La-Riva, M. E., Suyo-Vega, J. A., & Stephanie Gago-Chávez, J. J. (2023). Mental health problems of entrepreneurs during the covid-19 health crisis: Fear, anxiety, and stress. a systematic review. *F1000 Research*, 12, 1062. DOI: 10.12688/f1000research.139581.1

Ferrazzi, P., & Krupa, T. (2018). Remoteness and its impact on the potential for mental health initiatives in criminal courts in nunavut, canada. *International Journal of Circumpolar Health*, 77(1), 1541700. DOI: 10.1080/22423982.2018.1541700 PMID: 30384817

Finstad, G. L., Ariza-Montes, A., Giorgi, G., Lecca, L. I., Arcangeli, G., & Mucci, N. (2019). The JDCS Model and Blue-Collar Bullying: Decent Working Conditions for a Healthy Environment. *International Journal of Environmental Research and Public Health*, 16(18), 3411. DOI: 10.3390/ijerph16183411 PMID: 31540020

Fitzpatrick, J. M., Bianchi, L. A., Hayes, N., Da Silva, T., & Harris, R. (2023). Professional development and career planning for nurses working in care homes for older people: A scoping review. *International Journal of Older People Nursing*, 18, e12519. DOI: 10.1111/opn.12519

Foucault, M. (2008). *Madness and civilization: A history of insanity in the age of reason*. Routledge.

Foucault, M. (2013). *History of madness*. Taylor and Francis. DOI: 10.4324/9780203642603

Foucault, M., & Sheridan, A. M. (1973). *The Birth of the Clinic: An Archaeology of Medical Perception*. Routledge.

Frankfurt, H. G. (2005). *On bullshit*. Princeton University Press. DOI: 10.1515/9781400826537

Frishammar, J., Richtnér, A., Brattström, A., Magnusson, M., & Björk, J. (2019). Opportunities and challenges in the new innovation landscape: Implications for innovation auditing and innovation management. *European Management Journal*, 37(2), 151–164. DOI: 10.1016/j.emj.2018.05.002

Fritsch, M. (2013). New business formation and regional development: A survey and assessment of the evidence. *Foundations and Trends in Entrepreneurship*, 9(3), 249–364. Advance online publication. DOI: 10.1561/0300000043

Fritsch, M., & Mueller, P. (2004). Effects of new Business Formation on Regional Development Over Time. *Regional Studies*, 38(8), 961–975. DOI: 10.1080/0034340042000280965

Fritsch, M., & Storey, D. J. (2014). Entrepreneurship in a regional context: Historical roots, recent developments, and future challenges. *Regional Studies*, 48(6), 939–954. DOI: 10.1080/00343404.2014.892574

Fuller, M., Kamans, E., van Vuuren, M., Wolfensberger, M., & de Jong, M. D. (2021). Conceptualizing empathy competence: A professional communication perspective. *Journal of Business and Technical Communication*, 35(3), 333–368. DOI: 10.1177/10506519211001125

Gabay-Mariani, L., & Boissin, J. P. (2021). Commitment profiles of nascent entrepreneurs: Insights from an empirical taxonomy among French student entrepreneurs. *International Journal of Entrepreneurial Behaviour & Research*, 27(5), 1214–1240. DOI: 10.1108/IJEBR-09-2020-0652

Gabriel, A. S., Podsakoff, N. P., Beal, D. J., Scott, B. A., Sonnentag, S., Trougakos, J. P., & Butts, M. M. (2019). Experience sampling methods: A discussion of critical trends and considerations for scholarly advancement. *Organizational Research Methods*, 22(4), 969–1006. DOI: 10.1177/1094428118802626

Gabriel, K. P., & Aguinis, H. (2022). How to prevent and combat employee burnout and create healthier workplaces during crises and beyond. *Business Horizons*, 65(2), 183–192. DOI: 10.1016/j.bushor.2021.02.037

Galanis, P., Katsiroumpa, A., Vraka, I., Siskou, O., Konstantakopoulou, O., Katsoulas, T., & Graeber, D. (2019). *Bullshit jobs - the rise of pointless work, and what we can do about it*. Penguin Books Ltd.

Gampbell, J. T., & Pedersen, O. K. (Eds.). (1996). *Legacies of change: Transformations of postcommunist European economies*. New York: de Gruyter.

García-Martínez, J. A., Rosa-Napal, F. C., Romero-Tabeayo, I., López-Calvo, S., & Fuentes-Abeledo, E. J. (2020). Digital tools and personal learning environments: An analysis in higher education. *Sustainability (Basel)*, 12(19), 8180. DOI: 10.3390/su12198180

Garland, E. L., Farb, N. A., Goldin, P. R., & Fredrickson, B. L. (2015). The mindfulness-to-meaning theory: Extensions, applications, and challenges at the attention–appraisal–emotion interface. *Psychological Inquiry*, 26(4), 377–387. DOI: 10.1080/1047840X.2015.1092493 PMID: 27087765

Gavin, D., Gavin, J., & Quick, J. (2017). Power struggles within the top management team: An empirical examination of follower reactions to subversive leadership. *Journal of Applied Biobehavioral Research*, 22(4). Advance online publication. DOI: 10.1111/jabr.12100

Gbollie, E., Bantjes, J., Jarvis, L., Swandevelder, S., du Plessis, J., Shadwell, R., Davids, C., Gerber, R., Holland, N., & Hunt, X. (2023). Intention to use digital mental health solutions: A cross-sectional survey of university students attitudes and perceptions toward online therapy, mental health apps, and chatbots. *Digital Health*, 9, 20552076231216559. Advance online publication. DOI: 10.1177/20552076231216559 PMID: 38047161

Gelderen, M., Kibler, E., Kautonen, T., Muñoz, P., & Wincent, J. (2019). Mindfulness and taking action to start a new business. *Journal of Small Business Management*, 57(sup2), 489-506. https://doi.org/DOI: 10.1111/jsbm.12499

Genoa. InBates, R., Greif, A., Levi, M., Rosenthal, J. L., & Weingast, B. (Eds.), *Analytical Narratives: 23–63*. Princeton University Press.

Gérain, P., & Zech, E. (2021). Are caregiving appraisal and relationship quality key mediators in informal caregiving burnout? a structural equation modelling study in Belgium and France. *Health & Social Care in the Community*, 30(5). Advance online publication. DOI: 10.1111/hsc.13684

Gertler, M. S. (2010). Rules of the game: The place of institutions in regional economic change. *Regional Studies*, 44(1), 1–15. DOI: 10.1080/00343400903389979

Ghafoor, A., Qureshi, T. M., Khan, M. A., & Hijazi, S. T. (2011). Transformational leadership, employee engagement and performance: Mediating effect of psychological ownership. *African Journal of Business Management*, 5(17), 7391–7403. DOI: 10.5897/AJBM11.126

Ghasemi, A., & Zahediasl, S. (2012). Normality Tests for Statistical Analysis: A Guide for Non-Statisticians. *International Journal of Endocrinology and Metabolism*, 10(2), 486–489. DOI: 10.5812/ijem.3505 PMID: 23843808

Gilbreath, B., & Benson, P. G. (2004). The contribution of supervisor behaviour to employee psychological well-being. *Work and Stress*, 18(3), 255–266. DOI: 10.1080/02678370412331317499

Gjelsvik, M., & Trippl, M. (2018). Financial Organisations: An Overlooked Element in Regional Innovation Systems. In Isaksen, A., Martin, R., & Trippl, M. (Eds.), *New Avenues for Regional Innovation Systems–Theoretical Advances, Empirical Cases and Policy Lessons* (pp. 107–125). Springer International Publishing. DOI: 10.1007/978-3-319-71661-9_6

Goetz, L. H., & Schork, N. J. (2018). Personalized medicine: Motivation, challenges, and progress. *Fertility and Sterility*, 109(6), 952–963. DOI: 10.1016/j.fertnstert.2018.05.006 PMID: 29935653

Goldberg, R., Boss, R. W., Chan, L., Goldberg, J., Mallon, W. K., Moradzadeh, D., Goodman, E. A., & McConkie, M. L. (1996). Burnout and its correlates in emergency physicians: Four years' experience with a wellness booth. *Academic Emergency Medicine*, 3(12), 1156–1164. DOI: 10.1111/j.1553-2712.1996.tb03379.x PMID: 8959173

Gomes, H. S., Maia, Â., & Farrington, D. P. (2018). Measuring offending: Self-reports, official records, systematic observation and experimentation. *Crime Psychology Review*, 4(1), 26–44. DOI: 10.1080/23744006.2018.1475455

Gómez-Trinidad, M., Chimpén-López, C., Rodríguez-Santos, L., Moral, M., & Rodríguez-Mansilla, J. (2021). Resilience, emotional intelligence, and occupational performance in family members who are the caretakers of patients with dementia in spain: A cross-sectional, analytical, and descriptive study. *Journal of Clinical Medicine*, 10(18), 4262. DOI: 10.3390/jcm10184262

González-López, M. J., Pérez-López, M. C., & Rodríguez-Ariza, L. (2019). Clearing the hurdles in the entrepreneurial race: The role of resilience in entrepreneurship education. *Academy of Management Learning & Education*, 18(3), 457–483. DOI: 10.5465/amle.2016.0377

Goodrich, A. (2007). Peer mentoring in a high school jazz ensemble. *Journal of Research in Music Education*, 55(2), 94–114. DOI: 10.1177/002242940705500202

Gordon, J., & Schaller, T. (2014). The role of mindfulness in entrepreneurial market analysis. *Journal of Research in Marketing and Entrepreneurship*, 16(1), 7–25. DOI: 10.1108/JRME-02-2013-0005

Gorgievski, M. J., & Stephan, U. (2016). Advancing the psychology of entrepreneurship: A review of the psychological literature and an introduction. *Applied Psychology*, 65(3), 437–468. DOI: 10.1111/apps.12073

Gorgievski, M., Ascalon, M., & Stephan, U. (2011). Small business owners' success criteria, a values approach to personal differences. *Journal of Small Business Management*, 49(2), 207–232. DOI: 10.1111/j.1540-627X.2011.00322.x

Gorji, A. M. H., Ranjbar, M., & Darabiniya, M. (2016). Emotional Intelligence and Job Motivation of Member Faculties in Medical Sciences Universities. *International Journal of Advances in Agricultural & Environmental Engineering*, 3(2). Advance online publication. DOI: 10.15242/ijaaee.a0516001

Graham, S. (2019). *A history of the bildungsroman*. Cambridge University Press. DOI: 10.1017/9781316479926

Granovetter, M. (1992). Economic institutions as social constructions: A framework for analysis. *Acta Sociologica*, 35(1), 3–11. DOI: 10.1177/000169939203500101

Grawitch, M. J., Gottschalk, M., & Munz, D. C. (2006). The path to a healthy workplace: A critical review linking healthy workplace practices, employee well-being, and organizational improvements. *Consulting Psychology Journal*, 58(3), 129–147. DOI: 10.1037/1065-9293.58.3.129

Grecucci, A., Pisapia, N., Thero, D., Paladino, M., Venuti, P., & Job, R. (2015). Baseline and strategic effects behind mindful emotion regulation: Behavioral and physiological investigation. *PLoS One*, 10(1), e0116541. DOI: 10.1371/journal.pone.0116541

Greene, D. (2014). *The American worker on film: A critical history, 1909-1999*. McFarland.

Greif, A. (1998) Self-enforcing political systems and economic growth: Late medieval

Greiser, C., & Martini, J. P. (2018). Unleashing the power of mindfulness in corporations. [BCG]. *The Boston Consulting Group*, 15(2), 109–122.

Guercini, S., & Cova, B. (2018). Unconventional entrepreneurship. *Journal of Business Research*, 92, 385–391. DOI: 10.1016/j.jbusres.2018.06.021

Guidetti, G., Cortini, M., Fantinelli, S., Di Fiore, T., & Galanti, T. (2022). Safety Management and Wellbeing during COVID-19: A Pilot Study in the Manufactory Sector. *International Journal of Environmental Research and Public Health*, 19(7), 3981. DOI: 10.3390/ijerph19073981 PMID: 35409664

Guo, X., Guo, X., Wang, R., & Zhang, Y. (2022). Effects of perinatal cognitive behavioral therapy on delivery mode, fetal outcome, and postpartum depression and anxiety in women. *Computational and Mathematical Methods in Medicine*, 2022, 1–8. DOI: 10.1155/2022/8304405 PMID: 36199781

Gursoy, D., & Chi, C. G. (2020). Effects of COVID-19 pandemic on hospitality industry: Review of the current situations and a research agenda. *Journal of Hospitality Marketing & Management*, 29(5), 527–529. DOI: 10.1080/19368623.2020.1788231

Guthrie, D. (1999). *Dragon in a three-piece suit: The emergence of capitalism in China*. Princeton University Press. DOI: 10.1515/9781400823383

Guyo, D. M., Kero, C. A., & Kant, S. (2025). Is Marketing Intermediaries' Mediation Required for Livestock and Products Marketing to Improve the Economic Status of Pastoralist Communities in Ethiopia? In *AI in Agriculture for Sustainable and Economic Management* (pp. 216-234). CRC Press.

Guyo, K., & Kero, C. A. "Mediation of Marketing Intermediaries and AI Adoption Between Livestock Products Marketing and Economic Status of Pastoralist in Ethiopia," *2023 International Conference on Communication, Security and Artificial Intelligence (ICCSAI)*, Greater Noida, India, 2023, pp. 311-316, https://doi.org/DOI: 10.1109/ICCSAI59793.2023.10421261

Haddock-Millar, J., & Tom, E. (2019). *Coaching and mentoring for work-life balance*. Taylor and Francis.

Hahn, V. C., Frese, M., Binnewies, C., & Schmitt, A. (2012). Happy and proactive? The role of hedonic and eudaimonic well-being in business owners' personal initiative. *Entrepreneurship Theory and Practice*, 36(1), 97–114. DOI: 10.1111/j.1540-6520.2011.00490.x

Haider, Z., & Dasti, R. (2022). Mentoring, research self-efficacy, work–life balance and psychological well-being of doctoral program students. *International Journal of Mentoring and Coaching in Education*, 11(2), 170–182. DOI: 10.1108/IJMCE-07-2020-0036

Hair, J., Black, W., Babin, B., & Anderson, R. (2010). *Multivariate data analysis*. Prentice-Hall.

Halbesleben, J. R., & Wheeler, A. R. (2015). To invest or not? The role of coworker support and trust in daily reciprocal gain spirals of helping behavior. *Journal of Management*, 41(6), 1628–1650. DOI: 10.1177/0149206312455246

Hallonsten, O. (2023). We're All Entrepreneurs Now. In *Empty Innovation: Causes and Consequences of Society's Obsession with Entrepreneurship and Growth* (pp. 47–59). Springer International Publishing. DOI: 10.1007/978-3-031-31479-7_4

Haltiwanger, J., Jarmin, R. S., & Miranda, J. (2013). Who creates jobs? Small versus large versus young. *The Review of Economics and Statistics*, 95(2), 347–361. Advance online publication. DOI: 10.1162/REST_a_00288

Hameed, I., & Irfan, Z. (2019). Entrepreneurship education: A review of challenges, characteristics and opportunities. *Entrepreneurship Education*, 2(3), 135–148. DOI: 10.1007/s41959-019-00018-z

Hammett, R. D., Arenas, F., & Scherer, J. (2018). Facilitating full-range leadership with emotional intelligence in the USAF Squadron Officer College. The International Journal of Transformative Emotional Intelligence, 5.

Hammett, R. D., Hollon, C., & Maggard, P. (2011). Professional military education in the USAF SOS leadership course: Incorporating emotional intelligence. *The International Journal of Transformative Emotional Intelligence*, 1, 73–96. http://eitri.org/2015/11/13/professional-military-education- pme-in-the-usaf-sos-leadership-course-incorporating-emotional-intelligence/

Hamouche, S. (2020). COVID-19 and employees' mental health: Stressors, moderators and agenda for organizational actions. *Emerald Open Research*, 2(2), 15. DOI: 10.1108/EOR-02-2023-0004

Handa, P., Pagani, J., & Bedford, D. (2019). *Knowledge Assets and Knowledge Audits*. Emerald. DOI: 10.1108/9781789737714

Hannigan, T. R., Briggs, A. R., Valadao, R., Seidel, M. D. L., & Jennings, P. D. (2021). A new tool for policymakers: Mapping cultural possibilities in an emerging AI entrepreneurial ecosystem. *Research Policy*. Advance online publication. DOI: 10.1016/j.respol.2021.104315

Hansen, A., Buitendach, J., & Kanengoni, H. (2015). Psychological capital, subjective well-being, burnout and job satisfaction amongst educators in the umlazi region in south africa. *SA Journal of Human Resource Management*, 13(1). Advance online publication. DOI: 10.4102/sajhrm.v13i1.621

Hansson, J., Landstad, B. J., Vinberg, S., Hedlund, M., & Tjulin, Å. (2022). Small business managers and Covid-19—The role of a sense of coherence and general resistance resources in coping with stressors. *PLoS One*, 17(3), e0265029. DOI: 10.1371/journal.pone.0265029 PMID: 35302995

Harms, R., & Groen, A. (2017). Loosen up? Cultural tightness and national entrepreneurial activity Technological. *Technological Forecasting and Social Change*, 121, 196–204. DOI: 10.1016/j.techfore.2016.04.013

Harter, J. (2023, November 6). Is quiet quitting real? Gallup.com. https://www.gallup.com/workplace/398306/quiet-quitting-real.aspx

Hartl, G. (2001). *The World Health Report 2001: Mental disorders affect One in four people*. World Health Organization. https://www.who.int/news/item/28-09-2001-the-world-health-report-2001-mental-disorders-affect-one-in-four-people

Hartmann, S., Backmann, J., Newman, A., Brykman, K. M., & Pidduck, R. J. (2022). Psychological resilience of entrepreneurs: A review and agenda for future research. *Journal of Small Business Management*, 60(5), 1041–1079. DOI: 10.1080/00472778.2021.2024216

Hassan, N., Maon, S., & Kassim, E. (2018). Mental health predictors among malaysians during economic crisis: the 3fs influence.. DOI: 10.33422/8mea.2018.11.56

Hassannezhad, Z., Zali, M., Faghih, N., Hejazi, R., & Mobini, A. (2020). A process model of entrepreneurial alertness among technopreneurs. *International Business Research*, 13(3), 96. DOI: 10.5539/ibr.v13n3p96

Hechavarría, D. M., & Ingram, A. E. (2019). Entrepreneurial ecosystem conditions and gendered national-level entrepreneurial activity: A 14-year panel study of GEM. *Small Business Economics*, 53(2), 431–458. DOI: 10.1007/s11187-018-9994-7

Hechter, M. (1987). *Principles of Group Solidarity*. University of California Press.

Hedner, T., Abouzeedan, A., & Klofsten, M. (2011). Entrepreneurial resilience. *Annals of Innovation & Entrepreneurship*, 2(1), 7986. DOI: 10.3402/aie.v2i1.6002

Heigermoser, D., de Soto, B. G., Abbott, E. L. S., & Chua, D. K. H. (2019). BIM-based Last Planner System tool for improving construction project management. *Automation in Construction*, 104, 246–254. DOI: 10.1016/j.autcon.2019.03.019

Hernandez, R., Bassett, S. M., Boughton, S. W., Schuette, S. A., Shiu, E. W., & Moskowitz, J. T. (2018). Psychological well-being and physical health: Associations, mechanisms, and future directions. *Emotion Review*, 10(1), 18–29. DOI: 10.1177/1754073917697824 PMID: 36650890

Hess, F. M. (Ed.). (2006). *Educational entrepreneurship: Realities, challenges, possibilities*. Harvard Education Press.

Hidalgo, C. A., Balland, P.-A., Boschma, R., Delgado, M., Feldman, M. P., Frenken, K., & Zhu, S. (2018). The principle of relatedness. In Morales, A. J., Gershenson, C., Braha, D., Minai, A. A., & Bar-Yam, Y. (Eds.), *Unifying themes in complex systems* (Vol. IX). Springer. DOI: 10.1007/978-3-319-96661-8_46

Hoert, J., Herd, A. M., & Hambrick, M. (2018). The role of leadership support for health promotion in employee wellness program participation, perceived job stress, and health behaviors. *American Journal of Health Promotion*, 32(4), 1054–1061. DOI: 10.1177/0890117116677798 PMID: 27920214

Hofmann, S., Wu, J., & Boettcher, H. (2014). Effect of cognitive-behavioral therapy for anxiety disorders on quality of life: A meta-analysis. *Journal of Consulting and Clinical Psychology*, 82(3), 375–391. DOI: 10.1037/a0035491 PMID: 24447006

Högnäs, R., & Magnusson Hanson, L. (2020). Workplace violence and all-cause mortality. *European Journal of Public Health*, 30(Supplement_5), ckaa166.1200. Advance online publication. DOI: 10.1093/eurpub/ckaa166.1200

Holman, D., Johnson, S., & O'Connor, E. (2018). Stress management interventions: Improving subjective psychological well-being in the workplace. *Handbook of well-being*, 1-13.

Horn, D., Randle, N. W., & McNeil, S. R. (2020). A cross-disciplinary framework to measure workplace wellness program success. *S.A.M. Advanced Management Journal*, 85(1), 4–12.

Horowitz, A. (n.d.). Asher Horowitz: Department of political science: Faculty of liberal arts and professional studies: York University. Asher Horowitz | Department of Political Science | Faculty of Liberal Arts and Professional Studies | York University. https://www.yorku.ca/horowitz/courses/lectures/35_marx_alienation.html

Horta Reis Da Silva, T. (2022a). Muskuloskeletal minor injuries: assessment and treatment. In Curr, S., & Fordham-Clarke, C. (Eds.), *Clinical Skills at Glance* (1st ed., pp. 128–129). Wiley. [55]

Hosker, D. K., Elkins, R. M., & Potter, M. P. (2019). Promoting mental health and wellness in youth through physical activity, nutrition, and sleep. *Child and Adolescent Psychiatric Clinics of North America*, 28(2), 171–193. DOI: 10.1016/j.chc.2018.11.010 PMID: 30832951

Hosseininia, G., Aliabadi, V., Karimi, H., & Ataei, P. (2024). The interaction between exploratory behaviours and entrepreneurial opportunity recognition by agriculture students: The mediating role of strategic learning and mindfulness. *Innovations in Education and Teaching International*, 61(4), 649–664. DOI: 10.1080/14703297.2023.2192511

Huang, X. (2023). The roles of competition on innovation efficiency and firm performance: Evidence from the Chinese manufacturing industry. *European Research on Management and Business Economics*, 29(1), 100201. DOI: 10.1016/j.iedeen.2022.100201

Huffington, A. (2022, August 16). Arianna Huffington on linkedin: #joyfuljoining #work #culture: 753 comments. Arianna Huffington on LinkedIn: #joyfuljoining #work #culture | 753 comments. https://www.linkedin.com/posts/ariannahuffington_joyfuljoining-work-culture-activity6965397668625805312wsOR/?utm_source=share&utm_medium=member_de sktop

Hwang, J. H., & Jung, H. S. (2021). The effects of work characteristics related to work–life imbalance on presenteeism among female workers in the health and social work sectors: Mediation analysis of psychological and physical health problems. *International Journal of Environmental Research and Public Health*, 18(12), 6218. DOI: 10.3390/ijerph18126218 PMID: 34201286

Hwang, W., Ha, J., & Kim, M. (2021). Research trends on mobile mental health application for general population: A scoping review. *International Journal of Environmental Research and Public Health*, 18(5), 2459. DOI: 10.3390/ijerph18052459 PMID: 33801537

Iacobucci, D., & Perugini, F. (2021). Entrepreneurial ecosystems and economic resilience at local level. *Entrepreneurship and Regional Development*, 33(9-10), 689–716. Advance online publication. DOI: 10.1080/08985626.2021.1888318

Indrianti, Y., Abdinagoro, S. B., & Rahim, R. K. (2024). A resilient startup leader's personal journey: The role of entrepreneurial mindfulness and ambidextrous leadership through scaling-up performance capacity. *Heliyon*, 10(14), e34285. DOI: 10.1016/j.heliyon.2024.e34285 PMID: 39113945

Ingram, A., Peake, W. O., Stewart, W., & Watson, W. (2019). Emotional intelligence and venture performance. *Journal of Small Business Management*, 57(3), 780–800. DOI: 10.1111/jsbm.12333

Inzer, L., & Crawford, C. (2005). A review of formal and informal mentoring: Processes, problems, and design. *Journal of Leadership Education*, 4(1), 31–50. DOI: 10.12806/V4/I1/TF2

Iram, T., Bilal, A., Ahmad, Z., & Latif, S. (2022). Does financial mindfulness make a difference? A nexus of financial literacy and behavioural biases in women entrepreneurs. *IIM Kozhikode Society & Management Review*, 12(1), 7–21. DOI: 10.1177/22779752221097194

Irfan, M., Khalid, R. A., Kaka Khel, S. S. U. H., Maqsoom, A., & Sherani, I. K. (2023). Impact of work–life balance with the role of organizational support and job burnout on project performance. *Engineering, Construction, and Architectural Management*, 30(1), 154–171. DOI: 10.1108/ECAM-04-2021-0316

Isenberg, D., & Brown, R. (2014) For a booming economy, bet on high-growth firms, Not Small Businesses. Babson Entrepreneurship Ecosystem Project. Retrieved from http://blogs.hbr.org/2014/02/for-a-booming-economy-bet-on-high-growth-firms-not-small-businesses/

Isenberg, D. (2011). *The Entrepreneurship Ecosystem Strategy as a New Paradigm for Economic Policy: Principles for Cultivating Entrepreneurship.* Presentation at the Institute of International and European Affairs.

Isenberg, D., & Onyemah, V. (2016). Fostering scaleup ecosystems for regional economic growth (innovations case narrative: Manizales-Mas and Scale Up Milwaukee. *Innov. Technol. Governance. Innovations: Technology, Governance, Globalization*, 11(1-2), 60–79. DOI: 10.1162/inov_a_00248

Islam, M. S., Aso, K. A., & Azizzadeh, F. (2023). Workplace Bullying Causes Employee Turnover: A Responsible Human Resource Management Approach. *The International Journal of Organizational Diversity*, 23(2), 17–36. DOI: 10.18848/2328-6261/CGP/v23i02/17-36

Iyengar, S. S., & Lepper, M. R. (2000). When choice is demotivating: Can one desire too much of a good thing? *Journal of Personality and Social Psychology*, 79(6), 995–1005. DOI: 10.1037/0022-3514.79.6.995 PMID: 11138768

Jabo, B., & Kant, S. "Impact of Technical CRM on Ethiopia Bank Human-Computer Interface and Competitive Advantage as Mediators of Performance," *2024 IEEE International Conference on Computing, Power and Communication Technologies (IC2PCT)*, Greater Noida, India, 2024, pp. 679-682, https://doi.org/DOI: 10.1109/IC2PCT60090.2024.10486237

Jakupčević, K., Ercegovac, I., & Dobrota, S. (2021). Music as a tool for mood regulation: The role of absorption vs. mindfulness. *Primenjena Psihologija*, 14(2), 229–248. DOI: 10.19090/pp.2021.2.229-248

Jansson, N., Ahokangas, P., Iivari, M., Perälä-Heape, M., & Salo, S. (2014). The competitive advantage of an ecosystemic business model: The case of OuluHealth. *Interdisciplinary Studies Journal*, 3(4), 282–295.

Jiang, Y., Zilioli, S., Balzarini, R., Zoppolat, G., & Slatcher, R. (2021). Education, financial stress, and trajectory of mental health during the covid-19 pandemic. DOI: 10.31234/osf.io/tvry4

Jiang, Y., Zilioli, S., Balzarini, R., Zoppolat, G., & Slatcher, R. (2021). Education, financial stress, and trajectory of mental health during the covid-19 pandemic. *Clinical Psychological Science*, 10(4), 662–674. DOI: 10.1177/21677026211049374

Jiang, Z., & Park, D. (2012). Career decision-making self-efficacy as a moderator in the relationships of entrepreneurial career intention with emotional intelligence and cultural intelligence. *African Journal of Business Management*, 6(30). Advance online publication. DOI: 10.5897/ajbm11.1816

Jiménez-Ortiz, J. L., Islas-Valle, R. M., Jiménez-Ortiz, J. D., Pérez-Lizarraga, E., Hernández-García, M. E., & González-Salazar, F. (2019). Emotional exhaustion, burnout, and perceived stress in dental students. *The Journal of International Medical Research*, 47(9), 4251–4259. DOI: 10.1177/0300060519859145 PMID: 31311371

Jing, T., Dancheng, L., & Ye, Z. (2016). Study of impact on undergraduates' entrepreneurial failure based on the model of psychological resilience-knowledge acquisition. *English Language Teaching*, 9(8), 224–230. DOI: 10.5539/elt.v9n8p224

Johansson Sevä, I., Larsson, D., & Strandh, M. (2016). The prevalence, characteristics and well-being of "necessity" self-employed and "latent" entrepreneurs: Findings from Sweden. *International Journal of Entrepreneurship and Small Business*, 28(1), 58–77. DOI: 10.1504/IJESB.2016.075682

Jones, D., Molitor, D., & Reif, J. (2019). What do workplace wellness programs do? Evidence from the Illinois workplace wellness study. *The Quarterly Journal of Economics*, 134(4), 1747–1791. DOI: 10.1093/qje/qjz023 PMID: 31564754

Judge, T. A., & Kammeyer-Mueller, J. D. (2012). Job attitudes. *Annual Review of Psychology*, 63(1), 341–367. DOI: 10.1146/annurev-psych-120710-100511 PMID: 22129457

Kadowaki, H., Kayano, T., Tobinaga, T., Tsusumi, A., Watari, M., & Makita, K. (2016). Analysis of factors associated with hesitation to restart farming after depopulation of animals due to 2010 foot-and-mouth disease epidemic in Japan. *The Journal of Veterinary Medical Science*, 78(8), 1251–1259. DOI: 10.1292/jvms.15-0559 PMID: 27149890

Kaimal, G., Vidhukumar, K., & Padmam, M. (2021). Delinquent behaviour and emotional intelligence among inmates of juvenile homes in Kerala, India. *Kerala Journal of Psychiatry*, 34(1). Advance online publication. DOI: 10.30834/kjp.34.1.2021.230

Kaiser, H. (1974). An index of factorial simplicity. *Psychometrika*, 39(1), 31–36. DOI: 10.1007/BF02291575

Kallioniemi, M. K., Simola, A., Kaseva, J., & Kymäläinen, H.-R. (2016). Stress and burnout among Finnish dairy farmers. *Journal of Agromedicine*, 21(3), 259–268. DOI: 10.1080/1059924X.2016.1178611 PMID: 27081893

Kamberidou, I. (2020). "Distinguished" women entrepreneurs in the digital economy and the multitasking whirlpool. *Journal of Innovation and Entrepreneurship*, 9(3).

Kandilige, L., Teye, J. K., Setrana, M., & Badasu, D. M. (2023). 'They'd beat us with whatever is available to them': Exploitation and abuse of Ghanaian domestic workers in the Middle East. *International Migration (Geneva, Switzerland)*, 61(4), 240–256. DOI: 10.1111/imig.13096

Kang, Q., Li, H., Cheng, Y., & Kraus, S. (2019). Entrepreneurial ecosystems: Analysing the status quo. *Knowledge Management Research and Practice*, 19(1), 8–20. DOI: 10.1080/14778238.2019.1701964

Kant, S., & Adula, M. (2024). AI Learning and Work Attitude Mediation Between Reward and Organizational Support in Ethiopia. In Gomathi Sankar, J., & David, A. (Eds.), *Generative AI for Transformational Management* (pp. 109–136). IGI Global., DOI: 10.4018/979-8-3693-5578-7.ch005

Kant, S., & Adula, M. (2024). Human-Machine Interaction in the Metaverse in the Context of Ethiopia. In *Impact and Potential of Machine Learning in the Metaverse* (pp. 196–212). IGI Global., DOI: 10.4018/979-8-3693-5762-0.ch008

Karali, N., Mastrokoukou, S., & Livas, C. (2023). Mindful minds and entrepreneurial spirits in higher education: A scoping review. *Frontiers in Education*, 8, 1291845. Advance online publication. DOI: 10.3389/feduc.2023.1291845

Karimi, H., & Ataei, P. (2023). The effect of entrepreneurship ecosystem on the entrepreneurial skills of agriculture students: The mediating role of social intelligence and emotional intelligence (The case of University of Zabol, Iran). *Current Psychology (New Brunswick, N.J.)*, 42(27), 23250–23264. DOI: 10.1007/s12144-022-03479-z PMID: 35854700

Karimi, S., & Reisi, S. (2023). Satisfaction of psychological needs and entrepreneurial success: Mediating effects of well-being and work engagement (Case study: Nahavand County, Iran). *Journal of Agricultural Science and Technology*, 25(4), 847–862.

Karman, A. (2020). Flexibility, coping capacity and resilience of organizations: Between synergy and support. *Journal of Organizational Change Management*, 33(5), 883–907. DOI: 10.1108/JOCM-10-2019-0305

Kato, K., Matsumoto, Y., & Hirano, Y. (2022). Effectiveness of school-based brief cognitive behavioral therapy with mindfulness in improving the mental health of adolescents in a japanese school setting: A preliminary study. *Frontiers in Psychology*, 13. Advance online publication. DOI: 10.3389/fpsyg.2022.895086

Kauffman, J. M., & Badar, J. (Eds.). (2022). *Navigating students' mental health in the wake of COVID-19: Using public health crises to inform research and practice*. Taylor & Francis. DOI: 10.4324/9781003264033

Keim, A. C., Landis, R. S., Pierce, C. A., & Earnest, D. R. (2014). Why do employees worry about their jobs? A meta-analytic review of predictors of job insecurity. *Journal of Occupational Health Psychology*, 19(3), 269–290. DOI: 10.1037/a0036743 PMID: 24796228

Kelliher, C., Richardson, J., & Boiarintseva, G. (2019). All of work? All of life? Reconceptualising work-life balance for the 21st century. *Human Resource Management Journal*, 29(2), 97–112. DOI: 10.1111/1748-8583.12215

Kelloway, E. K., & Barling, J. (2010). Leadership development as an intervention in occupational health psychology. *Work and Stress*, 24(3), 260–279. DOI: 10.1080/02678373.2010.518441

Kell, S. (2024). University Students' Perceptions of a 30-Minute Break during Class: A Realistic Practice for Wellness? *Teaching & Learning Inquiry*, 12, 12. DOI: 10.20343/teachlearninqu.12.17

Kelly, L., & Dorian, M. (2017). Doing well and good: An exploration of the role of mindfulness in the entrepreneurial opportunity recognition and evaluation process. *New England Journal of Entrepreneurship*, 20(2), 26–36. DOI: 10.1108/NEJE-20-02-2017-B002

Khalid, A., Bashir, M., & Saqib, S. (2018). Collective impact of entrepreneurial self-efficacy and risk propensity on entrepreneurial intentions; mediating role of perceived social support. International Journal of Engineering & Technology, 7(3.21), 24. DOI: 10.14419/ijet.v7i3.21.17087

Khalid, U. B., Naeem, M., Stasolla, F., Syed, M. H., Abbas, M., & Coronato, A. (2024). Impact of AI-powered solutions in rehabilitation process: Recent improvements and future trends. *International Journal of General Medicine*, 17, 943–969. DOI: 10.2147/IJGM.S453903 PMID: 38495919

Khalil, R., Godde, B., & Karim, A. A. (2019). The link between creativity, cognition, and creative drives and underlying neural mechanisms. *Frontiers in Neural Circuits*, 13, 18. DOI: 10.3389/fncir.2019.00018 PMID: 30967763

Khammissa, R. A., Nemutandani, S., Feller, G., Lemmer, J., & Feller, L. (2022). Burnout phenomenon: Neurophysiological factors, clinical features, and aspects of management. *The Journal of International Medical Research*, 50(9), 03000605221106428. DOI: 10.1177/03000605221106428 PMID: 36113033

Khan, F., Siddiqui, M., Imtiaz, S., Shaikh, S., Tu, Y., & Wu, C. (2022). Determinants of mental and financial health during covid-19: Evidence from data of a developing country. *Frontiers in Public Health*, 10, 888741. Advance online publication. DOI: 10.3389/fpubh.2022.888741 PMID: 36117608

Khatri, S. (2018). Emotional intelligence in adolescents and its implications on their lifelong development. *International Journal of Indian Psychology*, 6(4). Advance online publication. DOI: 10.25215/0604.057

Khong, B. S. L. (2009). Expanding the understanding of mindfulness: Seeing the tree and the forest. *The Humanistic Psychologist*, 37(2), 117–136. DOI: 10.1080/08873260902892006

Kiefl, S., Fischer, S., & Schmitt, J. (2024). Self-employed and stressed out? the impact of stress and stress management on entrepreneurs' mental health and performance. *Frontiers in Psychology*, 15, 1365489. Advance online publication. DOI: 10.3389/fpsyg.2024.1365489 PMID: 38638509

Kildal, E., Stadskleiv, K., Boysen, E., Øderud, T., Dahl, I., Seeberg, T., & Hassel, B. (2021). Increased heart rate functions as a signal of acute distress in non-communicating persons with intellectual disability. *Scientific Reports*, 11(1). Advance online publication. DOI: 10.1038/s41598-021-86023-6

Kim, J., & Lee, J. C. (2020). Effects of COVID-19 on preferences for private dining facilities in restaurants. *Journal of Hospitality and Tourism Management*, 45, 67–70. DOI: 10.1016/j.jhtm.2020.07.008

Kim, J., Lee, M., & Lee, J. (2022). The effects of entrepreneurs' optimism and mindfulness on psychological well-being. *International Academy of Global Business and Trade*, 18(4), 123–137. DOI: 10.20294/jgbt.2022.18.4.123

Kim, K., Cundiff, N., & Choi, S. (2014). The influence of emotional intelligence on negotiation outcomes and the mediating effect of rapport: A structural equation modeling approach. *Negotiation Journal*, 30(1), 49–68. DOI: 10.1111/nejo.12045

Kim, K., Kim, J., Antonio, J., & Laws, J. (2021). Emotional intelligence, trust, and functional behavior: Longitudinal study of achievement approach to leadership emergence. *Journal of Organizational Psychology*, 21(4). Advance online publication. DOI: 10.33423/jop.v21i4.4552

King'ong'o, G. W. (2022). *Indigenous Entrepreneurship, Post-Conflict Reconstruction And Globalization Dynamics On Economic Development: A Case Of The Micro And Small Livestock Enterprises In Turkana County, Kenya* (Doctoral dissertation, University of Nairobi).

Kirzner, I. M. (2009). The alert and creative entrepreneur: A clarification. *Small Business Economics*, 32(2), 145–152. DOI: 10.1007/s11187-008-9153-7

Kniffin, K. M., Narayanan, J., Anseel, F., Antonakis, J., Ashford, S. P., Bakker, A. B., Bamberger, P., Bapuji, H., Bhave, D. P., Choi, V. K., Creary, S. J., Demerouti, E., Flynn, F. J., Gelfand, M. J., Greer, L. L., Johns, G., Kesebir, S., Klein, P. G., Lee, S. Y., & Vugt, M. V. (2021). COVID-19 and the workplace: Implications, issues, and insights for future research and action. *The American Psychologist*, 76(1), 63–77. DOI: 10.1037/amp0000716 PMID: 32772537

Komalasari, R. (2024). AI-Powered Wearables Revolutionizing Health Tracking and Personalized Wellness Management. *Timor Leste Journal of Business and Management*, 6, 42–50.

Kothgassner, O. D., Goreis, A., Kafka, J. X., Kaufmann, M., Atteneder, K., Beutl, L., Hennig-Fast, K., Hlavacs, H., & Felnhofer, A. (2019). Virtual social support buffers stress response: An experimental comparison of real-life and virtual support prior to a social stressor. *Journal of Behavior Therapy and Experimental Psychiatry*, 63, 57–65. DOI: 10.1016/j.jbtep.2018.11.003 PMID: 30454876

Koutsioumpa, E. (2023). Contribution of emotional intelligence to efficient leadership. a narrative review. *Technium Social Sciences Journal*, 48, 204–216. DOI: 10.47577/tssj.v48i1.9529

Kreiner, G. E., Hollensbe, E. C., & Sheep, M. L. (2009). Balancing borders and bridges: Negotiating the work-home interface via boundary work tactics. *Academy of Management Journal*, 52(4), 704–730. DOI: 10.5465/amj.2009.43669916

Krejcie, R. V., & Morgan, D. W. (1970). Determining sample size for research activities. *Educational and Psychological Measurement*, 30(3), 607–610. DOI: 10.1177/001316447003000308

Kring-Schreifels, J. (2019) Follow the path of least resistance: An oral history of 'office space', The Ringer. Available at: https://www.theringer.com/movies/2019/2/19/18228613/office-space-oral-history (Accessed: 30 August 2024).

Kritikos, A. S. (2015). *Entrepreneurship and Economic Growth. International Encyclopedia of the Social & Behavioral Sciences* (2nd ed., Vol. 7). Elsevier.

Kubzansky, L. D., Huffman, J. C., Boehm, J. K., Hernandez, R., Kim, E. S., Koga, H. K., Feig, E. H., Lloyd-Jones, D. M., Seligman, M. E. P., & Labarthe, D. R. (2018). Positive psychological well-being and cardiovascular disease: JACC health promotion series. *Journal of the American College of Cardiology*, 72(12), 1382–1396. DOI: 10.1016/j.jacc.2018.07.042 PMID: 30213332

Kuhn, K. M., Meijerink, J., & Keegan, A. (2021). Human resource management and the gig economy: Challenges and opportunities at the intersection between organizational HR decision-makers and digital labor platforms. *Research in Personnel and Human Resources Management*, 39, 1–46. DOI: 10.1108/S0742-730120210000039001

Kulkarni, A., & Mishra, M. (2022). Aspects of women's leadership in the organisation: Systematic literature review. *SA Journal of Human Resource Management*, 9(1), 9–32.

Kumar, A., & Ayedee, D. (2021). Technology adoption: A solution for SMEs to overcome problems during COVID-19. Forthcoming. *Academy of Marketing Studies Journal*, 25(1).

Kumar, A., Mandal, M., & Yadav, U. S. (2022). Motivation and challenges in career choice and well being of women entrepreneurs; experiences of small businesses of Lucknow, Uttar Pradesh. *Journal of Positive School Psychology*, ●●●, 10890–10906.

Kumar, P., Kumar, N., Aggarwal, P., & Yeap, J. A. (2021). Working in lockdown: The relationship between COVID-19 induced work stressors, job performance, distress, and life satisfaction. *Current Psychology (New Brunswick, N.J.)*, 40(12), 6308–6323. DOI: 10.1007/s12144-021-01567-0 PMID: 33746462

Kurtulmuş, B. E. (2020). Toxic leadership and workplace bullying: The role of followers and possible coping strategies. The Palgrave Handbook of Workplace Well-Being, 1–20. DOI: 10.1007/978-3-030-02470-3_24-1

Labrague, L. J., & Santos, J. D. L. (2020). Fear of COVID-19, psychological distress, work satisfaction and turnover intention among front line nurses. *Research Square*, 1–18. DOI: 10.21203/rs.3.rs-35366/v1

Lafuente, E., Acs, Z. J., Sanders, M., & Szerb, L. (2019). The global technology frontier: Productivity growth and the relevance of Kirznerian and Schumpeterian entrepreneurship. *Small Business Economics*, 55(1), 153–178. DOI: 10.1007/s11187-019-00140-1

Lafuente, E., Szerb, L., & Acs, Z. J. (2016). Country level efficiency and national systems of entrepreneurship: A data envelopment analysis approach. *The Journal of Technology Transfer*, 41(6), 1260–1283. DOI: 10.1007/s10961-015-9440-9

Lafuente, E., Vaillant, Y., Vendrell-Herrero, F., & Gomes, E. (2019). Bouncing back from failure: Entrepreneurial resilience and the internationalization of subsequent ventures created by serial entrepreneurs. *Applied Psychology*, 68(4), 658–694. DOI: 10.1111/apps.12175

Lan, X., Liang, Y., Wu, G., & Ye, H. (2021). Relationships among job burnout, generativity concern, and subjective well-being: A moderated mediation model. *Frontiers in Psychology*, 12, 613767. Advance online publication. DOI: 10.3389/fpsyg.2021.613767 PMID: 33716877

Lattie, E. G., Adkins, E. C., Winquist, N., Stiles-Shields, C., Wafford, Q. E., & Graham, A. K. (2019). Digital mental health interventions for depression, anxiety, and enhancement of psychological well-being among college students: Systematic review. *Journal of Medical Internet Research*, 21(7), e12869. DOI: 10.2196/12869 PMID: 31333198

Le Breton–Miller, I., & Miller, D. (2006). Why do some family businesses out–compete? Governance, long–term orientations, and sustainable capability. *Entrepreneurship Theory and Practice*, 30(6), 731–746. DOI: 10.1111/j.1540-6520.2006.00147.x

Lechmann, D. S. J., & Schnabel, C. (2014). Absence from work of the self-employed: A comparison with paid employees. *Kyklos*, 67(3), 368–390. DOI: 10.1111/kykl.12059

Lee, J., Lim, J. J., & Heath, R. L. (2017). Coping with workplace bullying through naver: Effects of LMX relational concerns and cultural differences. *International Journal of Business Communication*, 58(1), 79–105. DOI: 10.1177/2329488417735649

Lee, J., & Wang, J. (2017). Developing entrepreneurial resilience: Implications for human resource development. *European Journal of Training and Development*, 41(6), 519–539. DOI: 10.1108/EJTD-12-2016-0090

Lee, M., & You, M. (2020). Psychological and behavioral responses in South Korea during the early stages of coronavirus disease 2019 (COVID-19). *International Journal of Environmental Research and Public Health*, 17(9), 2977. DOI: 10.3390/ijerph17092977 PMID: 32344809

Leendertse, J., Schrijvers, M., & Stam, E. (2021). Measure Twice, Cut Once: Entrepreneurial Ecosystem Metrics. *Research Policy*, 104336. Advance online publication. DOI: 10.1016/j.respol.2021.104336

Lee, S. H., Patel, P. C., & Phan, P. H. (2023). Are the self-employed more stressed? New evidence on an old question. *Journal of Small Business Management*, 61(2), 513–539. DOI: 10.1080/00472778.2020.1796467

Lee, S. M., & Peterson, S. J. (2000). Culture, entrepreneurial orientation, and global competitiveness. *Journal of World Business*, 35(4), 401–416. DOI: 10.1016/S1090-9516(00)00045-6

Leibenstein, H. (1968). Entrepreneurship and development. *The American Economic Review*, 58, 72–83.

Lek, J., Vendrig, A. A., & Schaafsma, F. G. (2020). What are psychosocial risk factors for entrepreneurs to become unfit for work? A qualitative exploration. *Work (Reading, Mass.)*, 67(2), 499–506. DOI: 10.3233/WOR-203299 PMID: 33074213

Lenka, U., & Gupta, M. (2019). An empirical investigation of innovation process in indian pharmaceutical companies. *European Journal of Innovation Management*, 23(3), 500–523. DOI: 10.1108/ejim-03-2019-0069

León, J., Molero, F., Laguía, A., Mikulincer, M., & Shaver, P. (2021). Security providing leadership: A job resource to prevent employees' burnout. *International Journal of Environmental Research and Public Health*, 18(23), 12551. DOI: 10.3390/ijerph182312551 PMID: 34886276

Li, J. T., Tsui, A. S., & Weldon, E. (Eds.). (2000). *Management and organizations in the Chinese context*. St. Martin's Press. DOI: 10.1057/9780230511590

Lim, C., Kim, K. J., & Maglio, P. P. (2018). Smart cities with big data: Reference models, challenges, and considerations. *Cities (London, England)*, 82, 86–99. DOI: 10.1016/j.cities.2018.04.011

Lim, S., Han, S., & Joo, Y. (2018). Effects of nurses' emotional intelligence on their organizational citizenship behavior, with mediating effects of leader trust and value congruence. *Japan Journal of Nursing Science*, 15(4), 363–374. DOI: 10.1111/jjns.12206

Lin, J., & Reddy, R. M. (2019). Teaching, mentorship, and coaching in surgical education. *Thoracic Surgery Clinics*, 29(3), 311–320. DOI: 10.1016/j.thorsurg.2019.03.008 PMID: 31235300

Lin, Y.-M. (2004). *Between politics and markets: Firms, competition, and institutional change in post-Mao China*. Cambridge University Press.

Liu, X., & Li, J. (2013). Effects of team leader emotional intelligence and team emotional climate on team member job satisfaction. *Nankai Business Review International*, 4(3), 180–198. DOI: 10.1108/nbri-07-2013-0023

Liu, X., Wu, X., Wang, Q., & Zhou, Z. (2022). Entrepreneurial mindfulness and organizational resilience of Chinese SMEs during the COVID-19 pandemic: The role of entrepreneurial resilience. *Frontiers in Psychology*, 13, 992161. Advance online publication. DOI: 10.3389/fpsyg.2022.992161 PMID: 36275221

Liu, X., Yuan, Y., Sun, R., Zhao, C., & Zhao, D. (2023). Influence of entrepreneurial team knowledge conflict on ambidextrous entrepreneurial learning—A dual-path perspective of entrepreneurial resilience and fear of failure. *Journal of Innovation & Knowledge*, 8(3), 100389. DOI: 10.1016/j.jik.2023.100389

Li, W.-D., Fay, D., Frese, M., Harms, P. D., & Gao, X. Y. (2014). Reciprocal relationship between proactive personality and work characteristics: A latent change score approach. *The Journal of Applied Psychology*, 99(5), 948–965. DOI: 10.1037/a0036169 PMID: 24635530

Loewe, N., Araya-Castillo, L., Thieme, C., & Batista-Foguet, J. M. (2015). Self-employment as a moderator between work and life satisfaction. *Academia (Caracas)*, 28(2), 213–226. DOI: 10.1108/ARLA-10-2014-0165

Losana, Á. A., & Gallardo, C. F. (2019). Building Purpose-Driven Organizations. The Routledge Handbook of Positive Communication: Contributions of an Emerging Community of Research on Communication for Happiness and Social Change.

Louise, S., Fitzpatrick, M., Strauss, C., Rossell, S. L., & Thomas, N. (2018). Mindfulness-and acceptance-based interventions for psychosis: Our current understanding and a meta-analysis. *Schizophrenia Research*, 192, 57–63. DOI: 10.1016/j.schres.2017.05.023 PMID: 28545945

Lovell, B., & Wetherell, M. (2016). Behaviour problems of children with asd and perceived stress in their caregivers: The moderating role of trait emotional intelligence? *Research in Autism Spectrum Disorders*, 28, 1–6. DOI: 10.1016/j.rasd.2016.05.002

Low, G. R., & Hammer, R. D. with Nelson, D. B. (2019). Transformative emotional intelligence: Achieving leadership and performance excellence. Corpus Christi, TX: Emotional Intelligence Learning Systems.

Lowensteyn, I., Berberian, V., Belisle, P., DaCosta, D., Joseph, L., & Grover, S. A. (2018). The measurable benefits of a workplace wellness program in Canada: Results after one year. *Journal of Occupational and Environmental Medicine*, 60(3), 211–216. DOI: 10.1097/JOM.0000000000001240 PMID: 29200188

Low, G. R., & Hammett, R. D. (2021). *Transformative emotional intelligence for a positive career and life*. Emotional Intelligence Learning Systems.

Lubbadeh, T. (2020). Job burnout: A general literature review. *International Review of Management and Marketing*, 10(3), 7–15. DOI: 10.32479/irmm.9398

Luberto, C. M., Hall, D. L., Park, E. R., Haramati, A., & Cotton, S. (2020). A perspective on the similarities and differences between mindfulness and relaxation. *Global Advances in Health and Medicine : Improving Healthcare Outcomes Worldwide*, 9, 2164956120905597. DOI: 10.1177/2164956120905597 PMID: 32076580

Lubua, F. (2019). *From Innovation to Academic Entrepreneurship in Computer-Assisted Language Learning (CALL)*. Ohio University.

Luca, R., Pollicino, P., Rifici, C., Mondo, N., Iorio, S., Cassaniti, A., & Calabrò, R. (2023). Psycho-emotional well-being in caregivers of people with acquired brain injury: An exploratory study on the human immersion model during the omicron wave. *Clinics and Practice*, 13(2), 487–496. DOI: 10.3390/clinpract13020044

Luchman, J. N., & González-Morales, M. G. (2013). Demands, control, and support: A meta-analytic review of work characteristics interrelationships. *Journal of Occupational Health Psychology*, 18(1), 37–52. DOI: 10.1037/a0030541 PMID: 23339747

Lufkin, B. (2022, February 25). Office space turns 20: How the film changed The way we work. BBC News. https://www.bbc.com/worklife/article/20190205-office-space- turns-20-how-the-film-changed-work

Luo, M., Guo, L., Yu, M., & Wang, H. (2020). The psychological and mental impact of coronavirus disease 2019 (COVID-19) on medical staff and general public—A systematic review and meta-analysis. *Psychiatry Research*, 291, 113190. DOI: 10.1016/j.psychres.2020.113190 PMID: 32563745

Lyu, Y. (2024). Interplay of entrepreneurial failure experience, entrepreneurial resilience, and re-entrepreneurship performance: Evidence from China. *Environment and Social Psychology*, 9(3). Advance online publication. DOI: 10.54517/esp.v9i3.2069

Machovec, G. (2020). Selected tools and services for analyzing and managing open access journal transformative agreements. *Journal of Library Administration*, 60(3), 301–307. DOI: 10.1080/01930826.2020.1727280

Magnini, V., Lee, G., & Kim, P. (2011). The cascading affective consequences of exercise among hotel workers. *International Journal of Contemporary Hospitality Management*, 23(5), 624–643. DOI: 10.1108/09596111111143377

Mahand, T., & Caldwell, C. (2023). Quiet quitting – causes and opportunities. *Business and Management Research*, 12(1), 9. DOI: 10.5430/bmr.v12n1p9

Mahmoud, N. N., & Rothenberger, D. (2019). From burnout to well-being: A focus on resilience. *Clinics in Colon and Rectal Surgery*, 32(06), 415–423. DOI: 10.1055/s-0039-1692710 PMID: 31686993

Manga, J. P. A. (2023). Workplace Bullying Seen from the Perspective of Bystanders: Effects on Engagement and Burnout, Mediating Role of Positive and Negative Affects. *International Journal of Environmental Research and Public Health*, 20(19), 6821. DOI: 10.3390/ijerph20196821 PMID: 37835092

Mani, S., & Mishra, M. (2020). Non-monetary levers to enhance employee engagement in organizations–"GREAT" model of motivation during the Covid-19 crisis. *Strategic HR Review*, 19(4), 171–175. DOI: 10.1108/SHR-04-2020-0028

Marion, T. J., & Fixson, S. K. (2021). The transformation of the innovation process: How digital tools are changing work, collaboration, and organizations in new product development. *Journal of Product Innovation Management*, 38(1), 192–215. DOI: 10.1111/jpim.12547

Marshall, D. R., Meek, W. R., Swab, R. G., & Markin, E. (2020). Access to resources and entrepreneurial well-being: A self-efficacy approach. *Journal of Business Research*, 120, 203–212. DOI: 10.1016/j.jbusres.2020.08.015

Marshall, J., Dunstan, D., & Bartik, W. (2019). The digital psychiatrist: In search of evidence-based apps for anxiety and depression. *Frontiers in Psychiatry*, 10, 831. Advance online publication. DOI: 10.3389/fpsyt.2019.00831 PMID: 31803083

Martin, A. (2013). (Leuphana Universität Lüneburg, Institut für Mittelstandsforschung, Hrsg.). (2013). Die Beurteilung der Arbeitsbedingungen durch Unternehmer und Arbeitnehmer, Schriften aus dem Institut für Mittelstandsforschung, No. 43, Leuphana Universität Lüneburg, Institut für Mittelstandsforschung. Verfügbar unter: https://www. econstor.eu/bitstream/10419/71296/1/739971433.pdf

Martino, C. (2023). Organizational lay theories of intelligence and trust among minority women.. DOI: 10.14293/p2199-8442.1.sop-.prf7vg.v1

Maslach, C. Leiter, M. P., & Schaufeli, W. (2009). Measuring burnout. The Oxford Handbook of Organizational Well Being, 86–108. DOI: 10.1093/oxfordhb/9780199211913.003.0005

Maslach, C., & Leiter, M. P. (2016). Burnout. Stress: Concepts, Cognition, Emotion, and Behavior, 351–357. DOI: 10.1016/B978-0-12-800951-2.00044-3

Maslach, C., Schaufeli, W. B., & Leiter, M. P. (2001). Job burnout. *Annual Review of Psychology*, 52(1), 397–422. DOI: 10.1146/annurev.psych.52.1.397 PMID: 11148311

Mason, C. M., & Harrison, R. T. (2006). After the exit: Acquisitions, entrepreneurial recycling, and regional economic development. *Regional Studies*, 40(1), 55–73. DOI: 10.1080/00343400500450059

Ma, Y., & Fang, S. (2019). Adolescents' mindfulness and psychological distress: The mediating role of emotion regulation. *Frontiers in Psychology*, 10. Advance online publication. DOI: 10.3389/fpsyg.2019.01358

Mazzucato, M. (2014) Start-up myths and obsessions, *The Economist*, February 3 rd 2014. https://www.economist.com/blogs/schumpeter/2014/02/invitation-mariana-mazzucato

McFarland, D. C., & Hlubocky, F. (2021). Therapeutic strategies to tackle burnout and emotional exhaustion in frontline medical staff: Narrative review. *Psychology Research and Behavior Management*, 14, 1429–1436. DOI: 10.2147/PRBM.S256228 PMID: 34552358

McFarland, L., Bull, R., Cumming, T., & Wong, S. (2022). Workplace Bullying in Early Childhood Education Settings: Prevalence and Protective Factors. *International Journal of Early Childhood*, •••, 1–22. DOI: 10.1007/s13158-022-00341-y PMID: 36341082

Mertens, E. C., Deković, M., Van Londen, M., & Reitz, E. (2022). Parallel changes in positive youth development and self-awareness: The role of emotional self-regulation, self-esteem, and self-reflection. *Prevention Science*, 23(4), 502–512. DOI: 10.1007/s11121-022-01345-9 PMID: 35088219

Mikic, M., Horvatinovic, T., & Kovac, I. (2020). Climbing up the regional intellectual capital tree: An EU entrepreneurial ecosystem analysis. *Journal of Intellectual Capital*. Advance online publication. DOI: 10.1108/JIC-07-2020-0258

Miller, J. T., & Verhaeghen, P. (2022). Mind full of kindness: Self-awareness, self-regulation, and self-transcendence as vehicles for compassion. *BMC Psychology*, 10(1), 188. DOI: 10.1186/s40359-022-00888-4 PMID: 35906630

Miller, J., Davis-Sramek, B., Fugate, B. S., Pagell, M., & Flynn, B. B. (2021). Editorial commentary: Addressing confusion in the diffusion of archival data research. *The Journal of Supply Chain Management*, 57(3), 130–146. DOI: 10.1111/jscm.12236

Miller, P. J., & Cho, G. E. (2018). *Self-esteem in time and place: How American families imagine, enact, and personalize a cultural ideal*. Oxford University Press.

Mills, M. J., Fleck, C. R., & Kozikowski, A. (2013). Positive psychology at work: A conceptual review, state-of-practice assessment, and a look ahead. *The Journal of Positive Psychology*, 8(2), 153–164. DOI: 10.1080/17439760.2013.776622

Min, C. (1995). *Asian management systems: Chinese, Japanese, and Korean styles of business*. Routledge.

Miquel, C., Domènech-Abella, J., Félez-Nóbrega, M., Cristóbal-Narváez, P., Mortier, P., Vilagut, G., & Haro, J. (2022). The mental health of employees with job loss and income loss during the covid-19 pandemic: The mediating role of perceived financial stress. *International Journal of Environmental Research and Public Health*, 19(6), 3158. DOI: 10.3390/ijerph19063158 PMID: 35328846

Mishra, A., & Singh, P. (2024). Effect of emotional intelligence and cognitive flexibility on entrepreneurial intention: Mediating role of entrepreneurial self-efficacy. *Journal of Entrepreneurship in Emerging Economies*, 16(3), 551–575. DOI: 10.1108/JEEE-05-2022-0142

Moder, S., Jehle, E., Furtner, M., & Kraus, S. (2023). Short-term mindfulness meditation training improves antecedents of opportunity recognition. *Journal of Business Venturing Insights*, 19, e00381. DOI: 10.1016/j.jbvi.2023.e00381

Mohr, D., Lyon, A., Lattie, E., Reddy, M., & Schueller, S. (2017). Accelerating digital mental health research from early design and creation to successful implementation and sustainment. *Journal of Medical Internet Research*, 19(5), e153. DOI: 10.2196/jmir.7725 PMID: 28490417

Mokyr, J. (2002). *The Gifts of Athena: Historical Origins of the Knowledge Economy*. Princeton University Press.

Molek-Winiarska, D., & Żołnierczyk-Zreda, D. (2018). Application of mindfulness-based stress reduction to a stress management intervention in a study of a mining sector company. *International Journal of Occupational Safety and Ergonomics*, 24(4), 546–556. DOI: 10.1080/10803548.2018.1452843 PMID: 29578373

Molero Jurado, M. D. M., Pérez-Fuentes, M. D. C., Martos Martínez, Á., Barragán Martín, A. B., Simón Márquez, M. D. M., & Gázquez Linares, J. J. (2021). Emotional intelligence as a mediator in the relationship between academic performance and burnout in high school students. *PLoS One*, 16(6), e0253552. DOI: 10.1371/journal.pone.0253552 PMID: 34166434

Mónico, L., Mellão, N., Nobre-Lima, L., Parreira, P., & Carvalho, C. (2016). Emotional intelligence and psychological capital: what is the role of workplace spirituality?. Revista Portuguesa De Enfermagem De Saúde Mental, (Spe. 3). DOI: 10.19131/rpesm.0116

Monk, N. (2023). The Efficacy of an Automated Reminder System for Employee Clock-in and Clock-out Times. *J Curr Trends Comp Sci Res*, 2(3), 251–254. DOI: 10.33140/JCTCSR.02.03.06

Moosivand, S. (2023). Predictors of emotional intelligence among family caregivers of cancer patients: A cross-sectional study. *Cancer Reports*, 7(1). Advance online publication. DOI: 10.1002/cnr2.1943

Morrish, L. (2019). *Pressure vessels: The epidemic of poor mental health among higher education staff.* Higher Education Policy Institute.

Moss, J. (2021). *The burnout epidemic: The rise of chronic stress and how we can fix it.* Harvard Business Press.

Mouammer, L., & Bazan, C. (2021). Effect of mentorship on the early entrepreneurial journey of university students. *Proceedings of the Canadian Engineering Education Association (Ceea)*. DOI: 10.24908/pceea.vi0.14969

Mshilla, O. (2021). *Access the Role of the Youth in Peace Processes With a Focus in Mediation: a Case of Horn of Africa, Kenya Nairobi County* (Doctoral dissertation, University of Nairobi).

Muenks, K., Wigfield, A., & Eccles, J. S. (2018). I can do this! The development and calibration of children's expectations for success and competence beliefs. *Developmental Review*, 48, 24–39. DOI: 10.1016/j.dr.2018.04.001

Mukherjee, T. (2022). Performance, Discrimination, and Work–Life Interface: Perspectives in Workplace Health and Well-being. In *Handbook of Health and Well-Being: Challenges, Strategies and Future Trends* (pp. 295–321). Springer Nature Singapore. DOI: 10.1007/978-981-16-8263-6_13

Mulla, Z. R., Govindaraj, K., Polisetti, S. R., George, E., & More, N. R. S. (2017). Mindfulness-based stress reduction for executives: Results from a field experiment. *Business Perspectives and Research*, 5(2), 113–123. DOI: 10.1177/2278533717692906

Musiat, P., Goldstone, P., & Tarrier, N. (2014). Understanding the acceptability of e-mental health - attitudes and expectations towards computerised self-help treatments for mental health problems. *BMC Psychiatry*, 14(1), 109. Advance online publication. DOI: 10.1186/1471-244X-14-109 PMID: 24725765

Nahkamäki, R. (2018). *Living in the blurry zone: a study of the wellbeing and work-life balance of Finnish SME entrepreneurs* (Master's thesis).

Nambisan, S., & Baron, R. A. (2021). On the costs of digital entrepreneurship: Role conflict, stress, and venture performance in digital platform-based ecosystems. *Journal of Business Research*, 125, 520–532. DOI: 10.1016/j.jbusres.2019.06.037

Naseer, S., Raja, U., Syed, F., & Bouckenooghe, D. (2018). Combined effects of workplace bullying and perceived organizational support on employee behaviors: Does resource availability help? *Anxiety, Stress, and Coping*, 31(6), 654–668. DOI: 10.1080/10615806.2018.1521516 PMID: 30200787

Nasir, S., & Can, O. (2022). Workplace Aggression Profiles and Diverse Emotional Responses: Evidence from Pakistan. *Employee Responsibilities and Rights Journal*, 34(3), 335–359. DOI: 10.1007/s10672-021-09392-0

Nate, S., Grecu, V., Stavytskyy, A., & Kharlamova, G. (2022). Fostering entrepreneurial ecosystems through the stimulation and mentorship of new entrepreneurs. *Sustainability (Basel)*, 14(13), 7985. DOI: 10.3390/su14137985

Neal, A., & Griffin, M. A. (2006). A study of the lagged relationships among safety climate, safety motivation, safety behavior, and accidents at the individual and group levels. *The Journal of Applied Psychology*, 91(4), 946–953. DOI: 10.1037/0021-9010.91.4.946 PMID: 16834517

Nelson, D. B., Low, G. R., Hammett, R. D., & Sen, A. (2013). *Professional coaching: A transformative and research-based model*. Emotional Intelligence Learning Systems.

Neneh, B. N. (2024). Why peer support matters: Entrepreneurial stressors, emotional exhaustion, and growth intentions of women entrepreneurs. *Entrepreneurship Research Journal*, 14(3), 985–1019. DOI: 10.1515/erj-2021-0501

Ngalesoni, O., Mwakifwamba, G., & Pandisha, H. (2024). The effectiveness of mentoring programs on empowering women entrepreneurs in tanzania: A case of babati district council. *International Journal of Entrepreneurship and Project Management*, 9(2), 1–16. DOI: 10.47604/ijepm.2366

Ng, M., Firth, J., Minen, M., & Torous, J. (2019). User engagement in mental health apps. A review of measurement, reporting, and validity. *Psychiatric Services (Washington, D.C.)*, 70(7), 538–544. DOI: 10.1176/appi.ps.201800519 PMID: 30914003

Nicola, M., Alsafi, Z., Sohrabi, C., Kerwan, A., Al-Jabir, A., Iosifidis, C., Agha, R., & Agha, R. (2020). The socio-economic implications of the coronavirus pandemic (COVID-19): A review. *International Journal of Surgery*, 78, 185–193. DOI: 10.1016/j.ijsu.2020.04.018 PMID: 32305533

Nicotra, M., Romano, M., Del Giudice, M., & Schillaci, C. E. (2018). The causal relation between entrepreneurial ecosystem and productive entrepreneurship: A measurement framework. *The Journal of Technology Transfer*, 43(3), 640–673. DOI: 10.1007/s10961-017-9628-2

Ni, D., Li, N., & Zheng, X. (2024). Why do women entrepreneurs behave dominantly in the workplace, and what does it mean?: A family embeddedness perspective. *Group & Organization Management*, 49(4), 860–901. DOI: 10.1177/10596011221116729

Nightingale, S., Spiby, H., Sheen, K., & Slade, P. (2018). The impact of emotional intelligence in health care professionals on caring behaviour towards patients in clinical and long-term care settings: Findings from an integrative review. *International Journal of Nursing Studies*, 80, 106–117. DOI: 10.1016/j.ijnurstu.2018.01.006 PMID: 29407344

Nikolaev, B., Boudreaux, C. J., & Wood, M. (2020). Entrepreneurship and subjective well-being: The mediating role of psychological functioning. *Entrepreneurship Theory and Practice*, 44(3), 557–586. DOI: 10.1177/1042258719830314

Nisa, M., Srinivas, V., Rani, R., Prasad, K. D. V., & De, T. (2023). Analysing the Mental Health and Well-Being of Entrepreneurs. *Journal for ReAttach Therapy and Developmental Diversities*, 6(4s), 369–377.

Noguera, I., Guerrero-Roldán, A. E., & Masó, R. (2018). Collaborative agile learning in online environments: Strategies for improving team regulation and project management. *Computers & Education*, 116, 110–129. DOI: 10.1016/j.compedu.2017.09.008

Nooraie, F., Salehi, M., & Enayati, T. (2023). The effect of emotional and organizational intelligence on academic entrepreneurship. *Educational Researcher*, 18(73).

Noordin, M. (2021). *The Impact of Violent Extremism and Radicalization on the Political Economy of the Horn of Africa: a Case Study of Somalia and Eritrea* (Doctoral dissertation, University of Nairobi).

North, D. (1990). *Institutions, Institutional Change and Economic Performance*. Cambridge University. DOI: 10.1017/CBO9780511808678

Novak, I., & Honan, I. (2019). Effectiveness of paediatric occupational therapy for children with disabilities: A systematic review. *Australian Occupational Therapy Journal*, 66(3), 258–273. DOI: 10.1111/1440-1630.12573 PMID: 30968419

Nyoach, T. D., Lemi, K., Debela, T., & Kant, S. (2024). Does Organizational Commitment Mediate the Relationship between Employee Relationship Management and Bank Performance? The Case of Banks in Ethiopia. *International Journal of Organizational Leadership*, 13(2), 355–376. DOI: 10.33844/ijol.2024.60419

O'Connor, A. (2013). A conceptual framework for entrepreneurship education policy: Meeting government and economic purposes. *Journal of Business Venturing*, 28(4), 546–563. DOI: 10.1016/j.jbusvent.2012.07.003

O'Neill, R. (2024). By, for, with women? On the politics and potentialities of wellness entrepreneurship. *The Sociological Review*, 72(1), 3–20. DOI: 10.1177/00380261221142461

Oaten, M., & Cheng, K. (2007). Improvements in self-control from financial monitoring. *Journal of Economic Psychology*, 28(4), 487–501. DOI: 10.1016/j.joep.2006.11.003

Obschonka, M., Pavez, I., Kautonen, T., Kibler, E., Salmela-Aro, K., & Wincent, J. (2023). Job burnout and work engagement in entrepreneurs: How the psychological utility of entrepreneurship drives healthy engagement. *Journal of Business Venturing*, 38(2), 106272. DOI: 10.1016/j.jbusvent.2022.106272

Oi, J. C., & Walder, A. G. (Eds.). (1999). *Property rights and economic reform in China*. Stanford University Press. DOI: 10.1515/9780804764193

Oktalia, D., Irianto, A., & Sentosa, S. (2018). The influence of emotional intelligence and persistence on the income of small-scale peyek snack entrepreneurs in Padang. *Proceedings of the PICEEBA-2018.* https://doi.org/DOI: 10.2991/piceeba-18.2018.87

Ola, O. O., John, W. O., Simeon, O. A., & Mutiu, O. A. (2019). Impact of work life balance on the social life of workers living in Lagos metropolitan borders. [ACDMHR]. *Annals of Contemporary Developments in Management & HR*, 1(2), 50–59. DOI: 10.33166/ACDMHR.2019.02.006

Olberding, J. C. (2002). Does regionalism beget regionalism? the relationship between norms and regional partnerships for economic development. *Public Administration Review*, 62(4), 480–491. DOI: 10.1111/0033-3352.00201

Omrane, A., Kammoun, A., & Seaman, C. (2018). Entrepreneurial burnout: Causes, consequences and way out. *FIIB Business Review*, 7(1), 28–42. DOI: 10.1177/2319714518767805

Ordiñana-Bellver, D., Pérez-Campos, C., González-Serrano, M., & Valantinė, I. (2022). Emotions, skills and intra-entrepreneurship: Mapping the field and future research opportunities. *Management & Marketing*, 17(4), 577–598. DOI: 10.2478/mmcks-2022-0032

Orru, M., Biggart, N. W., & Hamilton, G. G. (1997). *The economic organization of East Asian capitalism*. Sage.

Ortiz-de-Mandojana, N., & Bansal, P. (2016). The long-term benefits of organizational resilience through sustainable business practices. *Strategic Management Journal*, 37(8), 1615–1631. DOI: 10.1002/smj.2410

Osabohien, R., Worgwu, H., & Al-Faryan, M. A. S. (2024). Mentorship and innovation as drivers of entrepreneurship performance in africa's largest economy. *Social Enterprise Journal*, 20(1), 76–90. DOI: 10.1108/SEJ-02-2023-0019

Osborne, S., & Hammoud, M. S. (2017). Effective employee engagement in the workplace. *International Journal of Applied Management and Technology*, 16(1), 50–67. DOI: 10.5590/IJAMT.2017.16.1.04

Ostrom, E. (1990). *Governing the Commons*. Cambridge University Press. DOI: 10.1017/CBO9780511807763

Ostrom, E. (2010). Beyond markets and states: Polycentric governance of complex economic systems. *The American Economic Review*, 100(3), 641–672. DOI: 10.1257/aer.100.3.641

Othman, N., & Muda, T. (2018). Emotional intelligence towards entrepreneurial career choice behaviours. *Education + Training*, 60(9), 953–970. DOI: 10.1108/et-07-2017-0098

Otto, M., Hoefsmit, N., Ruysseveldt, J., & Dam, K. (2019). Exploring proactive behaviors of employees in the prevention of burnout. *International Journal of Environmental Research and Public Health*, 16(20), 3849. DOI: 10.3390/ijerph16203849 PMID: 31614684

Overall, J. (2020). Mental health among entrepreneurs: The benefits of consciousness. *International Journal of Entrepreneurship and Economic Issues*, 4(1), 70–74. DOI: 10.32674/ijeei.v4i1.20

Overton, A. R., & Lowry, A. C. (2013). Conflict Management: Difficult Conversations with Difficult People. *Clinics in Colon and Rectal Surgery*, 26(4), 259–264. DOI: 10.1055/s-0033-1356728 PMID: 24436688

Owens, J., Kottwitz, C., & Tiedt, J. (2018). Strategies to attain faculty work-life balance. *Building Healthy Academic Communities Journal*, 2(2), 58–73.

Ozcan, N. A., Sahin, S., & Cankir, B. (2023). The validity and reliability of thriving scale in academic context: Mindfulness, GPA, and entrepreneurial intention among university students. *Current Psychology (New Brunswick, N.J.)*, 42(7), 5200–5211. DOI: 10.1007/s12144-021-01590-1

Ozili, P. K., & Arun, T. (2020). Spillover of COVID-19: impact on the Global Economy. *Available at SSRN* 3562570. DOI: 10.2139/ssrn.3562570

Page, K. M., & Vella-Brodrick, D. A. (2009). The 'what,' 'why' and 'how' of employee well-being: A new model. *Social Indicators Research*, 90(3), 441–458. DOI: 10.1007/s11205-008-9270-3

Paiva-Salisbury, M. L., & Schwanz, K. A. (2022). Building compassion fatigue resilience: Awareness, prevention, and intervention for pre-professionals and current practitioners. *Journal of Health Service Psychology*, 48(1), 39–46. DOI: 10.1007/s42843-022-00054-9 PMID: 35136862

Palmer, N. J., Davies, J., & Viney, C. (2023). Research Environment, Culture, Capacity, Capabilities and Connectivity. In *Business and Management Doctorates World-Wide: Developing the Next Generation* (pp.125-151). Emerald Publishing.

Palmer, C., Kraus, S., Kailer, N., Huber, L., & Öner, Z. H. (2021). Entrepreneurial burnout: A systematic review and research map. *International Journal of Entrepreneurship and Small Business*, 43(3), 438–461. DOI: 10.1504/IJESB.2021.115883

Panigrahi, A., Pati, A., Sahu, B., Das, M. N., Nayak, D. S. K., Sahoo, G., & Kant, S. (2023). En-MinWhale: An ensemble approach based on MRMR and Whale optimization for Cancer diagnosis. *IEEE Access : Practical Innovations, Open Solutions*, 11, 113526–113542. DOI: 10.1109/ACCESS.2023.3318261

Pan, T. H., & Lin, Y. N. (2022). Organizational Commitment Impact on Job Well-Being of SMEs Employees in Taiwan in Post-COVID-19 Era. *Education Quarterly Eeview*, 5(1). Advance online publication. DOI: 10.31014/aior.1992.05.01.407

Pappa, S., Ntella, V., Giannakas, T., Giannakoulis, V. G., Papoutsi, E., & Katsaounou, P. (2020). Prevalence of depression, anxiety, and insomnia among healthcare workers during the COVID-19 pandemic: A systematic review and meta-analysis. *Brain, Behavior, and Immunity*, 88, 901–907. DOI: 10.1016/j.bbi.2020.05.026 PMID: 32437915

Parasuraman, S., Purohit, Y. S., Godshalk, V. M., & Beutell, N. J. (1996). Work and family variables, entrepreneurial career success, and psychological well-being. *Journal of Vocational Behavior*, 48(3), 275–300. DOI: 10.1006/jvbe.1996.0025

Parker, S. C. (2013). Do serial entrepreneurs run successively better-performing businesses? *Journal of Business Venturing*, 28(5), 652–666. DOI: 10.1016/j.jbusvent.2012.08.001

Passey, D. G., Brown, M. C., Hammerback, K., Harris, J. R., & Hannon, P. A. (2018). Managers' support for employee wellness programs: An integrative review. *American Journal of Health Promotion*, 32(8), 1789–1799. DOI: 10.1177/0890117118764856 PMID: 29649899

Pathak, D., & Joshi, G. (2021). Impact of psychological capital and life satisfaction on organizational resilience during COVID-19: Indian tourism insights. *Current Issues in Tourism*, 24(17), 2398–2415. DOI: 10.1080/13683500.2020.1844643

Pathak, S., & Muralidharan, E. (2024). Contextualizing emotional intelligence for commercial and social entrepreneurship. *Small Business Economics*, 62(2), 667–686. DOI: 10.1007/s11187-023-00775-1

Paul, E., & Fancourt, D. (2022). Did financial interventions offset the impact of financial adversity on mental health during the covid-19 pandemic? a longitudinal analysis of the ucl covid-19 social study. DOI: 10.1101/2022.11.15.22282337

Pecino, V., Mañas, M., Díaz-Fúnez, P., Aguilar-Parra, J., Padilla-Góngora, D., & López-Liria, R. (2019). Organisational climate, role stress, and public employees' job satisfaction. *International Journal of Environmental Research and Public Health*, 16(10), 1792. DOI: 10.3390/ijerph16101792 PMID: 31117168

Pečiuliauskienė, P. (2021). Emotional intelligence and transformational leadership of gymnasium teachers'. *Society Integration Education Proceedings of the International Scientific Conference*, 2, 457-467. DOI: 10.17770/sie2021vol2.6194

Peñalvo, J. L., Sagastume, D., Mertens, E., Uzhova, I., Smith, J., Wu, J. H., Bishop, E., Onopa, J., Shi, P., Micha, R., & Mozaffarian, D. (2021). Effectiveness of workplace wellness programmes for dietary habits, overweight, and cardiometabolic health: A systematic review and meta-analysis. *The Lancet. Public Health*, 6(9), e648–e660. DOI: 10.1016/S2468-2667(21)00140-7 PMID: 34454642

Pesis-Katz, I., Smith, J. A., Norsen, L., DeVoe, J., & Singh, R. (2020). Reducing cardiovascular disease risk for employees through participation in a wellness program. *Population Health Management*, 23(3), 212–219. DOI: 10.1089/pop.2019.0106 PMID: 31513466

Pirsoul, T., Parmentier, M., Sovet, L., & Nils, F. (2023). Emotional intelligence and career-related outcomes: A meta-analysis *Human Resource Management Review*, 33(3), 100967. DOI: 10.1016/j.hrmr.2023.100967

Plana-Farran, M., Blanch, Á., & Solé, S. (2022). The role of mindfulness in business administration (B.A.) university students' career prospects and concerns about the future. *International Journal of Environmental Research and Public Health*, 19(3), 1376. DOI: 10.3390/ijerph19031376 PMID: 35162407

Podsakoff, P. M., MacKenzie, S. B., & Podsakoff, N. P. (2009). Recommendations for creating better concept definitions in the organizational, behavioral, and social sciences. *Organizational Research Methods*, 15(2), 192–207.

Prado, J., Zárate-Torres, R., Tafur-Mendoza, A., Prada-Ospina, R., & Sarmiento, C. (2022). Impact of leadership practices on manager's pathways to goal attainment: The mediating effect of emotional intelligence. *The International Journal of Organizational Analysis*, 31(7), 2889–2902. DOI: 10.1108/ijoa-01-2022-3110

Prahalad, C. K. (2005). *The Fortune at the Bottom of the Pyramid: Eradicating Poverty through Profits*. Pearson Education.

Prib, H., & Bobko, O. (2023). Psychological characteristics of entrepreneurs working in stress-related conditions. *Scientific Bulletin of Mukachevo State University Series. Pedagogy and Psychology*, 9(2). Advance online publication. DOI: 10.52534/msu-pp2.2023.57

Puertas Molero, P., Zurita Ortega, F., Ubago Jiménez, J. L., & González Valero, G. (2019). Influence of emotional intelligence and burnout syndrome on teachers well-being: A systematic review. *Social Sciences (Basel, Switzerland)*, 8(6), 185. DOI: 10.3390/socsci8060185

Pung, A., Fletcher, S., & Gunn, J. (2018). Mobile app use by primary care patients to manage their depressive symptoms: Qualitative study. *Journal of Medical Internet Research*, 20(9), e10035. DOI: 10.2196/10035 PMID: 30262449

Quintillán, I., & Legazkue, I. (2019). Emotional intelligence and venture internationalization during economic recession. *International Journal of Entrepreneurial Behaviour & Research*, 26(2), 246–265. DOI: 10.1108/IJEBR-08-2018-0521

Raabe, B., & Beehr, T. (2003). Formal mentoring versus supervisor and coworker relationships: Differences in perceptions and impact. *Journal of Organizational Behavior*, 24(3), 271–293. DOI: 10.1002/job.193

Ramani, S., Kusurkar, R. A., Lyon-Maris, J., Pyörälä, E., Rogers, G. D., Samarasekera, D. D., Taylor, D. C. M., & Ten Cate, O. (2024). Mentorship in health professions education–an AMEE guide for mentors and mentees: AMEE Guide No. 167. *Medical Teacher*, 46(8), 999–1011. DOI: 10.1080/0142159X.2023.2273217 PMID: 37909275

Ramos, E., Rodríguez, M., & Castaño, Á. (2021). Resilience in in-home caregivers of older adults during the covid-19 pandemic. *Revista Latinoamericana de Bioetica*, 20(2), 91–101. DOI: 10.18359/rlbi.4813

Randerson, A. K. (2020). Mindfulness, wellness, and spirituality in the workplace. *The Palgrave Handbook of Workplace Well-Being*, 1-22.

Rashid, S., & Ratten, V. (2021). Entrepreneurial ecosystems during [the survival of small businesses using dynamic capabilities. *World Journal of Entrepreneurship, Management and Sustainable Development*.]. *COVID*, •••, 19.

Rasool, S. F., Wang, M., Tang, M., Saeed, A., & Iqbal, J. (2021). How Toxic Workplace Environment Effects the Employee Engagement: The Mediating Role of Organizational Support and Employee Wellbeing. *International Journal of Environmental Research and Public Health*, 18(5), 2294. DOI: 10.3390/ijerph18052294 PMID: 33652564

Ratanavanich, M., & Charoensukmongkol, P. (2024). The interaction effect of goal orientation and mindfulness of entrepreneurs on firm innovation capability and its impact on firm performance. *VINE Journal of Information and Knowledge Management Systems*, (ahead-of-print).

Rathi, N., & Lee, K. (2016). Emotional exhaustion and work attitudes: Moderating effect of personality among frontline hospitality employees. *Journal of Human Resources in Hospitality & Tourism*, 15(3), 231–251. DOI: 10.1080/15332845.2016.1147935

Rauch, A., Fink, M., & Hatak, I. (2018). Stress processes: An essential ingredient in the entrepreneurial process. *The Academy of Management Perspectives*, 32(3), 340–357. DOI: 10.5465/amp.2016.0184

Raza, S. A., Tunio, M. N., Ali, M., & Puah, C. H. (Eds.). (2023). *Entrepreneurship and Green Finance Practices: Avenues for Sustainable Business Start-ups in Asia*. Emerald Publishing Limited. DOI: 10.1108/9781804556788

REBA (Reward & Employee Benefits Association). (2019). *Employee Wellbeing Research 2019*. June, Reba Group.

Rechstshaffen, M. (2022, February 19). "office space": Thr's 1999 review. The Hollywood Reporter. https://www.hollywoodreporter.com/movies/movie-news/office-space-review-1999-movie-1086336/#!

Reichl, C., & Spinath, F. (2014). Work–nonwork conflict and burnout: A meta-analysis. *Human Relations*, 67(8), 979–1005. DOI: 10.1177/0018726713509857

Reis da Silva Tiago. (2024a) The Value of Emotional Intelligence in Midwifery: Enhancing Care and Outcomes for Mothers and Infants through Sustainable Development Goals and Leadership. Journal of Womens Healthcare & Midwifery Research. SRC/JWHMR-133. Link: https://www.onlinescientificresearch.com/articles/the-value-of-emotional-intelligence-in-midwifery-enhancing-care-and-outcomes-for-mothers-and-infants-through-sustainable-developme.pdf

Reis da Silva, T. (2024f). The Evolution of Nursing for Older Adult: A Historical Perspective. Associative J Health Sci. 3(3). AJHS. 000561. 2024. DOI: . Link: https://crimsonpublishers.com/ajhs/pdf/AJHS.000561.pdfDOI: 10.31031/AJHS.2024.03.000561

Reis da Silva, T. H (2024h). Oncology and Cancer Medicine: Understanding the complexities in Older Patients. Biomed J Sci & Tech Res 55(3)-2024. DOI: DOI: 10.26717/BJSTR.2024.55.008720

Reis da Silva, T. H. (2024b). Chapter 6 – Navigating Healthcare Complexity: Integrating Business Fundamentals into Nursing Leadership. In Sedky, A. Resiliency Strategies for Long-Term Business Success. Pp. 145-168. IGI Global. DOI: 10.4018/979-8-3693-9168-6.ch006

Reis da Silva, T. H. (2024c). Chapter 11 - Integrating business essentials into Gerontological Nursing: Enhancing Care for Older Adults in Diverse Settings. In Sedky, A. Resiliency Strategies for Long-Term Business Success. Pp. 283-316. IGI Global. DOI: DOI: 10.4018/979-8-3693-9168-6.ch011

Reis da Silva, Tiago Horta (2024i). "Prevalence of elder abuse: a narrative review." British journal of community nursing vol. 29,9 (2024): 442-446. doi: DOI: 10.12968/bjcn.2024.0004

Reis da Silva. Tiago Horta (2024g). Death and Its Significance in Nursing Practice. Palliat Med Care Int J. 2024; 4(3): 555640. DOI: https://juniperpublishers.com/pmcij/pdf/PMCIJ.MS.ID.555640.pdf

Reis da Silva, T. (2024e). Can supplementing vitamin B12 improve mental health outcomes?: A literature review. *British Journal of Community Nursing*, 29(3), 137–146. DOI: 10.12968/bjcn.2024.29.3.137

Reis da Silva, T. H. (2023a). Ageing in place: Ageing at home and in the community. *British Journal of Community Nursing*, 28(5), 213–214. DOI: 10.12968/bjcn.2023.28.5.213

Reis da Silva, T. H. (2023b). Falls assessment and prevention in the nursing home and community. *British Journal of Community Nursing*, 28(2), 68–72. DOI: 10.12968/bjcn.2023.28.2.68

Reis da Silva, T. H. (2023c). Moving and Handling in the Community. *British Journal of Community Nursing*, 28(8), 369. DOI: 10.12968/bjcn.2023.28.8.369

Reis da Silva, T. H. (2024d). Loneliness in older adults. *British Journal of Community Nursing*, 29(2), 60–66. DOI: 10.12968/bjcn.2024.29.2.60

Reis da Silva, T. H. (2024j). Falls prevention in older people and the role of nursing. *British Journal of Community Nursing*, 29(7), 335–339. DOI: 10.12968/bjcn.2024.0005

Reis da Silva, T. H. (2024k). Understanding body fluid balance, dehydration and intravenous fluid therapy. *Emergency Nurse*. Advance online publication. DOI: 10.7748/en.2024.e2201

Reis da Silva, T. H. (2024l). Pharmacokinetics in older people: An overview of prescribing practice. *Journal of Prescribing Practice*, 6(9), 374–381. DOI: 10.12968/jprp.2024.6.9.374

Reis da Silva, T. H. (2024m). Chronic kidney disease in older adults: Nursing implications for community nurses. *Journal of Kidney Care*, 9(4), 174–179. DOI: 10.12968/jokc.2024.9.4.174

Reis da Silva, T. H., & Mitchell, A. (2024a). Integrating Digital Transformation in Nursing Education: Best Practices and Challenges in Curriculum Development. In Lytras, M., Serban, A. C., Alkhaldi, A., Malik, S., & Aldosemani, T. (Eds.), *Digital Transformation in Higher Education, Part B Cases, Examples and Good Practices*. Emerald Publishing Limited.

Reis Da Silva, T. H., & Mitchell, A. (2024b). Simulation in nursing: The importance of involving service users. *British Journal of Nursing (Mark Allen Publishing)*, 33(5), 262–265. DOI: 10.12968/bjon.2024.33.5.262

Reymen, I. M. M. J., Andries, P., Berends, H., Mauer, R., Stephan, U., & Van Burg, E. (2015). Understanding dynamics of strategic decision making in venture creation: A process study of effectuation and causation. *Strategic Entrepreneurship Journal*, 9(4), 351–379. DOI: 10.1002/sej.1201

Reynolds, C., & O'Dwyer, L. (2008). Examining the relationships among emotional intelligence, coping mechanisms for stress, and leadership effectiveness for middle school principals. *Journal of School Leadership*, 18(5), 472–500. DOI: 10.1177/105268460801800501

Rezvani, M. Q., Chaudhary, N., Huseynov, R., Li, M., Sharma, A., Jafarova, R., & Huseynova, C. (2021). Impact of organizational commitment on employee productivity during [evidence from Afghanistan and India.]. *COVID*, •••, 19.

Riegel, B., Dunbar, S. B., Fitzsimons, D., Freedland, K. E., Lee, C. S., Middleton, S., Stromberg, A., Vellone, E., Webber, D. E., & Jaarsma, T. (2021). Self-care research: Where are we now? Where are we going? *International Journal of Nursing Studies*, 116, 103402. DOI: 10.1016/j.ijnurstu.2019.103402 PMID: 31630807

Riyanto, P. and Sanjaya, P. (2020). Youth sports activities on emotional intelligence.. DOI: 10.2991/assehr.k.201014.088

Roberts, A., Davenport, T., Wong, T., Moon, H., Hickie, I., & LaMonica, H. (2021). Evaluating the quality and safety of health-related apps and e-tools: Adapting the mobile app rating scale and developing a quality assurance protocol. *Internet Interventions : the Application of Information Technology in Mental and Behavioural Health*, 24, 100379. DOI: 10.1016/j.invent.2021.100379 PMID: 33777705

Rocca, S., Sagiv, L., Schwartz, S. H., & Knafo, A. (2002). The Big Five personality factors and personal values. *Personality and Social Psychology Bulletin*, 28(6), 789–801. DOI: 10.1177/0146167202289008

Roche, M., Haar, J. M., & Luthans, F. (2014). The role of mindfulness and psychological capital on the wellbeing of leaders. *Journal of Occupational Health Psychology*, 19(4), 476–489. DOI: 10.1037/a0037183 PMID: 24933594

Rodrigues, A., Jorge, F., Pires, C., & António, P. (2019). The contribution of emotional intelligence and spirituality in understanding creativity and entrepreneurial intention of higher education students. *Education + Training*, 61(7/8), 870–894. DOI: 10.1108/et-01-2018-0026

Ronnie, J. B., & Philip, B. (2021). Expectations and what people learn from failure. In *Expectations and actions* (pp. 207–237). Routledge. DOI: 10.4324/9781003150879-10

Rothenberger, D. A. (2017). Physician burnout and well-being: A systematic review and framework for action. *Diseases of the Colon and Rectum*, 60(6), 567–576. DOI: 10.1097/DCR.0000000000000844 PMID: 28481850

Roundy, P. T., Bradshaw, M., & Brockman, B. K. (2018). The emergence of entrepreneurial ecosystems: A complex adaptive systems approach. *Journal of Business Research*, 86(1), 1–10. . jbusres.2018. 01. 032DOI: 10.1016/ j

Rovida, E., & Zafferri, G. (2022). *The importance of soft skills in engineering and engineering education*. Springer. DOI: 10.1007/978-3-030-77249-9

Rucker, M. R. (2017). Workplace wellness strategies for small businesses. *International Journal of Workplace Health Management*, 10(1), 55–68. DOI: 10.1108/IJWHM-07-2016-0054

Rudaleva, I. (2018). Research of organizational and personal factors of professional burnout of personnel in a consulting organization. *Helix*, 8(01), 2372–2376. DOI: 10.29042/2018-2372-2376

Ruiz Robledillo, N., & Moya Albiol, L. (2013). Self-reported health and cortisol awakening response in parents of people with Asperger syndrome: The role of trait anger and anxiety, coping and burden. *Psychology & Health*, 28(11), 1246–1264. DOI: 10.1080/08870446.2013.800517

Rupprecht, S., Koole, W., Chaskalson, M., Tamdjidi, C., & West, M. (2019). Running too far ahead? Towards a broader understanding of mindfulness in organisations. *Current Opinion in Psychology*, 28, 32–36. DOI: 10.1016/j.copsyc.2018.10.007 PMID: 30390478

Ryan, R. M., & Deci, E. L. (2000). Self-determination theory and the facilitation of intrinsic motivation, social development, and well-being. *The American Psychologist*, 55(1), 68–78. DOI: 10.1037/0003-066X.55.1.68 PMID: 11392867

Ryan, R. M., & Deci, E. L. (2001). On happiness and human potentials: A review of research on hedonic and eudaimonic well-being. *Annual Review of Psychology*, 52(1), 141–166. DOI: 10.1146/annurev.psych.52.1.141 PMID: 11148302

Ryff, C. (2019). Entrepreneurship and eudaimonic well-being: Five venues for new science. *Journal of Business Venturing*, 34(4), 646–663. DOI: 10.1016/j.jbusvent.2018.09.003 PMID: 31105380

Ryff, C. D. (2017). Eudaimonic well-being, inequality, and health: Recent findings and future directions. *International Review of Economics*, 64(2), 159–178. DOI: 10.1007/s12232-017-0277-4 PMID: 29057014

Saarni, S. I., Saarni, E. S., & Saarni, H. (2008). Quality of life, work ability, and self-employment: A population survey of entrepreneurs, farmers, and salary earners. *Occupational and Environmental Medicine*, 65(2), 98–103. DOI: 10.1136/oem.2007.033423 PMID: 17666452

Sachdev, N. (2023). Entrepreneurial resilience: What makes entrepreneurs start another business after failure. *Asian Journal of Economics. Business and Accounting*, 23(18), 46–58.

Sadoughi, M., & Hesampour, F. (2016). The relationship between mindfulness and cognitive emotion regulation and depression among university students. *International Journal of Academic Research in Psychology*, 3(1). Advance online publication. DOI: 10.46886/ijarp/v3-i1/2378

Sahni, J. (2020). Impact of COVID-19 on Employee Behavior: Stress and Coping Mechanism During WFH (Work From Home) Among Service Industry Employees. *International Journal of Operations Management*, 1(1), 35–48. DOI: 10.18775//ijom.2757-0509.2020.11.4004

Salari, N., Hosseinian-Far, A., Jalali, R., Vaisi-Raygani, A., Rasoulpoor, S., Mohammadi, M., Rasoulpoor, S., & Khaledi-Paveh, B. (2020). Prevalence of stress, anxiety, depression among the general population during the COVID-19 pandemic: A systematic review and meta-analysis. *Globalization and Health*, 16(1), 1–11. DOI: 10.1186/s12992-020-00589-w PMID: 32631403

Salas, E., Cooke, N. J., & Rosen, M. A. (2008). On teams, teamwork, and team performance: Discoveries and developments. *Human Factors*, 50(3), 540–547. DOI: 10.1518/001872008X288457 PMID: 18689065

Saleem, Z., Shenbei, Z., & Hanif, A. M. (2020). Workplace violence and employee engagement: The mediating role of work environment and organizational culture. *SAGE Open*, 10(2), 2158244020935885. DOI: 10.1177/2158244020935885

Saleh, T. A., Sarwar, A., Khan, N., Tabash, M. I., & Hossain, M. I. (2023). Does emotional exhaustion influence turnover intention among early-career employees? A moderated-mediation study on Malaysian SMEs. *Cogent Business & Management*, 10(3), 2242158. DOI: 10.1080/23311975.2023.2242158

Salgado, S. (2020). Job insecurity, financial threat and mental health in the covid-19 context: the buffer role of perceived social support. DOI: 10.1101/2020.07.31.20165910

Sana, H. A., Alkhalaf, S., Zulfiqar, S., Al-Rahmi, W. M., Al-Adwan, A. S., & AlSoud, A. R. (2021). Upshots of intrinsic traits on social entrepreneurship intentions among young business graduates: An investigation through moderated-mediation model. *Sustainability (Basel)*, 13(9), 5192. DOI: 10.3390/su13095192

Sánchez-García, J. C., Vargas-Morúa, G., & Hernández-Sánchez, B. R. (2018). Entrepreneurs' well-being: A bibliometric review. *Frontiers in Psychology*, 9, 1696. DOI: 10.3389/fpsyg.2018.01696 PMID: 30258384

Santos, L. L., Borini, F. M., & Pereira, R. M. (2021). Bricolage as a path towards organizational innovativeness in times of market and technological turbulence. *Journal of Entrepreneurship in Emerging Economies*, 13(2), 282–299. DOI: 10.1108/JEEE-02-2020-0039

Satici, B., Gocet-Tekin, E., Deniz, M., & Satici, S. A. (2021). Adaptation of the Fear of COVID-19 Scale: Its association with psychological distress and life satisfaction in Turkey. *International Journal of Mental Health and Addiction*, 19(6), 1980–1988. DOI: 10.1007/s11469-020-00294-0 PMID: 32395095

Satow, L. (2012). *Stress- und Coping-Inventar (SCI)*. Vollständige Test- und Skalendokumentation.

Saunders, D., & Kober, H. (2020). Mindfulness-based intervention development for children and adolescents. *Mindfulness*, 11(8), 1868–1883. DOI: 10.1007/s12671-020-01360-3 PMID: 33584870

Schermelleh-Engel, K., Moosbrugger, H., & Muller, H. (2003). Evaluating the fit of structural equation models: Test of significance and descriptive goodness-of-fit measures. *Methods of Psychological Research Online*, 8(2), 23–74.

Schmidt, A. T. (2016). The ethics and politics of mindfulness-based interventions. *Journal of Medical Ethics*, 42(7), 450–454. DOI: 10.1136/medethics-2015-102942 PMID: 27099360

Schmitt, A., Rosing, K., Zhang, S. X., & Leatherbee, M. (2017). A Dynamic Model of Entrepreneurial Uncertainty and Business Opportunity Identification: Exploration as a Mediator and Entrepreneurial Self-Efficacy as a Moderator. *Entrepreneurship Theory and Practice*. Advance online publication. DOI: 10.1177/1042258717721482

Schumpeter, J. A. (1976), Capitalism, socialism, and democracy. *George Allen & Unwin* Ltd [1943].

Schumpeter, J. A. (1934). *The Theory of Economic Development*. Harvard Univ. Press.

Schwartz, T., & Porath, C. (2014). Why you hate work. *Harvard Business Review*, 92(6), 58–66.

Seabrook, E., Kelly, R., Foley, F., Theiler, S., Thomas, N., Wadley, G., & Nedeljkovic, M. (2020). Understanding how virtual reality can support mindfulness practice: Mixed methods study. *Journal of Medical Internet Research*, 22(3), e16106. DOI: 10.2196/16106 PMID: 32186519

Seltzer, J., & Numerof, R. E. (1988). Supervisory leadership and subordinate burnout. *Academy of Management Journal*, 31(2), 439–446. DOI: 10.2307/256559

Septiani, H., Dwidiyanti, M., & Andriany, M. (2022). The influence of mindful thought on emotional regulation in adults: A literature review. *Nurse and Health Jurnal Keperawatan*, 11(1), 70–79. DOI: 10.36720/nhjk.v11i1.359

Seraj, A., Alzain, E., & Alshebami, A. (2022). The roles of financial literacy and overconfidence in investment decisions in saudi arabia. *Frontiers in Psychology*, 13, 1005075. Advance online publication. DOI: 10.3389/fpsyg.2022.1005075 PMID: 36248580

Serenko, A. (2024). The human capital management perspective on quiet quitting: Recommendations for employees, managers, and national policymakers. *Journal of Knowledge Management*, 28(1), 27–43. DOI: 10.1108/JKM-10-2022-0792

Severson, K., & Yaffe-Bellany, D. (2020, 20 March). Independent restaurants brace for the unknown. The New York Times. Retrieved from

Sexton, J. B., & Adair, K. C. (2019). Forty-five good things: A prospective pilot study of the Three Good Things well-being intervention in the USA for healthcare worker emotional exhaustion, depression, work–life balance and happiness. *BMJ Open*, 9(3), e022695. DOI: 10.1136/bmjopen-2018-022695 PMID: 30898795

Sforzo, G. A., Kaye, M. P., Harenberg, S., Costello, K., Cobus-Kuo, L., Rauff, E., Edman, J. S., Frates, E., & Moore, M. (2020). Compendium of health and wellness coaching: 2019 addendum. *American Journal of Lifestyle Medicine*, 14(2), 155–168. DOI: 10.1177/1559827619850489 PMID: 32231482

Shafiq, M., & Rana, R. (2016). Relationship of emotional intelligence to organizational commitment of college teachers in Pakistan. *Eurasian Journal of Educational Research*, 16(62), 1–14. DOI: 10.14689/ejer.2016.62.1

Shah, C., Chowdhury, A., & Gupta, V. (2021). Impact of COVID-19 on tourism and hospitality students' perceptions of career opportunities and future prospects in India. *Journal of Teaching in Travel & Tourism*, 21(4), 359–379. DOI: 10.1080/15313220.2021.1924921

Shanafelt, T. D., & Noseworthy, J. H. (2017, January). Executive leadership and physician well-being: Nine organizational strategies to promote engagement and reduce burnout. [). Elsevier.]. *Mayo Clinic Proceedings*, 92(1), 129–146. DOI: 10.1016/j.mayocp.2016.10.004 PMID: 27871627

Shanafelt, T., Goh, J., & Sinsky, C. (2017). The business case for investing in physician well-being. *JAMA Internal Medicine*, 177(12), 1826–1832. DOI: 10.1001/jamainternmed.2017.4340 PMID: 28973070

Shapero, B. G., Farabaugh, A., Terechina, O., DeCross, S., Cheung, J. C., Fava, M., & Holt, D. J. (2019). Understanding the effects of emotional reactivity on depression and suicidal thoughts and behaviors: Moderating effects of childhood adversity and resilience. *Journal of Affective Disorders*, 245, 419–427. DOI: 10.1016/j.jad.2018.11.033 PMID: 30423470

Sharif, K., Kassim, N., Faisal, M. N., & Zain, M. (2021). Impact of skill on bi-dimensional trust within small-to-medium sized enterprises upstream relationships. *EuroMed Journal of Business*, 16(1), 39–68. DOI: 10.1108/EMJB-03-2020-0020

Sharma, M., & Rush, S. E. (2014). Mindfulness-based stress reduction as a stress management intervention for healthy individuals: A systematic review. *Journal of Evidence-Based Complementary & Alternative Medicine*, 19(4), 271–286. DOI: 10.1177/2156587214543143 PMID: 25053754

Shenkoya, T., Hwang, K. Y., & Sung, E. H. (2023). Student startup: Understanding the role of the university in making startups profitable through university—industry collaboration. *SAGE Open*, 13(3), 21582440231198601. Advance online publication. DOI: 10.1177/21582440231198601

Shen, N., Kassam, I., Chen, S., Ma, C., Wang, W., Boparai, N., Jankowicz, D., & Strudwick, G. (2022). Canadian perspectives of digital mental health supports: Findings from a national survey conducted during the covid-19 pandemic. *Digital Health*, 8, 205520762211022. DOI: 10.1177/20552076221102253 PMID: 35646379

Shepherd, D. A., & Patzelt, H. (2018). Entrepreneurial Identity. In Shepherd, D. A., & Patzelt, H. (Eds.), *Entrepreneurial Cognition: Exploring the Mindset of Entrepreneurs* (pp. 137–200). Springer International Publishing., DOI: 10.1007/978-3-319-71782-1_5

Shepherd, D. A., & Patzelt, H. (2020). A call for research on the scaling of organizations and the scaling of social impact. *Entrepreneurship Theory and Practice*, 61(3), 104225872095059.

Sherman, C. L., Randall, C., & Kauanui, S. K. (2016). Are you happy yet? Entrepreneurs' subjective well-being. *Journal of Management, Spirituality & Religion*, 13(1), 7–23. DOI: 10.1080/14766086.2015.1043575

Shim, W., & Lee, S. W. (2019). An agile approach for managing requirements change to improve learning and adaptability. *Journal of Industrial Information Integration*, 14, 16–23. DOI: 10.1016/j.jii.2018.07.005

Shinbrot, X. A., Wilkins, K., Gretzel, U., & Bowser, G. (2019). Unlocking women's sustainability leadership potential: Perceptions of contributions and challenges for women in sustainable development. *World Development*, 119, 120–132. DOI: 10.1016/j.worlddev.2019.03.009

Shipman, K., Burrell, D. N., & Mac Pherson, A. H. (2021). An organizational analysis of how managers must understand the mental health impact of teleworking during COVID-19 on employees. *The International Journal of Organizational Analysis*.

Shir, N., Nikolaev, B. N., & Wincent, J. (2019). Entrepreneurship and well-being: The role of psychological autonomy, competence, and relatedness. *Journal of Business Venturing*, 34(5), 105875. DOI: 10.1016/j.jbusvent.2018.05.002

Sigala, M. (2020). Tourism and COVID-19: Impacts and implications for advancing and resetting industry and research. *Journal of Business Research*, 117, 312–321. DOI: 10.1016/j.jbusres.2020.06.015 PMID: 32546875

Simon, H. A. (1962). The architecture of complexity. *Proceedings of the American Philosophical Society*, 106, 467–482.

Simonse, O., Dijk, W., Dillen, L., & Dijk, E. (2022). The role of financial stress in mental health changes during covid-19. *Npj Mental Health Research*, 1(1), 15. Advance online publication. DOI: 10.1038/s44184-022-00016-5 PMID: 37521497

Singh, A. (2021). Anantshayi technique of meditation: An empirical evidence of strategic decision making by entrepreneurs and business managers. *International Journal of Indian Culture and Business Management*, 24(2), 189–213. DOI: 10.1504/IJICBM.2021.118897

Singh, A., Krishna, S. H., Raghuwanshi, S., Sharma, J., & Bapat, V. (2023). Measuring psychological well-being of entrepreneurial success–An analytical study. *Journal for ReAttach Therapy and Developmental Diversities*, 6(4s), 338–348.

Singh, N., & Kovid, R. K. (2023). *Women entrepreneur's emotional intelligence and firm performance: Mediating role of networking competencies*. FIIB Business Review., DOI: 10.1177/23197145231184307

Sitaridis, I., & Kitsios, F. (2020). Competitiveness analysis and evaluation of entrepreneurial ecosystems: A multi-criteria approach. *Annals of Operations Research*, 294(1), 377–399. DOI: 10.1007/s10479-019-03404-x

Smith, J. F. (2024). *Private Practice Mental Health Clinicians' Lived Experiences With Entrepreneurial Leadership, Social Learning, and Burnout Throughout the COVID-19 Global Pandemic* (Doctoral dissertation, The Chicago School of Professional Psychology).

Solomon, I. G. (2020). The influence of leadership based on emotional intelligence concerning the climate of an organization. *International Journal of Management Science and Business Administration*, 6(5).

Song, Z., & Baicker, K. (2019). Effect of a workplace wellness program on employee health and economic outcomes: A randomized clinical trial. *Journal of the American Medical Association*, 321(15), 1491–1501. DOI: 10.1001/jama.2019.3307 PMID: 30990549

Soren, A., & Ryff, C. D. (2023). Meaningful work, well-being, and health: Enacting a eudaimonic vision. *International Journal of Environmental Research and Public Health*, 20(16), 6570. DOI: 10.3390/ijerph20166570 PMID: 37623156

Sorenson, O. (2018). Social networks and the geography of entrepreneurship. *Small Business Economics*, 51(3), 527–537. DOI: 10.1007/s11187-018-0076-7

Sorkin, D., Janio, E., Eikey, E., Schneider, M., Davis, K., Schueller, S., Stadnick, N. A., Zheng, K., Neary, M., Safani, D., & Mukamel, D. (2021). Rise in use of digital mental health tools and technologies in the united states during the covid-19 pandemic: Survey study. *Journal of Medical Internet Research*, 23(4), e26994. DOI: 10.2196/26994 PMID: 33822737

Søvold, L. E., Naslund, J. A., Kousoulis, A. A., Saxena, S., Qoronfleh, M. W., Grobler, C., & Münter, L. (2021). Prioritizing the mental health and well-being of healthcare workers: An urgent global public health priority. *Frontiers in Public Health*, 9, 679397. DOI: 10.3389/fpubh.2021.679397 PMID: 34026720

Spigel, B., & Harrison, R. (2018). Toward a process theory of entrepreneurial ecosystems. *Strategic Entrepreneurship Journal*, 12(1), 151–168. DOI: 10.1002/sej.1268

Spilling, O. (1996). The Entrepreneurial System: On Entrepreneurship in the Context of a Mega-Event. *Journal of Business Research*, 36(1), 91–103. DOI: 10.1016/0148-2963(95)00166-2

Stam, E. (2015). Entrepreneurial ecosystems and regional policy: A sympathetic critique. *European Planning Studies*, 23(9), 1759–1769. . 2015. 1061484DOI: 10. 1080/ 09654313

Stam, E. and Ven, A. (2019). Entrepreneurial ecosystem elements. Small Business Economics, 56(2), 809-832. https://doi.org/ Cantner, U., Cunningham, J., Lehmann, E., & Menter, M. (2020). Entrepreneurial ecosystems: a dynamic lifecycle model. Small Business Economics, 57(1), 407-423. https://doi.org/DOI: 10.1007/s11187-019-00270-6\

Stam, E., & Spigel, B. (2018). Entrepreneurial ecosystems. Blackburn, R., De Clerq, C., Heinonen, J. (Eds.). *The SAGE Handbook of Small Business and Entrepreneurship*. DOI: 10.4135/9781473984080.n21

Stam, E., Hartog, C., Van Stel, A., & Thurik, R. (2011). Ambitious entrepreneurship and macro-economic growth. Minniti, M. (Ed.). *The Dynamics of Entrepreneurship. Evidence from the Global Entrepreneurship Monitor Data*. Oxford University Press, Oxford, pp. 231–249.

Stam, E., Van Stel, A. (2011). Types of Entrepreneurship and Economic Growth. Szirmai,

Stam, E. (2007). Why butterflies don't leave: Locational behavior of entrepreneurial firms. *Economic Geography*, 83(1), 27–50. DOI: 10.1111/j.1944-8287.2007.tb00332.x

Stam, E., & Bosma, N. (2015). Local policies for high-growth firms. In Audretsch, D. B., Link, A., & Walshok, A. (Eds.), *The Oxford handbook of local competitiveness*. Oxford University Press.

Stam, E., & Van de Ven, A. (2021). Entrepreneurial Ecosystem Elements. *Small Business Economics*, 56(2), 809–832. DOI: 10.1007/s11187-019-00270-6

Stangler, D., & Bell-Masterson, J. (2015). Measuring an entrepreneurial ecosystem. Kauffman foundation. Retrieved from https://www.kauffman.org/wpcontent/uploads/ 2019/12/measuring_an_entrepreneurial_ecosystem.pdf

Stankov, S., Brtka, E., Poštin, J., Ilić-Kosanović, T., & Nikolić, M. (2022). The influence of organizational culture and leadership on workplace bullying in organizations in Serbia. *Journal for East European Management Studies*, 27(3), 519–551. DOI: 10.5771/0949-6181-2022-3-519

Stephan, U. (2018). Entrepreneurs' mental health and well-being: A review and research agenda. *The Academy of Management Perspectives*, 32(3), 290–322. DOI: 10.5465/amp.2017.0001

Steyaert, C., & Katz, J. (2004). Reclaiming the Space of Entrepreneurship in Society: Geographical, Discursive and Social Dimensions. *Entrepreneurship and Regional Development*, 16(3), 179–196. DOI: 10.1080/0898562042000197135

Stinson, J., Kohut, S., Forgeron, P., Amaria, K., Bell, M., Kaufman, M., & Spiegel, L. (2016). The ipeer2peer program: A pilot randomized controlled trial in adolescents with juvenile idiopathic arthritis. *Pediatric Rheumatology Online Journal*, 14(1), 48. Advance online publication. DOI: 10.1186/s12969-016-0108-2 PMID: 27590668

Stoica, O., Roman, A., & Rusu, V. D. (2020). The Nexus between entrepreneurship and economic growth: A comparative analysis on groups of countries. *Sustainability (Basel)*, 12(3), 1186. DOI: 10.3390/su12031186

Stokes, V. (2022, August 29). Is "quiet quitting" really good for your health? what experts think. Healthline. http://www.healthline.com/health-news/is-quiet-quitting-really-good-for-your-health-what-experts-think#Quiet-quitting-and-health

Stumm, S., Chamorro-Premuzic, T., & Furnham, A. (2009). Decomposing self-estimates of intelligence: Structure and sex differences across 12 nations. *British Journal of Psychology*, 100(2), 429–442. DOI: 10.1348/000712608x357876

Sucharitha, S., Manoharan, A., Dhanuraja, V., Kasi, A., & Ezhilarasan, S. (2020). Digital mental health apps for self-management of depression: A scoping exploration on awareness, attitude, and user experience among professional course students. *International Journal of Community Medicine and Public Health*, 7(9), 3594. DOI: 10.18203/2394-6040.ijcmph20203928

Sull, D., Sull, C., Cipolli, W., & Brighenti, C. (2022). Why every leader needs to worry about toxic culture. *MIT Sloan Management Review*.

Sultan, M. F., Tunio, M. N., Aziz, A., & Shaikh, S. K. (2023). Social innovation and social entrepreneurship in the wake of COVID-19: A perspective from the developing side of the world. In *Frugal Innovation and Social Transitions in the Digital Era* (pp. 113–118). IGI Global.

Sutiyatno, S. (2023). The role of emotional, spiritual, and social intelligence on entrepreneurship intention of informatics and computer students: Self-leadership as a mediating variable. *Journal of Economics. Finance and Management Studies*, 6(4), 1482–1491. DOI: 10.47191/jefms/v6-i4-10

Su, Z., Cheshmehzangi, A., McDonnell, D., Chen, H., Ahmad, J., Šegalo, S., & Veiga, C. (2022). Technology-based mental health interventions for domestic violence victims amid covid-19. *International Journal of Environmental Research and Public Health*, 19(7), 4286. DOI: 10.3390/ijerph19074286 PMID: 35409967

Sweet, E., Nandi, A., Adam, E., & McDade, T. (2013). The high price of debt: Household financial debt and its impact on mental and physical health. *Social Science & Medicine*, 91, 94–100. DOI: 10.1016/j.socscimed.2013.05.009 PMID: 23849243

Szekeres, M., & Valdes, K. (2022). Virtual health care & telehealth: Current therapy practice patterns. *Journal of Hand Therapy*, 35(1), 124–130. DOI: 10.1016/j.jht.2020.11.004 PMID: 33568266

Szerb, L., Lafuente, E., Horváth, K., & Páger, B. (2019). The relevance of quantity and quality entrepreneurship for regional performance: The moderating role of the entrepreneurial ecosystem. *Regional Studies*, 53(9), 1308–1320. DOI: 10.1080/00343404.2018.1510481

Tahir, R. (2024). Work–life balance: Is an entrepreneurial career the solution? *Journal of Entrepreneurship in Emerging Economies*, 16(4), 845–867. DOI: 10.1108/JEEE-03-2022-0077

Taris, T. W., Geurts, S. A. E., Schaufeli, W. B., Blonk, R. W. B., & Lagerveld, S. E. (2008). All day and all of the night: The relative contribution of two dimensions of workaholism to well-being in self-employed workers. *Work and Stress*, 22(2), 153–165. DOI: 10.1080/02678370701758074

Tarrant, J., Viczko, J., & Cope, H. (2018). Virtual reality for anxiety reduction demonstrated by quantitative EEG: A pilot study. *Frontiers in Psychology*, 9, 1280. DOI: 10.3389/fpsyg.2018.01280 PMID: 30087642

Team, T. I. (2020.). Free rider problem: Explanation, causes, and solutions. Investopedia. https://www.investopedia.com/terms/f/free_rider_problem.asp Why quiet quitting is a bigger problem than you think. Why quiet quitting is a bigger problem than you think. | Randstad Australia. (2023, November 17). https://www.randstad.com.au/hr-news/talent-management/why-quiet-quitting-a- bigger-problem-you-think/

Teece, D. J. (2007). Explicating dynamic capabilities: The nature and microfoundations of (sustainable) enterprise performance. *Strategic Management Journal*, 28(13), 1319–1350. DOI: 10.1002/smj.640

Teece, D. J. (2014). The foundations of enterprise performance: Dynamic and ordinary capabilities in an (economic) theory of firms. *The Academy of Management Perspectives*, 28(4), 328–352. DOI: 10.5465/amp.2013.0116

Tee, S., Chin, S., Raman, K., Yeow, J., & Eze, U. (2014). The contributing roles of emotional intelligence and spiritual intelligence in entrepreneurial innovation and creativity. *World Journal of Management*, 5(2), 66–77. DOI: 10.21102/wjm.2014.09.52.06

Tereso, A., Ribeiro, P., Fernandes, G., Loureiro, I., & Ferreira, M. (2019). Project management practices in private organizations. *Project Management Journal*, 50(1), 6–22. DOI: 10.1177/8756972818810966

Terzimehić, N., Häuslschmid, R., Hussmann, H., & Schraefel, M. C. (2019, May). A review & analysis of mindfulness research in HCI: Framing current lines of research and future opportunities. In *Proceedings of the 2019 CHI conference on human factors in computing systems* (pp. 1-13). DOI: 10.1145/3290605.3300687

Tetterton, M. (2020). *Exploring the Challenges of Work-Life Balance of Female Leadership: A Qualitative Case Study.*

Thayer, Z., & Gildner, T. (2020). covid-19-related financial stress associated with higher likelihood of depression among pregnant women living in the united states. *American Journal of Human Biology*, 33(3), e23508. Advance online publication. DOI: 10.1002/ajhb.23508 PMID: 32964542

Thomas, K., Hu, C., Gewin, A., Bingham, K., & Yanchus, N. (2005). The roles of protégé race, gender, and proactive socialization attempts on peer mentoring. Advances in Developing Human Resources, Tshehla, B. and Costa, K. (2021). Exploring the relationship between mentorship and successful youth entrepreneurship at telkom, south africa. https://doi.org/DOI: 10.31730/osf.io/c5r4e

Thompson, C. A., Kopelman, R. E., & Schriesheim, C. A. (1992). Putting all one's eggs in the same basket: A comparison of commitment and satisfaction among self- and organizationally employed men. *The Journal of Applied Psychology*, 77(5), 738–743. DOI: 10.1037/0021-9010.77.5.738

Thompson, N., Gelderen, M., & Keppler, L. (2020). No need to worry? anxiety and coping in the entrepreneurship process. *Frontiers in Psychology*, 11, 398. Advance online publication. DOI: 10.3389/fpsyg.2020.00398 PMID: 32226405

Thompson, T. A., Purdy, J. M., & Ventresca, M. J. (2018). How entrepreneurial ecosystems take form: Evidence from social impact initiatives in Seattle. *Strategic Entrepreneurship, 12(1).Journal*, 12(1), 96–116. DOI: 10.1002/sej.1285

Thurik, A. R., Stam, E., & Audretsch, D. B. (2013). The rise of the entrepreneurial economy and the future of dynamic capitalism. *Technovation*, 33(8-9), 302–310. . technovation.2013.07. 003DOI: 10. 1016/ j

Thurik, R., Khedhaouria, A., Torr'es, O., & Verheul, I. (2016). ADHD symptoms and entrepreneurial orientation of small firm owners. *Applied Psychology*, 65(3), 568–586. DOI: 10.1111/apps.12062

Tisu, L., & Vîrgă, D. (2022). Proactive vitality management, work–home enrichment, and performance: A two-wave cross-lagged study on entrepreneurs. *Frontiers in Psychology*, 13, 761958. Advance online publication. DOI: 10.3389/fpsyg.2022.761958 PMID: 35310274

Tisu, L., Vîrgă, D., & Taris, T. (2023). Entrepreneurial well-being and performance: Antecedents and mediators. *Frontiers in Psychology*, 14, 1112397. Advance online publication. DOI: 10.3389/fpsyg.2023.1112397 PMID: 37928580

Tobias, J. M., Mair, J., & Barbosa-Leiker, C. (2013). Toward a theory of transformative entrepreneuring: Poverty reduction and conflict resolution in Rwanda's entrepreneurial coffee sector. *Journal of Business Venturing*, 28(6), 728–742. DOI: 10.1016/j.jbusvent.2013.03.003

Torp, S., Nielsen, R. A., Gudbergsson, S. B., & Dahl, A. A. (2012). Worksite adjustments and work ability among employed cancer survivors. *Supportive Care in Cancer*, 20(9), 2149–2156. DOI: 10.1007/s00520-011-1325-3 PMID: 22086407

Torp, S., Syse, J., Paraponaris, A., & Gudbergsson, S. (2017). Return to work among self-employed cancer survivors. *Journal of Cancer Survivorship: Research and Practice*, 11(2), 189–200. DOI: 10.1007/s11764-016-0578-8 PMID: 27837444

Torrès, O., Benzari, A., Fisch, C., Mukerjee, J., Swalhi, A., & Thurik, R. (2022). Risk of burnout in French entrepreneurs during the COVID-19 crisis. *Small Business Economics*, 58(2), 1–23. DOI: 10.1007/s11187-021-00516-2 PMID: 38624594

Totterdell, P., Wood, S., & Wall, T. (2006). An intraindividual test of the demands-control model: A weekly diary study of psychological strain in portfolio workers. *Journal of Occupational and Organizational Psychology*, 79(1), 63–84. DOI: 10.1348/096317905X52616

Tranfield, D., Denyer, D., & Smart, P. (2003). Towards a methodology for developing evidence-informed management knowledge by means of systematic review. *British Journal of Management*, 14(3), 207–222. DOI: 10.1111/1467-8551.00375

Tran, Q. N., Phung, T. M. T., Nguyen, N. H., & Nguyen, T. H. (2023). Financial Knowledge Matters Entrepreneurial Decisions: A Survey in the COVID-19 Pandemic. *Journal of the Knowledge Economy*. Advance online publication. DOI: 10.1007/s13132-023-01137-8

Trépanier, S.-G., Fernet, C., & Austin, S. (2015a). A longitudinal investigation of workplace bullying, basic need satisfaction, and employee functioning. *Journal of Occupational Health Psychology*, 20(1), 105–116. DOI: 10.1037/a0037726 PMID: 25151460

Tripathy, S., & Bisoyi, T. (2021). Detrimental impact of COVID-19 pandemic on micro, small and medium enterprises in India. *Jharkhand Journal of Development and Management Studies*, 19(1), 8651–8660.

Tsehayu, Y. G., & Østebø, T. (2020). Religious Entrepreneurship and Female Migration: The Case of a Muslim Religious Leader in Masqan, Ethiopia. *Africa Today*, 67(2-3), 63–83. DOI: 10.2979/africatoday.67.2-3.04

Tsvetkova, A., Pugh, R., & Schmutzler, J. (2019). Beyond global hubs: Broadening the application of systems approaches. *Local Economy*, 34(8), 755–766. DOI: 10.1177/0269094219897535

Tunio, M. K., Hamid, A. B. A., Latiff, A. S. A., & Hafeez, M. (2023). Unlocking organizational sustainability: The role of talent management through the lens of the AMO Theory. *Pakistan Journal of Humanities and Social Sciences*, 11(3), 3530–3547. DOI: 10.52131/pjhss.2023.1103.0634

Tunio, M. N. (2020). Academic entrepreneurship in developing countries: Contextualizing recent debate. In *Research Handbook on Entrepreneurship in Emerging Economies* (pp. 130–146). Edward Elgar Publishing. DOI: 10.4337/9781788973717.00014

Tunio, M. N., Chaudhry, I. S., Shaikh, S., Jariko, M. A., & Brahmi, M. (2021). Determinants of the sustainable entrepreneurial engagement of youth in developing country—An empirical evidence from Pakistan. *Sustainability (Basel)*, 13(14), 7764. DOI: 10.3390/su13147764

Tunio, M. N., Jariko, M. A., Børsen, T., Shaikh, S., Mushtaque, T., & Brahmi, M. (2021). How entrepreneurship sustains barriers in the entrepreneurial process—A lesson from a developing nation. *Sustainability (Basel)*, 13(20), 11419. DOI: 10.3390/su132011419

Tunio, M. N., Shaikh, E., Katper, N. K., & Brahmi, M. (2023). Nascent entrepreneurs and challenges in the digital market in developing countries. *International Journal of Public Sector Performance Management*, 12(1-2), 140–153. DOI: 10.1504/IJPSPM.2023.132244

Ucbasaran, D., Westhead, P., & Wright, M. (2001). The Focus of Entrepreneurial Research: Contextual and Process Issues. *Entrepreneurship Theory and Practice*, 25(4), 57–80. DOI: 10.1177/104225870102500405

Ugwu, D. I., Orjiakor, C. T., Enwereuzor, I. K., Onyedibe, C. C., & Ugwu, L. I. (2016). Business-life balance and well-being: Exploring the lived experiences of women in a low-to-middle income country. *International Journal of Qualitative Studies on Health and Well-being*, 11(1), 30492. Advance online publication. DOI: 10.3402/qhw.v11.30492 PMID: 27080016

Ukil, M., & Jenkins, A. (2022). Willing but fearful: Resilience and youth entrepreneurial intentions. *Journal of Small Business and Enterprise Development*, 30(1), 78–99. DOI: 10.1108/JSBED-03-2022-0154

Usai, A., Scuotto, V., Murray, A., Fiano, F., & Dezi, L. (2018). Do entrepreneurial knowledge and innovative attitude overcome 'imperfections' in the innovation process? Insights from SMEs in the UK and Italy. *Journal of Knowledge Management*, 22(8), 1637–1654. DOI: 10.1108/JKM-01-2018-0035

Uslay, C., & Erdoğan, E. (2014). The mediating role of mindful entrepreneurial marketing (MEM) between production and consumption. *Journal of Research in Marketing and Entrepreneurship*, 16(1), 47–62. DOI: 10.1108/JRME-11-2013-0034

Usoro, I. A., & Brownson, C. (2024). Creative Thinking, Adaptability and Entrepreneurial Development in Nigeria. *British Journal of Management and Marketing Studies*, 7, 69–77. DOI: 10.52589/BJMMS-96UF1ZBT

Utli, H., & Aydın, L. (2021). Perceptions of conscience of nursing students according to empathy levels. *International Journal of Health Services Research and Policy*, 6(2), 219–228. DOI: 10.33457/ijhsrp.916695

Uviebinené, E. (2021). The Reset: Ideas to Change How We Work and Live. Hachette UK.

Vaidyam, A. N., Wisniewski, H., Halamka, J. D., Kashavan, M. S., & Torous, J. B. (2019, July). *Chatbots and conversational agents in Mental Health: A review of the Psychiatric Landscape*. Canadian journal of psychiatry. Revue canadienne de psychiatrie. https://www.ncbi.nlm.nih.gov/pmc/articles/PMC6610568/

Valadkhani, S., Shariatpanahi, S., Atashzadeh-Shoorideh, F., & Tehrani, F. (2023). Investigating the relationship between the concepts of spiritual intelligence and entrepreneurship: a systematic review.. DOI: 10.21203/rs.3.rs-2061530/v1

Valliere, D., & Peterson, R. (2009). Entrepreneurship and economic growth: Evidence from emerging and developed countries. *Entrepreneurship and Regional Development*, 21(5–6), 459–480. DOI: 10.1080/08985620802332723

Van Bavel, J. J., Baicker, K., Boggio, P. S., Capraro, V., Cichocka, A., Cikara, M., & Willer, R. (2020). Using social and behavioural science to support COVID-19 pandemic response. *Nature Human Behaviour*, 4(5), 460–471. DOI: 10.1038/s41562-020-0884-z PMID: 32355299

Van de Ven, A. H. (1993). The development of an infrastructure for entrepreneurship. *Journal of Business Venturing*, 8(3), 211–230. DOI: 10.1016/0883-9026(93)90028-4

Van Stel, A., & Storey, D. (2004). The link between firm births and job creation: Is there a Upas tree effect? *Regional Studies*, 38(8), 893–909. DOI: 10.1080/0034340042000280929

Vázquez, F., Otero, P., Díaz, O., Sánchez, T., & Pomar, C. (2011). Emotional intelligence in women caregivers with depressive symptoms. *Psychological Reports*, 108(2), 369–374. DOI: 10.2466/09.13.14.pr0.108.2.369-374

Vedula, S., & Kim, P. H. (2019). Gimme shelter or fade away: The impact of regional entrepreneurial ecosystem quality on venture survival. *Industrial and Corporate Change*, 28(4), 827–854. DOI: 10.1093/icc/dtz032

Vermote, B., Aelterman, N., Beyers, W., Aper, L., Buysschaert, F., & Vansteenkiste, M. (2020). The role of teachers' motivation and mindsets in predicting a (de) motivating teaching style in higher education: A circumplex approach. *Motivation and Emotion*, 44(2), 270–294. DOI: 10.1007/s11031-020-09827-5

Verweij, H., Heijden, F., Hooff, M., Prins, J., Lagro-Janssen, A., Ravesteijn, H., & Speckens, A. (2016). The contribution of work characteristics, home characteristics and gender to burnout in medical residents. *Advances in Health Sciences Education : Theory and Practice*, 22(4), 803–818. DOI: 10.1007/s10459-016-9710-9 PMID: 27651045

Wach, D., Stephan, U., Weinberger, E., & Wegge, J. (2021). Entrepreneurs' stressors and well-being: A recovery perspective and diary study. *Journal of Business Venturing*, 36(5), 106016. DOI: 10.1016/j.jbusvent.2020.106016

Wagner, A., Tsarouha, E., Ög, E., Preiser, C., Rieger, M. A., & Rind, E. (2022). Work-related psychosocial demands related to work organization in small sized companies (SMEs) providing health-oriented services in Germany–a qualitative analysis. *BMC Public Health*, 22(1), 390. DOI: 10.1186/s12889-022-12700-4 PMID: 35209852

Waite, R. (2024). Embarking on an Entrepreneurial Journey: Top Advice for Start-Ups. https://www.robinwaite.com/blog/embarking-on-an-entrepreneurial-journey-top-advice-for-start-up-business-success

Wang, Q., Khan, S. N., Sajjad, M., Sarki, I. H., & Yaseen, M. N. (2023). Mediating role of entrepreneurial work-related strains and work engagement among job demand– resource model and success. *Sustainability (Basel)*, 15(5), 4454. DOI: 10.3390/su15054454

Wang, W., Huang, W., Liu, X., & Hennessy, D. A. (2021). Psychological impact of mandatory COVID-19 quarantine on small business owners and self-employed in China. *Current Psychology (New Brunswick, N.J.)*, 1–13. PMID: 34155428

Wang, Y. C., Lu, Y., Grunwald, S., Chu, S. L., Kamble, P., & Kumar, J. (2024). An AI Approach to Support Student Mental Health: Case of Developing an AI-Powered Web-Platform with Nature-Based Mindfulness. *Journal of Hospitality & Tourism Education*, 36(3), 1–14. DOI: 10.1080/10963758.2024.2369128

Wang, Z., Zaman, S., Rasool, S. F., Zaman, Q. U., & Amin, A. (2020). Exploring the Relationships Between a Toxic Workplace Environment, Workplace Stress, and Project Success with the Moderating Effect of Organizational Support: Empirical Evidence from Pakistan. *Risk Management and Healthcare Policy*, 13, 1055–1067. DOI: 10.2147/RMHP.S256155 PMID: 32821183

Wardana, L. (2018). Implementation of co-op learning model to increase students learning achievement and their active participation in entrepreneurship subject. *Jurnal Pendidikan Bisnis Dan Manajemen*, 4(1), 40–52. DOI: 10.17977/um003v4i12018p040

Wardana, L., Purnama, C., Anam, S., & Maula, F. (2020). Attitude determinant in entrepreneurship behavior of vocational students' entrepreneurship intention. [JPEB]. *Jurnal Pendidikan Ekonomi Dan Bisnis*, 8(1), 1–13. DOI: 10.21009/jpeb.008.1.1

Wasim, J., Youssef, M. H., Christodoulou, I., & Reinhardt, R. (2023). The path to entrepreneurship: The role of social networks in driving entrepreneurial learning and education. *Journal of Management Education*, 48(3), 459–493. DOI: 10.1177/10525629231219235

Webster, J., & Watson, R. T. (2002). Analyzing the past to prepare for the future: Writing a literature review. *Management Information Systems Quarterly*, 26(2), xiii–xxiii.

Wei, J. L., & Villwock, J. A. (2021). Balance versus integration: Work-life considerations. *Otolaryngologic Clinics of North America*, 54(4), 823–837. DOI: 10.1016/j.otc.2021.05.007 PMID: 34215359

Wei, J., Chen, Y., Zhang, J., & Gong, Y. (2019). Research on factors affecting the entrepreneurial learning from failure: An interpretive structure model. *Frontiers in Psychology*, 10. Advance online publication. DOI: 10.3389/fpsyg.2019.01304

Weingast, B., & Marshall, W. (1988). The industrial organization of Congress; or, why legislatures, like firms, are not organized as markets. *Journal of Political Economy*, 1(1), 132–163. DOI: 10.1086/261528

Weisel, K., Fuhrmann, L., Berking, M., Baumeister, H., Cuijpers, P., & Ebert, D. (2019). Standalone smartphone apps for mental health—A systematic review and meta-analysis. *NPJ Digital Medicine*, 2(1), 118. Advance online publication. DOI: 10.1038/s41746-019-0188-8 PMID: 31815193

Welter, F. (2011). Contextualizing entrepreneurship—Conceptual challenges and ways forward. *Entrepreneurship Theory and Practice*, 35(1), 165–184. DOI: 10.1111/j.1540-6520.2010.00427.x

Wendsche, J., & Lohmann-Haislah, A. (2017). A meta-analysis on antecedents and outcomes of detachment from work. *Frontiers in Psychology*, 7, 2072. DOI: 10.3389/fpsyg.2016.02072 PMID: 28133454

Wennekers, S., van Wennekers, A., Thurik, R., & Reynolds, P. (2005). Nascent entrepreneurship and the level of economic development. [Crossref. ISI.]. *Small Business Economics*, 24(3), 293–309. DOI: 10.1007/s11187-005-1994-8

White, J. V., & Gupta, V. K. (2020). *Stress and well-being in entrepreneurship: a critical review and future research agenda*. Res. Occu. Stress Well Being., DOI: 10.1108/S1479-355520200000018004

White, N., Packard, K., & Kalkowski, J. (2019). Financial education and coaching: A lifestyle medicine approach to addressing financial stress. *American Journal of Lifestyle Medicine*, 13(6), 540–543. DOI: 10.1177/1559827619865439 PMID: 31662717

Wiklund, J., Nikolaev, B., Shir, N., Foo, M. D., & Bradley, S. (2019). Entrepreneurship and well-being: Past, present, and future. *Journal of Business Venturing*, 34(4), 579–588. DOI: 10.1016/j.jbusvent.2019.01.002

Wiklund, J., Patzelt, H., & Dimov, D. (2016). Entrepreneurship and psychological disorders: How ADHD can be productively harnessed. *Journal of Business Venturing Insights*, 6, 14–20. DOI: 10.1016/j.jbvi.2016.07.001

Willard-Grace, R., Knox, M., Huang, B., Hammer, H., Kivlahan, C., & Grumbach, K. (2019). Burnout and health care workforce turnover. *Annals of Family Medicine*, 17(1), 36–41. DOI: 10.1370/afm.2338 PMID: 30670393

Williamson, A. J., Gish, J. J., & Stephan, U. (2021). Let's focus on solutions to entrepreneurial ill-being! Recovery interventions to enhance entrepreneurial well-being. *Entrepreneurship Theory and Practice*, 45(6), 1307–1338. DOI: 10.1177/10422587211006431

Williamson, O. (1975). *Markets and Hierarchies*. Free.

Williams, T. A., & Shepherd, D. A. (2016). Victim entrepreneurs doing well by doing good: Venture creation and well-being in the aftermath of a resource shock. *Journal of Business Venturing*, 31(4), 365–387. DOI: 10.1016/j.jbusvent.2016.04.002

Wilson, J. Q. (1980). The politics of regulation. In Wilson, J. Q. (Ed.), *The Politics of Regulation: 357–394*. Basic Books.

Wincent, J., & Örtqvist, D. (2009). A comprehensive model of entrepreneur role stress antecedents and consequences. *Journal of Business and Psychology*, 24(2), 225–243. DOI: 10.1007/s10869-009-9102-8

Wincent, J., Örtqvist, D., & Drnovsek, M. (2008). The entrepreneur's role stressors and proclivity for a venture withdrawal. *Scandinavian Journal of Management*, 24(3), 232–246. DOI: 10.1016/j.scaman.2008.04.001

Wirback, T., Möller, J., Larsson, J.-O., Galanti, M. R., & Engström, K. (2014). Social factors in childhood and risk of depressive symptoms among adolescents—A longitudinal study in Stockholm, Sweden. *International Journal for Equity in Health*, 13(1), 96–107. DOI: 10.1186/s12939-014-0096-0 PMID: 25384415

Wojujutari, A., Oladejo, T., Akanni, A., & Babalola, O. (2021). Spiritual intelligence, mindfulness, emotional dysregulation, depression relationship with mental well-being among persons with diabetes during covid-19 pandemic. *Journal of Diabetes and Metabolic Disorders*, 20(2), 1705–1714. DOI: 10.1007/s40200-021-00927-8

Wolters, C. A., & Brady, A. C. (2021). College students' time management: A self-regulated learning perspective. *Educational Psychology Review*, 33(4), 1319–1351. DOI: 10.1007/s10648-020-09519-z

Wong, P. K., Ho, Y. P., & Autio, E. (2005). Entrepreneurship, innovation, and economic growth: Evidence from GEM data. [Crossref. ISI.]. *Small Business Economics*, 24(3), 335–350. DOI: 10.1007/s11187-005-2000-1

World Bank Group. (2019, January 31). *About the Human Capital Project*. World Bank. https://www.worldbank.org/en/publication/human-capital/brief/about- hcp#:~:text=What%20is%20Human%20Capital%20and,as%20productive%20membe rs%20of%20society.

World Health Organization. (2019). Burn-out an "Occupational phenomenon": International Classification of Diseases. World Health Organization. https://www.who.int/news/item/28-05-2019-burn-out-an-occupational-phenomenon- international-classification-of-diseases

Worokinasih, S., Nuzula, N., Damayanti, C., Fauziah, S., & Syarifah, I. (2021). Is emotional intelligence matter in youth entrepreneur? *Proceedings of AEBMR-K*, 210928(012). Advance online publication. DOI: 10.2991/aebmr.k.210928.012

Wu, G., Wu, Y., Li, H., & Dan, C. (2018). Job burnout, work-family conflict and project performance for construction professionals: The moderating role of organizational support. *International Journal of Environmental Research and Public Health*, 15(12), 2869. DOI: 10.3390/ijerph15122869 PMID: 30558218

Wurth, B., Stam, E., & Spigel, B. (2021). Toward an Entrepreneurial Ecosystem Research Program. *Entrepreneurship Theory and Practice*. Advance online publication. DOI: 10.1177/1042258721998948

Xian, J., Li, B., & Huang, H. (2020). Transformational leadership and employees' thriving at work: The mediating roles of challenge-hindrance stressors. *Frontiers in Psychology*, 11, 1400. DOI: 10.3389/fpsyg.2020.01400 PMID: 32655458

Xie, Z., Wang, X., Xie, L., & Duan, K. (2021). Entrepreneurial ecosystem and the quality and quantity of regional entrepreneurship: A configurational approach. *Journal of Business Research*, 128, 499–509. DOI: 10.1016/j.jbusres.2021.02.015

Xu, Z., & Yang, F. (2021). The impact of perceived organizational support on the relationship between job stress and burnout: A mediating or moderating role? *Current Psychology (New Brunswick, N.J.)*, 40(1), 402–413. DOI: 10.1007/s12144-018-9941-4

Yang, A. (2023). Psychological resilience of entrepreneurial failure: An application of positive psychology to entrepreneurial failure repair. *Academic Journal of Management and Social Sciences*, 5(2), 17–21. DOI: 10.54097/ajmss.v5i2.06

Yang, E., Schamber, E., Meyer, R. M., & Gold, J. I. (2018). Happier healers: Randomized controlled trial of mobile mindfulness for stress management. *Journal of Alternative and Complementary Medicine (New York, N.Y.)*, 24(5), 505–513. DOI: 10.1089/acm.2015.0301 PMID: 29420050

Yang, H., Zhang, L., Wu, Y., & Shi, H. (2021). Benefits and costs of happy entrepreneurs: The dual effect of entrepreneurial identity on entrepreneurs' subjective well-being. *Frontiers in Psychology*, 12, 767164. Advance online publication. DOI: 10.3389/fpsyg.2021.767164 PMID: 34777177

Yang, Y., Liu, H., & Chen, X. (2020). COVID-19 and restaurant demand: Early effects of the pandemic and stay-at-home orders. *International Journal of Contemporary Hospitality Management*, 32(12), 3809–3834. DOI: 10.1108/IJCHM-06-2020-0504

Yan, J., Huang, T., & Xiao, Y. (2022). Assessing the impact of entrepreneurial education activity on entrepreneurial intention and behavior: Role of behavioral entrepreneurial mindset. *Environmental Science and Pollution Research International*, 30(10), 26292–26307. DOI: 10.1007/s11356-022-23878-w

Yao, K., Li, X., & Liang, B. (2021). Failure learning and entrepreneurial resilience: The moderating role of firms' knowledge breadth and knowledge depth. *Journal of Knowledge Management*, 25(9), 2141–2160. DOI: 10.1108/JKM-10-2020-0772

Ye, D., Liu, M. J., Luo, J., & Yannopoulou, N. (2024). How to achieve swift resilience: The role of digital innovation-enabled mindfulness. *Information Systems Frontiers*, 26(2), 551–573. DOI: 10.1007/s10796-021-10225-6

Yeh, T. (2020). An empirical study on how financial literacy contributes to preparation for retirement. *Journal of Pension Economics and Finance*, 21(2), 237–259. DOI: 10.1017/S1474747220000281

Yester, M. (2019). Work-life balance, burnout, and physician wellness. *The Health Care Manager*, 38(3), 239–246. DOI: 10.1097/HCM.0000000000000277 PMID: 31261191

Yin, J., Yuan, J., Arfaei, N., Catalano, P. J., Allen, J. G., & Spengler, J. D. (2020). Effects of biophilic indoor environment on stress and anxiety recovery: A between-subjects experiment in virtual reality. *Environment International*, 136, 105427. DOI: 10.1016/j.envint.2019.105427 PMID: 31881421

Yitshaki, R. (2012). How do entrepreneurs' emotional intelligence and transformational leadership orientation impact new ventures' growth? *Journal of Small Business and Entrepreneurship*, 25(3), 357–374. DOI: 10.1080/08276331.2012.10593578

Yoon, S., Goh, H., Low, X. C., Weng, J. H., & Heaukulani, C. (2024). User perceptions and utilization of features of an AI-enabled workplace digital mental wellness platform 'mindline at work'. *BMJ Health & Care Informatics*, 31(1), e101045. DOI: 10.1136/bmjhci-2024-101045 PMID: 39153756

YouTube. (2018, October 23). "Office Space" star Ron Livingston reveals movie joke he still feels "a little bad about" | today. YouTube. https://www.youtube.com/watch?v=SNyVsCeI6pA

Yusoff, Y., Anwar, I. F., Rahayu, S. B., Lajin, N. F. M., & Ridzwan, M. (2023). A review on integrating emotional intelligence with artificial intelligence in social media marketing among entrepreneurs. [JOCSSES]. *Journal of Contemporary Social Science and Education Studies*, 3(2), 44–50.

Yu, W., Cormican, K., Wu, Q., & Sampaio, S. (2021). In whom do we trust? critical success factors impacting intercultural communication in multicultural project teams. *International Journal of Information Systems and Project Management*, 9(3), 21–40. DOI: 10.12821/ijispm090302

Yuwono, W., Susanna, , Ramadhani, D. S., Sasmita, E. W., & Sihotang, W. H. (2023). Analysis of the influence of the role of financial literacy on personal financial management. *European Journal of Business Management and Research*, 8(3), 57–61. DOI: 10.24018/ejbmr.2023.8.3.1891

Zak, P. J., & Knack, S. (2001). Trust and growth, *Economic Journal,* vol. Ill, 295-321)

Zarchi, M., Nooripour, R., Oskooei, A., & Afrooz, G. (2020). The effects of mindfulness-based training on psychological wellbeing and emotion regulation of menopausal women: A quasi-experimental study. *Journal of Research and Health*, 10(5), 295–304. DOI: 10.32598/jrh.10.5.1669.1

Zhang, D., Lee, E. K., Mak, E. C., Ho, C. Y., & Wong, S. Y. (2021). Mindfulness-based interventions: An overall review. *British Medical Bulletin*, 138(1), 41–57. DOI: 10.1093/bmb/ldab005 PMID: 33884400

Zhang, H., Zhou, X., Nielsen, M. S., & Klyver, K. (2023). The role of stereotype threat, anxiety, and emotional intelligence in women's opportunity evaluation. *Entrepreneurship Theory and Practice*, 47(5), 1699–1730. DOI: 10.1177/10422587221096905

Zhao, H., & Wibowo, A. (2021). Entrepreneurship resilience: Can psychological traits of entrepreneurial intention support overcoming entrepreneurial failure? *Frontiers in Psychology*, 12, 707803. DOI: 10.3389/fpsyg.2021.707803 PMID: 34594271

Zhao, J., Qi, Z., & De Pablos, P. O. (2014). Enhancing enterprise training performance: Perspectives from knowledge transfer and integration. *Computers in Human Behavior*, 30, 567–573. DOI: 10.1016/j.chb.2013.06.041

Zhao, Y., & Sang, B. (2023). The role of emotional quotients and adversity quotients in career success. *Frontiers in Psychology*, 14, 1128773. DOI: 10.3389/fpsyg.2023.1128773 PMID: 36844276

Zhou, X., Rasool, S. F., & Ma, D. (2020). The Relationship between Workplace Violence and Innovative Work Behavior: The Mediating Roles of Employee Wellbeing. *Healthcare (Basel)*, 8(3), 332. DOI: 10.3390/healthcare8030332 PMID: 32927711

Zhou, X., Rasool, S. F., & Ma, D. (2020, September). The relationship between workplace violence and innovative work behavior: The mediating roles of employee wellbeing. [). MDPI.]. *Health Care*, 8(3), 332. PMID: 32927711

Дрібас, С., Makarenko, N., & Shumilina, I. (2020). Development of junior students' emotional intelligence in terms of new Ukrainian school: realities and prospects. SHS Web of Conferences, 75, 03008. DOI: 10.1051/shsconf/20207503008

About the Contributors

Muhammad Nawaz Tunio, an accomplished scholar in Entrepreneurship, Management, and Policy, brings much experience and expertise to the academic arena. With a Ph.D. in Entrepreneurship, Innovation, and Economic Development from Alpen Adria University, Klagenfurt, Austria, Dr. Tunio has established himself as a leading authority in his field. Currently serving as an Assistant Professor at the Department of Business Administration, University of Sufism and Modern Sciences, Bhitshah, Pakistan, he has also held positions at esteemed institutions such as Greenwich University and Mohammad Ali Jinnah University. Dr. Tunio's research interests include Entrepreneurship, Innovation, Economic Development, Youth Development, Career Development, and CSR. His scholarly contributions extend far beyond the confines of academia, with numerous research articles published in top-tier journals and prestigious book chapters with reputable publishers. Dr. Tunio has edited books with Springer, Emerald, and IGI Global Publishers on the different perspectives of entrepreneurship in collaboration with scholars worldwide. With an impressive research profile boasting over 1000 citations, an H-Index of 18, and an i10-index of 31, Dr. Tunio's work has significantly impacted the academic community. His consultancy experience includes projects with organizations such as the National Rural Support Program, the Small and Medium Enterprises Development Authority, Women Chamber of Commerce, SMEDA, and TRDP. He has provided invaluable expertise on issues related to small business restoration and brand management for men and women entrepreneurs. Dr. Tunio's dedication to academic excellence is further evidenced by his teaching and administrative roles at various universities, where he has mentored students, organized international conferences, and contributed to developing curricula in Business Administration and Management.

***

Rohit is a Research Associate at College of Healthcare Management and Economics, Gulf Medical University, UAE. He is MBA from Kurukshetra University Kurukshetra (A state government public university), India. He has published research papers in international journals and participated in various international conferences, workshops, and seminars. He worked as a management trainee and intern in the Thumbay Hospital, United Arab Emirates (UAE); Decathlon, Zirakpur, India; and Bajaj Allianz General Insurance, India. He completed various MOOCs from Copenhagen Business School, University of New Mexico, University of California, Irvine, University of London, and many other. His areas of interest are Entrepreneurship, consumer behavior, marketing strategies and strategic management. He is inspired with thought leadership and a regular contributor to educational magazines, debates, and cultural activities.

Ajay Chandel is working as an Associate Professor at Mittal School of Business, Lovely Professional University, Punjab. He has 14 years of teaching and research experience. He has published papers in

SCOPUS, WOS, and UGC listed Journals in areas like Social Media Marketing, E-Commerce, and Consumer Behaviour. He has published cases on SMEs and Social Entrepreneurship in The Case Centre, UK. He also reviews The Case Journal, Emerald Group Publishing, and International Journal of Business and Globalisation, Inderscience. He has authored and developed MOOCs on Tourism and Hospitality Marketing under Epg-Pathshala- A gateway to all postgraduate courses (a UGC-MHRD project under its National Mission on Education Through ICT (NME-ICT).

Shivani Dhand is an Associate Professor (14+ years of experience), a Certified SHRM (Society for Human Resource Management)faculty in the department of Mittal School of Business of Lovely Professional University. She is NLP(Neuro Linguistics Programming) Practioner She is also a member of the Indian Society for Training and Development (ISTD) and the Indian Society of Labour Economics. She is also a core committee member and Mentor of an NGO(Shalini Fellowship) Shivani Dhand has worked in an IT company as an HR. She has published 15 research papers in various journals which include Scopus-indexed, UGC care and peer-reviewed journals. She is a certified POSH trainer. She has worked with CPSC (Columbo Plan Staff College) Manila Philippines, and trained the faculty and Principals of various Institutions in Bhutan (2015). In 2016, She worked on one of the projects," Austria as an Innovation leader in EU in Austria and was awarded as best presentation and Excellent paper. Her research is situated in the field of Startups, HR Practices Human Resource Management, Entrepreneurship, and social entrepreneurship with a special focus on academic entrepreneurship.

Ridhoyanti Hidayah is a lecturer at the Nursing Department, Faculty of Health Sciences, University of Brawijaya, Indonesia. Her expertise is in psychiatric and mental health nursing. Autism spectrum disorder, psychosocial problems, and severe mental illness are her focus for research and community service.

Tiago Horta Reis da Silva is a Lecturer in Nursing Education (AEP) at King's College London, with a range of qualifications including BSc in Nursing, BSc in Traditional Chinese Medicine, MSc in Emotional Intelligence, Counselling and NLP, a Master of Business Administration, and MSc in Traditional Chinese Medicine. He has experience in other Higher Education Institutions and NHS and is a member of the Adult Nursing department, assisting with the running, development, and administration of BSc and MSc programmes. He also assists with teaching other modules' content and assists with interviews and assessment matters for other courses. Tiago is a Senior Fellow in Higher Education, a Fellow of the Royal Society of Medicine, and a Fellow for Faculty Nursing and Midwifery at the Royal College of Southern Ireland.

Preet Kanwal completed her Post-Doctoral Fellowship at the ESG, University of Quebec in Montreal, Canada, furthering research expertise in her field. During her Post Doctoral Fellowship, she worked on exploring demographic sensitivity and its impact on discrimination in HEIs while considering insights from Canada and India. Dr. Kanwal is an academician and researcher with over 20 years of experience in Human Resource Management. She holds a PhD in Human Resource Management from I.K. Gujral Punjab Technical University, Punjab, India, where she conducted an empirical study on the quality of work life in the textile industry of Punjab, India. She also has international experience teaching MBA students from Victoria University (Online), Australia, and Sunway University (Online), Malaysia. Dr. Kanwal's research interests revolve around the quality of work-life, work-life balance, industrial relations, labour laws, social security and labour welfare, organizational stress, and behaviour, particularly in the context of the textile industry. She has presented her research at numerous national and international conferences and published her work in Scopus-indexed and UGC-listed Journals. Additionally, she has authored several book chapters on related topics, underscoring her commitment to advancing knowledge in her field. Her contributions extend beyond teaching and research; she has been actively involved in organizing and leading training sessions, workshops, and conferences, both as a participant and as a session chair. Currently she is working on a funded project titled, "Empowering Women Artisans for Vision Viksit Bharat@2047: Financial Inclusion, Market Access, and Skill Development in Selected States of India".

Thi Minh Ngoc Luu is currently the Head of the Department of Economics and Management at the International School, Vietnam National University, Hanoi. She has over 17 years of experience in teaching and researching human resource management, management control, corporate governance, individual and organizational behavior, leadership, and sustainable development.

Shashank Mittal has done his FPM in Organizational behavior and Human Resource from Indian Institute of Management Raipur. He holds B. Tech from I.E.T. Lucknow. His post FPM work experience includes almost five years of industry and academics exposures in multiple roles. Prior to joining FPM, he has over two years of industrial experience and three years of teaching experience in various organizations. He has published multiple papers in ABDC ranked and SSCI indexed journals of international repute such as Journal of Knowledge Management, Journal of Behavioral and Experimental Finance, International Journal of Conflict Management, Journal of Management and Organization and Current Psychology. His current research interest includes Social identity, Knowledge exchanges, Status, Proactive helping, Employer branding, Organizational justice, and Humanitarian relief management. He enjoys badminton and cycling during leisure time.

Utsav Krishan Murari is a gifted writer, dedicated life coach, motivational speaker, passionate educator, and, above all, an exceptional mentor. He holds a doctorate in communication and media studies from the Central University of South Bihar. Graced with a vivid imagination, he is a genuine catalyst for ideas and is always open to trying new things. His one such initiative is Saarthi, which began as Saarthi Entertainment. Saarthi is a Delhi-based creative media production start-up that wants to leave a legacy of artistry in the production industry. Delivering content with a strong emotional connection and the potential to transform the world is what Team Saarthi is all about.

P. VidhyaPriya is a dedicated academician with a strong foundation in both computer science and business management. She holds an MBA from Avinashilingam Deemed University, Coimbatore, and earned her Ph.D. from Bharathiar University, Coimbatore, in 2010. Before transitioning to academia, she gained valuable industry experience working with a textile firm for over three years. In 2000, she joined Kongu Engineering College, where she has since built an illustrious career in research and teaching. With over 24 years of academic experience, Dr. VidhyaPriya's research interests lie in corporate finance, corporate governance, and behavioral finance. She has published 57 research papers in reputed national and international journals, including Scopus-indexed publications. Throughout her career, she has actively engaged with the academic community by attending numerous Faculty Development Programs (FDPs) at leading B-Schools, including IIM Bangalore, IIT Madras, Pondicherry University, and Mangalore

University. Dr.VidhyaPriya has also presented papers at 30 national and international conferences and has organized multiple conferences, seminars, FDPs, workshops, and training programs. She has successfully completed two ICSSR-sponsored projects focused on start-up entrepreneurship and the Stand-Up India Scheme for entrepreneurs.

Hemlata Parmar, a luminary in the field of computer Science and Engineering. Her Journey is defined by a constellation of achievements from prolific publications and patents to enlightening guest lectures. Yet, her brilliance is matched only by her unwavering commitment to human ethics. With a heart as vast as her intellect, she champions women's empowerment, bridging the gap with empathy and insight. In every endeavor, she embodies the perfect fusion of academic process and compassionate advocacy, inspiring generations to come.

Majdi Anwar Quttainah earned his Ph.D. degree in Management from Rensselaer Polytechnic Institute, Lally School of Management & Technology (USA); MBA degree with merits from the Business School & Entrepreneurship at Newcastle University (UK), and bachelor's degree in International Business from the American International University in London (UK). Dr. Quttainah is an associate professor of management in the College of Business Administration at Kuwait University. His research and teaching interests are corporate governance and strategies, entrepreneurship & small businesses, and organizational development. In addition, as a recognition of his research, he was awarded the Best Young Researcher academic year 2016/2017 Kuwait University. He is an active scholar, presently working as senior editor of FIIB Business Review (Scopus, WoS, Published by the Sage Publishing). His research won several recognition and awards including the Best Paper Award at the 76th Annual Meeting of the Academy of Management Anaheim, CA, the Best Paper Award at the AGBA's 12th Annual World Congress, Kuantan City (State of Pahang), Malaysia, and the Best Paper Award of the Gorontalo International Conference of Project Management (ICPM) - Gorontalo/Indonesia. Also, at the home country level the best paper award for the Kuwait Economic Researcher Award by the Central Bank of Kuwait; May 2019 and 2022.

SC Vetrivel is a faculty member in the Department of Management Studies, Kongu Engineering College (Autonomous), Perundurai, Erode Dt. Having experience in Industry 20 years and Teaching 16 years. Awarded with Doctoral Degree in Management Sciences in Anna University, Chennai. He has organized various workshops and Faculty Development Programmes. He is actively involved in research and consultancy works. He acted as a resource person to FDPs & MDPs to various industries like, SPB ltd, Tamilnadu Police, DIET, Rotary school and many. His areas of interest include Entrepreneurship, Business Law, Marketing and Case writing. Articles published more than 100 International and National Journals. Presented papers in more than 30 National and International conferences including IIM Bangalore, IIM Kozhikode, IIM Kashipur and IIM Indore. He was a Chief Co-ordinator of Entrepreneurship and Management Development Centre (EMDC) of Kongu Engineering College, he was instrumental in organizing various Awareness Camps, FDP, and TEDPs to aspiring entrepreneurs which was funded by NSTEDB – DST/GoI

Sandeep Kumar Singh is a faculty in the area of Information Systems and Analytics at Jindal Global Business School, O.P. Jindal Global University, Sonipat. Prior to joining Jindal Global Business School, he worked as an Assistant Professor at JKLU Jaipur for two years. He has earned his Ph.D. in computational physics from Antwerpen University, Belgium. His PhD work focused on mathematical modeling and simulation of two-dimensional materials. Post to his PhD, he worked as a research scientist in Sweden for four years in energy storage systems, bioelectronics. He also did MTech in industrial mathematics and scientific computing from IIT Madras, Chennai. His current research interests are to apply complex mathematical modeling in the business and financial world.

V.P. Arun is a driven and accomplished professional with a diverse educational background and extensive hands-on experience across various industries. Graduating with honors, Arun earned his Master of Business Administration (M.B.A) with a specialization in Human Resources and Marketing from the renowned Sona School of Management in Salem in 2018, where he excelled academically with an impressive 8.3 Cumulative Grade Point Average (CGPA).Throughout his academic journey, Arun displayed an unwavering commitment to learning and personal growth, actively seeking opportunities to expand his knowledge and skills beyond the confines of traditional education. He sought practical experiences to complement his theoretical understanding, such as a 45-day summer internship focused on conducting a feasibility study for R-Doc Sustainability in the market. Additionally, Arun broadened his horizons through a 7-day industrial visit to Malaysia and Singapore, immersing himself in diverse cultural and professional environments.Arun's academic pursuits were further enriched by his involvement in hands-on projects, including a comprehensive study on Employee Job Satisfaction at Roots Cast Private Limited. His professional trajectory includes serving as a Growth Officer at Parle Agro Private Limited, where he played a crucial role in driving sales growth and market expansion. Subsequently, Arun leveraged his expertise as a Sales Executive at PhonePe India Pvt Ltd and later as a Senior Executive at Indiamart Intermesh Limited, demonstrating exemplary business development skills.Arun's career path further diversified as he held positions in business development and sales at Sriniv Agencies and Axis Bank and Ujjivan Small Finance Bank in Erode, where he made significant contributions to organizational growth and success. Arun is a dedicated professional, currently employed at JKKN Engineering College in the Management Studies Department. He holds expertise in his field and has contributed significantly to academia through the publication of two journal articles.

Heni Dwi Windarwati is an esteemed nursing lecturer at the Faculty of Health Sciences of Universitas Brawijaya. She has an impressive educational background, having completed her undergraduate nursing program, nursing program, master's program specializing in psychiatric nursing, psychiatric nursing specialist program, and doctoral nursing program at the prestigious University of Indonesia.

Mohit Yadav is an Associate Professor in the area of Human Resource Management at Jindal Global Business School (JGBS). He has a rich blend of work experience from both Academics as well as Industry. Prof. Mohit holds a Ph.D. from Department of Management Studies, Indian Institute of Technology Roorkee (IIT Roorkee) and has completed Master of Human Resource and Organizational Development (MHROD) from prestigious Delhi School of Economics, University of Delhi. He also holds a B.Com (Hons.) degree from University of Delhi and UGC-JRF scholarship. He has published various research papers and book chapters with reputed publishers like Springer, Sage, Emerald, Elsevier, Inderscience etc. and presented research papers in national and International conferences both in India and abroad. He has many best paper awards on his credit too. He is reviewer of various international journals like Computers in Human Behavior, Policing etc. His areas of interest are Organizational Behavior, HRM, Recruitment and Selection, Organizational Citizenship Behavior, Quality of work life and role.

Index

A

Abuse 2, 3, 4, 5, 6, 7, 11, 15, 16, 17, 18, 20, 21, 24, 27, 147, 254, 423
Abusive 1, 5, 6, 16, 18, 23, 24, 25, 26, 27, 28, 64, 229
Accessibility 76, 78, 80, 88, 90, 118, 122, 124, 166, 360, 431, 438, 439, 443, 451, 453, 457, 459
AI 19, 20, 75, 76, 77, 78, 79, 80, 87, 88, 89, 90, 91, 93, 110, 111, 112, 137, 184, 185, 186, 187, 193, 195, 196, 197, 199, 287, 310, 312, 313, 319, 336, 338, 339, 358, 427, 438, 439, 443, 449, 450, 451, 452, 455, 457
AI-Driven Interventions 75, 457
Artificial Intelligence 19, 20, 75, 76, 77, 78, 79, 87, 89, 90, 93, 112, 115, 185, 186, 187, 193, 293, 310, 314, 336, 340, 358, 438, 445

B

Bullshit jobs 61, 62, 64, 71
Burnout 2, 15, 27, 30, 33, 34, 35, 36, 37, 38, 39, 41, 42, 43, 44, 45, 46, 47, 48, 50, 51, 54, 55, 56, 57, 61, 66, 69, 71, 72, 106, 118, 119, 120, 131, 136, 140, 153, 162, 164, 165, 173, 174, 175, 176, 177, 178, 179, 180, 183, 184, 185, 186, 187, 188, 189, 190, 194, 195, 196, 197, 198, 199, 202, 205, 206, 208, 211, 212, 215, 216, 217, 218, 220, 221, 230, 234, 235, 244, 245, 250, 251, 253, 254, 255, 256, 257, 258, 269, 293, 294, 296, 297, 298, 299, 300, 301, 302, 303, 304, 305, 306, 307, 308, 309, 310, 311, 312, 313, 314, 315, 316, 317, 318, 320, 322, 323, 324, 325, 326, 327, 328, 329, 330, 331, 332, 333, 334, 335, 336, 337, 338, 339, 340, 341, 342, 343, 344, 345, 346, 347, 349, 351, 353, 354, 355, 358, 359, 361, 362, 363, 364, 366, 369, 375, 377, 382, 384, 386, 387, 388, 394, 402, 407, 410, 411, 412, 415, 416, 419, 428, 432, 444, 445, 456, 457
Burnout Prevention 294, 305, 320, 331
Business 19, 21, 24, 26, 28, 29, 30, 31, 34, 35, 36, 37, 38, 39, 40, 41, 42, 43, 44, 45, 46, 47, 48, 49, 50, 51, 53, 54, 56, 64, 68, 71, 72, 93, 94, 95, 96, 97, 98, 99, 100, 101, 102, 103, 104, 105, 106, 107, 108, 109, 110, 111, 112, 113, 114, 118, 119, 120, 121, 122, 123, 127, 129, 130, 131, 132, 133, 135, 136, 137, 142, 146, 149, 151, 153, 154, 156, 158, 159, 163, 164, 165, 166, 167, 169, 170, 173, 174, 175, 176, 177, 178, 179, 180, 181, 182, 183, 184, 185, 186, 187, 188, 189, 190, 191, 194, 195, 196, 197, 198, 199, 202, 203, 204, 205, 206, 207, 208, 209, 210, 211, 212, 213, 214, 215, 216, 217, 218, 219, 220, 221, 222, 223, 225, 226, 227, 228, 231, 232, 234, 235, 237, 241, 242, 243, 244, 245, 247, 248, 249, 250, 251, 252, 253, 254, 255, 256, 257, 258, 259, 260, 261, 262, 263, 264, 265, 266, 267, 269, 270, 271, 274, 276, 282, 283, 284, 285, 286, 287, 288, 289, 290, 291, 292, 294, 295, 296, 297, 298, 299, 300, 301, 302, 304, 305, 306, 307, 308, 309, 310, 311, 312, 313, 314, 315, 316, 317, 318, 319, 320, 321, 322, 323, 324, 325, 326, 327, 328, 330, 331, 332, 333, 334, 335, 336, 337, 338, 339, 340, 341, 342, 343, 344, 345, 346, 347, 348, 349, 350, 351, 352, 353, 354, 355, 356, 357, 358, 359, 360, 362, 363, 364, 365, 366, 367, 368, 369, 370, 372, 373, 374, 375, 376, 377, 379, 382, 383, 384, 385, 386, 387, 388, 389, 390, 392, 393, 394, 395, 396, 397, 398, 399, 402, 403, 404, 406, 407, 408, 409, 411, 412, 413, 414, 415, 416, 419, 420, 421, 423, 427, 428, 429, 430, 431, 432, 433, 434, 435, 436, 437, 439, 440, 444, 445, 446, 448, 449, 453, 455
Business Success 34, 36, 37, 38, 40, 93, 94, 109, 156, 173, 177, 178, 181, 183, 202, 207, 209, 212, 214, 216, 218, 219, 223, 231, 249, 260, 261, 265, 297, 300, 323, 326, 375, 377, 407, 423

C

Chatbot 76, 77, 79, 80, 85, 87, 88, 89
Chatbots 75, 76, 77, 78, 79, 80, 85, 86, 87, 88, 89, 90, 91, 111, 185, 310, 336, 450, 459
Community Building 123, 236, 434
Community Networks 201
Community Support 122, 123, 166, 190, 191, 192, 193, 194, 225, 445, 448, 449
Computer 20, 55, 60, 63, 76, 114, 418
Computers 66, 292, 314, 316, 340, 342
Coping Mechanisms 7, 41, 130, 201, 202, 209, 210, 211, 223, 225, 231, 232, 233, 234, 250, 254, 310, 336, 353, 363, 369, 393, 395, 424, 448
Cultural Factors 84, 85, 233
Cultural Influences 235
Customer Relations 93, 94, 96, 100

D

Decision-Making 6, 16, 25, 33, 34, 35, 36, 38, 40, 42, 44, 51, 96, 103, 104, 105, 106, 107, 109, 110, 128, 137, 138, 146, 157, 167, 177, 178, 181, 186, 192, 205, 207, 208, 211, 212, 217, 221, 249, 250, 251,

253, 258, 260, 261, 263, 266, 267, 294, 295, 301, 307, 320, 321, 327, 333, 345, 347, 348, 349, 350, 351, 353, 354, 355, 358, 363, 366, 368, 373, 374, 377, 385, 388, 391, 393, 396, 405, 406, 407, 410, 411, 413, 414, 415, 416, 420, 428

Digital Age 78, 319, 437

Digital Mental Health 197, 357, 459, 460

Digital Solutions 173

Diversity 16, 18, 30, 53, 65, 79, 88, 89, 90, 102, 111, 128, 167, 230, 231, 234, 235, 241, 261, 277, 319

E

Economic Growth 235, 266, 273, 274, 275, 276, 277, 278, 279, 280, 281, 282, 283, 284, 285, 287, 288, 290, 291, 292, 381, 396, 397, 401, 414

EI 11, 44, 93, 94, 95, 96, 102, 107, 108, 109, 110, 260, 302, 303, 328, 329, 358, 391, 401, 402, 403, 404, 405, 406, 407, 408, 409, 410, 411, 414, 415, 416, 417

Emotional Intelligence 16, 33, 44, 45, 46, 47, 53, 54, 55, 56, 93, 94, 95, 96, 97, 98, 99, 100, 101, 102, 103, 104, 105, 106, 107, 108, 109, 110, 111, 112, 113, 114, 115, 120, 153, 156, 157, 167, 232, 233, 234, 235, 237, 249, 251, 254, 258, 259, 260, 261, 294, 302, 305, 320, 328, 331, 358, 381, 391, 392, 394, 395, 396, 401, 402, 403, 404, 405, 406, 407, 408, 409, 410, 411, 412, 413, 414, 415, 416, 417, 418, 419, 420, 421, 422, 424, 425

Emotional Resilience 5, 7, 16, 35, 40, 47, 50, 67, 94, 102, 104, 111, 146, 155, 157, 158, 159, 187, 251, 258, 314, 340, 345, 353, 355, 358, 360, 364, 412, 413, 416, 417, 432, 446

Emotional Support 36, 39, 43, 46, 49, 177, 181, 185, 191, 215, 216, 219, 236, 255, 301, 304, 327, 330, 368, 373, 392, 394, 409, 415, 430, 433, 437, 439, 448, 456

Emotional Wellbeing 1, 33, 38, 40, 47, 135, 136, 137, 139, 140, 141, 142, 143, 146, 147, 148, 149, 194

Emotional Well-Being 1, 5, 7, 8, 9, 10, 11, 13, 14, 15, 16, 17, 18, 21, 22, 23, 26, 33, 34, 38, 39, 40, 41, 43, 44, 47, 48, 50, 51, 66, 107, 135, 137, 139, 142, 146, 147, 156, 176, 181, 195, 221, 304, 309, 330, 335, 382, 394, 396, 401, 402, 403, 408, 409, 410, 412, 413, 414, 415, 416, 417, 421, 440

Empathetic Communication 239, 246, 247, 256

Employees 5, 21, 23, 25, 26, 28, 29, 34, 35, 36, 41, 45, 46, 56, 66, 67, 68, 69, 72, 94, 96, 97, 98, 99, 103, 106, 107, 108, 109, 110, 111, 130, 135, 136, 137, 138, 139, 141, 142, 145, 146, 147, 148, 149, 150, 151, 152, 153, 154, 161, 162, 166, 175, 176, 179, 180, 187, 188, 189, 190, 191, 193, 198, 206, 208, 213, 214, 216, 218, 222, 226, 232, 233, 234, 235, 236, 239, 240, 241, 242, 244, 245, 246, 247, 250, 251, 253, 256, 259, 260, 261, 262, 263, 265, 266, 269, 294, 295, 297, 298, 299, 301, 305, 306, 311, 313, 317, 320, 321, 323, 324, 325, 327, 331, 332, 337, 339, 343, 347, 348, 352, 361, 362, 365, 368, 375, 376, 378, 386, 392, 395, 396, 402, 403, 407, 409, 410, 411, 414, 415, 445

Employee Wellbeing 21, 28, 29, 31, 32, 110, 152

Entrepreneur 24, 34, 35, 36, 37, 38, 39, 40, 41, 43, 44, 46, 47, 51, 94, 95, 96, 97, 98, 99, 100, 101, 102, 103, 105, 106, 107, 110, 112, 114, 118, 120, 121, 123, 125, 127, 128, 131, 156, 157, 158, 159, 160, 161, 163, 164, 165, 167, 168, 174, 175, 176, 177, 178, 180, 181, 182, 183, 184, 185, 186, 187, 188, 189, 191, 192, 193, 202, 203, 204, 205, 206, 207, 208, 209, 210, 211, 212, 213, 214, 215, 216, 217, 218, 219, 220, 221, 222, 223, 224, 230, 250, 256, 271, 277, 286, 288, 294, 295, 296, 297, 298, 299, 300, 301, 302, 303, 304, 305, 306, 307, 308, 309, 310, 311, 320, 321, 322, 323, 324, 325, 326, 327, 328, 329, 330, 331, 332, 333, 334, 335, 336, 337, 346, 347, 348, 349, 350, 351, 352, 353, 354, 356, 357, 358, 359, 364, 365, 366, 367, 368, 370, 371, 372, 373, 374, 375, 376, 377, 382, 383, 384, 385, 386, 387, 388, 389, 390, 391, 392, 393, 394, 395, 398, 407, 418, 428, 429, 430, 431, 432, 433, 434, 435, 436, 437, 439, 444, 445, 447, 448, 449, 450, 452, 456, 457

Entrepreneurial Anxiety 345, 346, 347, 348, 350, 351, 352, 356, 357, 358, 360

Entrepreneurial Burnout 173, 174, 175, 176, 177, 179, 186, 188, 194, 198, 212, 297, 298, 300, 302, 307, 313, 316, 317, 323, 324, 326, 328, 333, 339, 342, 343

Entrepreneurial Failure 381, 382, 383, 385, 386, 387, 392, 397, 398, 399, 400

Entrepreneurial Leadership 96, 97, 135, 136, 137, 139, 140, 141, 142, 143, 145, 146, 147, 148, 149, 150, 199

Entrepreneurial Loneliness 427, 428, 429, 432, 439

Entrepreneurial Mental Health 181, 360, 363, 364, 377, 443, 444, 445

Entrepreneurial Mindset 220, 232, 233, 234, 235, 249, 252, 254, 355, 356, 367, 425

Entrepreneurial Stress 117, 125, 130, 131, 293, 294, 295, 300, 301, 304, 310, 312, 313, 320, 321, 326, 327, 330, 336, 338, 339, 412

Entrepreneurial Success 27, 35, 37, 47, 93, 94, 100, 103, 105, 110, 118, 120, 128, 130, 156, 169, 181,

185, 189, 195, 201, 202, 203, 204, 205, 206, 207, 208, 209, 211, 214, 216, 217, 218, 219, 222, 224, 225, 226, 227, 229, 232, 233, 234, 235, 261, 345, 346, 353, 359, 363, 367, 386, 390, 393, 403, 406, 407, 410, 411, 415, 416

Entrepreneurial Well-Being 199, 212, 214, 227, 228, 231, 319, 417, 460

Entrepreneurs 1, 2, 19, 20, 23, 24, 26, 27, 28, 30, 31, 33, 34, 35, 36, 37, 38, 39, 40, 41, 42, 43, 44, 45, 46, 47, 48, 49, 50, 51, 52, 54, 55, 56, 57, 93, 94, 95, 96, 97, 98, 99, 100, 101, 102, 103, 104, 105, 106, 107, 108, 110, 111, 112, 113, 114, 115, 117, 118, 119, 120, 121, 122, 123, 124, 125, 127, 128, 129, 130, 131, 132, 137, 138, 147, 148, 155, 156, 157, 158, 159, 160, 161, 163, 164, 165, 166, 167, 168, 169, 170, 171, 173, 174, 175, 176, 177, 178, 179, 180, 181, 182, 183, 184, 185, 186, 187, 188, 189, 190, 191, 192, 193, 194, 195, 196, 198, 199, 201, 202, 203, 204, 205, 206, 207, 208, 209, 210, 211, 212, 213, 214, 215, 216, 217, 218, 219, 220, 221, 222, 223, 224, 225, 226, 227, 229, 230, 231, 232, 233, 234, 235, 236, 237, 249, 250, 251, 252, 253, 254, 255, 256, 257, 258, 259, 260, 261, 263, 264, 265, 266, 267, 268, 269, 270, 271, 277, 278, 281, 282, 286, 289, 293, 294, 295, 296, 297, 298, 299, 300, 301, 302, 303, 304, 305, 306, 307, 308, 309, 310, 311, 312, 313, 314, 315, 316, 317, 318, 319, 320, 321, 322, 323, 324, 325, 326, 327, 328, 329, 330, 331, 332, 333, 334, 335, 336, 337, 338, 339, 340, 341, 342, 343, 344, 345, 346, 347, 348, 349, 350, 351, 352, 353, 354, 355, 356, 357, 358, 359, 360, 363, 364, 365, 366, 367, 368, 369, 370, 371, 372, 373, 374, 375, 376, 377, 378, 381, 382, 383, 384, 385, 386, 387, 388, 389, 390, 391, 392, 393, 394, 395, 396, 397, 398, 399, 401, 402, 403, 404, 406, 407, 408, 409, 410, 411, 412, 413, 414, 415, 416, 417, 422, 427, 428, 429, 430, 431, 432, 433, 434, 435, 436, 437, 438, 439, 440, 441, 442, 443, 444, 445, 446, 447, 448, 449, 450, 451, 452, 453, 454, 455, 456, 457, 458, 459

Entrepreneurship 19, 20, 21, 24, 26, 30, 31, 33, 34, 35, 36, 37, 38, 39, 40, 41, 43, 44, 46, 47, 48, 49, 51, 52, 53, 54, 55, 57, 93, 94, 98, 99, 101, 105, 106, 110, 112, 113, 114, 115, 117, 118, 119, 120, 121, 122, 123, 124, 129, 130, 131, 132, 152, 156, 157, 158, 159, 163, 167, 169, 170, 171, 173, 175, 176, 177, 179, 180, 181, 182, 183, 186, 190, 191, 192, 195, 196, 197, 198, 199, 202, 203, 204, 205, 206, 207, 209, 210, 211, 212, 213, 214, 215, 216, 217, 218, 219, 220, 222, 223, 224, 225, 226, 227, 228, 229, 231, 232, 233, 234, 235, 237, 249, 250, 251, 253, 254, 255, 256, 257, 258, 259, 260, 261, 263, 264, 265, 266, 267, 269, 271, 273, 274, 275, 276, 277, 278, 279, 280, 281, 282, 283, 284, 285, 286, 287, 288, 289, 290, 291, 292, 293, 294, 295, 296, 297, 298, 299, 300, 302, 303, 304, 307, 308, 309, 310, 311, 312, 314, 315, 316, 317, 318, 319, 320, 321, 322, 323, 324, 325, 326, 328, 329, 330, 333, 334, 335, 336, 337, 338, 340, 341, 342, 343, 344, 346, 347, 348, 349, 351, 353, 355, 357, 358, 359, 360, 362, 364, 365, 368, 369, 370, 371, 372, 373, 381, 382, 385, 386, 387, 389, 390, 391, 392, 393, 394, 395, 396, 397, 398, 399, 400, 401, 402, 403, 406, 407, 411, 412, 413, 414, 415, 416, 418, 422, 424, 425, 427, 428, 429, 430, 431, 433, 437, 439, 442, 445, 448, 449, 455

Entrepreneurship Ecosystems 131, 273, 274, 275, 276, 277, 278, 279, 280, 281, 282

F

Film Studies 60

Financial Literacy 169, 183, 194, 363, 370, 372, 373, 374, 377, 378, 379

Financial Stress 95, 175, 183, 186, 363, 364, 365, 366, 367, 368, 369, 370, 371, 372, 373, 374, 375, 376, 377, 378, 379

Future Research 27, 88, 129, 146, 149, 201, 222, 223, 224, 284, 315, 318, 341, 344, 398, 416, 422

Future Trends 56, 93, 110, 111, 155, 166, 167, 173, 192, 197, 293, 310, 313, 319, 336, 339

H

Healthy Work Environments 258, 401, 402, 403, 409, 414, 415, 416

Human Capital 59, 60, 68, 69, 72, 73, 280, 282

I

Inclusion 16, 19, 65, 85, 104, 111, 156, 231, 235, 241, 260, 319, 454

Inclusive Leadership 150, 223

Innovative Approaches 184, 262

Intervention 6, 15, 21, 29, 56, 82, 98, 117, 118, 119, 121, 122, 123, 125, 126, 127, 128, 129, 130, 132, 133, 134, 137, 211, 248, 317, 343, 357, 358, 359, 360, 374, 393, 394, 450

L

Leadership 5, 6, 16, 17, 18, 19, 21, 27, 29, 31, 47, 64, 65, 66, 67, 72, 93, 96, 97, 98, 102, 104, 105, 106, 107, 108, 109, 111, 112, 114, 135, 136, 137, 138, 139, 140, 141, 142, 143, 145, 146, 147, 148, 149, 150, 151, 153, 154, 161, 162, 167, 169, 174, 197, 199, 208, 218, 221, 223, 225, 237, 239, 240, 242, 245, 246, 247, 248, 253, 254, 258, 259, 260, 281, 294, 297, 305, 307, 320, 323, 331, 333, 358, 361, 383, 385, 388, 392, 402, 403, 404, 405, 406, 409, 413, 414, 415, 416, 417, 418, 419, 420, 421, 422, 423, 424, 428, 429, 433, 441, 446

Leadership Behavior 239, 245, 246

M

Mental Health 2, 3, 5, 7, 15, 16, 17, 21, 22, 27, 34, 36, 39, 41, 50, 51, 52, 54, 57, 67, 69, 71, 75, 76, 77, 78, 79, 80, 81, 82, 85, 86, 87, 88, 89, 90, 91, 110, 119, 120, 130, 131, 133, 137, 139, 147, 148, 151, 153, 156, 165, 166, 170, 174, 176, 177, 178, 179, 180, 181, 183, 184, 185, 187, 188, 189, 190, 191, 192, 196, 197, 198, 199, 201, 205, 206, 208, 209, 215, 217, 218, 219, 222, 223, 224, 225, 227, 229, 230, 231, 232, 233, 234, 235, 237, 240, 241, 246, 250, 254, 255, 257, 260, 265, 266, 267, 270, 293, 294, 296, 300, 306, 308, 310, 311, 312, 313, 316, 317, 319, 320, 322, 326, 332, 334, 336, 337, 338, 339, 342, 343, 345, 346, 348, 350, 352, 356, 357, 358, 359, 360, 363, 364, 366, 367, 368, 369, 371, 372, 373, 374, 375, 377, 378, 379, 381, 387, 393, 394, 395, 396, 397, 402, 408, 409, 411, 412, 413, 414, 420, 423, 428, 443, 444, 445, 446, 447, 448, 449, 450, 451, 452, 453, 454, 455, 456, 457, 458, 459, 460, 461

Mental Illness 77, 80, 81, 82, 85, 86, 87, 88, 357, 418, 449

Mental Peace 230, 231, 401, 402, 403, 407, 408, 409, 413, 414, 416, 417

Mental Wellbeing 35, 311, 337, 359, 367, 368, 446, 453

Mental Well-Being 34, 38, 41, 49, 50, 51, 77, 111, 119, 131, 139, 178, 181, 182, 184, 202, 207, 208, 217, 218, 219, 229, 230, 234, 235, 241, 249, 250, 254, 255, 256, 257, 258, 259, 261, 262, 263, 264, 265, 266, 267, 301, 305, 308, 310, 312, 327, 331, 334, 336, 338, 345, 348, 350, 357, 358, 359, 360, 364, 368, 369, 393, 394, 395, 396, 403, 404, 407, 408, 412, 414, 416, 425, 429, 443, 444, 446, 447, 449, 456, 458

Mentorship 16, 18, 36, 43, 49, 191, 211, 215, 223, 231, 234, 235, 242, 299, 306, 307, 308, 314, 315, 317, 325, 332, 333, 334, 340, 341, 343, 358, 370, 390, 394, 395, 396, 427, 428, 429, 430, 431, 432, 433, 434, 435, 436, 437, 438, 439, 440, 441, 442, 449

Mike Judge 59, 60

Mindfulness 33, 43, 44, 45, 47, 48, 53, 57, 103, 105, 117, 118, 119, 120, 121, 122, 123, 124, 125, 126, 127, 128, 129, 130, 131, 132, 133, 134, 148, 150, 155, 156, 157, 158, 159, 160, 161, 162, 163, 164, 165, 166, 167, 168, 169, 170, 171, 176, 177, 178, 180, 182, 185, 186, 188, 191, 193, 196, 198, 199, 202, 207, 208, 210, 211, 221, 231, 241, 249, 250, 251, 252, 254, 255, 256, 258, 259, 260, 261, 262, 263, 264, 266, 267, 269, 293, 294, 301, 302, 303, 304, 308, 310, 312, 313, 316, 320, 327, 328, 329, 330, 334, 336, 338, 339, 342, 349, 351, 352, 353, 354, 355, 357, 359, 360, 370, 378, 388, 390, 393, 394, 395, 403, 408, 409, 413, 420, 421, 424, 425, 444, 446, 450, 454, 455, 457

Mobile Applications 357, 443, 444, 446, 447

MSME 135, 139, 142, 147

N

Networking 49, 70, 104, 114, 123, 169, 188, 191, 193, 223, 235, 236, 242, 250, 255, 262, 266, 304, 330, 370, 390, 427, 431, 434, 437, 448, 449

Nursing 56, 237, 403, 412, 413, 415, 416, 418, 419, 421, 422, 423, 424, 441

O

Office Space 59, 60, 61, 69, 71, 72, 73

Organizational Support 20, 31, 150, 248, 293, 294, 305, 306, 307, 308, 313, 315, 318, 320, 331, 332, 333, 334, 339, 341, 344, 361

P

Personal Growth 163, 217, 221, 222, 261, 266, 381, 387, 405, 434, 441

Personal Well-Being 34, 37, 44, 120, 157, 178, 180, 183, 201, 202, 203, 204, 205, 206, 207, 209, 211, 213, 216, 222, 223, 224, 226, 249, 254, 266, 268, 294, 296, 300, 305, 320, 322, 326, 331, 401, 411, 445

Professional Fulfilment 155, 164

Psychological 2, 3, 4, 5, 6, 7, 11, 17, 19, 23, 28, 34, 35, 46, 48, 51, 54, 61, 64, 78, 79, 86, 87, 88, 89, 98, 99, 105, 111, 114, 118, 119, 120, 130, 133, 136, 138, 139, 147, 150, 151, 152, 153, 154, 162, 170, 174, 175, 176, 177, 182, 185, 188, 196, 197, 199,

201, 205, 206, 208, 209, 210, 211, 216, 217, 218, 219, 224, 225, 226, 227, 229, 231, 232, 233, 235, 239, 248, 250, 260, 263, 268, 269, 270, 271, 299, 302, 314, 315, 316, 325, 328, 340, 341, 342, 346, 348, 353, 357, 358, 359, 360, 361, 364, 365, 366, 367, 369, 370, 371, 372, 375, 378, 381, 382, 383, 384, 385, 386, 387, 388, 389, 391, 392, 393, 394, 395, 396, 397, 398, 399, 400, 405, 408, 415, 421, 422, 424, 425, 428, 429, 430, 432, 444, 445, 447

Psychological Resilience 130, 201, 209, 210, 211, 225, 353, 381, 382, 384, 393, 394, 395, 396, 397, 398, 399, 408

Psychology 17, 30, 31, 34, 53, 55, 57, 72, 80, 81, 82, 83, 85, 86, 113, 114, 115, 119, 131, 132, 133, 150, 151, 154, 170, 171, 198, 199, 224, 226, 227, 248, 268, 269, 270, 271, 314, 316, 317, 318, 340, 342, 343, 344, 361, 362, 369, 378, 379, 384, 394, 398, 399, 400, 405, 416, 420, 421, 422, 424, 425, 441, 460

Q

Quiet-quitting 59, 60, 61, 65, 66, 67, 68, 70, 71, 73

R

Recognition 2, 78, 97, 98, 102, 107, 121, 133, 138, 164, 169, 170, 176, 190, 230, 236, 239, 241, 266, 408, 416, 417, 446

Resilience 5, 7, 15, 16, 17, 18, 22, 33, 34, 35, 40, 44, 46, 47, 50, 51, 53, 56, 59, 67, 78, 94, 95, 98, 102, 104, 105, 107, 111, 117, 118, 119, 120, 121, 123, 129, 130, 131, 136, 146, 152, 155, 156, 157, 158, 159, 164, 165, 167, 168, 169, 170, 171, 173, 177, 181, 182, 187, 194, 198, 201, 202, 205, 207, 208, 209, 210, 211, 214, 217, 218, 219, 220, 222, 225, 231, 234, 237, 249, 250, 251, 253, 254, 255, 256, 257, 258, 259, 260, 263, 264, 265, 266, 267, 282, 287, 293, 294, 298, 301, 302, 303, 304, 305, 307, 308, 313, 314, 315, 316, 317, 319, 320, 324, 327, 328, 329, 330, 331, 333, 334, 339, 340, 341, 342, 343, 345, 346, 351, 353, 355, 357, 358, 359, 360, 363, 364, 369, 370, 371, 372, 374, 377, 381, 382, 383, 384, 385, 386, 387, 388, 389, 390, 391, 392, 393, 394, 395, 396, 397, 398, 399, 400, 402, 403, 404, 407, 408, 409, 411, 412, 413, 415, 416, 417, 419, 422, 427, 428, 432, 433, 435, 440, 444, 446, 447, 448, 449, 450, 451, 453, 457, 458, 459

S

Social Support 39, 46, 55, 169, 202, 207, 211, 212, 226, 234, 255, 319, 348, 364, 379, 382, 384, 388, 420, 449

Society 22, 37, 50, 51, 54, 60, 76, 77, 80, 81, 82, 83, 86, 87, 135, 156, 167, 169, 174, 204, 222, 278, 289, 290, 364, 378, 390, 396, 397, 405, 415, 422, 444

Stigma 75, 76, 77, 79, 156, 179, 234, 240, 265, 310, 336, 356, 357, 358, 360, 364, 389, 394, 395, 396, 397, 444, 446, 447

Stress Management 16, 43, 47, 57, 119, 121, 133, 134, 139, 166, 176, 177, 181, 182, 184, 192, 207, 210, 219, 229, 231, 239, 241, 255, 267, 293, 294, 300, 302, 306, 310, 312, 313, 315, 317, 320, 326, 328, 332, 336, 338, 339, 341, 343, 351, 358, 373, 374, 378, 394, 395, 405, 406, 407, 408, 409, 432, 444, 446, 449

Stress Reduction 117, 118, 120, 123, 125, 131, 132, 133, 134, 182, 196, 259, 294, 320, 351, 352, 393

Support Services 231, 234, 235

Support Systems 24, 36, 49, 175, 190, 191, 192, 201, 214, 216, 217, 224, 225, 232, 294, 299, 320, 325, 363, 364, 366, 372, 381, 382, 384, 389, 393, 395, 396, 434, 443, 449, 457

Sustainability 6, 7, 21, 43, 44, 114, 117, 125, 130, 131, 136, 137, 153, 164, 167, 169, 173, 174, 176, 178, 179, 180, 187, 188, 189, 190, 194, 204, 207, 219, 227, 237, 251, 256, 257, 260, 266, 267, 275, 290, 294, 307, 314, 315, 318, 320, 333, 340, 341, 344, 346, 348, 355, 364, 366, 371, 377, 395, 399, 409, 410, 414, 415, 441, 442

Sustainable Practices 6, 47, 51, 167, 178, 267, 310, 336, 414

T

Team Dynamics 93, 94, 96, 99, 108, 109, 112, 120, 166, 247, 255, 383, 396, 407, 409

Technology 15, 18, 26, 35, 41, 42, 49, 55, 65, 66, 76, 79, 87, 90, 93, 110, 111, 112, 113, 117, 122, 123, 124, 125, 129, 130, 131, 135, 151, 155, 166, 167, 168, 173, 176, 178, 182, 184, 185, 192, 193, 194, 195, 196, 201, 222, 223, 227, 248, 249, 252, 279, 283, 284, 285, 286, 287, 288, 298, 312, 319, 324, 338, 345, 357, 358, 360, 381, 385, 420, 439, 443, 444, 445, 446, 447, 448, 449, 451, 452, 453, 454, 455, 456, 457, 458, 460

Teletherapy 358, 394, 443, 444, 446, 447, 450, 451, 457

V

Virtual Platforms 427, 437
Virtual Reality 134, 166, 311, 317, 318, 337, 343, 344, 443, 455

W

Wellbeing 1, 21, 28, 29, 31, 32, 33, 35, 37, 38, 40, 47, 53, 56, 110, 118, 131, 135, 136, 137, 138, 139, 140, 141, 142, 143, 146, 147, 148, 149, 151, 152, 159, 182, 186, 191, 193, 194, 195, 196, 202, 207, 218, 240, 246, 269, 275, 304, 311, 330, 337, 346, 359, 367, 368, 376, 425, 444, 446, 453

Well-Being 1, 4, 5, 7, 8, 9, 10, 11, 13, 14, 15, 16, 17, 18, 19, 21, 22, 23, 25, 26, 28, 33, 34, 37, 38, 39, 40, 41, 43, 44, 47, 48, 49, 50, 51, 54, 56, 57, 65, 66, 67, 72, 77, 78, 93, 98, 107, 110, 111, 117, 118, 119, 120, 121, 122, 123, 125, 126, 127, 129, 130, 131, 132, 135, 136, 137, 139, 142, 146, 147, 152, 156, 157, 158, 160, 161, 162, 163, 164, 165, 166, 167, 170, 171, 173, 174, 175, 176, 177, 178, 179, 180, 181, 182, 183, 184, 186, 187, 188, 189, 190, 191, 192, 193, 194, 195, 196, 197, 198, 199, 201, 202, 203, 204, 205, 206, 207, 208, 209, 211, 212, 213, 214, 216, 217, 218, 219, 220, 221, 222, 223, 224, 225, 226, 227, 228, 229, 230, 231, 232, 233, 234, 235, 239, 240, 241, 243, 245, 246, 247, 248, 249, 250, 251, 253, 254, 255, 256, 257, 258, 259, 260, 261, 262, 263, 264, 265, 266, 267, 268, 269, 270, 271, 279, 293, 294, 296, 297, 300, 301, 302, 304, 305, 306, 308, 309, 310, 311, 312, 313, 314, 315, 316, 317, 318, 319, 320, 322, 323, 326, 327, 328, 330, 331, 332, 334, 335, 336, 337, 338, 339, 340, 341, 342, 343, 344, 345, 347, 348, 350, 352, 354, 357, 358, 359, 360, 361, 363, 364, 368, 369, 372, 377, 382, 393, 394, 395, 396, 397, 401, 402, 403, 404, 405, 406, 407, 408, 409, 410, 411, 412, 413, 414, 415, 416, 417, 418, 421, 425, 428, 429, 432, 440, 443, 444, 445, 446, 447, 449, 450, 451, 456, 458, 459, 460

Wellness Programs 173, 174, 176, 177, 178, 179, 180, 181, 183, 184, 187, 188, 189, 190, 191, 192, 193, 194, 195, 197, 198, 240, 241, 245, 247, 262, 306, 332, 393, 394, 395

Women 1, 2, 3, 4, 5, 7, 8, 9, 10, 11, 13, 14, 15, 16, 17, 18, 19, 20, 21, 22, 53, 55, 113, 114, 115, 149, 153, 169, 198, 223, 229, 230, 231, 232, 233, 234, 235, 237, 270, 316, 342, 361, 378, 379, 421, 424, 425, 441, 442

Work Environment 1, 21, 23, 25, 26, 28, 29, 30, 34, 45, 59, 64, 67, 95, 101, 102, 111, 120, 137, 139, 140, 146, 161, 162, 190, 216, 222, 229, 230, 231, 232, 233, 234, 235, 236, 242, 245, 246, 247, 257, 259, 260, 352, 403, 409, 410, 412, 413

Work-Life Balance 10, 11, 14, 33, 34, 35, 36, 37, 40, 41, 42, 43, 44, 45, 46, 47, 51, 53, 56, 57, 69, 120, 121, 138, 155, 162, 175, 180, 190, 191, 192, 201, 202, 203, 206, 208, 212, 213, 214, 216, 223, 225, 230, 235, 237, 239, 240, 241, 244, 250, 255, 257, 262, 267, 293, 295, 300, 302, 305, 306, 308, 311, 318, 321, 326, 328, 331, 332, 334, 337, 344, 351, 354, 355, 359, 368, 394, 407, 411, 415, 416, 434, 445, 449

Workplace Culture 2, 16, 17, 22, 26, 29, 34, 46, 65, 130, 232

Workplace Well-Being 72, 198, 239, 247